LITERARY IDEAS
in 18th Century France and England

LITERARY IDEAS
IN 18th CENTURY
FRANCE and ENGLAND

A Critical Survey

FREDERICK C. GREEN

FREDERICK UNGAR PUBLISHING CO.
NEW YORK

Republished 1966
with some changes by the author

By arrangement with E. P. Dutton & Co., Inc., New York
and J. M. Dent & Sons Ltd., London

First published in 1935 under the title *Minuet*

In this republished edition the original title
is carried on all left-hand pages.

Second Printing, 1970
ISBN 0-8044-2299-0
Printed in the United States of America
Library of Congress Catalog Card 65-23576

CONTENTS

DRAMA

POETRY

THE NOVEL

DRAMA

CHAPTER I

AFTER the Marlborough campaigns, it dawned upon a few French-men that England, which indubitably possessed a military machine, might also conceivably have a literature and a civilization of sorts.[1] The matter was at any rate worth investigation; and France of the Regency was in a speculative mood. At no period, indeed, in the cultural history of our two countries was the opportunity more ripe for an exchange or, maybe, an interfusion of ideas. And, as the century advanced, this intellectual *entente* developed with great rapidity. On both sides of the Channel a similar readjustment of opinions was in progress, a like reshuffling of literary values, an analogous effort to substitute a cosmopolitan for the old national outlook. Never had the translators been so active: never had there been so many borrowings and adaptations. The intellectuals of both countries crossed over to London or to Paris, carrying home the inevitable note-book crammed with impressions. New wars diverted, but did not interrupt, the two-way stream of books and periodicals which now entered both capitals by way of Holland. Contacts were made in every field; in science, in economics, in philosophy, in literature: even in more trivial things like fashions, gardening, and sport.

To describe this mutual curiosity as intellectual or literary interaction is tempting: whether that is justifiable is another question. Nations, like individuals, can be intensely curious about each other, and, having satisfied their curiosity, continue to behave as before. Besides, literary genius is essentially racial and the books which exercise an international appeal are very rare. To the foreign palate the art of a great writer will always seem strange and dis-concerting because of its native tang. Frenchmen have felt this in the works of Shakespeare and of Goethe: Anglo-Saxons, whilst ready to pay lip-homage to Racine, have never really assimilated his genius. Voltaire became a European figure not because he was a great artist but because he was a superb polemist. Literature,

[1] See Prévost's *Mémoires d'un Homme de Qualité*, tome v: 'The English are commonly regarded as a hard and proud race, fit only for war or navigation; cultivating the arts less from taste than from utility.'

if it will conform to alien taste, must almost of necessity sacrifice its essential beauties, which lie, not in ideas, but in their form of expression. Nevertheless, a curiosity so prolonged and so keen as that evinced by eighteenth-century England and France is seldom quite motiveless and is nearly always inspired by a dissatisfaction with existing domestic conditions. What caused this Anglo-French exchange of views? What was the precise nature of this *rapprochement*? What permanent influence, if any at all, did it exercise on the national spirit of French and of English literature? In what way did the French literary tradition differ from ours? These and kindred questions arise in the mind of every one who has consorted with the eighteenth-century writers of the two nations. And, like all matters that concern such elusive quantities as literary taste and influence, they are most certainly not 'problems' to be solved by any so-called scientific, critical method. They can only be discussed in a spirit of sympathetic and optimistic inquiry.

The obvious starting-point for a comparative survey of French and English literary taste and ideas is the theatre, which, despite the rapid development of the novel, continued throughout the eighteenth century to be the most direct expression of national taste in literature. At once, however, we are confronted by two sets of different conditions. In France the Catholic Church had never warmly encouraged the lay pursuit of letters. But the theatre it now regarded as a necessary evil. Besides, the Jesuits, in contrast to their Jansenist foes, had long cultivated the drama in the privacy of their colleges as an instrument of education. Again, by its nature—for what is more public than a play?—the stage could be, and indeed was, easily and effectively controlled by the censorship. The novel of manners, on the other hand, was a new and suspicious growth from which, as the Church shrewdly divined, no particular good could accrue to orthodox religion. So, at least in the early decades of the century, French novelists had to walk warily and as a rule, like the Abbé Prévost, frequently found it advisable to publish in Amsterdam works destined to be sold 'under the cloak' by Parisian hawkers. In England, no form of literature was subjected to a severe control of this sort. The Anglican Church, no doubt, had some vague idea that all imaginative writing was 'immoral,' and spasmodic pamphlets from its less comatose members condemned the stage as the high road to hell. On the other hand, as is only too painfully evident, many of the eighteenth-century dramatic poets were clergymen of the

Church of England. The State occasionally, as we shall see, made a feeble effort to gag the man of letters, but with no degree of success. Under these conditions, therefore, there was really no obstacle to check the swift rise of the English novel, with the result that this new genre challenged the supremacy of the stage much more quickly and effectively than it did in France. In England the popularity of the novelist was such that he soon forced the playwright to come to him for inspiration. Nevertheless, the eighteenth-century English theatre maintained its prestige, not merely because it pandered to the lovers of fiction, but because it remained, as it had always been, relatively democratic in contrast to the conventional and aristocratic stage of Paris. Shakespeare and the Elizabethans had always remembered the gallery, and so, . to a great extent, had the dramatists of the Restoration. In France the situation was very much less elastic. When, for example, a few years before the Revolution, the dramatist L. S. Mercier instituted a forcible campaign for a democratic stage, La Harpe,[1] stung by his reiterated references to the rights of the people, exclaimed: 'Why, then, is he so anxious that our tragedies should be written for the *peuple*? Why does he so constantly repeat the word, *peuple*, reproach us with not writing for the *peuple*, with despising the *peuple* . . .? Is it the *peuple* that comes to our plays? They have neither the time nor the means to do so.' And when, in conclusion, he adds that the fine arts are not for the uneducated, La Harpe but expresses the traditional attitude of the playwright of the old regime who did not, like his English colleague, cater to the taste of the mob. The London lower classes might appreciate Garrick in Shakespeare, but the Parisian plebs, as La Harpe points out, would certainly never dream of going to see Le Kain in Voltaire's *Mahomet* when it could roar at Taconet in the role of the cobbler at the theatre of the fair. Molière, it is true, had made a definite attempt to compromise between two extremes of taste, the popular and the aristocratic. He never, indeed, quite shook off the traces of his early experience as a strolling actor-playwright in the provinces, so that in the hey-day of his court successes there were plenty of kind friends like Boileau to remind him of the fact and to shrug a contemptuous shoulder at his lapses into 'vulgarity.' But all Molière's great work was conceived obviously in deference to the taste of a very cultured and sophisticated audience. There is no pandering to popular taste in the *Misanthrope* or in *Tartuffe*.

[1] *Réflexions sur le drame.*

To celebrate the birth of Madame Royale in 1779, and of the Dauphin, in 1781, the *Comédie française* and the *Opéra comique* gave free performances. It was only on such occasions that the French lower classes of the eighteenth century enjoyed the opportunity of seeing good plays, since, owing to the high prices and the limited accommodation of the royal theatres, even the *bourgeois* were driven to the cheaper establishments of the fairs and the boulevards. However, there is no reason to assume that the *peuple* would have welcomed a more classic repertoire had it been available. At the special, free performances the plays themselves were a mere excuse for public rejoicing. The theatre doors were opened at nine in the morning, and from then until late afternoon, when the curtain rose, the mob sang national and other ditties, ate, drank, and was thoroughly merry. According to a time-honoured custom, the fishwives and coalheavers lorded it in the two balconies beside the queen's and king's boxes respectively. In December 1779, we are told,[1] *Zaïre* was listened to in silence and with every apparent mark of appreciation. It is quite clear, however, from the same account, that the spectators turned in relief to *Le Florentin*, the comedy which followed Voltaire's tragedy. For then they could resume 'their noisy joviality and indulge to their heart's content in broad sallies and obscene innuendoes.' Another writer,[2] who was present when *Adélaïde du Guesclin* and Collé's *La Partie de Chasse* were offered to the plebs in 1781, remarks that these plays were far above its head. The prevailing sentiment, he says, was one of admiration, in the literal sense of the term. The fishwives and coalheavers, it is true, applauded at the right moments, but that was because they got their cue from the actors and the regular playgoers. Actually, they were quite insensible to the artistic merits of the plays. And, to prove his point, this eyewitness cites an interesting example. One of the most effective incidents in Collé's piece was that where the farmer's little daughter, who is ignorant of the king's identity, turns to Henri IV with the words: 'Avez-vous un couteau?' This remark, which never failed to excite applause from the ordinary aristocratic *habitués*, made not the slightest impression on the popular audience. 'The *naïveté*, the wonderful naturalness of this speech, which charms the connoisseur, says our writer disgustedly, 'left the *peuple* absolutely cold.' The *naïveté* lay, of course, in imagining that it would have any other result.

[1] *Gazette littéraire de l'Europe* (1779).   [2] *Journal de Paris* (1781).

On the whole there is a definite correlation, in England and in France, between the theatre and the social organism. The struggle in France to preserve the old hierarchic barriers against the pressure of wealth and talent is reflected, not merely in the French effort to maintain the traditional form of drama with its separation of tragedy and comedy, but also in the aid lent by the Government to the established State theatres. These were constantly menaced by the smaller, more popular establishments which now sought to encroach on the privileges of the royal theatres. This they did in response to the demands of a new public which was no longer satisfied by the gross *parades* of the fair theatres. In England we find, of course, a similar spread of education and, as a result, a similar improvement in theatrical taste, especially just after the Restoration. But this was not, as in France, a revolutionary change: if anything it was a reversion to tradition. Historically, therefore, the appearance of a play like *George Barnwell, or the London Merchant* [1] is no doubt interesting, but it is not nearly so significant as the production at the *Comédie française* of La Chaussée's *La Fausse Antipathie* [2] or, later, of Beaumarchais's *Le Barbier de Séville*. [3] Moreover, in this general movement towards a more democratic theatre, the English playwright had not to reckon with the chasm which in France separated the tastes of the upper and the lower middle classes. One has only to recollect the grossness and brutality of Restoration comedy to appreciate the fact. Men of the delicacy of Bolingbroke, Chesterfield, and Horace Walpole were exceptions and, in general, the taste of the English nobility of the eighteenth century was not noticeably different from that of the lower classes, whose sports and diversions they so often shared, and whose company, for political reasons, they were obliged to frequent. A French *seigneur* wintering in Paris could become really agitated about an infringement of the dramatic unities: his London *confrère* was much more likely to be exercised about rules of another sort, like those later devised, for instance, by the ingenious and immortal Marquess of Queensberry.

London, despite its larger population, had to content itself, as did Paris, with two theatres and an opera until well on into the seventies. In addition to the authorized houses in Drury Lane and Covent Garden there was, however, the Little Theatre in the Haymarket, a house with a chequered history which, from 1737 until 1762, had no legal right to exist, yet somehow did, thanks to

---

[1] By George Lillo (1731).　　　[2] 1733.　　　[3] 1775.

the ingenuity of the famous actor-author Foote, who advertised concerts, throwing in the play gratis. Prosecuted by the managers of the patent houses, he blandly substituted burlesques 'with a dish of tea.' After 1762, however, he was granted a patent for the Little Theatre, valid during the summer months. This favour he owed to the Teutonic humour of the Duke of York, who once conceived the exquisite joke of mounting poor Foote on a savage hunter, with the result that he lost a limb.

After 1720, in addition to the *Comédie française* and the *Opéra*, Paris once more possessed a third royal theatre, the *Comédie italienne*, since the regent, who liked broad farces, allowed Riccoboni's Italian troupe to use the Hôtel de Bourgogne with the title 'Les Comédiens de son Altesse Royale,' later changed to that of 'Les Comédiens Italiens du Roi.' Italian comedy was no novelty to the Parisians. From 1680 until 1697, when they were banished for an alleged slight to the pious Mme de Maintenon, the Italians had delighted the town with pantomime and *comédies de genre*. On their return they found, however, that the new generation knew no Italian, and were therefore obliged to enlist the services of French authors. Marivaux, Lesage, Boissy, Favart, and Fuzelier all wrote for the *Comédie italienne*, which soon became a formidable rival to the house of Molière.

Assuming for the moment that drama is something which has nothing to do with acrobats and performing dogs, it seems that the Parisian lower classes were more interested in dramatics than Londoners of the same social category. At any rate it is difficult to find in eighteenth-century London anything corresponding to the numerous theatres established annually at the great Parisian fairs of Saint-Laurent, Saint-Ovide, and Saint-Germain. These entertainments were a bugbear to the royal theatres, and the rivalry led to lawsuit after lawsuit. The fairs lasted for six months at a time and had well-built, excellently fitted theatres, the ancestors of the present-day *théâtres des boulevards*. The most usual type of show was the *parade*, and under the Regency it was fashionable to get up parties of the younger set to make the round of the fair theatres. *Parades* consisted originally of licentious scenes borrowed from the repertoire of the old Italian harlequinade, and they were recited in a comic jargon intended no doubt to imitate the 'pidgin' French of the foreign players. Collé, in his correspondence,[1] gives us a good idea of how it must have sounded and incidentally

[1] Edited by H. Bonhomme: *Origine de la Parade*.

discloses the fact that royalty did not disdain to amuse itself at the *parades*—though of course incognito.

'Il [1] me contait comme ça qu'il lui était zarrivé d'avcir mené plus de vingt fois en sa vie, entre quatre à cinq heures du soir MM. le chevalier d'Orléans, grand prieur de France, d'Argenson, *la guerre*,[2] les comtes de Maurepas et de Caylus, dans les préaux des foires Saint-Germain et Saint-Laurent. Ces gentilshommes étaient déguisés en reguingottes, leux chapeaux sur leux têtes, et là ces bons masques t'avaient le plaisir incognito de voir pour rien, représenter les parades que jouaient de dessus leux balcons, en dehors, Messieurs les danseurs de cordes, zavant qu'ils donnassent leux représentations véritables où l'on payait. . . . Ces scènes croustilleuses, la magnière dont elles étaient rendues, la franche gaieté qu'ils y mettaient, les ordures gaillardes, enfin jusqu'à leux pononciation vicieuse zet pleine de cuirs, faisaient rire à gueule ouverte et à ventre déboutonné tous ces seigneurs de la cour qui n'étaient pas tout à fait dans l'habitude d'être grossiers et de voir cheuz le roi des joyeusetés aussi libres. . . .'

As Collé indicates, the *parades* were at first offered merely as *hors-d'œuvre* by the mountebanks and tight-rope walkers to entice the public inside. But so popular did these entertainments become that, as early as 1706, says Parfaict, a contemporary historian of the stage, there were at the Foire Saint-Germain alone no fewer than seven theatres offering 'farces and comedies, half Italian and half French, interspersed with dances and intermezzos.' The latter were very like our modern revues for, to the huge delight of the audience and to the chagrin of the legitimate theatres, they parodied plays actually being produced at these houses. The management of the Foire Saint-Laurent, quick to scent business, obtained permission from the *Opéra* to introduce singers and musicians and built a new theatre, the original of the present *Opéra comique*. Here they produced their vaudevilles, but the *Comédie française*, as did Drury Lane in the case of the Little Theatre, instituted legal proceedings, forcing the fair actors to go back to their tumbling and their marionettes. Meanwhile the wily Italians tried to open at the fairs but were quickly repressed. At intervals, until 1752, the *Opéra comique* bobbed up irrepressibly, but on every occasion had to yield to the attacks of the other royal houses. To evade the law, the actors of the fair appeared with

---

[1] i.e. M. Sallé, secretary to the Comte de Maurepas and author of many *parades*.
[2] i.e. *ministre de la guerre*.

their parts printed on large placards and acted in dumb show; but even this ingenious subterfuge was of no avail. Finally Monnet, a manager whom we shall shortly find in close relations with his London colleague Rich, got permission, in 1752, to take over the *Opéra comique*. Monnet built a new theatre in thirty-seven days at a cost of twenty-two thousand francs, with ceilings by Boucher and stage decorations by the famous Deleuze of the *Opéra*. He engaged Le Sage and Vadé to write him comic operas in the modern manner, abandoning the *parades* to the meaner boulevard theatres and to the private stages of the great. Monnet's success ruined the *Comédie italienne*, which obtained leave in 1762 to merge with the *Opéra comique*. The joint spectacles were known officially as the *Théâtre italien*, but no one ever called it anything but the *Opéra comique*.

To the unprejudiced, or rather apathetic foreigner, one of the most amusing characteristics of the Third French Republic is the old-maidish attitude of its historians when they discuss the morals of the eighteenth - century nobility. Thus, when one of these gentlemen discovers that a minority of fashionable idlers not only frequented the *parades* but also had such plays written for their private stages and, moreover, that men like the Duc de Chartres actually took parts in them, he inevitably draws general conclusions pointing to a dreadful condition of perversity amongst the courtiers as a body. No one will dispute the fact so obviously reflected in the memoirs of the time and in the novels of the Crébillon school, that an immoral clique existed at the Court of Louis XV. But these *petits-maîtres* differed considerably from the English 'bucks,' or 'bloods.' Like the latter, they were badly educated and shared the literary tastes of the lower classes; but they were more sophisticated, more polite, and more class-conscious. The *académies* or military colleges under Louis XV resembled our English public schools in that they did not cultivate the intellect; yet they did teach their pupils to behave like gentlemen. Rarely, for example, do we find the French nobles making the people a witness of their viciousness.

The Abbé Le Blanc,[1] who was in London from 1737 till 1744, contrasts the two types, the English and the French *petits-maîtres*, at a period, be it remembered, when it was not yet the fashion for either nation to ape the manners of the other. Le Blanc is struck by the affectedly democratic manners and dress of the *milords*.

---

[1] *Letters on the English and French Nations* (translated in 1747).

'Is it not ridiculous,' he remarks, 'for a peer of the realm to appear cast in the same absurd mould as a brewer; and does the same sort of apron which orange - wenches wear in the playhouses fit well on a court lady?' How different from the exquisite clothes, the singular equipages, the jewels, the perfumes, the affected tone, and inane prattle of the French dandy! Contrast the general appearance of the latter with that of the English *petit-maître*, who wears a short bob without powder, a handkerchief round the neck instead of a cravat, a sailor's waistcoat, a strong, knotty stick, and affects the airs and the manners of the scum of the populace. What impressed Le Blanc most, however, as it did all French visitors to England, was the promiscuity of the English aristocracy, who shared regularly in the amusements of the mob; racing, cock-fighting, boxing, delighting even, says he, in bruising-matches with chairmen. No such democratic relations existed in France between the highest and the lowest classes. Indeed, apart from hunting, fencing, and tennis, which were essentially gentlemen's sports, the French nobility indulged little in physical exercises. Of course, in the seventies, when Anglomania became the fashion, racing and boxing were cultivated by a minority. And even when, as in the case of the *parades*, the tastes of the nobility happened to coincide with those of the lower classes, this mingling of the classes was more apparent than real. After the Regency the old hierarchy reasserted itself, and those gentlemen who liked *parades* got Collé, Vadé, Piron, and Sallé to write special ones for private performance. There is a distinct difference in tone between the really popular *parades* and such productions as Fagan's *Isabelle grosse par la vertu*, Collé's *Léandre*, *Étalon*, his *Alphonse l'Impuissant*, and the crude obstetrical humour of the *parades* of the boulevard shows. Moreover, the former were enacted behind closed doors to a select and limited audience. On the royal stages, obviously, we do not find evidence of any attempt at pandering to the dramatic taste of the mob, which, until the Revolution, had to content itself with the theatres of the fair or, as they were later called, the theatres of the boulevard. On the other hand, as we shall see, the *Comédie française* and the *Comédie italienne*, as early as the thirties, betray the growing pressure of middle-class influence.

It is very important to remember, in comparing the London and the Parisian theatres, that the French Government was autocratic and paternal to a degree impossible under the English constitution. The Parisian theatre, like all State institutions, was highly organized

* B

and strictly controlled, whereas in London, save for an occasional outbreak, the Lord Chamberlain's Office left the managers a fairly free hand. This was not the French way. From the ordinances governing the *Comédie française*, and they applied to the other houses, the whole administration, from the appointment and payment of actors to the choice of plays and the conduct of the players, was in the hands of a committee composed of the gentlemen of the king's bedchamber. An annual subsidy was granted from the king's privy purse. The actors constituted a business company and, as is the case to-day, full members or *sociétaires* drew a fixed salary with bonus; and on retirement, after twenty years' service, enjoyed a substantial pension. There was, however, another side to the medal. Regular fines were levied for breaches of discipline, failure to attend rehearsals or meetings of the casting committee, slackness in memorizing parts, missing one's cue, insubordination, or, more frequently, failure to show proper deference to the authorities or the audience. No doubt, in perusing the memoirs of the time, one must always recollect that the chronicler is attracted rather by the exception than the rule, yet it is clear that the French eighteenth - century actors were harshly disciplined. The old ecclesiastical prison of For-l'Évêque, which formerly stood on the Quai de la Mégisserie, more than once housed refractory players. Nor did their popularity or talent protect even the most celebrated stars against this indignity. The case of Mlle Clairon, one of the finest tragediennes of the century, is most illuminating, since it reveals the flaws of an administrative system too complicated to be efficient, let alone just.

Dubois, an indifferent actor, refused to pay his doctor's bill and was sued. His colleagues, for the honour of the profession, paid the leech, but expelled the actor for moral turpitude, after a trial approved by Richelieu, at that time one of the gentlemen of the bedchamber. But Dubois's daughter, who was pretty, and could act much better off stage than on it, persuaded Richelieu to reinstate her father. The actors therefore received an order to play with Dubois in Du Bellay's great hit, *Le Siège de Calais*. This was on 15th April 1765, and on the morning of that day Le Kain, the French Garrick, the famous Mlle Clairon, and others handed in their parts. At the last moment, to the disgust of the audience, it was resolved to cancel *Le Siège de Calais* and substitute Regnard's *Le Joueur*. Meanwhile, Mlle Dubois, accompanied by three very noble admirers, stirred up the public in the foyers so that, when the curtain rose, Mlle Clairon was greeted with shouts of 'Clairon au cabanon!' If I may use a well-rubbed phrase, pandemonium ensued. With difficulty the audience was restrained from setting fire to the theatre, the curtain was rung down, and the five recalcitrant players escorted to For-l'Évêque at the request of Mlle Dubois. For days the town was divided into two parties, for and against Clairon, and the great actress had at least the satisfaction of receiving most of fashionable Paris in her cell. But there are wheels within wheels. As Mlle Clairon indicates in her memoirs,[1] Mlle Dubois did her profession a grave disservice. By her action she played into the hands of a clique composed of the actor Préville, of the Lieutenant of Police, who wanted to control the *Comédie française*, and of the Intendant des Menus Plaisirs, who desired to manage, that is, to loot, the theatre treasury. The upshot of this disgraceful affair was that Paris lost its greatest actress, who very properly handed in her resignation. As for the rascal Dubois, he was retired with a small pension, so that, in the end, the actors did score a moral victory.

Our London theatres had their troubles also, but, at least after the passing of the Licensing Act of 1737, these difficulties were rarely due to Government interference. However, prior to that ordinance, the importance of which has been much exaggerated, there were conditions somewhat analogous to those existing in Paris. It is evident, for instance, from Steele's famous indictment of the lord chamberlain,[2] and from the reply to it, that the lord chamberlain had always reserved the right, exercised on several occasions, to interfere with the casting of plays. Colley Cibber was silenced by the Duke of Newcastle for a refusal to accede to his request that a certain actor should be given a part usually acted by one of the managers. There seems no doubt, too, that Steele was deprived of his patent because of a political quarrel with Newcastle, who was then lord chamberlain.

Until the passing of the Licensing Act, the royal patent did not, as in Paris, ensure protection against competition from rival houses. Betterton and some others, for instance, having quarrelled with the patentees, Skipwith and Rich, deserted their patent, but obtained a licence to act and to set up another theatre. Giffard's house in Goodman's Fields, the scene of Garrick's debut, was

---

[1] *Collection Barrière.*
[2] *The State of the Case between the Lord Chamberlain of His Majesty's Household and the Governor of the Royal Company of Comedians* (1720).

opened, in 1731, as a rival to the patent theatres in Drury Lane and Covent Garden. Ironically enough, it was Giffard who, by showing Walpole the manuscript of an anonymous seditious play, *The Golden Rump*, induced that minister to bring in the Act which limited the number of the metropolitan theatres to two and established an official censorship to control stage plays.[1] Until it closed, in 1742, the Goodman's Fields theatre managed to keep within the letter of the Act, but finally succumbed to the joint attacks of the patent theatres.

No doubt, in the abstract, the freedom of the press is a glorious and wholly admirable institution. Yet there must have been times when London managers envied their Parisian colleagues, who were legally protected against the mud-slinging of disgruntled authors. To-day, we are so accustomed to the gentlemanly reticence of the dramatic critic, we live in an age so unvituperative, that it is something of a shock to read an English eighteenth-century critique. Take this, for example, from the *Theatrical Monitor* of 1767. Referring to a performance of the *Oxonian in Town*, the reviewer writes: 'How cautious should authors and managers be not to exhibit such scenes. Nay, I will give a severe hint to the managers which, though unseen, shocks all decency, viz.: that the *corner* of the *green-room*, the *dark, narrow passage* next the end wall terminating with a scene to the stage; or a *silver key* to the wardrobe, may do more mischief and may be (I will not say are) *places* of more obscenity than any room at the *Shakespear*. Though the Oxonian may not be permitted to go there, yet the players are hunting one another about the theatre like rabbits at the mouth of a burrow, and from what appears from last *summer's productions*, they breed among one another. It is not unlikely that the example given by the late *dough-bak'd manager*, of calling one my *dear*, the other my *love*, the other my *charmer*, chucking them under the chin, patting their hands, caressing them with his blubber-mouth'd kisses, as false as Judas, might encourage such practices. . . . I hope there are none of the new managers who *do this*.' The same journal accused Garrick of jealousy towards his brother actors, notably of having suppressed Lee when he came to Drury Lane, of exploiting the fact that the players were not organized, and of foisting old pieces on the public to avoid expense. In its last number it calls upon him and Lacy to produce their receipts for public inspection.

Equally crude and scurrilous is the tone of the *Theatrical Review*.[2]

[1] Baker, *The History of the London Stage*, p. 67.   [2] 1771-2.

In addition to the usual abuse of Garrick we read that 'Mr. Hurst wades through the part of Sir Tom Evans with insufferable languor, insipidity, and affected importance,' that Mr. Owenson in *Tamerlane* (Covent Garden), 'having neither the accent of a Christian nor the gait of a Christian, must have been made by some journeyman of Nature, and that very carelessly too, he imitates Humanity so wretchedly. In short, the appointing such an Actor to represent so capital and so exalted a character as that of *Tamerlane* is one of the grossest insults upon common sense we ever remember to have met with at a *Theatre Royal.*' Even more pungently personal is the critic of the *Macaroni* (1772) when he comments on Bensley's rendering of the 'O Cromwell . . .' speech in the revival of *Henry VIII* at Covent Garden. 'Mr. Bensley drawled out those pathetic lines in a *tone* of *voice* and *roll* of *eye* at the apparent hazard of every pregnant woman in the house.' 'To crown the whole,' he pursues, 'Ned Shuter, not content with degrading the mitre by appearing in the character of a bishop, went a step farther in threatening to knock down Archbishop Cranmer with a clenched stick as he passed before him.' Nothing of this care-free manner is present in the French journals of the time, for the good reason that, even had they slipped past the censor, the printing of such scurrilities would have deprived the editor of his privilege and possibly landed him in jail. As a matter of fact, except in histories of the stage and in private memoirs and diaries, one finds very little valuable information as to the performance of individual players. To most of the journals, like the *Année littéraire* or the *Journal étranger*, it is the play and not its interpretation that interests the critic; and the occasional periodical, such as the *Mercure de France*, which does discuss the acting, confines itself, as to-day, to fulsome eulogy or remains discreetly vague. There was, however, no lack of venomous, clandestine publications grossly attacking the private lives of actresses in vogue, and written, for payment, by the Abbé Coignards of the time.[1]

Had the English press of the eighteenth century really reflected public opinion one might be inclined to wonder why London kept a theatre at all, so virulent and so persistent was the criticism levelled at managers, players, and plays. Numbers of the clergy, as in France, were fanatically hostile to the stage, and the echo of Jeremy Collier's famous indictment can be discerned in many a

[1] See, for example, G. de la Bataille's infamous book on Mlle Clairon, *L'Histoire de la vie et des mœurs de Mlle Cronel, dite Frétillon* (1739–40).

book and magazine throughout the century. It is hard to know sometimes whether this fanaticism had its origin in religious or in political prejudice, since it was possible to attack Restoration comedy or the Italian-French harlequinades from both motives. *The Stage the High-Road to Hell* (1767) and *Another High-Road to Hell* (1767), as their titles show, are of the good old Puritan vintage and contain the usual well-meaning, narrow views on the immorality of *Hamlet*, *Venice Preserved*, and *The Fair Penitent*, or the ordinary strictures on Restoration comedy, ending with the customary impassioned advice to rural husbands and fathers to guard their wives and daughters when strolling players come to the village.

At the end of Anne's reign a patriotic set was opposed to French fashions in general and in particular to French plays, 'for fear of popery and arbitrary power,'[1] but, as we shall see, the unwelcome reception accorded to French companies in the first half of the century was due to other reasons. Beyond question, the salacious savour of Restoration comedy was objectionable to many English playgoers of the thirties, and various issues of the *Grub Street Journal* contain angry protests against plays like *The Old Debauchee*, *The Covent Garden*, with their 'bullies, bawds, sots, rakes, and whores.'[2] That the spectators of two hundred years ago were not squeamish we know from their reception of Carey's *Chrononhotonthologos* at the Haymarket, where a certain obscene ditty 'went off with smiles from the fair and loud applause from the gentlemen.'[3] Later we shall note a marked change in the public attitude to licence on the stage, evidenced by numerous expurgations of Shakespeare and the Restoration dramatists. Looking back, in 1792, the *Thespian Magazine* mentions that *The London Cuckolds*, 'the most rank play that ever succeeded,' kept on appearing 'till taste and Garrick joining, banished it.' About the same time, that is, in the forties, it became no longer possible to show *The Rover*, 'one continued tale of bawdry,' the prime attraction of which was a scene in which a man in his shirt was to be viewed getting into bed with a *fille de joie*.

Yet not even Garrick could quite eradicate the contemporary taste for bawdry on the boards. The French, with their traditional respect for order, relegated obscenity to the theatres of the fair and to private stages, but this was not possible in London owing to the more democratic composition of the audience frequenting the patent

---

[1] *Grub Street Journal*, No. 58 (February 1731).
[2] Ibid. No. 133 (July 1732).   [3] Ibid. No. 221 (March 1734).

theatres. Plays may, of course, be censored by old gentlemen sitting in the licence office, but the 'funny business' of pantomime is a most elusive quantity. The *Connoisseur* [1] objected strongly to the grossness of Harlequin 'endeavouring to creep up Columbine's petticoats and at other times patting her neck and laying his legs upon her lap,' and one can imagine to what lengths this clownery could be carried. Curiously enough, by the way, though we have not taken up this critic's serious suggestion that writers of panto-mime should 'instead of *The Pantheon* or lewd comedies' derive their subjects from 'some old Garland, Moral Ballad, or Penny History Book,' we have adopted his proposal, couched in heavily sarcastic terms, to compose pantomimes about *Puss in Boots* and *Red Riding Hood*. [2]

In both countries it was an axiom that the audience was always right, or rather that the actor was always wrong. The deference shown to the audience by eighteenth-century mummers, in Paris and in London, amounted to self-abasement. It is sickening to read the prologues of English plays and to reflect that men like Garrick had to solemnly mouth these fulsome eulogies glorifying the taste, the intelligence, and the wit of an assembly made up to a great extent of individuals who were neither witty nor intelligent, and who possessed no taste save for the more degraded forms of alcohol. This particular form of humiliation the French actors and authors were spared, but they, too, came in for their full share of the abuse which was freely hurled at players by dissatisfied spec-tators. The root of all this mischief lay in the fact that the eighteenth-century actor was a social outcast. No doubt, both in England and in France, there were great actors and actresses whose company was sought by people of quality, but in these matters one had always to reckon with the dreadful snobbery of the lower classes and the pharisaic morality of the *bourgeoisie*. Even to-day in outlying tracts of England and America actresses are 'no better than they should be' and actors are regarded as vagabonds.

In eighteenth-century France the profession was automatically and permanently in a state of excommunication, and its members could approach the sacraments only as an act of favour and after due petition. Who can ever forget that the frail shell which once housed the purest comic spirit the world has ever known had to

---

[1] 1754.
[2] ''Twould be vastly pretty to see the pasteboard robin redbreasts let down by wires upon the stage to cover the poor innocent babes with their paper leaves.'

be smuggled to the grave by stealth? Long after the death of
Molière, Mlle Clairon, to her immortal fame let it be remembered,
had the courage to present a petition to Louis XV begging him to
remove the intolerable ban. Her advocate, De la Mothe, argued
with great common sense that, since the comedians were His
Majesty's servants, their excommunication was an indirect slight
on the king himself. The only reply was a decree that the memorial
be burnt by the common hangman and that the logical but hapless
De la Mothe be struck off the rolls. Nevertheless it would be
wrong to picture the acting profession in eighteenth-century France
as perpetually conscious of clerical oppression. Periodically there
arose a prelate of the stamp of De Beaumont, Archbishop of Paris,
a jealous guardian of the Faith who insisted on a rigorous application of the Church laws against actors; but, on the whole, the
ecclesiastical authorities were content to ignore occasional breaches
of the edict so long as the principle itself was not questioned, as it
was by Mlle Clairon. Actors were, for example, not allowed to
marry. So the practice was for the player to resign from the
theatre, whereupon the priest made no difficulty about admitting
him to holy wedlock. Next day he would receive an order from the
gentlemen of the bedchamber commanding him to resume his
functions. The famous Molé followed this procedure in 1769, but,
to the general surprise, De Beaumont threatened to annul his
marriage unless he permanently renounced the stage, and, moreover, suspended the *curé* who married him.[1] This from a man
like De Beaumont was a little Tartuffian, for, according to Collé [2]
and other writers, he was a 'gaillard' notorious in his youth for
his love of *parades*, on which, indeed, he was an authority. The
probable explanation is that Molé chose an unlucky moment to
flout Church regulations, since the archbishop was still smarting
from the effects of Rousseau's brilliant letter [3] and, besides, was
anxiously repelling the assaults of the *philosophes* at a critical period
in the history of French Catholicism.

When the French astronomer Lalande visited Covent Garden
Theatre in 1763 he was much impressed by the autocratic behaviour
of the gallery. The play was Mrs. Centlivre's *The Busybody*, and
Lalande notes, in his dry, staccato way: 'Mr. Woodward, an
excellent actor, played Marplot. Many people prefer him to
Garrick in comic parts. Mr. Shuter played Sir Francis Gripe very

---

[1] Grimm's *Correspondance* (1769).   [2] *Origine de la Parade.*
[3] *Lettre à Christophe de Beaumont, archévêque de Paris* (1763).

well. There are a great many changes of scenery and some agreeable dances. They played the pantomime of *Arlequin's Statue*: ended at ten, began at half past six. The theatre is wider but not so long as the Paris one. One hears the actors better and their acting is freer, more varied, and more individual. A great deal of barking and howling, throwing of orange peel at a man whose face displeased the gallery. The gallery controlled the acting and thanked the players. They sent off certain actors who were coming on so as to have Woodward's prologue.' [1] This was at a time, too, when, owing to the prestige of Garrick, much had been done to protect the actor and establish order in the house. What conditions had been earlier in the century we can surmise from sundry incidents related in the press and in private memoirs. When Macklin, in 1743, quarrelled with Fleetwood of Drury Lane, his friends for several nights organized riots and, defying Fleetwood's gang of paid bruisers, so interfered with proceedings that Macklin was reinstated. Such claques existed in Paris, but they were employed by authors, not by actors, and, as the pit was surrounded by soldiers, their activities were limited to applause and *sifflets* under the direction of an appointed leader. Voltaire in his early days had often a *chef de claque*, and Beaumarchais's Figaro speaks of these lusty mercenaries with great hands like paddles, who could make or mar a first night. The ineffable Joseph Andrews, it will be remembered, enjoyed quite a reputation in the footmen's gallery at Drury Lane as a fomenter of disturbances. That was before the famous riot of 5th May 1737, caused by the abolition of a custom introduced by Rich, who had allowed the footmen of gentlemen in the house free admission to the gallery. On this occasion the offended flunkeys, notwithstanding the presence of the king, who happened to be at the play, stormed the theatre and threatened to set fire to it. By the prompt action of a Colonel Eliot, the ringleaders were arrested and transported, but for three days the town blazed with excitement. [2] The same Rich, incidentally, was wellnigh killed in 1721 at his Lincoln's Inn Fields theatre by a nobleman. This gentleman, who, says Genest, [3] had been drunk for six years, was remonstrated with by the manager for crossing the stage during the performance, and at once prepared to run him through the body. A fracas broke out, during which the theatre was completely

---

[1] F. C. Green, 'The Journal of Lalande,' *Hist. Teacher's Miscellany*, September 1926.
[2] See *Correspondence of Mrs. Delaney*.   [3] *Some Account of the English Stage*, vol. iii.

wrecked and the military called in.   As a result a permanent guard
was established.   However, as the sentinels were few in number
and invariably lounged in front of the stage, their sole use seems to
have been to obstruct the view of the audience.

The scandalous outburst provoked by the appearance, in
November 1745, of a French troupe at the Haymarket, almost
became an international affair.   The details are curious.   Jean
Monnet, a well-known French impresario, who later founded the
Opéra comique and, by the way, was official pimp to the Duke
of Gloucester on the latter's unofficial trips to Paris, was invited
by Rich to bring a company of French players to the Haymarket.
Subsidized by various English noblemen, he opened in London
with a company which included elements from the *Comédie
française*.   One of these, Desormes, has left us, in a letter addressed
to Fréron, the editor of the *Année littéraire*, a very full account of
what occurred, with facts not cited in the English journals of the
day.   It seems that several English actors, mostly sons of French
Huguenot refugees, had been refused permission to play in Paris,
not because they were foreigners, but because they proposed
showing an execrable translation of Gay's *Beggar's Opera*.   'Now,'
argues Desormes, 'because French taste could not tolerate a farce
into which enter highway robbers, thief-catchers and trulls, and
other such persons, can one reasonably attribute this refusal to
national prejudice?   Had the French declined to accept a play
by Otway or Shakespeare, that might have been cited as a case
in point.'

At the first performance, an energetic cabal struck up a song
with the refrain: 'We don't want French players.'   Volleys of
missiles were hurled upon the stage, and one actress was struck on
the breast by two lighted candles.   Some English gentlemen, taking
the side of the players, dashed into the gallery among the rioters,
and after a scuffle in which candlesticks, pocket-knives, sheets of
iron, and wigs were used as weapons, Monnet's allies won the day.
At the second performance the rowdies again advanced, only to
be repulsed by a brewer who, at the head of a *posse* of butchers,
worked prodigies in defence of the French.   Monnet says, and no
one will doubt it, that meanwhile the terrified actresses took refuge
in the boxes, where they were reassured by some gallant English
officers.   The affair became a political one, and Lord Trentham
lost a by-election because he would not side with the mob against
the French players.   Poor Monnet, though Garrick got up a benefit

for him, was dunned by his own troupe and spent six months in a debtor's prison. Curiously enough, he remained a staunch admirer of the English.

The whole affair furnishes an interesting example of the chauvinism of the English eighteenth-century mob, which was then, as now, easily excited by the yellow press. The *Daily Advertiser*, indeed, claimed to see in the sending of French players to London a sinister move on the part of the French Government to sap the moral fibre of the English before undertaking their conquest by military methods! Desormes advances another reason for popular dissatisfaction. Having consulted various Englishmen who had lived in France, he was told that modern French comedy made them yawn; the new plays were difficult to understand and were not appreciated. Monnet, in relying upon his aristocratic protectors, overlooked the fact that the majority of English admirers of French comedy had been brought up in the cult of Molière's *comédie de caractère* by the French Protestants who took refuge in London after the revocation of the Edict of Nantes. Desormes very sensibly adds: 'Might it not be, sir, because the comedies of to-day are too subtle, too devoid of *action*, and deal only with a few ephemeral nuances peculiar to people of high society: whereas Molière presented general vices and foibles applicable to all nations and all classes?' Desormes pays our nation a compliment which, I fear, is undeserved. There were, as we shall see, instances in the eighteenth century where *French* playgoers got excited over questions of literary taste, and the considerations he mentions may have influenced the attitude of a minority in the Haymarket audience. But the mass did not riot for this reason. It was because England had just emerged from a war with France—peace had been signed in February—and, above all, because it felt obscurely that the 'furriner' was, as usual, robbing the English working man! A fair-minded writer pointed out that English pantomimes advertised by Francisque at the Parisian fairs were always enthusiastically received by the French lower classes; but his voice was drowned in the howls of the many.[1] The *British Magazine*,[2] though condemning the excesses of these anti-gallicans, observed with some justice that the Licensing Act limited the number of London playhouses to two, and asked why the law should be broken for the benefit of foreign actors. Unfortunately, it was always easy in troublous times to arouse and exploit the latent

[1] *An Impartial Statement of the Case of the French Comedians.*   [2] 1749.

patriotism of the London mob: the prologues of eighteenth-century plays and the plays themselves reek of jingoism. On the eve of the Seven Years' War Foote shamelessly commercialized the prevailing anti-French spirit in his *Englishman Returned from Paris*, for which he was very properly rebuked by the *Critical Review* [1] and the *Journal étranger*. [2] At a command performance of the *Chinese Festival* in 1755 a serious riot occurred owing to the presence in the cast of some French dancers, and, although the king was present, the gallery and pit did great damage to the theatre and nearly burned Garrick's residence. Happily the battle soon became merely one of words, and numerous pamphlets for and against the players were printed.

In the annals of the eighteenth-century French stage, it is difficult to find parallel examples of hooliganism in the audiences. One real riot, however, broke out in Molière's time. It was started by the king's household troops, who murdered the theatre porter and nearly massacred the actors because the privilege of free admission had been withdrawn. Louis XIV, however, dealt swiftly with the offenders and, in a royal ordinance, provided against the repetition of such scandals. Though no servants in livery were admitted to the theatre, save to hold boxes against the arrival of their masters, the pages and lackeys of princely houses appear to have given some trouble. At least this is what one gathers from an ordinance of 1769 relegating them to the parterre, and forbidding 'those who are present at these performances, and particularly those who are in the parterre, to commit any breach of the peace either on entering or on leaving, to shout or make a noise before the play begins and during the *entr'actes*, to whistle, make cat-calls, to keep their hats on their heads or to interrupt the actors during the performance in any way or under any pretext whatever.'

There was, of course, no gallery in the Parisian houses and, as Mercier points out, the mob did not frequent the royal theatres. However, in the parterre, which accommodated some six hundred standing and, says Riccoboni, 'bien pressés,' there were always obstreperous elements ever ready to give tongue. The same writer [3] suggests that in order to prevent disturbances it would be better if, as at the fair theatres or those of London, seats were provided in the parterre. This had been the case in the seventeenth century. But, compared to our English gallery, the French parterre seems

[1] 1756.   [2] 1756.
[3] *Réflexions historiques et critiques sur les différents théâtres de l'Europe* (1738).

to have been a good-humoured assembly, expressing its disapproval
by witticisms rather than by hurling missiles on the stage. When,
in 1751, the municipal police were replaced in Parisian theatres
by regular troops, seasoned playgoers like Collé were disgusted:
'This produces great tranquillity but casts a certain gloom over
the theatre which makes me fear sometimes that I am in some
foreign country. I miss our old French gaiety; the parterre has
a German air nowadays. These French guards are too pedantic
in their way of controlling a lively nation like ours, and then,
I don't know, but all this business has an appearance of servitude
and slavery and I don't like being annoyed like this in a place of
public amusement. Everything here has a nasty air of despotism
even in the smallest things. We are no longer allowed to feel
we are men.'[1]

A fertile source of disorder in the theatres of both London and
Paris was the presence of spectators on the stage. Every French
author alludes to the practice in order to condemn it, though
Riccoboni, whilst remarking that it interferes with the action of
the play, infers that the stage illusion was not impaired because
the spectators were so used to the custom.[2] Voltaire, on the other
hand, attributed the failure of his early plays to the lack of a clear
stage, and, curiously enough, contrasts the French with the English
practice, although from many sources it is certain that at Drury
Lane and Covent Garden there were often seats on the stage.
The *Connoisseur*, for instance,[3] wishes that the fops would leave the
performers a clear space on the boards, and an anonymous author
expresses the general feeling when he writes: 'No *Remonstrance*, I
doubt, will prevail upon the *Smarts* who oblige the *Town* with their
whole *Lengths* at the *Side-Scenes* to take their pretty Figures away.
To tell them that they take off the Effect of the Scenery, that they
make a motley figure among actors dressed in character; that they
discompose the performers by stopping up their entry and retreat;
that they interrupt the Drama by their giggling and grimace; that
the whole House look on them as a nuisance, and the more discerning
part as coxcombs, would, one think, shame them into decency
and retirement.'[4] In 1737 Garrick refused to take money for stage
seats, and in so doing was simply carrying out a seventeenth-century
regulation, never repealed but never observed, which forbade any
but actors on the stage. He was not successful in removing the

[1] *Journal* (1751).   [2] Op. cit.   [3] 1754.
[4] *Reflections upon Theatrical Expression in Tragedy* (1755).

nuisance till 1762, three years after it was abolished from the *Comédie française*. Barbier, in his *Journal*,[1] comments as follows on this revolution, which had an important influence on the future of French drama. 'In all times there have existed, for the use of spectators on the stage of the *Comédie française*, four rows of benches arranged amphitheatre-wise, on each side, reaching to the level of the boxes and enclosed by a balustrade and a gilt iron railing. At special performances another row of seats was added along the balustrade, whilst in addition there were more than fifty persons without seats who stood at the back of the stage in a semicircle. Usually the stage was occupied by men so that it was much restricted for the acting. To get an actor on the stage the people at the back of it had to make a passage for him. It was improbable that a king, speaking to his confidant, or holding a state council, or a prince conversing in secret with his household, should be surrounded by more than two hundred persons.' He adds: 'The Easter fortnight closure has been extended for three weeks. Work has been going on at the theatre and all the stage seats suppressed; part of the pit has been used to form a parquet holding one hundred and eighty people in addition to the orchestra. The amphitheatre has been made smaller to lengthen the pit.

'On Monday, the 23rd April, a performance was given on the new stage . . . there is no comparison . . . the action of the players is free and the illusion better preserved.'

In both countries the 'bloods' on the stage were a cursed pest. When not quarrelling with the rest of the audience, they meddled with the acting, and in some cases strolled across the stage at critical moments. When Voltaire risked his first ghost on the stage the apparition was observed elbowing its way through a knot of chattering dandies, and evoked shouts of 'Place à l'ombre!' So, too, when at the performance of *Childeric* the messenger struggled to deliver his missive to the king, he was hailed with ironic cries of 'Place au facteur!' It is not, perhaps, surprising that the French tolerated the nuisance for so long, since, owing to their larger stage and the observance of the unity of place, they were less handicapped than the English, who frequently had twenty-four scene-shifts in one play. The actors themselves, however, were really responsible for the persistence of the abuse because they hesitated to offend their wealthy patrons. Indeed, but for the generosity of the Duc de Lauraguais-Brancas, who gave the players

[1] April 1759.

twelve thousand francs, it is doubtful whether they would have instituted the reform of 1759. As a matter of fact, in London and in Paris, the old practice was continued on benefit nights till well into the nineteenth century. By the seventeen-sixties, there is no question, however, that the general desire for more realistic plays was accompanied by an urgent need for more space in which to display the new effects.

The lives of the famous actors and actresses of the age, French and English, have been recounted over and over again. Their loves, their jealousies, their triumphs, their *mots*, true and apocryphal, have been industriously recorded for the benefit of posterity. From the prints, we know how they looked and how they were costumed in their master-roles. In short, we know everything save what really matters—how they acted. Still, though their voices and gestures have faded into an irrevocable past, it is just possible from various references, annoyingly brief no doubt, to form a vague idea of what the eighteenth century understood by dramatic interpretation.

When the Abbé Le Blanc lived in London he saw Garrick and Barry in the much admired quarrel scene from *Julius Caesar*, and compared it to a brawl between street-porters. Garrick, says Davies,[1] never forgave Le Blanc, and on his visit to Paris refused to meet him. The latter, in his well-known *Letters*,[2] expresses his general disappointment with English acting. Our tragic declamation he found languid and, as he shrewdly remarks, since visitors are always apt to think foreign speech much quicker than it is, our tragedy heroes must have drawled most painfully. De Moivre, who knew French classic acting, told Le Blanc that Colley Cibber made the same criticism of the Parisian actors in their rendering of Corneille and Racine; whereupon De Moivre, by maliciously imitating Cibber in *Cato*, proved to him that English tragic declamation was exactly like the doleful cry of a London watchman chanting: 'Past twelve o'clock and a cloudy morning.' Cibber knew the stage of Paris, and, in order to study for the foppish parts in which he excelled, twice went to France to observe the *petit-maître* in his native haunt and, incidentally, to learn from the great veteran, Baron. According to Le Blanc, Cibber understood neither. Baron, like the Parisian fops, talked too fast, or so it seemed to Colley, whose French was none too good. However, says Le Blanc indulgently, his interpretation did well enough for the London tradesmen. Le Blanc's opinion of our comic actors was low: they

[1] *Dramatic Miscellanies.* [2] Op. cit.

lacked French subtlety and sought to convey humour by gestures rather than by inflexions of the voice. Riccoboni, on the other hand,[1] places the Italian and French actors behind ours both in tragedy and comedy. What impressed him deeply was the English attention to realistic detail, particularly in make-up. At Lincoln's Inn Fields, during the English rendering of *Crispin Médecin*, he was amazed to find that the part of the old man was taken by a comedian of twenty-six, whose make-up was so realistic that Mlle Sallé, then dancing at the same theatre, stepped politely aside for fear of knocking the 'old' man down. Our actors, observes Riccoboni, who is an authority on acting, understood the optics of the theatre. He does not use that expression, but it is what he means: 'Ils ont l'art d'enfler, pour ainsi dire, la vérité précisément comme il faut pour le faire paraître dans le lointain à me faire juger que c'est la pure vérité qu'ils m'exposent.'

Realism in acting, as Riccoboni indicates, was differently conceived in London and in Paris. The majority of French audiences, he says, were incapable of appreciating realistic acting, so accustomed were they to declamation. Though they knew that the heroes of classic tragedy were men with real passions, they yet expected from their actors a traditional, exaggerated, and unreal mode of speech, gesture, and behaviour. He adds: 'Almost all foreigners who hear tragic declamation for the first time are excessively disgusted by it. . . . I met several Frenchmen in Paris who abhor this sort of declamation and never go to see tragedy.' Riccoboni, as an Italian, was perhaps inclined to exaggerate the importance of pantomime in acting, but he is not alone in condemning the sing-song recitative of the *Comédie française*. The provincial heroine of Bridard de la Garde's novel of theatre manners [2] describes it as 'a peculiar method of pronunciation whereby, making the voice, so to speak, trot unevenly from syllable to syllable, the actor reins it in regularly at every alexandrine. The result appeared so queer to me that involuntarily I conceived a burlesque idea of it. I am sorry, however, that I could not find any pleasure in it, having noticed that the actors who most carefully observed this practice are the most applauded.' Mallet-Duclairon,[3] writing some years later, states that, particularly in comedy, but also in tragedy, the *Comédie française* is breaking with tradition. So 'abstract' are the rules of tragic declamation, so varied, he says,

---

[1] Op. cit.   [2] *Les Lettres de Thérèse, etc.* (1737).
[3] *Sur la Connaissance des Théâtres français* (1751).

are the recent interpretations of Corneille and Racine, that it is impossible to indicate now what method of interpretation is the most artistic. This revolution in the acting no doubt reflects the changes in drama itself, foreshadowed in the work of La Chaussée and Voltaire. The comic actors are clearly disconcerted by the crumbling of the old barrier which formerly distinctly separated comedy from tragedy. 'Since this queer taste for whining comedies has been introduced,' writes Mallet-Duclairon, 'the actors do not know how to act them; as they approach more closely to the tragic than the comic they have adopted all the tones and gestures of the former.' The French comic actors had never attempted to improve on the method of interpretation consecrated by Molière, but now, confronted by a greater variety of characters, which were no longer conceived with Molièresque vigour and clarity, they were obliged to change their style of acting in order to interpret roles less powerful but more subtly nuanced. That they succeeded we know from the applause given to Grandval, Sarrazin, Gaussin, and Clairon.

About the same time, David Garrick revolutionized English acting, not merely because he was a great actor but because he was a great producer. Vilified by the press, mercilessly attacked by scurrilous and interested pamphleteers, sneered at by his colleagues, he yet carried his reforms into every department of the theatre. From Murphy and Davies it is clear that Garrick raised the morale of the profession by his own prestige and by improving the economic and social status of the actor. His green-room was a virtual school of acting, where men like Bayes, Ryan, and Hall were shamed out of their old stupid ranting ways by their manager's diabolic gift of mimicry. Garrick's rendering of Richard III, a role in which Colley Cibber was supposed to have attained the acme of perfection, struck London with the force of a revelation. Even Pope crept from his grotto at Twickenham to see Garrick and to add his quota to the general flood of admiration. Every new role brought fresh proof of his originality. London and Paris quickly realized that here was an actor who had the genius to submerge his personality in that of the parts he interpreted. Wilks, Betterton, and Quin, great actors all, never succeeded in making the audience forget Wilks, Betterton, and Quin. Garrick *was* Richard or Macbeth or Lear. The greatest tribute one can pay him is to say that he tried to practise already what Diderot later preached in his admirable *Paradoxe sur le Comédien*.[1] He revealed that the art of the actor lies

[1] Circulated in manuscript in the eighteenth century but not published till 1830.

not in mere surrender to emotion; that, on the contrary, dramatic interpretation is the result of a long and careful study of the emotions to be portrayed on the stage. Garrick, I think, like Diderot, believed that the player can never afford to *feel* the passions which he expresses, though his business is to give the audience the illusion that he does. What little we can glean about Garrick's methods seems to indicate that he would have endorsed these words of Diderot's: 'What confirms me in my opinion is the unevenness of actors who act with their emotions. Do not expect from them any unity whatever: their acting is alternately strong or weak, hot and cold, insipid and sublime. They will fail to-morrow in the speech in which to-day they excelled; on the other hand, they will excel where yesterday they failed. On the contrary, the actor who plays, after reflection, from a study of human nature, from the constant emulation of an ideal model, from imagination, from memory, will be one and the same at all the performances, always equally perfect: all has been weighed, combined, learned, ordered, in his mind; in his declamation there is neither monotony nor dissonance.' Now, everything that has come down to us about Garrick the man, seems to indicate that Garrick the actor must have belonged to the category admired by Diderot.

'The generation of players that immediately preceded the present,' writes one English critic in 1754,[1] 'prided themselves on what they called *fine speaking*: the emotions of the soul were disregarded for a distinct delivery, and with them, as Mr. Johnson has observed of some tragic writers:

> Declamation roar'd, while Passion slept.

And indeed, to this uninteresting taste for acting we may partly attribute that enervate way of writing, so much in vogue among the *Frenchified* playwrights of those times; since nothing could be so well suited to the mouths of those actors as golden lines, round periods, florid descriptions, and a passionate amplification of sentiment. This *false majesty* was for a long time as much a characteristic of tragedy as the plumed hat and full-bottomed periwig.'

Of the rules which for many writers still governed dramatic composition there will be much to say in a later chapter. Meanwhile, we are reminded by at least one writer that acting also had its traditional rules.[2] The following hints upon the 'Management of the Feet and Legs' must have been a real help to beginners.

---

[1] *Connoisseur.*   [2] *Reflections upon Theatrical Expression* (1755).

'In *Astonishment* and *Surprise* arising from *Terror* the *left leg* is drawn back to some distance from the other: under the same Affection of the Mind, but resulting from an *unhop'd for Meeting* with a beloved Object, the *right leg* is advanced to some distance before the left. *Impatience* and *Regret* at being detected in an iniquitous Design may be heightened by shuffling of the *Feet* without moving from the *Spot*.'

Goldsmith [1] commented on the stiffness and formality of our English acting, and the *Connoisseur* [2] notes the same uniformity and the same rigidity in the interpretation of Shakespeare. 'Every line of Othello (a character remarkable for variety of passions) was drawn out in the same pompous manner.' However, by the late fifties, no doubt owing to the example set by Garrick, the old mechanical, strutting manner had begun to disappear. But bad actors are damnably fertile in discovering new ways of acting badly, and with the growing taste for melodramatic tragedies there arose a taste for convulsive acting, for 'unnatural startings, roarings, and whinings': a vice from which not even Garrick was quite free. 'The old actors used to strut with one leg before the other and wave their arms in a continual see-saw. The present ones go in for convulsed gestures as if afflicted with St. Vitus's dance,' and, adds the *Connoisseur*, 'actresses still roll the eye, stretch up the neck, and heave the chest.' What fortunes they would make to-day in Hollywood!

The writer just quoted, who is probably George Colman, thinks 'that the manner of elocution in a tragedy should not, on either hand, be more remote from our natural way of expressing ourselves than blank verse (which is the only proper measure for tragedy) is from prose.' It is interesting to compare with this the view expressed by a French actor, J. H. D'Hannetaire, [3] whose book on acting is little known but merits a brief resurrection. Wisely refusing to discuss the vexed question: 'Should tragedy be declaimed?' since 'several mistake it for that turgid recitative, that chant, as unreasonable as it is monotonous, which, not being dictated by nature, simply stuns the ear and never speaks to the heart or intellect,' D'Hannetaire proceeds: 'But whilst maintaining that tragic poetry cannot be recited too naturally, connoisseurs are careful not to proscribe majesty of utterance when it is appropriate to use it.

[1] *Remarks on our Theatres.* [2] 1754.
[3] *Observations sur l'art du Comédien* (1775). First published in 1764. In 1775 D'Hannetaire sent a very respectful letter to Garrick begging him to read his book on acting, and recommended the second edition as the only good one.

Too pompous recitation should be avoided wherever sentiments are to be expressed. It must be avoided also in simple narrative and in purely argumentative speeches.' It is clear from D'Hannetaire's remarks on gesture that the effect aimed at by French tragedians was one of great dignity and restraint. 'The frequent use of passionate gestures, not being admitted in *noble* comedy, should be still less so in tragedy. As much as a nobleman is above a man of the people, so much a hero is above a man who is merely a nobleman. If the latter is obliged to keep a certain respect for his rank, it is a duty still more indispensable for the other to maintain, by a grave exterior, the high idea we have of his character.' In passionate love-scenes, however, our author admits that tragedy demands a great many gestures but 'perhaps fewer than actors are accustomed to employ.' Certain of D'Hannetaire's criticisms give us an idea of how tragedy was usually acted in the France of his day, for D'Hannetaire knew the provinces as well as the capital. A common vice was the sounding of the final consonant of words like *état*, *détruit*, *effet*, and *horreur* as if they were followed by a voiced *e* ; or again, the sounding of the final *e* in words like *hyménée*, *envie*, *destinée*, a practice absolutely unknown off the stage. Those of us who have heard actors of the Irving school will understand what D'Hannetaire means by the *hoquet*, or hiccup, which the eighteenth-century French actor used to introduce at the end of each alexandrine, 'a vicious and monotonous aspiration by which they fondly believe that they can make up for their lack of soul or bowels, and which is no less painful to the player than disagreeable to the hearer.' An advanced school of French actors held the heretical view that poetry, either in tragedy or in comedy, should be spoken like prose, measure and rhyme being avoided as unnatural. La Noue, in fact, used to get the verse parts written out like prose for his troupe. One of the reasons, indeed, why the monotonous chanting recitative was so long retained on the French eighteenth-century stage was the reluctance of the dramatist to abandon verse, which the actors liked because it was more easily memorized than prose. Like one veteran, described by D'Hannetaire, many were lulled by the cadence of the couplets into a complete disregard of the sense. So, like this old actor, if one happened to forget one's lines it was easy to bridge the gap thus :

> Quand le sort ennemi m'aurait jeté plus bas,
> Vaincu, persécuté, *tati tatou, tata.*

In both countries the demand for more realistic or less conventional acting was accompanied by a new attitude towards stage decoration. In France, the rapid rise of the *drame* necessitated scenic reforms: the modest requirements of classic tragedy, with its inevitable temple or palace exterior, being now inadequate. But in London, where frequent changes of scenery had always been the rule, the chief need was not for more elaborate scenery or costume but for scenery and costume with some sort of relationship to the play, the period, and the characters. It is easy to be jocular about early eighteenth - century stage productions: it is less easy to be accurate and to avoid exaggeration. The French audience of those days saw nothing humorous in a Phèdre attired in the full court dress of the period, an Oreste in a short kilt, buskins, hose, and pasteboard helmet with nodding plumes. Nor did their London contemporaries appreciate Macbeth any less because he appeared in the dress uniform of a Hanoverian officer, or smile at Hamlet—this was to emphasize his feigned madness—strutting about with one black stocking rolled half-way down his leg to reveal the white one underneath.[1] However, as a reflection of the growing cult of experimental science, there arose in the theatre a desire for historical accuracy, or, as the Romantics later called it, local colour. As usual, both schools, the old and the new, were equally logical and right. If we regard the heroes of Racine and Shakespeare as incarnating passions or ideas that are universal and eternal, it is perfectly rational to demand that their interpreters should wear modern dress, as was the stage custom two hundred years ago. But, having modernized one element in the author's medium of expression, we are logically obliged to carry the reforms farther and to alter his original idiom so as to conform to present-day usage, as, for example, has been done in the revised version of the Bible. Otherwise, as we have recently seen, one anachronism is merely substituted for another. Hamlet, dinner-jacket by Poole and revolver by Smith and Wesson, is heard expressing himself in Elizabethan English. All that matters, of course, is the illusion of truth: happily the stage is not concerned with absolutes. The Parisians who went to *Tiridate* and saw Lecouvreur in the exaggerated panniers of 1727, like their children who years later saw the *Orphelin de la Chine*, with Le Kain as a Tartar chief dressed in a crimson and gold tunic and a head-dress of eleven nodding plumes playing against a Clairon resplendent in white satin with coloured *polonaise* of gauze, were satisfied that these costumes

[1] *Connoisseur* (1754).

appropriately expressed their idea of regal grandeur. If Tartars did not dress that way, they ought to have. After all Voltaire, who was the author, made no objection.

But there always is a Partridge at every play. If he is not cavilling at a perfectly good 'blood-boltered' ghost in armour there is always something else. So, for instance, we find a fellow writing in 1755: 'I have seen an *HERO*, whether *Greek* or *Roman*, I forget, who is to make nothing of *chining* whomever comes in his way with an *effeminate Plenitude* of *cherry-coloured Ribband* depending from the Tail of his Peruke; while the Princely Heroine of the same country has tottered in *State* upon a pair of *FRENCH HEELS*.' [1] With the same unbridled passion for accuracy he adds: 'If the *Streets*, *Buildings*, *Rooms* and *Furniture*, *Gardens*, *Views* of the *Country*, etc., be executed in the Taste of the Country where the Scene of the Action of the Play lies, and the *Keeping* of *Perspective* be *good*, the whole HOUSE never fails to give the most audible Evidence of their Satisfaction.' The *Connoisseur* [2] grudgingly allows that 'the hero now seldom sweats beneath the weight of a nodding plume of swan's feathers or has his face half hid with an enormous bush of horse-hair.' But weeping princesses still entered escorted by two mourning damsels in black; and heroines still dragged yards of black velvet train held up by little pages who, in the emotional passages, had to whisk about with some agility. Having once tasted realism, the English audiences became insatiable. Garrick put on a tin-foil waterfall with light effects and drew crowds to Drury Lane, whilst the *World* [3] humorously remarked that the 'pantomime of the genii narrowly escaped being damned by my Lady Maxim's observing that the brick-kiln was horridly executed and did not smell at all like one.' The same writer, however, reminded these innovators that it was Colley Cibber who first introduced the cult for naturalism by bringing some very personable geese into *Caesar in Egypt*.

In France the realists met with greater opposition. .Even Voltaire, who was in many respects something of a revolutionary, refused to allow Le Kain to drape the stage in black or to erect a scaffold for *Tancrède*. At the *Comédie italienne* in 1753, Mme Favart excited murmurs in the audience by appearing with a serge dress, hair in plaits, bare-armed, in sabots, and wearing a gold cross, as Bastienne in a parody of Rousseau's *Devin du Village*. But the Abbé Voisenon stilled the mutterings by exclaiming:

[1] *Reflections upon Theatrical Expression.*   [2] 1754.   [3] 1753.

'These sabots will pay for the actors' shoes.' Beaumarchais, in his *Eugénie*, gave elaborate stage directions, and elicited this jeer from the *Année littéraire*: [1] 'You are making a fool of the public, Sir, by entering into these wretched details as to *costume*. . . . Does the success of a good play depend on puerilities of this sort . . . does M. de Beaumarchais seriously believe that the audience will derive any pleasure from seeing a lackey yawning on a sofa, a man looking for a key in his vest-pocket, another smoking a pipe, etc.? Our theatre does not need these monkey tricks of which the Italians and the actors of the fair have so long been in possession: this sort of thing is plunging the French stage back into the low, popular manner of its infancy.' The writer,[2] as was his invariable habit, imputed these and all other new ideas to the sinister influence of the *philosophes*. So, when Lemierre's *Guillaume Tell* was produced in 1766, Fréron, commenting sarcastically on the Alpine setting, remarked: 'Formerly the stage used to represent a public square, a palace, or a temple. We have become contemptuous of this local pomp; this, perhaps, is one of the fruits of our new philosophy.' He was not so wide of the mark, since it was precisely the influence of experimentalists like Diderot that created the new vogue for realism.

It is evident from the tenor of D'Hannetaire's observations that, in the early seventies, although tragedy was now produced with an eye to local colour, very little had been done to reform either costume or setting in comedy. Molière was still played in modern dress except for the farcical characters, who retained the costume of Molière's day. But the heroes of classical tragedy no longer extinguished the candles overhead with their nodding plumes or played Mithidrates in breeches, buckles, and garters. With a clear stage it was possible also to provide more elaborate settings, as had always been the case at the *Opéra*. The introduction of footlights and reflectors further heightened the illusion of reality. 'How persuade oneself,' says D'Hannetaire, looking back at the old days, 'that one was in a garden, in the open country, or in Agamemnon's camp, when candles suspended from the ceiling greeted the eyes and noses of the spectators. With what face could an actor say in the midst of these guttering dips:

'Enfin ce jour pompeux, cet heureux jour, nous luit.'

De la Coste, a most alert observer [3] who was in London in 1783

---

[1] Vol. viii (1767).
[2] Fréron, the great anti-*philosophe* and arch-enemy of Voltaire.
[3] *Voyage philosophique d'Angleterre* (1786).

and 1784, has left us a very valuable impression of stage conditions at Drury Lane. For the costumes and settings he has nothing but praise. The scenery is varied, beautiful, and life-like, but, curiously enough, despite the progress made by other European countries and the perfection attained by England in the mechanical arts, the sets are still man-handled, so that the illusion is constantly destroyed by the crashing of stage furniture. The theatre itself he considers unworthy of a great metropolis. 'The boxes are flimsy, the decoration poor, and the ensemble has neither the gravity nor the dignity that befits a public edifice. The seating is not very different from that in our little boulevard theatres: a pit with benches, three tiers of boxes at the sides, and three galleries at the back. As for the tone, that of our fair booths is infinitely more decent. People sing, whistle, howl, drink, eat oranges and throw down the peel, without, by the way, any intention of insulting the person who gets it in the face. And nobody objects.'

La Coste has some interesting things to say about our acting. 'They (the players) almost always enter from the first wing, which is a door, and often together, from the two opposite sides, without anything previously having indicated the reason for their meeting at a given place. At the last couplet of the scene they begin to move backwards towards the entrance, if they have to leave separately; or shuffle towards it sideways if they have to leave together. The great art in these exits is to calculate the steps to be made so that the last word is articulated and heard by the spectator at the moment when the latter loses sight of the actor. Then you hear the sound of a bell warning the actors who are to come on, and they, after leaving the stage deserted for some minutes, enter like those whom they have replaced and leave in the same way. This casts a chill over the action, which is not dispelled even by the sublime monologues and really pathetic scenes with which the English theatre abounds. They seem to be ignorant of dumb-show, a defect all the more striking since their faces are extremely mobile; and their grimaces always exaggerate the sentiment and thought, because the facial play does not accord with the movements of their bodies, which are rarely natural, smacking always of study before the mirror, and are never agreeable. As for the asides, they are ridiculous to the last degree. When one of the actors wants to speak to himself, the others obligingly guess the fact and obligingly withdraw—sometimes to the back of the stage, where they walk to and fro, returning when the speech is

over. Finally, so ignorant are the English actors of the delicate
civility which constitutes good manners, that when one of the inter-
locutors leaves the stage, if he is not near the exit he takes the
shortest cut and, disregarding sex or rank, passes clumsily in front
of those he is leaving.'

If La Coste found our players lacking in *savoir-vivre*, English
visitors to Paris blamed the French actors for their excessive politeness, which, they claimed, made their acting unrealistic. Before
the present obsession for local colour it used to strike the French
spectator as quite natural to see Horace gravely don his gloves,
sheathe his dagger, and gallantly assist Camille to her feet when
she tripped over her pannier. An English visitor in 1772 observed
that 'the actors never forget they are acting . . . should despair
plunge a dagger into the hero's heart he must not fall; for the sake
of decency he is supported bolt upright even after he is dead.'
On the London stage, on the contrary, corpses thudded nightly
on the boards, but to prepare the audience for what Goldsmith
calls 'bloody work at Drury Lane,' a special carpet was always
laid down. D'Hannetaire infers that the French considered it
rather bad form to act seated, and puts in a timid plea for chairs
for tired actresses, especially 'in conversation supposed to last for
hours. It is an experiment which might be easily tried in the
next play.'

To imagine the eighteenth-century stage we must readjust our
twentieth-century minds to a smaller focus. The grandeur, the
light, and the dazzling colour of our modern spectacles could not
have been conceived by our ancestors even in their wildest dreams.
The French of those days were inordinately proud of the splendour
of their *Opéra*. On its stage, unhampered by unity of place, they
could indulge in an orgy of spectacular scenic effects. One went
to the *Opéra*, not so much for the music and singing, which were
bad, or even for the ballets, though French dancers had a European
reputation, but for the scenery, the costumes, and the *machines*, or
mechanical effects. Garrick, however, was not much impressed
by a visit he made to the *Opéra* in 1751. 'A very *raw* entertainment,' he notes, 'the scenes well conducted and had a good effect,
the habits seemingly rich, the singing abominable to *me*, and the
dancing very indifferent.' [1] But this was before the fire of 1762,
and even patriotic Parisians like Barbier were ill-pleased with the
old house. If we make due allowance for Rousseau's well-known

[1] *Diary* (ed. Oxford Press).

C

hatred of French music, the impression which he has left us, in *La Nouvelle Héloïse*, of the Paris *Opéra*, is most probably what ours would be if some necromancer's wand could whisk us suddenly back to the France of 1760.[1] 'Imagine to yourself,' writes his hero, Saint-Preux, 'the inside of a large box; about fifteen feet wide,[2] and long in proportion: this box is the stage; on each side are placed screens, at different distances, on which the objects of the scene are coarsely painted. Beyond that is a great curtain, bedaubed in the same manner, which extends from one side of the stage to the other and is generally cut through to represent caves in the earth and openings in the heavens, as the perspective requires. . . . The skies are represented by a parcel of bluish rags, hung up on lines or poles, like wet linen at the washerwoman's. The sun —for he is sometimes represented here—is a large candle in a lanthorn. The chariots of the gods and goddesses are made of four bits of wood nailed together in the form of a square and hung upon a cord like a swing. Across the middle is a board on which the deity sits astraddle. The bottom of this machine is illuminated by two or three stinking, unsnuffed candles which, as often as the celestial personage shakes his wings, smoke him deliciously. As in London, there are numerous trap-doors which fly open to emit devils, but the monsters are much more terrifying than our English ones—dragons, lizards, tortoises, crocodiles, and great toads, all of which stalk or crawl about the stage and bring one in mind of the temptation of Saint Anthony.' The performance itself is awe-inspiring. Imagine an orchestra and chorus, one hundred strong, the singers 'throwing themselves into convulsions, as it were to rend their lungs with squeaking . . . with fists clenched against stomachs, heads thrown back, faces red, veins swelled, breasts heaving like a pair of bellows,' and, like some infernal accompaniment, 'the continual clashing of jarring instruments attended by the drawling and perpetual groans of the bass'; finally, when a lively air is struck up, the whole audience 'thundering with its feet.'

[1] Several contemporary English journals translated and published Rousseau's famous letter, but, as they made no acknowledgment of their debt to the author, the casual reader is led to believe that he is reading the impressions of an English visitor to Paris. The abridged translation which is printed above I have taken from the *Macaroni* of May 1773.

[2] At first sight this seems very exiguous until we remember that it represents the distance between the *front* screens only. As these screens were arranged echelonwise, the width of the back of the stage might well have been almost forty-five feet. We know definitely, from the *Mercure* of 1770, that the stage of the rebuilt *Opéra*, which was considered vastly bigger than the old one, was only thirty-six feet wide in front.

CHAPTER II

IN no form of literature is the relationship between art and philosophy more clearly visible than in drama. Yet it would be a serious error to regard philosophy as the mother of drama; to seek, for instance, the genesis of Racine's *Phèdre* in Descartes's *Discourse on Method*, or even in his *Treatise on the Passions*. For although it frequently happens that the philosopher thus precedes the artist, nay, sometimes, as in the case of Bergson and Proust, appears to anticipate him, yet philosophy and literature are only interdependent: they represent, not cause and effect, but rather two effects of a common cause. Philosopher and artist, each in his peculiar idiom, is striving to express what we vaguely call the spirit of his times. Each, by his unique genius, divines the trend and contours of the contemporary mind as it drifts with deceptive aimlessness in a direction which, he can but hope, will lead to a closer vision of universal realities. Descartes's admirable *Discourse* is a valuable chart revealing very clearly the course laid by the seventeenth-century French mind in its voyage towards truth. But the same course may be discerned, though it is not so clearly demarked, in Corneille's later tragedies and in all the dramatic writings of Racine. Both of these giants, in their effort to approach reality, really adopt the method of thinking and of feeling which we call Cartesian, though it is actually the reflection of the mind of an era. The England of Shakespeare's time, if we except Bacon, produced no philosopher whom we can compare in originality to Descartes: yet the structure and the purpose of Shakespearian tragedy, so far as we have been able to divine it, reveals a way of thinking, an attitude towards life, which, although never formulated in any book comparable to the *Discourse on Method*, reflects, as does Cartesianism, the trend of a national or racial consciousness. It is the objective, experimental method which later led to the discoveries of Newton and of Locke; a process of reasoning by which principles or laws are induced from the consideration of observed facts. And this mode of reasoning was never codified or analysed with Cartesian thoroughness, for Bacon's *Novum Organum* is a superficial work, the texture of which must appear very loose to admirers of the *Discourse on Method*. Nevertheless, it satisfies our English temperament, and we have not, so far, betrayed any serious desire to abandon the Baconian approach to life.

In France, at the dawn of the eighteenth century, the Cartesian mode of thought was still in general favour—that *a priori* or hypothetical approach to natural truths which, as someone said, moves from the centre to the circumference, from the principle to illustrative facts. But in the new century there were many who, like Voltaire, were violently attracted by the doctrines of Newton and Locke and became openly contemptuous of Cartesian metaphysics. Still, though they rejected Descartes because of his *tourbillons*, they long continued to respect his *Discourse on Method*, partly because it was now marked with the seal of tradition, partly because they found it easier to erect their new religious, economic, and political systems on a purely rational basis than to face the laborious task of collecting the masses of facts from which the experimentalist induces his principles. Nevertheless, the adoption of Newton's findings meant that his method must eventually supersede that of Descartes: but, like all intellectual revolutions, this change proceeded very gradually. As a result, its repercussions upon literature were also gradual, as will be evident when we survey the evolution of eighteenth-century French drama. What must first be realized, if we are to understand the essential difference between French and English tragedy and comedy in this period, is the original dissimilarity of two mental attitudes, one of which produced a Bacon and a Shakespeare; the other a Descartes and a Racine.

The history of French literature in general since the French Revolution seems at first sight to indicate the overthrow of Cartesian rationalism and the triumph of empiricism. But is this really so? Balzac, no doubt, in theory is a Newtonian. 'Donnez-moi un gant et je reconstitue l'homme.' Still, there are novels of Balzac where, as in Hugo, Sand, and other Romantics, observation merely subserves creative intuition and illustrates preconceived ideas or principles; where the character does not necessarily evolve from the mass of realistic details presented; where, in short, it is the man who really explains the glove, or where the glove is simply a scrap of what the Romantics called local colour. The nineteenth-century Naturalists, for all their fine pretence of scientific objectivism, never advanced beyond the elementary stages of a method for which

they were temperamentally ill-adapted. They observed a corner
of the world with myopic minuteness but lacked the genius to rise
to any generalizations on life; and it is doubtful, in view of the
narrowness of their zone of observation, whether such generalizations would be of interest. Flaubert nearly exhausted himself in
a patient effort to approach human truths by empirical means and
triumphed over his temperament in *L'Éducation sentimentale*. Stendhal, on the other hand, like Racine and Proust, moves from the
idea to facts, but, unlike Racine or Proust, was prepared to admit
ideas, and therefore characters, which, from the traditional French
point of view, are irrational. To this we owe Julien Sorel and
the Countess Sanseverina. The Stendhalian mind is a blend of
Shakespeare and Racine, disconcerting alike to the English and the
French. Zola spent a lifetime in the happy illusion that he was a
scientific historian of human nature, whereas it is patent to the
most ingenuous reader that his magnificent and laborious docu-
mentation was amassed simply to reinforce certain *a priori* ideas
which in themselves were irrational to begin with. Zola presents
the unhappy spectacle of a man who just missed being a great
epic poet and, on the other hand, lacked the qualities of the great
thinker. It would almost seem, with M. Gide and his school, as
if there was a movement, at least in the novel, back to the seven-
tcenth-century outlook on life. That M. Gide desires this is clear
from the following remark: 'The novel has never known that
"formidable erosion of contours" of which Nietzsche talks, and
that deliberate turning away from life which gave style to the
works of the Greek dramatists, for example, or to the tragedies of
the French seventeenth century. Do you know anything more
profoundly human than these works? But exactly, they are
human only because they are profound; they do not pride themselves
on appearing human, or at any rate they do not pretend to be
real. They remain works of art. . . .' Unfortunately, with these
most laudable intentions, M. Gide has not yet presented us with
any work that can be said to illustrate his views, and it rather looks
as if, like Diderot, he will remain a writer fertile in suggestive
theories but without the creative genius to put them into practice.

Through all these vicissitudes, the reputation of Racine in France,
whilst it has been often questioned, has never been seriously disputed.
To the majority his tragedies still appear the supreme expression of
vital truths. It was so in the eighteenth century. And now, as
then, most Frenchmen continue to regard the creations of our

Shakespeare as puzzling, unreal, and perhaps grotesque, just as modern Englishmen look upon the heroines of Racine as lifeless, colourless, and abstract.

No doubt the initial difficulty here, as in all questions of comparative taste, is due to that language barrier which no translation, however good, can ever effectually surmount. But this is not an explanation that carries us much farther forwards, since language itself is but the cast from a mould fashioned by thought. The Germans, for instance, so far from being disconcerted by the fact that Shakespeare wrote in a foreign tongue, apparently understand him so well as to find it hard to believe that German was not his original medium. Possibly the best way to approach our problem, which lies much deeper, is to try to see what Shakespeare and Racine understood by dramatic structure and characterization.

The first striking point of difference between the two dramatists is Racine's refusal to mingle the comic and the tragic in one play. This seemed to Racine and to his public so natural and so reasonable as to merit very little discussion. And not only did he eliminate all comic elements but also any circumstance not immediately pertinent to his dramatic purpose, which was, not to show how a tragic situation arises, but, starting from the hypothesis that a situation *is* tragic, to demonstrate the terrible havoc produced in the souls of his characters by a passion which all reasonable people condemned as unreasonable. In *Phèdre* we have a typical example of Racine's method. The exposition is, as usual, brief; a curt outline of the situation. Thésée, Phèdre's husband, is absent, and Hippolyte, her stepson, has just returned from an exile into which he had been driven by his stepmother. Phèdre, we learn almost at once, is in love with Hippolyte. The tragic conflict is apparent. It is the battle between guilty, abnormal passion and reason. Thereafter, all that interests Racine is the logical, relentless demonstration of the tragic consequences of such a criminal love in the soul of a proud woman who happens to be a queen. Every nuance of horror, shame, fear, jealousy is exposed with lingering and ruthless realism. There is a minimum of external action, a fact which, of course, intensifies the ordeal of Phèdre, since any form of physical action would provide relief from the inner conflict. The final catastrophe, the violent act of self-murder, is made to seem inevitable. We have already witnessed the spiritual destruction of the woman: the death of her body follows fatally. In Racine the characters are few and the interest is thus concentrated

and deepened.   Phèdre indeed dominates the play.   No one else
matters very much : Hippolyte, Thésée, and Aricie are reflectors,
intensifying the illumination that floods the central figure.

In Racinian tragedy the objective is always thus deliberately
limited.   Racine shows his audience, not how a certain assemblage
of circumstances will inevitably give rise to a passion, as, for instance,
some combination of harmless ingredients will cause an explosion ;
but, taking as his hypothesis a passion which is already mature, he
demonstrates its inevitable effects, primarily on the person thus
obsessed, and then incidentally on that person's entourage.   Like
Descartes, like Molière, Racine moves from the general to the
particular : Shakespeare, on the other hand, works from the complex
and local to the universal.   In *Othello*, in *Hamlet, Lear*, or *Macbeth*
we do not acquire a complete realization of the hero's tragedy
until we have accompanied him through all the experiences and
circumstances that gave rise to it.   Now, in *Phèdre*, it is not vital
that we should see and hear Hippolyte and Aricie to comprehend
the heroine's terrible dilemma, yet there is hardly a character in
Shakespeare's tragedies whose presence is not in some degree
necessary to our full understanding of the tragic problem.   With
Shakespeare the awful import of the central situation emerges in
its full horror from a complex multitude of happenings, gradually
presented to our view.   And more often than in Racine, the
Shakespearian audience possesses a knowledge of the hero's situation
which he does not himself have, a dramatic device that can easily
degenerate into melodrama, yet somehow in Shakespeare seldom
does.   The elements of the tragedy, in Shakespeare, coalesce and
crystallize before our very eyes : Racine shows us a crystal which
we think is intact and transparent until by his marvellous art it
slowly glows with myriad secret fires, as illumination strikes it
from a number of cunningly chosen points.   Racine tells us wonderfully what passion does once it has attained its full maturity.
He does not, like Shakespeare, reveal its genesis.   How did a
woman of Phèdre's type come to conceive her guilty love for an
Hippolyte?   What social environment, what flux of events produced
this monstrous obsession we do not know.   In the English dramatist
we see the spiritual and physical climates where these strange
plants germinate and flourish : Racine is content to show us only
the blossoms and the fruits of passion.

In this an Englishman would maintain that Shakespeare is
greater than Racine, but for reasons that few Frenchmen would

admit. The elements that are absent from a Racinian play, the local circumstances explaining the genesis of a tragic obsession, are hard to translate into dramatic action: they belong really to the province of the novelist, and it is only by a *tour de force* of genius that Shakespeare contrives to dramatize these elements of the *milieu*, of the appropriate ambiance which shall determine the characters and explain their tragic problem. It is his way, the experimental way, of arriving at reality. It is the method of Fielding, of Balzac, of many great novelists, but in a dramatist it is unprecedented and unique. That is why, to a French spectator, the action of a Shakespearian play only becomes really interesting after the lapse of one or perhaps two acts. For him *Hamlet* begins to be intense only after the scene of the play inside the play, or *Othello* not until the reference to Michael Cassio. Racine always, Shakespeare practically never, opens his plays at a point very close to the crisis. His audience did not want a picture of the atmosphere that breeds jealousy, ambition, cruelty, or love: what interested them was to witness the behaviour of a character obsessed by these passions. So far as they were concerned, all that Shakespeare tells us in his opening scenes—which for us strike the first chord of a leitmotiv—might perfectly well be omitted or condensed into a retrospective phrase. And sometimes, to be just, the seventeenth-century Frenchman would be quite right. Only a fanatic will deny that there are passages in Shakespeare's introductory scenes which, even according to his conception of drama, are superfluous and undramatic.

It is evident from its very nature that Racinian tragedy was addressed to a highly cultured audience, well used to grasp psychological ideas directly, without the intermediate aid of imagery. The wealth of metaphor and simile which Shakespeare drew from the experience of everyday life and alchemized into language of immortal beauty is so utterly absent from Racine as to give English hearers an impression of chill severity, if not of drabness. That is, of course, because they cannot imagine the repercussions produced in the mind of the seventeenth- or eighteenth-century Frenchman by words the English equivalents of which are, indeed, cold and abstract. Words trail an aura, a secret perfume which vanishes in translation. It is apparent only to one who has lived in the *milieu* in which words were born and tasted the life that is secreted in them. To an Englishman there is always something amusing in Racine's reiterated use of terms like *feux, vos jours, flamme, forfaits*, because, even when he can dispense with the English rendering, they strike him as so inadequate to the situation which they describe as to be almost incongruous. But to a French mind not only are they completely adequate: to reinforce them by other images would mar their perfection. Boileau's line:

> La raison, pour marcher, n'a souvent qu'une voie,

contains many implications, one of which certainly is that the vocabulary required to express rational ideas must be limited, because, the fewer the words that intervene between the idea and the hearer's mind, the clearer will be the impression. Moreover, if vocabulary is thus deliberately limited, words gain in profundity and in suggestiveness. And if we reconsider the Cartesian structure of Racine's thought, departing as it does from a basic idea which he desires to illustrate by dramatic action, it is not surprising that in all his plays the course of destiny seems to be charted, rather than pictured in coloured exact relief. Yet presuppose a spectator who is perfectly familiar with the legend of the chart: he does not require the aid of a detailed vivid model in order to decipher the contours of the terrain. Indeed, the presence of such picturesque, complex detail would interfere with his enjoyment. At any rate, it would impress him as superfluous or trivial. A speech like Agamemnon's in *Troilus and Cressida*, or Hamlet's famous soliloquy on death, must strike him as not merely shallow in philosophy but choked with unnecessary metaphor. No doubt he would eventually discover the idea at the core of this verbiage, but he would consider it undramatically expressed, a mere excuse for a puzzling debauch in imagery.

In the age of Racine and of Boileau the vocabulary as well as the structure of tragedy was governed by certain fixed canons. No plebeians could be included in the dramatis personae, and it was equally impossible to introduce ignoble words into the style. Household, everyday words, the humble words we associate with all the ordinary manifestations of nature and the common acts of man, were banned from classic tragedy, just as farm-hands reeking of the byre were forbidden to tramp with clay-laden boots on the stainless marble steps of a palace. More, perhaps, than anything else, it is the absence in Racine of all that suggests fields, flowers, beasts, and trees which repels the English reader. This deliberate exclusion of landmarks which enable him to recognize his familiar world will always make Racine and Corneille difficult of access to

* c

an Englishman. How is it possible, he wonders, to take all these things for granted? Surely Frenchmen, too, must have sometimes known

> a bank whereon the wild thyme blows,
> Where ox-lips and the nodding violet grows,
> Quite overcanopied with luscious woodbine,
> With sweet musk roses and with eglantine.

How sober, restrained, and chill must the following lines from *Phèdre* sound to an ear attuned to the music, the imagery, the splendid abandon of Shakespeare's tragic verse!

> Tu le savais. Pourquoi me laissais-tu séduire?
> De leur furtive ardeur ne pouvais-tu m'instruire?
> Las a-t-on vus souvent se parler, se chercher?
> Dans le fond des forêts allaient-ils se cacher?
> Hélas! Ils se voyaient avec pleine licence.
> Le ciel de leurs soupirs approuvait l'innocence;
> Ils suivaient sans remords leur penchant amoureux,
> Tous les jours se levaient clairs et sereins pour eux.
> Et moi, triste rebut de la nature entière,
> Je me cachais au jour, je fuyais la lumière;
> La mort est le seul dieu que j'osais implorer.
> J'attendais le moment où j'allais expirer;
> Me nourrissant de fiel, de larmes abreuvée,
> Encor dans mon malheur de trop près observée,
> Je n'osais dans mes pleurs me noyer à loisir;
> Je goûtais en tremblant ce funeste plaisir;
> Et sous un front serein déguisant mes alarmes,
> Il fallait bien souvent me priver de mes larmes.

Is there in this passage a line which Shakespeare would not have magnificently elaborated, an idea which he would not have enmeshed in a shimmering net of imagery. Think of what he would have done with 'furtive ardeur,' or with the ineffably plaintive 'tous les jours se levaient clairs et sereins pour eux.' The mere thought of it fills an English reader with amazed pity for Racine's benighted compatriots! Yet these starved wretches would have doubted the sanity of an author who could interrupt the march of tragic action to brood over the spectacle of a bird winging homewards to the 'rooky wood,' or insult the intelligence and shock the taste of his audience with the drunken witticisms of a senile and incredibly lettered porter. To the French of Racine's day one of the touchstones of poetic excellence was condensation. A phrase like 'furtive ardeur' needs no elaboration: it is already perfect.   Every hearer could orchestrate it from his own imagination or experience.   Nor did he want a Shakespearian description of the sylvan glades where Aricie dallied with her lover.   Description, in his opinion, would only localize and restrict: it was for him a matter of supreme indifference whether a wood was in Arden, in Touraine, or in Greece.   'Dans le fond des forêts allaient-ils se cacher?'   What on earth did it matter where?   And what has natural environment got to do with the dramatic idea which is here to reveal the procession of emotions in Phèdre's tortured soul. Poetry, for the seventeenth-century connoisseur, was poetry only in so far as it directly served the dramatic purpose of the poet. If, as in *Iphigénie*:

> Les vents agitent l'air d'heureux frémissements,
> Et la mer leur répond par ses mugissements;
> La rive au loin gémit, blanchissante d'écume,

it is because the sea and the winds are actors in the drama, not merely elements of a poetic setting.

The unities had a considerable influence on the structure of French drama of the eighteenth century and, to a lesser extent, on English.   It is imperative, however, to remember that they were adopted by Racine because they happened to suit his conception of drama: they were not imposed on him by public opinion, as they were, originally, on Corneille.   To Racine, the unities provided a useful cadre within which his mind could work in comfort: a larger one would have embarrassed him.   He had not, like Shakespeare, the constant urge to let his imagination run glorious riot: the whole temper of his age was opposed to riot. Only by a nice compromise between the reason and the fancy could the work of art achieve balance, symmetry, purity of line: in short, plastic perfection.   The time had not yet come to doubt the infallibility of this rational aesthetic and to substitute sentiment for reason as the criterion of artistic beauty.   Descartes had mastered the laws of thought.   Boileau, in his *Art poétique*, formulated those which were supposed to govern literary taste.   He had never heard of Shakespeare, but it is certain that the Shakespearian theatre, had he known it, would have been contemptuously dismissed, like the Spanish, as 'un spectacle grossier' conceived by an ignorant rhymester who 'sur la scène en un jour renferme des années.'

Racine agreed with Boileau that if dramatic action is to be

handled with art, the law of the three unities must be observed because it is reasonable to do so. Reasonable, because drama cannot reproduce real life: at best, it can hope only to give the audience the illusion of real life. In this matter of the unities the difference between Racine and Shakespeare is not one of principle but solely of degree. Both enter into a tacit convention with their spectators that there are certain elements

> which cannot in their huge and proper life
> Be here presented.[1]

The actual time covered by events cannot be enclosed within the limits of the play, nor, of course, can the sites of the action be properly portrayed on the stage. But Racine would have laughed at Shakespeare's apologizing to the audience because he could not show Henry V crossing the Straits of Dover, the cheering crowds on the beach, and the journey up to London. All that and much more the French playwright was content to surrender to the 'wingèd thoughts' of his auditors. With a temple or a palace for his setting and the twenty-four-hour convention as to the duration of the play, Racine was free to apply himself to the essentials—the invention of plot, the conduct of the action, and the creation of characters. The question of historical accuracy did not interest him, though even the severe Boileau, in his *Art poétique*, had suggested:

> Des siècles, des pays, étudiez les mœurs:
> Les climats font souvent les diverses humeurs.

That, or something like it, was to be Voltaire's contribution to neo-classic tragedy. Meanwhile, borrowing his names and to some extent his plots from classical legend and history, Racine extracted from the manners of contemporary court society, not, indeed, the characteristic traits of that society, but those which are common to men and women of every class and climate. We must, however, make one important reserve; for he assumed always that reason, Cartesian reason, was a universal attribute. It was, for example, understood that civilized people do not as a rule hold intercourse with witches or ghosts. Occasionally, in a symbolic fashion and for purely poetic effect, he very discreetly opened the portals of drama to the supernatural. Thus Neptune is admitted into *Phèdre* and *Iphigénie*, but the fable of Iphigénie's metamorphosis into a fawn is excluded as 'trop absurde et trop invraisemblable.'

[1] *Henry V*, I. i.

The conventions governing the French theatre were at bottom, therefore, as elastic as those which obtained in England. The eighteenth-century critics used to attach inordinate importance to the question of their observation or neglect. The French proclaimed that Shakespeare might have been a great dramatist had he conformed to them: the English regretted that a writer of Racine's calibre should have allowed them to shackle his genius.

Both attitudes were, of course, wrong, since neither Racine nor Shakespeare was thus handicapped in any way. The former, had it suited him, would have ignored the unities for the same reason as Shakespeare actually did. Great artists make the conditions of their art, and no tradition, however strong, can fetter their genius for long. Such externals are never more than the surface reflection of a basic inner conception of art, though to contemporaries they always seem to possess an intrinsic value. So, for years after the passing of a genius, the literature of a generation is cluttered with mediocre imitations of the master's work; and they are mediocre, not because they lack talent, but because, by mistaking the husk for the kernel, their authors look for the secret of genius in what is merely accessory and not vital. Of this the French and English theatres of the eighteenth century can offer many examples.

Travelling by different routes, Shakespeare and Racine had a common objective: the discovery and the isolation of what in life is of universal moment. But by universal moment did they understand the same thing? The complexity of the world unfolded by Shakespeare tempts one to say that his universe surpasses and includes Racine's. Yet that would be unjust to the memory of one whose subtle and profound researches into the feminine soul discovered a domain which Shakespeare probably knew but did not enter. On the other hand, no Racinian hero approaches the Shakespearian in stature. Nor, as we have seen, does the Frenchman rival Shakespeare in the variety of his repertoire. The real difficulty in any attempt to compare the achievement of these writers is that Racine is primarily a dramatist and only incidentally a poet: in Shakespeare, poet and playwright are almost completely interfused. Yet no Frenchman will admit that Racine, the poet, is inferior to Racine, the dramatist—a hopeless impasse aggravated by the fact that in the present state of Shakespearian criticism it is equal heresy to suggest that some of the bard's scenes, though rich in glorious poetry, are what George III called 'sad stuff' from the point of view of drama. Presumptuous as it may sound, let us try to discover, in a general way, what each conceived to be the essence of tragedy.

The universe of Racine was not that of Shakespeare. To the former, Reason was an absolute, a universal: it was therefore the point of departure for any examination of the human soul. Reason is the norm, the gauge which enables the dramatist to plot the jagged graph of human destiny. To Racine's Cartesian mind there is a normal, universal psychology. An ancient Greek, acting rationally, will behave in the same way, under given circumstances, as a seventeenth-century Frenchman. Moreover, the same regularity will characterize his departure from the norm, since, even when he is swept away by passion from the rational course of conduct, he is always aware of its existence and its exact position. It is precisely this knowledge that renders him tragic. When a man reaches, like Molière's Harpagon, the stage where he fails to realize that his behaviour is irrational: when he acquires the illusion that the only really normal people are misers; he is, from the point of view of the seventeenth-century Frenchman, a monomaniac, but a comic monomaniac. At most he might be pitied, but more usually he is laughed at or ostracized. At any rate he is not tragic.

Shakespeare's world has no such clear-cut contours. As a result his drama is more suggestive, less didactic than Racine's. With him the survey of life starts with the observation of life: not from an *a priori* idea of its outline and organization. He works slowly from the consideration of human facts and slowly ascends to ultimate truths. That the latter should often tally with the conclusions arrived at by the method of Racine is no more surprising than that Descartes's formula for the refraction of light, discovered by a process of rational elimination, should later be confirmed experimentally by Newton. The two dramatists differ in their approach to truth, and in art, of course, it is the method of approach which is immensely important and interesting. Now, if we consider the relatively limited society from which Racine drew the illustrations of his universal theories, it is amazing that his characters should be so real, so human as they are. It is commonly said that Racine's theatre is a picture of the Court of Louis XIV, but it is obviously very much more. We have but to read the memoirs of Saint-Simon to realize how much of what is purely local and ephemeral has been omitted by Racine from his canvases. His theatre is an idealized expression of the polite society of his time: it is made up of traits selected for their durability, their essential, universal truth.

That is the secret of Racine's appeal. No Frenchman of his day and no Greek of antiquity evidently ever spoke or acted or felt so intensely as Phèdre, Bérénice, or Monime, yet the general tone of their speech and conduct is that which we can detect in the expression and the behaviour of any woman caught in a dilemma like theirs. This is surely what Racine meant once when he spoke of *la tristesse majestueuse* of tragedy. It is the note which in moments of crisis triumphs over local and superficial peculiarities of idiom or gesture, and creates the impression that we carry away from the spectacle of a woman in spiritual agony, no matter what may be her class or race. One cannot help feeling that the women Racine knew must have been more natural than the men, since the idealized reflection of them is so true and human. His tragedies convince us that the men of his time were less natural and more conventional: in their attitude towards women they were not being themselves, but merely adhering to an artificial, temporary standard. Racine's heroes have seldom that ring of veracity which is to be found in Corneille's.

Shakespeare, we have observed, rarely ventured into Racine's domain. Juliet is not, in the Racinian sense, an example of tragic love. Like Voltaire's Zaïre, she is pathetic rather than tragic. She has committed no tragic fault, and the obstacle to her happiness, the family feud, is an external one. Nor is there anything unnatural in Juliet's passion for Romeo: it is not shameful or abnormal like Phèdre's. It will not destroy her soul. She is simply a victim of an unfortunate combination of circumstances which she did nothing to create and is powerless to alter. To the French mind, therefore, only in the loose, undramatic use of the term is Juliet a tragic figure. Like Cleopatra, she would have made an excellent heroine for a novel, for there is none of that 'fighting' in her soul which is the essential characteristic of the Racinian heroine of tragedy. There is no actual conflict between her love for Romeo and her love for her parents. Like all Shakespeare's women, Juliet loves with no misgivings and no reserve. In most of his heroines love is tender, shy, strong, bold, or pathetic: it is never, in the Racinian sense, tragic. We know that Shakespeare's women will go on loving with the love 'that looks on tempests and is not shaken.' But that is because the tempests come from without. What they would do if their passion met with an obstacle from within, such as pride or shame or religious fervour, we do not know, for Shakespeare does not tell us.

Springing from a preconceived and very clear notion of a normal, well-ordered universe, the art of Racine, like that of Corneille and Molière, is much more social in its implication than Shakespeare's. Indeed, tragedy for Racine and Corneille is in essence the despairing consciousness of social abnormality, just as for Molière comedy lies in the monomaniac's illusion that his is the only normal mode of life. Shakespeare, approaching from another angle, discovers a more complex universe inhabited not only by people who, like Racine's, are haunted by the spectre of an ever-widening chasm which separates them from the many, but also by men so convinced of the validity of their unique and individual code as to ignore or despise the seamarks which preserve the ordinary man from spiritual disaster. Such men to Shakespeare are truly heroic or profoundly tragic. In them passion assumes the dimensions of an *idée fixe*: they see the course of their destiny, yet pursue it till inevitable catastrophe overtakes and crushes them. Maybe, as in the case of Macbeth, Brutus, and Hamlet, they nurse the splendid illusion that they are instruments of a higher power, and, fortified by this romantic conviction, follow their passionate ends with demonic energy. Or else, as with Richard III or Iago, this inner conviction of uniqueness is intellectual and not mystic, a cynical resolve to challenge the world-order, to prove by their immunity that the so-called moral laws are for the herd and not the genius. They are artists in evil. Lear and Othello are egotists of another brand, men in whom qualities fundamentally good, such as marital or paternal love, swiftly degenerate into hideous, cancerous growths because, through some innate defect of character, they flout the laws of spiritual hygiene.

Racine never leaves us in doubt as to what is the essence of his tragedies: we are kept in constant touch with each phase of the debacle. The characters analyse their emotions and passions, always reminding us of the extent of their aberration from what is rational or moral. For Racine has the Cartesian view that immorality is simply wrong thinking. How difficult it is, on the other hand, to know in Shakespeare what is really the core of his tragedy. We cannot here, as in the symmetrical Racinian drama, acquire that impression of certainty, of finality which is the natural product of a Cartesian mind. With Racine the visibility is such that his horizon, though distant, gloomy, and vast, is always clear-cut: in Shakespeare we see it only in spasmodic flashes, lit by the lightning of a random word.

Of all Shakespeare's works, there is none perhaps which more clearly reveals the difference between the English and the French conception of tragedy than *Hamlet*. Whether Hamlet's situation would have impressed Racine as matter for tragedy at all is most doubtful. It is almost certain, however, that he would have 'rationalized' or simplified it by making Hamlet's love for his mother the chief obstacle to his passion for revenge. That is a point of view which no English critic, and rightly so, has ever seriously advanced in order to explain Hamlet's tragic dilemma. To a Frenchman, filial love is a much more reasonable and fundamental source of tragedy than it has ever seemed to our writers. Its role in the French theatre is immense. But for Shakespeare it is only a source of pathos: it is never the pivot of his plays. For instance, Cordelia's tragedy is not that she loves her father but that she loves truth too much to pretend that filial love can ever be everything in her life. So, too, it would be quite wrong to assume that the tragedy of Hamlet is a conflict between two kinds of filial love, that which he cherishes for his dead father and the love he bears to his living mother. Now, although that would be a typically French conception of tragedy, it is not Shakespeare's. Profound as is Hamlet's love and sense of duty to his father, he has a higher duty towards himself. Is not that why so much of the play is devoted to the sole purpose of revealing Hamlet's effort to convince his own intellect, his reason, that his intuition regarding Claudius's guilt rests on something more relevant than an apparition? Everything in Hamlet, judged by ordinary standards, is abnormal—his melancholy, his intellect, his scrupulous sense of justice, his passionate love for his father, his hatred of Claudius, and his lust for revenge. Of irresolution in the accepted sense, that is, the inability to pass from willing to doing, there is none in Hamlet. It is clear from his dispatching of Polonius, from the remarks of Fortinbras, and Hamlet's own casual reference to grappling with the pirate ship, as if he were paying a friendly call, that he was not the man to baulk at killing an enemy. He has no irresolution of that sort.

Hamlet's conception of justice, like his hatred and his idea of revenge, is, for his times, unique. In the early stages, no doubt, he was conscious that his standards were not those of his entourage, and the consciousness drove him to outbursts of despair. These, however, he communicated to no one, not even Horatio. Unlike Laertes, Hamlet is an intellectual, not a *passionné*. But once an intellectual abandons himself to a passion he becomes more

dangerous than your 'rash and splenetic' type. And Hamlet's ultimate tragedy lies in the profound truth that no man can deliberately dedicate his intellectual faculties to the glutting of a passion
like revenge, however noble be the cause, without warping his
finer nature and eventually destroying his soul.

Hamlet's revenge, though he was not then conscious of the fact,
began with his feigned madness, a stratagem which he adopted to
conceal his emotions and to gain time to reflect on the question of
Claudius's guilt. But the audience can easily gauge by the king's
growing, nameless dread, how effective and vengeful are Hamlet's
strange utterances. Only an intellectual could have devised the
scheme of the play, and the first glimpse we have of a new Hamlet
is in his gloating appreciation of the artistic beauty of this plan.
Not quite convinced—that will come after the interview with his
mother—he deliberately arranges the form which that interview
will take. He will not kill her, as Nero did, though passion tempts
him to do so.

> Let me be cruel, not unnatural:
> I will speak daggers to her, but use none;
> My tongue and soul in this be hypocrites

—a vivid illustration of the growth of his new nature; for this is
the dialectic of a man wilfully dehumanizing himself in the interests
of a revenge compared to which a single dagger-thrust is trifling.
On the way to his mother's room he encounters Claudius at prayers,
and Hamlet toys with the idea of removing him then. But that
would not be revenge as he now conceives it: that would not be
sufficiently *raffiné*. The new tigerish quality in Hamlet is dreadfully
apparent in the interview with his mother, where he lashes himself
into a cold passion subserved by an imagination of incredible power,
torturing the queen as surely no mother was ever tortured by an
outraged son.

His soul now drained of sensibility, he drags the corpse of Polonius
from the room with grimly humorous comments. From this point
until the denouement he has no chance to kill Claudius, who is
strongly guarded, whilst Hamlet himself is under arrest. Now,
in taking leave of the king, he hardly troubles to keep up the
pretence of madness. Obviously, he sees himself as a master-mind
at grips with the master-mind of the king, whose abilities, in his
exaltation, Hamlet grossly exaggerates:

> O, 'tis most sweet
> When in one line two crafts directly meet.

For Claudius is at this stage simply a desperate, terrified man staking everything on a final throw.

Hamlet knows about the plot against his life, but he is now convinced that heaven is 'ordinant.'   The sinister, tigerish note of triumph is again evident in his mocking farewell to Claudius, as it is in the melodramatic letter with its cryptic, terrifying 'naked' and 'alone.'   But nowhere do we see the changed Hamlet so clearly as in his account to Horatio of his cunning in outwitting Claudius and hoisting his old school-fellows with their own petard.   Hamlet has now surrendered himself to a mystic force which cannot fail. His intellect is working smoothly, coolly, with beautiful rhythm.

> Ere I could make a prologue to my brains
> They had begun the play.

Claudius is doomed.   Hamlet, 'naked,' and 'alone,' will destroy him, since the king has no weapon to match the heaven-inspired genius of his stepson.   There is one brief reminder of the old Hamlet in the terrible outburst at Ophelia's grave.   Hamlet apologizes to Horatio, or rather to himself, for this regrettable but momentary lack of control.   The duel is announced.   Hamlet knows it is another pretext for an attempt on his life, but he accepts it serenely, confident that, whatever happens, Claudius is doomed.

Death comes, not only to the king but to all four.   Hamlet dies unhappy, knowing that the full splendour of his role will never be made clear to the world.   The tragedy, to him, is that in the eyes of all, save perhaps Horatio, he must seem (as he does to so many critics) a weak-willed John-a-dreams who, but for the king's blunder, would not have taken the latter's life.   What an intolerable thought to one who sees himself as *un homme d'élite*, the artisan of a unique revenge!

> Had I but time—as this fell sergeant, death,
> Is strict in his arrest—O, I could tell you—
> But let it be;

and in an anguished ejaculation:

> O God! Horatio, what a wounded name,
> Things standing thus unknown, shall live behind me?

That is, I feel, what Hamlet conceives to be his tragedy.   Possibly Shakespeare implies that it is something more awful.   It is the spiritual collapse, the destruction of a fine nature, which inevitably occurs if a man in his intellectual arrogance conceives himself as the instrument of divine vengeance.   To kill your father's murderer, as Laertes would, in a blind access of grief, is natural and human. It is a crime, but a pardonable one.   The Hamlet mode of revenge has in it something superhuman, akin to the slow grinding of the mills of divine vengeance.   Truly, Hamlet had within him 'something dangerous,' but the danger, as Shakespeare with fine dramatic irony implies, is to Hamlet's own immortal soul.

This faculty of overstepping the immediate present; of launching into an infinite future; of creating, as we say, for eternity, is, of course, the ultimate touchstone of all great dramatic art.   Englishmen deny it to Racine, but unjustly, for to-day, as in the seventeenth century, there are thousands of Frenchmen who derive from their great dramatist the same intellectual and emotional stimulus which Shakespeare gives us.   It is, of course, true that no Racinian play has given rise to so much conjecture as *Hamlet* or *Lear*: but it would be dangerous to conclude from this that, compared to Shakespeare, Racine is a lesser genius.   A great deal of recent English criticism of Shakespeare is, from the French point of view, illegitimate and valueless.   His greater distance from us, our almost complete ignorance of his life, the absence of any evidence as to his immediate purpose when he created his plays—all these circumstances have favoured the growth in England (and in Germany) of a body of purely subjective and mystic 'interpreters' who either disregard the actual text of Shakespeare's plays or arbitrarily distort it to make it fit into the mould of their *a priori* theories.   Completely objective, 'scientific' criticism of art is, happily, impossible.   Art cannot be 'proved'; and every individual and every age is bound to interpret a work of art in the light of his or its experience.   And art, of course, is only great in so far as it thus continues to respond to the questioning and satisfy the demands of posterity.   Its quintessential truth is sempiternal and inexhaustible: it offers a continual challenge to the critics of succeeding ages, inviting them to elaborate newer and more effective methods of unearthing its hidden riches.   There is, however, no need to 'salt' the mine, and that is precisely what some critics are doing with Shakespeare by substituting, for the universe which he created, a fantastic and mystic one that exists only in their own imagination. They submerge his pure gold beneath their glittering, coloured dross; offering us their mystic symbols for Shakespeare's human realities.

The French have not treated Racine in this way: they have

more respect for his memory, and still retain some leaven of reason in their interpretation of art. Yet we have only to read Proust to see that there are still discoveries to be made in Racine. Whether Shakespeare's lode is heavier or deeper only time can show. We like to think of both as immortal: yet a day may come when even they will cease to satisfy the demands of a future era. After all, there was a period in the eighteenth century when neither the works of Racine or of Shakespeare, as they stood, really satisfied the artistic ideals of their contemporaries, mainly because, as we now feel, those ideals were false, or, as we vaguely put it, their taste was bad. It may be profitable, therefore, to discover what was the dramatic taste of eighteenth-century England and France, and, in particular, to examine how they 'improved' on the art of their great models. It will be interesting also to see whether Racine and Shakespeare left any considerable mark on the theatres of their respective countries.

CHAPTER III

EVER since the eighteenth century it has been a commonplace of English criticism to regard Voltaire as an envious ingrate, a cynical plagiarist, whose noisy and ignorant abuse of our Shakespeare was a mere blind to conceal his furtive but extensive thefts from Shakespeare's plays. The old legend about Voltaire's fear lest a complete translation of our dramatist's works should reveal the extent of these larcenies has been accepted as a fact by a well-known Shakespearian scholar,[1] whose views are repeated and endorsed by the *Cambridge History of English Literature*. Cibber's preface to Hill's adaptation of Voltaire's *Zaïre* and a vague remark in the prologue to Miller's version of *Mahomet* are, for example, quoted as proof that Voltaire's 'own dramas borrowed from Shakespeare with a freedom that impressed even those who translated and adapted Voltaire's plays for the English stage.'[2] The use of the word 'even' in this context is a little ingenuous, since any one familiar with the prefaces to eighteenth-century adaptations from French dramas knows that almost invariably the author is anxious above all to show, for patriotic and personal reasons, how very English and how very un-French the original really is. The general tone of these introductions can be gathered from the following passage in the prologue to Murphy's *Zenobia*.[3]

> Yet think not that we mean to mock the eye
> With pilfer'd colours of a foreign dye.
> Not to translate, our bard his pen doth dip:
> He takes a play as Britons take a ship;
> Repair her well, and build with hearts of oak,
> To every breeze set Britain's streamers free,
> NEW-MAN her, and away again to sea.

Thus, when Cibber writes that:

> From English plays Zara's French author fir'd
> Confess'd his muse, beyond himself inspir'd;
> From rack'd Othello's rage he rais'd his style,
> And snatch'd the brand that lights this tragic pile,

---

[1] T. Lounsbury, *Shakespeare and Voltaire* (1902).
[2] *Cambridge History of English Literature*, x. 81.
[3] Adapted from Crébillon's *Rhadamisthe et Zénobie*.

one would be wise to read both *Othello* and *Zaïre* very carefully before blindly endorsing Cibber's opinion. The same caution is even more necessary in the case of Miller's

> Britons, these numbers to yourselves you owe;
> Voltaire hath strength to shoot in Shakespeare's bow:

lines which have, oddly enough, been construed to mean that Voltaire's *Mahomet* is indebted for its most critical scenes to Shakespeare's *Macbeth*,[1] a statement that betrays a profound misunderstanding of Voltaire's dramatic aims. To put it briefly, the attitude of the English critic towards the Shakespeare-Voltaire question has undergone no real change since the eighteenth century. On the other hand, there has been a complete revolution in English appreciation of Shakespeare. Now, modern English critics persist in exacting from Voltaire a respect for our master dramatist which they themselves have been disgracefully slow to evince and which the Frenchman could not be reasonably expected to show. After all, it was in some measure the resentment aroused by Voltaire's criticisms, prejudiced though they were, which stung our eighteenth-century Shakespearians to retaliate, and thus drove them to a closer study of a dramatist whose excellence they had hitherto taken for granted, though with reserves that showed a fundamental ignorance of his immense genius. Again, it is quite hopeless to discuss Voltaire's views on Shakespeare without some attempt to examine the trend and the scope of Voltaire's whole tragic theatre. To isolate his criticisms of Shakespeare from his other observations on drama, to segregate from his other plays those which seem to owe their inspiration to Shakespeare, is no doubt convenient, but it is not enlightening. The real vice of such a comparative method becomes still more apparent, however, when passages, scenes, or even lines are extracted from Voltaire's tragedies and, without any reference to their context, are set alongside seemingly analogous scenes, passages, and lines drawn from the plays of Shakespeare.[2]

Instead of marvelling at Voltaire's astounding blindness to the grandeur of Shakespeare, we ought to credit him with unusual originality and boldness of judgment. Of the tiny group of Frenchmen in the late seventeen-twenties who had even heard of Shakespeare, not one, save perhaps Prévost, would have ventured to

[1] T. Lounsbury, *Shakespeare and Voltaire*. Vide also *Cambridge History of English Literature*, xi. 352, where we encounter the following astounding remark: 'As many English readers know, he (Voltaire) had taken whole scenes from *Macbeth* for his *Mahomet*.'

[2] For examples, and a refutation of these conclusions, see Appendix I.

accord him 'un génie plein de force et de fécondité, de naturel et de sublime.' [1] On the other hand, few English writers of repute would have essentially disagreed with the spirit of the subsequent phrase, 'sans la moindre étincelle de bon goût et sans la moindre connaissance des règles.' Except that Pope rather loftily points out the injustice of judging Shakespeare by rules unknown to the crude Elizabethans, there is no substantial difference between his attitude and Voltaire's. [2] Like Dennis, [3] and Gildon, [4] Pope feels a patriotic urge to apologize for Shakespeare's shortcomings : Voltaire, on the contrary, fortified by the opinion of his hero, Bolingbroke, and serenely convinced, of course, that there is no dramatic salvation outside Paris, is obviously surprised that England possessed any tragedies at all. There was almost every reason why Voltaire should have condemned Shakespeare : there was scarcely one which should have induced him to be as indulgent as he originally was. Nor is it surprising that, with the passing of the years, Voltaire became more and more prejudiced against Shakespeare. His contempt for him grew with his knowledge of Shakespeare's works, and, besides, the more Voltaire studied Racine, the greater became his conviction that an unbridgeable chasm separated English and French drama. Liberal in everything pertaining to philosophy and science, Voltaire was in artistic matters an arrant Tory. His was, moreover, the worst brand of conservatism. He had the illusion that progress consists in tinkering with trifling externals or in making inconsiderable concessions to passing vogues. Strictly, Voltaire was never really influenced by Shakespeare, for the very excellent reason that he never understood his art. He did not for one moment suspect that a man of his stamp could learn from Shakespeare anything more than a few novelties like the presentation of ghosts, the omission of the love element in a tragedy, the introduction of crowds, and a few other theatrical tricks. These, if discreetly used by a skilled dramatist, might conceivably quicken the *tempo* of French tragedy and, incidentally, convince the world that France now possessed a greater playwright than Racine. Actually, Voltaire's chief contribution to the French theatre, and he certainly did not get it from either Shakespeare or Racine, was his annoying habit of using the play, as he did every form of literature, to express his anti-clerical and political propaganda.

[1] *Lettres philosophiques*, No. 23 (written *c.* 1729).
[2] Preface to Pope's edition of Shakespeare (1725).
[3] *Essay on the Genius and Writings of Shakespeare* (1711).
[4] *Essay on the Art, Rise, and Progress of the Stage, etc.* (1714).

When Voltaire arrived in England in the summer of 1727 there was no particular reason why he should have become wildly enthusiastic about Shakespeare or English drama in general. The French neo - classic theatre dominated Europe. Corneille and Racine had been translated, adapted, and played in London for fifty years. Troupes of French actors paid periodic visits to England, Holland, Poland, Germany, and Italy. Some indeed were permanently settled in foreign countries.[1] Saint-Évremond, who lived in London for forty-four years and was buried in Westminster Abbey in 1703, never found it necessary to speak English, and, although he was a dramatic critic whose views on Racine and Corneille were awaited with eagerness and quoted with respect, he never once mentions Shakespeare's name. By 1728, however, roughly one-fourth of the tragedies presented at Drury Lane and Covent Garden were from the pen of Shakespeare,[2] and Voltaire most probably saw performances of *Hamlet*, *Julius Caesar*, *Othello*, and *Macbeth*. It is doubtful whether he went to see *Lear*, *Richard III*, *Timon*, *Henry IV*, *Henry VIII*, or *The Merchant of Venice*, since he does not refer to them in his *Lettres philosophiques*. However, if he did not, it was not for lack of opportunity.

Several years before his English visit, Voltaire had frequented two famous exiles, Bolingbroke and Atterbury, Bishop of Rochester. With the latter he argued as to the superior merits of prose or verse in tragedy. Possibly, too, Shakespeare was discussed, but we do not know. It is, however, certain that Bolingbroke inspired his young admirer with a contempt for all English tragedy.[3] This corroboration of what was then a French prejudice, coming from a distinguished Englishman, explains to some extent why Voltaire, smarting under the cruel humiliation of the Rohan affair and disposed, therefore, to see every English institution in a rosy light, whilst lavish in his praise of English science, philosophy, and politics, finds in his study of our theatre simply a detailed confirmation of Bolingbroke's views. Besides, he was himself already a dramatist of some repute fired with the desire to show Europe that the new century of progress could reveal a dramatic genius superior to Corneille and Racine. It is clear from all his pronouncements that Voltaire intended to reform French tragedy. 'Your most irregular plays,' he wrote to Bolingbroke, 'have one great merit— action . . . excessive delicacy sometimes obliges us to put into

---

[1] Du Bos, *Réflexions sur la Poésie et la Peinture* (1719), tome ii.
[2] Genest, op cit., vol. iii.   [3] Preface to *Brutus*.

narrative what we should like to show to the eye. On our stage
we are afraid to risk new spectacles in the presence of a nation
prone to ridicule everything that is not customary.' Despite the
'barbarous irregularities,' the 'gross faults' of *Julius Caesar*, Voltaire
cannot help being impressed by the vision of Brutus clutching his
bloodstained dagger and haranguing the mob. But would the
Parisians tolerate plebeians on the stage? True, the Greeks risked
certain scenes no less revolting to eighteenth-century taste, for,
like the English, they erred in mistaking horror for terror; the
disgusting and the incredible for the truly tragic. Yet occasionally,
by this method, Shakespeare struck a note of true pathos : sometimes
he stumbled on 'peculiar beauties.' Often, too, Voltaire admits,
the French, in their timid anxiety not to 'overstep the limits,' fail
to attain the tragic. Voltaire's object, then, will be to strike a
happy mean between the excessive timidity of the seventeenth-
century French dramatists and the excessive brutality of Shakespeare. It is possible, he thinks, to discover situations which 'as
yet appear disgusting and horrible,' but 'if well arranged and
artistically presented; above all, if toned down by the charm of
beautiful poetry, might afford even the French a type of pleasure
which they do not suspect.' [1]

On the matter of the unities, however, Voltaire will admit no
compromise. In reply to La Motte [2] he expresses the opinion, and
he never changed it, that the Aristotelian unities, being founded
on reason, are essential to the creation of good drama. Even the
English have at last discovered this truth. 'To-day, even English
authors are careful to warn us at the beginning of their plays that
the duration of the action is equal to that of the play, and in this
go even farther than we who are their masters.' To Voltaire the
unities mark the close of barbarism and the dawn of enlightenment
in the European theatre; a fact so obvious as to require no elucidation. There must be one action because the human mind cannot
grasp more than one object at one time. That is reasonable and
natural. It is the same with the unity of place. 'If the people
I see are in Athens in the first act, how can they be in Persia in
the second?' As for the unity of time, it is clearly to the dramatist's
advantage to work on the established twenty-four-hour convention.
'Why not a fortnight? Because if the author makes the action last
a fortnight he must tell me what happened in that time; and he
finds himself writing, not drama, but history. The spectator does

[1] Preface to *Brutus*.   [2] Preface to *Œdipe*.

not go to the theatre to hear a hero's history but to see a single event in his life.'

Like his great predecessors, Voltaire adopted the unities because they suited his conception of tragedy, which was, and remained, essentially the same as that of Racine and Corneille. But there were other conventions, and these threatened to interfere with Voltaire's contemplated reforms. So, in the preface to *Brutus*, he questions the infallibility of such *règles de bienséance*. After all, if a hero is allowed to kill himself on the stage, why should he not be allowed to kill someone else? Is the stage any less bloody at the suicide of Atalide than at the murder of Caesar? He disposes similarly of the old tradition that not more than three persons should appear on the stage at one time—another *règle de bienséance*. In a word, Voltaire proposes to adhere to the three unities, but reserves the right to introduce whatever innovations he chooses. Such departures from accepted practice he is prepared to explain away with his customary skill in dialectic. There is, for instance, nothing improbable in a 'spectacle horrible.' All that is required is a 'great genius' who will make it acceptable by his poetry. Already, obviously, he has in mind the idea of introducing the supernatural into modern tragedy, but realizes that it will be hard to impart to an audience so sceptical about the existence of ghosts in real life the illusion that it is seeing one on the stage.

Another reform suggested itself. For many years Racine had been criticized, both in England and in France, for the excessive importance attached to love in his plays. Du Bos, perhaps the most original critic of his day, agreed with Dryden that Racine and his imitators frequently introduced love into tragedy, with unfortunate results. 'Indeed,' he wrote, 'the pit laughs almost as loudly as at a scene from comedy when it sees the performance of the last scene of the second act in *Andromaque*.' [1] The French, said English critics, depict as love 'any general inclination of a person for one of the opposite sex.' For them love is *galanterie* and, as in the seventeenth-century romances, is accompanied by a consecrated jargon dealing with 'fers' and 'chaînes.' 'In short, love, far from being regarded as a tragic weakness, is really treated as a virtue. Historical heroes like Brutus and Arminius are

[1] Op. cit. Note, also in this connection, the following comment on *Phèdre* taken from the *Journal Encyclopédique* (1772), vol. v: 'French spectators detest Phèdre's crime but secretly smile at the rôle played by Thésée: Racine, therefore, showed him as little as possible.'

represented as *tendres et galants*, a woeful travesty of the *amour-passion* portrayed by the Ancients.' Voltaire, on the whole, endorsed these views, but pointed out that for a century the English stage had been tarred with the same brush. 'For,' he wrote to Bolingbroke, 'you have always tended somewhat to adopt our fashions and our vices.' [1] In his new scheme of things love will be either all or nothing in tragedy. It will not, as in the modern English and French plays, be dragged in to fill up gaps in the action. Lcve, if employed at all, must henceforth be 'a really tragic passion, regarded as a weakness and combated by remorse.' Here, of course, he merely restates the traditional practice of Corneille and Racine, whose whole theatre pivots on this idea of tragedy. 'Love,' he continues, 'must lead either to misfortune or crime to show how dangerous it is; or else virtue must triumph over love to show that it is not invincible.' This moralizing, didactic conception of dramatic art prepares us for the views later formulated by Diderot on the social function of the theatre. Meanwhile, however, Voltaire was simply paving the way for two new types of tragedy: the play containing no love element at all, and that in which love is not sexual but something finer, as in *Mérope*. In these and other innovations, to what degree was he directly influenced by the art of Shakespeare?

Brutus, written in England, was not played till 1730, and the French actors were disconcerted, as was the audience, by a play largely devoted to politics. At the time of its first production, *Brutus* was quite devoid of actuality to spectators, who could conceive of no other possible regime than that which they had—an absolute monarchy. In 1790, of course, it gave rise to excited manifestations, but under Louis XV even a speech like 'Qui naquit dans la pourpre en est rarement digne' merely bored the hearers. Even the daring novelty, borrowed from *Julius Caesar*, of showing the senators proceeding to the council chamber in their red togas excited no comment, since the author, remembering the laughter excited by his chorus of Thebans in *Œdipe*, wisely gave his senators nothing to say at all. As a matter of fact, in the crucial scene, where Titus is accused of treason by his father, they were supposed to express their feelings in eloquent pantomime, but as the actors of the *Comédie française* were unfamiliar with this *jeu muet*, they remained completely inactive.

In the problem presented here by Voltaire there is nothing which remotely suggests Shakespearian influence. Titus, piqued at the

[1] Preface to *Brutus* (1731).

lack of regard paid by the senate to his merit, is persuaded by
Tarquin's ambassador to revolt against Rome. He is also in
love with Tarquin's daughter Tullia, .who is used as an added
means of seduction. Strictly speaking, there is no problem at all,
for Brutus discovers the plot. Tullia commits suicide, and Brutus,
having pardoned his son, has him executed *pro bono publico*.

Ériphyle (1732), on the other hand, suggests a definite attempt
to imitate Shakespeare's *Hamlet*. In reality, it shows how impossible
it was for Voltaire to understand what Shakespeare meant by a
tragic dilemma. *Ériphyle* is not a tragedy: it is a melodrama based
on an improbability. The heroine, Ériphyle, Queen of Argos,
had, at the age of sixteen, connived at the murder of her husband
Amphiaraüs, who was killed by Hermogide, an ambitious prince
of the blood. Filled with remorse, haunted by the spectre of the
dead king, she now fears and loathes her former lover, who is
king in all but name. Ériphyle's son is supposed to be dead.
Hermogide thinks he disposed of him unknown to the mother,
but in reality he was saved by one Théandre, and brought up
under the name of Alcméon.

Meanwhile, Ériphyle is tortured by the ghost of her late husband,
who haunts his own tomb. He holds a gory dagger over her head
whilst the blood streams from a gash in his side over the marble
sarcophagus. It becomes urgently necessary to appoint a king,
and Ériphyle's choice falls on Alcméon, whose valour stamps him
as a worthy opponent to Hermogide. The queen learns that her
son is alive, and that the gods have decreed that he shall kill her.
Hermogide now states that the boy was murdered by him. Ériphyle
makes Alcméon king and instructs him to avenge her son. In a
scene filled with supernatural mutterings and fearful gloom Théandre
tells Alcméon of the queen's guilt, in which he refuses to believe.
As he is about to be crowned in the temple the ghost of the king
appears, 'dans une posture menaçante,' calling on Alcméon to
avenge him. Finally, after an interminable tableau, featuring a
temple swarming with excited but voiceless Argives, old and young,
embracing the altar of Jupiter, Ériphyle confesses her crime.
There is a delirious muddle, in which, somehow, Ériphyle gets
killed by Alcméon, who is apparently not quite himself, his hand
having been impelled by 'une horrible force.' The play ends with
Alcméon's bitter words addressed to the shade of Amphiaraüs:
'Sois content, impitoyable père.'

What emerges from this queer chaos is that Voltaire could not realize Hamlet's problem as Shakespeare presents it. So he transposed it in terms of traditional French tragedy. But no French audience would have tolerated for one moment an Alcméon dallying even with the idea of killing his mother, whatever her guilt.

> Cruel Amphiaraüs! Abominable loi!
> La nature me parle et l'emporte sur toi.
> O ma mère!

he exclaims, and dashes off to kill Hermogide. The result is, no tragedy at all, but a farrago of *romanesque* and incredible situations; for, as we have seen, Voltaire dared not develop his hypothesis and present a son torn between a sense of duty to his murdered father and love for a guilty mother. Instead, he side-tracks the main issue and opens up a question which was to play a great part in the literature of the eighteenth century. No doubt it is natural to obey the commands of a wronged father, but the Mosaic law of an eye for an eye is 'abominable' and unnatural. So Alcméon-Hamlet indignantly refuses to kill his mother. Yet, according to Voltaire's formula, guilty love must lead to crime and catastrophe. The gods are therefore dragged in to assume responsibility for a deed which the author dared not impute to Alcméon without making him a monster and an illogical monster at that. To do Voltaire justice, he realized how bad the play was. 'I thought,' he wrote to Cideville,[1] 'that the best way to forget the tragedy of *Ériphyle* was to write another.'

The new play was *Zaïre*, his masterpiece. With *Mérope* it is perhaps the only dramatic work of Voltaire's which can attract a modern audience. In a dedicatory epistle addressed to his English friend Falkener, Voltaire says not a word about *Othello*, though no doubt the character of his hero, Orosmane, the generous but passionately jealous Mussulman, bears a resemblance to that of the Moor. However, the author confesses that from the English he borrowed the idea of introducing historic, national names. Here he was not a pioneer, since Du Bos speaks of a French play dealing with the death of Henri IV and witnessed by Louis XIII, who also figured in it.

Zaïre, far from revealing Shakespearian influence on Voltaire, is convincing proof of the impossibility of any real *rapprochement*, let alone a fusion of the two types of tragedy, English and French. Racine had portrayed the working of jealousy in the feminine soul.

[1] May 1732.

Almost certainly it was *Othello* which suggested to Voltaire the dramatic possibilities of the same theme, with a hero substituted for a heroine. But for the method of treatment, Voltaire never dreamed of consulting Shakespeare. The tragedy of Othello lies in the fact that a generous and noble soul is corrupted by the machinations of an intellectual villain. The play affords an excellent example of the English experimental, cumulative method of dramatic creation. But Voltaire, great as was his admiration of Newton and his often expressed contempt for Cartesianism, retained, nevertheless, till the end of his life, a quite Cartesian attitude towards art. Iago seemed to him, as to all his contemporaries, an incredible monster. What *rational* motive could be adduced to explain his deliberate, cold-blooded villainy? This objection, we shall see, persisted in France until the end of the century.[1] Moreover, according to French dramatic tradition, the action of a play must begin at a point where the passion to be presented has almost reached maturity; as close to the crisis as possible. Voltaire, here as in other respects, follows tradition. We know from the outset that Orosmane is passionately jealous and abnormally susceptible. In his case one spark will suffice to produce the explosion: there is no need for the patient, deliberate sapping of the master - engineer, Iago. Corasmin, his French counterpart, is the usual confidant, a complete cipher. His presence serves but to accentuate the fact that Voltaire considered Iago absolutely impossible as a character for tragedy. Indeed he has no parallel in the French tragic theatre. Tartuffe, who most nearly resembles him, belongs to comedy, and even Molière had great difficulty in getting the audience to laugh at the spectacle of a hypocrite who, by his scheming, almost destroys the peace of a household. It was only by exaggerating the ridiculous *naïveté* of Orgon and by his comic treatment of the Elmire-Tartuffe duel that he succeeded.

The fundamental difference between *Othello* and *Zaïre* becomes very marked if we examine the plot. Zaïre is Orosmane's captive. Of Christian family, she has been educated, however, as a Mohammedan, despite her confidante's efforts to inspire her with a reverence for Christianity. Her father, Lusignan, has been imprisoned for twenty years, but she does not know this till her brother Nérestan comes to ransom her. A cross which she has worn since childhood

---

[1] See, for example, the criticism of Dudoyer's *Le Vindicatif* in the *Journal Encyclopédique* (1774), v. The objection raised is that vindictiveness belongs to the category of vices that are 'too odious to be made bearable by any art.' For the same reason, it is said, Destouches's *L'Ingrat* revolted the French parterre.

is recognized by Lusignan, and this gives rise to a highly romantic *reconnaissance* scene. Zaïre's problem, which is the backbone of the play, is the favourite seventeenth-century conflict between filial love and passion. The only novel feature is Voltaire's thesis, based on the *a priori* idea that deism is the true rational religion. Zaïre appears, therefore, not so much as a tragic heroine but as the pathetic victim of circumstances which she has done nothing to create, and over which she has no control. She belongs really to the type of play condemned by Voltaire in his criticism of Racine's *Bérénice*, which to the French taste is elegiac rather than tragic, like Shakespeare's *Romeo and Juliet*. It is significant that for different reasons neither Shakespeare nor Voltaire attempted, in *Othello* or in *Zaïre*, to make dramatic capital out of the fact that their hero and heroine are of different race and religion. Shakespeare ignores it, for obviously it never enters Desdemona's mind. Voltaire's whole play is written to show the absurdity of attaching importance to such questions, and, to add spice·to his homily, he portrays Orosmane as an enlightened *philosophe* in his attitude towards matters of creed.

It is, however, in their treatment of the love theme that Shakespeare and Voltaire differ most strikingly. Desdemona is a married woman, loving and submissive. She goes to her doom still pathetically unable to understand Othello's jealousy. Such a situation would have seemed to a French audience undramatic, and, of course, Shakespeare does not make it the foundation-stone of his play, which rests on a more solid basis, the Iago-Othello problem. Voltaire tried, therefore, to create a dramatic conflict out of Zaïre's desire to obey her father's command that she be baptized, and her love for Orosmane, who cannot understand why she defers the marriage. Here is the real defect of the play: it is not in the episode of the intercepted letter arranging her rendezvous with Nérestan, whose relationship to Zaïre is unknown to the sultan. Granted that Orosmane's jealousy has reached a crucial point, the letter is no more absurd than Shakespeare's handkerchief, which, for reasons of *bienséance*, Voltaire could not employ.

Zaïre has something to conceal: Desdemona has not, and this fact enhances the pathos of her situation when she bows obediently to the fury of Othello's jealous rage. No French audience could have listened without protest to a scene in which a woman passively submits to the undeserved and brutal recriminations of a jealous lover. And even Orosmane, who has every reason for

his rage, melts at once at the sight of Zaïre's tears.   The famous
line: 'Vous pleurez, Zaïre,' never failed to produce an extraordinary effect at the *Comédie française*.   One can readily understand
the author's anger when he learned that at Drury Lane Mrs. Cibber,
as Zara, invariably at this point writhed on the ground, thus
featuring agonizing grief *à l'anglaise*.   Voltaire's comment is worth
preserving.   'For example, when, in the English play, Orosmane
comes to announce to Zaïre that he no longer believes he loves her,
Zaïre replies by writhing on the ground.   The sultan is not at all
perturbed to see her in this ridiculous, despairing posture, and the
moment after is quite astonished that Zaïre weeps.

'He says (Act IV, sc. i):
Zaïre, you weep!

'He should have said to her before:

Zaïre, you are rolling about on the ground.

The difference between French and English taste is evident in
the contrast between the language used by Othello to Desdemona
and by Orosmane to Zaïre.   Orosmane never forgets that he is
a sultan: Othello forgets everything save that he is a man in love.
An Orosmane calling Zaïre a strumpet would be as unthinkable
as his striking her.   Either incident, in France, would have reduced
the tragedy to the lowest level of farce.   And, apart from the
question of expression, Voltaire's portrayal of jealousy is, compared
to Shakespeare's, very inadequate.   Orosmane is really the victim
of a misunderstanding which one word from Zaïre would have
explained.   The jealousy of Othello is such that no explanation,
however reasonable, can conjure it away.   It is beyond reason,
an obsession that must inevitably find an outlet in murder.   The
great gulf separating *Zaïre* from *Othello* can only be partially accounted for by the superiority of Shakespeare's genius.   Only by
Shakespeare's dramatic method, which moves from particular facts
to massive, general truths, is it possible to base a whole tragedy on
jealousy.   Racine knew that when he made jealousy only one of
the elements in Phèdre's soul-drama.   What is really dramatic in
jealousy is its genesis and hideous development.   If, in the French
neo-classic manner, we assume at the opening of the play that the
passion already exists in all its maturity, it is difficult to imagine
how even a Racine or a Corneille could spend five acts revealing
its action on the human soul.   For, of all the great human passions
jealousy most urgently craves an outlet in action.   Voltaire

D

therefore, found himself obliged in *Zaïre* to link the jealousy *motif* with two other themes which deal with religion and politics. As a result, his tragedy lacks the greatest of all unities, that of tone.

It will be seen, then, that only in a very superficial sense can it be said that Voltaire's *Zaïre* is influenced by Shakespeare's *Othello*. Shakespeare probably suggested to him the idea of a tragedy based on male jealousy, though, of course, Calderon had treated a similar theme. Here, as in other Voltairian plays, I find it impossible to endorse the accepted view that Voltaire was indebted to our English dramatist for 'the general outline of the plot and its details.' [1]

Zaïre was an overwhelming success. Yet what attracted the audiences of 1732 was not simply the pseudo-national, historic colour produced by the presence of medieval paladins: it was, above all, the exotic element furnished by Orosmane. For at this time all French literature and art was tinged with a superficial lacquer of bogus orientalism. Influenced, no doubt, by the success in London of Shakespeare's historical plays, notably *Henry VIII*, which in 1727 had enjoyed a long run, Voltaire risked a complete national tragedy, *Adelaïde du Guesclin*, in 1734. Hissed at the first performance, it ran for a few nights, till withdrawn by the author. Not until 1765, when French taste had undergone a radical change, was *Adelaïde* received with applause. At its original appearance the audience objected strongly to the scene in which Vendôme, having ordered his brother's execution, listens for the cannon announcing his death. It was considered too melodramatic in 1732. The introduction of historic names excited only merriment. Thus at the phrase: 'Es-tu content, Couci?' a wag interjected: 'Couci-couci,' [2] with disastrous results. The failure of *Adelaïde* rather soured Voltaire for a time against English novelties: at least so we must judge from the prologue to his comedy *L'Échange*, produced in the same year. Speaking of the type of drama best suited to the French taste, the author exclaims:

> Eh quoi! des tragédies
> Qui du théâtre anglais soient d'horribles copies!
> *Madame de la Tour.* Non, ce n'est pas ce qu'il nous faut.
> La pitié, non l'horreur, doit régner sur la scène.
> Des sauvages Anglais la triste Melpomène
> Prit pour théâtre un échafaud.

---

[1] T. Lounsbury, *Shakespeare and Voltaire*, expounds a point of view with which cannot at all agree. My reasons will be found in Appendix I.
[2] So-so!

During his stay at Wandsworth, in 1728, Voltaire had planned
an adaptation of *Julius Caesar*, that 'mixture of the most terrible
tragedy and the lowest farce,' as he described it to a friend who
desired a free translation. His *Mort de César*, finally composed
in 1731, was not intended for public performance. It was to be a
play which, without resembling Shakespeare's, should yet be entirely
in the English taste. By that Voltaire meant a purely political
play with no love interest whatever. A comparison of the two works
illustrates once more the impossibility of any real contact between
the English and French conceptions of tragedy. The French
Brutus is a hot-headed young fanatic, who admires Caesar yet is
prepared to kill him for the public good. So far there is a resemblance to the Brutus of Shakespeare. But the French dramatist
obviously cannot discern any real tragedy in the English play.
So, in order to conform to French usage, he finds himself obliged
to introduce a *reconnaissance* scene which reveals that Brutus is
Caesar's son! This is out-Heroding Herod with a vengeance,
since the dilemma becomes not only incredible but revolting. It
is quite clear, also, that Voltaire utterly misunderstood the function
of the mob in *Julius Caesar*. True, he brings in the *peuple* as a sort
of afterthought—a gullible, almost mute *peuple* whose rage, as
Antony coolly states, may be employed to further his private scheme
of succeeding to Caesar. Obviously, in French dramatic tradition,
there was no place or precedent for a mob except as a sort of chorus.
The mass mind could not, as in Shakespeare, constitute an integral
part of the dramatic action, creating as it does in *Julius Caesar* that
necessary *milieu* which illuminates the characters of Brutus, Caesar,
and Antony, explaining their conduct and accentuating their problems. Again we see the workings of two differently adjusted minds,
the English and the French, experimental and Cartesian. In Shakespeare the problem emerges slowly from a maze of complexity: in
Voltaire it is defined at the outset; for we learn in Act I that Brutus,
the pupil of Cato, is Caesar's son. Voltaire was anxious, however,
to break new ground, to write a tragedy in 'le goût anglais.' What
he really had in mind was one that should reveal his superiority
over Corneille, whose *Cinna*, like *Julius Caesar*, deals with a conspiracy. But Cinna's tragedy is his battle between gratitude
to Augustus and his love for Aemilius, a traditional opposition
which Voltaire felt he must at all costs avoid. Yet he knew
the Parisian public better than to imagine they would accept the
central situation in the *Mort de César* without violent protest. It

was not publicly presented until 1743, when it dragged through six nights.

Mérope, the theme of which is mother-love, really marks a step forward in the evolution of French tragedy. Next to *Zaïre* it is Voltaire's most original play. In the preface he reads the English a short sermon on the treatment of love in tragedy. 'It must be confessed,' he states, 'that no nation in the world has portrayed this passion so badly . . . it seems as if the same cause which deprives the English of the genius of painting and music also deprives them of the genius of tragedy.' Yet, he observes, ever since the reign of Charles II, English authors have persisted in dragging love into their plays. Take, for example, the ridiculous *Merope*, produced in London in 1731, where the hero is ordered by the queen to drink a cup of poison to save the life of his mistress. This he does, but returns in Act V to announce coolly that he is the queen's son.

Voltaire had never forgotten the failure of *Ériphyle*: he was still haunted by the ghost. He could not understand why Shakespeare had succeeded where he had ignominiously stumbled. In the preface to *Sémiramis*, which was to dispel these unfortunate memories, he summarizes *Hamlet* with characteristic facetiousness. 'Hamlet goes mad in the second act, and his mistress in the third: the prince kills his sweetheart's father, pretending to kill a rat, and the heroine throws herself into the river. They make her grave on the stage: grave-diggers utter jests worthy of themselves, holding skulls in their hands. Prince Hamlet replies to their abominable crudities with no less disgusting stupidities. Meanwhile one of the characters conquers Poland. Hamlet, his mother, and stepfather, drink together on the stage: they sing at table, quarrel, and fight. They kill each other. One might take this for the work of a drunken savage. But amidst these gross irregularities, which to-day make the English stage so absurd and barbarous, one finds in *Hamlet*, and this is stranger still, sublime traits that are worthy of the highest genius. It seems as if it had pleased Nature to assemble in Shakespeare's brain the greatest imaginable force and grandeur with the lowest, most detestable, most witless elements.'

Yet, as Voltaire frankly admits, the ghost in Hamlet produces a more terrifying effect even than 'the apparition of Darius in Aeschylus's *Persae*. Shakespeare's ghost is not superfluous and it is not arbitrarily introduced: it serves to convince us there is an invisible power which is master of nature. Men, who have all a

germ of justice in their hearts, are naturally prone to desire that
Heaven should interest itself in the avenging of injustice.' Ghosts,
he concludes, in order to justify their existence in drama, should
always be a *necessary* element in the plot: they must not be brought
in, like the *deus ex machina*, to unravel a complicated intrigue.
Above all, the audience should be prepared for the apparition.
So much for Voltaire's theory.

In *Sémiramis* the ghost of Ninus, the murdered husband of the
queen, is, as in *Ériphyle*, a thoroughly crafty fellow, who takes
advantage of the obscurity of the final scene to outwit his son
Ninias. The latter, groping about in the murky tomb for his
intended victim Assur (the Claudius of the piece), is cunningly led
by the malevolent shade towards his mother, who has gone into
the mausoleum to save her son. Again, as in *Ériphyle*, the queen is
accidentally slain by her son, who is thus in the eyes of the audience
unfortunate but not guilty of matricide. Voltaire evades the tragic
struggle between the son's duty to his father and his love for his
mother. His Hamlet has indeed no problem at all. In Shakespeare's play the king orders the son to spare his mother, a fact
which must have puzzled a French audience. Voltaire eludes the
difficulty by keeping Ninias ignorant of his real identity till almost
the close of the play. Up to the fourth act, all he knows is that he
must kill someone in the tomb in order to avenge the murdered king.
Even after the *éclaircissement* he still thinks that his victim is Assur.

Sémiramis reveals Voltaire as an unoriginal dramatist. On the one
hand, he could not penetrate the secret of Shakespeare's art; on
the other, in his anxiety to improve on Racine and to introduce
more action, he was driven to invent elaborate and *romanesque*
situations. He really inaugurates the type of romantic melodrama
that was to be so popular in the early nineteenth century. The
disparity between his theory and his practice is startling, and, as
is evident from the preface to *Sémiramis*, he was wise only after the
event. We have already referred to the unfortunate contretemps
which marred the appearance of the shade of Ninus. Voltaire
seized on this to explain the failure of *Sémiramis*; adding that a
distinguished English actress who was present was amazed at the
crowds of spectators on the French stage. In his petulance, too,
he blamed his leading actor, Legrand, for being too fat; looking,
as he said, like 'the caretaker of the mausoleum.' What he failed
to realize was that an audience is much more horrified by murders
carried out in the gloom of a darkened mausoleum than by the

actual sight of the murder. How could a French audience of 1748, as yet unused to killing on the stage, not be revolted by the mysterious unseen doings inside the tomb? Voltaire could not understand why the English, who do not believe in ghosts, yet took 'a pleasure' in seeing the spectre of the king in *Hamlet*, 'an occasion *almost similar* [1] to that in which the ghost of Ninus was seen in Paris.' But he forgot that the audience at the *Comédie française* was very different from that of Drury Lane, which contained a large number of people who not only believed in ghosts but liked ghosts, and insisted on having ghosts. 'There is nothing,' said Addison, 'which delights and terrifies our English theatre so much as a ghost, especially when he appears in a bloody shirt. A spectre has very often saved a play, though he has done nothing but stalked across the stage, or rose through a cleft of it, and sunk again without speaking one word.' [2] There is a certain piquancy, by the way, in the spectacle of the rational Voltaire vainly trying to prove to himself on experimental and scientific grounds that the French *ought* to have accepted, indeed welcomed, the ghost in *Sémiramis*.

The play was, beyond doubt, like *Ériphyle*, immediately suggested by *Hamlet*. But in his treatment of the central idea Voltaire was influenced not by English but by Greek example. That is very natural. The *Critical Review*, [3] however, like many present-day English critics, was unable to see farther back than Shakespeare, and reproached Voltaire with imitating 'what he thinks most blameable in our immortal Shakespeare, namely, his fondness for the horrible.' It accused the author of *Sémiramis* of over-indulging in the marvellous, 'or at least what must appear so to a modern audience. Tombs gaping, ghosts stalking along the stage, thunder rattling, lightning flashing, and oracles delivered by a high priest,' forgetting that Voltaire, as he himself said, was modelling his supernatural, not on Elizabethan tragedy, but on that of Aeschylus. Much later, it did dawn on one writer, Davies, [4] that, though the idea of the ghost was immediately due to *Hamlet*, the spectre in *Sémiramis* was classic. 'As the ghost of Darius made his appearance before the whole Persian court, so does that of Ninus in the full presence of Semiramis and the court of Babylon.' Decidedly, Voltaire had no success either abroad or at home with his daylight spectre.

It may be pertinent, at this stage, to quote an extract from a criticism of *Zaïre* [5] which has a direct bearing on the point just

---

[1] My italics.   [2] *Spectator*, No. 44.   [3] 1760.   [4] *Dramatic Miscellanies*, iii. 16.
[5] *La Bibliothèque française* (1732), 'Extrait d'une Lettre écrite de Paris.'

raised in connection with *Sémiramis*. Voltaire, says this writer, is
obviously trying to make a reputation by breaking fresh ground in
drama. 'It seems to me that in his first play, *Œdipe*, as in *Ériphyle*,
his last but one, his intention was to resuscitate the Greek stage
and to oppose . . . the terror and pity of the Athenian theatre
to the sublime grandeur of Corneille and to the sentiment so happily
expressed by Racine. This really was opening up a third road,
and it is true to say that he has established a sort of triumvirate on
our stage and that M. de Voltaire is recognized by the connoisseurs
of the universe as our third master in good tragedy. Yet, despite
the applause and the success which has attended his plays, he
himself has admitted that these matters of taste may not and
cannot be transplanted and, in a word, that the French are not
constituted to appreciate the terrible. . . . He leaves it to our
scientists to explain the cause of this phenomenon: but I am persuaded that in things of genius there are national peculiarities
almost similar to those which we observe in the atmosphere and
the physique of different peoples.' In all this it will be noted that
there is no mention whatever of Shakespeare, though it is clear
from other articles in this magazine that the editor is most familiar
with our literature. A great deal of space, in fact, is devoted to
reviews of English works.

Rome sauvée (1752) contains no love interest. Apart from this it
was a play conceived deliberately in the neo-classic manner and
intended to show the superiority of French politico-historical
tragedy over the crude efforts of Shakespeare, in whose historical
plays 'there is neither unity nor reason, where all the tones are
confused, where history is meticulously observed, and the manners
altered to a ridiculous degree.' *Rome sauvée* was coldly received.
But Voltaire secretly hankered after the spectacular and the
original. The orientalism of *Zaïre* had drawn great applause, but,
since then, Voltaire the historian, working along experimental
lines, had written his famous *Essai sur les mœurs*, the first attempt
in France at a scientific history where, instead of the old *a priori*
generalizations, the author presented conclusions induced from
the consideration of observed facts. A contemptuous reference to
Shakespeare's histories in the preface to his next play, *L'Orphelin
de la Chine*, reminds us that he was determined to give France
something better than *Henry VIII*—coronation or no coronation.[1]

[1] 'L'action de la pièce chinoise [i.e. *L'Orphelin de Tchao*, which suggested
L'Orphelin de la Chine] dure 25 ans comme les farces monstrueuses de Shakespeare.'

What Voltaire wanted was to introduce local colour into the French theatre, and in this he was warmly abetted by Le Kain and Mlle Clairon, both of whom supported that movement for more realism on the stage which was being eloquently advocated by Diderot.[1] 'I wanted to depict the manners of the Tartars and the Chinese,' said Voltaire. 'The most interesting adventures are nothing if they do not depict manners.' The *Orphelin* is not Shakespearian. It is the product of a mind educated in the artistic creed of the French seventeenth century but bubbling with subversive ideas. As a result, this tragedy of manners becomes an excuse for disseminating Voltaire's cosmopolitan views on egalitarianism, humanitarianism, naturism, deism, tolerantism, and the other *-isms* of an age which still found it easier to build up speculative *a priori* systems than to submit to the laborious discipline exacted by experimental philosophy.

So far, what had Voltaire adopted from Shakespeare, or indeed from any other English dramatist? Very little, unless one can reckon an unsuccessful ghost, a smattering of national local colour, and the idea of a tragedy without love, though *Mérope*, his only successful application of that idea, was not in any sense inspired by Shakespeare. And this was in 1760, at a moment when England, thanks to the genius of Garrick, was in the grip of a Shakespearian revival. Surveying the French theatre, where a new type of play, *le drame*, was now being born, Voltaire, discouraged by his efforts to revivify and to reform neo-classic tragedy, felt justified in exclaiming: 'Le théâtre est épuisé.' The recent abolition of spectators from the stage inspired him, however, with the hope that now he could realize his old dream of introducing more action, more movement into tragedy. The result was his *Tancrède*, which was to be a great national tragedy, national in setting but essentially classic in structure. Its central idea, borrowed from the old novels of chivalry, was that the hero, though believing his lady criminal, yet enters the lists on her behalf and is killed. Ariosto was his source, not Shakespeare. The play failed, however, to appeal to an audience which long ago had ceased to enjoy the *romans pleurards* of the seventeenth century, and troubadours were not to come into vogue for another fifteen years.[2] Besides, the French theatre was

---

[1] See my *Eighteenth-century France*, p. 189.
[2] In 1732, however, Montaland had reprinted *Cassandre* and promised reprints of *Clélie, Cyrus, Pharamond*, etc., which, says the *Bibliothèque française*, 'had become very rare.'

becoming less heroic and more bourgeois. Possibly, too, Voltaire, now patriarch of Ferney, was, despite his voluminous correspondence and his constant stream of visitors, too remote from Paris to know what the public wanted.

So he gave them *Olympie* (1764), based on La Calprenède's novel *Cassandre*. This sensational melodrama culminates in a spectacular scene, in which Statire kills herself after ordering her daughter to marry Antigone. Olympie, in love with her father's slayer, Cassandre, leaps into her mother's funeral pyre. In his next work, *Le Triumvirat*, which was played once, in 1764, Voltaire, who remained incognito, attempted, as he tells us, to write a 'drame barbare un peu à l'anglaise.' In private he alluded to it humorously as *Les Roués*, a play in the 'genre terrible, perhaps in the English taste,' for, as he remarked: 'It is good to have works of every type.' Yet nothing could be less Shakespearian than *Le Triumvirat*. To a Frenchman of 1764 'the English taste' was not necessarily the manner of Shakespeare. By *le goût anglais* Voltaire means that *genre terrible* or *genre sombre* which is, of course, reflected in the gloomy setting of *Macbeth* and in the storm scenes of *Lear*, but which Voltaire's contemporaries derived more directly from the sepulchral writings of Baculard d'Arnaud.[1] To any one determined to see the hand of Shakespeare in every Voltairian play, the romantic opening scene of *Le Triumvirat*, with its rocks, precipices, its thunder and lightning, would naturally suggest perhaps *Julius Caesar*, but it would be mere conjecture to carry the parallel farther. The play is most undramatic, consisting really in a series of violent incidents. Antony is deserting his wife, Fulvia, in order to marry Octavia. Fulvia tries to kill Antony. Meanwhile Octavius is in love with Julia, the wife of Pompey, who attempts to murder Octavius. This ignoble imbroglio is ended by the repentance of Octavius. Actually, the alleged English influence is limited to inessentials. Certainly the curious blend of crime and voluptuousness which passes for love in this play is not of Shakespearian origin. It is neo-classic, corresponding, as a matter of fact, somewhat to Diderot's conception of the sublime in art.[2] Speaking of the effect produced upon his mind by the statue of Cleopatra, he writes: 'Great effects arise everywhere from voluptuous ideas interlaced with terrible ones; for example, from half-naked, beautiful women offering us a delicious beverage in the

---

[1] Fragments of Ossian, too, had been recently translated.
[2] *Lettres à Sophie Volland*, ed. Babelon, ii. 201 (1762).

bleeding skulls of our enemies. Here we have the model of all sublime things. It is then that the soul drinks in pleasure and shudders with horror. These mixed sensations hold it strangely in thrall; the sublime has the peculiar property of penetrating it in a most extraordinary fashion.' Voltaire does not, of course, rise to such romantic peaks, but like his rival, the elder Crébillon, he touches in *Le Triumvirat* a sensational, melodramatic chord. *Les Pélopides*, written in 1771, but never staged, further emphasizes the *romanesque* trend of Voltairian tragedy, which though neo-classic in structure is melodramatic in tone. This play represents an attempt to improve upon Crébillon's dark *Atrée et Thyeste*. 'I have never believed,' Voltaire explains apologetically, 'in rose-water tragedy. . . . Tragedy must have furious passions, great crimes, violent remorse.' And indeed *Les Pélopides* is not *à l'eau rose*, for it ends with the triple murder, by the sinister Atreus, of Thyestes and the latter's wife and child at the altar where the rival brothers met to swear eternal friendship.

We now approach 1776, the year when Voltaire, in his notorious *Letter to the Academy*, delivered final judgment on the dramatic art of Shakespeare. In reality it was but a detailed restatement of views which he had always held and frequently expressed. But now Shakespeare was better known in Europe through the adaptations of Ducis and by the fame of Garrick, an actor known to many Parisian *salons*. Anglomania was at its height and Shakespeare was to be translated. The very fact that enough subscriptions could be collected for this undertaking indicates a growing curiosity as to Shakespeare's art. It would be wrong, however, to conclude that his works were well known to French *literati*. Prior to 1769, when Ducis presented his Racinian version of *Hamlet*, it would be hard to find more than half a dozen important references to our national dramatist in French writings. And except for La Place's preface to his *Théâtre anglais*,[1] there is, in the utterances of this handful of critics, no substantial disagreement with Voltaire's opinion of Shakespeare. Only a very small number of Frenchmen knew Shakespeare, and the adaptations of La Place and Ducis were ill calculated to give a very accurate impression of his genius. The purpose of the Le Tourneur-Catuelan translation was to make Shakespeare known in France: the work did not represent the homage paid by admirers to an author of established fame and recognized influence. This is precisely what Voltaire resented.

[1] 1745.

No one better than he knew the impossibility of translating Shakespeare without doing violence to French taste. Referring to his own rendering of *Julius Caesar*,[1] which, as he rightly avers, is extremely faithful, he implies that he has already sufficiently demonstrated the incompatibility of French and English canons of taste. But what chiefly enraged him was that Le Tourneur, in his one-hundred-and-thirty-page preface, scarcely mentions the French masters of drama, and Voltaire not at all—Voltaire, whose work had been translated and produced in all civilized countries! Moreover, Le Tourneur was indiscreet enough to gibe at the 'petits Aristarques' who, without knowing Shakespeare, dare to criticize him. Voltaire was, of course, careful not to identify himself with 'these impudent little judges,' but without doubt thought himself indirectly attacked. Incidentally, he was not sorry to have an opportunity to reply to Elizabeth Montagu's *Essay on the Genius of Shakespeare*,[2] in which Voltaire, with Corneille and Racine, was vigorously attacked. Most unjustly, too, pouncing on a minor slip in his translation of *Julius Caesar*,[3] the Queen of the Blue-stockings had roundly taxed him with ignorance of English and given the impression that his whole rendering was a mass of 'miserable mistakes and galimathias,' which, as she well knew, was grossly untrue.

Now Voltaire's criticism of Shakespeare had always been largely directed against the 'low' tone of his work. In the *Dictionnaire philosophique* (1765) he had given a literal translation of *Antony and Cleopatra* (Act v. sc. ii), of *Henry V* (Act v. sc. ii), and of sundry passages from *Julius Caesar* and *Othello*,[4] to illustrate the incredible coarseness of Elizabethan taste. To be quite fair, however, he also cited excerpts from *Julius Cæsar* and *Hamlet*, including a free rendering of the 'beau monologue' on suicide, to show that Shakespeare could write lines 'which uplift the imagination and penetrate the heart.' The *Letter to the Academy* merely furnishes more examples in support of his opinion that Shakespeare's style is a vicious model for young French playwrights. Scenes from *Hamlet, Lear, Romeo and Juliet*, and *Henry V* are translated or summarized to reveal the irreconcilable contrast between English and French dramatic taste as exemplified in Shakespeare and Racine. Garrick is congratulated on having suppressed at Drury Lane the infamous grave-diggers'

---

[1] In his *Théâtre de Corneille* (1764).   [2] 1769.
[3] He rendered the word 'course' by its French homonym, which means 'a race.'
[4] *Art dramatique*. The reference is to 'the beast with two backs.'

scene, which Le Tourneur, incredible as it may seem, has retained because it is still put on at Covent Garden. Voltaire is merciless to *Hamlet* because Home had dared to compare the first scene of this 'monstrous and anachronistic' production with that of Racine's *Iphigénie*. What possible comparison can exist, he asks, between the phrase 'Not a mouse stirring' and 'Tout dort, et l'armée, et les vents, et Neptune.' Why is this a great line? Because, says Voltaire, 'it is the harmonious expression of great truths which are the basis of the play. There is no harmony, no interesting truth in the soldier's *quodlibet*: "Je n'ai pas entendu une souris trotter." Whether the soldier did or did not hear a mouse stir is a matter of no moment to the tragedy of *Hamlet*: it is a clown's speech, a low proverb that cannot produce any effect. There is always a reason why every beauty is beautiful and every stupidity stupid.'

This little skirmish is worth noting because it shows the fundamental impossibility of Le Tourneur's scheme, which was to make Shakespeare better understood through the medium of a literal translation. There is no need to attribute any malicious motive to Voltaire for rendering 'stir' by 'trotter,' which, in this context, is quite proper. From the eighteenth-century French standpoint Voltaire was perfectly right. What he could not know was that Shakespeare, in selecting this metaphor, hit upon the swiftest route to the understanding of his English hearers. He might have said 'As still as death,' which would perhaps have been more noble according to the French view. But by selecting a familiar domestic image he communicates the idea of profound silence to every class of auditor. Voltaire once told Bolingbroke, just after his return from London, that he had learned to think so well in English as to find it hard to write in French. That, however, was fifty years before. In 1776 he still knew how to translate English but no longer thought in English. As a matter of fact, it was foolish of Home to parallel the two passages, since Shakespeare's phrase was not intended to have the same repercussion as Racine's. In *Hamlet* the soldier's words are used to accentuate the silence that precedes the entrance of the ghost; in *Iphigénie* the author employs a phrase calculated to remind the audience of the elements on which the fate of the heroine depends. If the gods are angry, if Neptune withholds the winds, a sacrifice will have to be made.[1]

---

[1] In justice to Shakespeare the phrase should not have been literally translated: an analogous one should have been substituted. In that case, however, Voltaire would have been accused of tampering with the original.

There are, no doubt, ungenerous and petty outbursts in Voltaire's letter, as when he perfidiously dissents from Rymer's [1] remark that an African ape or baboon had less taste than Shakespeare. But it must be remembered that the whole document was composed in a spirit of fuming irritation by a moribund octogenarian never celebrated for his tolerance and appalled, moreover, at his countrymen's growing infatuation for the art, manners, and institutions of the English. His last words on Shakespeare are more dignified, though the convictions are, if anything, more settled. He openly replies here to Mrs. Montagu. One can discern a tone of underlying hopelessness in his patient, laboured attempt to explain once more that whilst Shakespeare is great in certain 'natural and energetic' passages, these are invariably disfigured by 'low familiarity.' The French tragic masterpieces enjoy international fame: Shakespeare is appreciated only in England. Mrs. Montagu attacks Corneille, but she has not discovered as many defects as Voltaire did in his own commentary. She 'tries to be touched by the beauties of Euripides so as to try to be insensible to the perfection of Racine.' And she obviously does not know Euripides any more than did Brumoy, whom she plagiarizes; and Voltaire proves that the famous line in *Iphigénie*, 'Vous y serez, ma fille,' which Mrs. Montagu, after Brumoy, attributes to Euripides in order to show Racine's inferiority, is not by the Greek but by the Frenchman. With a politeness that thinly veils the exasperating urbanity of the savant addressing a half-wit, Voltaire explains the dramatic defects of Shakespeare: the mixture of low comedy and high tragedy, the absence of 'exposition, *nœud*, or denouement,' the scenes where princes converse like street-porters and street-porters like princes. But why this deplorable international squabble over a literary matter? The English are superior to the French in philosophy and in science; but Shakespeare? Well, La Harpe has just proved what every one feels, that 'Shakespeare is a savage with sparks of genius which shine out in a horrible night.' [2]

Had Voltaire been less sincere and really afraid, as spiteful Parisians alleged,[3] lest Le Tourneur's translation should reveal the true extent of his unacknowledged debt to Shakespeare, he would

[1] *Tragedies of the Last Age Considered* (1678).
[2] On Mrs. Montagu's knowledge of the classics, see Johnson's remark to Boswell: 'Sir, she has not read them: she shows none of this impetuosity to me: she does not know Greek and, I fancy, knows little Latin. She is willing you should think she knows them; but she does not say she does.'
[3] *Correspondance de Grimm, etc.*, xi. 217 (1776).

have welcomed a work which pleased few and, because of its literalness, horribly misrepresented our English genius. London critics were chagrined, and said it was inaccurate in parts. This was not surprising, since no two English editors of Shakespeare could agree upon the text of certain passages. The 'impartials' proclaimed that Shakespeare was still a genius but badly translated. 'This translation,' said Grimm, 'has met with success only amongst those who did not know the poet and were burning to read him.' Now Grimm, though not a creative mind, had the gift of assimilating and collating the views of men wittier and more original than himself. His opinions on the repercussions evoked by the Voltaire-Shakespeare controversy are therefore valuable. A Frenchman by culture, he was a German by race and temperament, and this explains his appreciation of Shakespeare's more profound qualities. For all the disorder of his plays, Grimm finds in them a sense of the theatre, a compelling note of vigour and originality which the French, with their more finished execution, often miss. The English are apt, he says, to exaggerate nature: the French often embellish it beyond recognition. Both are frequently unnatural, but in different ways; for, if it is absurd to make valets talk like heroes, it is still more so to make them speak like plebeians. Shakespeare, he infers, is a dangerous model, since by his genius he transcends all rules. 'Who else but he can hope to preserve in his greatest, most complex compositions that marvellous light which constantly illuminates their steady march and, so to speak, spontaneously irradiates every aspect of his subjects? Who can ever flatter himself that he can sustain that great fund of interest which Shakespeare himself seems to interrupt deliberately and yet is always certain to resume with the same energy? What genius ever penetrated so deeply into all the characters and passions of human nature?'

Yet Grimm feels that Le Tourneur's translation might do great harm in France by distracting young writers from the only models which can be imitated without danger. 'It would invite them to vain experiments in a genre that can never suit the *mœurs* or the spirit of the nation. Of course it is much easier to violate all the rules of art than to observe one. Of course, too, it is not difficult to pile up a mass of events one on top of the other, to mingle the grotesque and the terrible, to pass from a cabaret to a battlefield or from a cemetery to a throne.' In these prophetic words Grimm forecasts the excesses of French Romantic melodrama. He is convinced of the inveterate incompatibility of French and English dramatic taste. Possibly, he thinks, a great genius like Voltaire might succeed in transposing the beauties of one literature to another, but it is a delicate and risky business. 'I know very well that up to the present the object of the English theatre has seemed totally different from ours. The whole effort of the one appears to tend towards exciting the most lively passions; the whole effort of the other is to assuage them and restore them to their natural trend. One seems wholly occupied in reinforcing the character and the manners of the nation; the other in softening them. The one presupposes a sort of inertia in the imagination which has need of violent, extraordinary shocks; the other postulates a great suppleness, a great facility for receiving outside impressions, a soul naturally sympathetic and therefore strongly disposed to imitate anything that strikes it vividly.' Grimm's notion that the sensational tone of English drama is due to the torpor of the racial temperament is an echo of Riccoboni's well-known remark: [1] 'The essence of the English character is to plunge in reverie; . . . it is because they are continually engaged in thinking, that the highest scenes are treated by the writers of this nation with great profundity; and the arts are carried to that degree of perfection we know, because their thoughtful nature furnishes the patience and exactness lacking in other nations. . . . According to my reasoning, I think that if any one presented on their stage tragedies in the best and most correct taste, i.e. denuded of those horrors which stain the stage with blood, the spectators would perhaps fall asleep.' The theory was an old one, as old indeed as Du Bos's views regarding the influence of climate on the national temperament later elaborated by Montesquieu and others. By Grimm's time it was generally accepted, along with the traditional French notion that every November witnessed a queue of Londoners waiting on the bridges of the metropolis to end their *spleen* in the murky waters of the Thames.

Grimm, who disliked Voltaire, gleefully opined that the *Letter to the Academy* would arouse trouble. He speaks, indeed, of a 'fermentation des esprits.' The Shakespeare adepts were busily agitating for a translation of Mrs. Montagu's famous *Essay on the Writings and Genius of Shakespeare*,[2] and La Harpe, who, according to

---

[1] *Réflexions historiques et critiques sur les différents théâtres de l'Europe* (1738).

[2] It duly appeared, in 1777, under the title: *Apologie de Shakespeare en réponse à la Critique de M. de Voltaire. Londres (Paris).*

the malicious German, did not know a word of English, was furiously working at a critique of *Othello*. The first reply to the *Letter* came from the son of an Irishman, the Chevalier Rutlidge, born in France. But his *Observations à Messieurs de l'Académie française*,[1] though discreetly hinting at Voltaire's debts to the English dramatist, only repeat the commonplace that Shakespeare dramatizes incidents, such as the conduct of the mob in *Julius Caesar*, which a French author would have narrated and not shown. Much more spirited was the *Discours sur Shakespeare et sur M. de Voltaire* of the Italian Anglomaniac, Joseph Baretti.[2] In general, he hangs to the skirts of Mrs. Montagu, accuses Voltaire of not knowing English and of 'murdering' *Julius Caesar*. Inevitably the question of the unities crops up, and Baretti trots out the now hoary arguments of the eighteenth-century moderns. Corneille is, of course, attacked, and Baretti, in his heavy way, jeers at 'the confidants and confidantes who listen so patiently to long stories so that the audience may know in advance what the subject will be; the cups of poison now swallowed by accident, now by design; the dagger-thrusts which at the fifth act so regularly kill off the tyrant or the heroine behind the scenes . . . and other such-like happenings which never occur in ordinary life.' Above all, he criticizes Corneille's style, 'overladen with big sentiments suitable only to imaginary heroes; or else maxims too often embodied in an antithesis. There will come a time when no one will be able to stand him, when the works of Corneille will be exiled to the library.' Here again he but echoes Elizabeth Montagu.

Baretti's discourse reads suspiciously like a document prepared in some London drawing-room in collaboration with English friends. He makes no effort to excuse Shakespeare's lapses into 'coarseness,' and is naïvely angry with Voltaire for not pointing out 'that nowadays every *gaillardise* is excised from these plays when they are performed, and there are even some which are no longer played because the defects somewhat counteract their beauties.'[3] With the same querulous simplicity he accuses Voltaire of giving as typical examples of Shakespeare's genius passages which were obviously written for the mob. We gather, too, that Le Tourneur's translation had not been a success in England. 'One

---

[1] 1777.

[2] He was a friend of Dr. Johnson's. The latter, in 1762, sent him Shakespeare's plays, 'that you may explain his work to the ladies of Italy and tell them the story of the editor.'

[3] Voltaire did, as a matter of fact, mention that Garrick had altered *Hamlet*.

must not judge of the merits of a foreign work,' says Baretti, 'through translation, especially in the case of poetry, which is so difficult to render because words are poetic in one language and not in another.'

The one really interesting passage in Baretti's discourse is that where he compares Shakespeare's handling of the ghost in *Hamlet* with Voltaire's unfortunate experiments in *Ériphyle* and in *Sémiramis*. The English ghost appears in 'circumstances corresponding to the average man's idea of a ghost: the French author starts by ignoring every popular notion which might in some sense have made his phantom credible. He simply follows his own whim in making him appear on the stage. He is too far above ordinary ideas to conform to them.' The bitterness with which Baretti attacks Voltaire for his arrogance in departing from the good old British custom of staging ghosts only at night is funny, but nevertheless he is right. The shade of Ninus had no business to appear at noon. Yet, if a timid word may be inserted in defence of Voltaire, it is only fair to point out that he was careful to bring on his apparition to the accompaniment of darkness, thunder, and a minor earthquake.[1]

Apparently no Frenchman was interested enough to take up the glove thrown down by Voltaire. Ignoring Baretti, the latter, now in his eighty-third year, was busy with his tragedy *Irène*, in the preface to which he said his very last word on Shakespeare. Of the intellectual fermentation predicted by Grimm there was no sign. The press commented on the replies, but not in a manner hostile to Voltaire or favourable to our dramatist. Mrs. Montagu's letters,[2] naturally enough, give a one-sided version of the affair. By an odd coincidence she was in Paris when the *Lettre à l'Académie* was read to the Immortals and, in fact, was actually present on the occasion. The tenor of Voltaire's protest surprised none, not even Mrs. Montagu, who, like every one else, had seen a copy of Voltaire's private letter to D'Argental, a letter couched in his most vituperative style, in which he cries aloud for vengeance on that *maraud*, that *faquin*, that *impudent imbécile*, Le Tourneur. Metaphorically Voltaire lashes himself for having, by displaying the fair pearls in Shakespeare's 'enormous dunghill,' unwittingly helped to trample on the laurels of Corneille and Racine in order to

[1] The spectre of Ninus, as Voltaire informed D'Argental, was 'quite white, in gilt armour, a sceptre in its hand, and a crown on its head.' It closely resembles, indeed, the statue of the commander in Molière's *Don Juan*. It was, in fact, a neo-classic, not an Elizabethan spectre.

[2] Published by R. Blunt, vol. i.

crown the brow of a 'barbaric histrion.' The Duc de Nivernais, whom she had entertained when he was ambassador in London, introduced Mrs. Montagu to 'Russian princes, French princesses, *beaux-esprits*, etc.' In excited letters she rattles on complacently about Paris and the *bon ton*, the magnificent residences, the squalid theatres, the dresses, the bugs, dirt, and smells, the charm, the wit, the politeness of the capital. She writes home a full account of the proceedings at the Academy. Voltaire's 'trash,' his 'blackguard, abusive invective' raised a momentary laugh, but 'the Academy and the audience seemed displeased at the paper read,' many declaring it unjust and unworthy of the *Académie française*. This is somewhat different from D'Alembert's version dispatched post-haste to Ferney. 'Your reflections gave great pleasure and were much applauded . . . several parts I was made to repeat. I need not tell you that the English who were there went away displeased.' Horace Walpole in a letter to Mason [1] refers to Voltaire's 'paltry, scurrilous letter,' which he does not consider worth sending, and later writes: 'Voltaire has lately written a letter against Shakespeare (occasioned by the new paltry transaction,[2] which has still discovered his miraculous powers), and it is as downright Billingsgate as an applewoman would utter if you overturned her wheelbarrow. Poor old wretch! How envy disgraces the brightest talents . . . It hurts one when a real genius like Voltaire can feel more spite than admiration, though I am persuaded that his rancour is grounded on unconscious inferiority. I wish you would lash the old scorpion a little and teach him awe of English poets.' Walpole, by the way, had felt the 'old scorpion's' sting in the little affair of his preface to the *Castle of Otranto*, but there is a startling difference between the tone of the letter to Mason and the grovelling obsequiousness of his reply to the old man.[3]

M. Jusserand [4] is convinced that Le Tourneur's translation was a 'European event.' This is perfectly true. But every French work in the eighteenth century that was published by subscription was a European event, since its subscription list invariably included the names of all French and European aristocrats who possessed libraries. Le Tourneur's translation was no exception. Obviously those who purchased the first volume bought the others. Voltaire

---

[1] September 1776. [2] i.e. Le Tourneur's translation.
[3] *Correspondence*, ix. 414.
[4] In his excellent *Shakespeare en France*, a pioneer work and a classic.

claimed that some withdrew their subscriptions; M. Jusserand, on the other hand, maintains that volume three attracted one hundred and fifty new subscribers. Both are most probably correct. Ducis said that the translation was in everybody's hands, but Ducis, the adapter of *Hamlet* and *Othello*, is hardly a reliable judge. 'Numerous symptoms,' according to M. Jusserand, 'had foreshadowed the event from the middle of the century. Imitations intended for the stage had multiplied; studies more and more minute, and judgments more and more eulogistic, had come out.' It is with great diffidence that one ventures to disagree with the statement of a scholar of such brilliance and industry, yet it is to be feared that in this case M. Jusserand's sympathy for our literature has affected his habitual and exact sense of balance. The affair of the *Lettre à l'Académie* certainly aroused much curiosity, because it came from the pen of Voltaire. Are we justified, however, in concluding that Shakespearian drama had now definitely and profoundly metamorphosed French traditional taste? Was it not simply yet another symptom of Anglomania, the current form of *snobisme*? What were those 'imitations intended for the stage,' the 'eulogistic studies and judgments,' and to what extent do they reveal that the French of the second half of the eighteenth century understood and admired the real Shakespeare? In this connection it is very easy to confuse two almost separate movements: the evolution of *le drame*, which was the product of the new attitude towards society, and the gradual disintegration of neo-classic tragedy which announces the Romantic theatre of the nineteenth century. The partisans of either movement might well use Shakespeare in order to justify changes of a revolutionary sort, but it does not follow that such reforms were of a nature to produce even a partial fusion of the French and English schools of drama. These are questions that demand very close scrutiny.

CHAPTER IV

SHAKESPEARE AND FRENCH DRAMATIC TRADITION

FOR information regarding the English theatre, the French reading public of the seventeen-fifties would naturally turn to Voltaire, Prévost, La Place, or to Le Blanc, a French abbé who had lived in our country from 1737 to 1744. His *Letters*,[1] addressed to men like Crébillon the dramatist, La Chaussée, the protagonist of *la comédie larmoyante*, Buffon, and other Frenchmen of note, enjoyed a considerable vogue. Voltaire's opinions we have already discussed. They had behind them all the weight of his great reputation. Prévost, the author of *Manon Lescaut*, recorded in 1728 his first impressions of the English stage.[2] He finds our plays irregular in structure, but adds: 'For the beauty of their sentiments, whether tender or sublime, for that tragic form which stirs the depths of the heart and infallibly excites passions in the most torpid soul, for the energy of the expressions and for the art of leading up to the incidents, and for the handling of situation I have read nothing in Greek or in French to surpass the English theatre. Shakespeare's *Hamlet*, Dryden's *Don Sebastian*, Otway's *Orphan* and *Venice Preserved*, several plays by Dongrew [Congreve], by Farghar [Farquhar], etc., are excellent tragedies in which you find a thousand beauties assembled. Some are rather disfigured by a mixture of buffooneries unworthy of the buskin, but that is a defect recognized by the English themselves, and one which they are beginning to correct. They are no less successful in the comic genre. Apart from the question of regularity, I doubt if one can find in any country anything more agreeable and more ingenious than their *The Constant Couple*, *The Provoked Husband*, *The Recruiting Officer*, *The Careless Husband*, and *The Way of the World*, which are the work of their best authors, and at the performance of which I had infinite satisfaction.' Little comment is necessary. Prévost's enthusiasm strikes a new note, but he can scarcely be said to single out Shakespeare for special mention. He is more explicit in his magazine, the *Pour et Contre*,[3]

[1] Op. cit.
[2] In the *Mémoires d'un Homme de Qualité*, in which he enshrined his immortal *Manon*.
[3] 1733–8.

the purpose of which was to make English literature and English ideas better known to the French. Prévost was in London in 1731 and saw some of the earliest performances of Lillo's *George Barnwell, or the London Merchant*. This melodrama, with its sombre theme, the corrosive effects of passion on a naturally virtuous soul, made an instant appeal to the author of *Manon Lescaut*. No doubt, in the character and history of Barnwell there was much to remind the romantic, gloomy abbé of his own passionate, chequered life. He devotes three numbers of the *Pour et Contre* [1] to a summary of the plot and to translations of outstanding scenes, notably those introducing the courtesan Millwood, who, though so different from Manon, yet plays the same role in the life of Barnwell as did the French courtesan in that of the Chevalier des Grieux. We shall return to this subject in discussing Prévost, the novelist. Meanwhile, the abbé notes the effect of the play on the Drury Lane audience of 1731 : 'Astonishment and horror were visible, at every performance, on the faces of the spectators. The silence was so profound and so mournful that in order to form an exact idea of it, one would have to experience something of the sentiment that caused it. Of course, the art of a clever actor helps a great deal to produce these extraordinary impressions from which not one spectator is immune.' Even from the little we know about the abbé's love tragedies, it is not difficult to enter into his emotions. Here was a new type of dramatic art, untrammelled by any classic *bienséances* and thus capable of realistic effects unknown to French drama. Even in 1748 when Clément produced his translation, *Le Marchand de Londres*, he dared not render the final scenes where the unhappy Barnwell and his demonic mistress die on the scaffold. Raynal,[2] commenting on the play, relates a conversation he had with Prévost, who told him he had never been so impressed by any dramatic work. Raynal was obviously puzzled at his enthusiasm, and remarks: 'I did not experience this emotion on reading this tragedy, but on the other hand, it did not appear to me as ridiculous as a play must naturally be in which a prostitute is the chief character.'

Raynal's criticism enables one to gauge the extent, not only of Prévost's originality, but also of the prejudices yet to be overcome by later writers like Diderot, in the effort to make the French stage a medium for the discussion of social problems. His casual words make us realize very sharply the historical importance of *Manon*

[1] 1734, Nos. xcix, c, cix.
[2] *Correspondance littéraire de Grimm, Raynal et Diderot*, i. 229 (1748).

Lescaut.   In this novel, by sheer art and with unparalleled audacity
Prévost conquered national prejudice, and enlisted popular sympathy for a work of imagination in which a prostitute is a heroine.[1]
But there was a vast difference between exhibiting such a theme in
a novel and presenting it to a theatre audience.   So many years
were to elapse ere *George Barnwell*, even in the diluted adaptation
of L. S. Mercier,[2] was allowed on the boards of the *Comédie française*.
Even in 1775 the French actors refused to play Palissot de Montenay's
Les Courtisanes, a most chaste treatment of the courtesan theme based
on Mme Riccoboni's novel, *Les Lettres du Marquis de Roselle*.[3]

On the question of Shakespeare, however, Prévost is curiously
disappointing.   Only two numbers [4] of the *Pour et Contre* are devoted
to our greatest playwright, and of these the first is but a translated
abridgment of Rowe's preface to his edition of Shakespeare's works.
At the outset of the second article, Prévost promises us his 'own
reflections on the character and merit of Shakespeare,' and tells us
that in deference to the wishes of several 'amateurs du Parnasse,'
he has selected and 're-read' those plays which continue to interest
the English public.   They comprise *The Tempest*, *The Merry Wives*,
Othello, and *Hamlet*, all of which are briefly summarized.   But of
the promised critical reflections there is scarcely any trace.   With
Rymer, Prévost agrees that Desdemona's love for the Moor is
improbable, and that no satisfactory motive is adduced for Othello's
terrible jealousy.   On the other hand, he is perhaps the only
eighteenth-century Frenchman to refute the current objection that
Iago is a character too revolting and too shockingly vicious to be
shown upon a stage.   *The Tempest* and *The Merry Wives* are briefly
dismissed with the comment that, at least in a literal translation,
they could have no appeal to French taste.   On *Hamlet*, Prévost
is even more explicit, and in summarizing the plot, reminds
one strangely of Voltaire in his most facetious vein.   'This
strange rhapsody,' concludes the abbé, 'in which one can discern
neither order nor probability, wherein comedy and tragedy
are confusedly mingled, is considered to be the masterpiece of
Shakespeare.'   This incredible fact Prévost offered to explain in
a future number of his journal.   But, though the *Pour et Contre*
continued to appear for a further two years, until 1740, its editor

---

[1] Not, however, without falling foul of the censorship.   Details will be found
in Harrisse's biography of Prévost.
[2] See Chapter v.
[3] For an account of this work see Green, *French Novelists*, i. 189–91.
[4] 1738, xciv, cxv.

failed to redeem his pledge, and indeed, never again mentioned Shakespeare's name.

The explanation is, I think, that Prévost's admiration for Shakespeare, like his knowledge of the latter's works, was but a fleeting reflection of the opinions expressed by his English friends. Again, as a novelist of manners, he was primarily interested in the psychology of his contemporaries and, therefore, much more attracted by modern drama than by the plays of the Elizabethan period. Had he really been a fervent admirer of Shakespeare he would have translated some of his plays, but the only English dramatic work he rendered into French was Dryden's *All for Love*. His translations of Richardson's novels, a heroic achievement, indicate clearly the eighteenth-century trend of his taste. A classic by education, like Diderot, Prévost was not temperamentally equipped to grasp the immense complexity of Shakespearian tragedy. Save in *Manon Lescaut* he could not rise above melodrama, and the tone of all his novels betrays the *âme sensible*, the humanitarian who, had he turned to the theatre, would have inevitably written *drames*, not tragedies.

La Place, on the other hand, while modestly laying no claim to originality as a Shakespearian critic, was the first Frenchman to attempt a translation, though an abridged one, of Shakespeare's tragedies. Perhaps the most sympathetic and certainly the most competent review of his *Théâtre anglais*, is by Desfontaines,[1] who, as a bitter enemy of Voltaire, is, if anything, predisposed in favour of Shakespeare. 'Everybody agrees,' says he, 'that the English theatre is, in general, ridiculous and absurd. That is the opinion of enlightened Englishmen and especially of those who know ours. Such as it is, however, this theatre has peculiar beauties: the tragedies of Shakespeare, for instance, strange as they are, contain admirable scenes the pathos of which carries one away.' La Place's contention that Shakespeare's plays must be great because they have held the stage for one hundred and fifty years and still draw large audiences does not impress Desfontaines. 'The taste of the English plebs is not taste but a defect in taste.' After all, he argues, did not Pope admit that Shakespeare pandered too much to the mob though he redeemed himself in his later works? Desfontaines is annoyed when La Place pleads for tolerance in matters of literary taste on the ground that the English temperament differs from the French. 'Do not the English have,' he asks, 'a share of reason like other nations?' The rules of drama are founded on reason. No

---

[1] *Jugements sur quelques ouvrages nouveaux*, vol. ix (1745).

doubt, as La Place maintains,[1] tragedy may be perfected, but only by retaining those rational, fundamental principles which are crystallized in the unities. To La Place's diffident suggestion, that just as a new type of novel, the novel of psychological analysis, has evolved from a closer study of the heart, so we may expect a new type of tragedy based on new rules; Desfontaines replies sarcastically that 'it would be most singular if the art of splitting hairs should produce such a marvellous result.' [2] On the matter of the rules Desfontaines is intransigent. He contemptuously brushes aside La Place's timid objections to the unities as 'specious,' though he allows that those of time and place need not be mathematically observed. Rather illogically, he then accuses La Place of inconsistency and timidity for not daring to translate Shakespeare's *Hamlet* and *Richard III* completely. In a sense, however, Desfontaines was right, for La Place is too apt to sit on the fence, and the whole tone of his preface reveals him as a writer who harboured revolutionary views on drama, yet lacked the courage to give them public expression. La Place neither speaks of Shakespeare nor translates him with conviction. Take, for instance, his rendering of the famous bedchamber scene from *Othello*, beginning: [3]

> It is the cause, it is the cause, my soul.
> Let me not name it . . .

La Place:

> Arrête, malheureux, c'est ici que ton cœur
> Va faire triompher, ou l'amour ou l'honneur!
> Sauve-toi! de l'amour crains les douces amorces:
> De ta faiblesse seule il emprunte ses forces:
> Et sa moindre étincelle allume le flambeau,
> Qui de l'honneur d'un homme éclaire le tombeau.
> Songes-y: cet instant, ou fatal ou propice,
> Te conduit à la gloire, ou dans le précipice.
> Élève-toi, mon âme, écarte loin de moi
> Tout ce qui peut causer la tendresse ou l'effroi. . . .

La Place appears to have undertaken his *Théâtre anglais* in the spirit of a hack translator faithfully carrying out his contract to a speculative publisher. This suspicion is confirmed by the preface, where we learn that the idea of issuing a French collection of English

[1] Both La Place and Desfontaines were 'moderns,' and strongly imbued with the eighteenth-century ideas of progress and perfectibility.
[2] La Place was thinking of Marivaux's novels, *La Vie de Marianne* and *Le Paysan parvenu.*
[3] Rowe's edition, which Prévost and La Place used.

plays was suggested by the recent success of Brumoy's *Théâtre des Grecs*. Nevertheless, curiosity was excited by the first two volumes, which contained *Othello, Henry VI, Richard III, Hamlet*, and *Macbeth*. Thus encouraged, La Place published two more volumes, offering what he termed his translations of *Cymbeline, Antony and Cleopatra, Julius Caesar*, and *Timon of Athens* together with very brief plot-summaries of the remaining plays. As may be gathered from the specimen given from *Othello*, which reveals La Place at his best, the translations are incredibly bad. Every scene which, in the opinion of La Place, might offend French taste is ruthlessly omitted or summarized in drab prose; whilst the most superbly poetic speeches are gravely prostituted and recostumed in alexandrines. An eighteenth-century Frenchman, on reading the *Théâtre anglais*, would get a vague outline of the physical action of the plays; otherwise there is nothing remotely to suggest the Shakespearian spirit.

'A very timid translation, attenuated, toned down, full of mistakes, but nevertheless meritorious for its time,' is M. Jusserand's indulgent comment on a production which is not a translation at all; it is the pale shadow of the shadow of Shakespeare. That it is meritorious for its time there is no doubt, since, apart from a few extracts by Voltaire, there is nothing with which to compare it. All that can be concluded from La Place's experiment is that a small section of the French public of 1745 was curious to know Shakespeare. But if a faithful translation had been presented to them they would have recoiled in horror as at some frightful monster.[1]

Prévost and La Place rely very much on English critics for their impressions of the English theatre, particularly in the case of Shakespeare. The Abbé Le Blanc, on the contrary, betrays a first-hand knowledge of our stage.[2] The real weakness of our late seventeenth-century and early eighteenth-century tragedy, as he shrewdly notes, is a vicious tendency to rant; to drown ideas and action in a spate of irrelevant images. 'A prince, racked by the most violent passion, interrupts himself in the middle of a thought to make a most ample and frothy description of a storm. At the end of it, whatever jealousy or fury he is possessed with, he must close it with a flowery

---

[1] Ficquet du Bocage, in the *Lettres sur le Théâtre anglais* (1752), thinks that the result of La Place's *Théâtre anglais* will be to produce few admirers but 'beaucoup de curieux.' Patu, probably the most enthusiastic French supporter of Shakespeare in the eighteenth century, wrote to Garrick (unpub. letter, Forster MSS.) in 1755 that La Place 'translated the defects and left the genius in the original.'

[2] Described by the *Museum* (1746) as 'very fair and candid. We can learn from him.'

simile.' Even Addison, most French, most correct of all English dramatists, is not free from this in his *Cato*. As Le Blanc infers, this abuse is the defect of a quality; it arises from the boldness of the English genius and the peculiarity of the English imagination. We make a virtue of this fault, and accuse the French of slavishness and servile imitation. But the fact remains, says Le Blanc, that an observance of Aristotle's rules would at least help to restrain this luxuriance of the English fancy. Even Shakespeare, genius though he be, 'for want of knowing the rules of the ancients or at least for neglecting to follow them, has not produced a single play that is not a monster of its kind: if there are admirable things in all his pieces, not one of them will bear reading throughout.' [1] He prophesies that 'entire translations of Shakespeare would do much prejudice to his reputation in France. . . . The admirable productions of his genius are a perpetual contrast to those of his bad taste; at the conclusion of one of his finest scenes you must expect something excessively ridiculous. In favour of these fine passages, the English pardon him for all the trash which his works are full of; we should not be so indulgent.' The English, he points out, admire Shakespeare so extravagantly that 'if the French translated him they would not praise him enough, and the French would be justly displeased to see the force and sublimity of the great Corneille continually joined with low and immoral crime, puns, playing with words, and all the pitiful jests of our ancient tragedies on the mysteries of our Saviour's passion.' [2] In his comic scenes, Shakespeare is often happy, but 'Falstaff, so famous on the English stage, is commonly speaking a buffoon like *Don Japhet d'Arménie*; [3] except that the one talks of nothing but empires and crowns, and the other of cutting purses and robbing passengers.'

Perhaps Le Blanc's most acute observation is that it was impossible to translate Shakespeare into eighteenth-century French. We are prone, I think, to forget what an extraordinary revolution in the French language resulted from the Romantic movement. And Le Blanc was the first Frenchman to discern the genius of Shakespeare the poet. 'Style,' he says, 'is Shakespeare's great distinction; it explains everything. It is a language peculiar to himself . . . he cannot be translated without mutilating him in every page, and when he is mutilated 'tis no longer himself.' [4] Le Tourneur, in his

---

[1] *Lettres sur les Anglais* (1745). I quote from a contemporary English translation, Letter XXXI.
[2] Letter XXXIX.   [3] A farce by Scarron.   [4] Letter LIX.

Anglomania, chose to disregard these sensible remarks. It is regrettable, for his famous translation is one of those indiscretions which cannot be excused even by the best of intentions.

Le Blanc saw *Hamlet*, which he considers to be an imitation of *Electra*, and he was much impressed by the terror of the audience at the ghost scene. 'In such scenes Shakespeare is a great poet; the more unnatural they are, the more art and force he makes use of to bear himself up in them.' What also struck him was the superstition of the English, and he infers that the audience of the *Comédie française* would be harder to convince in these supernatural matters. The *Electra-Hamlet* comparison was suggested by Prévost, who saw a like resemblance between the Greek and the English tragedies. 'I remember,' says Le Blanc, 'that the Abbé Prévost in his comparison of the tragedies of *Electra* and *Hamlet* commends the English poet because, wiser than Sophocles, he forbids young Hamlet, by the appearance of the ghost in the first act, to attempt anything against his mother's life.' Le Blanc was, however, as a priest, shocked at Hamlet's desire to kill his father's murderer simply in order to damn him. 'I don't know whether there is not as much childishness as indecency in this thought of refined vengeance.' [1]

It is disconcerting, just as one is about to congratulate Le Blanc on being an unusually enlightened and precocious critic of Shakespeare, to find in a letter to Hénault, that he discovers a resemblance between the latter and the author of *Henry V* and *Antony and Cleopatra*. To savour the irony of this one must glance at Hénault's *François II*, a worse than mediocre effort at a French national tragedy. Our confidence is further shaken by an epistle [2] to the elder, the bloodthirsty Crébillon, whose *Atrée et Thyeste*, says Le Blanc, shows just to what a pitch terror should be carried without shocking good taste. Shakespeare, no doubt, is unrivalled for the force of his expressions, yet with him terror is chiefly due to the frightful objects, e.g. the strangling of Desdemona, which he shows on the stage. 'Fletcher succeeded better in moving the passions than Shakespeare,' says Le Blanc, and concludes: 'Corneille made men greater and more virtuous than they are, but Shakespeare has made them worse perhaps than is consistent with human nature.' [3]

Now these are the views of a man who knew the English theatre. With Prévost and La Place one is never quite sure. The former in

---

[1] Letter LXX.   [2] Letter LXXIII.
[3] A remark which really condenses the objections raised by eighteenth-century France to the art of Shakespeare.

the *Pour et Contre* was obviously in his search of copy indebted, as he admits, to second-hand English sources. La Place, as we have seen, tries to hunt with the hounds and run with the hare. The case of Le Blanc is quite different, since he was familiar enough with our theatre, ancient and modern, to write the shrewdest, the best informed, and the most devastating criticism of our dramatic manner ever penned by a Frenchman.[1] M. Jusserand dismisses it amusedly as Le Blanc's 'sham warfare against Shakespeare.' In reality, it is the well and long deserved French *riposte* to Dryden's jingoistic attack on the seventeenth-century French theatre. With great urbanity and wit, the abbé touches unerringly on all the defects of modern English drama, proving, as it were, Voltaire's theorem that 'le mérite de Shakespeare a perdu le théâtre anglais.' This is the gist of all his remarks, which for greater effect he attributes to an imaginary Englishman. That is the only 'sham' element in his satire; for it is and was meant to be most serious.

The first axiom, says Le Blanc, is to attack the rules, but to base your tragedies on Corneille and Racine. 'The French furnish the materials, but we are the architects and we alone know how to make a proper use of them. Like their language, the genius of the French is frivolous and trifling in comparison with the English.' Your first act can remain as in the original, but as the French are too cold and too natural you must season the narrative with bold and strong epithets filched from Shakespeare. Do not forget Dryden's profound remark to the effect that we can as easily conquer the French with the pen as with the sword. To make your kings really regal give them two or three guards in order to raise the grandeur and the dignity of their character; they will need it. Do not hesitate to use the candle-snuffers as princes or ministers in a council, or to swell the numbers in mobs or popular commotions. Avoid the meanness of the French theatre in this respect: remember *The Heroic Daughter* and Cibber's *Ximena*, where the heir to the throne is allotted twelve guards; a common prince, six; and a queen or princess of the blood, gets four: 'one to answer her or simply to hear her and the other three to support her in case you think it proper to let her fall into a fit.' It is always safe, also, to end your first act with a concert of music 'which will supply the want of pathetic in the expressions.'

In the second act the author should provide something really

[1] See his *The Supplement of Genius, or the Art of Composing Dramatic Pieces as it has been Produced by Many Celebrated Authors of the English Theatre.*

striking in the way of setting, for example, as in *Montezuma*, a magician's grotto with demons; or else as in *Cleomenes*, a temple crowded with people attending the priestly rites. Shakespeare will, of course, furnish suggestions for 'the conjuration and magic.' As the original French play may be too simple, another plot and a few extra characters should be added. It is quite unnecessary, says Le Blanc, to bother about consistency in dialogue and action; the hero will be much more interesting if he is vicious and virtuous at the same time, as in Fletcher's *Rollo*. Besides, since a scene can be changed at will, it will be easy to introduce new characters without warning just as Dryden does in *All for Love*. This invariably excites the curiosity of the audience and gives them something to wonder at. Remember Dryden's injunctions regarding variety of sentiment. As he so rightly points out: 'Our spectators do not like to be too long employed in the same sentiment; they must laugh and cry alternately.' Therefore, change abruptly from verse to prose, from tragedy to comedy, especially to low comedy for which, naturally, the Elizabethan dramatists will provide inexhaustible matter.

There is absolutely no excuse in English drama for letting the interest wane. Should the action flag, the British playwright can always 'bring in some florid comparison taken from the most delightful objects of nature, or some pompous description of a torrent or hurricane, in emphatical or jingling verses.' Rowe's *Fair Penitent* or Otway's *Venice Preserved* are good models here. Once again, exhorts Le Blanc, remember Dryden's spirited words. Our men and our verses can always conquer the French 'by weight.' The slavish Racine hampers himself by rules. Lose no time upon these puerile conventions; keep the scene moving from Rome to Constantinople, from London to Carolina. Do not let the time-factor cramp your style. 'If a week is not sufficient, take a fortnight,' urges Le Blanc, 'take a month, a year.' As the author of *Love Triumphant* so justly observes: 'Tho' such licences are faults, commit them boldly; they suit the English genius.' [1]

Nothing lends more vivacity to a tragedy than a night-scene with appropriate meteorological effects. Avoid, too, mere narrative. 'Nothing is so terrible that it cannot be exposed to the eyes of the audience.' Think, says Le Blanc, of that effective plague scene in the English *Oedipus*, where the stage is strewn with dead and dying—a lofty scene.

[1] Dryden.

The third act is to be reserved mainly for killing. The English gallery loves bloodshed. Besides, now is the time to lay in a stock of ghosts for the last two acts. A word, too, about love. Here, the chief error to be avoided is the absurd French idea that rank and love have anything in common. Dryden, who, as he tells us, is too good an Englishman to lose what his ancestors have won for him, makes Octavia and Cleopatra 'natural': that is, he makes them scold like fish-wives. Do not be prudish either in the discussion of intimate and sexual matters. Imitate Dryden in *Aureng-Zebe*, where the heroine prattles about her comfortless nights and reproaches her spouse with 'his icy age and impotence.' Rowe, too, has a fine bit in *The Ambitious Stepmother*, where the senile Mirza tries to rape Amestris but 'wearies himself in fruitless efforts.' For the more romantic and sentimental scenes, introduce music and songs, angels and demons to while away the moments when the hero, weighed down by care, falls asleep.

French fourth acts are not sufficiently brisk. Brighten them up with a battle or so, and, of course, bring on the ghost in a bloody sheet to the accompaniment of thunder and lightning. Here your foresight in killing off a few characters in the third act will be rewarded. The slain in the foregoing battles will provide you with a few 'inferior ghosts.' Now, too, is the moment to bring on the army with stirring martial music. Should the heroine hang on your hands, make her mad and dress her like a shepherdess; or else introduce a prison scene.

The last act rightly belongs to the ghost, who should appear at least once in each scene. In *The Duke of Guise* and in *Henry VI* there is a devil, and this devil pact is not a bad idea. Now, too, is the time for fine speeches—it does not matter about what—speeches against kings, ministers, and, above all, a rousing panegyric of the government in power. Any characters not previously disposed of must now be killed off, or kill each other, observing, of course, the the proper precedence, since the most guilty must die first. It is unnecessary to add that bells, axes, daggers, scaffolds, and black velvet should be lavishly employed. Finally, as Le Blanc puts it: 'If you have any unhappy, disarmed hero left on your hands, whom pains have been taken to save from killing himself, let him follow the example of our Oedipus and throw himself out of a window to put an end to the affair.' So much for Le Blanc's 'sham warfare.'

Prior to 1750, then, there was no particular reason why an intelligent and curious Frenchman should suddenly have evinced an infatuation for Shakespeare. The remarks of Prévost and Le Blanc perhaps corrected the severity of Voltaire's more biting gibes, but left the kernel of his criticism intact. La Place's so-called translations, which, until 1776, were the most direct medium between Shakespeare and French intellectuals, could only confirm the traditional view that he was interesting, nay fine, in isolated passages but, considered as an artist, completely monstrous. And, after all, no Frenchman was called upon to be 'plus royaliste que le roi'; more enthusiastic about Shakespeare than the English themselves. 'Of all the eighteenth-century English critics previous to 1779,' says Mr. Ralli, who has given us a useful précis of their views on Shakespeare, 'only Morgann recognizes that he was a supreme dramatic artist. Otherwise it is held that he pleased by accident.' Now, however incompetent the French may have been to form a judgment on Shakespeare's poetry, since this demanded a knowledge of English possessed by very few, they could at least claim the right to judge of his merits as a dramatist, if only in the bowdlerized version furnished by La Place. And naturally, the criterion by which they measured him was the only one they knew—the neo-classic. It is not, therefore, inordinate to assume that to the few Frenchmen of 1750 who were interested enough to examine his plays, Shakespeare appeared crude and barbarous. The only conceivable point of contact between his tragedy and that of the age of Louis XIV was Corneille, the Corneille of the early regrettable manner: and here the analogy was so faint as to be almost negligible. No: interest in Shakespeare, if it was to become more general and more real, was to evolve slowly and indirectly.

A new dramatic genre, new at least in France, was developing in both countries. Neither tragedy nor comedy, this type of play was concerned, not with the destinies of the great, but with those of the middle classes. It was strongly tinged with bourgeois sentimentality; it was melodramatic in expression, and didactic or social in its intention. Proceeding upwards—or is it downwards?—from the sentimental comedies of the early decades of the century, the new dramatic genre developed into what was called in France *le drame*, and was sponsored by Diderot, who composed its dramaturgy. From 1760 onward, France was flooded with *drames*, or, as they were loosely called in England, domestic tragedies. In London, however, despite the precarious success of *George Barnwell* and Moore's *Gamester*, the domestic tragedy, which was not such a novelty as it was in France, made very little progress, for reasons that may be discussed later. At the moment, however, it is interesting to note that each nation attributed the origin of this new genre to the other. The French traditionalists thought that the *drame* was an English importation because of its sombre note and its unheroic, familiar tone. The English said it was a French growth, mainly because of the reputation of Diderot's *Entretiens* and his *Essay on Dramatic Poetry*. It is easy to understand, therefore, why, in the thick of this dramatic revolution, French curiosity which was now concentrated on the contemporary English stage, was once more directed towards Shakespeare, whose tragedies were being revived at Drury Lane and Covent Garden. The *dramatistes* or *dramomanes*, as they were dubbed by their enemies, did not, of course, work according to a cut-and-dried plan. A few, like L. S. Mercier, were determined to abolish the neo-classic tradition and to make a clean sweep of the unities. These composed a very small minority. Others, inspired by the example of Voltaire and the success of Du Bellay's *Siège de Calais*, tried, as did Baculard d'Arnaud, to compromise between the *drame* and traditional tragedy. As a result they produced melodramas with an historical, national flavour. A group, headed by Sedaine, faithfully carried out the spirit of Diderot's injunctions and, whilst endeavouring to observe the unities, wove their plays round domestic and social problems. Now, all of these could obviously find in Shakespeare a precedent or justification for their several conceptions of dramatic art. In *Romeo and Juliet*, *Julius Caesar*, *Othello*, *Macbeth*, or *Hamlet* could be found characters or situations which, with some considerable alteration, might be adapted to the French taste. Certainly, too, the more modern plays like *George Barnwell* and *The Gamester*, however violent and crude, offered much to interest the didactic spirit of these timid French innovators in the field of social and dramatic reform. But it would be most inaccurate to assume, as has been done, that French *drame* owed its inception to the influence of Lillo, and that French *comédie larmoyante* had its origin in Steele's *The Conscious Lovers*. Leaving this point to be elucidated later, let us return to Shakespeare and his reputation in France until the close of the century.

Referring to the appearance, in 1776, of the Le Tourneur translation of Shakespeare, M. Jusserand says: 'The event had been announced since the middle of the century. Isolated imitations written for the stage had multiplied. More and more detailed studies, and judgments more and more flattering to Shakespeare, had appeared.' Here, I fear, our author is guilty of exaggeration.

No 'études minutieuses' of Shakespeare appeared in France between
1750 and 1776. And M. Jusserand himself finds it very difficult
to find examples of the 'jugements de plus en plus flatteurs' to which
he rather sweepingly alludes. He quotes Marmontel's reserved
eulogy and Diderot's one important pronouncement on Shakespeare,
in which, writing to Tronchin, in 1774, he compares our dramatist
to 'a Gothic colossus, but between whose legs we could all pass.'
Mercier's opinion comes in for lengthy mention, but, as we shall see,
Mercier was not always wholly inspired by an intelligent understanding of Shakespeare's art. M. Jusserand ought to have devoted
more attention to the correspondence between Patu and Garrick;
for Patu was a genuine lover of Shakespeare, and perhaps the only
Frenchman of his age capable of appreciating our Elizabethan
master. It was Patu [1] who bearded Voltaire in his Genevan retreat,
and made a desperate attempt to convert him to his own religion.
For hours he bombarded his host with Shakespearian quotations
but with not much success. Voltaire admitted that Shakespeare
was 'un barbare aimable, un fou séduisant,' but no more. Finally,
however, Patu came to the speech from *Romeo and Juliet*, beginning:

> 'Tis torture and not mercy: heaven is here
> Where Juliet lives . . .

To his delight, Voltaire suddenly became serious, and ejaculated:
'Cela est très beau, très touchant, très naturel.' With that Patu
had to be content.

But Patu was a great exception. Much more typical is the
judgment on Shakespeare which is to be found in a letter written
to Garrick by Suard. M. Jusserand refers briefly to it in a footnote, but quotes only two lines of a criticism that deserves to be
reproduced in full because it reflects, I think, what the majority of
enlightened Frenchmen thought about Shakespeare in the last
thirty years of the eighteenth century. Suard, it should be noted,
was a thorough Anglomaniac, and it was he who first introduced
Ossian into France. He writes to Garrick in 1766: 'And, above all,
what does it matter to the illustrious Garrick, whose fame is independent of the reputation of the English theatre, whether we prefer
Corneille to Shakespeare or Racine to Otway? All we owe to the
dead is the truth. I am one of the men of this country who admire
Shakespeare most; but I admire him as a barbarian full of genius.
You had fired my imagination with the beauties of this poet. I

---

[1] Garrick's *Correspondence* (1827), Patu to Garrick, 1755.

E

wanted to write an article on his character and I began to re-read him; but I was so appalled at the extravagance and puerilities which disfigure his best passages that the pen dropped from my fingers. Let me say once more that a man must either renounce every principle of taste, of nature, and decency and burn the models of the ancients or else agree that the dramas of Shakespeare are monstrous, and that his genius is like gold encrusted in the mine. *Vitium non hominis sed temporis.* I have one more thing to say to you. It is that there is not a single scene by this extraordinary man, the literal and complete translation of which can be success-fully given in any language or played on any theatre. Shake-speare owes much to the famous men who have praised him, but the man to whom he owes most is yourself.'

And even Ducis, on the eve of producing his French *Hamlet*, writes to Garrick in the following vein: 'I imagine, sir, that you must have thought me very bold to put a play like *Hamlet* on the French stage. Apart from the wild irregularities in which it abounds, the self-confessed ghost who speaks at length, the strolling players, and the duel seemed to me absolutely inadmissible on our stage. How-ever, I was very sorry not to be able to take over the terrible spectre who exposes the crime and demands vengeance. I have, therefore, been obliged, in some sort, to create a new play. However, I tried to make an interesting part out of a parricidal queen, and, above all, to depict in the pure and melancholy soul of Hamlet a model of filial tenderness. In treating this character, I looked on myself as a religious painter working at an altar-piece. But why, sir, do I not know your language?' Here, indeed, we have enthusiasm: whether the judgment of Ducis is flattering to Shakespeare is, however, open to doubt.

Now, what of the imitations which, according to M. Jusserand, had multiplied between 1750 and 1776? He does not mention a verse comedy said to be based on *The Merry Wives* which, in 1761, was put on at the *Théâtre italien*, 'but,' says a contemporary historian of the stage, 'did not succeed at all, so great is the difference in our taste, owing to the difference in manner.' An appallingly literal prose translation of *The Merchant of Venice*,[2] which escaped the notice of every eighteenth-century reviewer, was published in 1768. The anonymous perpetrator of this crime has the grace to admit that,

---

[1] D'Origny, *Annales du Théâtre italien.*
[2] '*Le Marchand de Venise.*' *Comédie. Traduite de l'Anglais de Sharkespeare* [sic]. *A Londres et se trouve à Paris chez Grangé, De Lalain et Valade* (1768).

on re-reading the translation, he 'was struck with the singularity of the style.' As a specimen of his manner, let us take the famous speech on mercy: 'Le caractère de la clémence est de n'être jamais forcée. Elle tombe comme la pluie du ciel sur les lieux inférieurs. Elle produit une double félicité. Elle rend heureux celui qui donne et celui qui reçoit. Elle est plus puissante dans le plus puissant. Elle sied mieux au Monarque que le diadème. Son sceptre montre la force d'une autorité temporelle: il est l'attribut de la vénération et de la majesté que les Rois sont redoutés; mais la clémence est au-dessus du pouvoir attaché au sceptre; elle a son trône dans le cœur des Rois.' How right was Suard!

Ducis adapted *Hamlet* (1769) and *Romeo and Juliet* (1772). Douin's *More de Venise* appeared in 1773. In 1774, the chevalier de Chastellux produced, on Savalette's private stage at La Chevrette, an adaptation of *Romeo and Juliet*.[1] According to Madame Riccoboni, who had considerable experience in turning English plays into French, he bowdlerized the original, and gaily converted tragedy into sentimental comedy by marrying Romeo to Juliet and making them live happy ever after. Thus, in the sixteen years preceding 1776, only five plays can be traced which are directly or indirectly attributable to the influence of Shakespeare, and of these only two can be said to have attracted the attention of the limited public which was interested in English literature.

Nor can it be said, as is implied by M. Jusserand, that the Le Tourneur translations gave rise to a Shakespeare cult in France. Let us examine the imitations which appeared between 1776 and the Revolution. Luckily, Collot d'Herbois, the author of *L'Amant Loup-Garou* (1780), has told us that this play is based on *The Merry Wives*; otherwise it would defy the wit of the most zealous source-diviner to discover the fact. In 1782, Mercier, the *dramomane*, published his *Tombeaux de Vérone*, a domesticated version of *Romeo and Juliet*. In the following year, eleven years after his *Romeo and Juliet*, Ducis adapted *Lear*; whilst in 1785, Butini, a Swiss lawyer, gave to oblivion a tolerably close imitation of *Othello*. Another *Othello*, never printed, was written by one Leriget, somewhere between 1775 and the end of the century.[2] To sum up, the Le Tourneur translations produced exactly five Shakespearian

---

[1] In an unpublished letter to Garrick (Forster MSS., vol. xxx), Chastellux says: 'I have changed most of the plot and cut out all the comedy. I am proud to have had the approval of some English people.' His *Roméo et Juliette* was apparently never printed, and, so far as I know, no manuscript exists.

[2] Not mentioned by M. Jusserand. Bib. Nat. MS. Anc. sup. fr. 9263 (3067).

imitations in thirteen years, and of these only one, that by Ducis, appeared on the stage.

With the Revolution and the advent of a free stage, much might have been expected; but the French public betrayed no desire to see much of Shakespeare. The faithful Ducis, in 1784, produced *Macbeth*, and in the following year, *Jean sans Terre*, based on *King John*. The revolutionary Mercier published in 1792, a queer version of *Lear*, entitled *Le Vieillard et ses Trois Filles*, and followed it up with an imitation of *Timon of Athens* in 1793. This represents the last attempt, in the eighteenth century, to adapt Shakespeare to the French taste. Of these four plays only two were acted. A critical analysis of all these so-called imitations will show to what extent, if any, French traditional ideas on drama were influenced or altered by this contact with Shakespeare.

Ducis attempting to adapt Shakespeare to the taste of an eighteenth-century audience reminds one of a village architect trying to make a Gothic cathedral look like the Trianon. To do him justice, one must remember that, knowing no English, he had to base his *Hamlet* and his *Roméo et Juliette* on La Place's versions, than which nothing could be less like the originals. There are, however, degrees of badness, and Le Tourneur's translation did help to give the author of the French *Lear*, *Macbeth*, and *Othello* a more accurate idea of Shakespeare's dramatic purpose. Ducis's real stumbling-block, however, was the inherent dissimilarity of English and French dramatic taste. Was a reconciliation possible? If not, what were the limits of a *rapprochement* such as that attempted by Ducis? Now, if ever, the moment was ripe for, despite the American war, anglomania was at its height. English poetry and English novels, if not really understood in France were much admired and copied *à la française*. The new dramatists were in a particularly receptive mood. The legend of the Englishman, the melancholy, upright, independent, *honnête homme* of the *Nouvelle Héloïse* was now firmly embedded in the French imagination. Descartes was now discredited, ousted by Locke and Newton. Du Bos's warnings as to the possible effect of Cartesianism on civilization had borne fruit,[1] and since his time a new generation has been trying hard to think experimentally. 'I shall content myself,' Du Bos had said, 'with the remark that the philosophic spirit which makes us so reasonable, so *logical*, will soon do to a great part of Europe what formerly the Goths and Vandals did, supposing

[1] Op. cit. (1719).

it continues to make the progress it has achieved in the last
seventy years.   I see the necessary arts neglected, those prejudices
so necessary to the preservation of society abolished, and speculative
reasoning preferred to prejudice.   We are behaving without regard
to experience—the best master the human mind ever had.'   There
is no doubt, then, that the experimental spirit had invaded history,
philosophy, and, to some extent, literature.[1]   The novel, comedy,
and to a lesser degree, tragedy, showed traces of it.   Was not the
drame largely an attempt to escape from the hegemony of the
esprit géométrique?   Yet, when we examine Ducis's adaptations of
Shakespeare's plays, it is abundantly evident that the seventeenth-
century conception of a clear-cut universe governed by a well-
defined law, *la raison universelle* of Descartes, is still predominant.

To Ducis, the *Hamlet* of Shakespeare is not really tragic.
After a certain point Hamlet's course is clear.   Filial duty obliges
him to kill Claudius and to forgive his mother: only thus can
the universal order be readjusted.   So Ducis obligingly presents
Hamlet with a tragic problem, such as Corneille or Racine would
have conceived.   Claudius is a cynical usurper, but he has a
daughter, Ophelia, with whom Hamlet is in love.   We have thus
an inner conflict between love and filial duty and, to heighten the
interest, a typical palace intrigue directed by Claudius, who spreads
the rumour that Hamlet's distemper is due to remorse—he has
killed his own father!   To accentuate the horror, Ducis goes
farther than Shakespeare, and leaves Hamlet long in doubt as to
the meaning of the ghost's instructions.   The shade, which is, by
the way, visible only to the bereaved son, vaguely tells Hamlet to
remove the paternal dagger and urn from the tomb and not to replace
them till he has avenged his father.   Does this mean that Hamlet
must kill his mother?   The thought is too revolting, too unnatural.

> Quoi?   Moi?   j'accomplirais ce décret inhumain!
> Ou change de victime ou cherche une autre main:
> Sur un vil criminel je cours venger mon père,
> Mais je n'attente point aux jours de ma mère.[2]

---

[1] See Marmontel's *Discours sur la force et la faiblesse de l'esprit humain* (1763), in
which, contrasting Newton with Descartes, he says of the former:
> 'Newton, plus sage en sa timidité,
> Autour de lui cherche la vérité.
> Il a saisi le fil du labyrinthe;
> Mais, pas à pas, il s'avance avec crainte,
> Et, pénétré d'un juste étonnement
> Il suit des faits le long enchaînement.'

[2] II. iii.

The supernatural element evidently embarrassed Ducis. The ghost is not visible save to Hamlet, and its orders are indirectly narrated. Moreover, we are constantly reminded that it may be but a figment of Hamlet's imagination. The prince's friend, Norceste, had written from England a graphic account of a crime similar in every way to that which preoccupies Hamlet. The English king had been killed by his consort in league with an ambitious lover. Back once more in Denmark, Norceste now suggests that very possibly his letter is the cause of Hamlet's fearful nightmares. As in Shakespeare, the latter tries to obtain proof by an artifice. But obviously the Shakespearian idea of 'reconstructing the crime,' however popular it may be to-day with French criminologists,[1] could not be shown to an eighteenth-century French audience as yet hardly accustomed to the sight of killing, even in hot blood. It would certainly have recoiled from, or derided, the representation of a deliberate, imaginary crime.

Very cleverly and, I think, very plausibly, Ducis substitutes another scheme. While Norceste relates the story of the English regicide, Hamlet watches its effect on his auditors. The queen is violently agitated, but the Tartuffian Claudius urbanely dismisses the matter with an appropriate platitude:

> Laissons à l'Angleterre et son deuil et ses pleurs,
> L'Angleterre en forfaits trop souvent fut féconde.

The discovery by Claudius and Gertrude that Hamlet is in love with Ophelia momentarily suspends their alarm. Here, of course, is the reason for Hamlet's melancholy. However, they are soon deprived of this 'flattering unction,' since Hamlet, after a prolonged struggle, renounces his love for Ophelia; it must be sacrificed to filial duty. Now he proceeds to his final purpose, the extorting of a confession from Gertrude. This was for Ducis a delicate situation. Nothing even remotely approaching Shakespeare's treatment of the theme was possible on a French stage. The audience would not for a moment have tolerated the scene where Hamlet tortures his mother with innuendoes.

In retaining this situation at all Ducis risked the success of the whole play. As it is, he displays great ingenuity. Of course, his Gertrude has not married Claudius, and technically is not guilty of murder, because, although at her lover's instigation she had left a cup of poison by her husband's bedside, she repented and went

---

[1] According, at least, to the authors of detective stories. I have no closer acquaintance with French criminal procedure.

back to remove it—too late. Obviously, Ducis's purpose in thus
boggling at the issue was to render Gertrude less revolting. Further,
all through the play she is shown as anxious to atone for her sin
by aiding her son against the plots of Claudius. Nevertheless,
Ducis showed great courage in introducing the scene where Hamlet
bluntly accuses Gertrude of complicity, and forces her to swear on
his father's ashes that she had no part in the crime. The queen,
naturally, breaks down, and Hamlet, in an access of filial tenderness, forgives her. As Diderot [1] malicious observes, he talks to
her like a confessor:

> Ne désespérez point de la bonté céleste:
> Rien n'est perdu pour vous si le remords vous reste.
> Votre crime est énorme, exécrable, odieux:
> Mais il n'est pas plus grand que la bonté des dieux. [2]

The ghost again appears, adjuring Hamlet to kill both Gertrude
and Claudius, and the distraught son begs his mother to go:

> Eh bien! ma mère . . . ah! dieux! . . . mon cœur peut-être,
> D'un transport renaissant ne serait plus le maître.

Norceste, who has aroused the mob in defence of Hamlet, saves
him from Claudius and his conspirators. Hamlet kills Claudius;
Gertrude makes public confession and commits suicide. The
curtain falls on a Hamlet who is now king and resolved to live, but
only for the sake of his subjects:

> Mais je suis homme et roi: réservé pour souffrir
> Je saurai vivre encor; je fais plus que mourir.

Ducis's *Hamlet*, un-Shakespearian though it is, yet represents the
closest approach to Shakespeare achieved by an eighteenth-century
French dramatist. Largely because of Molé's frenzied acting it
drew crowds. Collé called it a 'stale abomination,' and accused
Ducis of having murdered Shakespeare with 'rare bonhomie.' In
the scene when Hamlet raises his dagger on his mother, 'covering
his face with his mantle like a good son who wants to kill her without
seeing her,' the audience hooted him. [3] Diderot said he would
rather see Shakespeare's *monster* than this scarecrow. [4] Fréron, in
the *Année littéraire*, sardonically twitted Ducis with his solicitude in
sparing the French certain scenes. 'M. Ducis need not have feared
our so-called delicacy. Have we not seen on our stage horrors
which the English stage would not perhaps have admitted?' [5] He

---

[1] *Œuvres*, viii.   [2] v. iv.   [3] *Journal*, iii. 235–9.
[4] *Œuvres*, viii.   [5] A 'palpable hit' at Voltaire.

objects also to the handling of the ghost which is bungled as in Voltaire. Voltaire was, of course, Fréron's *bête noire*, so that we cannot trust his opinion too much on Shakespearian matters. It is clear, however, from all accounts that Ducis had gone even farther than the audience would have wished. On the whole, his *Hamlet* was rather a *succès de scandale* than a real indication that French taste was radically converted.

Roméo et Juliette marks a greater departure from the original. As was to be expected, Ducis could see nothing actually dramatic in Shakespeare's presentation of the unhappy love affair. He therefore concentrates on the hostility between the rival houses, and imagines a Roméo (called at first Dolvédo) who is ignorant of his true parentage and, moreover, has been brought up by the Capulets. Quite surprisingly we learn in Act III that he had killed Juliette's brother, Théobaldo, in order to save his own father, who as it transpires, is an outlaw. Capulet asks Roméo to help him avenge his son's death and Roméo then reveals his secret. Thanks to the intercession of the Duc Ferdinand, it looks as if the enemy houses will be reconciled, but old Montaigu is merely dissembling. He reveals to Roméo the ghastly secret that he had been committed by the Capulets with his sons to a tower and, like Ugolino, was eventually forced to drink his children's blood. In revenge, he now orders Roméo to kill Juliette. The son pleads for pity and the old man seems to yield.

The sham reconciliation between the enemy houses is to take place at the family vaults of the Montaigus and Capulets, and this gives Ducis an opportunity for a scene which would have delighted Dr. Young, the author of the popular *Night Thoughts*.

> *Juliette.* Dieu, quel jour effrayant dans l'épaisseur des ombres
> Au sein de ces tombeaux répand ses clartés sombres !
> Les Manes enchaînés sous ces marbres poudreux
> Semblent tous m'inviter d'y descendre avec eux.
> Je vois avec plaisir, au sein de ces ténèbres,
> Le jour pâle et mourant de ces lampes funèbres.
> Cet astre des tombeaux, plus affreux que la nuit,
> Vient mêler quelque joie à l'horreur qui me suit.

She disillusions Roméo by showing a letter which reveals that Montaigu intends to turn the reconciliation ceremony into a bloody ambuscade. To end the vendetta Juliette, as she confesses, has taken poison. In despair, Roméo also kills himself. At this moment, the parents arrive accompanied by Ferdinand and his escort. Montaigu draws his dagger, but suddenly perceives the dying Juliette. As he is gloating over her, Capulet shows him the corpse of Roméo, whereupon Montaigu commits suicide.

In all this there is little or nothing of Shakespeare, except for the idea of the family feud, which for Ducis is the core of the tragedy. Of the ineffable lyricism with which Shakespeare conceals the incredibility of his plot, not the smallest echo can be surprised in the French version. It is simply bad melodrama. Once more Ducis is caught in the net of tradition. A Juliet like Shakespeare's, who unhesitatingly sacrifices filial duty to love, could not yet appear sympathetic to a French audience. The 'rights' of individual passion were not yet recognized and, despite the *Nouvelle Héloïse*, fifty years were to pass before this romantic theme invaded the theatre of France. Still, *Roméo et Juliette* does mark an advance on the seventeenth-century conception of parental authority. The whole of Ducis's play rests on the thesis that this authority is not absolute: that parental rights become criminal when they conflict with the natural law of humanity. No seventeenth-century author would have dared to present the spectacle of a son preaching such a doctrine to his father, and adjuring him to sacrifice his hatred to his natural sensibility. Essentially, *Roméo et Juliette* is the criticism by a new generation, the generation of the *âmes sensibles*, of the rigid code of so-called family honour which governed the age of Corneille.

Certain elements in the original were automatically excluded from Ducis's play. Without absolutely reducing his tragedy to the level of a *drame*, Ducis could not, of course, retain the realistic, domestic atmosphere of Shakespeare's play. He therefore omits Juliet's mother and, not surprisingly, the bawdy old nurse who was impossible, even in comedy. The English were equally prudish, for at Drury Lane her more savoury utterances were excised by Garrick. To make it possible for Romeo and Juliet to converse without a chaperon, Ducis had to assume that the hero was a protégé of Capulet's, thus introducing a fresh complication. Apart from the fact that the censorship would not have accepted him, Friar Lawrence is excluded for other reasons. It would have shocked the audience to see a monk on the stage, and in any case, in the role allotted to him by Shakespeare he would have aroused derision. One writer [1] who had seen the famous funeral scene in London, where it was the great attraction of the play, says that

[1] Probably Grimm. *Correspondance*, x. 25 (1772).

to his surprise he was as impressed as any child of ten. But as someone else remarked, it is doubtful whether a French audience would have observed the proper awe at the sight of so much pomp for one they knew to be not dead.

Roméo et Juliette ran for seventeen nights, which was in those days considered a great success. However, it was severely criticized, both in the *Année littéraire* and in Grimm's *Correspondance*. Fréron maintaining that only Brissard's acting and a few excellent passages saved it from disaster.[1] Grimm pointed out the folly of copying a model 'so remote from French tragedy.' The gigantic crimes which appealed to the Elizabethans, he says, are not in tune with the spirit of eighteenth-century France. Why teach our children tales 'borrowed from a coarse and stupid race which for a thousand years has been the object of our hatred and contempt, and can only inspire us with a love of fanaticism, of religious intolerance, and corruption by their details of licence and debauch.' In any case, he adds, Ducis has not the genius to imitate Shakespeare. He omits, for example, a certain balcony scene which the writer recalled having witnessed with delight in London. Commenting on the love-passages in the original, Grimm marvels at Shakespeare's art in expressing these delicate nuances of emotion, a striking contrast to the morbid inventions of Ducis.

So far no great triumph can be claimed for Shakespeare, because what the French audience had applauded in *Roméo et Juliette* and in *Hamlet* was certainly not English. This is equally true of *Le Roi Léar*, the appearance of which, after the long interval of eleven years, does not denote any pressing anxiety on the part of the French actors to interpret, or of the audience to see, more 'Shakespeare.' As usual, Ducis selects a 'family' play. In order to supply his Léar with some rational motive for disowning Helmonde (Cordelia) he supposes that, prior to the opening of the play, Volnérille (Goneril) had convinced her father that Helmonde, who is in love with Ulric, King of Denmark, was plotting the death of her father and the overthrow of England. Ducis omits those early scenes where Shakespeare gradually reveals the ferocity and ingratitude of the two evil sisters. When we first see Léar he is searching for Helmonde, and he meets Kent who is sad because of the supposed desertion of his two sons Lénox and Edgard. Kent is a confirmed Rousseauist, believing, despite everything, in man's natural goodness: 'L'homme est compatissant, il n'est pas né barbare.' He

[1] *Année litt.* v (1772).

invites Léar to return with him to nature, to his country estate,
where:

> . . . la terre avec usure,
> Par des trésors certains, nous paiera sa culture.

All through the play Ducis, as far as possible, avoids confronting
Léar with the two evil daughters. Only indirectly do we learn of
Volnérille's atrocities, and in the scene where Régane and Léar
come face to face, the former scarcely speaks. Shakespeare's way
of presenting the situation would have been received with horror
and incredulity. Similarly, Edmund is completely omitted, the
role of the villain being discharged by Oswald. Consequently,
too, there is no mention of the sinister love affair between Edmund
and Goneril. Shakespeare's Edmund was, from the French point
of view, rationally inadmissible. His crimes are of such a monstrous
sort that it would overtax the imagination to conceive a motive
sufficiently plausible to account for them.

Ducis's Léar is simply a pathetic, white-haired old gentleman,
the innocent victim of a conspiracy. It is rather difficult to know
when he is sane and when he is not. The author, of course, had to
remember that Léar, as a king, must always be dignified even in his
madness, which in Ducis's version resembles the absent-mindedness
of the stage professor, rather than the heart-rending babblings of
Shakespeare's king. The fool, naturally, was excluded in deference
to the classic rule forbidding the mingling of comedy and tragedy.
Despite all this, we learn from Collé [2] that the audience furiously
applauded one scene,[1] that in which the king, on recovering his
reason, recognizes Helmonde. This episode, by the way, is a
ghastly travesty of Shakespeare, comparable in the banality and
falseness of its sentiment to the worst slobberings of Marmontel's
Moral Tales which were at the time extremely popular. The truth
of the matter is, that the France of 1783 was less than ever disposed
to assimilate Shakespeare's stupendous conception of human nature.
It is interesting in this respect to read the letters of Madame du
Deffand, whose Platonic passion for Horace Walpole is one of the
saddest and most curious events in the social history of the age.
With a pathetic anxiety to refashion her taste in conformity with
her lover's, this blind, witty lady, whose intellect completely dwarfs
that of Walpole, devoted herself piously to the worship of Horace's
English god. So long as she sticks to La Place, Shakespeare seems

---

[1] *Journal*, iii. 364.   [2] IV. v.

to her admirable. *Othello* and *Henry VI* cause her to utter naughty
heresies against the rules. She says: 'There are, I admit, a great
many things in bad taste, which could easily be excised: but, as
to the lack of the three unities, far from being shocked by it, I
approve.'[1] She and Horace go to see *Hamlet*, but her comments
are chiefly directed at Molé's acting, which is terrific: 'He will kill
himself.' In 1773 she humbly confesses, being a sincere woman:
'I cannot feel the merit of Shakespeare. I have great deference for
your judgment. I think it must be the fault of the translation.'
In reply to Walpole's attacks Madame du Deffand defends Racine,
and points out that a Frenchwoman does not need the shock of great
passions to interest her. 'The play—it is not the right word but
I can find no other—of ordinary interests, tastes, and sentiments,
when they are graduated as in Richardson, is sufficient to interest
and to please me.' Le Tourneur's translation, to Walpole's great
delight, pleased her and her friend the Abbé Barthélemy.[2] But two
years later she finds *Coriolanus*—saving Horace's respect—frightful,
and lacking in common sense. *Macbeth* she reads with horror, fear,
and interest, turning with relief to *Cymbeline*, which is 'pleasant and
interesting.' In 1779, she writes: 'Talking of madmen, I have
just read *King Lear* by your Shakespeare. Ah! Good heavens!
What a play! Really, do you find it beautiful? It smirches my
soul to an inexpressible degree: it is a mass of all the infernal
horrors.' Answering Horace's remonstrances, she says: 'I won't
reply about *Lear*. You see nature in *King Lear*, but apparently in
so far as she sometimes produces monsters.' Shakespeare's style,
by its audacity, reminds Madame du Deffand of Homer. 'What
I like in Homer is that the gods have all the vices and defects of
men, just as in Shakespeare all the kings and great noblemen have
the tone and the crude manners of the plebs.'

Madame du Deffand's experience was certainly typical of that
of many intelligent French people of her time, though few, I imagine,
had the same incentive to conversion. Many, of course, went to
see Ducis's adaptations much in the same way that they went to see
the giraffe which had recently appeared in Paris. They were actuated
by a fashionable desire to be in the swim. Such was the Duc de
Brancas, who was heard asking, after a performance of *Roméo et
Juliette*: 'Who *are* those Montaigus and Capulets that nobody has
ever heard of?' A minority of anglomaniacs, a fairly large number
of *dramomanes* in revolt against the rules like Mercier, and a handful

[1] 1768.   [2] 1776.

of inquisitive cosmopolitans seem to have composed the audiences
for whom the earnest Ducis mutilated Shakespeare.

A cruelly malicious skit on *Le Roi Léar* was acted to delighted
crowds at the *Théâtre italien*.[1]   Certain lines of Ducis's original were
transferred to the parody, where in their new context they produced
a droll effect.   Léar is described as a

> Moraliste chagrin, un conteur ennuyeux,
> Lassé de n'être rien, et surtout d'être vieux.

With diabolic accuracy, the author reproduces the insipid vapourings of Ducis's Léar:

Le Roi. [*In a frenzy.*] La Nature, l'amour . . . l'amour, la Nature.
Le Comte. [*To the king.*] Ménageons ces mots-là, trop répétés pour nous.
Le Roi. C'est le cas, ou jamais, de les prodiguer tous.

The storm breaks in all its fury.   Léar enters with an unopened
umbrella:

> Que cet abri léger tous les deux nous ombrage.
> Philosophons à l'air sur ce terrible orage.
> On est roi, c'est égal, tu vois, il pleut sur tous.
> La Nature, en fureur, n'a point d'égard pour nous,
> La foudre, mon ami, n'est pas respectueuse.
> *Le Comte.* Cette réflexion me paraît très heureuse.

After a decent interval of seven years, Ducis undertook the hard
task of accommodating *Macbeth* to the French taste.   This was in
the year after the Revolution, and France was more saturated
with humanitarianism and dangerous sentimentality than it had
ever been.   Ducis had qualms.   'First of all,' he tells us, 'I set
myself to the task of eliminating the always revolting impression
of horror which would certainly have ruined my play; I then tried
to lead the soul of my spectator to the first stages of tragic terror
by artistically mingling it with what would render it tolerable.'
The whole fate of his play, he felt, depended on the sleep-walking
scene, 'that singular scene, risked for the first time on our stage.'
The setting is the 'Palace of Inverness,' and the first act takes place
near the palace 'in the most remote spot in an ancient forest, rocks,
caves, precipices, a frightful site.   The sky is threatening and
gloomy.'

Duncan's son, Malcolm, has been brought up by an old Scottish
Highlander, Sévar, and is known as Loclin.[2]   He is unaware of his

---

[1] *Le Roi Lu, parodie du Roi Lir ou Léar* (Paris, 1783).   (According to Quérard it
is by J. P. D. Desprès.)
[2] Shade of Ossian!

noble origin, and Duncan awaits the outcome of his war against
Cador before acknowledging his son. His allies are Macbeth,
Herifort, and Menteth. Herifort is mortally wounded. Menteth,
when the play opens, is about to be executed for treachery. Macbeth suspects Glamis, a prince of the blood and apparently the
successor to the throne, of poisoning the old king's mind against
him.[1] Frédégonde (Lady Macbeth) excites her husband against
Glamis, whom she accuses of complicity in an attack by brigands
during which her son was almost burned alive. Macbeth has seen
a supernatural creature called Yphyctone, bearing a sceptre and
diadem. Moreover, in a horrible nightmare he perceived three
witches bending over a new-slain child; and in their flight towards
the castle the hags prophesied that he would be king. These
events are interpreted by Frédégonde as favourable omens.

In the third act, Frédégonde spurs on her unwilling husband to
murder Duncan and Glamis. News arrives of the execution of
Menteth, but Macbeth still hesitates:

> Mais l'honneur, mais la reconnaissance,
> Mais ce vieillard, un roi, mon parent, mon ami . . .

His wife urges that it would be easy to accuse Glamis of the murder
and upbraids him for his childish fears. Suddenly, news arrives
that Cador's friends are ready to attack the castle and slay Duncan
and Glamis:

> *Frédégonde.* Ils vont pour nous, Macbeth, immoler nos victimes.
> A leurs coups, cependant, s'ils allaient s'échapper,
> Au défaut de leurs bras, il est à toi de frapper.

We next see Macbeth a prey to remorse, haunted by the vision
of Duncan's corpse, and accusing his wife of having 'borrowed his
hand' to commit the crime.

Loclin and the people make Macbeth king but, since this is in 1790,
he has to swear that he will only be 'le premier citoyen.' Sévar,
however, arrives with the news, which none questions, that Loclin
is Malcolm and the true owner of the crown. Frédégonde begs
Macbeth to destroy the title deeds and retain the throne, and on
his refusal resolves to get rid of Malcolm and Sévar. Macbeth
now urges Malcolm to take the crown, which gives rise to a typical
eighteenth-century dialogue on the beauties of the 'state of nature,'
contrasting the democratic rustic innocence of Malcolm's life with

---

[1] Ducis throws in an optional scene with witches at the end of Act I. It
might, he dubiously suggests, 'help to increase the terror of the subject.'

the remorse of the haunted Macbeth. Sévar and Malcolm witness
the sleep-walking of Frédégonde in which it is clear that she intends
to murder them. At dawn, Macbeth re-enters and publicly confesses his guilt. At this moment Frédégonde, dishevelled and distraught, rushes in to announce that she has slain her own boy in
mistake for Malcolm. In an alternative version Ducis, who felt,
oddly enough, that the first ending was perhaps far-fetched, now
makes it clear that Frédégonde killed her child in her sleep—the
vengeance of the gods !

Now Ducis was, no doubt, a poor dramatist, but he was not an
imbecile. He must have had some rational object in this amazing
distortion of Shakespeare's *Macbeth*. Presumably, in order to soften
the monstrous character of Lady Macbeth, he emphasizes the fact
that her crimes are due to abnormal mother-love, and with some
hazy idea of inventing a fitting punishment, alters the sleep-walking
scene as he does. This, I suppose, might be called extracting the
last ounce of drama from a situation. Like all timid innovators,
in seeking to avoid what he calls the horrors of Shakespeare, he
reveals others more horrible and incredible. Perhaps his worst
crime was in prostituting the character of Macbeth, who now appears
as a weak-kneed amateur in crime, the spineless instrument of his
wife's ambition. Ducis is saturated with the mephitic humanitarianism of his age, which, as Grimm rightly said, was ill-fitted to
serve as a background to Shakespeare's demonic heroes.

One need do no more than mention Ducis's travesty of *King John*,[1]
written first in five acts and later reduced to two, because, as the
author ingenuously admits, the audience lost interest after Arthur
loses his sight. This is not a play at all; it is an account of John's
effort to defend his throne against the intrigues of Arthur, the
people's favourite. John is simply a puppet dressed up as a king,
whilst Hubert and Constance exist merely as the vessels of Ducis's
maudlin sensibility. Right triumphs in the end, and the sentimental Hubert devises a suitably lingering death for the 'tigre'
John.

Othello [2] was Ducis's last affectionate onslaught on Shakespeare,
and it is particularly interesting because of the re-casting of Iago,
who, more than any other character of English drama, seems to
have disconcerted the French admirers of Shakespeare. Ducis
is most emphatic on this point. With lyrical horror he speaks
of the 'execrable character of Iago,' the 'frightful suppleness' with

[1] *Jean sans Terre* (1791).   [2] 1792.

which 'this serpent caresses and seduces the generous, confiding Othello. How he infects him with all his poisons! How he envelops him in his folds! Finally, how he crushes, stifles, and tears him in his rage! I am quite persuaded that, if the English can quietly observe the manœuvres of such a monster on the stage, the French could not for one moment suffer his presence, much less watch him reveal the whole scope and depth of his villainy.' Ducis's simple way out of the difficulty is to keep the audience in ignorance of Iago's true nature till the *dénouement*, when he suddenly draws back the veil. He is careful, moreover, to point out that Iago dies in the agonies of the most refined torture. Had the spectator once suspected Iago's perfidy in the course of the play, the horror inspired by him, adds Ducis, would have detracted from the sympathetic interest aroused by Othello and Desdemona.

From our point of view, of course, Ducis, by this method, ruins the play before the curtain rises, since he deprives the tragedy of its generating, dynamic force. It is childish, also, to imagine that the true cause of Othello's jealousy can be casually revealed as an afterthought. It is like a *Hamlet* where, after portraying the hero's attitude towards Claudius and Gertrude, the author were to explain nonchalantly in a footnote to the last scene: 'By the way, Claudius, abetted by the queen, had killed Hamlet's father.' Still trapped in the revolving cage of neo-classic tradition, Ducis lays great stress on the question of Desdemona's filial duty. She is not yet married to Othello, though he has asked her to wed him secretly. To complicate her problem, her mother had secretly predicted on her deathbed that Desdemona was fated to meet an unhappy death.

Othello, a stout loyalist, is contrasted with the 'nobles sans gloire ou connus par leurs vices,' those enemies to the state with whom Odalbert, the heroine's father, is hand in glove. To complicate the situation there is a young man, Lovédan, a great admirer of Othello's. The Moor [1] discovers Desdemona at Lovédan's feet,[2] and does not know, of course, that she is simply trying to enlist his help to save her father. Not unnaturally, Othello's African jealousy is aroused, and as Lovédan and Desdemona are obliged to see each other a great deal, Othello's worst suspicions are excited. Ducis, in the classic manner, assumes at the outset that Othello is noted

---

[1] 'Not to revolt the public,' Ducis made him ochre-coloured, not black.
[2] She is called Hédelmonde, but to avoid confusion I retain Shakespeare's name.

for his jealousy. To the annoyance of Desdemona, Lovédan is indiscreet enough to make her a declaration of his love. In the fourth act there is some very confusing business about a compromising letter written by Desdemona to Lovédan under duress. This she gives to Lovédan in order to save her father. She also parts with a diadem so as to raise money for the now outlawed Odalbert. During all this time Iago (Pézare) conceals his perfidy, and not until the close of the fourth act does he produce the diadem and the letter as proof of Desdemona's guilt. The last act, as in Shakespeare, takes place in the heroine's bedchamber. The early scenes are full of her forebodings, for she remembers her mother's prophecy. Desdemona falls asleep and is awakened by Othello. But—and it is in these critical situations that one realizes the advantages of a good upbringing—she merely remarks:

'Quel sujet (pardonnez ma surprise inquiète)
Vous fait chercher si tard ma paisible retraite?'

Despite her very lucid and convincing explanation regarding the letter and the diadem, Desdemona, invoking the *Être suprême*, is slain. There is one delicious touch. Othello, after the murder, and still amazed that a girl so young should be such a hardened dissembler, concludes that it must be the effect of the climate and the environment:

'C'est l'effet du climat. Il faut pour tant d'horreur,
Que tout l'art de Venise ait passé dans son cœur.'

At this moment, a crowd of officers and soldiers bursts in with the intelligence that Pézare was a false friend who secretly burned for Desdemona. Othello commits suicide. In an alternative ending, however, the tender Ducis averts the murder at the eleventh hour. All are happy and Othello pardons Pézare.

This was not the first French *Othello*. That honour goes to Douin, who in 1773 translated the play and made it conform to the unities of time and place. Douin's sins are mostly negative. He cuts out what he calls the 'incidental' scenes, that is, those which contain licentious or comic passages. This chaste pruning notwithstanding, he was advised that the play could not be shown on a French stage. The objections, all of which he answers, are most interesting. The hero is black. There are references in the play to sorcery, which 'has no longer any credit in France.' [1] Iago is

---

[1] This of course is inaccurate. Belief in sorcery, in the guise of science (Mesmer, Cagliostro), existed.

unnaturally wicked, and no actor should be exposed to the hatred
of the audience for two and a half hours, a remark which confirms
a statement by D'Hannetaire,[1] that in those days the parts played
by an actor considerably influenced his social standing. Besides,
it was objected, even if we admit Iago, it is impossible to make him
the mouthpiece of the noble sentiments attributed to him by
Shakespeare, an extraordinary and illogical objection revealing a
complete misunderstanding of Iago's character, which is the essence
of duplicity. Again, Cassio's drunkenness cannot be decently
shown on a public stage—a natural objection when we reflect
that, even in French comedy, drunkenness was rarely shown because of the prejudice against this vice in real life. The scene where
Othello is supposed to think that Cassio is speaking of Desdemona
when he is actually referring to Bianca is criticized, and rightly,
as far-fetched. The murder scene is considered too long. Finally,
the French stage cannot admit, in profane tragedies, the use of terms
like *Ciel*, *Ange*, *Diable*, *Être souverain*: 'one ought to employ general
expressions relating to the gods of mythology.'

Douin points out that in making Othello black, Shakespeare is
merely imitating his Italian source. Sorcery does appear, it is
true, but only to be refuted. Iago is not *unnaturally* wicked, 'for
he is never wicked for the mere pleasure of being so, a character
which for the sake of humanity I prefer to think could not exist.
Iago does not commit any wickedness or villainy without the
audience being apprised beforehand of his motives and object.'
Here Douin appreciates the fundamental difference between the
English and French conception of character. According to him,
and he is simply following Cartesian tradition, even vice must be
rational. Descartes had pointed out that moral evil was due simply
to incorrect thinking. Correct the mind and you correct the heart.
Douin, who had lived in England, realized the full force of the
French attitude and, in defending Shakespeare, misinterprets Iago,
who really does commit his crimes for the sheer love of evil. In
one respect, however, Douin is a heretic, since he defends Shakespeare against the *style noble* of traditional French tragedy and,
moreover, does so with audacity. Where before, he confesses,
he had thought like every one else that it was ridiculous to hear
a tragic hero complain of a headache, what now strikes him as
absurd is the elaborate gymnastics performed by French dramatists
in their anxiety to avoid 'vulgar' or 'trivial' expressions. Think

[1] *Observations sur l'art du comédien.*

of how one of these would have rendered Othello's simple
remark:

> Depuis que le soleil m'a fermé la paupière
> D'insolites vapeurs mes yeux sont obscurcis.
> Et je sens que chez moi le siège des esprits
> Ressent incessamment les douleurs les plus vives.

Why not say simply: 'J'ai mal à la tête,' just as one says: 'Je me
meurs.' This is quite revolutionary; it is, in fact, as we shall see
later, the reflection of a great movement now in progress, inspired
by *âmes sensibles* like Rousseau, who were determined to substitute
for the conventional in thought and in expression, emotions and
language of a simpler, warmer, and more real sort.

Douin agrees that drunkenness is improper on the stage, and
alters Shakespeare so as to imply that Cassio is not drunk but
poisoned. The Bianca scene, he maintains, is quite probable if we
recollect Othello's excited state of mind. As to the murder, it is a
masterpiece: it fills one with pity and horror. He adopts the
same uncompromising attitude to the affair of the 'profane' exclamations which shock his pious friends. 'Is it possible that one
must write nonsense in a tragedy so as to dress it in the costume of
the French theatre?' Of all the imitators of Shakespeare in
eighteenth-century France, Douin is the most intelligent, and
therefore the most daring. He could not, however, get his *Othello*
produced on the stage, not even privately.

Much could legitimately be expected from L.S. Mercier's associa-
tion with Shakespearian drama. His violently professed enthusiasm
for our dramatist, his heretical attitude towards Racine, his criticism
of the whole traditional conception of tragedy, and his campaign
for a more democratic theatre seem to stamp him as the Moses
who was to lead his French compatriots out of the desert of neo-
classicism into the promised land which he himself so vividly
describes.[1] Theoretically, Mercier ought to have bridged the gulf
between English and French dramatic taste: actually, for two
excellent reasons, he did nothing of the sort. Firstly, the gulf
could not be bridged; secondly, Mercier regarded Shakespearian
art not as an end in itself, but as a means to his real object, which
was to carry Diderot's ideas to their logical, inevitable conclusion.
In his hands *le drame*, which had evolved from sentimental comedy,
degenerates into bad melodrama with a strong admixture of
philosophic propaganda. Voltaire, setting out from Racinian

[1] In his *De la littérature*.

tragedy, had drifted also in the direction of melodrama; but his *tragédies de mœurs*, despite their load of improbable sensational incidents, and the transparent attacks on religion and on the administration which was their *raison d'être*, still preserved the armature of the neo-classic play. Mercier, on the contrary, began by denying the unities and all the conventions so greatly prized by the traditionalists. Like Molière, but in a very different sense, he might have said: 'Je prends mon bien où je le trouve.' But his was the case of a polemical writer, actuated by an uncontrollable desire to give artistic, public expression to his hatred of social abuses, yet devoid of dramatic gifts. Whatever material came his way was bound to be twisted and refashioned in one direction. This is painfully apparent in his *Tombeaux de Vérone*, which is an eighteenth-century French *drame* suggested by *Romeo and Juliet*. Not only do the hero and heroine assume a mere secondary importance compared to the role of Benvoglio, the *médecin-naturaliste*, but all the characters are sacrificed to the ideas which form the chief interest of the play. But that Rousseau had already come and gone, Shakespeare's lyricism would have embarrassed Mercier. As it is, he ruthlessly rips up the web of Shakespeare's poetry, and claws out a few strands which he weaves into the stringy fabric of his own dreadful sentimental moralizings.

Romeo and Juliet are here secretly married. Théobald's death, however, prevents the hoped-for reconciliation between the enemy houses. The lovers meet secretly, in a 'salon opening on to a garden'; it is for the last time, since Romeo is now exiled. They are abetted by the *philosophe* Benvoglio, for he is 'l'ami des hommes.' This is how he describes himself: '. . . Il faut des lumières pour oser être bon contre l'opinion qui gouverne les hommes. Sans la science, il n'est point de courage, il n'est point de véritables amis de l'humanité.' Benvoglio is the man of Rousseau's dreams: 'scrutateur assidu de la nature, à qui il a dérobé plusieurs secrets, après avoir lu dans nos cœurs, il est devenu notre véritable père.' Mercier's romantic puppets are infatuated with Benvoglio, who announces that long line of terribly earnest and often terribly boring thinkers who will crop up periodically in nineteenth-century plays. Brieux or Ibsen would make him, as does Mercier, a doctor. Later he becomes a social worker, an engineer, or a labour member. In any case, his invariable mission is to talk a great deal and to criticize existing social institutions. In the *Tombeaux de Vérone* he stands for tolerance and, of course, abets the children against their harsh parents. Shakespeare's poetry holds no terrors for Mercier. His rendering of the superb dawn scene makes us realize what a debt we owe to Ducis for having left it alone:

Roméo. N'entendez-vous pas la messagère du matin, l'alouette qui s'élève en chantant à travers les ombres qui fuient devant le crépuscule du jour!

Juliette. Non, non, c'est le rossignol qui se plaît à percer les ténèbres de ses accents.

Roméo. Tous les flambeaux de la nuit sont éteints: vois la lune qui pâlit à l'approche de l'aurore.

Juliette. Non, c'est un nuage qui la voile. . . . Le jour est encore loin de paraître.

Roméo. Une lueur blanchâtre s'éteint sur le sommet de cette colline. Ces traits de lumière qui percent les nuages vers l'orient!

Juliette. C'est quelque météore. Ah! mon cher Roméo, un instant! C'est le dernier peut-être.

Inevitably, since he is converting Shakespearian tragedy into *drame*, Mercier stresses the domestic scenes but alters the character of Juliet's mother. She becomes here an eighteenth-century bourgeoise in secret rebellion against a brutal, authoritative husband. She is, needless to say, cordially supported by Benvoglio, who gives his views on the question of women's rights, and invokes the 'natural law' to prove that no human institution can stand in the way of 'precious sensibility.' He declaims: 'As soon as the voice of sentiment makes itself heard, the profane clamours of prejudice vanish, yielding to the most legitimate as well as to the most sacred of all laws.' Mercier is already a full-fledged romantic: Juliet, he regards as an *incomprise*. 'You have walked,' Benvoglio tells her, 'in the midst of a blind world which was not made to appreciate you.'

Indeed, Juliet scarcely needs these exhortations. She is a convert to Rousseauism, and, with delicious anticipation, pictures her father's grief when he shall learn of her suicide. 'When Count Lodrino (Paris), accompanied by my venerable father, comes to seize the trembling Juliet he will find only a cold and trembling hand. The pallor of death will be imprinted on her colourless cheek; soon, the funeral bell will resound through the air . . . my father will weep perhaps . . . his power will exist no longer. I shall be with death which restores to all, equal once more, their primitive liberty.'

For censorship reasons, there is no Friar Lawrence in Mercier's version, but Benvoglio supplies the magic drug. There is a harrowing scene when Capulet discovers his daughter's 'corpse.' And Benvoglio curses 'the tyranny, under the name of paternal authority, which weighs upon this amiable sex.' As in Ducis, the graveyard episode provokes an outburst of 'night thoughts.' Benvoglio had written informing Romeo where he should find Juliet, carelessly forgetting, however, to mention that she would be drugged but not dead. As a result, Romeo's suicide is averted just in the nick of time. On the arrival of the parents, Juliet miraculously awakes. Benvoglio, striking while the iron is hot, delivers a little sermon. It *is* a miracle, but not in the accepted sense. The true miracle is Juliet's courage, born of a great love. Love is the great solvent of hatred and evil. 'If it reigned supreme, how many evils would be spared to the world by its universal empire.' The former enemies fall on each other's necks; Romeo and Juliet are happy, and the world is made safe for democracy and humanitarianism.

In a preface to his *Le Vieillard et ses Trois Filles*, published in *L'An quatrième de la Liberté*,[1] Mercier reminds his readers that as early as 1773 he had praised Shakespeare's *drames* as 'a mine rich in strong and vast ideas, in eloquent, vivid impressions: in short, as most calculated to kindle our timid conceptions and enlarge the *parloir* of the French stage.' He adds: 'I flatter myself that in *Le Vieillard et ses Trois Filles* you will find the true manner of Shakespeare: yet the plan and details almost entirely belong to me.' Nothing could be more true than the final words of this remark, for Mercier, in an access of republican zeal, dethrones Lear and makes him an ordinary citizen. 'I preferred to offer a moral picture, closer to ourselves, and above all, applicable to domestic life. The new *Lear* shall be an object lesson to all ungrateful children who have abused, forgotten, or insulted their benefactors.' Goneril, Regan, and Cordelia are rebaptized Judith, Sara, and Caroline, while the Earl of Kent becomes Jones, the faithful old retainer. La Manon (Lear) divides his property between the three daughters, but is displeased with Caroline who is not a demonstrative girl. Sara's butler is rude to the old man and this leads to painful scenes. Mercier pursues throughout his dreadful plan, closely following the action of the original, but reducing each situation, like each character to a republican level. The storm, however, remains unchanged. Reluctantly, one feels, the author resigns himself to the *ci-devant* lightning, thunder, and rain. Not even the Terror can change those.

Le Vieillard et ses Trois Filles is possibly the greatest atrocity ever

[1] 1792.

committed in the name of Liberty, Equality, and Fraternity. It
is, however, instructive because it reveals the danger of attaching
too much significance to the so-called 'appreciations' of Shakespeare
by eighteenth-century French writers. To read Mercier's early
eulogies, and the same thing is true of Marmontel, La Place, and
Ducis, one might readily have the illusion that they reflect an increasing understanding of Shakespearian art and point to a possible
fusion of French and English taste. Mercier's version of *Lear* is
a timely reminder of the folly of any such idea: and, miserable
artist though he was, Mercier, after all, actively supported the
most vigorous and the most revolutionary movement in the French
eighteenth-century theatre. If there was to be any real approach
to Shakespeare in France, it was much more likely to come from the
writers of *drames* than from men like Ducis, who were still wedded
to the neo-classic formula. In this dreadful pollution of a great
tragedy, one realizes vividly the fallacy of the argument advanced
by English and French admirers of 'domestic tragedy,' namely
that greatness of rank or the magnitude of the interests involved
have nothing to do with the tragedy of a situation or character;
that, on the contrary, a tragedy will be all the more impressive if
it is presented as happening to persons of middling social status in
circumstances appropriate to that class. To do Diderot justice,
never once in all his discussions of the new genre, 'le genre sérieux,'
does he suggest that it might usurp the function of heroic or traditional tragedy. Nevertheless, as we know, that is what actually
occurred. The eighteenth-century *drame* was taken as a model by
the successors of Diderot. To-day tragedy, as Shakespeare or
Racine conceived it, is extinct.

In considering Mercier's ludicrous attempt to reduce Shakespeare
to the stature of eighteenth-century *drame*, we mentioned his idea
that to make the theatre more realistic it must be made more
democratic. By stripping Lear of his regality, and abolishing the
atmosphere of momentous political events with which Shakespeare
enveloped his play, Mercier destroys it, and reduces the tragedy
to the dimensions of a tawdry family squabble about money.
Diderot wisely limited himself to saying that this kind of play can
be interesting and moral because of the obvious analogy between
its situations and those of everyday life: Mercier and his friends
claimed that, on this account, the *drame*, by touching our immediate
experience, must leave the spectator with a deeper impression of
tragedy. Now, even if Mercier had been a good and not an abject

dramatist, he could never have aroused the same pity for Lear the bourgeois as for Lear the monarch. For, if it is true that in the lovely and pitiful words used by Shakespeare to express the anguish of the old king, we catch an echo of the language and the accents of any father deserted by his children, it is false to assume that, conversely, the grief of an ordinary man will strike us with the same tragic intensity, since it is the peculiar essence of all great tragedy to give us a momentary illusion of the Absolute: that, to take the case of Lear, never again can we imagine a grief so boundless, so completely unlimited by time or *milieu*. No man of imagination, gazing on the spectacle of Lear's anguish, can utter the truism that the passing of the years, the change of environment, will blunt the keen edge of his sorrow. And Shakespeare, as Racine had done, with an exquisite sense of fitness, imagines as a cadre for these splendid emotions and passions one which by its dignity and grandeur will harmonize with the dignity and grandeur of the theme. A transposition like that devised by Mercier cannot be effected without committing a crime against art. It is aesthetic incest. The novelist, moving on a different plane and by employing other means, may produce a tragic illusion of another sort, as does Balzac in *Père Goriot*. But that opens up another question.

To dispose of Mercier it is enough simply to mention his *Timon*,[1] a pale, neuter adaptation of the Shakespearian original. Mercier, who was in prison during the Terror, has lost all enthusiasm for revolutions, political or literary. He now admits the difficulties of subjugating Shakespeare to our theatrical rules, and especially to the severe taste of a Parisian audience. His *Timon* is amusingly polite, and the *bienséances* are sedulously observed. Even in 1795, it was apparently indecorous for a 'citoyen' to hurl dishes at the heads of his guests or to speak his mind to the ladies of the town—at least on the stage.

Farmain de Rozoi strenuously denies that his *Richard III*[2] owes anything to Shakespeare, and there is no reason to doubt him. Envious contemporaries, however, insisted that it did, possibly basing their accusations on occasional passages like the following:

[*Richard paraît sur le haut du côteau, les cheveux hérissés, n'ayant à la main qu'une moitié de son épée. Il entre en courant et paraît égaré par la rage.*]

> Une épée! une épée! ô désespoir! ô rage!
> La mienne s'est brisée au milieu du carnage.
> Une épée! . . . ou je perds et le Trône et l'Honneur.

---

[1] 1795.   [2] 1782.

With some eagerness we hasten to say that there is practically
nothing else in this imbecile production to suggest the influence
of Shakespeare.[1] Butini's *Othello* [2] claims to be 'imitated from
Shakespeare,' and apart from the omission of the most powerful
speeches and the most essential scenes, Butini follows the original
closely. There is a Moor in his play who is jealous of his wife and
stabs her. Being a Swiss and a former 'procureur de Genève,'
Butini has not the French squeamishness about portraying drunkenness on the stage and retains the Cassio scene. In a fit of recklessness
he also keeps the ignoble 'mouchoir.'

The MS. *Othello* already referred to is most probably by Leriget.
It was never played, and was most probably rejected by the reading
committee of the *Comédie française*. It is, however, unique in many
respects. The author is prepared to present the original almost
intact. He recognizes that all other so-called adaptations really
omit what is essentially English in their models. Leriget uses an
English edition,[3] because he finds that Le Tourneur's translation
does not render the 'finesse and energy' of Shakespeare. Leriget,
we learn from an interesting document appended to his manuscript, wrote to London for information as to the Drury Lane
production of *Othello*.

His general remarks on the whole question of Shakespeare in
France are most valuable. It would not be difficult, he says, to
prove that *Romeo and Juliet*, *Hamlet*, and *King Lear* are 'absolutely
unknown' in France for the following reasons. Some Frenchmen,
content to judge Shakespeare by hearsay, that is through translation,
and accustomed to their own 'symmetrical plays,' see in him nothing
but cemeteries, gravediggers, deaths, etc., and they believe that it
is these horrors which endear him to the English. Others, like
Ducis, have committed the stupidity of trying to regularize Shakespeare's plays, forgetting that the movement, the action, and the
variety of his work must disappear if we try to reduce him to the
rule of the three unities. If, for instance, *Othello* is treated in
this way, 'the first two acts, like all the first acts of tragedies, will
consist in explanations, description of characters, preparation
scenes, etc. After that, what will be left for the remaining acts,
the tragic and difficult part of the subject, which will not, as in the
original, have been softened by the preparatory scenes? In a word,
Leriget is really the first Frenchman to suspect the fundamental

---

[1] He seems to have read Cibber's popular version of *Richard III*.
[2] 1785. Never played.   [3] Bell's.

difference between the slow, cumulative, experimental method of the English dramatist and the concentrated, tense, swift manner of French tragedy. What the French called Shakespeare's 'irregularity,' his apparent lack of definite plan, is vital to the development of his gigantic passions. The French way was not to portray the genesis of passion, but, assuming its maturity, to reveal the dire effects of passion on the human soul. Shakespeare does both.

Even Leriget, however, feels it necessary 'to tighten up the action, to put more continuity into the scenes: in short, to soften what in the strong situations might seem too harsh for the French.' In this manner he finally manages to cut down the acting-time from the English four or five to the French two hours. But, like all his compatriots, he finds Iago a bugbear. 'I have deemed it indispensably necessary,' he confesses, 'to give a comic aspect to the character of Iago so as to get the audience amused at the subtlety of his very villainies; otherwise, he would not have been bearable.' In this, the closest approach to the real Shakespeare achieved by an eighteenth-century French author, we do, in places, catch some faint echo of the Shakespearian *motif*, but, of course, it is without the orchestration of his poetry.

Had Leriget been able to fulfil his ambitions it would have meant, as he points out, that for the first time a French audience would have witnessed a tragedy that did not observe the unities: 'The attempt has not yet been made. Why should it not be? Perhaps it might succeed, but without trying it one cannot be sure. What a new mine could be exploited by the theatre appropriating such a genre!' Leriget wanted to make his *Othello* as English as possible. From a London correspondent he learns that 'the practice of the English theatre has been to dress all the characters in modern habits: Othello and his officers in their regimentals; Roderigo as much like a coxcomb as tragedy will admit of; Brabantio at first in his *robe de chambre*, and afterwards, like a senator, i.e. in loose, flowing robes such as were worn three hundred years ago and perhaps still. But the English theatre has been so remiss in its practice that I have frequently seen the senators dressed in very mean, black gowns and tie-wigs, with a red gown, if I remember rightly, for the duke, rather like beggarly lawyers than with any richness of costume. . . . The truth is that, in preparing the play at Paris, the actual costume of Venice ought much rather to be studied than the practice of the English theatre.' The writer obligingly supplies various hints as to the usual method of London actors in interpreting *Othello*. Thus

Brabantio addresses Iago and Roderigo from his balcony. In the third scene of the first act, when the duke and senators rise and retire, it has been the custom to drop a kind of curtain scene. Desdemona and Othello show their love 'by the energy of their looks.' 'The habitual reserve of the English stage requires that stage embraces should be more cold, more conformable to the natural manners than on the French theatre.[1] Cassio, even drunk, should be a gentleman. Iago should be very careful as to how he recites his asides—a difficult business. Othello stabs, not strangles, Desdemona, first forcing her down on the pillow.' Poor Leriget's meticulous preparations—he had even decided that the playbills must have 'Othello, comme on le joue à Londres'—were all for naught. His play met that most inglorious and dustiest of deaths: it now reposes in a dossier of the Bibliothèque Nationale.

The only conclusion to be induced from these experiments is that Shakespeare could not be adapted to suit the French dramatic taste of the eighteenth century, even at that favourable moment when the French theatre was in a most receptive mood. To any lover of Shakespeare, the adaptations themselves are, of course, painful to contemplate: to those, however, who wish to discover what distinguished French from English dramatic taste they are interesting. Before damning them completely, it might be well to consider how Shakespeare was being presented in his native country. For if the French took insupportable liberties with his plays, so did their English contemporaries, and none more than Garrick, whose interpretation of the great tragedies was the wonder of his age. Yet I doubt if a twentieth-century audience could stand ten minutes of Garrick in his favourite roles without leaving the theatre. Such, at least, is the impression one gathers from the utterances of the few serious contemporary critics of his art.

As is well known, Garrick preferred Tate's version of Lear, which he altered somewhat, keeping, however, the happy ending in which Cordelia marries Edgar and the old king is restored to the throne. Sir John Hill[2] has some very pertinent remarks to make on Garrick's acting in the scene where Lear curses Goneril. He did it 'solemnly and with premeditation,' whereas, as Hill points out, he should have been in 'a rage almost equal to phrenzy.' Nor could Hill pardon the tears shed at the end of this passage which is 'a climax of rage.' Yet this 'unmanly snivelling' was apparently

[1] Here he is in error, since embraces were taboo on the French tragic stage.
[2] British Magazine (1747).

noisily applauded by the 'groundlings.' More interesting is the glimpse of Garrick as the mad Lear pulling at his rags, and playing with his straws as he consults mad Tom whom he takes for a learned Theban. What Garrick completely missed, according to Hill, is that Lear, mad, is still Lear the king. 'All his expressions are full of the royal prerogative.' There should be no 'sign of equality, no familiarity, no sitting down cheek by jowl; this might be the proper representation of a mad tailor, but by no means corresponds to my idea of King Lear.' On the other hand, Hill is full of admiration for Garrick's rendering of the recognition scene, 'a masterly blend of joy, tenderness, grief and shame, worthy of Rubens and Angelo.' Hill, by the way, was one of the few to take exception to the altered version of *Lear*: [1] others felt that Shakespeare's original made Cordelia too coarse. The public expected alterations and excisions. In almost every Shakespearian tragedy, says one writer, there are scenes 'which it has been since found necessary to retouch in the action.' [2] The same author finds fault with Shakespeare's portrayal of the character of Hamlet, who 'should love a more distinguished woman than Ophelia. This love is a defect in his character.' Also, he should not, as a prince, give instructions to the players. He expresses the hope that Garrick will 'take the piece in hand,' because it might be made much superior to the *Electra* of Sophocles.

Shakespeare is more severely criticized in the *Dramatic Censor*.[3] Lady Macbeth's speech beginning: 'Was the hope drunk?' is considered offensive because of its 'vulgar and nauseous allusions.' She should be excluded from the stage. The porter interlude is dismissed as 'an insult on the judgment.' The murder of Lady Macduff is 'farcically horrid,' and therefore rightly omitted in representation. We learn, incidentally, that Donalbain's exclamation: '*To Ireland I* nine times out of ten, raises a horse laugh.' *Othello* is described as 'unhappily loaded with indelicate passages,' and Act v, scene i, as 'a strange jumble of events.' We gather that the Covent Garden audience was spared the sight of Bianca 'howling over her gallant.' Quin, as the hero, used to appear 'in a large, powdered major wig which, with his black face, made such a magpie appearance of his head as tended greatly to laughter; one stroke, however, was not amiss; coming on in white gloves, by putting off which the black hands became more realized.'

[1] *The London Magazine* also objected.
[2] *Essay on the Present State of the Theatre in France, England, and Italy* (1760).
[3] 1770. The writer is Francis Gentleman.

The *Romeo and Juliet* of T. Cibber, which was a cross between the
original and Otway's strange adaptation called *Caius Marius*, was
replaced at Drury Lane by Garrick's version with intercalated
lyrics from his own pen.   Here Juliet awakens in the tomb in time
to converse with Romeo before she dies.   Shortly after this innovation, we find a critic in the *London Magazine* [1] complaining that
'we do not know about Romeo's first love, Rosaline.'   By representing him as in love with Juliet before they meet on the
stage half the pathos is lost.   In the scene, too, where Romeo takes
leave of Juliet, the lovers 'are brought *tête à tête* on the platform of
the stage,' and instead of Romeo descending by a ladder of ropes
from his mistress's window, he is 'made to walk off the stage coolly,'
a circumstance which, as the critic remarks, takes all the point from
the lines:

> O God . . .
> As one dead in the bottom of a tomb . . .

The 'grand raree-show at the end of Act IV,' i.e. the much-
admired funeral scene, is properly condemned as 'a ridiculous
piece of pageantry.'   Both at Drury Lane and at Covent Garden
the coffin of the drugged heroine was accompanied by a long procession of monks to the strains of liturgical music by Dr. Boyce.

Francis Gentleman,[2] referring to the same production, raises
objections of another sort, though, like the previous critic, he admires
Garrick's *dénouement*.   The 'mobbish scuffling' of the opening scenes is
deplored and Gregory's 'low comedy message' which concludes Act I,
scene iii, is condemned as 'totally inconsistent with common English decorum, much more the pride and distance of Italian quality.'
As might have been expected, Gentleman is prudishly disgusted with
Garrick for retaining the nurse's frank references to sexual matters.
More enlightening is his observation that when she goes to awaken
Juliet her remarks 'commonly make an audience laugh when they
should cry.'

Garrick's great friend, Patu, has some sensible and interesting
things to say about Garrick's *Romeo and Juliet* in the *Journal étranger*.[3]
The poetry of the garden scene strikes him as very beautiful,
'though somewhat in the style of Oriental love stories.'   He shows
with what genius Shakespeare recasts Bandello's tale, but prefers

---

[1] 1749.   [2] In the *Dramatic Censor* (1770).
[3] 1755.   In a review of Mrs. Lenox's *Shakespeare Illustrated*.   Patu's letter to
Garrick (23 Sept. 1755 in the Forster MSS.) makes it clear that he is the author
of this article, though at the moment Fréron edited this paper.

the Italian ending where Romeo dies in Juliet's arms. Garrick he finds superior to Otway, who did not realize the dramatic possibilities latent in the new *dénouement*, in which Juliet awakens before Romeo's death. At Covent Garden, the original Shakespearian ending was retained, and Fréron seems to agree with 'many connoisseurs' who prefer it to Garrick's. He also defends Romeo's speech to Balthazar which, he considers, 'portrays a hundred times better the cruel state, the trouble and agitation of Romeo, than the sangfroid, the deliberate actions, the carefully drawn-up will, the considered commands, in brief, everything that denotes the *amiable despair* of the unfortunate young man in the original novel.' Patu points out, however, that in *Romeo and Juliet* there is much that French taste cannot accept: the multiplicity of interests, the continual changes of scene, and, above all, the low comedy characters—Mercutio and the nurse. These are, however, minor flaws reflecting the manners of Shakespeare's age. Even in Corneille, there are traits which make an eighteenth-century Frenchman laugh because of the change that has come over language and manners. Patu, who is one of the most enthusiastic Anglophiles of the eighteenth century, concludes very sensibly, that in examining foreign works such local details do not matter, provided the great passions are handled with genius and strength.

Garrick's object in 'revising' *Hamlet*, we learn from the *Macaroni*,[1] was to rid the play of certain 'monstrous incongruities and absurdities which displeased both French and English critics.' To effect this, he postponed the meeting between Hamlet and his father's ghost to Act II. Thus Shakespeare's Act II became Act III, his Act III became Act IV, and the original fourth and fifth Acts were fused into one. Hamlet's return from England, 'instead of being accidental,' we read, 'and thereby defeating his pre-determined purpose of killing the king, is now an act of his own; arising from the recollection of the much superior business he had to do in revenging his father's death than going upon a needless expedition.' The gravediggers' scene is 'very properly expunged.' The fencing-match with Laertes becomes a duel, though the critic feels that it should have been left out altogether. Hamlet kills the king and is killed by Laertes. From another source we gather that the queen turns insane and dies.[2] Ophelia quickly disappears from the play, and the customary funeral scene is consequently omitted.

[1] 1772–3.
[2] According to Professor Odell, *The English Stage from Betterton to Irving*.

It is not surprising to learn that the eighteenth-century actors permitted themselves such gross liberties with Shakespeare's text, though several editions of his works had been recently made available. Even a writer of Voltaire's reputation and well-known irascibility complains, again and again, that he was powerless to prevent the numerous excisions and the stupid additions and alterations made by the *Comédie française* before it staged his plays. Shakespeare was long dead and, unfortunately, despite the lip-homage paid to his name, and the labour expended by successive editors in annotating his works, practically none protested against the systematic and public prostitution of his genius which was practised nightly on the boards of Covent Garden and Drury Lane. It was considered natural for Garrick to add a long dying speech to *Macbeth* because, says Davies,[1] 'he excelled in the expression of convulsive throes and dying agonies.' Is it not ironical when we read of the indignation inspired in England by Voltaire's observations on Shakespeare, to reflect that Garrick, instead of being hissed off the stage, was rapturously applauded? Johnson, one of Shakespeare's editors — and he was not alone — admired the modern travesty of *Lear* because he could not bear the cruel *dénouement* of the original. One or two timid souls objected; but their voices were drowned in the applause of the majority. Indeed, the only protest worthy of the name which I have so far enountered was made, not by an Englishman, but by De la Coste, a French visitor to London in 1783.[2] It may not be amiss to quote it in full if only for the well-deserved rebuke with which it concludes. De la Coste is speaking of the acting version of *Lear* but, in general, is attacking the abuse of allowing actors to tamper with plays. 'When I see her (Cordelia) travestied by the actors as a vagabond shepherdess, wandering in the mountains, solely in order to confess her romantic love to her lover whom she there finds hidden under the rags of a mad beggar; when, instead of seeing the octogenarian Lear succumb finally and with dignity beneath the ultimate blow of fate which deprives him of Cordelia, I see this prince in the depths of a dungeon, stretched on the straw like a vile scoundrel with his daughter a prisoner also; shuddering at the aspect of the wretch who appears, followed by three servants with ropes to strangle him; when I see these ruffians seize him from Cordelia's arms and twist him, and yet this combat, or rather this disgusting scuffle, end with the deaths of two or three of these vile characters, slain

---

[1] Op. cit., iii. 73.   [2] *Voyage philosophique d'Angleterre* (1786).

by an old man who can scarcely stand; in short, when I see all these disjointed, improbable, and revolting scenes finish coolly with the marriage of the princess to her lover, I say that Shakespeare is felt, neither by the actors who mutilate him, nor by the spectators who not only suffer but applaud them—and often with enthusiasm. I say that the honours of the apotheosis decreed to this great man were offered by pride and not by sentiment; on the word of a few men of letters and foreigners and not by the heart and genius of a nation obviously insensible to his real beauties.' De la Coste is perfectly right. Strictly speaking, the eighteenth-century English audiences never saw Shakespeare acted in the original. From what we know of the productions at Covent Garden and Drury Lane it is clear, too, that what was actually Shakespearian in the revised plays had to be reinforced by a good deal of spectacular pomp and stupid clownery. As this elicited little protest, references to it are sparse though illuminating. Davies speaks of the actor who was the bishop in *Henry VIII* pretending to aim a blow at Cardinal Wolsey as he passes him.[1] Gentleman [2] protests at the 'funny' business in *Henry IV* when Falstaff sits down on the same drum as the king, tumbles down as Henry gets up and vice versa; and again at the 'farcical incident' of Kent going to sleep in a pair of movable stocks, while a gentleman usher makes a 'very pantomimical stroke' by prodding him with a stick whilst his legs are fast. With these facts in mind, I cannot disbelieve Voltaire when he talks of the gravediggers playing with the skulls and singing drinking-songs in *Hamlet*.[3] Nothing is more likely.

In writing these chapters my object was not to apologize for the failure of the eighteenth-century French to understand or to assimilate the art of Shakespeare. That would be ridiculous. It was rather to indicate how little actual significance attaches to statements about the profound influence exercised by Shakespeare on French dramatic taste. It was also to show the unreasonableness of supposing that the contact with Shakespeare at this period could possibly affect, in any real fashion, the spirit of French drama. In one sense, the moment was a favourable one, since French

---

[1] Op. cit. [2] *Dramatic Censor* (1770).
[3] This makes Professor Lounsbury angry. He writes: 'Even in the simple report of what he had before his eyes Voltaire was enabled to free himself from the tyranny of exactness. The gravediggers sing songs: but they are not drinking-songs. In the exercise of their calling they throw up skulls; but they do not play with them' (*Shakespeare and Voltaire*, p. 51). The author obviously forgets that Voltaire not only read, but probably saw, *Hamlet*.

dramatists were in a peculiarly receptive mood: in another, it was inopportune, since the English themselves were by no means unanimously convinced of Shakespeare's perfection. In an un-published diary [1] kept by Lady Crewe, who was in Paris from 1785 to 1786, we discover these comments on the question. They are suggested to her by an argument she overheard between Guibert and Goldburne as to the merits of Corneille and Shakespeare. It will be a long time, she thinks, before the wisest of the French under-stand Shakespeare. 'For I observe they hardly even attempt to learn the *familiar* parts of our language and such as are used in conversation even *now*. How then, for God's sake, can they seize upon the pith of several sentences which hang perhaps on the spelling of a word, and at which we ourselves can often only guess from the context?'

[1] B. M. MS. 37926, folios 19–129.

F

CHAPTER V

CONTACTS IN TRAGEDY

'Le mérite de Shakespeare,' wrote Voltaire, 'a perdu le théâtre anglais,'[1] unconsciously uttering a profound truth. What he really meant was that Shakespearian tragedy was beneath contempt: what he should have meant was that Shakespeare, because of his uniqueness and perfection, is a dangerous model. How true that is we know from the tragedies of Otway, Rowe, and Lillo. It is possible to imitate Racine and be guilty merely of dullness and insipidity; but none has ever copied Shakespeare without lapsing into crude melodrama and turgid rant.[2] Bad Racine produces in the mind of a cultivated Frenchman much the same impression as does Racine himself on an Englishman with a schoolboy's knowledge of French. It is soporific and meaningless; sometimes it maddens by its rhythmic regularity. But it has dramatic shape. That is because the literary ape is usually a methodical animal. He can always be trusted to imitate what, in his model, is most obvious and least essential. As a result, even the worst travesty of a Racinian tragedy contrives somehow to possess a clear-cut problem, a well-marked crisis, and a *dénouement* of sorts. It manages, somehow, to look like a tragedy, whereas an imitation of Shakespeare is almost always a chaotic nightmare. By sheer genius, Shakespeare alchemized incredible fiction into brilliantly convincing drama. He conferred splendid actuality upon creatures of godlike, or demonic passions. So, in the works of his imitators, we inevitably discover incidents that are impossible, situations both complicated and absurd, and strutting, roaring manikins who pretend to be human.

On the whole, if we except Lillo and Young, the author of the *Revenge*, the eighteenth-century English tragic writers did not consciously or strenuously seek to imitate Shakespeare. This is natural enough in an age which was doing its best to produce the original works of the master. Yet it would be hard to find a single tragedy outside Addison's *Cato*, the timbre of which does not evoke

---

[1] *Lettres philosophiques* (1734).   [2] Except Miss Clemence Dane.

130

memories of Shakespeare just as some cheap and foul synthetic scent will occasionally recall the pristine freshness of a woodland flower.

In France, Voltaire was making a furious attempt to hide his real impotence by introducing into the traditional *cadre* of neo-classic tragedy elements that were superficial and meretricious. Several of his English contemporaries who lacked even Voltaire's specious originality, but were still impressed by the prestige of the French theatre, tried to blend the two conflicting dramatic traditions, the English and the French. To effect this, they employed a formula which has been, perhaps, most naïvely expressed in Aaron Hill's prologue to his translation of *Zaïre*:

> The French, howe'er mercurial they seem,
> Extinguish half their Fire by Gothic Phlegm:
> While English writers Nature's Freedom claim,
> And warm their Scenes with an ungovern'd Flame.
> 'Tis strange that Nature never should inspire
> A Racine's Judgment with a Shakespeare's Fire.

The popularity of Shakespeare, Dryden, Otway, Lee, and Southerne protected Racine and Corneille, who were not much molested by eighteenth-century translators or imitators. The age of Anne, however, produced Colley Cibber's *Ximena*, 'an improvement' on the *Cid*; and Ambrose Philips's *Distrest Mother*, a popular, though nerveless, rendering of *Andromaque*. *Ximena* is much the more interesting of the two, as revealing what can happen to a French masterpiece at the hands of an English dramatist brought up on a mixed diet of ill-digested Shakespeare and Otway. One example of Cibber's style will be enough:

Corneille:

> Va contre un arrogant éprouver ton courage:
> Ce n'est que dans le sang qu'on lave un tel outrage.
> Meurs, ou tue: Au surplus, pour ne te point flatter,
> Je te donne à combattre un homme à redouter:
> Je l'ai vu, tout couvert de sang et de poussière,
> Porter partout l'effroi dans une armée entière.
> J'ai vu par sa valeur cent escadrons rompus: . . .[1]

Cibber:

> Pursue him, Carlos, to the world's last bounds
> And from his heart tear back our bleeding honour.
> Nay, to inflame thee more, thou 'lt find his brow

---

[1] I. v.

Cover'd with laurels and far-famed his prowess.
Oh! I have seen him, dreadful in the field,
Cut through whole squadrons his destructive way,
And snatch the gore-dy'd standard from the foe: . . .

This is sufficiently bad, but it is nothing to the liberties which Cibber takes with the original plot. In an epilogue that is a masterpiece of bad taste, he tells us, with the naïve complacency of the intrepid blockhead, how he has improved on Corneille. Ximena speaks:

Well, Sirs!
I 'm come to tell you that my fears are over,
I 've seen papa, and have secured my lover.
And, troth, I 'm wholly on our author's side,
For had (as Corneille made him) Gormaz died,
My part had ended as it first begun,
And left me still unmarried, and undone,
Or what were harder far than both—a nun.
The French, for form indeed, postpones the wedding,
But gives her hopes within a year, of bedding.
Time could not tie her marriage-knot with honour,
The father's death still left the guilt upon her:
The Frenchman stopp'd her in that forced regard,
The bolder Briton weds her in reward:
He knew your taste would ne'er endure their billing,
Should be so long deferr'd, when both were willing.
Your formal Dons of Spain an age might wait,
But English appetites are sharper set. . . .

With equal sang-froid, but perhaps more respect for his original, Edmund Smith mutilated Racine's *Phèdre* in his *Phaedra and Hippolitus* (1707). Smith approached his task with a mind full of addled impressions gleaned from *Venus and Adonis*, and further confused by vague memories of the two Cleopatras, Shakespeare's and Dryden's. In this mood, he evolves a Phèdre who resembles a drunken Madame Bovary with her hat awry. In that superb scene—one of the glories of French literature—where Phèdre confesses her love for Hippolyte, Smith excels his own worst. The English Hippolitus gives Phaedra a good talking to: whilst she, in her eagerness to seduce him, mentions that her 'proffered bed,' to which she frequently refers, has always been denied to the absent Theseus. Smith substitutes for Œnone a male confidant called Lycon, an intriguing minister who for political reasons encourages Phaedra's guilty passion. It is safe to say, however, that no prime minister was ever so scurvily rewarded for his zeal as this pimping old rascal. Here are Theseus's orders to the guards who hale Lycon off:

> Haste, haste, away with him,
> Drag him to all the torments earth can furnish.
> Let him be rack'd and gash'd, impaled alive.
> Then let the mangled monster, fix'd on high,
> Grin o'er the shouting crowds and glut their vengeance.

To make up for Nature's failure to blend 'A Racine's judgment with a Shakespeare's fire,' Aaron Hill, James Miller, and Arthur Murphy undertook to brighten up Voltaire's plays for Drury Lane audiences. The results are curious but interesting. All three adopt much the same method. Every speech over ten lines in length is ruthlessly cut, and the effect of all Voltaire's lapidary, crucial utterances is ruined by the addition of meaningless interpolations. Thus, where in *Zaïre* Orosmane commands his servant to give him the letter that seals the heroine's fate he says simply:

> Donne. Qui la portait? Donne.

Hill elaborates:

> Come nearer, give it me.—To Zara!—Rise!
> Bring it with speed—Shame on your flattering Distance.
> Be honest—and approach me like a subject
> Who serves the Prince, yet ne'er forgets the Man.

To this spirited author, Orosmane seems a poor substitute for his own idea of a full-blooded British hero. In the critical scene where, convinced of Zaïre's guilt, the Sultan turns to his minister, Corasmin, with the words:

> Eh bien! cher Corasmin, que dis-tu?

Hill, glowing with the 'ungovern'd Flame,' translates:

> Hell! Tortures! Death! and Woman!—What, Orasmin!
> Are we awake? Heard'st thou? Can this be Zara?

Nor is the Indian hero of *Alzire* allowed to retain his French phlegm.

> Cruel! les tyrans de ces lieux
> T'ont fait esclave en tout, t'ont arraché tes dieux,

says Voltaire's Zamore, reproaching his countryman for having adopted the religion of the Spaniards.

Not so the British Zamor:

> Hell blast 'em! What! These sons of rapine,
> They have not robbed thee of thy faith alone,
> But pilfered even thy reason!

So, too:

> J'entends l'airain tonnant de ce peuple barbare,

becomes:

> Hark! From their iron throats [*Guns.*] yon roaring mischiefs
> Pour their triumphant insult . . .

Equally impressive is his rendering of Alzire's

> O toi qui me poursuis, ombre chère et sanglante,
> A mes sens désolés ombre à jamais présente . . .

> O thou soft-hovering ghost, that haunt'st my fancy!
> Thou dear and bloody form that skims before me!
> Thou never-dying, yet thou buried Zamor . . .

The Miller flame is equally ungovern'd and as rousingly British.

> Faut-il donner mon sang? Faut-il porter leurs fers?

asks Voltaire's Séide in *Mahomet*. Contrast this puling meekness
with Miller's:

> Or if my streaming blood must be the purchase,
> Drain every sluice and channel in my body,
> My swelling veins will burst to give it passage.

For a clerical gentleman this is not bad. But the palm must go,
I think, to Arthur Murphy's *Chinese Orphan*. Here, showing Voltaire
how the *Orphelin de la Chine* should have been written, he provides
us with a full-grown orphan who, after a stirring combat with the
Tartar, Gengis-Khan, staps his vitals with the memorable words:

> Die, bloodhound, die!

Yet this colourful exuberance is offset in places by a curious
reticence. Hill gallantly omits in *Zaïre* the words:

> Ce sexe dangereux qui veut tout asservir,
> S'il règne dans l'Europe, ici doit obéir.

But is it from gallantry or perhaps rather because his female spectators did not reign in that part of Europe called England? In the
English *Zaïre*, no mention is made of the baptismal ceremony to
which Voltaire frequently, and with hidden malice, refers. Hill
apparently considered, too, that Fatima's last speech to Orosmane
was too blasphemous for a London audience. In the original, it
will be remembered, she expresses the romantic hope that God will
pardon Zaïre because of the very intensity of her passion. This
Hill omits along with the really fine line:

> Tu balançais son Dieu dans son cœur alarmé.

Yet in *Merope* the same author outdoes Voltaire in his attacks on the priesthood.   Indeed, he adds a tirade of his own invention:

Merope.   Out of my sight,
   Ye sanctified deceits!   You whose bold arts
   Rule rulers and compel ev'n kings to awe—
   Begone, fly, vanish!—
   Ye mouths of mercy and ye hearts of blood—

a truly Voltairian sentiment, though perhaps Voltaire might have expressed it differently.

The author of the English *Mahomet* is prudishly anxious to emphasize the sisterly nature of Palmira's love for Zaphna (Séide) who later turns out to be her brother:

   My affection for thee
 Is of that pure, disinterested nature,
 So free from passion's taint, I have no one wish
 To have thee more than thus, have thee my friend,
 Share thy loved converse, wait upon thy welfare,
 And view thee with a sister's spotless eye.

Nothing of this is in Voltaire, and his audience would not have welcomed it, so accustomed were they to situations of this sort.   We gather from Davies,[1] however, that 'a play founded on incest or anything repugnant to nature, even in supposition, can never please an English audience.'   This, he adds, was the reason for the failure of Dryden's *Don Sebastian* and Massinger's *Unnatural Combat*.[2] Even with a cast including stars like Betterton, Booth, Barry, and Anne Oldfield, in Smith's *Phaedra and Hippolitus*, it was impossible to overcome the prejudices of the spectators or arouse any real interest in the play.

Imitation is said to be the sincerest form of flattery: in literature it is often a sure sign of ignorance, of the failure to recognize that inexorable ring of finality which is the character of perfection or of genius.   Eighteenth-century England, when it began to produce the original Shakespeare, instead of trying to 'improve' upon or imitate his manner, entered on the first stage of its artistic salvation. But this process was of necessity slow and, to some extent, unconscious.   It was slow because the temper of the age was un-Shakespearian.   The great Elizabethan is not a sentimentalist, nor is he, in the eighteenth-century sense, ethical.   His theatre is not a sounding board for didactic, social ideas, nor is his imagination fettered by convention.   Awed by their own fetishes, the eighteenth-

---

[1] *Dramatic Miscellanies*, i. 27.
[2] And of Beaumont and Fletcher's *A King and No King*.

century critics and producers, as we have observed, praised him
with reserves, and doctored, mutilated, or revised those of his plays
which they deemed fit for the stage.   What then is the explanation
of the Shakespearian revival which, from the forties and right
through the century, grew steadily in force until it finally assumed
the lineaments of that national cult upon which time had set the
seal of permanence?   Every great change in national taste reflects
a social upheaval, and the effect of a social revolution can be
esthetically good or bad.   While the English were resurrecting
Shakespeare, a large body of the French was doing its utmost to
forget Racine.   Both movements can be traced to an almost
identical social phenomenon, the rise of the lower middle classes.
And if it is no doubt true that this class had never in England been
so completely submerged, politically and intellectually, by the
aristocracy as was the case in Frence, yet we have only to consider
the type of drama produced in Caroline England to realize that
its general appeal was not bourgeois but aristocratic.   With the
'purification' movement under Anne comes evidence that the
stage must henceforth cater to a different, a more varied public.
Defoe, in the novel, reflected this change.   Fielding did, too, and
Richardson dedicated himself completely to the taste of the middle
classes.   In the theatre, Lillo made a bid for its applause but, save
for Moore, found no successor.   This is not surprising, since Garrick
was already scoring his first successes in Shakespeare, whose plays
had matter to satisfy the tastes of all, especially if produced
with sufficient pomp and acted with enough licence and emphasis.
That is why 'domestic tragedy' never flourished in eighteenth-
century England as did the *drame* in France.   There was, in fact,
no need for a dramatic revolution in England: it was enough to
resurrect Shakespeare, and in doing so the English public was
actuated, not by any widespread urge to improve its aesthetic sense,
but by a general desire to see plays which, however irregular, would
hold its interest and stir its emotions as Hamlet's father's ghost
did with Fielding's Partridge.

In French neo-classic tragedy, on the contrary, there was little
meat for Partridges.   The mass of the petty bourgeoisie had never
frequented the royal theatres, so that really they had no serious
plays.   In comedy their choice lay between the coarse popular
parades of the fairs, where they could laugh at the Rabelaisian antics
of the Docteur and Isabelle, the comedies of Molière, Regnard,
and Dancourt in which they themselves were ridiculed for the

benefit of their social and intellectual betters, or, finally, the harlequinades of the Italian players which, but for the music, were as
unedifying as the *parades*, at least until well after 1750. The immediate response to the *comédies larmoyantes* of Destouches, and
especially of his pupil, La Chaussée, showed what was to be the tone
and trend of the new drama. It was to be moralizing, sentimental,
didactic, mildly tragic, but rarely, until after the Revolution, was
it to approach the horror and realism of *George Barnwell*, *The Fatal
Discovery*, or *Arden of Feversham*. Despite certain analogies with
English 'domestic tragedy,' certain outward similarities which
reflect the class consciousness and the simple psychology of the
English middle class and the French petty bourgeoisie, the *drame*,
viewed as a form of art, was essentially different from the dramatic
genre cultivated by Lillo and Moore.

Particular incidents have been seized upon and exaggerated by
English historians of literature, so as to suggest that French sentimental comedy is descended from Steele,[1] and that the *drame* owes
its origin to the direct influence of Lillo.[2] There should be no need
to repeat here what has been so admirably demonstrated by M.
Lanson as to the rise of sentimentality in French comedy.[3] But,
unfortunately, Destouches, like Voltaire, lived for a time in London,
and this has given rise to the legend that he wrote his *Philosophe
marié* under the influence of Steele's *Conscious Lovers*. Apart from
the fact that there had already been many French comedies written
in a strongly moralizing vein, and that Destouches, like Steele, was
most certainly familiar with Terence, other considerations must be
borne in mind. The first is that the experience dramatized in the
Philosophe marié was a personal one. The author had married a
Lancashire girl, but, like his hero, was obliged to hide the fact from
his parents. Again, to any one who has read Destouches's prefaces,
in which he expresses a very low opinion of our comedy, it is clear
that he was little tempted to regard English comic authors as
possible models. One must not overlook, either, the close affinity
between drama and the novel in the eighteenth century. And when
we peruse the fiction of the closing seventeenth century, it is not
surprising to find in the plays of the next generation some echo
of that sensibility and that wearisome insistence on *la morale* and
la vertu which characterize the romance, of the 'grand siècle.' That

---

[1] Notably Professor Bernbaum, in his book on sentimental comedy in England.
[2] *Cambridge History of English Literature*, x. 78–9.
[3] In his *Nivelle de La Chaussée*.

* F

there were, in the course of the eighteenth century, many contacts between the French and English theatre we have already seen in the case of Voltaire, and there were many others.   However, what must be avoided is the temptation to rush from these to sweeping generalizations, which are not corroborated by a comparison of English and French dramatic taste or ideas.

A great deal of the comparative literary history written in the last twenty years is stamped by this very weakness, and too often studies of this kind have been undertaken by writers who, though authorities on the literature of their own country, are unfamiliar with the spirit of the foreign works they discuss.   This is very evident in the case of Shakespeare and Voltaire: and on the question of Lillo's alleged influence on Diderot and the *drame* the same tendency is to be observed.

Diderot makes three references to Lillo's *George Barnwell*.   The first is to justify his use of prose instead of the traditional verse in bourgeois drama; [1] the second is to illustrate his thesis that tableaux or pantomime can be employed with great realistic effect in serious plays. [2]   Here he gives four examples of scenes which could be enhanced by the use of pantomime: the entrance of Maria into Barnwell's cell; [3] the meeting in prison between Trueman and Barnwell; [4] the spectacle of Philoctetes [5] writhing at the entrance to his cave, uttering inarticulate cries, and the anguish of Clytemnestre when she learns that her daughter Iphigénie is to be sacrificed. [6]   The third allusion is again to the pathetic meeting between Barnwell and his friend.   Diderot quotes, as an instance of good technique in dialogue, Trueman's reply to Barnwell. [7]

> *Barnwell*. . . . Thus, good and generous as you are, I should have murdered you.
> *Trueman*. We have not yet embraced and may be interrupted.   Come to my arms.

This, as Diderot rightly says, is excellent theatre because, though unexpected, it has the ring of veracity.

Now, all that can be induced from this is that Diderot admired two situations in Lillo's play because they happened to illustrate his dramatic theories.   But it is quite unwarrantable to assume that Lillo's whole play appealed to him as good dramatic art.   All his other pronouncements on the nature of the *genre sérieux* show con-

---

[1] *Œuvres*, vii. 119–20 (1757).   [2] *Œuvres*, vii. 95–6.
[3] *George Barnwell*, Act v.   [4] ibid.
[5] Sophocles.   [6] Racine's *Iphigénie en Aulide*.
[7] *Œuvres*, vii. 365.

clusively, as do his own two plays, the *Fils naturel* and the *Père de Famille*, that he and Lillo are in essential respects utterly at variance.

In the first place, Diderot did not intend, as is often said, to substitute his new style of drama for the heroic tragedy of neo-classic tradition. And it is equally false to infer that even in the *drame* he was prepared to sacrifice the famous three unities, because, both in theory and in practice, he always defends them. Diderot's two plays reveal just what we might expect from his dramaturgy. They touch very timidly on social questions such as illegitimacy and the dignity of commerce, but consist largely of long-drawn-out sermons on filial duty, paternal obligations, and equality. The action, such as it is, occupies a series of pathetic situations designed to offer full scope to the author's ideas on the dramatic value of effective pantomime. The speeches are surcharged with sensibility which too often lapses into mawkish platitudes, the whole being interrupted by inarticulate, despairing exclamations obviously suggested by his beloved Philoctetes. Except that, along with Lillo and a hundred other English and French contemporaries, he celebrates the beauties of virtue and *bienfaisance*, there is absolutely nothing in Diderot's dramatic theory or practice to justify the assumption that he or the later writers of *drames* were directly influenced by the art of Lillo. Nothing is, however, more natural than that he should quote a foreign dramatist as a precedent for views which to his contemporaries sounded revolutionary and impracticable. Mercier did the same with Shakespeare, yet one cannot say that Shakespeare influenced his art—if it may be called art.

Now, if there was one eighteenth-century French dramatist heretical enough to imitate Lillo's *George Barnwell* it was not Diderot, but Mercier. As a matter of fact he did so, but as we shall see, his imitation, which was considered too audacious to be played at the *Comédie française*, simply emphasizes the fact that, even in 1781, the French were not prepared to assimilate English domestic drama any more than they were prepared to accept Shakespeare.

Lillo's *George Barnwell, or the London Merchant*, based on an old ballad, portrays the spiritual debacle of an upright young apprentice whose passion for a bad but beautiful courtesan leads him to murder his uncle. For this brutal crime he is very properly hanged, along with his accomplice. First played at Drury Lane in 1731, Lillo's melodrama had a great success, and was acted periodically throughout the century as a warning to the young. Whether these performances were subsidized by the London merchant companies as a sort of insurance propaganda is not quite clear. Cumberland, writing late in the century, says: 'We act it once a season with the same relish as we eat salt fish on Good Friday, and who can be a greater object of pity than the poor unhappy Millwood of the night? I can hardly suppose there is a writer now living who has fortitude enough to attempt such a play or interest enough to get it acted if he had written it. Jonas Hanway had moral zeal enough for the undertaking, but his genius did not carry him quite so high up as the apprentices; he got no farther than the chimney-sweepers: and he, good man, is no more. He warned us against drinking tea and shooting London Bridge; but he did not live to dissuade us from shooting our uncles and drinking wine with bad women.' [1]

The Abbé Prevost, who had just treated a similar theme, though, of course, in a different way, in his *Manon Lescaut*, was obsessed by Lillo's Millwood. And from what little we know of the abbé's tempestuous career, he had some affinities with Barnwell. He never, indeed, committed murder, but it has been conclusively proved that he was guilty of forgery, most probably because of a woman. [2] But even in a novel Prévost could not possibly adopt the realistic English method in telling the story of his rake's progress. As it was, *Manon Lescaut* created a scandal, and was suppressed by the authorities, who not only objected to his theme, but, above all, considered it outrageous that he should choose as his hero a man already practically wedded to the Church, and a heroine who was a courtesan. Prévost could afford to laugh at the censorship, the natural result of which was to increase his sales, but he was careful to avoid shocking the traditional taste of his countrymen, who had hitherto never admitted that a courtesan could be tragic or pathetic. That is why his Manon moves in an aura of impenetrable, mysterious vagueness. Always we see her through the eyes of her lover, for it is he who tells her story. Like an alabaster vase in a twilit room, she glows only in the effulgence of the chevalier's passionate presence: only then can we discern the contours or the radiance of her personality. As it happens, Prévost's timidity, his classic reluctance to 'define' Manon in the Balzac manner, has made her one of the most perfect examples of the novelist's creative art. By

[1] Cumberland's *British Drama*, vol. i.
[2] See Dr. Mysie Robertson's preface to her edition of vol. v. of Prévost's *Mémoires d'un Homme de Qualité*.

her alluring stillness, her enigmatic charm and clinging sweetness, she becomes the incarnation of romantic love : she is the woman of every man's dreams—elusive, passive, and lovely. Unlike Millwood, she does not deliberately excite her lover to crime, because, if we may whisper it without sacrilege, she was probably not intelligent enough to be a criminal had she wanted to. It is enough that Manon should seem to be unhappy, that she should seem to want something. To gratify her unsatisfied, unformed desires Des Grieux would tear the stars from the firmament.

It would be hard to find a greater contrast than Manon and Millwood. Lillo's courtesan is Shakespearian in conception; she is a type which was not to appear in French literature until Balzac and Sand. She is the deliberate enemy of society, the self-appointed avenger of down-trodden women, the Romantic 'doomed before the world began to endless pain.' To make her really credible would require the poetic genius of Shakespeare and the heroic setting of *Antony and Cleopatra*. In *George Barnwell*, speaking Lillo's bastard blank verse, Millwood accentuates the melodrama of the play and throws it out of focus. She seems unnatural, like a Pavlova in the chorus of a third-rate revue. The real tragedy of *George Barnwell* is that Lillo, having conceived a Millwood, was too impotent to provide her with an adequate artistic *milieu*. The lamentable George can only be found admirable by an audience of sentimental costermongers, or of ardent 'students of the English drama' on the hunt for paradoxes. To have presented him, as he was conceived by Lillo, to a French eighteenth-century audience would have been out of the question. George is too inanely naïve, too incredibly fresh from the nest. To see him in the hands of the urgent, 'snowy-bosomed' Millwood, makes one want either to shout with laughter or to write a strong letter to the S.P.C.C. And even if we allow for the mawkish sensibility of the French eighteenth-century public, there were other elements in Lillo's domestic tragedy which they could not admit. The hanging of Millwood and Barnwell in full view of the audience was, of course, out of the question, and so was the murder of the innocent old uncle, whose morbid night thoughts are so rudely stopped by George's dagger-thrust. Millwood's pungent comments on the 'suburb magistrates who live by ruined reputations,' her coarse remarks on religion and its ministers, and the picturesque description of her appearance before the court would not have passed the French censor. In short, a character like Millwood, in order to conform to French taste, had first to be shorn of everything that made her interesting or dramatic to the audience of Drury Lane.

George Barnwell was translated by Clément in 1748, but, as he tells us, he could not at first bring himself to write the closing scenes. This version, further emasculated by the omission of the bourgeois setting, was converted into sentimental comedy by Anseaume, and played, to music by Duni, at the *Théâtre italien* in 1765 under the title of *L'École de la Jeunesse*. But for a note by an eighteenth-century writer it would be hard to recognize its English origin.[1] A poetic, chastened revision by Lemierre was refused by the censorship in 1768, apparently because of certain comments on the administration of justice. It was acted after the Revolution when the *Comédie française* was handed over to the plebs. Apart from an adaptation called *Jenneval*, first played in a boulevard theatre[2] and, later, in 1781, on the stage of the *Théâtre italien*, nothing remotely like *George Barnwell* was offered to an eighteenth-century French audience.[3] The closest imitation, that by La Harpe, was confessedly a closet study, never intended for the stage and never performed.

If we remember that Mercier was the most advanced of the *dramomanes*, his *Jenneval* provides a rough criterion of the extent to which French dramatic taste was influenced by that of England. In his preface he points out the impossibility of reproducing the crudity of character and action which distinguishes the original, 'so different from ours is the English genius.' The hanging scene is, of course, omitted, as indeed it was in English acting versions after 1759. Moreover, the whole atmosphere is altered. Thoroughgood becomes a barrister and Barnwell a law student: Trueman, as Bonnemer, remains the faithful friend, a character now long familiar to French readers of sentimental comedies. Millwood, as Rosalie, is scarcely recognizable, though she does talk about the secret war between the sexes. There is a *lettre de cachet* episode suggesting that Mercier had read *Manon Lescaut*. Rosalie, unlike Millwood, does

---

[1] Anseaume makes his hero, Cléon, almost succumb to the suggestions of the heroine, Hortense, who is a conventional coquette. He recoils, however, from the crime.

[2] In 1776, by the troupe called 'Les Associés.' It was also acted in the provinces.

[3] Except, perhaps, Blin de Sainmore's *Orphanis* (1773). The author admits having got from Lillo the idea of a hero led into crime by a wicked woman. Otherwise, as he says, there is absolutely no resemblance between his tragedy, which is conceived in the neo-classic manner, and *George Barnwell*. De Sainmore's remark on Millwood is typical: 'Certainly such a character, exhibited on a French stage, would make all the spectators flee in horror and indignation.'

not get George to consent to murder his uncle, and, in fact, the
dénouement is achieved by his saving the uncle from the daggers of
Rosalie's hired assassins. Ducrone, the uncle, is so impressed by
his nephew's frank confession, that he is converted into a *bienfaisant*,
and closes the play with the astounding remark to Jenneval: 'Votre
caractère vaut mieux que le mien.' Even this diluted travesty, as
we learn from an eye-witness, 'inspired less interest than horror'
when it was produced in 1781 at the *Théâtre italien*. Yet this was
the Mercier who talked of putting the *Hôpital général* on the stage,
and predicted that if French drama was to survive it must be
entirely revolutionized.

Ironically enough, it was Mercier's most pitiless critic, La Harpe,
who first discerned Lillo's originality, and showed why his play
could not be adapted to French taste without sacrificing that
originality. The seduction scene, said La Harpe, 'would seem to
us merely indecent and ridiculous. All that the spectator would see
in it is a brazen creature who wants to get a young man's virginity.
The idea of showing a prostitute at all on the stage is disgusting and
intolerable.[1] We admit only on the stage that *selected nature*, which
is the object of all the imitative arts, and whatever you say about
it I think we are right.' La Harpe now discusses the situations
which he considers 'strong and touching.' These are: the death
of the uncle, not the actual murder, but the episode where the uncle
forgives his murderer; the meeting in prison between Trueman and
Barnwell, 'a masterpiece'; finally, the powerful scene where Millwood betrays Barnwell—*Quelle punition du crime!* In his own version, which, he insists, is intended only for the reader, La Harpe
'risks' the murder. With many apologies he makes Barnwell a
criminal and Millwood a *monstre*. Yet she is not, as in Lillo, a
courtesan; she is a widow, once respectable but reduced to poverty
by a rascally husband.[2]

Lillo, then, had no direct influence on the trend of the *drame*.
What interested the French in *George Barnwell* was the moralizing,
sentimental element to which they were already well accustomed.
The essence of the English tragedy escaped them. 'Perhaps,' says
La Harpe vaguely, 'there is in the English author's plan a truth
which the decency of our manners does not allow us to develop,
and which is possible on a freer, English stage.' His subsequent

---

[1] Even Palissot de Montenay's *Courtisanes*, a satire on the profession, was refused
in 1775 by the *Comédie française* as too indecent to be shown.
[2] Preface to *Barnevelt* (1778).

remarks make it clear that the fatality brooding over the whole play simply did not exist so far as French readers were concerned. It is not, of course, surprising that Lillo's other play, *The Fatal Discovery*, aroused no interest at all across the channel. This is a crude melodrama consisting of four acts of nonsense designed as a prelude to a bourgeois travesty of the famous scene in *Macbeth*, where Lady Macbeth incites her husband to murder Duncan. To compare it to Greek tragedy or refer to it as a *Schicksalstragödie* [1] betrays a strange lack of the sense of proportion. Old Wilmot and his wife, rendered desperate by poverty, murder a guest and steal his jewels. Curiously enough, the guest turns out to be their son whom they had supposed to be drowned. If this is a *Schicksalstragödie*, then every Chicago gangster who ever existed is a victim of destiny and a tragic hero. I can hear Molière's comment; we have it in Argante's reply to Scapin: 'On n'a plus qu'à commettre tous les crimes imaginables, tromper, voler et assassiner, et dire pour excuse qu'on y a été poussé par sa destinée.' [2]

The production of Saurin's *Béverlei* at the *Comédie française* in 1768 represents the most serious attempt made by a French eighteenth-century playwright to acclimatize English drama in France. This piece is a tolerably close imitation of Edward Moore's *The Gamester*, which was played in London in 1753 with great success. A few years later, Garrick took it up and it remained a favourite until well into the nineteenth century. The French dramatists of the new school, who regarded the stage as an instrument of moral and social reform, were attracted by Moore's theme—gambling. In 1760, Diderot discussed the play with his mistress, Sophie Volland, and, in reply to her objections, said that he did not think it would require many changes to conform to the new French taste. He translated it to please his friends, and except for some minor additions designed to throw the viciousness of gaming into stronger relief, did not materially depart from his original. In 1762, Bruté de Loirelle, one of the royal censors, rendered it into bad verse, but Saurin, when he adapted it, most probably used Diderot's translation. We know from Grimm that Diderot offered Saurin advice on *Béverlei* which the dramatist did not, however, always accept. Moore weaves the story of his hero's downfall into an elaborate plot of the 'thriller' type. The false friend, Stukely, assisted by two wicked confederates, arranges to kill Beverley's comrade, Lew-

---

[1] *Cambridge History of English Literature*, vol. x.
[2] *Les Fourberies de Scapin*, I. vi.

son, and have the gamester hanged for murder. Saurin entirely omits this exciting melodrama and concentrates on the pathos of the Beverley family. For greater effect he invents a new character Tomi, the gambler's infant son. Obviously the Frenchman is embarrassed by Stukely, Béverlei's *âme damnée*. In Moore's play Stukely ruins Beverley out of jealousy and in the hope that he may win Mrs. Beverley. Saurin supposes that he is actuated by wounded *amour-propre*, having been once rejected by the gambler's wife: his Stukely does not make love to the heroine. Oddly enough, the French author, whilst rejecting the scene in the gambling den, invents another which is much more repulsive than anything imagined by Moore.[1] At the end, Béverlei, who is in a debtors' prison, not only takes poison but raises his dagger to kill his sleeping child. This repelled the audience and the critics, as did also the suicide of the gamester. Nevertheless, large crowds, drawn by curiosity, flocked to the early performances. Collé [2] and Grimm [3] confirm this. 'This piece,' writes the latter, 'is one of those that are rarely played, but attract people by their lack of resemblance with the plays produced every day.' Collé, commenting on its original success notes: 'Despite this, I fear it will not have many performances. It attracts, but in no way holds, the interest. It does not excite pity, it oppresses. You do not weep at it. It stifles you; gives you a nightmare. That evening it made me physically ill.' Collé hoped that there would be no more of these barbarous, Ostrogothic productions and, like many, attributed the importation of such horrors to the insensibility of the *philosophes*, who, he said, required shocks of this kind to arouse them. The most sensible criticism came, as it happened, from that hammer of the Encyclopaedists, Fréron, who, though condemning the atrocities of the *dénouement* and the intrinsic lack of action, yet admired the Greuze-like pathos of the scenes introducing little Tomi and Jarvis the faithful old retainer. Above all, he praised the situation where Lewson, although aware that Henriette has been ruined by the gamester, asks her to marry him. It is, however, significant that Saurin, when he issued a second edition of *Béverlei*,[4] provided an alternative and rose-coloured ending in which the gamester is saved from death in the nick of time.

Collé, in holding the *philosophes* responsible for this dramatic

---

[1] In a letter to Garrick (1768), Madame Riccoboni points out that Saurin got the idea from Prévost's novel, *Clèveland*. She adds: 'The public say horrible things about the play, but run to see it.'

[2] *Journal*, iii. 194.   [3] *Correspondance*, ix. 226.   [4] 1771.

innovation, but echoed the public opinion of his age which imputed every novelty, in art, science, or in philosophy, to the Encyclopaedists. Public opinion was very nearly right. Still, there were many of the intelligentsia like Voltaire who, though ready to use the theatre as a channel for their social propaganda, yet frowned on the artistic heresies of extremists so violent as Mercier. Voltaire preferred writers of the La Harpe type, whose *Mélanie* (1770), whilst based on the theme of the enforced profession of religious vows, adhered in form and in tone to neo-classic tradition. This play, it is scarcely necessary to add, was rejected by the censorship, now more alert than ever. Two years previously, a special committee, presided over by the Archbishop of Paris in person, had sat in judgment on Fontanelle's *Éricie ou la Vestale*, which was condemned, as was also Baculard d'Arnaud's still more sombre drama on the convent question, *Euphémie ou le Triomphe de la Religion*. This lugubrious production, in Baculard's most typical manner, is full of gloom, vaults, and skulls: in every sense of the term it is *macabre*. The eighteenth-century French censors were not normally concerned with aesthetic questions, yet the most ardent apostles of the liberty of the press must be convinced, after reading these forbidden works, that, after all, there is something to be said in favour of tyranny.

The existence of a strong censorship goes far to explain the unusual energy and industry of the new French school of dramatists. The absence of any such repression in England left the playwright free, if he chose, to exploit the success of Lillo. That he failed to do so was owing to the fact that the rising middle class found in Shakespeare, as he was then presented, ample satisfaction of its dramatic needs.

The growing French mania for everything English did undoubtedly influence their theatre. How superficial this influence was we can judge, however, from the nature of these French imitations of Lillo and Moore. The real trend of the new French stage was in the direction of social reform, and here, naturally, the affinities with English drama could only be of the slightest. The theses which provided the *raison d'être* of so many *drames*, focusing as they did on questions of religious tolerance, judicial reform, and social equality, were inspired by conditions almost peculiarly French. For instance, Garrick refused Fenouillot de Falbaire's *L'Honnête Criminel* on the grounds that it could have no possible interest for English audiences. And indeed, on laying it down, one wonders why Diderot ever advised its author to submit it to Garrick at all. *L'Honnête Criminel* is based on an actual occurrence. A French Protestant pastor in Languedoc was condemned to the galleys for preaching in public. His son gallantly took his place, and was later pardoned when a senti-mental public and a still more sentimental administration learned of his noble deed. This play was not, however, permitted on the stage till 1790, when the *Comédie française* ceased to be French and became *nationale*, i.e. plebeian.

The Anglo-French *rapprochement* of the second half of the eighteenth century was confined to a limited set, composed largely of a few advanced intellectuals and a handful of fashionables. On the literature of neither country was its influence profound. In drama, as in the novel, a hasty observer, surveying the titles of works without examining their content, is apt to acquire the erroneous impression that the traditional literary taste of each nation was radically changed by contact with foreign models. Nothing could be more misleading.

To regard the *drame* as an art-form which Diderot and his col-leagues intended to substitute for the traditional, neo-classic tragedy, is to misunderstand the nature of the new genre and its origins. Diderot did not, as has been said, 'set himself in direct opposition to the classical standards which, despite some inconsistencies, Voltaire maintained.' [1] That would be like saying what is equally inaccurate, that sentimental comedy, because of the achievements of a La Chaussée, supplanted the old pure comedy, the *comédie gaie*. Far from setting himself in direct opposition to neo-classical standards, Diderot, both in theory and in practice, adhered to the so-called Aristotelian unities, and in advocating his new genre, the *genre sérieux*, evinced no intention of challenging the prestige of heroic or Racinian tragedy. On the contrary, he remained convinced that tragedy and comedy are separated by a 'natural' barrier. [2] We must not, therefore, look upon the *drame* as merely Racinian tragedy with the characters reduced in social status and emancipated from the tyranny of the unities of time and place. Actually, it represents a normal stage in the evolution of neo-classic comedy, a natural process in the development of a literary form which, after all, has always closely followed the contours and reflected the changing colours of the social organism. Nothing, then, was more

[1] *Cambridge History of English Literature*, x. 79.
[2] *Œuvres*, vii. 137.

inevitable than for French comedy gradually to reveal, as it did by its increasing emphasis on sentiment, and by the growing gravity of its criticism, the existence of a new and clamant public opinion, the voice of the lower middle classes. In his *Tartuffe* and in his *Misanthrope*, Molière reached the frontier beyond which comedy ceases to be comic and becomes tragic. But here Molière was moving on a plane already almost inaccessible to the mind of the petty bourgeoisie. This *haute comédie* was too high, too philosophical ever to become really popular, though the author, by the introduction of certain scenes, notably in *Tartuffe*, made a fine attempt to communicate the true inwardness of his satire to the parterre as well as to the boxes. Nevertheless, the *Misanthrope*, possibly his finest comedy, long remained caviare to the general. Now, what the new rising class wanted was not criticism of life but criticism of society; it desired not philosophy but facile moralizing. It wanted the sententious platitudes, crystallized into proverb form, which are handed down from generation to generation; the sagacious dictums which every parish priest or village wiseacre delivers upon serious occasions. These sentimental commonplaces writers like Destouches and La Chaussée worked into the fabric of their comedies with great success. As the philosophic movement spread, sentimental moralizings gave way to humanitarian propaganda, and sentimental comedy, gradually shedding its comic elements, developed into that serious type of play later called the *drame*, the chief object of which was the dramatic representation and the discussion of situations or problems closely touching the destinies of the middle classes. An effort has been made [1] to draw certain fundamental distinctions between the *comédie larmoyante* and the *drame*. Yet if we compare, let us say, a sentimental comedy by La Chaussée with one of Falbaire's dramas, it is evident that there is no essential difference in the artistic methods of the two writers. The social criticism is more emphatic; its expression and purpose more definite. Sentiment degenerates into flamboyant *sensiblerie*; the characters sacrifice their individuality to the ideas of which they are the ciphers, but in structure and in characterization there is no real change. As was to be expected, this type of play declined aesthetically until after the Revolution, when it sank into melodrama. In the hands of professional demagogues, like L. S. Mercier, it ceased to reflect the moods and preoccupations of the middle classes and pandered to the tastes and prejudices of the mob.

[1] By M. Gaiffe in his scholarly thesis, *Le Drame*.

CHAPTER VI

THE SURVIVAL OF COMEDY

BUT meanwhile the spirit of true comedy was not quite dead, though indeed it sometimes appeared to be moribund. Humanity, like Figaro, 'se presse de rire de tout, de peur d'être obligé d'en pleurer.' So laughter did not vanish from the French theatre when Molière left it. On the other hand, it was Molière's genius that paralysed two generations of French comic dramatists. The annals of French eighteenth-century comedy display a sad array of third-rate works cast in the mould created by the master. Genius, we are told, exercises a fertilizing effect on posterity; yet we have only to glance at the plays in any eighteenth-century *Répertoire d'auteurs de deuxième rang* to realize the poverty of the minds which conceived them. *L'Irrésolu, L'Indiscret, Le Dissipateur*—and there are dozens of the same calibre—all confirm the impression that the effect of Molière's genius was not to fertilize but to sterilize French comedy for well-nigh a century; to produce, not a galaxy of lesser geniuses, but a cortège of third-rate hacks. Molière had subjected the great universal vices and foibles to the play of his deadly satire, and, baffled by this fact, his mediocre imitators tortured their ingenuity to dramatize, in his manner, characters that were not universal types but the products of a restricted social *milieu*. There existed, happily, glorious exceptions to this rule, but the majority of French eighteenth-century comic writers betray a real lack of originality, an ingrained reluctance to abandon a code which genius had emptied of its treasures, or to relinquish a form now unsuited either to their talents or to the spirit of their civilization. For the inclination of the eighteenth century was no longer to regard society as a nicely balanced organism governed by a universal, eternal Reason. The old, clear-cut hierarchic barriers, thanks to the growing importance of wealth and commerce, had begun to crumble, and this produced a rich confusion of classes and conditions, entailing a revision of the old comic values. At the opening of the century it seemed, indeed, as if comic authors had already awakened to this fact. The plays of Dancourt, for instance, furnish a vivid, varied, though sketchy panorama of contemporary social life. But Dancourt lacked the creative gift: he gives us a journalist's hurried commentary on the idiosyncrasies of his time, yet never seizes their underlying, human significance. As if aware of his limitations, he rarely pauses to exploit the dramatic possibilities of a situation or to probe the depths of a character. With exasperating virtuosity he ranges in his fifty comedies over a France which, we know, was crowded with raw material of the most attractive and promising kind.

In one comedy, his only memorable one, Le Sage almost leads one to regret that he was a great novelist. *Turcaret* (1709) is, in a sense, the swan-song of neo-classic comedy, the last public manifestation of that virile contempt for the gross, purse-proud *parvenu* which is the true index of a nation's spiritual health. The time had not yet come when wealth was to be pandered to and exalted by the *philosophes*; when the greatest houses of France were to regard an alliance with rich *fermiers-généraux* as a privilege, and when intellectuals like D'Alembert, Marmontel, and Diderot were to consider it an honour to be the pensioners of a Madame Geoffrin or a Baron d'Holbach. It is not in this temper that Le Sage approaches his *financier*, but rather in the mood of that glorious reprobate and splendid humanist, the Abbé Coignard of immortal memory, when he invites the 'vile publican,' De la Guéritaude, to engrave over the entrance to his residence the appropriate inscription, *Aceldama*. No doubt, as the century advanced, Turcarets became rarer and their progeny less distinguishable from the nobles alongside whom they received their education. Still, their places were filled by a steady upward pressure from below. But the real reason why comedies of the acid, Turcaret brand had no true successors is to be found in the preface to Beaumarchais's *Mariage de Figaro*: 'All conditions of society have managed to escape the censorship of the dramatist. You could not put Racine's *Plaideurs* on the stage to-day without hearing the Dandins and Bridoisons, and even more enlightened people, crying out that there is no longer such a thing as morality or respect for the magistrates.' Under Louis XIV, when comedies were written to please a select, aristocratic audience, the dramatist had a wider and freer field. Owing to social changes under Louis XV and his successor, no one class dared offend another by abetting a writer who exposed the vices of any particular profession. We have only to think of the subjects satirized by Molière to realize that we are now dealing with an age whose influential classes were so imbued with respect for *la science*, so steeped in bourgeois sentiment and humanitarianism as to look askance at jokes on doctors, lawyers, blue-stockings, cuckolds, and parvenus. In Molière's day there were few heads in his audience which his caps might fit, and if they did, what did it matter? The contrary was now the case. It is in the eighteenth, not in the nineteenth century, that we must seek the Victorian era of French literature.

Few men of letters managed to preserve their intellectual integrity in this age of coteries and literary cliques. A Voltaire, and he was an exception, could snap his fingers at society because he had ample private means. For the others, patronage or some other form of dependence was an economic necessity; and volumes could be written about the ignominious practices to which even the finest writers had to stoop to obtain the privilege of publishing a magazine, or else to extract a well-paid sinecure from some ignorant jack-in-office. Under these conditions, the launching of a comedy was an affair fraught with anxieties. Alexis Piron, one of the rare, independent spirits of his century, the Piron 'qui ne fut rien, pas même académicien,' tells us in a foreword to his *Métromanie* of the pitfalls that lurked in the path of young aspirants to fame: the envy and malice of established cliques; the Tartuffes 'sous le dehors plâtré d'un zèle spécieux' who rake up some boyish indiscretion which a lifetime will not live down; the insolent caprices of petted favourites of the stage, and above all, the dangerous, incredible allusions which some fool in the audience is sure to discover in the most innocent comedy. In a society so class-conscious, so mildewed with discretion, so horrified of anything that looked like the shadow of a personality, the comic author had an uphill battle. True comedy cannot exist on ideas alone: to be vital it must cling to actuality, and that was precisely what the French playwright of the eighteenth century found it hard to do. Serious comedy and *drame*, on the other hand, flourished on a windy diet of inoffensive abstractions. Their admirers could sit for hours listening to prosy sermons on the dignity of the merchant, of the judge, of the *père de famille*; to lectures on duelling, tolerance, egalitarianism, patriotism, and gaming, loosely stitched to the tissue of an impossible, romantic intrigue, and presented by characters who, praise God, never existed in the eighteenth or any other century. This sentimental blight left its spots everywhere. By destroying the unity of tone of Destouches's *Le Glorieux* it spoils an otherwise excellent comedy which might have been a brilliant satire, contrasting the lot of the ruined nobility with that of the ambitious parvenus. Even Voltaire, for all his contempt of 'whining comedy,' surrendered to the prevailing vogue in *L'Enfant prodigue*, in *Nanine*, and in *L'Écossaise*, where his deliberate introduction of eccentrics or 'humorists,' as the English called them, only draws attention to the fact that the comic and the sentimental will not coalesce. Such authors as tried to escape the contagion, like Gresset in *Le Méchant* or Piron in *La Métromanie*, are content to trail in the wake of Molière, but their plays, though written in flowing, witty verse, are pallid productions. They lack comic force because they are not inspired by Molière's demonic scorn for the foibles and vices which they satirize. The subjects bear a spurious likeness to those which the seventeenth-century master incarnated and immortalized in his Harpagon, Alceste, and Tartuffe, but the eighteenth-century imitators failed to realize the secret of Molière's genius. To them it seemed sufficient to select from the category of human manias some odd psychological trait overlooked by Molière and by inventing a few situations to illuminate it from every angle. Their fallacy is well illustrated by Piron's rueful reflection as to what Molière could have done with the subject of *La Métromanie*. 'What flowers would he not have made to bloom, what fruits to grow on a field better known to him than to any other?' He was wide of the mark. Molière would not have dreamed of basing a whole comedy on a little mania like the itch for versifying, a mania which is quite personal and has no social repercussions. At most, Molière might have hung Piron's hero in the gallery of *Les Fâcheux*. And the same is true of all these *Irrésolus*, *Dissipateurs*, *Indiscrets*, *et hoc genus omne* who jostle each other in eighteenth-century repertoires. They have no cosmic import, and so do not fit into the Molièresque conception of comedy. Handled according to the seventeenth-century manner, such characters revolve about themselves like squirrels in a cage; they do not evolve in any dramatic sense because one situation is enough to reveal their shallowness. An English author of the eighteenth century would have called them 'humorists' and bundled half a dozen into one play, compensating for their insipidity by a complicated intrigue rich in varied situations; but situations amusing in themselves, apart altogether from their relation to these eccentrics.

This is exactly what did happen when an English dramatist, either from indolence or lack of imagination, adapted one of these spurious *comédies de caractère* to our London stage. Let us take, for

example, Murphy's handling of Destouches's *L'Irrésolu* (1713) which
he presented, in 1777, under the title *Know your own Mind*.   To begin
with, the Frenchman's choice of subject was a mistake.   Irresolution, on the stage as in real life, when prolonged over three hours
is not funny but maddening.   Again, unless treated tragically,
when it involves the destinies of others, it is a purely individual
affair.   When Destouches's hero flits from the brunette to the blonde
we are amused.   And when he veers back from the blonde to the
brunette our amusement persists, though more mildly.   But when
he proceeds to go back from the brunette to the blonde we reach
for our hat and quietly tiptoe out.   Any one who thinks that a
character of this sort can be spun out to provide five acts of comedy
should be forced to serve on a committee for advising students
as to their choice of a curriculum.   Murphy borrows Destouches's
main idea and works it up into a quite amusing farce.   But he
completely alters the French comedy by adding several new characters, and he shifts the interest from character to situation.   The
hero, for instance, becomes not so much irresolute as inconstant and,
since Murphy fuses three love intrigues into an interesting picture
of contemporary manners, the whole atmosphere is transformed.
Moreover, pandering to the taste of his decade, the English playwright indulges rather heavily in sentiment and introduces, in the
person of Miss Neville, the now indispensable character of the poor
girl of gentle birth, who is obliged to serve as companion to an ill-
natured, rich old harridan.

What Molière's French imitators did not grasp, then, is the fact
that his great characters are essentially static; that all his comedy is
born of the clash between the irrational, obdurate individualism of
his monomaniacs, and the rational resistance opposed to them by
the society in which they move.   At the fall of the curtain, Harpagon and Tartuffe have been temporarily ousted.   They have
ceased to disturb the harmony of the immediate social *milieu*
imagined by the dramatist.   But Harpagon is still a miser and Tartuffe is still a hypocrite.   Literally, all that happens is that they
have been 'exposed' in the light of certain situations.   But these
great figures are composed of very different stuff from the demi-
types or eccentrics who fill the title-role in the comedies of Molière's
eighteenth-century imitators.   Diderot, I know, used to maintain
that such *caractères* could be revised every fifty years, but this,
again, is to misunderstand the genius of Molière.   No doubt, the
situations required to illuminate the character would be different,

but the traits exposed by Molière are universally and eternally true. A modern Harpagon might not switch off half the lights in a room or steal his own petrol; Tartuffe to-day might not finger the lace on Elmire's corsage, but the one would retain that everlasting suspicion of his fellow-men and the other would still contrive to use the truth to destroy truth.

Except for Beaumarchais, Marivaux is the only French comic author of the eighteenth century who recognized the finality of Molière's genius, and the only author, therefore, in the realm of pure comedy who himself deserves the name of original genius.

Marivaux began to write for the stage in 1720, some fifty years after the death of Molière. Most of his plays, it is worth noting, were written not for the *Comédie française*, but for the *Théâtre italien*, whose players, having been exiled some years previously by Louis XIV, had now been brought back by the Regent. It was not, of course, new to find a Frenchman writing for the Italians. Regnard and Dufresny had done so, but only to the extent of isolated scenes. These were interspersed through the Italian farces, which consisted largely of pantomime. Marivaux was the first French author of note to supply them with entire comedies. The Italian manner of acting, more subtle, less rigid than that of the House of Molière, and relying for most of its effect on expressive gesture, was admirably suited to interpret the delicate *nuances* of sentiment and emotion, the vivacious wit, the fluid action of Marivaux's comedies.

Marivaux created the psychological comedy of love. Now love, unless we take it in its extreme form, passion—which rules it out of comedy—is much less a social than an individual affair. Molière, who specialized in the extreme expressions of human nature, did not, therefore, regard love as a possible central theme of comedy. In all his plays it has a purely subsidiary role, and even in the *Misanthrope* is simply one of the devices employed to emphasize the hero's mania, his inordinate love of sincerity. Nor is Molière unique in this respect. So accustomed are we to associate love with comedy, that we rarely pause to reflect that there are very few comedies devoted wholly to the theme of love. Love has provided the dramatist with inexhaustible matter for tragedy, pathos, and farce, but not often for pure comedy. All the world, no doubt, loves a lover, and all the world is ready to pity or to sympathize with him but very seldom to laugh at him. Yet we laugh at the snob, the miser, the parasite, the hypocrite. It is scarcely pertinent to object that in farce love provides food for laughter. What we laugh at here is not love, but an exaggerated and irrational form of it, like insane jealousy or maudlin romanticism. In this matter the playwright's difficulty seems to arise from the following fact: we are prepared to see comedy only in what we think ourselves to be immune from, and no one can sincerely cherish that illusion about love. There is another difficulty. How can the playwright dramatize love and retain it on the plane of pure comedy? A love comedy is obviously bound to consist largely of the analysis of the lovers' sentiments and emotions, their hopes, doubts, fears, repressions, and disagreements —excellent material for the leisurely pen of the novelist, but hard to translate into action for the purpose of the comic stage.

All this Marivaux realized and more. Up to his time love as portrayed on the stage had been almost always tragic or pathetic, since the dramatist had invariably imagined it as persecuted or thwarted. Always it encountered some strong external obstacle to its fulfilment. But was this really so in life? No doubt in France of the seventeenth and eighteenth centuries parental authority was very much of a reality and *mariages de raison* were very common, not only in the nobility but in the bourgeoisie. On the other hand, it is difficult to conceive a France peopled entirely by harsh, unrelenting parents. Certainly Marivaux did not so conceive it, and one of his great claims to originality is that he broke completely with the 'heavy father' tradition, and created a new type of comedy based on the hypothesis that the chief obstacle to love is not external but internal, since it is usually to be found in the lovers themselves. That obstacle is *amour-propre*, and all Marivaux's great comedies are born of the conflict between *amour-propre* and love, a conflict from which love inevitably emerges victorious. This was an artistic discovery of the first importance, for it opened the way to a more credible, more realistic treatment of love in the theatre, and indeed, for the first time made love possible as a theme for pure comedy. The old adage that 'the course of true love never did run smooth' received a new interpretation.

The stereotyped conception of the society of Marivaux's time as consisting entirely of frail ladies, lecherous noblemen, and downtrodden peasantry still persists, and is likely to continue so long as the critics assume that the memoirs and correspondence of the eighteenth century represent the life of society as a whole. As a matter of fact, they reflect the manners of the small section of the French people who composed the court and town nobility. Yet writers of the eminence of Lanson shared that illusion, and, to explain the discrepancy between Marivaux's picture of manners and their own, they created the legend that his comedies, to quote Lanson, 'are enacted in an ideal society, in the land of dreams.' More indulgently Larroumet compares the atmosphere of Marivaux's plays to that of Watteau's paintings. *'L'Embarquement pour Cythère,'* he says, 'is, as it were, the apotheosis of Marivaux's theatre.'

Both judgments are completely false, unless indeed we confine ourselves to Marivaux's scanty mythological plays, which are frankly *féeries*, and make no pretence at anything more. The opinions expressed by these critics, however, concern Marivaux's well-known comedies, which, on the contrary, present very real characters moving in a real *milieu*. Marivaux was not interested in the life of the *haute noblesse*. His heroines are drawn from the bourgeoisie and the provincial nobility, where forced marriages and cases of forced profession of vows were not the rule but the exception. His women are free to follow the inclinations of their hearts unhampered by external interference, and this for various but very probable reasons. His *jeunes filles*, like Silvia of *Le Jeu de l'Amour et du Hasard* or Lucile of *Les Serments indiscrets*, have reasonable and indulgent parents. Sometimes his heroines, as in *La Surprise de l'Amour* or the *Fausses Confidences*, are rich young widows, or again, as in *L'Heureux Stratagème* or *Le Legs*, they are independent ladies of the manor, old enough to manage their estates and their matrimonial affairs. Nor is there anything unreal or Watteau-like about the setting of the plays, which is usually the garden or the park of a country house. A brief discussion of the comedies themselves will show, I think, the fallacy of the traditional opinion consecrated by Lanson and Larroumet.

Marivaux was primarily an expert in everything connected with the psychology of love, and it was not for nothing that he frequented the *salons* of Madame de Lambert and of Madame de Tencin where the analysis of the passions, emotions, and sentiments was practised as a fine art. Madame de Lambert was an ardent Platonist. It was she, indeed, who suggested that a school should be established to cultivate the soul, and to purify love by bringing it closer to the Platonic ideal. Marivaux, however, was too much a realist to follow her into these regions, and in fact rarely misses a chance of scoffing at those who regard love as a mystic fusion of twin souls. The early stages of love, he noticed, are characterized by needless but inevitable complications, all traceable to *amour-propre*. Here, he felt, was ample material for comedy, since there is nothing quite so amusing as to observe other people entangled in a network of quite unnecessary and complicated activities, whether of an intellectual or physical sort. The drawings of Mr. Heath Robinson, and the antics of the inimitable clown Grock, are extrem eillustrations of this truth. So, in most of Marivaux's comedies the characters live and move in a state of illusion as to their actual situation. Their *amour-propre* will not permit them to believe that they are falling in love and, assuming the guise of reason, invents amusingly rational and complicated explanations for their irrational behaviour. It is the contrast between the lovers' anxiety to be reasonable in their conversations and actions, and the complete futility of the latter, which Marivaux seizes upon and exploits for the purpose of comedy. An excellent example can be found in the *Fausses Confidences* (1737), whose heroine, a rich young widow called Araminte, prides herself on her reasonableness. But, as the author suggests, nothing is more dangerous for a woman's peace of mind than this combination of pride and reason.

Dorante. Et tu me dis qu'elle est extrêmement raisonnable?
Dubois. Tant mieux pour vous, et tant pis pour elle. Si vous lui plaisez, elle en sera si honteuse, elle se débattra tant, elle deviendra si faible, qu'elle ne pourra se soutenir qu'en vous épousant . . .

Events justify Dubois's prediction. A weaker, more sentimental woman would have admitted the danger of falling in love with the handsome, impecunious secretary and dismissed him before it was too late. Araminte, sure of her reasonableness, and, moreover, piqued by her mother's interference, persists in keeping Dorante and finds perfectly rational motives for doing so despite incidents which show her that he is hopelessly in love. The essence of the comedy lies, however, in the fact that, as she is completely independent, she could at any moment have led up to a declaration and married Dorante. There is no obstacle to her happiness save this illusion that she is not the irrational type of widow who becomes infatuated with secretaries. So she passes from one complication to another, until a letter written by Dorante to a friend and intercepted by her mother makes it quite impossible to feign further ignorance of the situation.

For Marivaux, *amour-propre* corresponds in our sentimental life to what in the physical domain is called self-preservation. It is the natural instinct which leads us jealously to guard our ego intact, and, of course, is opposed to love, which implies at least to some extent the surrender of our individual will. The whole comedy of existence for Marivaux, then, lies precisely in this illusion that we can keep our individuality intact and live a happy social life. In our effort to escape love we yield to our *amour-propre*, and thus mortgage our liberty both of action and of speech. In *La Seconde Surprise de l'Amour* (1727), the hero, a chevalier, has just lost his fiancée, who has taken the veil. The heroine, a marquise, is a widow. Both regard themselves as unique examples of perfect constancy in a world where, as they agree, 'il n'y a plus de mœurs, plus de sentiments.' And when they fall in love their *amour-propre* will not allow them to admit that they could be so inconsistent as to change. Maliciously, the author plunges them into a series of complications. Jealousies and doubts arise, but still they cling desperately to the illusion that these are the natural results of their *parfaite amitié*. In a delightful scene they unconsciously make love to each other by using that convenient verb *aimer* in its purely Platonic sense.

Swiftly and smoothly they arrive at the critical point where they must definitely choose between *amour-propre* and love. The chevalier's friend and rival, the count, does not believe in Platonic friendship, and the chevalier, to save his pride, is driven to say that he is not in love. That being so, says the wily count, the chevalier will not mind approaching the marquise on his behalf since it is practically certain she will consent to become madame la comtesse. Despair and jealousy of the poor chevalier, who, in a fit of pique, offers to marry the count's sister. The interview, the *scène obligatoire*, between the chevalier and the marquise reveals Marivaux in one of his happiest moments. The chevalier tells of the count's questions.

> *La Marquise.* Ah! il parlait d'amour? Il est bien curieux. A votre place je n'aurais pas seulement voulu les distinguer. Qu'il devine.

Unfortunately, explains the chevalier, savouring his revenge, equivocation was not possible; therefore he was obliged to point out that there was no question of love, merely of friendship. But, inquires the marquise anxiously:

> Croyez-vous l'avoir bien persuadé, et croyez-vous lui avoir dit cela d'un ton bien vrai, du ton d'un homme qui le sent?

Here is the chevalier's chance to soothe his wounded pride and jealousy.

> Oh, ne craignez rien . . . j'y ai mis bon ordre et cela par une chose tout à fait imprévue: vous connaissez sa sœur; elle est riche, très aimable et de vos amies même.
> *La Marquise [froidement].* Assez médiocrement.

Marivaux is a perfect artist. The action flows along limpidly and inevitably, always in harmony with the character of the actors. Now, unless the chevalier and the marquise are prepared to sacrifice their whole future happiness to their absurd *amour-propre*, love must have its way. The man, of course, will make the *dénouement* possible, but how, without too much damage to his pride? Marivaux cleverly compromises. The chevalier's servant hands the marquise a note written by the chevalier and then thrown away. In the final interview the lady produces this note at the opportune moment, thus sparing her embarrassed lover the complete humiliation of a prolonged declaration:

La Marquise. Tenez, chevalier, n'est-ce pas là le mot qui vous arrête?
Le Chevalier. C'est mon billet. Ah! marquise, que voulez-vous que je devienne?
La Marquise. Je rougis, chevalier; c'est vous répondre.

Every conceivable *nuance* of *amour-propre* is reflected in Marivaux's theatre. In the first, *Surprise de l'Amour*, he brings together a misogynist and a man-hater; in *Les Sincères*, a man and a woman who pride themselves on their unique candour, and, of course, quickly detest each other. The *Préjugé vaincu*, a charming satire on pride of rank, shows snobbery vanquished by love, and the heroine practically driven to propose to her bourgeois lover. In *Le Legs* we meet a brusque and somewhat terrifying lady who has no patience with sentimental nonsense. So well has she convinced her admirer, the marquis, of her sincerity that he dares not propose. Yet she wants him to, though now he is so accustomed to being hopelessly in love that it never occurs to him to ask for her hand. He assumes, of course, that she would be furious. So when the countess tries to lead him to the question, he draws back cautiously, fearful of ridicule, and with a comic blend of indulgence and annoyance treats the affair as a joke. Here are the closing lines of a scene that in its way is almost unique in comedy:

La Comtesse. Apprenez donc, lorsqu'on dit aux gens qu'on les aime, qu'il faut du moins leur demander ce qu'ils en pensent.
Le Marquis. Quelle chicane vous me faites!
La Comtesse. Je n'y saurais tenir; adieu.
Le Marquis. Eh bien! madame, je vous aime; qu'en pensez-vous? Et encore une fois qu'en pensez-vous!
La Comtesse. Ah! ce que j'en pense? Que je le veux bien, monsieur; et encore une fois, que je le veux bien; car si je ne m'y prenais pas de cette façon-là nous ne finirions jamais.

Marivaux remains undisputed master in the genre which he created, the psychological comedy of love. To understand all that this implies, one must remember the extraordinary difficulties which he had to overcome. It is no easy task, even in the ample and elastic cadre of the novel, to unravel the tangle of emotions, sentiments, and ideas which motivate the behaviour of those whom we vaguely describe as 'falling in love.' How much harder is the task of the comic author. For his effects must be instantaneous. The phrase which charms us in a novel, subtle and pregnant with secret significance, the phrase one lingers over and re-reads with delight, becomes when heard over the footlights, drab, meaningless, and maybe, absurd. That is why the comedy of psychological analysis is so difficult to write and, of course, difficult to act. In Ròsa Benozzi (Silvia) Marivaux was fortunate enough to discover an actress ideally qualified to interpret the charm and subtlety of his heroines. Unhappily, she has had few successors. In France, the two national theatres, the *Français* and the *Odéon*, have a virtual monopoly of the 'classics,' and these famous schools of acting, admirable in many respects, cultivate in comedy a certain rigidity of manner, whereas Marivaux's roles require, above all, fluidity and spontaneity.

For another reason Marivaux's comedies, though they are the reverse of 'high-brow,' appeal only to a certain section of the public. As they deal almost entirely with the analysis of love, they alienate both the *épicier du coin* and the Voltairian intellectual. Most people demand that love shall be treated on the stage as tragic passion, as a pathetic weakness, as namby-pamby sentimentalism, as howling farce, or more recently as scientifically disguised erethism. They are disconcerted by Marivaux's matter-of-fact and realistic attitude. He has no *coups de foudre*, no duels, elopements, irate parents, abductions, or wicked guardians; no sneering, polished villains, or persecuted, ravished, compromised, or seduced heroines; no nymphomaniacs, Lesbians, or ladies oozing with 'life-force.' For him, falling in love is not a mystic or devastating phenomenon like religious conversion, but an imperceptible, natural process which is not, however, achieved without a struggle. His women are delightfully real with a human spice of caprice and quick temper. His lovers are equally intelligent; ardent without being sensual, and, like the women, easily wounded in their *amour-propre*.

None of Marivaux's characters is, like Molière's, incurable. He is not, like Molière, a specialist in abnormal psychology. Marivaux's characters overcome their particular form of the malady, *amour-propre*. His older people are usually sensible bourgeois, like M. Orgon, whose splendid philosophy—which is that of the author—is summed up in that priceless line: 'Va, dans ce monde, il faut être un peu trop bon pour l'être assez.' Occasionally, however, we run across amusing elderly irascibles like Madame Argante and M. Remy of the *Fausses Confidences*. And when they clash, the audience can expect an authentic *mot pour rire* like this:

Monsieur Remy. Comment donc! m'imposer silence! à moi, procureur! Savez-vous bien qu'il y a cinquante ans que je parle, madame Argante?
Madame Argante. Il y a donc cinquante ans que vous ne savez ce que vous dites.

Or, more subtle:

Dorante. Je vous demande pardon, madame, si je vous interromps. J'ai lieu de présumer que mes services ne vous sont plus agréables, et dans la conjoncture présente il est naturel que je sache mon sort.
Madame Argante. Son sort! Le sort d'un intendant; que cela est beau!
Monsieur Remy. Et pourquoi n'aurait-il pas un sort?

There is a comic crescendo in the reiteration of that word *sort* which gives one the measure of Marivaux's force. It takes a first-rate writer to realize the comedy that is latent in an ordinary colourless word, but emerges if we remove it from its habitual context or *milieu*. It is easy, of course, by this method to create farce, either by puns or malapropisms. The bigger men, however, like Marivaux in the above example and Molière with his 'Il sait du grec!' contrive to achieve by this device a purely comic effect.

In the comedies of Marivaux's French contemporaries or successors there is almost nothing that can be said to resemble his comic manner. Perhaps in Barthe's flimsy *Les Fausses Infidélités* we catch a fleeting echo of his subdued laughter, yet it is but an echo. His English colleagues, whose habit it was to ransack the latest French successes for ideas and situations, left Marivaux severely alone. In this they showed unusual wisdom, for his comedies are like those 'petits vins du pays,' those sparkling and delicious vintages from Saumur and Vouvray which somehow lose their bouquet half-way between Calais and Dover. Isaac Bickerstaffe's operetta, *Love in a Village*, which, it is alleged,[1] owes its inspiration to Marivaux's *Le Jeu de l'Amour et du Hasard*, contains only one situation

[1] Professor Allardyce Nicoll in *A History of Early Eighteenth Century Drama, 1700-1750.*

G

that might justify this assertion. Rosetta, like Silvia, in the disguise of her maid, is wooed by a young man of family. In all other respects, the two plays are ludicrously unlike. Bickerstaffe's Rosetta and his Lucinda would have been hooted off the French stage for indecency. Imagine one of Marivaux's *jeunes filles* calmly announcing, like Lucinda, that she has run away from home to escape 'a preposterous gouty father and a superannuated maiden aunt,' or asking in the silvery accents of Rosetta: 'I desire to know what I can do with this wicked Justice of the Peace, this libidinous father of yours? He follows me about the house like a tame goat!' Lucinda, bursting with laughter at her 'whimsical' girl friend, retorts: 'Nay, I'll assure you he has been a wag in his time—you must take care of yourself.' Badinage of this sort would not for one moment have been allowed on the stage of the *Comédie française*, and even at the fair theatres, which were quite Rabelaisian, it is certain that such sentiments would never have been put into the mouth of an *ingénue*. Eighteenth-century France, as I have said, was very Victorian.

Before we proceed to discuss what essentially differentiates English and French eighteenth-century comedy, it might be well to discover precisely what modern English writers have in mind when they speak of Anglo-French interaction in the comic theatre of our period. It is possible, from prefaces to plays and from eighteenth-century reviews, to compile a most imposing list of English comedies 'borrowed' from French ones, and, to a lesser extent, a companion list of French plays 'influenced' by English models. It would be, however, quite wrong to infer from such literary statistics that there was any real interfusion of dramatic taste: most of these so-called imitations, on the contrary, like Bickerstaffe's *Love in a Village*, simply confirm the impression, already gleaned from our comparison of English and French tragedy, that authors of both nations were interested in the works of their foreign colleagues, from whom they borrowed occasional scenes and characters. But in order to utilize these, they were almost invariably obliged to refashion them to the taste of their nation. It is rare, for instance, to find a literal translation of a French comedy offered, even in abridgment, to an English audience, and I know of no example of an English comedy being thus transferred from the London to the Parisian stage.

A few examples selected from a recent list of English comedies 'borrowed' from French models will indicate what connotation we are to apply to the term 'influence,' which is so often and so vaguely

used in this connection.[1] Destouches's five-act *L'Amour usé* (1742)
deals with a situation which, at best, might provide material for
a one-act farce. Lisidor, an old colonel, has been engaged for
fifteen years to an old maid, Isabelle. Both, meanwhile, have been
separated and have fallen in love elsewhere: Isabelle with a young
chevalier, and the colonel with Angelique, whom they pass off
respectively as their nephew and niece. Thanks to the intervention
of a generous but crusty old friend of Lisidor's, called Davies,
the natural order of things is restored. Thomas Francklin in *The
Contract* cuts down the French play considerably, but in the main
roughly follows the plot of the original. Yet the whole tone of
Francklin's play is English, not French. Davies becomes Commo-
dore Capstern, the bluff, coarse old sea-dog already well known to
English admirers of Smollett. As to the expression, contrast the
manner of Destouches and Francklin in the following scene, where
the colonel after a long absence meets his elderly fiancée. Each is
heartily sick of the other but both pretend to be still in love.

> *Isabelle.* Est-ce bien lui? Ne m'a-t-on pas flattée? Non, c'est une
> vérité. Vérité charmante! Je vous revois donc, mon cher, mon
> bien-aimé Lisidor!
> *Lisidor.* Ma belle, mon aimable, ma charmante Isabelle.
> *Isabelle.* Je suis dans une folie . . .
> *Lisidor.* Et moi dans un transport . . .
> *Isabelle.* Qui me bouleverse le sens.
> *Lisidor.* Qui me fait extravaguer.
> *Isabelle.* Je n'en puis plus.
> *Lisidor.* Je me meurs.

Now turn to the English version:

> *Colonel.* She comes, she comes, the charmer of my heart.   O Eleanora!
> > [*They embrace.*
> *Eleanora.* My dearest colonel, is it then given me once more to
> behold—— [*Aside.*] He's a horrid creature!
> *Colonel.* After so many years of tedious absence, again to look on those
> dear eyes, to taste those balmy lips. [*Embrace again.*] She stinks
> like a polecat. [*Aside.*]

Conway, in the preface to *False Appearances* (1758), parts of which
he translates almost literally from Boissy's *Les Dehors trompeurs*
(1740), points out, however, that 'it wanted some of the *cayenne*
humour which makes the necessary seasoning for an English audi-

---

[1] For this list I am indebted to Professor A. Nicoll's useful series of books on
the history of the English theatre. From a score of plays I have chosen only
those which suggest that the English dramatist had a first-hand knowledge of
the French model.

ence; especially those in the higher regions whose appetite a manager must of necessity consult.' He brings in, therefore, a farcical abbé, a ridiculous poetaster, who is persuaded to dress up as a cavalry officer. In this role he is questioned as to his alleged campaigns in North America, is exposed, of course, and ignominiously booted downstairs. Like so many of his confrères, Conway glosses over his borrowings, and lays great store by his abbé, who does not appear in Boissy's play:

> An abbé, too, a sight you 've seldom seen,
> A parrot clothed in black instead of green.
> Half church, half lay, half clerk, half militant,
> Though in a band, the creature will not cant.

In one or two scenes, Murphy's *Citizen* (1761) is closely modelled on Destouches's *La Fausse Agnès* (1759), an excellent play based on a really fertile situation.[1] In the French, as in the English comedy, a girl, in order to avoid an unpalatable marriage, pretends to be a congenital idiot. But Murphy misses half the savour of the original by altering the character of the unwelcome suitor, who in the French, is an intellectual snob and a conceited amateur poet. His English understudy, George Philpot, is a rascal and a rake. As a result, the *Citizen*, though funny, is funny in a quite different way. Murphy invents, for instance, a typically English episode heavily redolent of Restoration comedy at its worst. Young Philpot surprises his 'liquorish' old father in the house of his favourite trull, Corinna, an incident which is used to precipitate the *dénouement*.

One English writer states that in the second half of the century, Diderot 'exercised his old fascination' on our dramatists.[2] It would have comforted Diderot to hear this, for as a playwright he made very little impression on his own countrymen. However, I fear that the statement contains an exaggeration. Sophia Lee, in 1780, wrote a complicated, sentimental comedy entitled *The Chapter of Accidents*, which is said to be modelled on Diderot's *Père de Famille*. There is no resemblance at all between the French hero and Miss Lee's Woodville who has seduced his sweetheart, Cecilia, or between the latter and the painfully chaste Sophie of Diderot's play. There is, indeed, a misunderstanding and a quarrel between the hero and his friend as in Diderot, but, of course, Steele's *Conscious Lovers* had hinged on the same idea. This pleasant game of chasing sources has, no doubt, its attractions; it has, however, if properly

---

[1] Suggested obviously by Molière's *L'École des femmes*.
[2] Nicoll, *A History of Early Eighteenth Century Drama, 1750–1800*.

played, the disadvantages of leading one a merry dance sometimes backwards and forwards over the Channel. Beaumarchais's *Eugénie* is a good case in point. The characters are all dressed in English garb. The heroine, by means of a bogus marriage, has been seduced by a Lord Clarendon. Obviously, one would say, Beaumarchais has gone straight to *Clarissa Harlowe*. But the French critic, Grimm, who was most familiar with our literature, states unhesitatingly that the plot is taken from a story in Le Sage's *Le Diable Boiteux* entitled *L'Histoire du comte de Belflor*. He is perfectly right, and Beaumarchais follows his model with remarkable fidelity. However, let us return to Diderot. General Burgoyne, the 'gentlemanly Johnny' of Shaw's *Devil's Disciple*, is alleged to have based his *Heiress* (1786) on the *Père de Famille*. Once more, the connecting link, if there is one, is almost invisible. First of all, there is in the *Heiress* no *père de famille*, and the heroine is the usual very English, very genteel, but persecuted governess. It is true that Burgoyne has a theatrical duel between two friends, but Diderot's main theme, the relations between father and son, does not interest him at all. His is a comedy of manners, a vigorous attack on parasites and parvenus. Besides, although his play is tinted with sentiment it is far from being, like the *Père de Famille*, an emotional debauch punctuated with rifty and maudlin ejaculations.

One of the minor pests of the French eighteenth-century theatre was the surreptitious gentleman in the parterre who quietly jotted down the text of new plays at their first performance. Usually he was an indelicate publisher eager to launch a pirated and garbled edition of the latest success. Sometimes he was an unscrupulous English author, like Thomas Holcroft, who in this way filched Beaumarchais's *Mariage de Figaro*, and staged it shortly afterwards in London under the name of *The Follies of a Day*. The English version is a three-act play. It has no Bartholo and no Marceline. The dialogue is wooden, and the omission of several scenes reduces the *Mariage de Figaro*, which is a masterpiece, to the level of a tenth-rate farce. That Holcroft should then have heaped infamy upon injury by cynically taking out a patent for his stolen goods, is an illuminating reflection on the literary ethics of eighteenth-century England. This is, however, what happened, and we are told by George Colman the younger that *The Follies of the Day* was one of the biggest successes at Covent Garden under his father's management.

It will serve no useful purpose to continue this examination of English comedies, the authors of which, either from laziness or more probably from lack of brains, went to French contemporaries for situations, scenes, and sometimes for characters.   Nearly always, this borrowed metal was resmelted and refashioned into something that no Frenchman would have acknowledged as a work of art. Such pilfering was not entirely reciprocal, but it was not entirely one-sided either.   Occasionally throughout the century, but particularly during the Anglomania vogue, we can find French comedies which, if they do not reveal the influence of the English comic genius, show at least that their authors were familiar with certain English plays or novels.   It is interesting if not remarkable to note that nearly all such works are sentimental comedies.   Obviously, our comedies of manners, which, like those of the Restoration, were highly localized, could offer little to attract a foreign audience. Our plays were held by the French to be exceedingly free, if not coarse, both in dialogue and in situation, a reputation not altogether undeserved despite the growing English fashion for purity.   After Voltaire, Destouches, who had also seen our London comedies, expresses amazement that 'virtuous and modest ladies' could witness these licentious plays with 'their lively but too faithful pictures of contemporary manners.' [1]   Indeed, the only comedy which he felt could possibly be adapted to the French taste was Addison's *The Drummer*, and that, by the way, was never staged in France.   Le Blanc, whose caustic and shrewd remarks on our tragedy have already been quoted,[2] is equally outspoken as to our Restoration pilferings from Molière, and almost loses his usual urbanity at the scurvy way in which Frenchmen are caricatured on our stage.   But what really shocks this good churchman and fervent royalist is the English playwright's attitude to Church and State.   'If you bring in a parish priest or nobleman's chaplain,' he writes sarcastically, 'be sure to make an atheist of him, or at least place him in a low, ridiculous light, preferring even a pimp before him.' Le Blanc is disconcerted by our fondness for taverns, whores, highwaymen, duels, and disguises on the comic stage, which seems to him primarily intended to suit the taste of the mob.   The Licensing Act of 1737 he welcomed as a salutary, much needed measure to curb the licentiousness of a theatre where 'the honour due to the sovereign is trampled under foot, the authority of the Parliament

---

[1] Preface to *Le Tambour nocturne*, adapted from Addison.
[2] op. cit.

vilified and degraded, the wisest laws turned to ridicule, and the
sanctity of religion vilified with impunity.' [1] With distressing
unanimity these and similar views are repeated by later French
writers, and though many of them envied our comparative freedom
of speech in social and political matters, all agree as to the indecency
of our comic stage.   Indeed, until the end of the century our comic
dramatists were regarded by the French with that blend of shocked
prudery and sneaking admiration with which our Victorians used
to look on the French novelists of their time.   From our fiction and
the novels of Prévost, eighteenth-century France derived the idea
of an Englishman who was a high-souled philosopher, an *honnête
homme*, a sort of cross between Sir Charles Grandison and Hamlet:
from our sentimental comedies they drew the picture of an Englishman who was comically eccentric and brutal, but at heart good-
natured and generous.   Rousseau's Lord Edward Bomston [2] may
be said to typify the former, whilst the latter is to be found depicted
in the Freeport of Voltaire's *L'Écossaise*.

Richardson's *Pamela*, translated by Prévost in 1742, dealt at some
length with the themes already known to French literature through
the novels of Marivaux: unprotected innocence harried by aristocratic vice and the problem of marriage between noble and
commoner.   Boissy [3] put a French Pamela on the stage, but despite
the care he took to adapt her to the French taste she was a dismal
failure.   Undeterred by this example, La Chaussée presented his
Pamela at the *Comédie française*,[4] but also with no success.   It did,
however, inspire an outrageous pun.   At the original performance
a late-comer inquired of a friend who was already on his way out:
'Comment va Paméla?' and received the reply: 'Je viens de la
voir.   Elle pâme, hélas!' [5]   This double failure gave a *fermier-
général*, D'Aucour, the idea for his *Déroute des Paméla*, a poor skit
but one which had several performances.   It is possible, as Grimm
says, that Voltaire's *Nanine* (1749) was suggested by Richardson's
novel, but in its general tone it echoes the moralizings of Destouches
or La Chaussée, rather than the crude whinings of the English
novelist.   Moreover, Voltaire's central situation was almost certainly suggested by Marivaux's *Vie de Marianne*.   Nanine's lover,
the count, who is utterly different from the boorish Mr. B., sends
her away in a fit of jealous pique, but she finds an ally and admirer

[1] op. cit., Letter LXXXII, to La Chaussée.
[2] In *La Nouvelle Héloïse*.   [3] 1743.   [4] 1743.
[5] D'Origny, *Annales du Théâtre italien* (1788).

in the count's mother, who, like Marivaux's Madame de Miran, consents to their marriage with the rueful remark:

> . . . La famille
> Étrangement, mon fils, clabaudera.

Voltaire's *L'Écossaise* [1] is set in a London coffee-house. In the choice of characters, such as the wicked Lady Alton, the eccentric Freeport, and the impetuous Lord Murray, there is an evident desire to give the French audience an authentic picture of London manners. The melodramatic love affair which constitutes the plot is, however, merely an excuse for Voltaire's real object, which was to satirize his detested enemy, Fréron, here thinly disguised as Frelon, a rascally journalist. All the characters are 'stage' Englishmen and Englishwomen, who express their sentiments and passions in a style which Voltaire would not have dared to attribute to his own compatriots. That this play did receive a hearing was due partly to its scandalous attack on Fréron, and partly to the real ignorance of English manners so characteristic of this period of Anglomania.

The sentimental royalism of Dodsley's *Miller of Mansfield* exploits the popular idea that the king is a sort of father who protects his people from the vicious nobles. As such, it was bound to appeal to the French shopkeepers of the reign of Louis XV for whom the king was never wrong: he was always in their eyes the innocent dupe of wicked ministers or designing mistresses. Dodsley's one-act piece inspired two French plays: Sedaine's comedy-operetta, *Le Roi et le Fermier*, [2] and Collé's *La Partie de Chasse d'Henri IV*, both signal successes. In its passage from London to Paris, however, Dodsley's work underwent several changes. His plot, it will be remembered, is as follows. The king, whilst hunting, is arrested as a poacher by a miller, who is also a keeper of the royal demesnes. In the course of conversation the king learns that Lurewell, one of his courtiers, has seduced the sweetheart of the miller's son, Dick. This he managed by a forged letter accusing Dick of having had a child by another woman. One can guess at the *dénouement*. Lurewell is forced to settle £300 a year on Dick, who marries the seduced girl. The miller is knighted.

Collé, in refashioning the play, [3] said that he could not possibly retain this ending. A French audience would have been repelled by a hero who not only accepts damaged goods, but is indelicate

---

[1] Adapted by Colman as *The English Merchant* (1767).
[2] Produced at the *Théâtre italien*, 1762.
[3] Produced at the *Comédie française* in 1774, written in 1760.

enough to take money from a seducer. Collé, therefore, arranges
that his heroine, Agathe, shall be abducted by the villain, in this
case an Italian favourite of the queen's. Agathe, who is very
different from Dodsley's village maid, escapes through an upper
window. Collé introduces, too, an historical plot dealing with the
situation of the minister Sully, whom the villain, the marquis de
Concini, is trying to drive into exile. Dodsley's key-scene is, however, retained. The king drinks and chats with the country folk,
and in the French play there are certain piquant incidents not in
the original. Henri, for instance, is pictured as a gay old dog who
turns a 'covetous eye' on a pretty kitchen wench, and in an amusing
scene he is made to listen to a ribald song about his gallant adventures with a certain *belle jardinière*, then a legendary character. The
whole episode is handled with great dramatic effect and with a just
blend of emotion and comedy.

Sedaine, who had a different audience in mind, is more naïvely
rustic, and in the sentimental scenes inclines to mawkishness. But
he is more familiar with the psychology of the peasant. Signifi-
cantly enough, his hero, whom the king wants to ennoble, declines
the honour, and as in Collé's version, is able to marry the girl
because she escaped from the clutches of the lecherous villain.

Collé's *Journal* tells of the obstacles he had to overcome before
his adaptation saw the footlights. 'I transported the play to France,'
he writes, 'and chose a period which might be piquant and agreeable. The subject made this quite natural and I chose that of our
Henri IV. In the details of this comedy, not only was I obliged to
depart from the English version, but even to take a route directly
opposed to Dodsley's, seeing that the moral of the English play is to
satirize the vices and foibles of the court, whereas in mine I hardly
permitted myself the slightest moral or critical allusion in this
connection.' [1] Though *La Partie de Chasse d'Henri IV* was played
on private stages with astounding success and also in the provinces,
Louis XV, influenced, it is said, by Madame de Pompadour,
stubbornly refused permission for the Paris theatre, and it was not
produced at the *Comédie française* until fourteen years later. Sedaine's *Le Roi et le Fermier*, on the other hand, contained no historical
allusions, and thus passed the censor without trouble. However,
his most celebrated work, *Le Philosophe sans le savoir*, the only one
out of some three hundred *drames* that can still be played, was the
occasion of an extraordinary meeting of the censorship committee.

[1] II. 247.

* G

Indeed, only because it drew tears from the wife of the lieutenant-general of police was it finally allowed on the stage. Here the objection was moral rather than political. Sedaine made the whole interest of his play hinge on a duel, and it was feared that by sanctioning it the Government would be gravely lacking in its duty to the police. This is yet another instance of the paternalism that characterized the attitude of the French administration in its dealings with the people.

Both Collé and Sedaine went to Patu's *Théâtre anglais* (1756) for their text, but Collé had a closer link with English comedy in Garrick, whom he entertained twice in Paris, once in 1751 and again in 1765. On the first occasion, the famous actor delighted Collé by his rendering of the dagger scene from *Macbeth*, but on the second, disgusted him by flatly refusing to repeat the performance. Collé, at Garrick's request, had read him his *Henri IV*, sung his songs, and given him an edition of his works. To quote from his *Journal*: 'The day I was silly enough to receive him at my house I paid attention only to him and his wife, and bored myself to extinction by talking only about England and everything that might interest these two animals.' Garrick, however, on the plea that he never acted just after meals, declined to grant Collé's request. The latter extorted a promise for another day, and, as he admits, deliberately importuned Garrick, till one day the latter received him in a manner which left no doubt as to his annoyance, thus convincing the enraged Collé that English actors were even more insolent than French. 'The sixty thousand francs a year he got from managing the London theatre, the intoxicating praises showered upon him, must have completely turned his head. He forgot that he is, and never will be, anything but an actor, and that, however far the talent may be developed, it is still a very little thing to be a good actor. I do not consider that Mr. Garrick has very much wit; I saw one of his comedies which was translated in the *Journal étranger*, and found in it neither wit, genius, nor talent.' Another English author-manager, George Colman the elder, was also well known in Paris. And his *Clandestine Marriage*, turned into a comedy-operetta by Madame Riccoboni and the Bohemian composer, Kohaut, was put on in 1768 at the *Comédie française*, where it was an abject failure.

Mme Riccoboni, who left the stage to write novels, and very good ones, was well acquainted with English literature. In 1768 she published her *Nouveau Théâtre anglais*, containing translations of

Kelly's *False Delicacy*, Colman the elder's *The Jealous Wife*, Moore's
The Foundling, and two farces by Murphy, *The Way to Keep Him*
and *The Deuce is in Him*.   As one who had unrivalled knowledge of
the French stage, Mme Riccoboni knew that these plays could not
be presented in Paris.   'The sole object of this work,' she states,
'is to offer to young authors who intend to work for the theatre,
not models, but an opportunity of enlarging their ideas by placing
before their eyes new and varied scenes.' [1]   At this particular
moment, since Beaumarchais had not yet written his joyous *Barbier
de Séville*, French comedy was literally in a sad state.   The *comédie
larmoyante* was gradually shedding its few remaining comic elements
and degenerating into *drame*.   Even the *Théâtre italien* was infected
by the fashion for pathos.   Rochon de Chabanne's *Le Deuil anglais*,
a vague imitation of Steele's *The Funeral*, had drawn applause
by the sensibility of its verses. [2]   A cult for artificial rusticity set in
and was consecrated by the success of *Annette et Lubin*, *La Laitière*,
Rose et Colas, and similar operettas, all of which offered an idealized
and highly sentimental picture of country life.   Marmontel had
done the same thing in his immensely popular *Contes moraux*, and
these were freely ransacked by Favart, Sedaine, and other pur-
veyors to the *Théâtre italien*.   For the first time, too, it seemed as if
France would have to look across the Channel for gaiety.   'As the
English continue to brighten their stage,' wrote Mme Riccoboni,
'we are getting more sombre.   The sensitive French, once so easily
moved, who used to mingle their tears with those of Bérénice and
Alzire, seem now to disdain the sweet and natural passions.   They
desire, not so much to be interested, as to be made sad.   They no
longer want to have their hearts touched, but rent.'

Collé, in 1770, reviewing Beaumarchais's money drama, *Les Deux
Amis*, enlarges on the same topic. [3]   'True comedy,' he says, 'comedy,
properly speaking, is out of fashion: the nation has become sad.
Besides, women have got the upper hand so completely in France
that Frenchmen now model their thoughts and feelings entirely
on theirs.   Women want a play that will touch them, that will
make them snivel.   They have, besides, a natural aversion to the
criticism and satire of their foibles, even when it is kept within the
most permissible bounds as is fitting in true comedy.   On the other
hand, they love *drames* in which there is endless, insipid conversation addressed to their sex: where love is paramount, where the

---

[1] Preface to *Le Nouveau Théâtre anglais* (1768).
[2] *Annales du Théâtre italien* (1757).   [3] *Journal*, iii. 241.

virtue, honour, disinterestedness, grandeur of soul, sentiments, and delicacy of their sex are exalted in an incredibly romantic fashion. They allow the lovers in these wishy-washy plays to be accorded the same perfections to an overwhelming degree. They must have passions—I do not mean tender ones—but violently insane passions in which everything is sacrificed to women. . . . They come to the theatre to witness their triumph over man and their prodigious ascendancy over our sex.' Collé is perfectly right, too, when he notes that the French theatre is now merely an annexe of the novel, as, indeed, it had been before Molière rescued it by creating character-comedy. Under the influence of Destouches, of La Chaussée, of Diderot and his *dramomanes*, the central interest of comedy, which had formerly lain in the exposition of character by means of well-chosen situations, now consisted in the narration of complicated adventures selected for their pathos and sensation. In other words, what now appealed to the playgoer was not the dramatic or comic, but the *romanesque*.

If Mme Riccoboni's choice of English comedies was influenced by a desire to counteract this irrational sensibility, her models were not unaptly selected. Was it from accident or design that she gave first place on her list to Hugh Kelly's *False Delicacy*, a play which scored a great success at Drury Lane and, in our day, has been curiously misrepresented as 'essentially a sentimental comedy'? [1] In reality, as its name implies and as can be judged from its plot, it is an amusing satire on romantic sensibility, so much so, indeed, that the reviewer of the *Gentleman's Magazine* [2] was moved to protest: 'Though the situations render it extreamly [*sic*] entertaining . . . yet the sentiments are so managed as to destroy the merits of their use. The piece as it stands is more a satire on true delicacy than on false . . . and indeed there does not appear to be one instance of false delicacy in the dramatic action.' On the other hand, it contained one pathetic scene which was much applauded: that in which the heroine's father, Colonel Rivers, discovering his daughter's projected elopement, makes no effort to assert his parental rights and, indeed, assures her financial future. This moves her so strongly that she abandons her idea. No doubt, for many of the spectators it was this sort of pathos which constituted the chief merit of the comedy. Yet Kelly's intention was obvious, and it is repeatedly

[1] Professor Nettleton, *English Drama of the Restoration and Eighteenth Century*, p. 268.
[2] Vol. xxxviii, p. 80.

expressed by the characters, Cecil and Mrs. Harlay, whose robust common sense disentangles the sensitive souls from the absurd situations created by their romantic delicacy. As Cecil points out: 'It is extremely happy for your people of refined sentiments to have friends with a little common understanding.'

Kelly, in this play, comes as close to the spirit of Marivaux as is possible in a second-rate dramatist, educated in a school which, despite various contacts with the French, yet remained at the core thoroughly English. *False Delicacy* made no impression in Paris, where a feeble adaptation by Marsollier was produced in 1776 under the title, *La Fausse Délicatesse*. Colman's *Jealous Wife* had even less success, though Mme Riccoboni had carefully bowdlerized Lord Trinket's attempt to rape the heroine, and completely altered the scene where Charles Oakly, in his cups, joyously insults her father, Squire Russet. Earlier in the century, Destouches and Dancourt had experimented with drunkenness on the stage in a farcical way, but it was still a French tradition that gentlemen in a state of inebriety should not come into the presence of ladies. This was an unwritten law in real life as on the stage. For a lover like Charles Oakly in the *Jealous Wife* to appear roaring drunk in the presence of his sweetheart was to forfeit the sympathy of an eighteenth-century French audience. Beaumarchais, it is true, gives us an amusing drunken scene in the first act of the *Barbier de Séville*, but here Almaviva's intoxication is feigned, and moreover, he is disguised as a veterinary officer, it being an accepted fact, of course, that veterinary officers were seldom sober. The *Jealous Wife* was too flagrantly English to make any appeal to the French. Desforges's *Femme Jalouse* (1785), as the author truthfully protested, owes nothing at all to Colman. What happened was that Desforges, like Colman, went to Fielding's *Tom Jones* for his ideas.[1]

Diderot, when he admired a work, admired it exuberantly. He was delighted with *False Delicacy* and its 'mad, sweet, pathetic scenes, full of verve and truth.' He said: 'It is here that you see lovers who have wit, but no common sense; honour, but no reason; too much delicacy to be happy; genius enough to be extravagant. They do not know what they want, what they are saying, or what they are doing. Walk up, walk up, ladies and gentlemen, and admire their wisdom.' Because of its pathetic scene, he preferred it, of course, to Colman's *Jealous Wife*. 'You laugh and sigh

[1] He produced with success, in 1782, a *Tom Jones à Londres*, at the *Comédie française*.

alternately at *False Delicacy*; you laugh all the time at the *Jealous Wife*. But Diderot's enthusiasm for the matter of these comedies was tempered by severe criticism of our English slovenliness in regard to construction. 'It is almost impossible to follow,' he says of Kelly, 'the complicated intrigue of the drama; not the slightest continuity in the scenes, endless changes of setting; a jumble (the word is harsh but I will not alter it), a jumble of scenes thrown together.'[1]

The cult of sensibility, so sharply reflected both in English and French comedy during the second half of the eighteenth century, would seem at first sight to indicate a common attitude towards social relations and ideas. Necessarily, one feels, there must have resulted a type of comedy almost wholly shorn of traditional, national traits and, in its choice of subjects and characters, displaying a common desire to inculcate the beauties of sensibility, virtue, tolerance, equality, with their manifold variants and derivatives. Actually, such was not the case. By habit and by temperament, the French comic dramatists were incapable of achieving that fusion of the comic and the sentimental which we discover in plays like Sheridan's *The Rivals*, in Kelly's *False Delicacy*, and in Colman's *Clandestine Marriage*. One has but to read Voltaire's *Nanine* or Diderot's *Père de Famille* to observe that French sensibility and the French comic spirit were incompatible elements. Sensibility, as understood by the eighteenth-century writers, degenerated inevitably into *drame*. The moral, sentimental comedy of La Chaussée, raised by Diderot to the dignity of a separate genre, was merely a transitional stage on the downward course which led to the democratic melodramas of L. S. Mercier. Indeed, but for the timely arrival of Beaumarchais's *Barbier de Séville*, the old *comédie gaie*, so brilliantly cultivated by the seventeenth century, might have been temporarily submerged. For Beaumarchais opened the shutters wide and flooded a darkened house once more with sunlight and laughter. Now despite all that has been said to the contrary, Goldsmith performed no such miracle when he produced *She Stoops to Conquer*, because at no time in the eighteenth century had the English stage ceased to be comic. With Steele, no doubt, during a period of immediate reaction against the brutality of Restoration comedy, the English stage threatened to become maudlin. It is also true that, relatively, English comedy became more 'genteel,' and that in several plays there is evidence of a

[1] *Œuvres*, viii. 465.

mawkish harping on the beauties of the sentimental life. Yet even in a work like Cumberland's *West Indian*, which is generally held up as the most typical and most successful example of English sentimental comedy, we find as in all its predecessors, situations which keep alive the spirit of pure comedy and agreeably temper the pathetic incidents, The impetuous, quixotic Belcour, the breezy Major O'Flaherty, and the transparently knavish Fulmers could have no counterpart in a French play dealing with a similar theme. The *drame* is completely different in tone from the English sentimental comedy of the period, and although in a few *drames*, like Voltaire's *L'Écossaise* or Beaumarchais's *Eugénie*, we can observe a belated attempt to retain an air of comedy, the usual effect of such a compromise is one of extreme artificiality. The comic characters strike a jarring note. They resemble those waggish friends who are vastly entertaining at weddings, but somehow never score a real success at funerals.

Beneath this surface froth of occasional borrowings and apparent *ententes* the parallel currents ran as strong and as steady as of old. In basic matters, in the aspects of life which they reflected and in their way of reflecting them, English and French comedy kept their individuality. Even under the Restoration there never had been any real Gallicising of the English theatre, nor during the eighteenth-century vogue for Anglomania was the comic stage of either country really influenced by the other. Both theatres, however, became in time more democratic. In the case of Paris, the evolution was more marked because it met with more resistance. There seems, indeed, no doubt but that French comedy, had it been allowed to develop normally and unimpeded by the censorship, would never have degenerated into *drame*. By its excessive paternalism, the administration forced the French dramatist to take himself seriously; and, incidentally, by depriving comedy of its birthright, which is social satire, wellnigh destroyed its spirit. It was this dogged adherence to a principle that kept the *Mariage de Figaro* off the public stage for five years, and not, as is so often said, the fear of a political revolution.

Now if we ignore, as we must, the French *drames* of the second half of the century, since these are for the most part quite devoid of comic elements, it will be seen that from the death of Marivaux to the appearance of the *Barbier de Séville* (1775) there was very little true comedy in France. And with the decline of Panard, Fuzelier, and Le Sage, even comic opera became, with Sedaine and Favart, lumpish and sentimental. Collé, the author of that wickedly sophisticated *La Vérité dans le Vin*, reserved this and other amusing indiscretions for private stages, whilst in public, as we have seen, he pandered to the reigning vogue. For the space of some thirty years, then, there is only a trickle of mediocre plays to prove that the springs of French traditional comedy were not wholly dried up. Meanwhile, across the Channel the plays of Foote, Hoadly, Bickerstaffe, Murphy, and Colman, the revivals of Shakespeare, and the revised versions of Restoration comedies show that there still was a Merrie England, though merry in its own peculiar way.

The whole of English comedy, during and after the Restoration, derived its comic effect largely from the portrayal of eccentrics or 'humorists.' Marmontel [1] noted the fact: 'A State in which every citizen takes a pride in thinking independently was bound to furnish a great number of originals to be depicted. The affectation of not resembling any one else has often the result that a man no longer resembles himself and exaggerates his own character for fear of adapting himself to that of his fellows. It is not current crazes, but personal singularities which provide food for amusement. The dominant vice of society is unsociableness. This is the source of English comedy—in which probability is rigorously observed even at the expense of modesty.' In other words, the English accepted their eccentrics gladly, nay with joy, whereas in France, again to quote Marmontel: 'The moment a man wants to live for himself, he is condemned to live alone.' Nowhere is the English attitude more obvious than in the plays of Vanbrugh, Wycherley, and Farquhar, which are crowded with what we call 'characters,' but whom the French would dismiss as 'originaux,' that is, people with amusing idiosyncrasies, either of conduct or speech, yet not sufficiently interesting to lend themselves to prolonged analysis on a stage. The English comedy of the Restoration and of the eighteenth century abounds in 'humorists' and displays a great variety of comic situations. Of characters in the French sense there are very few. Once Sir John Brute has revealed himself in that splendid opening scene of the *Provoked Wife*, Vanbrugh is forced to invent the rowdy, improbable incident of the drunken frolic and the noisily amusing Spring Garden masquerade. Wycherley's Horner in the *Country Wife* has practically no character at all; he is simply a man tied to an unusual and farcical situation, for, dramatically speaking, it is no evidence of character to have the sexual appetites of a stud stallion. What gives the play its brutal

[1] *Œuvres*, xii. 492.

verve is the central situation, Horner's pretence that he is a eunuch. It is this that makes it possible for Wycherley to introduce us to a group of urgent ladies assembled in circumstances so odd as to make their talk and behaviour remarkable and piquant.   Farquhar, whose *Beaux' Stratagem* is, I think, our best Restoration comedy, holds an even balance between character and situation.   In this, and in his breezy, open-air quality he recalls Dancourt but not in an imitative sense.   Like Vanbrugh and Wycherley, he has the gift of individualizing his creations, but he is a better artist than either because his people, though well defined, are not oddities. Squire Sullen, that lesser Brute, is in his way a perfect example of character portrayal equal to anything ever achieved by Beaumarchais, outside Figaro.   Sullen's retort to his wife and sister when they reproach him for his inveterate sottishness is really great. 'I can afford it, can't I?'   It is just this sort of repartee, illuminating and condensing a character in a flash, that is so sadly lacking in our comedy.   We do not get it even in Congreve, though in all conscience it is not for want of trying.   It is actually painful to watch Congreve panting after wit through the five acts of *The Way of the World*.   He almost persuades one to believe that a man can become a good dramatist by taking pains.   Why Hazlitt in that brilliant essay finds Congreve witty and Millamant enchanting must remain a mystery.   Like so many others, Hazlitt was taken in by this author's disingenuous trick of using Mirabell, Fainall, and Petulant as advance publicity agents for Millamant, who, as soon as she opens her mouth, utterly fails to justify their exaggerated eulogies.   It is, in a way, the technique adopted by the mountebank—a preliminary roll on the kettledrum rising in excitement to announce what?—a vulgar double somersault that any street-arab will do for a penny.   Millamant's suburban platitudes on love and marriage remind one of the conversation anybody can overhear in a London tea-room after a Noel Coward matinée.   She is not witty; simply dull and perhaps a little irritating.   Because Congreve is not so bawdy as his contemporaries, some critics have acquired the illusion that his work has a French flavour.   As a matter of fact, it has not the slightest trace of *esprit*, and Congreve would have been a much better dramatist if he had been less obviously 'genteel,' and infused a little of Lady Wishfort's gusto into his other creations. Hazlitt rightly calls them 'mere machines,' but adds that they can all speak well.   That is precisely their weakness.   Like Oscar Wilde's puppets, they speak too well, but Wilde, at least, has wit whilst Congreve merely seems to have it. What is more serious, he is a striking instance of the truth of Diderot's saying, that the business of a comic dramatist is not to *lend* wit to his characters, but to place them in circumstances where they would naturally *be* witty.

Still, in all these Restoration comedies, and it is also true of their eighteenth-century successors, we get a closer contact with human nature than we do in most French plays of the same period. They are much more public. For, although the characters are usually most superficial, we know exactly how they would behave and what they would say in every conceivable situation. No doubt, this impression of more intense actuality is due in a large measure to the great variety of settings and of social *milieux* reflected in our English plays; but it springs, too, from the haphazard English method of building plays. Nearly always your French dramatist is over-anxious to achieve form and symmetry; to keep the central situation or character always in the foreground. As a result, he often misses that life-like effect of casualness which, in our English comedies, accompanies the introduction of characters and events. Almost certainly the mixed composition of the London eighteenth-century audience as opposed to the more select nature of the Parisian one had its influence on play construction. 'We reproach the English,' said Mme Riccoboni,[1] 'for introducing vicious and contemptible characters on their stage. They do have this defect, it is true, but perhaps less from choice than from necessity. In Paris, the rich and great are assiduous theatre-goers. In London, persons of distinction rarely go to the playhouse: the employment of their time and the hours of their meals seldom permit them to be free when it opens. Managers are obliged, therefore, to please the bourgeoisie and even the plebs.' Whatever be the cause, the comedies of both countries possess distinctive traits that persisted throughout the century and remained impervious to what is called 'interaction.'

Viewed in the mass, English comedy of the eighteenth century becomes a cavalcade of changing fashions in manners and morals. Each play is a picturesque social document, dated almost to a decade by some obvious allusion to a current foible. In this, the English playwright differs sharply from his French colleague, who seems, on the contrary, to avoid anything that might localize his work and thus compromise its permanence. It would be possible,

[1] Preface to *Le Nouveau Théâtre anglais* (1768).

for instance, in the absence of any other clue, to indicate at once from its oaths and expletives whether an English comedy belongs to the Restoration or the reign of George III.   But we should find it very hard, indeed, to tell merely from its style that Collin d'Harleville's *Le Vieux Célibataire* was written in 1789 and not in 1720. This indifference to local colour in the choice of plot, of incident, is very marked in French comedy up to the eve of the Revolution. In English plays, constant emphasis is laid on those traits of a character which, it was assumed, are stamped on a man by his social condition or his profession.   Long before Balzac, these English playwrights are imbued with the experimental attitude towards life : they would have cordially endorsed his axiom that, as the tortoise can be identified by its shell, so a man's psychology is to be inferred from his habitual environment, since his calling lends a distinctive bias to his character.   Prior to the Regency it looked as if Dancourt and Le Sage were approaching such a conception of drama, but they had no real successors in the eighteenth century. One of Diderot's reforms, it is true, aimed at the substitution of *conditions* for *caractères* on the stage : his object, however, was not comic but serious drama.   It was to discuss the problems that confront the doctor, the lawyer, the merchant, the officer, the judge, the paterfamilias in the exercise of his professional or social functions : it was not, as in English comedy, to make us laugh at professional *tics*.   Diderot's error lay in thinking that the critical actions of a man's life are shaped by professional habit.   But a doctor does not perform an illegal operation because he belongs to the medical profession : it is because he is an individual with criminal desires. On the contrary, when the *Punch* curate at the dinner-table of the purple-faced major-general replies, on being asked his opinion of the '98 port, that it is 'most refreshing,' the humour does depend on the fact that he is a curate.   Attributed to a barrister, the remark would be incredible and not funny.

Now the French tended, as a rule, to individualize their characters from within rather than from without; to dissociate them almost completely, sometimes, from their habitual social environment. Thus a *procureur* in an eighteenth-century French comedy is rarely comic primarily because he is a lawyer.   To take one instance: Marivaux's M. Remy in the *Fausses Confidences* is always amusing, but only once is he comic because of his profession.[1]   It is for this reason that French eighteenth-century comedy seems, to the

[1] See p. 161.

English, lacking in actuality. Dramatic action, for French authors, is psychological and very seldom physical. It does not matter to them, ordinarily, whether their characters talk in the park of a chateau or in a drawing-room, whether France is at peace or at war, whether their servants hail from Poitou or Auvergne, or whether crinolines are going out or panniers coming in. One can read all Marivaux's plays without finding a solitary clue as to the material situation of the charming people whose conversation reveals, so naturally and so wittily, the ultimate recesses of their mind and soul. It would, of course, be a gross exaggeration to say that Marivaux is, in this respect, typical of his century, but it is true that, from our point of view, French comedy of this period portrays changes in thought and feeling, rather than the more superficial fashions and manners which give such a topical air to English plays.

One cannot, for instance, see a performance of *The Rivals* without being at once aware of the constant intrusion of contemporary, everyday life and its passing modes. The whole of the first scene, indeed, owes its actuality to the vogue for circulating libraries. Lydia Languish is not simply vaguely presented as a romantic; we are given a detailed list of her favourite authors. Again, the effectiveness of the scene where young Absolute, muffled to the chin with sword hidden under greatcoat, suddenly meets Sir Anthony, hangs on the fact that duelling is forbidden in Bath. In *She Stoops to Conquer* the choice of *milieu*, a remote country-house, is vital to the credibility of the idea on which the play is based. Moreover, much of its delicious humour springs from the contrast between the rustic idiom of the loutish, cunning Tony Lumpkin and the sophisticated language of the hero, who is a fashionable man about town. Lumpkin's name reminds us, too, of a practice adopted by every other English playwright. One can scarcely find a single comedy of this period in which half the humour is not already obvious as soon as the curtain rises. The character is partly completed before he utters a word, for we know that Sir Harry Beagle,[1] Captain O'Cutter,[1] Lord Trinket,[1] Jerry Sneak,[2] Sir Brilliant Fashion,[3] Sir Archy MacSarcasm,[4] and Sergeant Circuit[5] will in general act up to their labels both in conduct and language. Only to a very minor extent is this the case in French comedy. In comic opera and in the comedies of the Regency, Arlequin and Sganarelle, those

---

[1] Colman, *The Jealous Wife.*   [2] Foote, *The Mayor of Garratt.*
[3] Murphy, *The Way to keep Him.*   [4] Macklin, *Love à la Mode.*
[5] Foote, *The Lame Lover.*

immigrants from the Italian *commedia dell' arte*, persist until close on
the Revolution, but they are Italian only in name.

On the whole, our comic authors of the eighteenth century employ
situation to disguise the shallowness of their characters, the French
use it to elucidate character. In Molière—and his influence long
persisted in France—it is the character which colours the situation and makes it comic. Take one instance from *L'Avare*. Two
candles on a table and a man: there is nothing necessarily comic
in that. But if the man is Harpagon and blows one candle out we
are immensely amused. Again, there is nothing outrageously funny
in the spectacle of an old man in love with a young girl. But if he
is Harpagon he will create an irresistibly comic scene by putting
her through an anxious *interrogatoire* as to the amount she costs
to feed and dress. Now, in *She Stoops to Conquer* the leading situation
is comic in itself; for no matter who the characters are, they cannot
help making us laugh if they mistake a manor house for an inn.
And the same is true of Horner's situation in the *Country Wife*, and
of Sir John Brute's in that scene where he appears before the
magistrate disguised as a woman.

This English tendency to subordinate character to situation gives
our comedy a farcical bias. Without the aid of physical action, as
we see in Congreve, the shallowness of the characterization becomes almost painfully marked. Even Sheridan, whose Faulkland
and Julia come very close to the French manner, is driven to invent
a farcical duel episode in order to sustain the interest of *The Rivals*.
In the *School for Scandal* he prolongs a very good situation, the picture
sale, until it becomes tedious. The object of that scene was to
illustrate the generosity of Charles, but, not content to leave well
alone, Sheridan brings in Rowley to elucidate the same trait. And
Charles could have been made a much more complex, more dramatic
character, for example, like Colman's Charles Oakly in the *Jealous
Wife*. Sheridan could have learned much from Marivaux or even
Destouches about the art of character projection. Compared with
the former's Dorante in the *Fausses Confidences*, or the latter's Comte de
la Tufière in *Le Glorieux*, Charles Surface seems a trifle crude. In
the French comedies every speech and every situation contributes
its quota to our growing conception of the hero's personality.
There is nothing static in the psychological action, and, as each
fresh situation looms, we become really curious to know how the
character will meet it. In Joseph Surface, Sheridan achieves this
suspense and intellectual excitement, yet in that justly celebrated

interview between Joseph and Lady Teazle one always wonders how far the author was inspired by memories of Tartuffe and Elmire.

Still, in the last analysis it must be confessed that the French method of character portrayal has its dangers and defects. To be effective, psychological analysis must have an object both complicated and profound, a Tartuffe, an Harpagon, or an Alceste. Molière, of course, postulates a character so obsessed by a particular vice or foible as to be a monomaniac, and his genius makes these monomaniacs seem quite human. But when we descend the scale of human weaknesses it becomes more and more difficult for the author to interest his audience during five acts by the exposition of a minor mania. It is this, as we have seen, that explains the weakness of so many of Molière's imitators, and helps us to understand the originality of Beaumarchais. For Beaumarchais does not really continue the Molière tradition: he is a creator in the field of comedy. Interesting as such a comparative study would have been, we have unfortunately no comic dramatist in the English theatre of our period who can properly be set up alongside Beaumarchais. Beside him, Sheridan and Goldsmith are merely talented and agreeable, and their works do not stand up to the ordeal of a prolonged critical analysis. In Beaumarchais, on the contrary, it is still possible to make interesting discoveries.

Beaumarchais possessed to a high degree the true dramatist's protean gift of self-abandonment. 'When my subject seizes me,' he wrote, 'I evoke all my characters and I *situate* them. "Take care, Figaro, your master is about to find you out." "Quick! Chérubin. It's the count you are touching." "Ah! countess. How rash of you. With such a violent husband, too." What they are going to say I 've not the least idea: it is what they will do that concerns me. Then, when they are thoroughly animated, I write at their rapid dictation, sure that they will not deceive me . . . each one speaks his own language.'

Here already we have the clue to Beaumarchais's technique—action, swift and progressive, arising almost wholly from change of situation rather than from character development. He does not, like Molière, X-ray the depths of his people's minds in the light of a number of carefully chosen situations. Nor does he, like Marivaux, delight in those charming conversational duels which reveal subtle nuances of emotion and sentiment. His comic spirit is more brilliant than Marivaux's, less searching than Molière's. In these two earlier authors what happens to the characters is infinitely less important than what the latter think about these happenings. In Beaumarchais, on the contrary, it is the situations that really matter, and above all, the adroitness with which the characters adapt themselves, chameleon-like, to a series of changing circumstances. His comedy thus becomes a tissue of cleverly arranged *coups de théâtre*, an exciting succession of scenes, each arousing our suspense and eliciting a gasp of amused relief, as at the eleventh hour once more victory is snatched from almost certain catastrophe.

To achieve this Beaumarchais realized that there is no duel unless the opponents are well matched. The snuffling, ill-tempered old guardian who plots to marry his ward for her money was a stock figure on the French comic stage. Beaumarchais re-creates him in Bartholo, who is no longer the facile dupe of tradition, but a shrewd, damnably suspicious cynic endowed, as Rosine says, with 'l'instinct de la jalousie.' Bartholo is Molièresque in conception, but not exploited with Molièresque thoroughness. The great seventeenth-century dramatist would have added *Le Jaloux* to his repertoire had he not realized the impossibility of exploiting jealousy whilst still remaining on the comic plane. In Bartholo suspicion is the dominant note, but Beaumarchais is content to remain on the surface. The chief use he has for Bartholo is to complicate the situation of Almaviva and of Rosine: above all, it is to present Figaro with an opponent worthy of his steel.

There is an illuminating remark of Figaro's which, like nearly all of that joyous rascal's observations, is applicable to Beaumarchais himself: 'Je me presse de rire de tout de peur d'être obligé d'en pleurer.' Now when Beaumarchais takes himself seriously he is really insufferable. *Eugénie* and the *Mère Coupable* are monuments of mawkish *sensiblerie*. In the *Mariage de Figaro* there are some maudlin, Richardsonian moralizings by Marceline which the actors wisely insisted on excising. How right they were! After all, there is a certain unity of tone which is almost as important in a play as unity of character or of action. It would scarcely, indeed, be necessary to mention it were critics not for the moment befogged by the vapourings of a few illuminists for whom the intellect is the very devil, and who profess to interpret literature solely by the smoky glare of their private repressions. When this phase passes we shall once more realize that every work of art, above all, a play, which is art in its most condensed form, must possess unity of some sort: for unity is the very essence of artistic perfection. The *Barbier de Séville* is a work of art. For all its apparent spontaneity it is, like every good comedy ever written, the product of an exuberant imagination controlled by a lucid intelligence. It is not by mere chance that Rosine is the only woman in it, for her maid, Marceline, is deliberately kept off the stage. Beaumarchais supposes she is ill. Now what would have happened if Rosine's confidant had been retained? We should have had much more talk about love. With all deference to Bartholo, notes would have been smuggled and clandestine meetings with Almaviva arranged. The love element, actually almost negligible, would have transformed the whole atmosphere of the comedy, necessarily conducting Beaumarchais into a realm with which he was quite unfamiliar, the world so deliciously described by Marivaux, the heart of a young girl in love. There are two ways of being a great artist. One is to be aware of one's limitations; the other is to be, like Shakespeare, serenely unconscious of any limitations whatever.

Beaumarchais's great limitation is his ignorance of feminine psychology, and in his comedies he seems aware of it. Had he always been so sensitive he would never have written his *drames*. In comedy, like Le Sage, he confines the activities of his women to intrigue, so that his deficiency is not very noticeable. But in *Eugénie* and in the *Mère Coupable* his embarrassment is pitifully obvious. The truth is that the only type of woman he could understand was the 'fine mouche,' the artful minx, but a minx who is normally placid till her interests are threatened. Then she is suddenly galvanized into action, revealing an unsuspected and instinctive genius for duplicity. Even then, like Rosine or Suzanne or the Countess Almaviva, she is content to leave the initiative to Figaro. Nowhere does Beaumarchais show that he is interested in women, and we need not read his biography to guess that, though he had amours, he certainly never fell in love. He belongs to the numerous category of men who have literally no time for women. Primarily he was a man of action. Speculation, intrigues, polemics, and the exciting business of matching his wits against the wits of others: such for Beaumarchais was the true savour of life. So, in his comedies, where situation predominates, women are a mere excuse for the play: they are never, as in Marivaux, an integral, indispensable part of the play itself. Rosine, Suzanne, and the countess are little more than bones of contention, desirable possessions for which Bartholo, Almaviva, and Figaro plot and counterplot.

As a matter of fact, women are a cause of embarrassment to authors of *comédies gaies*. Molière fought shy of women in his lighter

plays, and even in his character comedies, Celimène and Elmire,
to take two notable examples, are not explored with the intensity
and skill which went to the creation of Alceste and Tartuffe.   It is
only within relatively recent times that authors have discovered a
comic element in woman since, owing to her economic position,
she had not hitherto enjoyed that social freedom which all of us must
have if we are to make fools of ourselves.   The first evidence of it
is in Molière's *Les Femmes savantes* and in *Les Précieuses ridicules*, where
he shows how ludicrous women could be when they were first
admitted into a domain previously reserved for males.   And, were
he writing now I am sure that his typical snob would be Madame,
not Monsieur Jourdain, simply because to-day the French middle-
class *père de famille* has no time to concern himself with the social
side of domestic life.   Still, woman is not yet completely emancipated.   We cannot yet imagine a funny female Harpagon or see
ourselves laughing at a Madame Tartuffe.   Yet avarice and
hypocrisy are not exclusively male vices.   The explanation surely
is that it is difficult to imagine really efficient, full-blooded female
hypocrites and misers.   Love, in some of its forms, would most
certainly prevent them from carrying their obsession to that degree
of exaggeration which makes it comic.   To the man of the old
regime, with its highly simplified and rigid social system, woman's
sole obsession was love, and that, for the comic writer, meant
intrigue; because, owing to the unique authority then enjoyed by
parents, love was normally represented as thwarted.   Marivaux's
originality lies in the fact that he broke with this convention, and
evolved a more subtle and more realistic comedy where the sole
obstacle to the fulfilment of the lovers' desires was their own *amour-
propre*.   Even then his heroines are not comic in the ordinary sense.
The comic spirit in Marivaux is muted into something very exquisite and charming, something which provokes not laughter but
an almost wistful sympathetic amusement.   His older women, his
Madame Argantes, however, are less complex and therefore more
obviously comic, because in them the comic element is not compromised by the presence of any profound sentiment like love.
To be really comic or tragic a character must possess a certain rigidity
of outlook on life, a sclerosis, so to speak, of the mental faculties.
In Molière, of course, it takes the form of an obsession, but Marivaux's elderly women are the victims not of an obsession but merely
of a strong prejudice.   Beaumarchais, as we have seen, adheres
to the old tradition.   The theme of both his tragedies is thwarted

love. The subject of the *Barbier* is, indeed, a hoary one, but he infuses new life into it by re-creating Bartholo. He is more original in the *Mariage*, though the *droit du seigneur* idea no longer possessed —if it ever had—any foundation in reality. His attitude is briefly this: Women are apparently a necessary evil. By all means let us have them in our comedy, but beware of letting them talk or think too much about love. A woman in love is only comic when she is busy with intrigue.

A great deal too much has been made of the political significance of Figaro. To some critics the *Mariage* is the first knell of the tocsin of '89. It would be just as foolish to have concluded in 1915 from the singing of *I'm on the Staff* at the Alhambra that the British Army was riddled with Bolshevism. On the other hand, there is no doubt that for Beaumarchais's contemporaries the secret of Figaro's appeal lay in what Beaumarchais himself called *disconvenance sociale*, the inherent contrast between his hero's social condition and his inexhaustible genius for intrigue. To see in him, however, a staunch and audacious champion of the *tiers état* is to be wise after the event. Figaro schemes for the love of scheming; because he is an artist. As for his altruism, remember his reply to the count in the *Barbier*: 'Moi jaser! Je n'emploierai point pour vous rassurer les grandes phrases d'honneur et de dévouement dont on abuse à la journée; je n'ai qu'un mot: mon intérêt vous répond de moi.' But what of his satires on the courtier whose *métier* can be summed up in the three words: 'recevoir, prendre et demander'? What of his biting comments on social inequality, and the famous remark addressed to the absent Almaviva: 'Vous vous êtes donné la peine de naître, rien de plus'? Is not the long monologue in the fifth act of the *Mariage* the noble outburst of a true republican smarting under years of tyrannical repression? May we not, like so many imaginative humanitarians, detect in it the spirit which on the 14th of July swept the mob of Saint-Antoine to the Bastille? I can imagine Beaumarchais's comment: 'Chansons que tout cela!' How does the *Mariage* end? Listen to Brid'oison:

> 'Or, Messieurs, la co-omédie,
> Que l'on juge en cé-et instant,
> Sauf erreur, nous pei-eint la vie
> Du bon peuple qui l'entend.
> Qu'on l'opprime, il peste, il crie;
> Il s'agite en cent fa-açons;
> Tout fini-it par des chansons . . .' [*Bis.*]

Beaumarchais was not a revolutionary. Revolutionaries do not write comedies.[1] He was like Gil Blas, *un homme universel*, artist, financier, journalist, man of the world, a Parisian, that is to say, a born *frondeur*, instinctively restless under authority, and only really happy when he is flouting it. For nothing in the world would he change places with an Almaviva, a Brid'oison, or a Bartholo, but he must have the luxury of cracking a joke at the expense of the courtier, the doctor, and the judge. What an error to take him seriously when he rails at the injustice which refuses a post to Figaro and gives it to a gigolo! Reward him according to his merits and you will deprive Figaro of the joy of life—intrigue. Remember that in the famous monologue Figaro is surprised in one of his rare moments of pessimism. Suzanne, he is sure, has deceived him: he, Figaro, is a dupe—intolerable thought. Even then, it is fate and not the social order he rails at. What he wants is not that the social order should be reversed, but that there should be room at the top for an *homme d'élite* like himself. Imagine Figaro sharing authority with a Bazile or an Antoine: he would go mad with rage. Of course, as Marceline says, it is a grave injustice that Brid'oisons should be able to buy their judgeships. But this is not an indictment of the French judicial systems. It is addressed to Beaumarchais's old enemy, the judge Goezman, here thinly disguised as Don Guzman Brid'oison. Is it not lucky for Dickens that we had no English revolution in 1870, otherwise the creator of Mr. Justice Stareleigh and Mr. Nupkins would most assuredly have been held responsible for it. None of Figaro's gibes was new, since a hundred others had indulged in similar criticisms of current institutions— though never on the stage. Beaumarchais was a privileged person. He consorted with ministers who consulted him on financial matters, and he had dozens of friends amongst the court nobility. Like our Mr. Shaw he was a national jester. People expected him to say and do the unexpected thing and he rarely disappointed them. Yet no one took his satirical remarks any more seriously than we take Mr. Shaw's humorous sallies on vaccination. No one, that is, except Louis XVI, who was not an 'animal risible,' and a few of the court inner circle. Yet on the strength of a remark of Madame Campan's we assume that the king, with preternatural omniscience, foresaw the Revolution, and, in the *Mariage*, the spark which was to explode the mine. Louis XVI's obstinate refusal to allow the play was not, of course, based upon any such belief.

[1] Consider, for example, the case of Mr. Bernard Shaw.

For him it was simply a frivolous production, the tone of which was an offence to good taste, gravely lacking, besides, in that respect for traditional authority which a monarch then had the right to demand of each of his subjects, even though he was called Pierre Caron de Beaumarchais.

But political satire, however piquant it may be to contemporaries, does not confer immortality on a play. What is it then to-day which crowds the *Comédie française* at performances of the *Barbier de Séville* and of the *Mariage de Figaro*? It is, of course, that great and original comic creation, Figaro. To call him, as some do, a comic type is to speak loosely, for his originality lies precisely in the fact that he is not, like Harpagon and Tartuffe, primarily a type but an individual. Note the difference in Molière's and Beaumarchais's method of projecting and developing character. Harpagon emerges gradually in the light of successive situations until the ultimate recesses of his nature are illuminated. There is nothing abnormal in these situations; it is Harpagon's response to them that is abnormal and comically so. Beaumarchais's technique is very different because his object is different. It is not to use situation as a means of exploring character but to show us how an unusual individual can dominate circumstances which would leave an ordinary man speechless, stupid, and humiliated. Moreover, Figaro is handicapped by his social position, a point persistently emphasized by Beaumarchais the better to reveal his hero's resourcefulness and dexterity. We laugh at Molière's characters because circumstances get the better of them. Society outwits the miser, the snob, the hypocrite. It is exactly the opposite in Beaumarchais. The unique individual called Figaro, despite heavy odds, defeats the jealous Bartholo and the arrogant Almaviva.

Now the various situations from which Figaro emerges triumphant do not profoundly enlighten us as to his character. Were it not for what he himself tells us about himself and his past, notably in the monologue, he would be even more superficial than he is. None of that information, strictly speaking, emerges from the action, to which, indeed, it is almost extraneous. The monologue passes successfully in a long play crammed with movement. Its sole justification is that it is credibly introduced and at an opportune moment, since Figaro has already captivated his audience. Figaro, then, is not a 'type' in the Molièresque sense. One does not say of a man: 'He is a Figaro,' as one says: 'He is an Harpagon.' Yet, complex and highly individualized though he is, Figaro has universal appeal.   He arouses, in fact, that sympathy which normal men feel for the optimist and sportsman who refuses to submit to 'the bludgeonings of chance.'   He does not even whine about his bloody head.   Like the funny man in the medieval farce, he leaps up and gives the Devil a swift kick on the posterior, which is the earliest, and perhaps the profoundest, expression of the dramatic.

Beaumarchais is not deeply interested in the psychology of his characters, but they are boldly presented and sufficiently individualized.   One quality they all possess, however, and that is wit.   Even Brid'oison, that incarnation of grave imbecility, has his *bon mot*.   Remember his stammering rejoinder to Marceline's comment on the abuse of selling posts to judges: 'Oui, l'on ferait mieux de nous les donner pour rien.'   Beaumarchais simply cannot resist the *mot pour rire*.   He extracts wit from situations as naturally as a magnet draws steel filings from a dust heap.   He has a genius for it.   But he has also a genius for inventing the situation which will yield the maximum of comedy, and an amazing talent for creating an atmosphere of excitement and suspense.   He quickened the tempo of French comedy.   No wonder he disconcerted the actors at the original performance of the *Barbier*.   According to Grimm, they could not at first play fast enough.   Le Sage and Regnard have swift and brilliant scenes, but they remain isolated.   Molière, more concerned with character than situation, does not produce this effect of speed, save occasionally in his farces.   In the *Barbier de Séville*, to my mind the more perfect of the two comedies, Beaumarchais produces an illusion of credibility by the rapidity and smoothness with which he fuses a series of incredible situations into a plot.   It is a veritable *tour de force*, an exciting, breathless game in which the author is always one point ahead of the spectator. Yet the *Barbier* is not a pure farce: every character remains indelibly stamped on our minds as the curtain falls.   It is, perhaps, the most completely French comedy in existence, a splendid example of *furia francese*.

We have already mentioned a quality peculiar to all perfect works of art, unity of tone.   Like most attributes of artistic perfection it is usually most conspicuous by its absence, or when for some reason the author compromises it, as does Beaumarchais in the *Mariage de Figaro* by introducing Marceline.   Unity of tone does not exclude variety—far from it.   Like the theme in a sonata, it suffuses the whole composition, emerging clearly at intervals. Yet, let the artist introduce one element of dissonance and the oneness of the creation, the unity of tone is seriously affected. The *Barbier de Séville* possesses that unity to a supreme degree. We saw how the author deliberately excludes any chance of prolonged conversation between Rosine and Almaviva, and by getting rid of Marceline gives Rosine little opportunity of enlarging on her sentiments. The prevailing tone of this play is one of comic disillusionment. All the characters are tinged by it. Figaro's opening conversation with Almaviva is strongly coloured by that spirit of light-hearted cynicism, that instinctive willingness to believe the worst of one's fellows which in varying manner is reflected in every person of the play. Bartholo's attitude is deliciously defined in his comment on Rosine's explanation as to how her note disappeared. 'Le vent, le premier venu! . . . Il n'y a point de vent, madame, point de premier venu dans le monde; et c'est toujours quelqu'un posté là exprès qui ramasse les papiers qu'une femme a l'air de laisser tomber par mégarde.' The sombre and sardonic Bazile with his: 'Qui diable est-ce qu'on trompe ici?' needs no more illuminating gloss. As for Almaviva, we have only to recollect that when he first pursues Rosine his intentions are thoroughly dishonourable, since he has no idea that she is not married to Bartholo. Rosine herself, despite all Beaumarchais's heroic efforts to make her an *ingénue*, is a most unconvincing one. On the flimsiest possible evidence, supplied by the detested Bartholo, she is quite willing to believe that her lover is a pimp. Even the alcade, with only three remarks to make in the whole play, gaily interprets Bartholo's very natural objection to Rosine's marriage as 'sa frayeur sur la mauvaise administration de ses biens.'

It is just because this unity of tone is not preserved in the *Mariage* that I consider it less perfect than the *Barbier*. At the outset, the tone is that of the earlier play; but the introduction of Chérubin, that enigma for the critic, is surely a mistake. Of course, Beaumarchais uses him as he uses all the others, to complicate an already complicated plot. But the reason which he alleges is that the countess's resistance to Chérubin's charms emphasizes her conjugal fidelity. We need not take this weak argument very seriously, since elsewhere he is careful to insist that the infatuation of a boy of thirteen for a married woman can only be exquisitely pure and amusingly naïve. No; the true explanation of Chérubin is obvious to any one familiar with the delicately suggestive pictures of Fragonard and his contemporaries, those experts in the perverse art of blending the erotic and the sentimental. You will find Chérubins

and Fanchettes in a dozen eighteenth-century prints and in sur-
roundings where they are more at home than in the *Mariage de
Figaro*. Now that our critics of the Proudhon school have finished
depicting Beaumarchais as the hidden hand behind the French
Revolution, the door is open to the Freudian symbolists, who
will, no doubt, furnish a much more mystic and more satisfactory
explanation of Chérubin than I have been able to produce. Surprisingly enough, none of these illuminati has yet interpreted him
as a symbol of 'eonism.' Yet think of the dressing-up scene (Act II,
sc. vi), and, of course, Beaumarchais's well-known friendship for the
Chevalier d'Éon him- or is it her-self! In the meantime, may we
not regard Chérubin simply as an experiment and a not very
successful one? After all, we have our beloved Figaro and that is
all that really matters.

POETRY

CHAPTER VII

THREE CLASSICS

IF a passion for truth, a love of clarity, an instinct for moral and intellectual neatness could make great poetry, Boileau would rank with Shakespeare and Racine. But something happened at his birth to rob him of that glory. The fairies, doubtless already discerning in him the future enemy of their charming chronicler, Charles Perrault, cruelly but justly denied poor Boileau the gifts of poetic imagination, of sensibility, and of fancy. So, like many another frustrated poet, he turned to satire. And, as a satirist is always a legislator in disguise, he wrote an *Art poétique* codifying the poetic practice of a generation whose prestige was already on the wane, though no one at the time had the temerity to state this blunt truth. The *Art poétique* is a masterpiece of lucidity and a miracle of condensation; but, like every treatise on poetics that was ever penned, it has one grave failing. It does not tell its reader how to become a genius, nor even what poetic genius is. Apart from this, however, it excels abundantly in common sense, and will always remain a most interesting historical document.

There remains Boileau, the satirist. Now, the art of satire, when all is said, is simply the art of embalming a numskull in an epigram. At this Boileau was an expert. The epigram was his natural mode of expression and there never is any real shortage of numskulls. Even Pope, by no means an amateur at this pleasant game, never quite attains to the Frenchman's imperturbable and untiring precision of execution. The *Dunciad* has its moments, and they are superb; yet its lapses into stercoral invective must always exclude it from a place of honour beside Boileau's seventh and ninth Satires. Boileau, as is well known, wrote his satires in cold blood. His was what Rousseau used to call 'staircase wit,' revised and polished to produce a perfect illusion of spontaneity and naturalness. Personal satire, to be effective, must carry a certain air of nonchalance and good-humoured disdain. It is a crystallization obtained only

after the fumes of ill-temper and rancour have evaporated.   Pope,
with his unfortunate habit of losing his temper in the mêlée, is
possibly more human but less artistic.   Boileau does his work
cleanly.   With a deft stroke he snaps the spine and passes on.
Pope can rarely drop his kill; he must almost always worry it and
drag it through the mire.

In the satire of a more general and more moralizing sort, we begin
to detect an essential difference of method in the two men.   Pope
might have been thinking of Boileau when he wrote:

> Pictures like these, dear Madam, to design,
> Asks no firm hand and no unerring line;
> Some wand'ring touches, some reflected light,
> Some flying stroke, alone can hit 'em right.
> For how should equal colours do the knack?
> Chameleons who can paint in white and black? [1]

The retort to this is to be found in Boileau's tenth Satire.   Here
we find inimitable black and white etchings of feminine types: the
married harlot, the miser, the scold, the false prude.   In drawing
these, Boileau follows the practice of his country and his age,
eschewing local colour in the attempt to isolate and express universal
truth.   Compared to his portraits, Pope's are curiously impressionistic and sometimes disconcertingly vague in a genre where
vagueness is a serious artistic fault.   The Frenchman, once he has
grasped his central idea—here the essence of a character—clings
to it tenaciously, and all his apparent digressions are in reality
subservient to his main purpose.   As a result, the finished work,
like an elm-tree, has *galbe* as well as variety.

Boileau's artistic method reflects the philosophic attitude, the
habit of thought peculiar to his race and time.   Like all the great
writers of the French neo-classic period he adhered consciously or
unconsciously to the Cartesian view that if we can discover the basic,
rational motive for human behaviour, the explanation of individual
psychology is a mere matter of deduction.   Pope, it will be remembered,[2] could not bring himself to believe that human conduct
can be so easily explained.   In the manner of Racine or Molière,
he searches, no doubt, for 'the ruling passion,' but with this vital
difference, that he does not approach it by 'the high-priori road'
of Descartes.   His is the more circuitous, more thorny path traced
by Bacon.   Once again, therefore, we encounter that almost im-
passable barrier separating English and French tradition, that

[1] *Moral Essays*, Epistle II, 'Of the Characters of Women.'   [2] *Moral Essays.*

H

obstacle we have already alluded to in our consideration of the drama of these two races.

To Boileau and his school, even passion obeyed the dictates of reason: its motive, therefore, must be commensurate with its intensity. Irrational passion, the passion that can be diverted from its course by something as irrelevant as Pope's shifting 'east wind' was unthinkable. Such a conception of human nature was inadmissible in French art. Pope, and in this he is as truly a poet as Boileau was not, discerned and expressed most nobly something of that mystery in life which is of the very essence of great poetry. In an unwonted flash of genius he anticipated, indeed, some of those Bergsonian ideas so perfectly illuminated in Proust's *Recherche du Temps perdu*. Pope sensed, though he did not develop, the Proustian views that reality is not a mere matter of objective observation, a 'mere cinema vision'; that the true reality of life is subjective and extra-temporal, and that, to quote Proust himself: 'We cannot narrate our relations with a being, however little we may have known him, without picturing the succession of the most different sites of our lives.' Such, admittedly in embryo, is what we find already in Pope's fine lines:

> Yet more; the diff'rence is as great between
> The optics seeing as the objects seen.
> All manners take a tincture from our own,
> Or come discolour'd thro' our passions shown;
> Or fancy's beam enlarges, multiplies,
> Contracts, inverts, and gives ten thousand dyes.
>   Nor will life's stream for observation stay,
> It hurries all too fast to mark their way:
> In vain sedate reflections we would make,
> When half our knowledge we must snatch, not take.
> Oft in the passions' wild rotation toss'd,
> Our spring of action to ourselves is lost:
> Tir'd, not determined, to the last we yield,
> And what comes then is master of the field.
> As the last image of that troubled heap,
> When sense subsides, and fancy sports in sleep
> (Tho' past the recollection of the thought),
> Becomes the stuff of which our dream is wrought,
> Something as dim to our internal view
> Is thus, perhaps, the cause of most we do.[1]

In passages like these Pope is lifted beyond himself. Intellect and imagination fuse into poetry. Such moments Boileau never

[1] *Moral Essays*, Epistle I.

knew; nor did he ever attain to Pope's profound wisdom on the rare occasions when he laid down the lash of satire and tried to understand, not castigate, human frailty. To him human nature was never, as it was to Pope, a bright flux of complexities, but an organism endowed with free will subjected to the dual force of passion and reason. He would have vigorously rebutted the assertion contained in the lines of Pope:

> Our depths who fathoms, or our shallows finds,
> Quick whirls and shifting eddies of our minds?
> On human actions reason tho' you can,
> It may be reason, but it is not man.

Boileau delights us by the subtlety of his wit, the keenness of his observation. There is in his satirical portraits a manly vigour and that firmness of texture which derives from a robust, logical mind. He has the 'firm hand,' 'the unerring line,' the limitations of which Pope was quick to suspect. Yet in all his works there is not one couplet vibrant with poetic feeling. Really Boileau was a *conteur*, not a poet. One has only to glance at those admirable third and sixth Satires to know that he is the lineal descendant of the medieval writers of fabliaux, without, however, any of their grossness. When he is describing a lunch with an importunate bore [1] or comically cursing the din and confusion of Paris, his verses are alive with actuality, charged with dynamic energy. We have nothing by Pope to compare with them or with the *Lutrin*, that masterpiece of anti-clerical satire in the heroic-comic vein. It is illuminating to pass from the *Lutrin* to the *Rape of the Lock*, Pope's essay in the same manner. At once we move in a different ambiance. The Englishman wafts us into a land of faëry, into 'the crystal wilds of air'; with Boileau our feet are planted always on the solid earth. Even the latter's symbolic characters, *La Renommée*, *La Discorde*, *La Mollesse*, are comically and earthily human. Not of them can it be said:

> Some in the fields of purest ether play,
> And bask and whiten in the blaze of day.

The *Rape of the Lock* is bathed in happy light and laughter. It has the diaphanous, summery joyfulness of the *Midsummer Night' Dream*, tinged, however, with eighteenth-century boudoir artificiality. In fact, if Pope were alive to-day one doubts very much whether he could honestly answer Peter Pan's famous question in the

[1] Satire III.

affirmative.　Boileau, of course, would not even pretend to.　His prevailing note is one of comic Gothic gloom keenly edged with satire.　Thus:

> . . . la Discorde, encor toute noire de crimes,
> Sortant des Cordeliers pour aller aux Minimes
> Avec cet air hideux qui fait frémir la Paix,
> S'arrêta près d'un arbre au pied de son palais
> Là, d'un œil attentif contemplant son empire,
> A l'aspect d'un tumulte elle-même s'admire.

> Quoi! dit-elle d'un ton qui fit trembler les vitres,
> J'aurai pu jusqu'ici brouiller tous les chapitres,
> Diviser Cordeliers, Carmes et Célestins:
> J'aurai fait soutenir un siège aux Augustins:
> Et cette église seule, à mes ordres rebelle,
> Nourrira dans son sein une paix éternelle![1]

One must first read Boileau to acquire the illusion that Pope is a poet of great imagination, and the conviction that these two writers have very little in common.　It is time, surely, to jettison the comfortable legend that Pope is the English Boileau and Boileau the French Pope.　It is easy, however, to see how it arose; for, if one but selects his passages with reasonable care from the *Essay on Criticism* and the *Art poétique*, it is possible to write a convincing comparative thesis on the classicism of the two authors.　So, when Pope says that

> Those rules of old discover'd, not devis'd,
> Are nature still, but nature methodiz'd,

he sounds more dogmatic than Boileau himself.　But read on until you light upon the passage opening with these lines:

> Some beauties yet no precepts can declare,
> For there 's a happiness as well as care.
> Music resembles poetry; in each
> Are nameless graces which no methods teach.[2]

Boileau goes so far as to admit that, under vigilant supervision, an *esprit vigoureux* may once in a while kick over the traces and learn from Art herself to defy the prescribed rules.　Yet never does he remotely suspect that 'happiness' which Pope so often tried to grasp and sometimes did.

All through Pope's writings we can glimpse these strivings to escape from the bondage of the intellect into a more luminous and happy climate of the soul.　Pope is obsessed by the idea of

[1] Satire VI.　　　　　　　[2] *Essay on Criticism.*

light and cherishes the words that suggest it. Like wildfire, it flashes fitfully low on the horizon of his mind. He is haunted by 'the bright idea of the skies,' by visions of 'heavens bespangled with dishevelled light,' by the fiery glow of diamonds in 'the flaming mine.' There is a strange pathos in Pope's reluctant surrender to these and kindred dreams of sensuous beauty. For music and colour and perfume obsessed him, too. Yet by its very rarity, the luminous word, when it appears in Pope's verse, lights up the sombre austerity of his moralizings like a smile on the face of a sad woman. And when he abandons himself to the rare ecstasy of a musical, condensed phrase, it is with the ascetic voluptuousness of his own Eloisa:

> Soft as the slumbers of a saint forgiv'n,
> And mild as op'ning beams of promis'd heav'n.
>
> .   .   .   .   .   .
>
> Thy image steals between my God and me.

Here, the marriage of sentiment and expression is complete and inevitable. But when, elsewhere, he writes:

> She said, and melting as in tears she lay,
> In a soft silver stream dissolved away.
> The silver stream her virgin coldness keeps,
> For ever murmurs, and for ever weeps,[1]

Pope, the intellectual and the moralist, is simply indulging in the illicit joy of dabbling in lovely sounds. Or was it an illicit joy? Are we to regard Pope as one who felt within him the surgings of a fine Shakespearian frenzy yet dared not run counter to the accepted canons of his day, canons which by precept and practice he had done much to sanctify? Or must we see in him a great *poète manqué*, a poet whose brief and sudden flights but indicate an inveterate lyrical impotence? The habitual trend of his mind was critical and analytic. In the art of expressing noble sentiments in fluent and fitting numbers he has few equals in the English language. In the domain of abstract ideas his intellectual grasp and power of penetration is stronger often than Shakespeare's. But he is utterly lacking in Shakespeare's genius for irradiating ideas, and, by sheer poetry, of investing them with an aura of eternal suggestiveness. Pope can make an idea transparent as glass; but it takes a master craftsman to endow it with the crystalline fire, the purity, and the far-echoing ring of great poetry.

Of this he was, I think, conscious, and that, not his much

---

[1] *Windsor Forest.*

advertised physical disability, was his tragedy. Perhaps this is what he tried to express when he wrote:

> Is there no bright reversion in the sky
> For those who greatly think or bravely die?

> .　　.　　.　　.　　.　　.

> Most souls, 'tis true, but peep out once an age,
> Dull, sullen prisoners in the body's cage;
> Dim lights of life that burn a length of years,
> Useless, unseen, as lamps in sepulchres.[1]

Poetic fire is a good master but a bad servant. Voltaire made poetry, and, indeed, every form of literature, the servant of his propaganda. With him the heroic couplet, the expressive medium of Corneille's generosity of soul and Racine's passionate sensibility, became an instrument of precision. It derived a new power from Voltaire's dynamic genius for destructive raillery. Outwardly, the alexandrine remained the same, but in the process of a subtle change it really acquired a swifter, more urgent rhythm to harmonize with the purpose for which it had been refashioned. There are, however, passages, sometimes whole poems, where Voltaire abandons his terrible drilling into the concrete crust of human cruelty, intolerance, and stupidity. Then, indeed, when satire yields to a hopeless sense of despair, he is momentarily a great poet. No longer is he Voltaire, the Hammer of the Church, but Everyman:

> Dans nos jours passagers de peine, de misères,
> Enfants du même Dieu, vivons au moins en frères:
> Aidons-nous l'un et l'autre à porter nos fardeaux.
> Nous marchons tous courbés sous le poids de nos maux:
> Mille ennemis cruels assiègent notre vie,
> Toujours par nous maudite, et toujours si chérie:
> Notre cœur égaré, sans guide et sans appui,
> Est brûlé de désirs, ou glacé par l'ennui:
> Nul de nous a vécu sans connaître les alarmes.
> De la société les secourables charmes
> Consolent nos douleurs, au moins quelques instants:
> Remède encore trop faible à des maux si constants.
> Ah! n'empoisonnons pas la douceur qui nous reste.
> Je crois voir des forçats dans un cachot funeste,
> Se pouvant secourir, l'un sur l'autre acharnés,
> Combattre avec les fers dont ils sont enchaînés.[2]

He is Everyman, appalled by the mystery of human evil, humbly appealing to his fellow-men for the help and courage which all of

---

[1] *Elegy to the Memory of an Unfortunate Lady.*
[2] *Poème sur la Loi naturelle*, iii (1752).

us need on that fearful voyage between two eternities. Had Voltaire always thus leavened reason with sensibility and pity, he would have been immensely greater as a poet, and, it must be said in fairness to his memory, infinitely less effective as a social reformer. For it is not only the way to hell that is paved with good intentions. A chasm separates the poet from the writer who, like Voltaire, makes it his life's work to outwit and smash the sinister tyrant, to strip the hypocrite and expose him naked and shivering in the market-place of public obloquy, to set the dogs of satire and ridicule joyously snapping at the heels of privileged fools. The poet, in a thousand ways, in language we had never dreamed could be, can echo all the heartache and the sorrow of a humanity that suffers daily from these and similar evils; echo, too, the love of freedom and happiness that is man's birthright. He can, in words of unspeakable loveliness, mirror our souls, hold up to them the divine consolation of a beauty far transcending our earthly ills, and thus rob life of its bitter sting. But he cannot, like a Voltaire, argue with the imbecile, cajole the greedy place-seeker, and vilify the charlatan without smirching his immortal soul and destroying our illusion.

But quite aside from this, Voltaire had one great handicap which in itself was enough to exclude him from the company of the Parnassians. His *amour-propre* was so sensitive, his irascibility so easily aroused by purely personal matters, that he never could surrender himself to his noble and impersonal dreams of universal justice and tolerance. Always in his highest flights he is distracted by the sight of a Fréron, a Desfontaines, a Lefranc de Pompignan. Then, irritably descending to earth in a series of astonishing spirals, he swoops to the attack with a scream of rage, leaving us saddened and puzzled to see our eagle transformed into a rather disreputable kite.

It is, for instance, difficult to forgive a man who can close an inspired attack on atheism, an impassioned plea centring round the now famous line:

> Si Dieu n'existait pas, il faudrait l'inventer,

with the miserable couplet:

> Entre les beaux esprits on verra l'union,
> Mais qui pourra jamais souper avec Fréron?

Now it is precisely because in the famous reply to Pope, the *Poème sur le Désastre de Lisbonne*, there is not one word of personal satire, that this, with the *Poème sur la Loi naturelle*, must rank as Voltaire's greatest achievement as a poet. Their author, whilst unable to share the English poet's comfortable optimism, wrote of the *Essay on Man* that it was 'the most beautiful, the most useful, and the most sublime didactic poem ever written in any language.' [1]   In his reply to Pope, he reveals the passionate intensity of a De Vigny, and for once we can believe him when he writes:

> Croyez-moi, quand la terre entr'ouvre ses abîmes
> Ma plainte est innocente et mes cris légitimes.

The great earthquake of November, 1755, which destroyed Lisbon and its surrounding towns was the immediate source of Voltaire's inspiration. But for years he had been awaiting an occasion to express his scorn for a doctrine which seemed to him rotten with falsehood and scabbed with cant. Greatly as he admired some of Pope's deistic utterances, his whole being revolted against the mellifluous smugness of lines like these:

> But errs not Nature from this gracious end,
> When burning suns with livid deaths descend,
> When earthquakes swallow, or when tempests sweep
> Towns to one grave, whole nations to the deep?
> 'No,' 'tis replied, 'the First Almighty Cause,
> Acts not by partial but by general laws.'

This was mere pulpit rhetoric and Voltaire knew it. In words white-hot with indignation, in epithets that erupt from the volcano of his anger, he evokes a merciless picture of the actuality so vividly present to his imagination:

> Philosophes trompés qui criez: 'Tout est bien,'
> Accourez, contemplez ces ruines affreuses,
> Ces débris, ces lambeaux, ces cendres malheureuses,
> Ces femmes, ces enfants, l'un sur l'autre entassés,
> Sous ces marbres rompus ces membres dispersés:
> Cent mille infortunés que la terre dévore,
> Qui, sanglant, dechirés et palpitant encore,
> Enterrés sous leurs toits, terminent sans secours
> Dans l'horreur des tourments leurs lamentables jours!
> Aux cris demi-formés de leurs voix expirantes,
> Au spectacle effrayant de leur cendres fumantes,
> Direz-vous: 'C'est l'effet des éternelles loix
> Qui d'un Dieu libre et bon nécessitent le choix'?
> Direz-vous, en voyant cet amas de victimes:
> 'Dieu s'est vengé, leur mort est le prix de leurs crimes'?

With a majesty for once in harmony with the gravity of his theme, in accents touched with the glow of deep emotion, he explodes, one by one, the arguments advanced by theologians to explain the

[1] *Lettres philosophiques*, xxix

enigma of human suffering in a universe created and governed by
a God of justice and pity. In words that are often an ironical and
acid parody of Pope's, he violently rejects the optimistic fatalism
implied in the famous couplet:

> And spite of pride, in erring reason's spite,
> One truth is clear, Whatever is, is right.

The *Poème sur le Désastre de Lisbonne* is superior to the *Essay on Man*
because it bears the stamp of sincerity. It rises inevitably in a clear
crystal jet from a well of pure conviction. Pope, in certain passages,
is admirably, nay, brilliantly inspired, but his *Essay on Man* has not
the integrity of conception and execution of Voltaire's work. One
feels, like Johnson, that 'the poet was not sufficiently master of his
subject.' It would be true to say, perhaps, that Pope was essentially
untouched by its gravity. He smothers his theme in a rich em-
broidery of memorable aphorisms, illustrations, and comments,
leaving one with the inescapable impression that he chose the
Leibnizian explanation of human destiny, not from mature reflection, but because, as themes go, it is as good as any other. It
had, too, the added lustre of Bolingbroke's approval. Had Pope
never written the *Dunciad* or the beautiful *Eloisa* it might be possible
to think of him as a sincere believer in the doctrine of *whatever is,
is right*. But all that we know of his writings and his temperament
points to the contrary. With Voltaire, on the other hand, we have
no such misgivings. In the *Poème sur le Désastre de Lisbonne* there is
no suggestion of acquiescence or resignation. He vindicates the
dignity of human reason, and in that final outburst of revolt, where
he anticipates the noble spirit of De Vigny's *Mont des Oliviers*, hurls
defiance at the God of Leibniz:

> Je t'apporte, ô seul roi, seul être illimité,
> Tout ce que tu n'as pas dans ton immensité,
> Les défauts, les regrets, les maux et l'ignorance.
> Mais il pourrait encore ajouter, l'espérance.

Perhaps it is this dramatic quality that most clearly distinguishes
the art of Voltaire from the art of Pope; this, and the pungent irony
which imparts form and vitality to his abstractions. One can
best realize the contrast between the genius of the French and the
English poet by comparing the seventh *discours* of Voltaire's *Poème
sur l'Homme* with the fourth epistle of the famous *Essay*. Here they
have a common theme—virtue. For Pope it is self-love enlarged
so as to embrace God and the world in one 'close system of benevolence.' For Voltaire it is *bienfaisance*. But what is really interesting

*H

is not their respective ideas of virtue so much as their manner of expressing them. With the discursive Englishman we travel by a mazy, circuitous road through brooding, philosophic groves suffused with the 'calm sunshine' of familiar thoughts nobly uttered. That there may be an end to this journey is not apparent till we reach it. Nor does it seem to matter; for, in a subfusc, elusive way Pope has already suggested all that he shows us in the final vision. Voltaire's way is very different. It is the dramatic method of a Molière, or a Racine, by which a central idea is illuminated from several chosen points till it emerges in its full radiance. In a series of vivid portraits graven by the acid of satire, he exposes the various masks which hypocrisy wears when it counterfeits true virtue; the stoicism of the pagan, the stupid asceticism of the monk, the corybantic exaltation of the fanatic, the inhuman austerity of the professional judge. Towering above these is the figure of the Christ, the divine simplicity of whose every act and word shines forth with an accentuated purity, as each new image of falsehood is added to the group clustered round His feet.

The presence of this dramatic quality in Voltaire's satires lends them a tone and tempo utterly different from Pope's. Much of this, no doubt, is due to the inherent different between the English and the French heroic couplet and the relative monotony of the former.

The English line is essentially stately; the French, if handled by a Voltaire, can acquire a variety of moods. By adopting this metre for his *Dunciad*, Pope was unconsciously committed to satire of the mock heroic sort employed by Boileau in the *Lutrin*. For example:

> High on a gorgeous seat, that far outshone
> Henley's gilt tub or Flecknoe's Irish throne,
> Or that where on her Curlls the public pours,
> All bounteous, fragrant grains and golden showers,
> Great Cibber sat: the proud Parnassian sneer,
> The conscious simper, and the jealous leer
> Mix on his look.[1]

This is excellent—for a time. But note what Voltaire can achieve in *La Vanité* by using the metre of Boileau's *Lutrin* or Racine's *Phèdre*:

> Qu'as-tu, petit bourgeois d'une petite ville?
> Quel accident étrange en allumant ta bile
> A sur ton large front répandu la rougeur?
> D'où vient que tes gros yeux pétillent de fureur?
> Réponds donc! — L'univers doit venger mes injures;
> L'univers me contemple, et les races futures

---

[1] *Dunciad.*

Contre mes ennemis déposeront pour moi.
— L'univers, mon ami, ne pense point à toi,
L'avenir encore moins : conduis bien ton ménage,
Divertis-toi, bois, mange, sois tranquille, sois sage.
De quel nuage épais ton crâne est offusqué !

Who can fail to note the flexibility of the line, the perfect ease
with which it follows every modulation of the syllables, now long
and lingering, now short and biting as the whip alternately strokes
or lashes its victim's back?

Though Pope rarely achieved or indeed conceived this refinement in satire, when he abandons the heroic couplet for the
decasyllabic his verses acquire an almost Voltairian note.   The
epithets rise and fall in flail-like, thudding cracks, terrible epithets
tinged with a picturesque hideousness that is English and not French :

Yet let me flap this bug with gilded wings,
This painted child of dirt, that stinks and stings ;
Whose buzz the witty and the fair annoys,
Yet wit ne'er tastes, and beauty ne'er enjoys.
So well-bred spaniels civilly delight
In mumbling of the game they dare not bite.
Eternal smiles his emptiness betray,
As shallow streams run dimpling all the way,
Whether in florid impotence he speaks,
And, as the prompter breathes, the puppet squeaks ;
Or at the ear of Eve, familiar toad,
Half froth, half venom, spits himself abroad . . .[1]

This is invective tinged with the hue of poetic fancy, and, as I have
said, it is not to be found in French poetry.   To Voltaire it would
have been repellent, a brutal and needless prostitution of poetry ;
to borrow Pope's own words, 'beauty that shocks you.' Many
would no doubt agree, yet none will deny that it is effective ; its
images sear themselves on the memory.   Contrast this manner
with that of Voltaire in equally brutal vein.   He is dealing with
Jean-Jacques Rousseau.

C'est de Rousseau le digne et noir palais.
Là se tapit ce sombre énergumène,
Cet ennemi de la nature humaine,
Pétri d'orgueil et dévoré de fiel ;
Il fuit le monde et craint de voir le ciel :
Et cependant, sa triste et vilaine âme
Du dieu d'amour a ressenti la flamme :
Il a trouvé pour charmer son ennui
Une beauté digne en effet de lui :

---

[1] *Épistle to Arbuthnot.*

C'était Caron amoureux de Mégère.
Cette infernale et hideuse sorcière
Suit en tous lieux ce magot ambulant,
Comme la chouette est jointe au chat-huant . . .[1]

This is corrosive and deadly acid, but it is pure acid. Pope's satiric verse is almost always coloured with imagery and flavoured with the bitter honey of his moralizings.

One need not, then, frequent Boileau, Pope, and Voltaire for long to realize the ineptitude of the common label 'classicism' which has been carelessly applied to them. The fact that Pope translated the *Iliad* and the *Odyssey* does not make him a classic of the Boileau persuasion. And Voltaire, with all his respect for the formal canons codified in the *Art poétique*, when he made poetry an instrument of intellectual propaganda obviously moved at once into a region of which Boileau never dreamed, though Pope had furtively slipped across its borders. Of the latter's innate distrust of reason and his search for the 'happiness' that great poets have found only in a complete surrender to the seemingly irrational urgings of their subconscious self, Voltaire knew little. Yet even he had his moments of doubt:

On a banni les démons et les fées.
Sous la raison les grâces étouffées
Livrent nos cœurs à l'insipidité;
Le raisonneur tristement s'accrédite:
On court, hélas, après la vérité.
Ah! croyez-moi, l'erreur a son merite.[2]

And a few years before his death he has belated and heretical misgivings as to the infallibility of the medium which he did so much to perfect and to polish. We find him, in 1771, complaining bitterly of

Cette loi si dure
Qui veut qu'avec six pieds d'une égale mesure
De deux alexandrins, côte à côte marchants,
L'un serve pour la rime et l'autre pour le sens:
Si bien que, sans rien perdre, en bravant cet usage
On pourrait retrancher la moitié d'un ouvrage.[3]

But these are rare, isolated digressions. In no way do they bring him even within sight of the course followed by Pope. The art of each is a tree that has its taproot deep in the traditional genius of his race. No doubt, the Hybla bees visited the blossoms of each, but they made their flights on separate days. At any rate they carried no English pollen into France.

[1] *La Guerre civile de Genève,* chant iii (1768).   [2] *Ce qui plaît aux dames* (1763).
[3] *Épître au Roi de Chine* (1771).

CHAPTER VIII

THE FEARFUL MUSE

'It is idle,' wrote Shenstone, 'to be assiduous in the perusal of inferior poetry.' And what author is more qualified to speak on this subject than Shenstone, who produced more consistently bad verse than any other poet of his time? Now, but for several considerations, one might very well endorse his truism, and leave the lesser poets of eighteenth-century England and France to that oblivion from which they are unearthed only by the authors of doctoral theses. As something resembling a mass disinterment is here projected, it may be necessary to state very firmly, at the outset, that my purpose is neither to tabulate Dorat's reactions to the weather nor even to prove that Young is a greater poet than Milton. It is rather, if possible, to picture the stages of that sea-change by which the arid, shrivelled verse of two different countries was prepared for the rich and strange renascence which we call romantic poetry. Both in France and in England poetry had to shake off the rustling cerements of a dry, false, conventional classicism. In both it had to strive against the hegemony of prose because, in a century so preoccupied with social and moral progress, it was felt by many quite intelligent Frenchmen and Englishmen that, for the dissemination of didactic ideas, poetry was at best but an inferior medium. So we find D'Alembert, one of the editors of the *Encyclopédie*, candidly admitting that for intellectuals the chief attraction of poetry resided, not in its emotional appeal, but in the fact that though, like prose, it expresses thought, poetry 'adds to this merit, the merit of a difficulty overcome.' Now it should be remembered that D'Alembert is here dissociating himself from the philistines. Did he not stoutly maintain that poetry *is* an imaginative art? He saw himself indeed as a reformer; since, after La Motte, he advocated the abolition of rhyme in lyric poetry and applauded those moderns who desired to jettison the outworn fictions, the verbal *clichés* derived from classic mythology. Yet he concludes: 'The less we soften the rigour of our poetic laws, the greater will be the glory in surmounting them. Do not let us be afraid to assert that there is more value in ten good lines of French poetry than in thirty English or Italian. . . . A poet is a man whom we oblige to walk gracefully with fetters on his feet.'

That a number of the *philosophes* were definitely opposed to imagery of any sort in poetry we know from Dorat, who composed an ode to their confusion, and in one of his prefaces said: 'It is no use declaiming, arguing, or invoking the feeble help of reason; images will always be the essence of poetry as rhythm is its form.' [1] He agrees, however, that the old classic, 'tawdry' mythology must go. The 'zephyr wings,' the 'garlands of Flora,' the 'tresses of blond Ceres,' 'the rosy fingers of that eternal Aurora whom we never see but always quote,' are doomed. On this point the critics of his time, French and English, would have agreed. Indeed, ever since the beginning of the century, the moderns of London and Paris had stormed and jeered at their poets for this slavish but dogged imitation of classic language. Yet we have but to glance at any anthology of English or French eighteenth-century poetry to realize the comparative futility of such protests. 'Except for Thomson,' said Thomas Warton, 'every painter of rural beauty copied his images from Theocritus without ever looking into the face of nature.' Aikin [2] held that this was not 'strictly just,' having in mind the achievements of Gray and Collins, but admitted that 'descriptive poetry has degenerated into a kind of phraseology, consisting of combinations of words which have been so long coupled together, that, like the hero and his epithet in Homer, they have become inseparable companions. Incidentally, Aikin reminds us that the eighteenth-century poverty of poetic imagination was reflected not merely, as was the French, in its servile repetitions of classic images, but also in its constant echoes of Shakespeare. Aikin gives us illustrations. The 'shard-borne beetle,' which 'wheels his droning flight' in Gray's *Elegy*, again 'winds his small but sullen horn' in Collins's *Ode to Evening*. Had he wanted to, he could no doubt have quoted whole passages from Young's *Night Thoughts*, from Mallet's *Excursion*, from Thomson's *Seasons*, and from a host of smaller fry to reveal the persistence of Shakespeare's influence. It would, indeed, be fair to say that three factors: Shakespeare, the Bible, and the Classics, helped to paralyse the originality of our eighteenth-century poets. They did not as yet realize the folly of trying to improve on these models,

[1] *Œuvres* (1776), Preface to *Les Lettres d'une Chanoinesse de Lisbonne.*
[2] *Essay on the Application of Natural History to Poetry* (1777).

because they were not fully alive to their amazing beauty and genius. Only with such an awareness, which did not come till very late, could there be a new blossoming. For the poetry of our Romantics is great, not in so far as it reminds us of Shakespeare or the Bible, or Spenser or Milton, but precisely inasmuch as it reminds us of nothing that ever happened in literature before.

Meanwhile, however, of such a renascence there were few visible signs. No doubt, the general will to shake off the thraldom of the classics was widespread and sincere, though not many poets had the strength to execute it. Naturally, in an age where, in the absence of wealth or rank, a smattering of the classics was a valuable social asset, the temptation to display classical knowledge was irresistible. There exist to-day quaint people who think that a man who can quote Greek must be a gentleman. An enormous quantity of the verse turned out in France and in England was written, therefore, with the sole object of extracting coin from wealthy, ignorant peers and successful business men who would have felt insulted by the omission of the traditional, classical trappings. Statesmen, princes, and generals enjoyed being compared to their predecessors of ancient Greece and Rome; and even actresses had to be placed on a level with the pagan goddesses. Having then contracted this vicious trick, it was difficult even for poets of original talent to escape it when they were writing, not begging letters, but poetry. The example set by Pope did much to perpetuate this abuse, since he gave his successors the illusion that eighteenth-century sentiments and thoughts could be harmoniously and gracefully expressed in classic terms. They were too close to him to see that Pope is only really a poet when he breaks away from classic domination, as he does in *Eloisa* and the *Epistle to an Unfortunate Lady*. His *Essay on Criticism* was eagerly read, not for the reserves it contains, which, as we have seen, absolve it from the dogmatism of Boileau, but for couplets like:

> Those rules of old discover'd, not devis'd,
> Are nature still, but nature methodiz'd.

Even a reformer like Thomas Warton maintained, for example, that 'to attempt to understand Poetry without having diligently digested Aristotle's *Poetics*, would be as absurd and impossible as to pretend to a skill in geometry without having studied Euclid.' Yet Warton was furiously attacked by the Rousseauist Stockdale for daring to suggest that there was nothing 'transcendently sublime' in Pope. Said Stockdale: 'Warton's Gothic soul is stimulated only with the transcendently sublime; or, in other words, with the unnatural, the gigantic, the incoherent. . . .' The poetry of the Warton brothers, according to Stockdale, was extravagant in its sentiments and displayed all the 'madness of ill-imagined passion.' He compared it to the new Chinese gardens introduced by Sir William Chambers, since in the Warton poems he discerned the same grotesque colouring and disorder, the same 'huddle and crash of objects.'[1] The situation was paradoxical and piquant; for, whilst Pope in the seventies is championed by the men of feeling, he is belittled by Romantics like Warton who swear by the poetry of the bardic Gray. One remembers Gray's holy horror of Rousseau, whose *Nouvelle Héloïse* he condemned as immoral or absurd, and whose *Confessions* he could not even finish.[2] In the meantime, however, let us simply record that after the lapse of nearly eighty years, the prestige of what the seventeenth century called classicism was, in England, at least, severely compromised. Yet Aristotle was still a name to conjure with.

Now with all this growing disgust in France and, above all, in England, for the artificial, conventional jargon of the neo-classics, the fate of poetry was by no means decided. The spirit of the new century was prosaic. Poetry was therefore called upon to sing the scientific achievements of the men of progress: and a large anthology could be made of poems, in French and English, which were compsed solely to celebrate their discoveries in science, in the arts and crafts, in agriculture and commerce. Masses of verse appeared, too, devoted to the discussion and elucidation of theological and humanitarian problems. In a word, poetry became for many a mere annexe to prose. Dorat, the very writer who had defended the rights of the imagination, defines the new function of poetry very well in the following words: 'Every time a new discovery is made in physical or in moral nature, it must, if possible, be pictured and rendered *sensible*. Images will remain when reasoning is forgotten.' The poetic imagination, then, was to be an accessory to intellectual propaganda. The poet was to be an encyclopedist, not a singer. More crudely, perhaps, than Dorat, we find the same ideal expressed by Aikin,[3] who dogmatically asserts that if English poetry is to come out of the rut, poets must acquire an exact knowledge of the natural sciences: botany, zoology, and

---

[1] *Inquiry into the Nature and Genius of the Laws of Poetry* (1778).
[2] *The Correspondence of Gray*, ed. by Paget Toynbee, vol. ii, pp. 208, 235.
[3] loc. cit.

geology. His argument is that our nature poets were bad, simply because they had never learned the art of accurate observation.

This new trend was inevitable, and it raises a point which is of interest to readers of twentieth-century poetry. Is it true, as is sometimes asserted, that there are no essentially unpoetic ideas? Certainly there is nothing in the experiments of the eighteenth-century French and English poets to convert one to this opinion. When, for example, we read John Dyer's *The Fleece* (1757) it is hard to see how even a fine poet could write poetically of the castration of rams, the dipping of sheep, and their treatment for maggots. And Dyer, though very far from being a good poet, yet displays in his fourth book a real sensitiveness to colour, and to the music of resonant, exotic names. But there he is dealing with poetic ideas, with a theme that would delight Sir Henry Newbolt: the sailing of the wool armada and its adventures in tropic seas, the arrival on foreign shores, and the chaffering in

> . . . the wealthy marts
> Of Ormus or Gombroon, whose streets are oft
> With caravans and tawny merchants thronged.

Again, there may be poetry latent in sugar, or even in that delectable word 'marmalade,' which none of our moderns, however, dares to use; but if so, it somehow escaped the eager questings of Dr. Grainger, whose *Sugar Cane* (in four books) has won a place in Chalmers's *Works of the British Poets*. Poor Grainger was most unlucky with his Muse. When invited to sing of rats and their depredations on the young plantations, she failed to respond,[1] and one is prepared to wager that even Mr. T. S. Eliot would find rats a tough morsel. To do Grainger justice, he does his utmost, in a series of audacious attempts, to prove, experimentally, that there is no idea which cannot be alchemized into poetry. Thus, on constipation, he sings of cassia:

> . . . See what yellow flowers
> Dance on the gale and scent the ambient air;
> While thy long pods, full fraught with nectared sweets,
> Relieve the bowels of their lagging load.

Reluctantly, one is driven to the conclusion that the theory is unsound. However, it would be unfair to condemn it without,

[1] The ineffable line, 'Now, Muse, let's sing of rats,' aroused hilarity even in Sir Joshua Reynolds's *salon*, where Grainger read his poem.

as someone once neatly put it, 'exploring every avenue.' The eighteenth-century French raised periphrasis to the level of a fine art, and prided themselves on being able to express in the *style noble* almost anything from an earthquake to a wooden arm. This is literally true. Lebrun's *Ode sur les causes physiques des tremblements de terre* and Delille's *Épître à l'occasion d'un bras artificiel* were, in their day, much admired. Greater scope for poetic originality was offered, however, by the less circumscribed theme of inoculation—a favourite subject, too, with our own singers. In 1774, the abbé Roman composed a poem in four cantos called *L'Inoculation*, and Dorat followed in the same year with his *Ode sur l'Inoculation*. Both received the thanks of the *Journal encyclopédique*, which expressed the gratitude of France to these gentlemen for 'forcing' the language 'to render ideas which had at first appeared to resist poetic expression. The merit of the difficulty overcome adds a new lustre to the beauties born of the writers' pens.' Yet, oddly enough, one can read these and other effusions of the same type without that bristling of the epidermis which is, according to Professor A. E. Housman,[1] an infallible sign that we are in contact with great poetry.

In England, this subordination of poetry to science and philosophy was never quite so widespread or so systematic as it became in France, where, after the sixties, the Encyclopaedists dominated the *Académie française*, and thus, to some extent, were able to impose their taste on aspiring poets. D'Alembert makes this painfully clear when he writes: 'In a word, here it seems to me is the rigorous but just ideal which our century imposes on the poet; it no longer recognizes anything as good in poetry except what it would consider excellent in prose. This way of thinking, if I may venture here to indicate the unanimous dispositions of my colleagues, will eventually direct more than ever the judgment of the *Académie française* on the poems submitted for competition.' This was serious, but, as we shall see, D'Alembert's party was by no means as omnipotent as he imagined. In England, on the other hand, one can discover no such unity of purpose on the part of any single group, simply because our literature, like our Protestant Church, throve, not on order, but on schism. Besides, compared to French, our language was extremely elastic, both as regards construction and vocabulary. Indeed, one of the earliest foreign critics of our poetry[2] is struck by the contrast between our tongue and his own in this respect. 'The

---

[1] *The Name and Nature of Poetry*, p. 47.
[2] *Journal littéraire*, ix (1717), 'Dissertation sur la poésie anglaise.

refinement of the purists has impoverished our language; a great many old, expressive words have been eliminated and only necessary terms introduced.' But English, he adds, is very different. 'Never, on the other hand, was a language more unscrupulous in adopting foreign expressions; appropriating not merely words but turns of phrase.' And the English are constantly inventing new expressions. 'There is no limit to the boldness of their metaphors.' Rather enviously this writer goes on to contrast our 'licence' with the rigidity of the French rules, finally touching on a matter very pertinent to our present topic. 'Besides, an inviolable rule of French style forbids the reappearance of the same term in neighbouring periods; so, as we have few synonyms, it is often difficult to vary the style except by means of circumlocutions which replace one word by a whole phrase, produce an emptiness in the sense, and absolutely enervate the diction.' One could cite hundreds of cases. Let two suffice. This is from Dorat's *L'Inoculation*, and is interesting because Dorat was a tireless opponent of the *philosophes*:

> Faut-il forger l'acier en glaive parricide,
> De l'airain bouillonnant faire un tube homicide?

When Colardeau, another anti-*philosophe*, wants to say 'un baromètre' or 'un thermomètre,' he is obliged by the rules to write:

> Là de l'antique Hermès le minéral fluide
> S'élève au gré de l'air plus sec ou plus humide:
> Ici par la liqueur un tube coloré
> De la température indique le degré.[1]

English poets were infected with the same virus, but to a relatively small degree. Thomson was one of our worst offenders. But, on the whole, our didactic or scientific poets made no scruples about calling a spade a spade. As a result, however execrable the poetry was, it had at least the virtue of putting into circulation large numbers of terms hitherto unknown to the average layman. A good example is Falconer's *The Shipwreck* (1766), which, though it is full of reminiscences of the *Aeneid*, has, on the other hand, hundreds of sinewy nautical words and expressions. Our didactic poets in general aimed at realistic description: the French on the contrary, imitated an ideal, neo-classic model, the so-called *style noble*. Everything which they observed in real life around them had, therefore, to be recast in terms of that ideal. This phenomenon had its origin in the seventeenth-century tendency to universalize immediate realities, to strip them of their local colour, and restate them in

[1] *Épître à M. Duhamel.*

terms of fixed, immutable norms — *le beau* and *le vrai*.   Here
Prévost scented the influence of Descartes, and, as early as the
thirties, scoffed at these poems on 'Agriculture, Mirrors, and Por-
celains,' [1] asserting that Cartesian philosophy 'had annihilated the
taste for belles lettres in France and in all Europe.' [2]   The Cartesian
spirit, he maintained, was fatal to poetry.   'The geometric poet
will always be a cold, insipid poet.' [3]   One might, indeed, have
assumed that with the growing admiration for Newton and experimental science the French would have enlarged their poetic vocabulary; yet we have but to remember the persistence of tradition in
Voltairian drama to realize that such conservatism in esthetic
matters was not incompatible with the greatest liberalism in science
and in philosophy.

It was not till about 1728 that the French began to translate
English poetry.[4]   Prior to that date, however, we do find odd references to Butler, Prior, Rochester, Dryden, and Pope in papers
edited by French refugees resident in England and Holland.   The
Journal littéraire, already cited, refers briefly to the above poets, and
incidentally contains the first French remarks on Chaucer and
Shakespeare.[5]   The general tenor of these early comments on our
poetry is reflected by Prévost in his review of a new translation of
Pope's *Essay on Man* in the *Pour et Contre*.[6]   Defending us against
criticisms of our poetic licence, Prévost very kindly points out that
this is but a natural step in the development of a race which has still
'a trace of barbarism,' and 'is still at the stage of the simple and
crude productions of a primitive mind and of that common sense
with which indeed it is very well endowed, pending the time when
it will please Heaven to grant it the taste for order, elegance, sweetness, and harmony.'   Without a vestige of arrogance and in the
most matter-of-fact way, French critics, whilst admiring our 'fire'
and 'liberty,' continue till late in the century to express the same
views.   Dorat, in a poem to Hume, his great friend, writes:

> Nous aimons vos graves chimères
> Et vos jeux tristement sensés,
> Nous ornons ce que vous pensez;
> Nous savons de nos mains légères
> Polir vos goûts et vos talents.
> Vous avez quelques diamants,
> Mais vous manquez de lapidaires.

---

[1] *Pour et Contre*, lxiv.   [2] ibid., lxv.   [3] ibid., lxxiii.
[4] *Bibliothèque française* (1743).   [5] loc. cit. (1717).   [6] ccl.

Ce négligé qui nous déplaît
Nous l'égayons par la parure;
Et notre France est le creuset
Où l'or de l'Europe s'épure.

Until about 1750, the only eighteenth-century English poet really known to cultured Frenchmen was Alexander Pope. It was he, said Prévost, who did more than any one else to purify English verse and to lend it those qualities associated in France with good poetry. The proof of this he adds, is that no English poems are easier to render into French than Pope's—a criterion typical of the age. Pope's *Rape of the Lock*, before 1750, had enjoyed three translations in prose and two in verse; that of Marmontel being most celebrated. The *Essay on Criticism* was rendered into French by three different writers, the most noted of whom was Du Resnel, whose translation ran through four editions before 1750. The *Essay on Man* was thrice turned into French, and Du Resnel's version was reprinted. It is significant that the *Eloisa to Abelard* did not attract a translator until 1758, for reasons that will later become evident. Pope, then, for some fifty years remained in French eyes the sole representative of our eighteenth-century poetry, though it would be more correct to say that our poetic genius was not represented at all. What interested the French in Pope was his thought and not its manner of expression.

In 1749 it occurred to one Trochereau to offer a small anthology of English poetry, but Pope's *Essay on Fame* was the only eighteenth-century selection.[1] In the same year, the abbé Yart published his *Idée de la Poésie anglaise*, a book that sadly belies its title since it contained only a prose version of Philips's *Cyder*, *The Splendid Shilling*, *Hochstedt*, and a few poems by Swift.[2] Yart pointed out that his countrymen had exhausted the classic resources and needed to turn to the modern foreign poets for inspiration. 'Do not,' he said of us, 'allow ourselves to be repelled by the queerness of some of the metaphors, the confusion and disorder which reign in their books, or, finally, by the unevenness of their style. Let us delve in these deep mines. Let us separate the gold from the dross. Let us embellish our gardens with these exotic plants, and by our art give them a beauty which nature has denied them. . . . We have been to them for a long time in some sense what the Greeks were to the Latins. None of the polished nations of Europe has made

[1] The others were Buckinghamshire's *Essay on Poetry*, Roscommon's *Essay on Translated Verse*, Dryden's *Alexander's Feast*, and Pomfret's *Choice*.
[2] The latter, I think, at the suggestion of Prévost.

so much use of our works, but none is able to make us richer amends.'
Now all things considered, this was very handsome of Yart: but the
French were curiously unmoved.

From another source [1] we get some light on Yart's motives in
coming to our poetry for fresh energy. The good abbé was a man
of feeling, an ardent disciple of the school of sensibility that was
beginning to make its influence felt on the stage. 'Sensibility,'
he wrote, 'is perhaps poetry itself. . . . French poetry under Louis
XIV was the triumph of sentiment, but of a purified, ennobled, and
perfected sentiment. Never had any one seen more elegance in
verse, more originality in the choice of subject, more skill in the
execution. But never, too, had sentiment spoken a more touching
language. The intellect did but polish the verses: they were animated by sentiment.' But now Yart felt that the intellect, the
esprit géométrique would soon abolish sentiment altogether. 'A
precious style, far-fetched thoughts, metaphysical dissertations are
taking hold of our poetry and invading every genre. Sentiment,
which should be everywhere, is found nowhere.' Poetry, he urged,
should be subjective. 'The true poets are those who withdraw
within themselves, examine their emotions, draw their inspiration
from that fertile source, explore the causes, the springs of human
passion and submit these to the judgment of sentiment and experience. Their hearts, prepared by nature, illuminated by study, and
warmed by reflection, will not be slow to catch fire.' For Yart,
poetry is 'a sublime art which by harmonious language represents
objects that excite the passions.' The qualities he would bring
back to French poetry are lyricism, sensibility, enthusiasm, the very
qualities, indeed, which English poets like Gray and Collins were
even then restoring to our own literature.

Unfortunately, in Yart's book, which ran into eight volumes,[2]
there is no mention of Gray, Collins, or even Young. The only
eighteenth-century poets are Pope, Akenside, and Addison, and
these only in fragments. Moreover, as even the orthodox Fréron
complained in his *Année littéraire*, Yart rectifies and cuts down his
originals to such an extent as to prevent the French from forming
any 'real idea' of English poetry. In fact, Yart's method was that
employed by La Place in his strange *Théâtre anglais*.

Nevertheless, it is clear that the moment was ripe in France for
essential poetic reforms. The tone of the theatre and of the novel,
thanks to La Chaussée, Destouches, Prévost, and Madame de

[1] *Le Petit Réservoir* (1750).   [2] The last two were published in 1771.

Tencin, had already altered: it now echoed a new note of brooding sensibility, in sharp contrast to the cynical, witty writings of the *libertins*, the boudoir novelists, and the satirical playwrights of the Regency. In England and in France there arose in poetry a tendency to dwell upon the theme of death. In the former country it found expression in verse of a morbid colour: in the latter it produced eventually a melodramatic species called the *héroïde*. In both cases, this change in poetic taste, just as in the contemporary theatre and novel, was the reflection of a social transformation. It echoed, indeed, a spiritual change, a new consciousness not simply of the complexities of social life, but of life's deeper mysteries: tragic love, death, and immortality. These could find really adequate expression only in poetry; but first of all the eighteenth-century poets had to learn a new language. For the French this implied a revolution, because, under the prolonged influence of neo-classicism they had deliberately thrown away the treasures amassed by their medieval forbears. We, on the other hand, suffered from an *embarras de richesses*. The vocabulary of the English version of the Bible, and of Shakespeare's theatre, was, in part, now embedded in the living language. These words had, indeed, become such current coin that some wondered, like Gray, whether they were worthy to express poetic thoughts. 'The language of the age,' he wrote to West,[1] 'is never the language of poetry, except among the French, whose verse, where the thought or image does not support it, differs in nothing from prose. Our poetry, on the contrary, has a language peculiar to itself: to which almost every one who has written has added something by enriching it with foreign idioms or derivatives, nay, sometimes, words of their own composition and invention. . . . And our language, not being a settled thing (like the French), has an undoubted right to words of a hundred years old, provided antiquity have not rendered them unintelligible.' With the re-discovery of Shakespeare in England, there was a danger lest her new poets might lose whatever creative power they possessed, and in place of original poetry, offer up a mere rehash of Shakespeare. Gray was alive to this. 'However, the affectation of imitating Shakespeare may be carried too far; and is no sort of excuse for sentiments ill-suited or speeches ill-timed, which I believe is a little the case with me.' Never was a warning more in season, though, of course, it went unheeded by many. Still, there were in the new spirit elements which could not be expressed in Elizabethan

[1] Gray's *Correspondence*, ed. cit., ii. 27.

language.   Universal as Shakespeare is, his attitude to man, to
nature, and to God was not that of the eighteenth century nor of its
spiritual heirs, the Romantics.

Anglo-Saxons have somehow managed to convince the rest of
the world that they hold a monopoly in the domain of serious
thought.   And there is something almost coquettish in the persistence which which the French writers of the eighteenth century
defer to us on certain literary topics, reserving for themselves the
more elegant, artistic qualities.   To understand this one must
remember their violent rejection, late in the seventeenth century,
of all that smacked of Pascal and Jansenism.   The razing of Port-
Royal has a profound symbolic meaning.   It was the desperate
gesture of a powerful minority to shut the door on a grim and unpleasant reality that the Jansenists had considered it their duty to
keep always before men's eyes.   This reality is death, which implies,
among other things, self-examination.   However, Jansenism did
not expire with the destruction of Port-Royal.   True, the site was
sown with salt so that nothing should grow upon it.   But the
ideas for which Jansenism stood were not so easily exterminated.
Throughout the new age their influence on the middle classes was
very marked.   The famous affair of the 'Unigenitus' Bull, the mystic
religious enthusiasm aroused by the miracles supposed to have been
enacted at the grave of the Jansenist François de Paris, and the
eventual downfall of the Jesuits in 1762, clearly reveal how numerous
were the adherents of this austere sect, particularly, says Barbier,
amongst the people, the bourgeoisie, and the parish priests.[1]   The
novels of Prévost and Tencin are steeped in the spirit of Jansenism.
The latter's popular *Comte de Comminges*, the scene of which is laid in
a Trappist monastery, has for its theme the tragic contrast between
love and religion, a subject which was now to become most popular
with French reformers of literature.

The Jansenists had no more active opponent than Chaulieu,
the uncrowned laureate of the *libertins* and the spiritual godfather
of Voltaire.   It is therefore odd, at first sight, to connect this
Epicurean with the sombre, moralizing poets of the later period.
Nevertheless, Chaulieu's pagan, voluptuous *joie de vivre* is fraught
with the terror of death.   There are, of course, Epicureans who
savour the sweetness of life more acutely by wilfully recalling its
fugacity and inevitable term.   But with Chaulieu the spectre of
death rises unbidden.   He tries to exorcise it by invoking reason,

[1] *Journal*, August 1729.

and failing that, by the reflection that the God of the Deists is merciful:

> Ainsi dans ce moment qui finira mes jours,
> Qu'il te faudra quitter, La Fare, et mes amours,
> Mon âme n'ira point flottante, épouvantée,
> Peu sûre de sa destinée,
> D'Arnaud et d'Escobar [1] implorer le secours. [2]

And when sickness clutches him he shrinks in horror from the sight of death:

> J'ai vu de près le Styx, j'ai vu les Euménides.
> Déjà venaient frapper mes oreilles timides
> Les affreux cris du chien de l'empire des morts;
> Et les noires vapeurs et les brûlants transports
> Allaient de ma raison offusquer la lumière. [3]

All his later poetry is touched with this dark solemnity. Even at his beloved Fontenay he is troubled by the thought that soon he must leave his sunlit fields and the cool shade of his beautiful elms, 'pour ce manoir terrible et sombre.' [4] On the death of his dear friend, La Fare, Chaulieu bitterly confesses the futility of philosophy and reason:

> A leurs belles leçons insensé qui se fie!
> Elles ne peuvent rien contre le sentiment.
>
> .   .   .   .   .   .
>
> En vain je cherche encore ici quelque agrément;
> Mes jours sont un tissu de douleur et de peine. [5]

He thinks of suicide, but instinctively recoils: even that solace is denied him:

> Pourquoi n'osé-je rompre une fatale chaîne
> Qui m'attache à la vie et m'éloigne du port?
> Il faudrait du moins que le sage,
> Quand il le veut, eût l'avantage
> D'être le maître de son sort. [6]

The cold, didactic Louis Racine, the translator of *Paradise Lost*, could not resist a little sneer at Chaulieu in his *La Religion*:

> Du mépris de la mort il me parle à chaque pas;
> Il m'en parlerait moins s'il ne la craignait pas.

But this frigid bigot was only half right. Chaulieu was too sensitive

---

[1] Well-known Jansenists.   [2] *Sur la Mort*, 1708.   [3] *Sur la Mort*, 1695.
[4] *Louange de la vie champêtre.*   [5] *Sur la mort de La Fare*, 1712.   [6] ibid.

a poet to despise death.   Louis Racine, though he never, I think,
had heard of our Dr. Young, offers a certain chill resemblance to
the author of the *Night Thoughts*, in the orthodox, long-winded
verses that compose *La Religion*.   Of Pope he had certainly read the
Essay on Man, which he attacks with pedantic gusto.

Louis Racine, as has been said, translated Milton's great epic
and did it very badly.   But his introduction contains the first
important French criticism of *Paradise Lost*.   It is not my intention
here to enlarge upon the interest displayed by the eighteenth-
century French in Milton, or to rediscuss Voltaire's views on him.
All this ground has been very completely covered by Mr. Telleen
in his classic work on Milton in France, and again in a paper [1]
by that fine scholar, the late Professor J. G. Robertson.   As my own
inquiries lead to the conclusions reached by the latter I cannot do
better than quote them.   'In spite of the interest which the French
showed in Milton, the influence of this poet on French literature
remained small and unimportant. . . . It was clear that Milton's
genius had, after all, no very firm hold on the French mind of the
eighteenth century.'   Yet, it is worth noting at this point, that
Dupré de Saint-Maur's translation of *Paradise Lost*,[2] which was more
popular than Louis Racine's wooden rendering, was twice reprinted
before the Revolution.   Besides these, there appeared during the
same period four other versions of this poem, two in prose and two
in verse.   That an epic written by a Protestant should have found
many readers amongst orthodox Catholics does not necessarily
mean that they overlooked his heresies.   In its great campaign
against irreligion, the Catholic Church welcomed pious literature
of every sort.   This alarmed the *Monthly Review*,[3] and provoked a
long article on the insidious nature of Popish propaganda ending
with this warning: 'What can tend more to reconcile Protestants
to the errors of the Church of Rome than the plausible manner in
which its clergy unite their friendly labours with ours against the
common enemy of religion in general?'

Like Racine, Lefranc de Pompignan was concerned with Biblical
subjects, and also contributed to that generous stream of odes
inspired by the Psalmists and Prophets which runs uninterrupted
through the century.   Despite Voltaire's merciless gibes, however,
there is a rare sincerity and sensibility in Lefranc that is quite absent

---

[1] *Proceedings of the British Academy*, vol. iii (1908).
[2] First published in 1729.   Reprinted in 1755 and 1772.
[3] Vol. xxxi (1764).

from the poetry of the younger Racine.[1] More perhaps than any
one, Lefranc de Pompignan, by his ceaseless attacks on the freethinkers, bolstered up the shaky prestige of the Church.

The terrible earthquake which destroyed Lisbon in 1755 made a
profound impression on the French imagination. Voltaire, as we have
seen, profited by this to deliver a fierce attack on the Leibnizian
conception of the world order. But for others, like Lebrun, it was
the occasion for a fanatical outburst of Old Testament frightful-
ness.[2] His *Ode sur la ruine de Lisbonne* pictures the catastrophe as
a dramatic manifestation of the divine anger at human pride.
With ill-concealed and grisly relish Lebrun thus apostrophizes
our globe:

> Un jour les siècles, en silence
> Planant sur ton cadavre immense,
> Frémiront encore de terreur.

Lebrun was absolutely classic in his style, but when we read him
there is no longer any need to wonder why Young's *Night Thoughts*
later received a hearing. In his minatory, melodramatic vein he
appealed, as did Young, to those who extract a perverted delight
from sensational poetry whatever their class or creed. Lebrun has
been scurvily treated by his countrymen, in particular by M.
Potez, who asks us rather unfairly to condemn the poet because the
man's life was scabrous. Lebrun rants unconscionably, and, with
a very hazy notion of the genius of Pindar and Homer, professes
to imitate them. His real masters are Crébillon and the darker
Voltaire. Lebrun cherished a violent, physical conception of love,
which he regards as a desperate refuge from the obsession of death:

> Préviens l'affreuse nuit qui n'aura point d'aurore.
> Entrelaçons nos bras, et qu'un lien si beau
> De la Parque jalouse affronte le ciseau.[3]

Yet by its intensity his eroticism is immensely remote from that
of boudoir poets like Bernis, Gentil-Bernard, and Malfilâtre. On
the other hand, he is too brutally passionate to be classed with his

---

[1] See his *Ode à Louis Racine sur la mort de son fils*, which has some fine lines:
> 'Loin de tes yeux, loin de sa mère,
> Au sein d'une plage étrangère,
> Son corps est le jouet des flots . . .

[2] See Warburton on the same topic. In a letter to Hurd he said: 'The affair
of Lisbon has made men tremble, as well as the Continent shake from one end of
Europe to the other. To suppose these desolations the scourge of Heaven for
human impieties is a dreadful reflection; and yet to suppose ourselves in a forlorn
and fatherless world, is ten times a more frightful consideration.'

[3] *Élégies*, i. 4.

mortal enemy, Baculard d'Arnaud, that 'gravedigger of Parnassus,' whose *Lamentations de Jérémie* and versified *drames* justify his claim that he invented the *genre sombre* in France. None of these could have written anything so realistic as the following lines from Lebrun's *Élégie faite pendant une hémorragie violente*:

> Le sang baigne à longs flots mes lèvres palissantes,
> Et mon Tibulle échappe à mes mains défaillantes.
> De mon sein oppressé les pénibles efforts
> Tourmentent la vie et brisent ses ressorts.
> Dans ce combat mortel et de glace et de flamme
> Fanni seule, Fanni retient encor mon âme.

Eighteenth-century France had her first real contact with our poetry in 1758 when Colardeau published his adaptation of Pope's *Eloisa*. The great success of this poem, said Palissot,[2] was due to its theme. 'This passion of Eloïsa's is one of the most beautiful monuments we possess in the history of love. Ovid would have envied the barbarous race which gave it birth. Nothing, indeed, is more touching than this contrast between love and religion, which the poets of antiquity did not know.' There are other reasons. The theme was already well known in France through the famous, but apocryphal,[3] *Lettres d'une Religieuse portugaise*, which first took the country by storm in 1669 and since that date had been constantly reprinted. As early as 1699, these love-letters had already been published in the same volume as a French translation of the original letters from Abelard to Eloisa, which were almost equally popular.[4] Prévost and Tencin had treated the same theme with overwhelming success; and by its very nature it was bound to appeal to a variety of tastes. The *philosophes* were able to exploit it for anti-clerical purposes, the fashionables of the Crébillon school felt that the convent setting lent an added piquancy to eroticism, and the sentimentalists found in it an ample source of pathos.

As a comparative study in Anglo-French poetic taste it is interesting to watch what Colardeau does with Pope's *Eloisa*. Writing with an eye on the censor, the Frenchman is, of course, obliged to modify Pope's grim picture of convent life. Convents are no longer

> Shrines where their vigils pale-ey'd virgins keep,

---

[1] *Élégies*, i. 6.
[2] *Mémoires littéraires. Œuvres*, vi. 369.
[3] See my article on the subject in *Mod. Lang. Rev.*, vol. xxi, p. 2.
[4] *Recueil des lettres galantes et amoureuses d'Héloïse à Abélard, etc.* (Amsterdam, chez François Roger, 1699).

but retreats,

> Où les cœurs asservis à de sévères lois,
> Vertueux par devoir, le sont aussi par choix.

Omitting, no doubt as blasphemous, the line:

> Where mix'd with God's his lov'd idea lies,

Colardeau gives a subtle Racinian turn to the original, and shows us an Eloisa who has sinfully sacrificed duty, honour, and virtue to nature:

> Je cède à la nature une indigne victoire,

but who, unlike Racine's Phèdre, has at least the solace of tears. The French poet does not yet dare to follow Pope in his romantic

> Fame, wealth, and honour, what are you to love?

This, in his vague, diluted rendering, becomes:

> Abélard, qu'il est doux de s'aimer, de se plaire!
> C'est la première loi, *le reste* est arbitraire.

The hot, brutal passion of the verses in which Eloisa describes the physical frustration of her lover and her own persistent longings, is dwelt upon by the French poet with lingering pleasure.   Pope writes:

> Still on that breast enamour'd let me lie,
> Still drink delicious poison from thy eye,
> Pant on thy lip and to thy heart be press'd;
> Give all thou canst—and let me dream the rest.

Colardeau's lines express the same thoughts with greater gusto, and perhaps with greater audacity.

> Viens, nous pourrons encor connaître le plaisir,
> Le chercher dans nos yeux, le trouver dans nos âmes.
> Je brûle; de l'amour je sens toutes les flammes.
> Laisse-moi m'appuyer sur ton sein amoureux
> Me pâmer sur ta bouche, y respirer nos feux. . . .
> Quels moments, Abelard! les sens-tu? quelle joie!
> O douce volupté, plaisir où je me noie!
> Serre-moi dans tes bras, presse-moi sur ton cœur . . .
> Nous nous trompons tous deux; mais quelle douce erreur!
> Je ne me souviens plus de ton destin funeste,
> Couvre-moi de baisers. . . . Je rêverai le reste.

When Pope is romantic in the English sense; when he speaks of:

> These moss-grown domes with spiry turrets crown'd,
> Where awful arches make a noon-day night,
> And the dim windows shed a solemn light,

or, again, in the famous passage ending:

> Deepens the murmur of the falling floods,
> And breathes a browner horror on the woods,

Colardeau is obviously disconcerted. I doubt, indeed, whether he quite understood these lines, so foreign are they to the stock vocabulary at his command. He, therefore recasts the whole passage in the classic manner. The effect is curious.

> But o'er the twilight groves and dusky caves,
> Long-sounding aisles and intermingled graves,
> Black Melancholy sits, and round her throws
> A death-like silence and a dread repose,

becomes,

> L'ennui, le sombre ennui, triste enfant du dégoût,
> Dans ces lieux enchantés se traîne et corrompt tout . . .
> Il sèche la verdure, et la fleur pâlissante
> Se courbe et flétrit sur sa tige mourante.
> Zéphyr n'a plus de souffle, Écho n'a plus de voix,
> L'oiseau ne sait plus que gémir dans nos bois.

It is difficult here to criticize Colardeau, who is really doing his best for Pope with the limited means at his disposal. Sometimes, indeed, he really improves on his model—for example, by mercifully omitting Pope's luscious and treacly references to the unfading roses of Eden, the wings of seraphs, and the heavenly harps. Rightly, too, he condenses the rhetorical ending of *Eloisa* with its

> . . . roseate bowers,
> Celestial palms and ever-blooming flowers,

all of which smacks of stale incense and bad Milton.

The poetic splendour of the Catholic ritual, exquisitely suggested by Pope in the following lines, completely eludes Colardeau:

> When from the censer clouds of fragrance roll,
> And swelling organs lift the rising soul,
> One thought of thee puts all the pomp to flight;
> Priests, tapers, temples, swim before my sight.
> In seas of flame my plunging soul is drown'd,
> While altars blaze and angels tremble round.

Not until Chateaubriand shall we find in the French language words sensuous enough to express such images.

With all its limitations, Colardeau's rendering of *Eloisa* is more than adequate. Less romantic, however, than Pope, he has no words to express the Gothic eeriness, the sinister hush which broods

over the English conception of the nunnery. From Prévost or
Tencin he has learned how to picture the tragic conflict between
sensual and divine love. But his Eloisa, even in her most passionate
moments of abandon, remains always rational. In Pope's poem
the heroine's words and gestures, tinged as they are by the prevailing atmosphere of sombre, religious awe, acquire therefrom
a hallucinatory intensity and colour. This tone is absent from
Colardeau's version. In her moments of erotic abandon, the French
Eloisa is superb; the Eloisa haunted by remorse and by visions of
death is less convincing. To reproduce the strange sweetness of
Pope's elegiac and susurrant lines:

> Come, sister, come! it said or seem'd to say,
> Thy place is here; sad sister, come away,

is clearly beyond Colardeau's powers. The words:

> Arrête, chère sœur, arrête, me dit-elle,
> Ma cendre attend la tienne, et ma tombe t'appelle,

are in the nature of an anticlimax. In a word, when the Frenchman moves outside the sphere of rational passion or sensibility
into the twilight of the supernatural, he is ill at ease, because he is
confronted by a new array of poetic values. Pope, classic though he
was on the surface, had behind him all the pressure of a tradition
shaped by Shakespeare and Milton. For him, the cloister suggested
not merely tragic love and renunciation, but something deeper and
darkly mysterious. It is this penumbra which Colardeau's imagination cannot pierce, however hard he tries.

Colardeau's *Héloïse* was successful, not because it was adapted
from an English model, but because it blended with the mood of
Prévost's novels and the *drames* of men like D'Arnaud. French
literature, as we have seen, was already darkly tinted with tragic
sensibility. But the success of Colardeau prepared French readers
for a new species of poetry, the *héroïde*, the main theme of which
was, originally at least, that of unhappy love. One can best grasp
its nature by regarding it as the poetic counterpart of the *drame*
in which the general tendency was to substitute prose for poetry.
'There are subjects,' wrote Dorat, the most famous composer of
héroïdes, 'of which we are daily deprived by the delicacy of our
manners, the timidity of our taste, and the conventionalism of our
stage. These are the especial property of the *héroïde*.' It is significant that Fréron, commenting on Dorat's famous *Lettre de*

Barnvelt, an *héroïde bourgeoise* based on Lillo's play, discovers no peculiarly English flavour in it. On the contrary, he says in his *Année littéraire* (1764) : 'The author reveals the same genius as does Racine in his *Phèdre,* and the abbé Prévost in *Manon Lescaut,* i.e., the art of making crime interesting, and, if one may use the expression, of exciting horror and pity ; of making us in some sense pardon Barnvelt for the horrible murder with which his unnatural hands are fouled, and of forcing us to pity him.'

The object of the *héroïdes* was to harrow the sensibilities by the portrayal of passionate and pathetic love. In these dramatic narrative poems, one seems to rediscover, indeed, something of the tone of the medieval *romans courtois*; except, of course, that the *héroïdes* are very eighteenth-century in their sophistication. Colardeau chose as the subject of his *Armide à Renaud,* the unhappy passion of a pagan girl for a crusader who abandons her from a sense of religious duty and knightly honour. Here, however, I do not think that he was directly indebted to medieval literature. More possibly he had just read Voltaire's *Tancrède,* or novels like Madame de Grafigny's *Lettres d'une Péruvienne* (1747) and Godard d'Aucour's *Mémoires turcs* (1753), both of which deal with the conflict between love and religion.

Reference has been made to Lillo's *George Barnwell,* on which Dorat based his *Lettre de Barnvelt dans sa prison à son ami Truman* (1763). His purpose here was, he says, to 'familiarize the French with the cup of Atreus,' [1] or, less grandly, to accustom them, by the medium of narrative poetry, to scenes from which in the theatre they would have recoiled in horror. This was easier to say than to do, and immediately we find Dorat nonplussed by the irrational ferocity of Millwood. Unable to understand how a civilized race like the English could tolerate such a character, the French poet assumes that they did so because of the beauty of the final scene where Barnwell takes farewell of his friend, Trueman. To conform to French tradition, he tries to invent some rational motive for Barnwell's crime and for Millwood's savagery. Not for a moment did he see her as a demonic figure, as the self-appointed avenger of women's wrongs. Of all the French writers who encountered Millwood, only Prévost understood this aspect of her character. Dorat's Millwood (Fani) is completely incredible. She appears at one moment as a meek little *midinette*; then, suddenly possessed by ambition and by a spiteful desire for revenge on Thoroughgood,

[1] A reference to Crébillon the elder's *Atrée et Thyeste.*

she urges her lover to kill his uncle. Diderot [1] angrily damned this sudden metamorphosis as absurd, and he was right. Dorat, he said, should have pictured Millwood's 'incredible and frightful address,' the cunning with which she plays on Barnwell's sentimental chivalry and infatuation. 'The failure to depict this scene of mingled horror and voluptuousness was not,' he added, 'due to any lack of colour in the French language, but in the poet's mind.' And again, like Fréron, he is reminded of Racine. 'Remember all the Clytemnestra scenes in Racine.' But what enraged Diderot most was Dorat's omission of the famous reply made by Trueman to Barnwell's frenzied assertion that, had Millwood ordered, he would have murdered his friend also.

> *Trueman.* We have not yet embraced and may be interrupted.
> Come to my arms.

'A man must be made of stone,' exclaimed Diderot, 'if he does not burst into tears at these words.'

Dorat softens Lillo's melodrama by sparing us the uncle's musings on death, which are in the best manner of the gloomy Dr. Young. He respects his reader's anguish, too, by making Thoroughgood recognize and pardon his assassin before he dies. Yet, on the other hand, when he describes the old man's death it is in language of almost physical brutality.

> Ma bouche en sanglotant s'attache à sa blessure,
> De son sang qui bouillonne et sort avec murmure
> Je comprime les flots, j'en repais ma douleur,
> Et des flots de ce sang ont coulé dans mon cœur.

This haemorrhagic style reminds one of the elder Crébillon or of the Pindaric Lebrun. And when Dorat pictures Barnwell's hallucinations in the scene where he is haunted by the spectre of Thoroughgood with its open, blood-streaming wounds, he is certainly not inspired by Lillo or by any English writer. Here we have the manner of Voltaire in *Mahomet* and in *Sémiramis*, the bloody realism of which derives from Greece and not from England. What in the first place attracted Dorat to Lillo was not the latter's display of brooding, melodramatic horrors but his moralizings on friendship. Most of all, it was the opportunity to present, what Lillo never suggests, a prolonged psychological conflict between passion and gratitude. That explains why, in order to complicate the dilemma, Dorat makes Fani offer George the choice between killing

---

[1] *Correspondance de Grimm, Diderot et Raynal.*

I

his uncle and her suicide. Such a form of moral blackmail did not cross to the Englishman's mind.

In the *Lettre de Zéïla à Valcour* and in the *Réponse* to it, Dorat felt the need, he says, to give his public 'a few roses' after the 'cypresses of *Barnvelt*.' Now the *motif* is one of pathetic resignation. Once again, however, his model is English, a tale from the *Spectator*, called 'Inkle and Yarico.'[1] Thomas Inkle, an English trader, was saved from savages by a West Indian girl whom he seduced. Thomas's business instincts, however, got the better of his love and he sold Yarico into slavery, demanding, moreover, a double fee because she was with child. Naturally, Dorat omits this revolting episode, and, in deference to the existing craze for the Orient, transports the setting to Turkey. The result is a curious pot-pourri in which we can descry several of the ingredients that went to make up the popular taste of his age. He first offers a glowing picture of primitive life *à la Rousseau*. Valcour, the hero, and Zéïla, the French Yarico, make love in a dreamland peopled by *bons sauvages*. Zéïla hunts in order to feed and clothe her lord; whilst the latter, in a theatrical, Fragonard setting, plays with the tangles of her hair:

> Près de nous, mille oiseaux, jaloux de nos transports,
> Entremêlant leurs becs et leurs plumes nouvelles,
> Au-dessus de ta tête ils agitaient leurs ailes.
> Que de tendres baisers dans ce riant séjour,
> Multipliés, donnés et rendus par l'amour!

But Valcour tires of Zéïla and abandons her. For though she is the incarnation of primitive artlessness, her French lover's natural goodness has been tainted with the disease of modern civilization, ennui:

> L'ennui, ce monstre affreux, dont la triste présence
> Répand sur les objets une sombre influence.

Here and elsewhere, Dorat insists on defining what he means by ennui, and if we are to understand the eighteenth-century origins of French Romanticism, and, above all, discover in what way it differs from ours, it might be well to listen to his words. *L'ennui* reflected a literary taste, and produced a kind of literature somewhat akin to the English, but, as Dorat points out, it is not the same thing as *la tristesse anglaise*. To confuse the two is to adopt a fallacy that

[1] Dramatized under this title in 1742, probably by Weddel. I notice, too, from a playbill in a Richmond shop-window, that it was later turned into an operetta and produced in Richmond Theatre in 1795.

has been perpetuated by every well-known student of comparative literature. The melancholy that came into our poetry with the Pope of *Eloisa*, with Young, Hervey, and the Wartons, is something deeply embedded in the Anglo-Saxon character: the melancholy born of French eighteenth-century ennui is a new growth, much more sophisticated and more *raffiné*. To cite Dorat: 'Like our neighbours we must have massacres, rapes, death's-heads, ghosts cloaked in their shrouds, in short, all the exaggerations of Drury Lane, in order to revive our burnt-out souls and excite minds that are empty rather than melancholic. For we affect sadness when we are merely bored. It is this incurable ennui which has been the object of so many vain attacks, and it arises essentially from our mode of life. Disgust germinates always in the womb of facile sensuality. Surrounded by pleasures, we are driven to cadge for sensations without the aid of which we are no longer able to experience pleasure. . . . After every outburst of convulsive gaiety we are quite surprised to find ourselves sinking back into sadness. We seek more novel, more attractive, and more sophisticated pleasures; then, to escape the ennui of laughter we rush off to weep deliciously at the performances of *Ariane*, *Alzire*, and *Mahomet*.'

The *Lettre de Zéila* and its sequels reveal as in a prism the subtle nuances of a taste born of ennui, which is a restricted form of French pre-Romanticism. Zéila is seduced and deserted by her lover; captured, then persecuted by an amorous sultan. Inevitably, therefore, we are offered a voluptuous, exotic picture of the interior of a harem. Zéila's letters, tenderly reproachful, tell pathetically of her child and appeal to her lover's parental instinct. Finally, in Valcour's father we have the moralizing humanitarian of Diderot's *Père de Famille* and Sedaine's *Philosophe sans le savoir*. On his deathbed he learns his son's secret and orders him to rejoin Zéila. Greuze might have painted this tableau—the erring son who must repair the wrong he has done to society or suffer the curse of the stern old patriarch whom he will never see again. How differently Hogarth would have handled it!

In Dorat's *Lettre de Comminges à sa mère* we have a more sombre note, derived from Madame de Tencin's famous novel. The heroine is separated from her lover by a family feud, but disguises herself as a Trappist novice so as to live beside him. Comminges, who has accidently wounded her husband, is expiating his crime in this gloomy refuge of dead souls. The poem, which smells of the charnel house, is written in the convulsive style affected by Diderot and other composers of *drames*. Here is what Fréron describes as the 'beau moment,' the crisis of 'surprise, terror, and tears':

> Je m'entends appeler par ces sons effrayants,
> Lamentable signal de nos derniers moments.
> J'accours. . . . Dieu! quel spectacle, et que vais-je t'apprendre?
> Je trouve un malheureux étendu sur la cendre;
> Nous l'environnons tous; l'observons de plus près.
> Dans l'ombre de la mort je distingue ses traits. . . .
> Je crois le voir encor . . . J'en frissonne. . . . Ma mère . . .
> C'était . . . le croiras-tu? . . . Ce même solitaire,
> C'était . . . . Tu me préviens; tu vois mon sort affreux . . .
> C'était Adélaïde . . . expirante à mes yeux.[1]

In an *héroïde* based on the exquisite *Lettres d'une Religieuse portugaise*,[2] Dorat veers once more from sombre tragedy to pathos. But these poems did not all deal with the theme of unhappy love. In one collection, for instance, we find a poet mourning over Philoctetes in the island of Lemnos; another weeps at Milton's blindness, or pathetically recounts the death of Socrates. Any subject, if it were sufficiently harrowing, found favour with the select public which sought a relief from its ennui in these works. The *héroïdes* were emotional cocktails, as swift in their effect and as evanescent; unworthy, in any case, to be compared for one moment with the true and noble wine of fine poetry. They were concocted obviously for the unhappy few, the minority of sensation-hunting intellectuals who could afford to pay for these costly 'slim volumes,' with their expensive engravings by Longueil after Eisen.[3]

Dorat's poetry draws its energy from several currents of ideas; from the frank sensualism of *libertins*, like Chaulieu, whose pagan *joie de vivre* is sharpened by the vision of death; from the growing awareness of the beauties of a sensibility which as yet had not passed beyond the stage of refined sensationalism; from the contemporary lust of moralizing on social questions, and finally, from the powerful fallacy consecrated by Rousseau, that civilization had poisoned the wellsprings of natural human goodness. However, there is in Dorat very little trace of sincere feeling, though no one more violently attacked the *philosophes* for their lack of sentiment. He did, however, accustom a section of the French public to the accents of a language in which later poets were destined to express true

---

[1] *Année littéraire*, vii (1764).

[2] *Lettre d'une Chanoinesse de Lisbonne à Melcour, officier français* (1770).

[3] I should say that the editions were limited, but in view of our general lack of information as to the habits of eighteenth-century French publishers, my statement is based on conjecture.

and profound emotions. Moreover, he reinforced and extended the reputation of writers like Prévost and Tencin by recasting their themes in a form that appealed to the fashionable *ennuyés*, to the very class which was afterwards attracted by the 'barbarian' Shakespeare, the 'delicious' Dr. Young, and the 'romantic' Ossian.

Such was the result of the first important impact made by an eighteenth-century English poet on the poetry of eighteenth-century France. Pope's *Eloisa* cannot, then, be said to have changed the direction of French tradition; but it aided indirectly to release and strengthen certain tendencies which, although present in other literary genres, had not yet succeeded in entering poetry. It is true that the *héroïdes* enjoyed only a brief vogue. Yet the mood that inspired them was to colour the verse of a new generation. Neither Pope nor any other foreigner begot this new poetry, though Pope was one of its accoucheurs. And one fact is undeniable. It is that this contact with the author of *Eloisa* was much more fertile than any other achieved in this century, for the simple reason that Pope's mode of expression made him easier of access to the French than any other of our poets.

But before discussing Thomson, Young, and 'Ossian,' whose influence on the poetry of eighteenth-century France has been, I feel, much over-rated if not actually misunderstood, we must form some clear idea of the general tone of English and French poetry before the seventies, before the period which roughly marks the wane of the vogue for *héroïdes* and the dawn of interest in the three English poets just mentioned. The poetry of the *héroïdes* was bad, no doubt, but their authors performed at least one good service. They battered one more breach in that bastion of prejudice called *le bon goût*, which, for nearly a century, had resisted all efforts to free the French poetic spirit from the tyranny of false classicism.

CHAPTER IX

THE DAWN OF ENTHUSIASM

WHEN the English and French critics of the early eighteenth century have occasion to use the word 'enthusiasm' or 'enthousiasme,' it is almost always in a tone of thinly-veiled contempt. In literature, enthusiasm was regarded as a vice; in philosophy, it was despised; in religion, barely tolerated. Very broadly speaking, then, the ultimate object of all the attacks levelled against classicism by the English and French poets of the new movement was really to vindicate the rights of enthusiasm and of imagination in literature. For this desire to remove the stigma from enthusiasm was not, of course, confined to poetry. In France it was reflected in the novel and in the theatre before eventually spreading to poetry. In England, on the other hand, the defenders of enthusiasm seem to have invaded every branch of letters almost simultaneously. Indeed, our tragedy, degenerate though it was from the aesthetic standpoint, can scarcely be said ever to have lost its fire; so brief is the interval between the plays of Dryden and Otway and those of Rowe, Southerne, and Lillo. On the other hand, half a century separates *Paradise Lost* from *Eloisa* and the *Elegy on an Unfortunate Lady*, the publication of which, in 1718, really announces the revival of enthusiasm in English poetry.

Thomas Parnell, who was unfortunately later used by Goldsmith as a whip to scourge the 'innovators' whose 'pristine barbarity' he deplored, actually gave a powerful stimulus to the new spirit. The dreadful and pedantic *Essay on the Different Styles of Poetry* should not be held up against the author of the *Hermit* and the *Night-Piece on Death*. Parnell is, no doubt, flashy, echoing the melodramatic Rowe, but he has the stuff of which true poetry is made. With him we move into a new climate:

> A fresher green the smelling leaves display,
> And glittering as they tremble, cheer the day.[1]

Parnell's moods are various, capricious, and sudden; but almost always they are beautifully expressed. He is a poet of disconcerting

---

[1] *The Hermit.*

230

transitions, passing swiftly from facile melodrama to the poetry
which sheds rays of dark light:

> Ye Ravens! cease your croaking din,
> Ye tolling clocks! no time resound
> *O'er the long lake and midnight ground.*[1]

In the brief compass of the *Hermit*, there is as much evidence of a
true sensitiveness to natural beauty as in the whole of Thomson's
Seasons.   Thomson could not have written these lines:

> Down bend the banks, the trees depending grow,
> And skies beneath with answering colours glow;
> But if a stone the gentle sea divide,
> Swift ruffling circles curl on every side;
> And glimmering fragments of a broken sun,
> Banks, trees, and skies, in thick disorder run.
>
> .   .   .   .   .   .
>
> The morn was wasted in the pathless grass,
> And long and lonesome was the wild to pass.

Here is the impression of a mind which, like Proust's, could see
nature as something alive, excited, and never still.   Thomson, on the
other hand, usually persists in viewing nature as part of an immutable
theological system.   That is why his *Seasons* reminds us always of
one of those didactic mid-Victorian landscapes, with a factory and
a church in the background and a fox-hunt careering across the
meadows, just to emphasize the fact that nature, though beautiful,
is strictly subordinated to the hierarchic order as represented by
Commerce, the Church, and what Dickens's lady in red called Blood.

One of the most fascinating qualities of our English poets is their
astounding unevenness.   When a French poet is bad he is consistently
so; but I know of no eighteenth-century bard save, perhaps, Shenstone, who betrays this geometric constancy in his badness.   Our
Wordsworth is, of course, the classic example of such irregularity.
Mention of Wordsworth, by the way, recalls Mallet, who also wrote
an *Excursion* (1728), though, to be quite fair, there is no further
analogy between the two poets.   In Mallet we can already guess
from various reminiscences what an important and baneful role will
be played by Shakespeare in the revival of enthusiasm.   Here is *Macbeth* seen through the distorting glass of the eighteenth-century mind:

> Here night by night, beneath the starless dusk,
> The secret hag and sorcerer unblest
> Their sabbath hold and potent spells compose,
> Spoils of the violated grave.[2]

[1] My italics.   [2] *The Excursion.*

With growing uneasiness, too, we realize what will be the effect of Milton's epic imagination coupled with the style of the *Essay on Man* upon minds like that of Dr. Young. This is again from Mallet:

> When unknown suns to unknown systems rise,
> Whose numbers who shall tell? stupendous host!
> In flaming millions through the vacant hung,
> Sun beyond sun and world to world unseen,
> Measureless distance unconceived by thought.[1]

Mallet, who was a bad poet, knew, however, where good poetry lurked. He was one of the first to sense the beauty of our old ballads, and we can forgive him a great deal for the second stanza of his *William and Margaret* (1724):

> Her face was like an April morn
> Clad in a wintry cloud,
> And clay-cold was her lily hand
> That held her sable shroud.

The rest of the ballad is sufficiently dreadful. As an example, take the regal imbecility of this couplet, which Wordsworth, at his ineptest, never bettered:

> Pale William quak'd in every limb,
> And raving left his bed.

Yet it is no paradox to say, even after this, that Mallet foreshadows Gray. After all, pearls do grow in oysters and water-lilies in mud. Take the lines:

> . . . And now in lowing train
> Were seen slow-pacing westward o'er the vale
> The milky mothers; foot pursuing foot,
> And nodding as they move.[2]

But for the Thomsonian 'milky mothers' we have already the opening chord of the famous *Elegy*, except, of course, that Mallet, having shot his bolt, tumbles backwards head over heels into sheer bathos.

The Warton brothers, in particular Thomas Warton, have been rightly praised for the capital part they played in helping to bring back enthusiasm and imagination to our poetry. Neither was a great poet, but both were acutely alive to the beauties of fine poetry, and, moreover, both possessed a rare knowledge of our ancient literature. Thomas Warton's *History of English Poetry* (1774–87) remained, indeed, for more than half a century our only authoritative survey of English poetry. Its influence on the poets of the latter

---

[1] *The Excursion.* [2] *Amyntor and Theodora* (1747).

years of the eighteenth century was profound. Joseph Warton,
the editor of Virgil and, above all, of Pope, showed not merely, as
Johnson rather heavily put it, 'how the brow of criticism may be
smoothed,' but also exploded the legend that no one could be a
great classical scholar and at the same time a connoisseur of our
native or 'Gothic' poetry. His *Enthusiast* (1740), though couched
in the stiffly classical language of the day, strikes a blow for poetic
freedom, and he bluntly asks:

> What are the lays of artful Addison,
> Coldly correct, to Shakespeare's warblings wild?

In further poems, in the *Ode to Liberty*, the *Ode to Fancy*, and in
Solitude, we catch the same accent of romantic admiration, no longer,
indeed, for 'Shakespeare's warblings wild,' but rather for the
gloomy, eerie, and 'Gothic' aspects of Shakespeare and Milton
and Pope:

> Let us with silent footsteps go
> To charnels and the house of woe,
> To Gothic churches, vaults and tombs,
> Where each sad night some virgin comes
> With throbbing heart and faded cheek
> Her promised bridegroom's urn to seek.[1]

It must be remembered, however, that these verses were written
after his brother Thomas had given the lead with his *Pleasures of
Melancholy*, published in 1747, but written when the author was
nineteen—a remarkable essay for a youth. When Joseph wrote
defending enthusiasm he meant by enthusiastic poetry simply poetry
which is spontaneous and imaginative. But when we read the
Pleasures of Melancholy it is clear that for Thomas Warton, and for
many others, enthusiasm has acquired a more definite connotation
and now signifies something much more complex. As a reflection
of the various poetic moods and manners of English romanticism
about the middle of the century, the *Pleasures of Melancholy* deserves
to be read. It displays all the nuances of the new poetic spirit,
the dominant feature of which was a morbid hankering after the
sensational. With loving care Thomas Warton amasses his hoard
of images and impressions, all of which are tinged with sombre
gloom. With the passion of the collector he lets these dark jewels
slowly trickle through his fingers. We know already what are to
be the themes of the young Romantics. They are catalogued here
in verses that would be excellent if they were not so reminiscent;

[1] *Ode to Fancy.*

*I

Gothic, owl-haunted, ivy-covered towers; December's foggy glooms; the Eloisan 'religious horror' of the convent; Macbethian witches; the dusk and shadows of silent woods; the rush of distant waters; the dim and solemn light that filters through cathedral naves; the pathetic melancholy of Juliet and of Otway's Monimia; the chill stillness of frozen solitudes; the spectacle of ruined grandeur, of grass-grown streets once thronged by 'tradeful' merchants; forests that saw the dread, mystic rites of ancient Druid priests.   Not until much later, when he was writing his *History of English Poetry*, did Warton reach farther back in our literature for his inspiration, and by that time, thanks to Hurd, Macpherson, and Percy, the vogue for troubadours, skalds, and bards was already launched, and Gothic melancholy was no longer the only source of poetic inspiration.

Thomas Warton was, however, one of our first eighteenth-century writers to see the poet as a brooding, introspective, and solitary soul; as an artist who is content to penetrate the secrets of nature, and thence to extract impressions which he can relate in words of lasting beauty.   Unlike Young and Gray, Thomas Warton is untouched by social or religious considerations.   Solitude for him is the poet's sanctuary, the retreat where he can alchemize nature into beauty.   Warton evokes the past, for example, not in the moralizing vein of his fellows, but simply because it harbours 'the fair image of ancient things.'   No doubt

> Severer Reason forms far other views
> And scans the scene with philosophic ken,

but that for Warton is not the concern of the poet.   The same mood is visible in his poem *The Suicide*, which is fine only in the stanzas picturing the sinister wildness of the madman's gestures.   When the poet begins to moralize on suicide his fire vanishes, and he shambles along in the conventional track which leads to religion and metaphysics.   Thomas Warton's first inspiration was his best.   *The Crusader* and *The Grave of King Arthur* (1777) smell of the lamp save for an occasional flashing line like:

> . . . the ponderous spear,
> Rough with the gore of Pictish kings.

The strange enthusiasm for images of death and decay which we find in the *Pleasures of Melancholy* was shared by many English poets of this period.   To express it, they had recourse largely to the vocabulary of Shakespeare, Milton, Pope, or Spenser, though many affected to invent new words of their own.   'I have known some of my contemporary poets,' said Walter Harte,[1] 'who have coined their one or two hundred words a man; whereas Dryden and Pope devised only about three score words between them, most of which turned out to be perennials.' To some extent this was comprehensible, since these necromantics approached their themes in the didactic and moralizing temper so typical of their age. Moreover, in their zeal to be original and strange, they misused the words they stole from the old poets. Wrenched from their pristine settings, these jewels from Shakespeare and Milton still shone forth bravely in their new lack-lustre environment: but their original, secret fire had vanished.

The arch-priest of the necromantics was Dr. Edward Young, who, as has been seen, was largely responsible for the masses of 'sacred and devotional' poems, 'elegant extracts' from which continued until mid-Victorian times to sadden and twist the souls of English children. I refer to such abominations as the sadistic outpourings of the 'gentle' Dr. Watts, to Dr. Porteous's popular *Ode to Death*, Fitzgerald's *Thoughts upon Death*, and Cotton's *Visions for the Entertainment and Instruction of younger Minds*. In this rational and philosophic age, those who were struggling to shake off the gyves of a false, classic convention soon found that the quickest escape to poetry of a more imaginative and spontaneous sort could best be contrived by way of religion, since no race which, like ours, was brought up on the Old Testament could readily or openly frown upon an enthusiasm dedicated to the service of the Almighty. James Thomson was well aware of that fact when he disguised his pagan enthusiasm for nature by constant references to the Protestant Author of all these beauties. Hence it is, too, that so many of our most fiery odes of this epoch are inspired by the Psalmists and Prophets. Hence, too, on the other hand, the quantities of metaphysical poems concerned with the Deity and His attributes; with the abstract vices and virtues and with the mystery of immortality. The necromantics really staged a minor counter-Renaissance. For not only did they attack the formal imitations of classicism, which was an excellent things, but also the humanistic spirit of the classic writers, and that was very serious. Writers like Young and Hervey tried to substitute for the humanistic attitude towards life the old Calvinist conception which regards life, not as an experience fraught with joy and beauty, but as a stolid preparation for death and immortality. Whilst claiming to destroy Deism because, as they

[1] The author of *Religious Melancholy*, an 'emblematical elegy.'

insisted with some truth, it was a product of reason, they defended religion largely by rational arguments when, of course, the proper appeal was to the heart. So, on the whole, their poetry, though fiery and minatory, lacks sensibility; when these men write of the mystery of death and of the resurrection it is with none of that white-hot sincerity which in a Marlowe erupts in dazzling lines like:

> The stars move still, time runs, the clock will strike,
> The devil will come, and Faustus must be damned.
> Oh, I'll leap up to my God; who pulls me down?
> See where Christ's blood streams in the firmament. . . .

The necromantics had fanaticism of a sort, but it was cold and rational; they had sensibility of a kind, but it was pale and watery, like Dr. Young's moon.

Now Robert Blair, whose *The Grave* (1743) was written before the *Night Thoughts*, ought not to be associated, as he always is, with these moralizing versifiers. Blair is a necromantic, too. He sets out to 'paint the gloomy horrors of the tomb,' but not to preach sermons on immortality. Yet incidentally, by the sheer brutality of its images, *The Grave* produces a much more vivid impression of death than a hundred sermons. There is a directness of utterance and of observation, a pictorial power in Blair which takes us back to the old Scots poets of the Dunbar type. His age found his expressions 'mean' and 'vulgar,' and recoiled in genteel horror from lines like these:

> The sickly taper,
> By glimmering thro' the low-brow'd musty vaults
> (Furr'd round with mouldy damps and ropy slime),
> Lets fall a supernumerary horror
> And only serves to make thy night more irksome.

or the Villonesque violence of his picture of beauty in decay:

> Methinks I see thee with thy head low laid,
> Whilst, surfeited upon thy damask cheek,
> The high-fed worm, in lazy volumes roll'd,
> Riots unscared.

Here, of course, was the reality of death unadorned by the sentimental prettiness of lilies, cypresses, and moonlight. Nor did Blair's contemporaries relish his sardonic gibes at the pomp and ceremonial of eighteenth-century funerals, or the bitter taste of his sneers at wealth and tyranny. Yet this Scotsman is the only poet of the sombre school who displays originality; for his visions of death are direct and intense, unblurred by any memories of Milton. Had

Blair given us more, he would assuredly have taken a unique place amongst the poets of his country.

When, like poor Collins, an English poet has the ill luck to die insane his critics automatically divide into two groups. One hails him as a genius, and discovers strange beauties in what strikes the other simply as the vapours of a disordered mind. Dr. Johnson, who resembles so many supremely sensible people in that he was haunted by an inordinate fear of madness, wrote of Collins's poems that they were 'the productions of a mind not deficient in fire, nor unfurnished with knowledge either of books or life, but somewhat obstructed in its progress by deviation in quest of mistaken beauties.' Not for one moment did it occur to him that Collins might have written his verses when he was eminently sane, or that the 'mistaken beauties' heralded the dawn of a new poetry which, by its very imaginativeness, lay outside the scope of the Johnsonian understanding. Collins, though prone to melancholy, is anything but a necromantic. He is a Romantic striving to free himself from the wheel of classic tradition. When, as in the *Ode to Evening*, he has the courage to surrender to his own genius, Collins creates poetry which is not only melodious but is clouded in mystery. And this mystery results from a real experience tinged and softened by fancy. As an imaginative poet, however, he is essentially lacking in power and sweep. That is to be observed in the odes to *Pity*, *Fear*, and *Liberty*, and even, too, in *The Passions*. For in these he imitates the Thomsonian trick of labelling the abstract virtues and vices with banal and prosaic epithets; like 'brown Exercise'; 'Sport leap'd up and seized her beechen spear'; 'Cheerfulness, a nymph of healthiest hue'; 'pale Melancholy,' etc. Now no one minds this in Thomson, who was born like that; but it angers one to see such a beautiful poem as the *Ode to Evening* trailing a last stanza of this sort:

> So long, regardful of thy quiet rule,
> Shall Fancy, Friendship, Science, rose-lipp'd Health,
> Thy gentlest influence own,
> And hymn thy favourite name.

It is like creating an exquisite flower and calling it Mrs. Sadie Goldstumpf!

But this is rankly ungrateful to the sensitive poet 'of the quick, uncheated sight.'[1] who could surprise the smallest stirrings of nature; whose fancy could focus her moods and landscapes in

[1] *The Manners.*

phrases bright and perfect as drops of morning dew. The 'weak-ey'd bat,' the 'quaggy moss'; the 'hum of sedgy weed'; the 'cool gleam' have all that 'novelty of extravagance,' as Johnson sourly puts it, which fill the reader of eighteenth-century poetry with surprise and delight. To meet them after rising from Glover's *Leonidas* or Akenside's oddly-named *Pleasures of Imagination* is to see the first spring flowers on a Canadian prairie. Collins was a frustrated Romantic. One has but to read the ode to John Home,[1] the *Epistle on Hanmer's Shakespeare*, or *Hassan* to realize that he was born out of his proper time. Fifty years later he would have found a spiritual *milieu* which, by its warmth and sympathy, would have released the rare perfumes that lay half-frozen in his poetic soul. The chill rationalism of his own day seldom favoured such an effluence. But there is enough in Collins to make us long for more.

Collins, for all his timidity and lack of imaginative strength, helped along with Thomas Warton to accustom the English public to the sound of Romantic poetry. Had he possessed, like Gray, the doubtful gift of tinging his Romanticism with social sensibility, his true merit might have been more quickly perceived. But Collins lived in an era when what he called 'enthusiastic heat' was looked at askance. There were plenty of critics to admire it in a Shakespeare, as interpreted by a Garrick; or in Milton, because of the sacred nature of his theme. But then Shakespeare and Milton were not moderns. Now, Gray's odes *To Spring*, *To Adversity*, *On a Distant Prospect of Eton College*, and the *Elegy* (1751) were well and even warmly received. But, as Warburton tells us, the *Progress of Poesy* and *The Bard* 'were not understood any more than were Shakespeare and Milton.' [2] Johnson, who was apparently vexed at not being able to attribute Gray's violence to insanity, confessed rather naïvely that he could not find any meaning in the first stanza of the *Progress of Poesy*. As usual, he was here on the side of the majority. Indeed, his enormous popularity with his age lay precisely in this wonderful knack of articulating the prejudices of the ordinary man in language graven with the seal of judicial authority.

For various reasons, the *Elegy in a Country Churchyard*, although a fine poem, did not give offence to traditional taste. It achieved, in fact, the miracle of pleasing nearly everybody. Its melancholy was

[1] *Ode on the Popular Superstitions of the Highlands of Scotland Considered as the Subject of Poetry.*

[2] See also Gray to Hurd in the *Correspondence*, ed. Tovey, ii. 346 (1757): 'In short, I have heard of nobody but a player and a doctor of divinity that profess their esteem for them—Garrick and Warburton.'

expressed in the mellifluous and haunting manner of Pope's *Elegy to the Memory of an Unfortunate Lady*, and the whole poem was imbued with that social warmth, as Thomson might have phrased it, which could not fail to appeal to humanitarians. Never did it depart, like the *Bard* or the *Progress of Poesy*, from the avenue trodden out by reason and common sense through the dark forests of enthusiasm. Yet the *Elegy* lives. Its conventional discreetness is redeemed by qualities that were new to our poetry, and, like *The Bard*, though in a different way, it is an historic poem. In their broodings on death, the necromantics betrayed no genuine sensibility, and in their pulpity, hell-fire threatenings there is not a trace of Gray's humanity. Gray does not harp on immortality, but he made his age aware for the first time that there is a poetic grandeur in the spectacle of a humble life devoted to unflagging labour. And if he speaks of death it is really to look backward on life, not forward to eternity. Life is the real theme of the *Elegy*: death is the poet's coign of vantage, the high hill from which life can be seen in its true and proper perspective. Gray took his age away for a moment from 'the madding crowd's ignoble strife' to a new and quiet place; and thus he gave it a new conception of society, a saner vision of humankind. With no hysteria, and with none of that exaggeration or maudlin sentimentality which was later to colour the democratic literature of the nineteenth century, he spoke nobly and tellingly of the place of the common man in the social scheme. No one in our period, save Cowper, viewed the people with so much sense and sensibility. For the first time, too, a great poet frankly confessed a wistful longing for human sympathy, and lyrically expressed the intolerable anguish of loneliness, the poet's haunting fear lest he should pass from this world's scene unnoticed and unwept. The closing stanzas harbour a plea for poetry and foreshadow the romantic idea of the poet visualized as the champion of oppressed humanity, the sweet mediator of divine compassion. And in expressing this idea Gray reveals an exquisite tact and sincerity that rob his poetry of all taint of sentimentality.

The *Pindaric Odes* appeared in 1757, one year after Burke's illuminating *Philosophical Enquiry into the Origin of our Ideas of the Sublime and Beautiful*. Once again literature and philosophy reflected, but independently, the trend of a national spirit. Gray seems never to have mentioned Burke's work, but we know from his remarks on Hutcheson what he thought about the aesthetic 'jargon' of that philosopher and of Shaftesbury. The fact that he ignored

Burke has little significance, since poets do not create their poetry by reading treatises on the nature of beauty. What is interesting, however, is to observe Burke unerringly plotting the course that was to be followed by our English poets for two generations. Naturally, he had not seen the *Odes* when he wrote: 'In reality a great clearness helps but little towards affecting the passions, as it is in some sort an enemy to all enthusiasm whatsoever.' And not till the lapse of a decade, when English poets went medieval and Ossianic, could Burke realize how prophetic had been these words: 'In general, the languages of most unpolished peoples have a great force and energy of expression; and this is but natural. Uncultivated people are but ordinary observers of things, and not critical in distinguishing them; but, for that reason, they admire more, and are more affected with what they see, and therefore express themselves in a warmer and more passionate manner.'

Burke's *Enquiry* was more than the *Art poétique* of eighteenth-century England, since an *Art poétique*, like a royal commission, simply reaffirms a long-established practice. Burke anticipated, without directing, the poetic art of England from 1760 to the close of the Romantic period. This thinker, whose influence on Diderot, though never acknowledged, was at a certain period most profound,[1] thus indirectly helped to sap the prestige of neo-classicism in France. The Diderot of the sixties, even if he recanted later, once shared Burke's conception of the 'sublime' in art. To Burke great poetry is impressionistic. It appeals to the senses, not by the symmetry and clarity of its form, but by its lack of form, by its suggestion of the infinite. Sublime poetry, by its very obscurity, inspires awe; it is gigantic, rugged, cleft with silences more eloquent than the noblest rhetoric. And even when it is not sublime but merely beautiful, it retains the same careless disorder and is fraught with the same melancholy.

The *Progress of Poesy* was suggested to Gray by his reading of Pindar. It may not be Pindaric, but in these exultant marching lines, which astounded all by their audacity, he carries on the lyric spirit of Shakespeare and of Milton. With the *Progress of Poesy* 'the rich stream of music,' so long frozen into immobility by the cold chill of common sense, begins once more to surge and eddy. Soon, favoured by the genial warmth of a new spiritual climate, swelling in volume and in power, it will hurl itself down the crags of Romanticism, crashing into a thousand fractured hues of light and sound

---

[1] See M. Folkierski's luminous *Entre le Classicisme et le Romantisme*.

and ecstasy.   But as yet with Gray, we see only the early swirlings
of the flood, the mere promise of future delights:

> Nor second he, that rode sublime
> Upon the seraph-wings of Extasy,
> The secrets of th' abyss to spy.
> He passed the flaming bounds of place and time:
> The living Throne, the sapphire-blaze,
> Where Angels tremble while they gaze,
> He saw; but blasted with excess of light,
> Closed his eyes in endless night.

Here we are in mid-stream, moving magnificently.   But in other
places there is still a hint of frostiness, as in the lines:

> Man's feeble race what ills await,
> Labour and Penury, the racks of Pain,
> Disease, and Sorrow's weeping train,
> And Death, sad refuge from the storms of Fate.

But why cavil?   In the superb stanza where Gray celebrates the
glory of Milton, he achieved immortality for himself.   The pedants
shuddered and sneered at

> . . . blasted with excess of light,
> Closed his eyes in endless night.[1]

but here was great poetry, sure and strong enough to brush aside
the peevish carpings of the rationalists.

The same trumpet note rings out in the *Bard*.   Once more, in
language wedded to the grandeur of his thought, Gray brings back
to our poetry something of its lost, high valour.   Here he reminds
us, not of Milton or Shakespeare, but of the wild, menacing spirit
of the *makars*.   Here is the strong, pulsing beat that Burns will later
introduce into his *Bannockburn*; a relentless, grim, weaving measure
through which we seem to hear the clack of Fate's loom.   It is
heard again in the *Fatal Sisters*, but with a new accent of primitive
ferocity, a savage, Northern, gloating cry.   In this, as in the other
Norse-inspired *Descent of Odin*, Gray tapped a well which was to
refresh the imagination of a generation.

The achievement of Gray, Collins, and their fellow-poets did
not, of course, bring a sudden revolution.   Such *débâcles* do not
occur in literature.   That is an illusion which is invariably cherished,
however, by the triumphant and ungrateful rebels who walk into
the captured citadel.   Like the nineteenth-century Romantics, they
are apt in their excitement to forget the debt that they owe to
the pioneers, to the Wartons and the Grays.   In reality, the road

[1] The *Critical Review*, vol. iv (1758), found this 'a puerile conceit unworthy of
the author.'

leading from the arid desert of pseudo-classicism to the splendours
of the new Parnassus was beset with obstacles that necessitated
many digressions and apparent backslidings.   Imagination, in order
to win her freedom, had to pay lip homage to her bastard but powerful sisters, Science and Humanitarianism, who also claimed liberty
as their goal.   A confirmed classic like Glover, for instance, was
sure to win the popular applause, because of the public-spiritedness
and the love of liberty which he flaunted in his epic *Leonidas* (1737)
and in his *London, or the Progress of Commerce* (1759).   Yet so far as
poetry is concerned, Glover never budged an inch from the old rut.
The true enemies of poetry were men like Mark Akenside, who
employed the language of an enthusiasm that was not always
wholly uninspired in order to discredit the work of the incipient
Romantics.   For in the *Pleasures of Imagination* (1744), the fame of
which spread to the Continent, Akenside sought to ridicule what
he called the 'monkish horrors' of the new poets, accusing them
of perpetuating 'the poisonous charms of baleful Superstition.'
His own ideal he expresses in the lines:

> Genius of ancient Greece! whose faithful steps
> Well pleas'd I follow through the sacred paths
> Of Nature and of Science . . .

The trouble was that the majority of Akenside's readers were also
'well pleased.'   The exquisite lines where Thomson had evinced
a true and delicate appreciation of natural beauty were passed
over by most of his successors, who followed Akenside in admiring
the dreadful passages offered up to the scientists and theologians.
It is, therefore, with no surprise that we find in the *Pleasures of
Imagination* descriptions of this sort:

> . . . the sunbeams gleaming from the west
> Fall on the wat'ry cloud, whose darksome veil
> Involves the orient; and that trickling shower
> Piercing through every crystalline convex
> Of clustering dew-drops to their flight oppos'd,
> Recoil at length where concave all behind
> The internal surface of each glassy orb
> Repels their forward passage into air.

Yet when he chose, Akenside could see nature outside a test-tube:

> The brown woods wav'd; while ever-trickling springs
> Wash'd from the naked roots of oak and pine
> The crumbling soil; and still at every fall
> Down the steep windings and the channel'd rock,
> Remurmuring rush'd the congregated floods
> With hoarser inundation.

There were too many Akensides in the eighteenth century:

> Intent with learned labour to refine
> The copious ore of Albion's native mine,[1]

or, in a word, to pass the 'crude' imaginings of Shakespeare, Milton, or Spenser through the filter of reason and morality. Francis Fawkes, for instance, castrated Gavin Douglas's dark and brutal *May* and *Winter* in the following typical manner:

> The hollow ditches, swelled with sudden rains,
> Poured a black deluge on the lowland plains,
> And every road received its sordid flood,
> Swam with the swell and stiffened into mud.[2]

which sounds like Burns's *Tam o' Shanter* recited by the top girl in an English preparatory school. Henry Brooke, who, though he died insane, can hardly be called a great poet, similarly bowdlerized Chaucer's *Man of Law's Tale*. Ironically enough, even the classics themselves were not immune from this eighteenth-century mania for rational emendation. Mason's *Elfrida* (1752), 'written on the model of the ancient Greek tragedy,' is a delicious example of a conventional poet's attempt to improve on the taste of Aeschylus. Here is an elegant extract from one of the choruses:

> Hail to thy living light,
> Ambrosial Morn! all hail thy roseate rays,
> That from young Nature all her charms display
> In varied beauty bright,
> That bids each dewy-spangled floweret rise
> And dart around its vermeil dyes.

The later 'Druidic' fire of the same author's *Caractacus* is equally impressive.

By the sixties the curiosity in regard to old English poetry had become epidemic. On every hand one could espy contented and scholarly poetasters grubbing in the pleasaunces of medieval and of Elizabethan literature. Unconsciously following the path traced out by Burke, they moved farther afield, ransacking the libraries for old ballads and for the epics of Scotland, Ireland, and Scandinavia. It is not easy to-day to appreciate the exact nature of this extraordinary interest in ancient poetry. To a great extent

---

[1] *The Remonstrance of Shakespeare.*

[2] Compare with the original (Prologue to Douglas's *Aeneid*, Book VII):
> 'The dowy dichis war all donk and wait,
> The law vaille flodderit all wyth spait,
> The plane stretis and every hie way,
> Full of fluschis, doubbis, myre and clay.'

it was quite superficial, a mere craze like the contemporary mania for Gothic furniture and Chinese pagodas. It was also scientific, and, in fact, began with the historians and philosophers, who, ever since the end of the seventeenth century, had been interested in the psychology of the 'natural' or 'primitive' man. That, as we shall see, was the chief reason why Macpherson's Ossian appealed to the French intelligentsia. But, for poets like Gray and Chatterton, the old poetry was a genuine source of aesthetic delight. Gray, the *Gelehrte*, knew perfectly well that Ossian was a fraud, yet Gray, the Romantic, strenuously shut his ears to the philologists. Underneath all this can be discerned the fermenting of that idealism which was the Romantic protest against the cult for Newtonian reason. The vogue for 'Gothic' literature, if we may use the word in its loose eighteenth-century sense, was, of course, the denial of that fetish of the rationalists called Perfectibility or intellectual Progress. It involved the eternal question: 'What is human nature?' The wedge of Cartesianism had separated mind from matter, since Descartes conceived human nature as pure intelligence. The Newtonians conceived it as pure sensation. Between these two extremes there was room for another view, that of the Rousseauists who saw man as 'une âme sensible,' the English 'man of feeling.' Primitive man, they said, was naturally good, though his original perfection had been slowly corrupted by centuries of civilization. The idea was an old one, but interpreted by genius, it acquired a devastating force and range of influence, the vibrations of which can still be perceived in our world to-day. Yet before Rousseau, the claims of feeling, as opposed to those of reason, had been urged in eighteenth-century France and England. So, to many who now for the first time gained contact with medieval poetry, it seemed as if Rousseau were right. Here, at last, surely was true beauty, the spontaneous reactions of men who were all feeling, untainted by rational inhibitions, to the world around them. Here was the true Promethean fire, the original flaming torch of poetry before it was dimmed by its passage through the gusty corridors of civilization.

Had these enthusiasts listened more closely to Jean-Jacques Rousseau, they would have heard a warning to the effect that the hands of the clock cannot be put back. Only Romantics could hope in the eighteenth century to see Nature and God with the faith and candour of the Middle Ages. But then they *were* Romantics, and that is where Rousseau's wisdom went astray. By sheer feeling, by sheer imagination, the nineteenth-century poets did eventually attain to a fresh and unsullied vision of Nature and of God. And thus we have the lyric poetry of Romanticism, which is glorious, so long as it remains unsmirched by romantic morality, romantic politics, and romantic theology. For art is not, as Voltaire said, just nature; it is the power which seems to create a gorgeous illusion about nature. It is not an imitation of nature; it is what reconciles us to the nature we see through the eyes of reason. Poetry neither improves nor reforms life; it illuminates it with a soft radiance in which every hard and ugly contour disappears. It does to life what a sunset does to a town in the Black Country. And if, after the sunset fades, we whine illogically that poetry distorts reality and that we have been cheated, the obvious answer is, to paraphrase Proust, that realistic art is not a mere summary of lines and surfaces, a mere cinema vision of life. Now what the poets of our period were beginning in a fumbling way to see, was that reality in poetry, as in every art, is essentially subjective. It is a unique affinity between the sensations which hourly besiege our soul and the memories that seethe within it. When, as Proust suggests, that affinity can be expressed in language of appropriate beauty, poetry is born, art is born. Poetry *is* a reality, though it masquerades as a glorious illusion. But that is only so long as we insist in dredging it through the reason. Absorbed by the soul and by the senses— presuming that the two can thus be separated—this apparent illusion emerges as a profound and vital reality. To such a conception of poetry the eighteenth century did not attain; though by emphasizing the importance of sentiment as a criterion of aesthetic beauty, the poets of this age had already dragged themselves half out of the slough of rational convention. The windows were now open, and men could directly experience the tonic effects of light and air. First England, followed much later by France, stepped through these windows into the garden. But gardens, however artfully wild, but poorly resembled the natural *milieu* which must have surrounded and inspired the poets of olden times. So, very soon the bolder spirits of the dying eighteenth century found their way to the mountains and to the sea. And because these things were to them a revelation, the visions they recorded were luminous and beautiful too.

CHAPTER X

GARDENS AND GRAVEYARDS

The new cosmopolitan spirit of eighteenth-century France vented itself in a series of crazes. Of these, perhaps, the most durable was the vogue for 'English gardens.' It was also one of the most significant, because it expressed in a concrete and picturesque way that reshuffling of aesthetic values which is visible in the drama and in the poetry of the period. It is, indeed, no exaggeration to say that the evolution of the eighteenth-century French garden reflects a profound spiritual change. Is not every man who designs a garden a creative artist, in the sense that he gives to raw material a form which corresponds to his ideal of beauty? A rational, utilitarian age will find complete aesthetic satisfaction in a garden composed of shrubs, vegetables, and fruit-trees arranged in neat, geometric patterns. In a more rational and less material age, the designer may strive to express the ideas of nobility and order by means of long, straight avenues of elms or chestnuts, interrupted by circular lakes, adorned with classic fountains. This was, in fact, the fashion immortalized by Le Nôtre at Versailles, and, like the architecture of the period, it imaged the Cartesian ideal of order and of reason. It symbolized the conquest of nature by human intelligence. On a smaller scale such, too, was the type of garden favoured by Englishmen at the close of the seventeenth century, except that, with the accession of William of Orange, it was modified by the Dutch spirit, which tended to subordinate the spaciousness of classic beauty to materialism. From Holland, too, came the odd custom, still to be met with in Kew and elsewhere, of clipping evergreens into the shape of grotesque animals, birds, and what not. The Dutch were also responsible for the vogue for the sombre yew, a tree that lent itself admirably to the whims of the topiarist. Good Whigs, we are told,[1] imitated the king's gardens, and imported many plants from Holland. In the *Critical Review* [2] there is a good description of one of these 'Gothic' gardens, as they were later called by those who saw in them a fancied likeness to the sombre

[1] *The World* (1753). [2] Vol. xliv (1777).

poetry of the necromantics. 'The mansion house was immured in front by a high, dead wall; and surrounded by a moat well-covered with duck-weed, by sculptured pyramids, giants and monsters in yew. The garden was laid out with the utmost formality, presenting to the eye the unbending line, the acute angle, the trim alley, the tonsil'd box, the scrolled parterre, the dead-brown terrace, the gloomy labyrinth.'

Pope and even the classic Addison were amongst those who laughed at such monstrosities and pleaded for a more natural type of garden. Thomas Whately, in his famous *Observations on Modern Gardening*, propounded the metaphysical principles on which gardens should be laid out; and finally Kent, a great practitioner, showed how gardens could be made charming by introducing a certain wildness and irregularity. It was this revolutionary who created the style afterwards known in French gardening circles as English, though our gardeners, like our poets, did not rest content with mere disorder. Sad to say, however, Kent had been forestalled by a Frenchman. The *Année littéraire*,[1] in reviewing a French translation of Whately's book, pointed out that Dufresny, the comptroller of Louis XIV's grounds at Versailles, 'used to work at his ease only on an uneven terrain; he had to have obstacles to conquer, and when nature did not give him any, used to make them. Out of a flat and regular site he would construct a hilly one, so as to vary the objects, he said, and to multiply them.' Dufresny left several specimens of his art, which was in advance of contemporary taste. Thus, when he submitted to the king a plan for transforming the Versailles gardens it was rejected as too unconventional and too costly.

With the publication of Chambers's book on Chinese gardens, the departure from classic regularity became even more marked. The line of beauty, like Hogarth's, was now sinuous. Moreover, tiny rivers, miniature bridges, and mazes were to be found cheek by jowl with Gothic grottoes and little temples dedicated to the classic gods. A French writer, Marnésia,[2] looking back on our horticultural taste, wrote: 'In an enlightened century, the English have too often planned their gardens as Shakespeare wrote tragedy in a barbarous age. They have mingled the sublime and the low, the abject and the noble, the finicky and the grand; and sometimes the hideous.' Save for the typical reference to Shakespeare, Marnésia was perfectly right. In our gardens, as in our poetry, there was a queer conflict of tendencies. The moralizing, meta-

[1] 1771. [2] *Essai sur la nature champêtre* (1787).

physical spirit of Young completed the chaos. Placards, embellished with serious sentiments from the *Night Thoughts* and similar poems, were hung on trees. In a Surrey garden,[1] for example, there was a temple of death containing a lectern at which one could read and meditate to the mournful clank of a passing-bell. Paths, symbolizing the avenues of life, led to an iron gate beyond which lay the valley of the shadow. Two stone coffins flanked the entrance. In one reposed the skeleton of a highwayman; in the other the remains of a prostitute. But this by no means exhausted the attractions. Passing on, one arrived at a great alcove with a statue of the Unbeliever dying in the agonies of fear and despair, surrounded by the evil books that had led him to this sorry plight, books written by Toland, Tyndale, and Collins. The orthodox Fréron, who read this account in an English paper, admired the general idea, but remarked that 'a man must have a soul deeply absorbed in melancholy to have imagined such a garden.'

Neither in their gardens nor in their nature poetry were the French disposed to copy the excesses of our English enthusiasts. Marnésia,[2] and he echoes the general opinion, is full of respect for our energy, our initiative, and our love of liberty, but adds that this new genre, though created by the English, can only be brought to perfection by 'a nation accustomed to go back to the principles of the arts, a nation whose observant and delicate mind has made her taste sure.' Naturally, there were a few excessive Anglomaniacs who cluttered their gardens with weird and symbolic edifices. Delille, in his famous poem, *Les Jardins* (1780), condemned this

> . . . amas confus
> D'édifices divers prodigués par la mode,
> Obélisque, rotonde, kiosk et pagode;
> Ces bâtiments romains, grecs, arabes, chinois;
> Chaos d'architecture, et sans but et sans choix. . . .

In the same way he laughed at the cult for artificial ruins, vestiges of which may still be found at Kew and at Bagatelle.

> Mais loin ces monuments dont la ruine feinte
> Imite mal des temps l'inimitable empreinte,
> Tous ces temples anciens récemment contrefaits,
> Ces débris d'un château qui n'exista jamais,
> Ces vieux ponts nés d'hier et cette cour gothique,
> Ayant l'air délabré sans avoir l'air antique.

In gardens, as in poetry, eighteenth-century French taste was

---

[1] *Année littéraire* (1767), 'Description du Jardin de M. Tyers à Denbies.'   [2] loc. cit.

shaped by the traditional genius of the race. Very early in the period, Chaulieu, it will be remembered, had discreetly tinged his verse with sadness, and by evoking images of death, had accentuated its voluptuousness. Now Delille, who quotes him admiringly, suggests that the smiling beauties of the perfect garden may be enhanced by 'the melancholy sight of urns and tombs dedicated to friendship and to virtue.' This was quite in harmony with the aesthetic ideas of Diderot, who might, indeed, have penned the following words: 'These contrasts of sensations that are half voluptuous and half sad, by agitating the soul in opposite ways, always produce a deep impression.' However, one can discern in the new French gardens the influence of another tendency which was inspired by Rousseau's *Nouvelle Héloïse*. Less gloomy and less violent than Delille's, the *jardin anglais* of the Rousseauists, whilst favouring the picturesque disorder of certain English models, was designed to express emotions that were dreamier, more wistful, and more definitely humanitarian. The *Hameau* at Trianon is an excellent example of what I mean. Winding paths invite the friend of man to solitary meditations on the charms of a vanished golden age; and the snug rusticity of its thatched farm-buildings recalls the ideals of the *bons seigneurs* who sighed for a happy patriarchal state where every one, from Louis XVI down to the humblest citizen, was to find peace and joy in a return to the occupations of primitive man—to that sunny Arcadia where Adam delved and Eve span. Such, indeed, was the ideal that shaped the most celebrated gardens of the time, at Auteuil, Bagatelle, Limours, Montreuil, and Maupertuis, all of which were created by aristo-cratic admirers of Jean-Jacques Rousseau, with, of course, the help of English gardeners. Some political historians, armed with all the 'facts' as to the economic situation of France in those years, have made short work of these and similar aspirations. Knowing so much more than did any Frenchman at the eve of the Revolution, they impute to the nobles of that period a prescience which they did not, naturally, possess. In consequence, the creation of these beautiful gardens is made to seem like the cynical, brutal gesture of blasé egoists. In reality they were absolutely and pathetically sincere. Their gardens, like their poetry, artificial as they now appear to us, expressed the sensibility of a group educated in the school of classic convention and striving to shake off the bondage of reason. The ideal to which they aspired has been well described by Marnésia, who was one of their number:

Sous un paisible ciel, je connais une terre
De fertiles coteaux, un vallon solitaire;
Ils n'attendent que vous; ils seront les jardins
Que l'Éternel créa pour les premiers humains.
Sur la croupe d'un mont dont la pente adoucie
Vient mollement se perdre au sein de la prairie;
Où le chêne robuste et l'orme vigoureux
Opposent un rempart à l'aquilon fougueux;
Où le printemps fleuri s'empresse de sourire,
D'où l'automne fécond à pas lents se retire.
Ce songe, hélas, si vain, du charmant âge d'or
La sensibilité le renouvelle encor.

But these lines were written in 1787, and we must now retrace the origins of this new attitude to the poetry of nature.

Thomson's *Seasons* (1726–8), was ideally framed for the object which it eventually achieved. But for Thomson, indeed, our Romantic renascence, which was, in essence, the recovery of our lost sense of natural beauty, might easily have been delayed. Possibly, too, its aesthetic integrity might have been compromised by the intrusion of too many didactic elements. Of these, there are remnants enough in Wordsworth to inspire us with a salutary sense of gratitude towards Thomson, and his imitators whose poetry acted as a safety valve for what the author of the *Seasons* called 'philosophic melancholy.' The *Seasons* pandered to all the moralizing tendencies of the age, the majority of which were absolutely incompatible with poetry as we now conceive it. Somehow or other the eighteenth century had to work these out of its system; this it did through the Thomsonians, the last of whom was Wordsworth, who, however, had one foot in a new and promised land.

The prevailing tone of Thomson is heavily and artificially classic. He is in turn a pedant, a preacher, and a demagogue. But he is also sometimes a great artist. We yawn our weary way through scientific disquisitions on the nature of frost and the origin of rivers; with this terrible Scot we clamber over rocks, whilst he, with his little geological hammer, chips off topazes, opals, and amethysts for our inspection; we flounder through 'reluctant streams,' and do obedient homage with him to the 'efflux divine' of 'the prime cheerer light'; we listen to his windy, impassioned descriptions of what the 'foodful earth' can do when she erupts, quakes, or sideslips; we admire the angry elements, and are duly impressed by the sad stories of the lovers killed by lightning and of the poor man frozen to death in winter snows. All this the reader of the *Seasons* must endure, and his patience will be well repaid. For suddenly he will light upon passages that recall the dewy freshness and fragrance of Milton's *L'Allegro*. And in those lines where Thomson describes a summer dawn—the great test of the nature poet's mettle—he discovers a quality which is absolutely his own. In the *Allegro*, the dawn-dispelling things are sounds; the song of the lark, the crow of cock, the hunter's horn. Thomson surprises an earlier dawn: and, before man or beast have time to wake, he has caught, in a few swift, unerring strokes, the secret rhythm of that lovely moment, of that ineffable, brief silence when only nature breathes.

> The meek-ey'd Morn appears, mother of dews,
> At first faint-gleaming in the dappled east;
> Till far o'er ether spreads the widening glow,
> And from before the lustre of her face
> White break the clouds away. With quickened step
> Brown Night retires. Young Day pours in apace
> And opens all the lawny prospects wide,
> The dripping rock, the mountain's misty top
> Swell on the sight and brighten with the dawn.
> Blue, through the dusk, the smoking currents shine.

That is a painter's vision. Here Thomson reveals the painter's quickness of observation, sense of colour and of perspective, coupled with the poet's power to suggest movement. What he lacks is the superb imaginative force of Shakespeare:

> Full many a glorious morning have I seen
> Flatter the mountain-tops with sovereign eye,
> Kissing with golden face the meadows green,
> Gilding pale streams with heavenly alchemy.

And Thomson's absence of 'heavenly alchemy' is always most flagrantly visible when he deliberately imitates Shakespeare. For example:

> But yonder comes the powerful King of Day,
> Rejoicing in the east. The lessening cloud,
> The kindling azure, and the mountain's brow
> Illum'd with fluid gold, his near approach
> Betoken glad.

Thomson's misfortune was to have been born in a philosophic, didactic, scientific, mawkishly sentimental epoch. Usually, he sees nature through the windows of that age; then he is unbearable. Occasionally, however, he achieves a more personal vision, and then he is exquisite because he gives us impressions untarnished by conventional moralizings. But alas! how rare with Thomson is 'the cool, the fragrant and the silent hour,' the hour of pagan, Keatsian, and sensuous abandon. From nearly every page of the *Seasons* the pulpit philosopher wags his pow at us; Thomson the artist is very seldom glimpsed. Yet those glimpses leave us with the impression of one who with all his faults did something really fine. He rent the veil and let the morning sun filter in through into the dusty rooms of a prosaic century.

Thomson's successors were slow to discover his essential poetic beauties. For a long time they admired in him what we detest— his dreadful faculty of deforming natural loveliness by clothing it in the jargon of the theologian or scientist. As we have seen, even a genuine poet like Collins imitated Thomson here. So did many lesser ones. England, even after the *Seasons*, was far from being a nest of singing birds: it resembled rather a nest of owls. Few of her poets dared to look nature straight in the eyes and tell what they saw there. Gray was often distracted by humanitarian problems. So were Goldsmith and Cowper. John Cunningham, a minor poet, gives us flashes of a brief, but direct and complete experience, in his *Day* and *Evening*.

> From the low-roof'd cottage ridge
> See the chattering swallow spring;
> Darting through the one-arch'd bridge
> Quick she dips her dappled wing.

and

> Now the hermit howlet peeps
> From the barn or twisted brake;
> And the blue mist slowly creeps
> Curling on the silver lake.

Equally picturesque, equally minute, but even more superficial is the manner of John Scott, the Quaker poet, who wrote *Winter Amusements in the Country*:

> And oft steep dells or rugged cliffs unfold
> The prickly furze with bloom of brightest gold.
> Here oft the redbreast hops along his way
> And midst grey moss explores his insect prey;
> Or the green woodspite flies with outcry shrill
> And delves the sere bough with his sounding bill.
> Or the rous'd hare starts rustling from the brake,
> And gaudy jays incessant clamour make.

There was a good deal of this rustic verse in the eighteenth century. It is pleasant and charming, yet lacks the fervour of poetry.

Now in France, with the notable exception of La Fontaine, no poet had shown any feeling for external nature since the *Pléiade*. The neo-classic writers, as is well known, fought shy of lyricism and thus gave us no nature poetry. Cartesianism had pitchforked external nature from French literature, but she did not come back with the proverbial rush. Her return, which was very gradual, was achieved by way of Virgil and eighteenth-century rationalism, an odd combination. Thomson had also a hand in the process, but here, again, this English influence played a secondary and not a leading role. Two Latin poems, René Rapin's *Hortorum Libri* (1665) and J. Vanière's *Praedium Rusticum* (1707), enjoyed a great vogue, and throughout the eighteenth century were constantly reprinted. These didactic and almost botanical works eventually drew attention to the fact that Virgil had written the *Georgics* as well as the *Aeneid*. Besides, the increasing demand for instructive literature brought forth poetical treatises, not merely on commerce and science, but on rural economy. Of such *poèmes champêtres*, as they were called, one of the most popular was Rosset's *L'Agriculture* (1774). However, the French enthusiasm for agriculture really dates from 1764, the year in which the government, abandoning its traditional policy, allowed the free export of wheat and began to encourage farming. The physiocrats, who had been most active in the polemical battle that led to this revival, now seriously turned their attention to rural matters, under which category they included the *poèmes champêtres* and Thomson's *Seasons*. To be quite fair, they had every reason to be disgusted with the old artificial stuff imitated from the classics, which had hitherto passed muster as pastoral poetry. These *bergeries* repeated the insipidities of Racan, Segrais, and Fontenelle, but they still had admirers. In 1772, for instance, we find in Calvel's *Encyclopédie littéraire* a solemn account of the 'rules' governing the composition of pastoral verse. The action of the idyll or eclogue, says this authority, must always take place in a rustic or solitary spot: the bank of a stream, a field enamelled with flowers, a grotto, and, very occasionally, at the seaside. The fields, too, must always be green, the myrtles ever in leaf, and the trees always in fruit. Statues of Pan or Venus may be sprinkled about. The characters, of course, are invariably shepherds and shepherdesses, but they must be prosperous. No suggestion of poverty can be allowed to enter the poem. The object of this sort of poetry, we are told, is to depict the golden age, 'that happy time when man must have been naturally good.' To-day,

Calvel strikes us as merely funny; yet when he wrote there was a real danger lest nature poetry, in the true sense of the term, might never have a chance to develop. The rationalists regarded *la poésie champêtre* as useful propaganda designed to entice landowners back to their estates; while misguided admirers of Rousseau's *Nouvelle Héloïse*, like Calvel, yearned to revive their moribund pastoral poetry and to sentimentalize over rustic joys. The craze for gardens, too, was symptomatic. A garden, as T. E. Brown brightly said, 'is a lovesome thing, God wot.' It can also, God wot, be very hideous, like the one in Surrey described by Fréron. Eighteenth-century France, too, could show some rather terrible specimens. For, though with many Frenchmen this love of gardens might, and did, lead to a love of nature, it was for many others a mere fashionable whim. The latter regarded the garden as a substitute for nature and emulated those Englishmen who, finding that mountains and forests were disturbingly huge, preferred to contemplate them in miniature within their own grounds. Rousseau himself was not an Alpine enthusiast, and the scenery he describes is usually very pastoral and civilized. One powerful *motif*, however, which was later to inspire beautiful poetry, is to be discovered in his *Nouvelle Héloïse*. It is the romantic conception of nature as the reflection of man's deepest emotions; of nature viewed as the ideal setting to romantic passion. Readers of this novel will recall the magnificent passage describing the meeting of Saint-Preux and Julie at Meillerie, a superb nocturne which found no worthy echo in French poetry till Lamartine. Rousseau's own generation did not associate nature with unbridled passion but with a sensibility that was sincere although mawkish. Like the winding walks of their gardens, the woodland paths and valleys were haunted by *âmes sensibles* rapt in solitary meditation or engaged in earnest moral converse. As Marnésia puts it: 'The French, tired of being merely ingenious children, have felt the emptiness and ennui of their futile societies. Amongst them an important revolution is in progress; the sexes, who used to be gathered together by idleness, luxury, and frivolity, are beginning to separate. This separation, which is still sad for women unused to their touching duties, and who do not know the charms and the interest they could enjoy in their homes, is already raising men above what they were. Living more among themselves, they are getting accustomed to stronger ideas and to more sinewy conversations. They are more self-sufficing, their conceptions are greater, and they are building up

more real pleasures for themselves. A pure and amiable taste
for the country is being reborn in them. And how can one live
in the country and not want to fertilize and beautify it? The rich
will become gardeners . . . they will surround themselves with sweet
and grand images; and amidst these compositions they will hear the
voices of their souls which, perhaps, they have never questioned.'

In all this, what was Thomson's share? His *Seasons* first appeared
in a very literal prose translation by Mlle Bontemps, in 1759. The
English poet is described as being equally good as a scientist and as
a painter.[1] Mlle Bontemps praises the force and energy of Thomson's imagination, but deplores his penchant for hideous and unnecessarily gloomy pictures. However, as she naïvely concludes:
'If he were not inordinate he would not be English, or rather he
would not be a genius.' Fréron [2] attributed this enthusiasm to the
fact that Thomson only wrote when he was drunk! He admired
the Miltonic aspect of his pictures of the golden age, but found him
hopelessly chaotic, though undoubtedly a genius. Grimm,[3] on
behalf of the *philosophes*, stated bluntly that the translation had no
chance of success because the *Seasons* was too rich in images and
poetry, an odd, but quite typical and logical objection. 'By sheer
richness and floridity it becomes monotonous and tiring.' The
Cardinal de Bernis, or as Voltaire called him, 'Babet the flower-
girl,' was moved to write a poem called *Les Quatre Saisons* [4] (1763),
but except for its title it has little to remind us of our poet. Bernis
is a boudoir poet of the Chaulieu school, yet without a trace of that
profound emotion we find in the latter's most nonchalant verses.
Except in *L'Hiver*, Bernis is just a clever versifier, playing at the
pretty game of ransacking classic mythology for new words with
which to describe rustic objects without shocking the taste of his
fashionable readers. Like Madame Deshoulières [5] and Thomson,
he is sentimentally erotic about the amours of the birdies and
beasties in early spring:

> Voyons ces taureaux mugissants
> Poursuivre Io dans les prairies;
> Voyons ces troupeaux bondissants
> Donner par leurs jeux innocents
> Aux bergères des rêveries
> Aux bergers des désirs pressants.

[1] 'Aussi bon physicien que peintre.'   [2] *Année littéraire* (1760).
[3] *Correspondance*, iv. 248 (1760).   [4] Or, *Les Géorgiques françaises*.
[5] A contemporary of Chaulieu's and one of the most urgent devotees of
sensibility.

Occasionally in *L'Hiver* Bernis strikes a natural and almost poetic chord, as when he tells of the poverty of the peasants, and calls on the nobles to leave the luxury of Paris and return to the aid of their tenants. But he is not a Rousseauist:

> Quelle âme inhumaine et grossière
> Du notre ignorance première
> Regrette les temps évolus?

He is a social reformer who gave practical lessons in *bienfaisance* to those who wanted to know how to employ the leisure of their peasants on idle, winter days. In Bernis, too, we catch the first signs of that return to the Middle Ages which was already being voiced in English literature:

> Nos donjons, nos tours délabrées,
> Monuments antiques des Goths,
> Sont moins affreux que les magots
> Dont nos maisons sont décorées.
> Sans aimer la grossièreté
> De nos aïeux encore barbares,
> Leur aimable naïveté
> M'attache à leurs travaux bizarres.
> Le chevalier, le paladin
> Viennent remplir mes rêveries.

Saint-Lambert, whom Voltaire calls a *poète-philosophe*, was also the accepted lover of Rousseau's 'Julie.' In 1769 he published his *Saisons*, a loose adaptation from Thomson. Voltaire, whose verdict may have been coloured by Saint-Lambert's footnotes,[1] immediately placed his poem far above its English model. Thomson, he said, describes the seasons: Saint-Lambert tells what should be done in each. The French poem has that finish which is so sadly lacking in Thomson's. Besides, Saint-Lambert had the harder task, since Thomson wrote only in blank verse, which 'is so easy to do that it has scarcely any merit.' Indeed, says Voltaire, it is because he used blank verse that Thomson, in order to avoid 'prosaic languor and mediocrity,' was obliged to resort to 'gigantic expressions and ideas,' and thus make up for an inevitable absence of harmony. In a word, Saint-Lambert had achieved something hitherto deemed impossible. To quote this poet's own words: 'Thomson sang of nature to a people by whom nature is known and loved; but I sing of her to a nation which either knows her not or

[1] In which Saint-Lambert ranked Voltaire's tragedies above those of Corneille or Racine.

regards her with indifference.' To perform this feat he had not only to pander, as did Thomson, to the scientific and utilitarian proclivities of his time, but also to surmount the traditional prejudice against words and expressions which were not considered 'noble' or appropriate to poetry. Like Thomson, Saint-Lambert regards nature poetry from the viewpoint of the social moralist: unlike Thomson, however, he avoids direct contact with the poor countryman. So, very seriously, he explains: 'One must not introduce wretched peasants. They interest us only by their misfortunes; they have no sentiments or ideas; their morals are not pure. Necessity obliges them to deceive. They have that trickery, that exaggerated cunning with which nature endows those weaker animals which are ill-provided with weapons. Speak of them, but only rarely. Show them in action. And, above all, speak *for* them. There are scattered about the country rich husbandmen and peasants who live in ease and plenty—men who lack only theory to be philosophers. Representations of their conditions and sentiments cannot fail to give pleasure to every man of sense, virtue, and knowledge.'

Saint-Lambert writes with a *but moral*: it is to interest the nobility in country life, to induce them to return to their estates, and so, indirectly, to improve the lot of the wretched peasant. His sensibility, like Thomson's, is largely social, although he has none of the English poet's romantic longing for the return of a golden age. The Frenchman is a *philosophe*, a social reformer with no illusions as to the character of the French peasant whose lot he deplores. For him the golden age is the age of progress, the eighteenth century. Admittedly, there are abuses, such as the *corvée* and other seigneurial rights which Saint-Lambert attacks with vigour and courage. But he lives in the happy illusion that a new era has already dawned, where, thanks to the efforts of the physiocrats, agriculture has come into her own. Even the nobles have become *philosophes*, that is to say, humanitarians. The *bons seigneurs* of Marmontel's tales and of the *Opéra comique* are now to be met with in real life. The theatre and the novel were reflecting the secret ideals of a new generation; and reflecting them in glowing colours that aroused a growing desire to emulate and realize these fictitious virtues. Poetry, therefore, must not lag behind. So, in the *Saisons* we find sentimental pictures of country life, good old patriarchs, benevolent landowners, sweetly innocent village lads and lasses, whose chaste loves are consecrated by dear old *curés*. Saint-Lambert, for

K

instance, sees nothing comic in the following description of a grape-harvest:

> Bacchus a suspendu la haine et la vengeance.
> Il fait régner l'amour, il répand l'indulgence.
> Deux vieillards attendris se tiennent embrassés;
> Dans leurs yeux entr'ouverts brillent d'humides flammes,
> Ils font de vains efforts pour épancher leurs âmes.

They are intoxicated, not with wine, but with sensibility.

Where Thomson is maudlin, scientific, and moral, the French poet will faithfully copy him. But in the rare passages where the former saturates his senses in the colour, the scents, and the vital saps of nature, Saint-Lambert shrinks back in wonder and alarm. And even where he is merely picturesque, the French poet's palette has none of Thomson's richness and brilliance. Saint-Lambert has an eye for colour, but his expressive medium is limited. One must remember that as yet Saint-Pierre had not unladen his sacks of nuanced and iridescent epithets, the rich booty from his voyage to the tropics and his wanderings in the French countryside. So when Saint-Lambert describes the glories of a sunset or of an autumn wood, it is in the artificial words he learned from the erotic, boudoir poets. His pages, therefore, are stuffed with rubies, diamonds, sapphires, and opals. No doubt, a great creative artist would have forged a new vocabulary of his own, but Saint-Lambert was not a creative artist. At best, he was a poet who knew and loved the country, yet had moved always in a circle where man and not eternal nature was the chief topic of conversation. Whether the men of that time were really nature-blind it is hard to know; at any rate, there is little evidence to the contrary. Even in those intimate letters of Diderot to Sophie Volland, most of which were written from D'Holbach's beautiful country-house near Boissy St. Léger there is scarcely a line to show that the writer was in the least affected by the changing pageant that passed before his window. However, there are in the *Saisons* certain passages which reveal a sensitive lover of nature. The silence of the forest inspires in Saint-Lambert a joy mingled with terror, followed by a sigh of relief as the fresh wind rises and rustles in the tree-tops:

> Le feuillage frémit, se soulève et murmure,
> Chaque arbre est animé. Les chênes, les ormeaux
> Sont devenus pour moi des compagnons nouveaux.
> Je rentre dans ces moments dans le monde sensible;
> Et les bois, dépouillant leur majesté terrible,
> Ne sont plus à mes yeux qu'un paisible séjour
> Où ne pénètrent point le tumulte et le jour.

Fréron's comment on these lines is illuminating: 'I confess I do not know what the author means.'[1] And when Saint-Lambert observes the light undulating over the backs of the oxen, Fréron sharply rebukes him for introducing this 'little detail which is neither noble nor touching and not worth anybody's attention.' In trying to communicate his forest experience Saint-Lambert was courting ridicule, for here was an emotion wholly personal and sensuous, unrelieved by the usual moralizings on man or by the customary references to the Great Architect. His contemporaries could understand him better when he wrote:

> Ce concert monotone et des eaux et des vents
> Suspendant ma pensée et tous mes sentiments,
> Sur elle-même, enfin, mon âme se replie,
> Et tombe par degrés dans la mélancolie.
>
> .   .   .   .   .
>
> Je crois me retrouver à ces moments horribles
> Où j'ai vu mes amis que la faux du trépas
> Menaçait à mes yeux ou frappait dans mes bras.

And this, at least, marks an advance in the eighteenth-century French attitude towards nature. Something which was vitally to affect the destiny of poetry had occurred since Pascal jotted down this thought: '*Lustravit lampade terras*. The weather and my mood have little connection. I have my foggy and my fine days within me.'[2] Gone now is that serene aloofness; nature can now, at least, arouse sensibility, even if that sensibility be immediately transmuted into the social consciousness we call humanitarianism. Of that other sentiment which we find in Rousseau, the gorgeous romantic conviction that nature is a mere theatrical setting designed by a divine stage-manager as a background to the play of individual passion, we discover no trace in Saint-Lambert. Usually he is simply descriptive. Only seldom is he ever alone with nature, and then, as if afraid, he returns to his true theme, which is man. That is what Marnésia and others admired in him. 'The poet,' said Marnésia, 'must never leave *man* out of his pictures. How cold would his landscapes be if he left them without inhabitants!'[3]

Some little time was to elapse after the appearance of the *Saisons*, ere French and English poets went to the mountains or to the sea for inspiration. The eighteenth century had a horror of uncivilized nature, and Gray's letter on the Grande Chartreuse reveals a precocious and unique emotion.[4] 'Not a precipice, not a torrent, not

---

[1] *Année littéraire*, ii (1770).   [2] *Pensées*, No. 107.   [3] loc. cit.   [4] To West, 1739.

a cliff but is pregnant with religion and poetry. There are certain scenes that would awe an atheist into belief without the help of argument. One needs not to have a very fantastic imagination to see spirits there at noonday.' But the grandeur of Mont Cenis is too much even for Gray's romantic soul : 'Mont Cenis, I confess, carries the permission mountains have of being frightful rather too far ; and its horrors were accompanied with too much danger to give one time to reflect upon their beauties.' By Joseph Vernet's paintings the French were gradually induced to overcome their dread of desolate nature, but it was long ere the word *désert* ceased to be applied to forest and mountain scenery that we should consider beautiful, but which was looked on by the eighteenth century as arid and repulsive simply because it was not inhabited. On the eve of the Revolution there appeared several travel books on Switzerland, notably H. B. de Saussure's *Voyages dans les Alpes* [1] and Sinner's *Voyages historiques et littéraires dans la Suisse occidentale,* [2] which, by their popularity, testify to the dawning romantic love of mountain scenery among stay-at-home Frenchmen.

The vogue for gardens and the growth of the new feeling for natural beauty ensured for Delille's *Les Jardins* and for his *Géorgiques* (1770) a most favourable reception. In the latter, by sheltering under the wing of Virgil, he smuggled in large numbers of rustic words and expressions formerly banned from poetry as being common, unharmonious, and ignoble. Delille, whose reputation in his day was equal to that later enjoyed by Victor Hugo, was essentially a classic and a descriptive poet. For these reasons his poetry was ideally suited to the taste of a people who, whilst eager to discover new sources of poetic inspiration, were reluctant to leave the path of tradition. We have only to read Delille's poem entitled *L'Imagination* [3] to realize that he was not the man to lead his compatriots towards anything remotely resembling the lyrical enthusiasm of the nineteenth-century Romantics. Yet, on the other hand, if only by describing nature, he provided the rebels with the raw material which they fused in the crucible of genius and refashioned into stuff of lasting virtue. At times, too, Delille evinces a feeling for nature in verses where we can already detect the accents of a Lamartine.

> Les eaux sont ta ceinture, ô divine Cybèle !
> Non moins impérieuse, elle renferme en elle
> La gaieté, la tristesse et l'effroi.
> Eh ! qui l'a mieux connu, l'a mieux senti que moi !

[1] 1779–96.   [2] 1781.   [3] 1806.

Souvent, je m'en souviens, lorsque les chagrins sombres,
Que de la nuit encore avaient noirci les ombres,
Accablaient ma pensée et flétrissaient mes sens,
Si d'un ruisseau voisin j'entendais les accents,
J'allais, je visitais ses consolantes ondes.
Le murmure, le frais de ces eaux vagabondes
Suspendaient mes chagrins, endormaient ma douleur ;
Et la sérénité renaissait dans mon cœur,
Tant du doux bruit des eaux l'influence est puissante.[1]

To Thomson, Delille owed nothing; to Virgil a great deal. The
only English poet he really admired was Pope: and an eloquent
passage of *Les Jardins* was composed in honour of the author of
Eloisa and of *Windsor Forest*.

Roucher's *Les Mois*,[2] however, was certainly suggested by the
Seasons, though in his preface this poet attributes his love of the
country to solitary rambles with his father in the Jura and to his
memories of Tasso and Fénelon. Roucher's sensibility, however,
such as it is, comes from Rousseau. Like Saint-Lambert he follows
Thomson in the latter's geological flights, and, of course, in the
half-erotic, mawkish passage where he sings of the amours of the
birds and beasts in spring. *Les Mois* is a queer hotch-potch of
erudition, social propaganda, and genuine nature worship concocted
by an enthusiast who is apt at one moment to lapse into incredible
bathos, and at the next to reel off pages which seem to have been
lifted bodily from some treatise on rock formations. Yet in his
délire extatique, as he calls it, Roucher often stumbles on images of
pagan sensuality. Thus, describing the fertilizing of the earth by
spring, he writes :

La terre, devant lui frémissant d'allégresse,
S'enfle, bénit l'époux qu'implorait sa tendresse,
L'embrasse, le reçoit dans ses flancs entr'ouverts :
La sève de la vie inonde l'univers.[3]

Again, in alert, simple words which foreshadow Lamartine's
Jocelyn he breaks ground tilled by no poet since Remy Belleau.

Dans nos champs, en ce mois, voyez de tous côtés
Ces animaux, fumants de sueur, de poussière,
Ouvrir et renverser la glèbe nourricière.
Cependant que leur guide, au chant vif et joyeux,
Sur le soc reluisant la main appesantie,
Presse de l'aiguillon leur marche ralentie.

Awkward and stilted in expression, no doubt. Yet to any one who

---

[1] *Les Jardins*, Chant II.   [2] 1779.   [3] *Mars*.

has ever perused an anthology of French eighteenth-century poetry it is heartening to read these lines and to recapture the smell of good, honest earth. The poets of the nineteenth century owed Roucher more than they could guess, for one must be familiar with the spirit of his age to realize the courage required to pen inoffensive and banal words like these:

> De canetons rameurs ces étangs sont couverts.
> La compagne du coq, les yeux sans cesse ouverts,
> De ses nombreux poussins, marche et glousse entourée.

Who had ever heard of *canetons* or *poussins* outside a farmyard? As Roucher tells us himself, no poet, in singing the praises of the great Henry IV, had ever dared even to repeat his famous saying about the hen in the pot on Sundays. 'Such is the caprice of our language that it is impossible to make it adopt into good poetry the words *dimanche*, *poule*, and *pot*, which we love and admire on the lips of Henry IV.' Roucher was ridiculed for using homely terms like these, and censured, too, for neologisms like *s'aviver*, *bleuir*, *ravageur*, *punisseur*, *bronzé*, all of which, as he pointed out to the French Johnsons, had been resurrected from the vocabulary of the sixteenth century. The critics frowned also at the liberties he took with rhyme—for example:

> La trombe, comme une épouvantable masse
> Tombe—

and with the position of the caesura, which he shifted frequently from its half-way house in the alexandrine, thus smoothing the path for the Romantics who achieved a revolution in prosody by following Roucher's lead.

Les Mois is a vast store-house of miscellaneous knowledge. It is crammed with allusions to ancient customs and superstitions, Greek, Roman, and Celtic. Roucher knows his Newton and his Linnaeus, his Thomson, his Young, and his Haller. He has read in Pope of the Man of Ross, and pens a stanza in honour of the latter's French counterpart, Lucien Pannelier. After Saint - Lambert, but with keener feeling, he attacks the cupidity of the throne and of the Church, reminding them bluntly that

> . . . le peuple est avant vous.
> Si par nous vous régnez, régnez aussi pour nous.

In realistic, scathing words he tells of the havoc wrought by war in the French countryside, and boldly rebukes the reckless monarchs

> dont l'orgueil sanguinaire
> Arma ces meurtriers d'un glaive mercenaire.

With restless curiosity he examines every natural phenomenon, reinforcing his text with enormous and learned footnotes. Thus he discusses the two current theories of the golden age, Bailly's and De Pauw's, and ends by preferring Plutarch's. He has a hundred lines on the slave traffic, *à propos de bottes*; for Roucher's transitions, though quite logical, are bewildering to follow. For example, he is led from a description of the harvest moon to Newton's theory of light. Newton suggests superstition, and so we get a vivid account of the massacre of St. Bartholomew. One of the eighteenth-century objections to poetry was that it was not sufficiently instructive. Roucher's business will be to remove that reproach. 'What!' he exclaims, 'we live surrounded by the rich discoveries which the naturalists and physicists have made and are making daily, and our poetry remains indigent!' The poet, then, he claims, must be the instructor of humanity, a title which Roucher certainly strives to deserve. Indeed, for that very reason, there is very little true poetry in the *Mois*. Roucher is an excellent example of the man who knows all about nature and her ways without ever experiencing the sense of wonder, awe, and exultation that has transformed men less learned into 'nurslings of immortality.' Yet he is not exactly a Peter Bell. The primrose by the river's brim did mean something to Roucher. Unhappily, it meant something that is too material, too scientific ever to be distilled into poetry. A rationalist who tried to be a poet, Roucher possessed a habit of mind that was normally analytic. He could never surrender himself to the fleeting impressions made on his senses by the things he saw and loved in nature. He could watch bees at work, and tell us all that is to be known about their ways, yet never once did he see, like Shelley,

> The lake reflected sun illume
> The yellow bees in the ivy bloom,[1]

or note with Richard Church that

> The bourdon bee from grass
> To grass heaved his brown sacks.[2]

It may be argued that Roucher flourished at a time when poetry was almost wholly descriptive; yet what are Keats's *Fancy* or Leconte de Lisle's *Midi* but descriptive poems? No; Roucher's defect lay not in any dearth of seeing power: the *Mois*

---

[1] *The Poet's Dream.*   [2] *News from the Mountain.*

is full of observation. It lay in his inability to escape from his reason. To take one instance. Roucher describes the arrival of the northern birds in the south of France, where these migrants always rest ere winging their way to Africa. And all that they inspire in him is a tedious philosophical digression on the nature of animal instinct, and a frowsily sentimental appeal to the nobles to follow the birds south from Paris! Every sensuous impression is evaporated and desiccated in this fashion. The poet is regularly strangled by the rationalist.

This process is occasionally interesting to observe. Thus, autumn fills Roucher with a sombre melancholy, and he writes: 'The *Night Thoughts* of Young, read in the country on autumn evenings while the winds are whistling through the woods, have always filled me with a profound sentiment of sadness . . . for, it must be confessed, this state of languor and melancholy which is aroused in us by the sight of the leafless countryside has its charms. We dwell on it with pleasure. We think of what we have lost, and that is an added source of delight. Our life is then completely in the past.' But here, surely, are the thoughts of a Romantic. And so they are until the *philosophe* reasserts his power. For Roucher continues: 'And, as distance always adds to the illusion, the voice of the birds, the perfume of the flowers, the brightness and coolness of the verdure, the pleasures which animate the scene of rural labours, seize upon our imagination and paint themselves in enchanting colours *which they really do not possess*.' This passage with its characteristic closing words gives the exact measure of Roucher's weakness as a poet. He could not really suffer illusions. With him 'facts are chiels that winna ding.' Yet he could warmly agree with Bougainville that nothing is so conducive to sublime and poetic thoughts as long and solitary communion with nature. Momentarily inspired by that idea, he writes:

> Sur la roche sauvage où le chêne a vieilli
> J'irai m'asseoir; et là, dans l'ombre recueilli,
> A l'aspect de ces monts suspendus en arcades,
> Et du fleuve tombant par bruyantes cascades,
> Et de la sombre horreur qui noircit la forêt,
> Et de l'or des épis flottant sur les guérets . . .

But in reality his was not a contemplative soul. He speaks indeed of 'la sensibilité que nourrit la retraite,' yet so inveterate was the social bent of his mind that he never actually remained alone with nature. All his reveries were brief. Their calm was constantly invaded by the swarm of rational and humanitarian ideas that infested his century with their clamorous drone.

The opening lines of Roucher's *Mars* remind us that in France, as in England, a new conception of poetry had taken shape:

A la voix du tonnerre, au fracas des autans,
Au bruit lointain des flots se croisants, se heurtants,
De l'inspiration le délire extatique
Versera dans mon sang la flamme poétique.

And as we re-read *Les Mois* this impression is strengthened. For example, in *Décembre*, Roucher, plunging back into pre-Christian times, evokes the procession of the Druids led by their bards, moving into the dark forest where they will offer up sacrifices to their sacred plant, the mistletoe. And in one of his erudite footnotes, he touches upon a question which for some years had been exercising the minds of poets and *philosophes* in France and in England. What was the nature and the aesthetic value of primitive poetry? To what extent could a rational century, a century of intellectual progress, benefit from the bold imaginings of barbarians? We know Burke's answer to that question, and Diderot, in his erratic weathercock fashion, veered for a time towards the poetic ideal of Burke. In Dorval [1] he sketched the poet of the future, wandering in silent forests, lulled by the roar of the mountain torrent, listening to the inner voice of his genius in the hush of solitary meditation. In a famous passage Diderot defines enthusiasm as the soul of poetry. 'Enthusiasm is born of nature. If the mind has seen a natural object under striking and diverse aspects, it is possessed, shaken, tormented by it. The imagination warms; passion is aroused.' Then, in words which offer a strange contrast to the views he afterwards expresses in his *Paradoxe sur le Comédien*, Diderot pictures the swift delicious shudder that announces the dawn of poetic frenzy, 'the strong enduring fervour which fires the poet, makes him pant for breath, consumes him, kills him, but gives life and soul to all he touches.' Again, in the *Salons*,[2] he applauds the grandeur of a poetry inspired by wild, dark and solitary nature, 'the fall of distant invisible waters, silence, solitude, the desert, the beat of muffled drums.' 'Poetry,' he says in his *Essai sur la Peinture*, 'demands something enormous, barbaric, and wild.' Much of this was, of course, pure literature, the froth of impressions gleaned from his readings of Shaftesbury and Burke. Diderot the poet had a

---

[1] *Entretiens* (1757). [2] 1767.

*K

habit of jotting down such white-hot thoughts: Diderot the philosopher was quite as apt in cooler mood to revise them. Such was the case here. Still, these extracts reflect what was his attitude to poetry in the sixties, at a time when Turgot and Suard, in the *Journal étranger*, were translating fragments from Macpherson's *Works of Ossian*, that extraordinary bogus antique which excited the curiosity of English and French eighteenth-century connoisseurs, and, during the Romantic period, left its imprint on the poetic style of Europe.

The *raison d'être* of this journal, as its name implies, was to collect and diffuse in France all available information regarding the latest foreign books of note. Its Ossianic extracts met with a mixed reception, and, as the editor confessed, this type of poetry displeased many readers by its monotony and vagueness. Its chief appeal was to the historic, scientific minds of the Encyclopedists. 'Those who possess a sensitive soul and a philosophic mind,' said one correspondent, 'those who love to observe new and extraordinary *mœurs*, to go back to the source of the arts, and to follow the spontaneous outbursts of the human spirit when it is abandoned to its natural forces, have been struck by a primordial crudity which conceals a multitude of great, energetic, and pathetic beauties, and have regarded these poems as curious monuments in which poetry reveals herself with the pomp and energy she derives from pure nature, unaided by art or culture.' It was not, indeed, to be expected at this stage that the French eighteenth-century poets would go to these *chansons erses*, as they were called, for inspiration. Yet it was quite possible that Imagination, having been driven out of French poetry by Reason, might in time slip back again by the same route. Meanwhile, the English scholars, led on the one hand by Dr. Johnson, and on the other by Dr. Blair, waged a bitter polemic battle over the authenticity of *The Works of Ossian*, now published in their complete form by the arch-charlatan, James Macpherson. In France, they were comfortably received as genuine —a sound procedure; for, if one admired the poems it really did not matter who wrote them, and if one thought them idiotic it mattered still less. To the group which found them interesting, the Ossianic poems furnished fine matter for scholarly discussions on 'primitive' psychology, at a moment when Rousseau's thesis on the so-called natural goodness of man was the object of repeated and venomous attacks by freethinkers and orthodox Christians alike. Another question was debated. Was there a difference between the Oriental or Biblical and this Celtic poetry? One result of these controversies was that now, in France as in England, scholars began to extend their researches to Scandinavian literature, but as yet only in a very tentative and superficial way. Sainte - Palaye, by his *Mémoires sur l'ancienne Chevalerie* (1759), had already provided Hurd with material for his famous *Letters on Chivalry and Romance* (1762), which did much to stimulate Romanticism in England. Yet though it was a Frenchman who wrote the first important history of chivalry, the interest in medieval and in Scandinavian literature was slow to develop in France, and, as M. Baldensperger has shown, did not affect her poetry till the Empire.[1]

We have been using the term 'romantic' to indicate a new spirit now animating English poetry. To apply the same word to the French poetry of our period would be, for several reasons, unjustifiable. It is correct to say, very generally, that the literatures of both countries were evolving in the same direction; that their imaginative writers were departing from an outworn, classic or rational conventionalism, and, in various ways, expressing themselves with increasing sensibility and enthusiasm. Yet though they were at this time moving roughly in the same direction, we know, as a matter of fact, that their goals were not identical; for there is a great difference between the romantic literature of France and of England in the nineteenth century. So, too, despite certain analogies and contacts, there is little *essential* similarity between the new spirit displayed by the eighteenth-century French poets and the 'romanticism' of their English coevals. There was in the *drames*, in Voltaire's tragedies, in several novels, and in the *héroïdes*, an element which the English would have called 'romantic.' An eighteenth-century Frenchman would have used the adjective 'romanesque,' meaning literally, 'pertaining to the manner of novels or romances.' In Le Sage's *Gil Blas*, for example, there are intercalated short stories, full of passionate and strange adventures, which by their *romanesque* tone offer a striking and odd contrast with the cynical realism of the novel itself. Le Sage, in introducing such attractions, was pandering to the taste of those who, for a time, at least, long to escape in imagination from the actuality of everyday existence. That, in essence, is the *romanesque* spirit. With the rise of the middle classes it grew in scope and in intensity. Two of its crudest expressions were the *comédie larmoyante* and the *drame*. A third was the erotic novel of the Crébillon school, in which, for the benefit of the fashionables, the *romanesque* element was given an Oriental,

[1] *Études d'Histoire littéraire*, série i.

Arabian Nights or fairy setting. Madame de Tencin and Prévost, in another way, catered for the same craving; Voltaire, who closely observed the trend of the reigning taste, freely exploited this desire for the *romanesque* by situating his plays in far-off climes and ages, cramming them, moreover, with exciting situations that might have been taken from a seventeenth-century romance. This was the pleasant anaesthetic he administered before inoculating his audience with the serum of his subversive ideas.

Now, in recent years, a great deal of emphasis has been laid on certain apparent resemblances between French and English eighteenth-century writers. It is, therefore, very easy to lose sight of the normal or general tone of the two literatures. On the whole, the Romantics of our country sought to appeal to the sensations rather than to the sensibilities. Their necromantic poetry, with its physical images of death, their 'bardic' poems evoking violent pictures of war and slaughter, their admiration for the melodramatic elements in Shakespeare, all point to an ideal, *l'idéal du terrible*,[1] as Marnésia called it, which was really at variance with traditional French taste. Only exceptionally, did the *romanesque* assume a sensational form: its normal expression was gentler and more elegiac. To this fact must be attributed the failure to acclimatize the plays of Shakespeare and Lillo, even after they had been copiously emended and diluted. This was even more evident in poetry. Feutry, for instance, had little success with his *Tombeaux*, though it contains only a very discreet echo of the harsh, physical imagery of Hervey's *Meditations* or of Blair's *The Grave*. In nature poetry, also, as we have observed, the French could never bring themselves to imitate the sensuous delight evinced by Thomson, sometimes, in the colours, scents, sounds, and light of a shimmering summer's day. The 'romanesques' preferred subtler, pastel tints reflecting a quieter, sweetly sentimental mood; a sensibility that still retained the contours of a rational habit of mind. For, despite the influence of Rousseau, sentiment was not yet paramount. Always in the background, like a North Sea mist, there loomed the spectre of *la Raison*, and its shadow haunted the French soul. Rousseau himself, in the passionate *Nouvelle Héloïse*, stopped in mid-career and quietly rationalized his passion into mere sensi-

[1] 'The English run after the *idéal du terrible*, which is easy to seize and not pleasant to find. Therefore where our admirable Racine depicts in beautiful lines the death of a hero and draws tears from our hearts, Shakespeare drags before the eyes of the spectators a corpse soiled with blood and dust, covered with livid wounds, and makes grief howl.'

bility. A Julie 'all for love,' would have estranged even his most sentimental readers.

What were the favourite themes of eighteenth-century French literature? Virtue, friendship, paternal or filial love, renunciation, honour, and, above all, *bienfaisance*. These are essentially rational, and their artistic expression is apt to produce a literature fraught with sadness and regret rather than with lyrical frenzy. The French thinkers of the period, Rousseauists and *philosophes*, dreamed of a world governed by the qualities I have mentioned. The former, indeed, visualized this golden age as a renaissance, as a harking back to nature, a return to attributes innate in the human soul, though smothered and smirched by centuries of civilization. With that idea the *philosophes* violently disagreed. Their golden age was to be the inevitable outcome of intellectual progress, a perfecting of human nature, not its rehabilitation. Not, therefore, until after the excesses of the Terror, which were committed in the name of liberty, humanity, fraternity, and all the other virtues; not until Reason had absolutely lost her former prestige did the French surrender to the dictates of individual passion and give us a truly Romantic literature. Then only did French poetry escape from its cage and soar into the empyrean. That is why, in the eighteenth century, Ossian appealed only to the curious minority, to the handful of precocious spirits whom French critics have christened the 'pré-romantiques.' And if, as we are about to see, the *Night Thoughts* of Young attracted a somewhat larger group, it was because these poems, for all their sentimentality and enthusiasm, are yet at the core extremely rational. Had they been really romantic, in the later eighteenth-century sense of the word, they would have encountered that apathy with which France greeted *The Bard* or the *Ode to Evening*.

To-day, Edward Young is known only to foreign students of comparative literature and to a minority of English readers. For these reasons he perhaps deserves some comment here. Beyond doubt, the *Night Thoughts* is one of the many threads in that rich skein which the English and German nineteenth-century Romantics wove into the glittering pattern of their literature. What part it played in the formation of Spanish, Italian, Dutch, and Scandinavian Romanticism only one critic, M. Van Tieghem,[1] is competent

[1] A most valuable study of Young's vogue on the Continent is to be found in M. Van Tieghem's *Le Préromantisme*, vol. i. With the influence said to have been exercised by the *Night Thoughts* on the French Romantic poets we are not here concerned. I might, however, express my reluctance to accept the views

to say, and he concludes that it was very great indeed. Relatively, the influence of Young on French Romanticism was very small, smaller perhaps than this eminent scholar would care to admit. In these pages, however, we are concerned, happily, only with the repercussions produced by the *Night Thoughts* in the minds of eighteenth-century Frenchmen.

What really attracted the first French admirers of Young was the picturesque story that crystallized round his name. And though many English had doubts as to its genuineness the French had none. For them, Edward Young was like a character straight from the pages of Prévost, a venerable, saintly man struck down in rapid succession by three bereavements. In presenting Young to French readers his translator, Le Tourneur, drew a touching picture of this dear old broken clergyman spending whole nights in the churchyard at Welwyn lost in holy contemplation. By many, too, he was regarded as the victim of Catholic fanaticism. The following account, which I take from my Scots edition of the *Night Thoughts*, was widely disseminated: [2] 'The priests refusing the doctor leave to bury his daughter in one of their churchyards, he was obliged, with the assistance of his servant, to dig a grave in a field near Montpellier, where they deposited the body without the help of any of the inhabitants, who considered Protestants in the same light as they do brutes.' A good part of this pathetic history has since been disproved, but this much is true: the *Night Thoughts* owed their inception to the author's sorrow over a personal loss. It would be wrong, however, to regard them as the lyrical, romantic effusion of a grief-tortured soul. The first *Night* appeared in 1742, the ninth in 1745, that is to say, at a time when it was bad form to lay bare one's inmost soul for the benefit of the curious reader. Indeed, had Young used poetry in this way, it is safe to say that he would have alienated the sympathy of his English public. As for the French, they would have looked on him as *un exalté*. In fact, however, Young is really most discreet in his references to his private experiences. These emerge only at intervals from the thick clusters of his sombre moralizings. The author's chief desire, as he

advanced by M. Baldensperger and accepted with some reserves by M. Van Tieghem. To quote his words: 'With Lamartine, the current which came from Young was merged and lost in the great flood of Romantic poetry.' I cannot find in the poetry of Lamartine any elements that would not have been there had Young never written. Perhaps what I have to say in this and in the next chapter will justify my misgivings.

[2] 1795.

tells us in the first fifty lines, is to escape from his personal woe to
nobler themes:

> . . . O lead my mind
> (A mind that fain would wander from its woe),
> Lead it through various scenes of Life and Death,
> And from each scene the noblest truths inspire.

Like Pope's *Essay*, the *Night Thoughts* is a didactic poem, yet its
subject is not merely man, but 'immortal man.' It is, in fact, a
long sermon in blank verse composed by an earnest fundamentalist
who, in the heat of his fervour, is liable to sink at one moment into
balderdash and in the next to rise to lines touched with the majesty
of great poetry. As every one who has ever read him has complained, Young is garrulous and morbid. Nevertheless, he has an
uncanny knack of carrying the reader along with him in those
nocturnal rambles through the dark forest of his meditations on
human vice and sorrow, or on the mysteries of death and immortality. The master-theme of the *Nights* is to be found condensed
in the following couplet:

> This is the desert, this the solitude:
> How populous, how vital is the grave!

The whole poem is, in fact, a passionate *memento mori*. There is
no escaping from death with Young. The reader, like some
Trappist monk, turn whither he will, is forced to contemplate the
grim symbols of his own mortality. All Young's thoughts are
directed to that end. He discourses solemnly on friendship, on
conscience, on time and eternity, on sensibility false and true, on
sincerity and hypocrisy. But he is only really enthusiastic when he
fulminates against atheism, and triumphantly proves the existence
of God and the certainty of a future day of judgment.

Now all these themes were familiar both to Englishmen and
Frenchmen of his time. English and French divines had dealt with
them in a hundred sermons. But Young, cleric though he was,
wisely employed the more spectacular methods of the lay preacher,
in order to drive home his lessons. This he tells us frankly in the
eighth *Night*:

> Since verse you think from priestcraft somewhat free,
> This, in an age so gay, the Muse plain truths
> (Truths which at church you might have heard in prose)
> Has ventur'd into light; . . .

Owing to a variety of causes, the chief of which was her scandalous system of appointments, the Church of England sank in the eighteenth century into a slough of apathy and spiritual sloth. 'The clergy,' said Goldsmith in one of his essays, 'are nowhere so little thought of by the populace as here; and though our divines are foremost with respect to abilities, yet they are found last in the effects of their ministry.' In France, too, the great days of Massillon and Bourdaloue had gone. In both countries the pulpits were filled with what Young calls 'cold-hearted, frozen formalists' and 'downy doctors.' The time was, therefore, ripe for a work like the *Night Thoughts*, in which commonplace truths were exhibited in language of passionate and sincere conviction. Young was also shrewd enough to realize the persuasive power of 'the human touch' which was supplied by his discreet but reiterated references to a pathetic and personal experience. His insistence on the theme of friendship appealed also to a generation whose theatre was beginning to sentimentalize on the moral beauties of friendship, and on conjugal and filial love, a generation that was heading straight for the maudlin humanitarianism of the late eighteenth century.

Young was very proud of his originality as the first poet to cele-brate the poetic grandeur of night and of death. Yet it would be wrong to regard him as the precursor of that Romantic group which, in the ecstatic joy of solitary communion with nature, was 'half in love with easeful death.' Young is a man of the seventeenth century in his attitude to solitude and to nature. Like the French *philosophes* who afterwards attacked Rousseau, he regarded the desire for solitude as sinful, morbid, and egotistic. In some of his worst lines he says:

> Joy is an import; joy is an exchange;
> Joy flies monopolists. It calls for *two*.
> Rich fruit, heav'n-planted! never pluck'd by *one*.
> Needful auxiliars are our friends to give
> To *social* man true relish of himself.[1]

Solitude for Young is to be indulged in only after social intercourse. It is not to be employed in selfish introspection but in the con-templation of universal, moral problems. For Young, solitude is no romantic ivory tower: it is 'the felt presence of the Deity.' He sees nature in the same unromantic, objective spirit. For him external nature, in the warm, exultant, romantic sense, simply does

[1] Note the metaphors, well calculated to melt the hearts of contemporary shopkeepers.

not exist, because nature for him is not day but night.   The pageant
of the stars, the moon, the

> . . . clouds, in Heaven's loom
> Wrought thro' varieties of shape and shade,

do, indeed, to quote his dreadful expression, 'claim a grateful
verse.'   In point of fact they claim several grateful verses, but that
is simply because Young's didactic, earnest mind sees these things
as the chief proof of God's omnipotence.   They compose an
'orrery,' reflecting the order and relentlessness of the divine will.
With this in mind, Le Tourneur, and every critic since his time,
have always compared Young to Pascal, forgetting that Pascal
would have absolutely disapproved, on principle, of the whole of
Young's *Night Thoughts*.[1]

Young enlarges on his 'lunar' theme,[2] choosing the moon and
night as his Muses until, like MM. Baldensperger and Van Tieghem,
we might be tempted to see in him a pre-Romantic, a precocious
Lamartine, expecially after reading the opening lines of the third
Night.   But how can any one possibly impute Lamartinian sensibility to a man who, in his invocation to Cynthia or Cyllene, begins
by calling her 'fair Portland of the skies'?

So far it has not been suggested that Young is a great poet, and
he is not.   But he has flashes of greatness.   In his love of imagery
he recalls Shakespeare if only to remind us of the gulf which
separates the imagination of the eighteenth century from that of
the Elizabethans.   Still, so ardently does Young pursue the elusive
and dazzling metaphor that, by sheer taking of pains, he occasionally
forges lines of rare value:

> This is the bud of being, the dim dawn,
> The twilight of our day, the vestibule.
> Life's theatre as yet is shut, and Death,
> Strong Death, alone can heave the massy bar.

These have the true Shakespearian ring, but one guesses that
Young, though he knew his Shakespeare and remembered him,[3]

---

[1] See his *Pensées*, section iv, beginning: 'I admire the boldness with which these
persons undertake to speak of God.   In addressing their arguments to infidels
their first chapter is to prove Divinity from the works of nature. . . .'

[2] loc. cit.

[3] Cf. Young's:
> 'Insidious Death! should his strong hand arrest,
> No composition sets the prisoner free,'

which is a typical example of his 'Shakespearian' style.   The original is, of
course:
> 'This fell sergeant, death,
> Is strict in his arrest.'

was, as a rule, closer to the spirit of Shakespeare's eighteenth century-
imitators. Nevertheless, his thought finds its most natural expression in bold, passionate, and concrete images. Too often, however,
they lack spontaneity. They diffuse no aura, and, like spent
rockets, fizzle out ingloriously in mid-air. The once much admired
address to Night furnishes a typical illustration and so do the
chaotic lines:

> What numbers, sheath'd in erudition, lie
> Plunged to the hilt in venerable tomes,
> And rusted in; who might have borne an edge
> And play'd a sprightly beam, if born to speech!

Pope he often imitates, but nearly always in a tone of disgusting
priggishness:

> . . . to teach us to be kind,
> That, Nature's first, last message to mankind.

or of idiotic sagacity, as in:

> All men think all men mortal but themselves.

Yet once, at least, he strikes a note which Pope never attained:

> The melancholy ghosts of dead renown,
> Whispering faint echoes of the world's applause.

Admittedly, such passages are relatively infrequent if we consider
that there are some ten thousand lines in the *Night Thoughts*. Yet,
quite apart from other considerations, they are numerous enough
to explain the popularity of the author in an age which was not
surfeited with an excess of good poetry. It was not Young's poetry,
however, that captured the interest of his French contemporaries;
for they knew him almost exclusively through the translation
of Le Tourneur, first published in 1769. This was the only
complete rendering of the *Night Thoughts*. The others were
fragmentary essays,[1] only one of which is the work of a writer of
any note.

Before commenting on the reception accorded by the French to
Le Tourneur's *Nuits*, it might be well to recount the latter's reasons
for having translated Young at all. In Germany, the English poet
was already well known, and in his own country had many admirers

---

[1] See Appendix II for a detailed account of these, which, according to M. Van
Tieghem, 'attracted attention and excited much interest.' I have not been able
to find much evidence of this, either in the French journals of the period or
elsewhere.

as well as detractors. A eulogy by his first French translator, De Bissy, had been printed in the *Journal étranger* (1762).[1] This nobleman and dilettante admired Young's sombre style, which was so closely attuned to the solemn grandeur of such themes as Time, Space, Eternity, and the Immensity of God. These, said De Bissy, demand 'sombre coloured words, words that make us shudder even before reflection makes us tremble.' Le Tourneur, who is obviously more *romanesque*, sees Young's poetry always through the mirage of the story which clung to his name. And the whole of his version of the third *Night* ('Narcissa') is strangely and subtly tinted by the translator's preconceived idea of Young. In what is, after all, a free paraphrase rather than a faithful translation, it is extremely difficult, naturally, to set the French side by side with the English original and thus definitely show where Le Tourneur's idea of poetry diverges from that of the Englishman. There is, however, one tangible difference. Le Tourneur constantly makes Young address Narcissa as 'ma fille' and so emphasizes his paternal grief. 'O ma fille, ma fille, je voudrais t'oublier'; 'Le nom de père me cause plus de tristesse qu'il ne m'a jamais donné de joie'; 'En quel état j'ai vu ma fille.' He causes Young to invoke the sympathy of all other 'pères sensibles' when he describes the secret burial of Narcissa. 'Mes bras paternels la portèrent plus près du soleil.' 'Je ne peux renoncer,' he exclaims, 'à songer à ma fille; je ne peux en détacher mon âme.' The cumulative result of these expressions, none of which appears in the original, is to make Young very much more subjective than he is, and to lend him an intensity of feeling which English readers will not find in the *Night Thoughts*. Moreover, Le Tourneur sedulously omits all Young's pompous, rhetorical images, and condenses the latter's moralizings so as to concentrate on the theme which really interests him—the father's grief over the tomb of a daughter 'carried off in the flower of her youth, at the nuptial hour.'[2] There is no need to go outside French literature in order to account for the elegiac spirit of Le Tourneur's version. More than a hundred years before, a French poet, in language of great beauty, in accents laden with deep

---

[1] In the foreign correspondence of Garrick (Forster MSS., vol. 30) occurs the first French reference to the *Night Thoughts*. It has not, I think, appeared in print. Patu, writing to Garrick in June 1755, thanks him for his views on 'the lugubrious *Night Thoughts*, which I have begun to read every evening before taking my night-cap. There are worse soporifics.'

[2] Here I paraphrase Le Tourneur's 'enlevée à la fleur de tes ans, à ton heure nuptiale.'

sensibility, had tried to console a friend whose daughter had died young. Who can forget Malherbe's lovely lines:

> Mais elle était du monde, où les plus belles choses
>   Ont le pire destin;
> Et rose, elle a vécu ce que vivent les roses,
>   L'espace d'un matin.

tempered by the manly dignity of

> Mais d'être inconsolable, et dedans sa mémoire
>   Enfermer un ennui,
> N'est-ce pas se haïr pour acquérir la gloire
>   De bien aimer autrui?

Malherbe expresses, in a few words, sentiments which Young in his peculiar garrulous way elaborates, and, by elaborating, robs of their simple, forceful appeal. Le Tourneur, who belonged to the age of La Chaussée and of Diderot and was infected by the larmoyant style of the *drame* and the *héroïde*, where no subject was more popular than that of paternal love, naturally accentuates this aspect of the third *Night*. The *romanesque*, almost macabre episode of the burial by night attracted a man who had certainly read his *Manon Lescaut* and his *Doyen de Killerine*. It is interesting, though, to see how Le Tourneur recoils from Young's more violent and morbid broodings on death, and from the brutality of his contrasts between life and death. The style of Le Tourneur, in this connection, foreshadows rather the faded languor of *Paul et Virginie*, where Bernardin de Saint-Pierre writes: 'Les pâles violettes de la mort se confondaient sur ses joues avec les roses de la vertu.' It is true, of course, that at times Young himself displays a similar artificiality, though not often:

>   . . . The sun
> (As if the sun could envy) check'd his beam,
> Deny'd his wonted succour, nor with more
> Regret beheld her drooping than the bells
> Of lilies; fairest lilies, not so fair!

In these moments, Le Tourneur will faithfully transcribe him. But when Young, with a plethora of heroic images echoing the rant of contemporary tragedy, fulminates against the superstitious priests who denied Narcissa a Christian burial, Le Tourneur is obviously embarrassed and becomes discreetly reticent. That is why it is difficult to agree with M. Van Tieghem that Le Tourneur paraphrases Young so as to make him 'almost a Deist.' Our critic bases this assertion apparently upon one passage taken from the French translation of Lorenzo's blasphemous speech in the seventh *Night*. Le Tourneur, he says, inserts the following words, addressed to the Deity: 'car je ne vois plus que ton pouvoir odieux.' This is a little far-fetched. As it happens, Le Tourneur, according to his invariable habit, is here simply condensing and transposing a passage which occurs earlier in the text:

> *Know my Creator?* climb his blest abode
> By painful speculation, pierce the veil,
> Dive in his nature, read his attributes,
> And gaze in admiration—on a *foe*, etc.

Had he desired, as M. Van Tieghem thinks, to metamorphose Young into a 'chrétien sans dévotion et presque déiste,' he would certainly not have omitted the whole of this violent diatribe. The French critic misunderstands Young when he represents him as another Lamartine in revolt against God. There is no analogy at all between the terrible despair voiced by Lamartine in *Le Désespoir* and Lorenzo's rebellious rhetoric, which was invented in order to allow Young to direct the long blast of his invective at the freethinkers.

In general, Le Tourneur adhered to the plan outlined in his preface. He paraphrased most of the *Night Thoughts* but rearranged them under twenty-four chapters, the titles of which are suggested by Young's own rubrics or by the subject-matter of the *Thoughts*. Also, again according to plan, he altered Young's poetic language or excised it so as to conform to the style of his time, which, as we have seen, was tinged with sensibility and with humanitarianism of an exaggerated sort. The group that favoured writing of this type was still in a minority. In Young it found, as it did later in Shakespeare, an author of repute albeit a foreigner, who exemplified to some extent that freedom of expression at which they aimed. But only to some extent, for Young was too violent, too disorderly and pungent for the average French taste. To have revealed pure Young to this public would have defeated the purpose of the reformers. So the *Night Thoughts* were watered down, 'chastened,' as Prévost said of his Richardson translation. Even in this form, diluted *à la française* and submitted to the general reader by Le Tourneur, is it true that French poetry assimilated the *Nuits*?

In France his translators praised Young: it would have been odd if they had not. Fréron, in the *Année littéraire*, admired his moral tone, but was only really interested in the pathetic story of his life

related in Le Tourneur's introduction. As to the merits of the
Night Thoughts he was discreetly vague.   Voltaire, on the other hand,
congratulated the translator on having reduced Young's 'mass of
turgid and obscure platitudes' into some sort of order, and
inferred that these sermons had little chance of interesting a nation
which would not even read Racine's *Religion*.   Diderot humorously
scolded Grimm for ridiculing Young, and claimed that the *Night
Thoughts* were popular with the *petits maîtres*.   Grimm, in his reply,
said he was 'hanged' if he could find any evidence to support
Diderot's statement. Rousseau was obviously not interested in
Young, and when he quotes him it is solely to find arguments in
favour of the solitary life.[1]   It will be remembered that Diderot had
incurred Rousseau's bitter enmity for saying that it is only the
wicked man who shuns society, an innocent generalization which
Jean-Jacques applied to himself. Reformers like Baculard d'Arnaud
and L. S. Mercier naturally praised the *Night Thoughts*, firstly,
because they were foreign, secondly, because they were utterly
different in tone to the traditional French poetry which they were
trying to displace. But Young had the majority against him.
Roucher, it is true, mentions him, but in no flattering terms:

> Tais-toi, farouche Young, ta sublime folie
> Remplit d'un fiel amer la coupe de la vie.
> Et qu'apprend aux humains ta lamentable voix?
> Que de la mort un jour il faut subir les Lois
> Et cette vérité, sans toi, tout me l'enseigne.[2]

La Harpe, in his advice to young poets, tells them to steer clear of
the 'melancholy swarm of Young's bastards' amongst whom he
includes the authors of *drames*, thus rather unfairly saddling our
poet with a paternity of which he was quite innocent.   However,
the quickest and most effective way to discredit the *genre sombre* was
to attack it as un-French.   So, for example, the cheery Augustin
de Piis reviles the 'apes of gloomy Young' in these words:

> Mère du désespoir, fille de la folie,
> Recule loin de moi, noire mélancolie!
> Recule loin de moi! je n'oublierai jamais
> Que tu conduis au crime et que je suis Français.

Ironically enough, at this very time, in England, the 'whining
comedies' were being attacked by many as a French importation.

---

[1] Rousseau knew Young only through Le Tourneur's translation. Had he
read the original he would have found that Young did not approve of the solitary,
misanthropic life.   See p. 272.

[2] *Les Mois: Février.*

The truth seems to be that Le Tourneur's translation found favour only with the small group which was darkening the French stage with its *drames*. And the chief of this *cénacle*, Baculard d'Arnaud, went for his inspiration, not to England, but to France. Indeed, his greatest success, the *Comte de Comminges*, was based on a novel by Madame de Tencin. But Baculard, though he admired Young, did not imitate him, nor did any French poet of repute. Philippe Bridel's *Les Tombeaux* (1779) and *Poésies helvétiennes* were the work of a Swiss; besides, they were influenced by Parnell just as much as by Young. Bulidon's *Méditations sur la Mort* (1782) is a tenth-rate poem composed by an amateur about whom nothing else is known.[1]

[1] Both cited by M. Van Tieghem in *Le Préromantisme*, ii.

CHAPTER XI

THE PERSISTENCE OF TRADITION

AT the close of 1776, the indefatigable Le Tourneur, translator of Richardson and of Young, published a French version of the so-called *Works of Ossian*, a really brave undertaking. For even to English readers, Macpherson's idiom offered associations of words and syntactical audacities which, to put it mildly, sounded odd and far-fetched. However, there are no chartable limits to the gullibility of connoisseurs in antiques or novelties, so that qualities which in a modern book would be dismissed as aesthetically grotesque and monstrous are always certain to enjoy a vogue, however brief, at given periods in social development. And the enthusiasts who were littering their gardens with bogus Chinese and Gothic ornaments welcomed *Ossian* with rapture. In the late fifties of the eighteenth century, the Highlands of Scotland were something of an *ultima Thule* to the English Romantics. I note, for instance, in the *Journal étranger*, an account copied from some London magazine and relating to the habits of the northern Scots. Its general tone recalls that of a modern treatise on the Australian aborigines. The Scots, we are told, are small, and their wives, especially, are remarkably so. 'As from their infancy they are accustomed to be wet to the skin, when they are obliged to sleep in the open air in dry and windy weather, they wet their cloaks and, wrapping themselves up in them, throw themselves down on the heather.' The same writer describes the daring exploits of four English officers who nearly reached the summit of Ben Nevis, which is 'seven miles, not to the top, but simply to the place where it begins to be accessible.' These gallant fellows, after fighting their way for four miles against amazing difficulties due to weather and terrain, gave up the attempt, and, one is happy to record, came safely back though 'glad to have escaped death by starvation.'

Johnson's matter-of-fact *Journey to the Western Islands of Scotland* was not printed till 1775. Yet even had his book appeared before the *Works of Ossian*, I doubt whether Macpherson would have lost a single admirer. As it was, he encountered an English public whose imagination had already enshrouded the Highlands in mystery and romance. So, on their arrival, the 'Ossianic' poems were greeted with cries of rapture but not of astonishment: here was no revelation, but simply the unhoped-for confirmation of a romantic belief.

In the present age of specialization, a hoax like that successfully engineered by Macpherson would be hard to achieve. The author of the *Works of Ossian*, to do him justice, was no cold-blooded mystificator, and from first to last his heart was never really in the business. His weird fabric was erected upon a flimsy substructure of fact, and, but for Macpherson's silly vanity and the naggings of his enthusiastic friends, would never have been completed. As things were, this inventive but unscrupulous Scot quickly found himself committed to a task which he lacked the moral courage to renounce. Besides, he dared not disillusion his romantic public. The fanatics who devoured the early poems of Ossian experienced 'a rising of the hair upon the flesh,' and decided, therefore, that this was great poetry. They wanted more of it. So, in response to their clamours, Macpherson desperately took up his pen with the grim resolve to give them more Ossian or perish in the attempt. Certain doubting Thomases there were; but, as their cavillings were unsupported by scientific evidence, the father of Ossian could afford to ignore them. The immediate problem was to provide fresh thrills for the true believers. Consequently, in *Fingal*, in *Temora*, in *Cath-Loda* and in numerous 'fragments,' we encounter cohorts of fiery warriors with 'red-rolling' eyes; of yellow-haired, white-armed, sonsy Scottish amazons complete with lances, armour, and shield, slaughtering wild boars and 'brither Scots' on the banks of foaming 'burns' that hurtle down the barren mountain-sides. What really astonishes the modern reader of Ossian is that, in spite of endless repetitions of incidents couched in epithets which nauseate by their recurrence, he is yet swept along in a bemused spirit of dazed optimism; hoping feebly, always, to light again upon one of the really poetic passages which do, from time to time, rise out of the chaos. Caught in a whirlpool of 'dark-bosomed ships,' 'dark-rolling deeps,' of 'ridgy' hosts and 'dark-browed' heroes, he listens over and over again to the same bards singing the same weird songs to the spirits that lurk in the eternal mists. With an uncanny air of being about to give us something new, Macpherson envelops his readers in a gyrating circle of storms, blood affrays, darkened moons, red stars, and lightning-skirted clouds. For those of a melancholy cast he invents long-winded laments on death and on the fugacity of life. To the sentimental he offers, as in the *Songs of Selma*, a fleeting picture of love. But it is love drained of eroticism and washed in the murky waters of Lethe. To the pious, however, he gives nothing, and as he himself points out, there is no religion in Ossian. Apparently the only remnant of conscience still possessed by Macpherson was a superstitious fear of the Old Testament, jealous god which restrained him from inventing a Celtic theogony. But the success of *Ossian* had little to do with its ideas or even with its sentiments. It came from the peculiar language invented by Macpherson to conceal his fundamental poverty of ideas. *Ossian* appealed to the young romantics because it had qualities which are to be found in poetry that really *is* lyrical and fine—suggestiveness, mystery, and a supreme disregard for the stereotyped, rational clarity of conventional verse.

Since Macpherson, who had no epic gifts, was hopelessly vague as to what he wanted to say, he was driven to repeat himself. Still, he was obliged to introduce some apparent variety into his expressions. What he really did, therefore, was to ring the changes on his small stock of imaginative epithets, and in consequence, occasionally hit upon a strange combination which enthusiasts had no difficulty in identifying as the lilt of weird and unearthly music. A great deal of our dadaist or Bloomsbury verse is forged in much the same manner. But the palm is still held by James Macpherson. Take, for example, the word 'dark' and its variants. 'Cornuel darkened as he went'; 'he saw him rolled, dark in a blast'; 'I darkened in my place'; 'dark-browed Fuldath'; 'joy rose darkly in his face'; 'darkly laid in his narrow house'; 'her soul is darkly dead'; 'the dark heads of pine'; 'darkened into wrath'; 'in two dark ridges bent the hosts'; 'he rolls his darkening eyes'; 'the dark-red rage of Fuldath'; 'with darkening doubt'; 'dark in his grief' . . . but why go on? These are taken at random from a few consecutive pages of *Temora*. Macpherson played much the same game with other epithets and with much the same effect. That is to say, once in a dozen shots, by sheer perseverance he hit the mark and stumbled into poetry. Had he been really as clever as he thought he was, or his audience less gullible, he would have thrown the failures into the waste-paper basket and, out of the remainder, composed quite a tolerable poem or two.

Now Le Tourneur's problem was harder than Macpherson's.

It was to foist this stuff as great poetry on a race that had fixed
ideas about poetry, and was, on the whole, more critical and better
read than the English. The fragments in the *Journal étranger* had
attracted the attention of the demi-savants and *philosophes*. Would
the complete works appeal to the Anglomaniacs and to the adventurers who were tired of the Racinian tradition? Might they not
also find favour with the Rousseauists, now a goodly band? Were
they too bloodily violent, too lacking in the true French *romanesque*
quality? The scales were not too heavily weighted against Le
Tourneur. Ossian possessed *désordre*, though perhaps he was more
disorderly than the English gardens. In his poems one caught a
glimpse of a far-off land, not, indeed, blooming with citron trees,
but enchantingly different in its uncouth wildness from the pastoral
scenery of France. In the Ossianic heroes, too, one could discover
that chivalrous magnanimity and that fierce quick sense of family
honour celebrated by Voltaire in *Tancrède*, in *Zaïre*, and in *Adélaïde
du Guesclin*. Then there was an undoubted elegiac ring in the
laments of the aged Fingal about his vanished youth and his
approaching death—a Marmontelesque and patriarchal touch.
Moreover, this was a poem by an Englishman (or rather by a
Scotsman, but that made no difference, for, as Mlle Bontemps had
pleasantly implied in regard to Thomson, all these islanders were
queer or *démesurés*). In a word, there were enough literary snobs
in France to make a fuss about the quaintness of the 'too, too
precious' old bards, and there was enough in Ossian to give them
something to rave about. Yet, somehow, they did not catch fire,
or, at least, not until the Empire. Two or three enthusiasts tried
their hand at translating fragments. The press was guardedly
polite; occasionally eulogistic, often, however, openly hostile.
There was no imminent sign of Ossian merging into the stream of
traditional French poetry. The only poet who seriously 'Ossianed'
—one can ignore Léonard's *Chant d'un Barde*—was Fontanes, and he,
after a visit to England, hastily turned his back, not merely on
Ossian, but on all foreign importations. This was the Fontanes
who, in a letter to Bonaparte, revealed that the latter kept Ossian
as a bedside book, presumably, as Fontanes suggested, because he
was a soldier's poet—in fact, the Kipling of his age. That was, of
course, much later. Meanwhile, in 1783, Fontanes wrote a *Chant
du Barde*, a mosaic of words and phrases lifted from the Le Tourneur's
translation and deeply embedded in eighteenth-century *sensiblerie*.
In this poem, Fontanes sings of the larmoyant generosity of Fingal

to his slain foe, Cathmor. Here is an example of his 'Ossianic' manner:

> Il expire à ces mots. Fingal s'attriste et pleure:
> 'Le brave, hélas! vient de tomber,'
> Dit-il; 'gloire à son nom dans la sombre demeure.
> Tout passe, et je vois venir l'heure
> Où je dois aussi succomber.
> Ma main, si longtemps indomptée,
> S'affaiblit sous le poids des ans injurieux.
> Prends ma lance, ô mon fils! lance redoutée
> Que nos pères jadis ont fait craindre en cent lieux;
> Soutiens-en tout l'honneur; tant que je l'ai portée,
> On vit trembler l'audacieux,
> Et l'infortune respectée
> De ses persécuteurs osa braver les yeux.'
> Il se tait; je m'avance et des mains de mon père
> Je prends avec respect la lance héréditaire.
> O mon père! O Fingal! O mes braves aïeux!
> Je n'en ai point flétri l'éclat victorieux.
> Mais des plus grands héros qu'il reste peu de trace!
> Que font au siècle ingrat nos travaux glorieux?
> La main du froid oubli par degrés les efface.

This, of course, is Ossian at third hand, and, to realize what a gulf has yawned between Macpherson and Fontanes, we must glance at the original passage in *Temora* which inspired the above effusion:

Why speaks the king of the tomb? — Ossian! the warrior has failed! Joy meet thy soul, like a stream, Cathmor, friend of strangers!—My son, I hear the call of years; they take my sword as they pass along. Why does not Fingal, they seem to say, rest within his hall? Dost thou always delight in blood? In the tears of the sad?—No: ye darkly-rolling years, Fingal delights not in blood. Tears are wintry streams that wash away my soul. . . . Ossian, take thou thy father's spear. Lift it in battle when the proud arise, etc.

Yet, under the Directoire, Fontanes's *Le Chant du Barde* was accepted as pure Ossian. In reality, its author's infatuation for the 'bard' was short-lived, a youthful enthusiasm. At one period, in 1779 to be exact, he looked to northern literature as a promising source from which the French might draw fresh vitality, and in an *Épître à Ducis* referred to the 'Germains' as

> . . . nos modèles,
> De la simple nature interprètes fidèles.

This was, however, afterwards omitted from his published works. In an *envoi* appended to the *Chant du Barde*, Fontanes expressed a

poetic nostalgia for the winter gloom, the rugged, desolate scenery
of the Ossianic poems.

> L'enthousiasme qui m'anime
> S'éveille plus ardent au milieu des hivers.
> Que ne puis-je habiter les monts couverts de neiges
> Où l'Écosse enferme ses citoyens heureux,
> Et, contemplant les mers qui baignent la Norvège,
> Rêver au bruit des vents sous un ciel ténébreux?

But this, too, was a fleeting mood, and, with *La Grèce sauvée*, he
went back to the traditional source of French poetry—classicism.
The Ossian essay was an escapade to which little importance can
be attached. Fontanes was, nevertheless, permanently influenced
by one of our poets. Sainte-Beuve's quick ear caught in the *Jour
des Morts* (1783) and in *La Chartreuse* (1783) a note of religious
melancholy which he attributed to the influence of Gray's *Elegy*.
For once, apparently, his *flair* deserted him, since the romanticism
of these two poems derives much less from Gray than from Pope,
whose *Essay on Man* Fontanes was actually at the moment turning
into French. In the *Forêt de Navarre* (1780) he had already imitated
Windsor Forest, transposing the setting to Normandy. And it was
natural that Pope rather than Gray or Macpherson should serve as a
medium for the transfusion of the English romantic spirit into French
eighteenth-century poetry. No doubt, the lines in *La Chartreuse*:

> Mais quel lugubre son, du haut de cette tour,
> Descend et fait frémir les dortoirs d'alentour?

present a superficial resemblance to Gray's lines about the curfew,
and in the *Jour des Morts* there is an unmistakable echo of the
'village Hampden.' But Gray was not a cloister poet, and the
claustral gloom, the religious air which envelop *La Chartreuse*, come
straight from Pope's *Eloisa*. The lines:

> Déjà de feux moins vifs éclairant l'univers,
> Septembre loin de nous s'enfuit, et décolore
> Cet éclat dont l'année un moment brille encore.
> Il redouble la paix qui m'attache en ces lieux;
> Son jour mélancolique est si doux à nos yeux,
> Son vert plus rembruni, son grave caractère,
> Semblent se conformer au deuil du monastère.
> Sous ces bois jaunissants j'aime à m'ensevelir;
> Couché sur un gazon qui commence à pâlir,
> Je jouis d'un air pur, de l'ombre et du silence.[1]

[1] *La Chartreuse.*

and

> Et le lierre embrassant ces débris de murailles
> Où croasse l'oiseau chantre des funérailles;
> Les approches du soir et ces ifs attristés
> Où glissent du soleil les dernières clartés;

reflect not so much the Sunday evening calm of the *Elegy* as the 'browner horror' of Pope's *Eloisa*. And similarly, although the *Jour des Morts* suggests at moments the humanitarian and faintly sententious manner of Gray, in general it is Pope whom Fontanes remembers.

> Cet orgue qui se tait, ce silence pieux,
> L'invisible union de la terre et des cieux,
> Tout enflamme, agrandit, émeut l'homme sensible;
> Il croit avoir franchi ce monde inaccessible
> Où, sur des harpes d'or, l'immortel séraphin
> Aux pieds de Jéhovah chante l'hymne sans fin.

Here it is absolutely impossible to think of Gray. This is Pope, but with none of the erotic passion which, in *Eloisa*, is so strangely blended with ritualistic fervour. The same accents can be heard in *La Chartreuse*:

> . . . sous ces voûtes antiques
> Parviennent jusqu'à moi d'invisibles cantiques;
> Et la Religion, le front voilé, descend;
> Elle approche: déjà son calme attendrissant
> Jusqu'au fond de votre âme en secret s'insinue;
> Entendez-vous un Dieu, dont la voix inconnue
> Vous dit tout bas: Mon fils, viens ici, viens à moi;
> Marche au fond du désert, j'y serai près de toi.'

This is infinitely less haunting, however, than Pope's:

> From yonder shrine I heard a hollow sound.
> 'Come, sister, come!' it said, or seemed to say;
> 'Thy place is here, sad sister, come away.'

Fontanes's verses reveal a mood long absent from French poetry and anticipate Chateaubriand, who was inspired by the same profound sense of religious beauty.[1] And if we have any lingering doubts as to the spring from which Fontanes refreshed his imagination they are set at rest by the following lines in *La Chartreuse*:

> Héloïse! à ton nom quel cœur ne s'attendrit?
> Tel qu'un autre Abélard tout amant te chérit.
> Que de fois j'ai cherché, loin d'un monde volage,
> L'asile où dans Paris s'écoula ton jeune âge. . . .

[1] Chateaubriand and Fontanes met in England during the emigration, and the former afterwards inserted his friend's *Chartreuse* in *Le Génie du Christianisme*.

Fontanes was indebted to Pope and also to Madame de Tencin's *Le Comte de Comminges*, which he mentions in the same breath. He speaks, too, of Rancé, that sombre nobleman who buried himself in La Trappe to escape the spectre of a tragic love affair. Rancé, Pope, Tencin, Fontanes, and Chateaubriand: these are suggestive names. And to round off the list, we must add that of Guilleraque, the author of *Les Lettres d'une Religieuse portugaise*. Here we have a striking illustration of the delicate and complex process which governs literary interaction. Some twenty years earlier than Fontanes, French literature made contact, through Colardeau and Dorat, with the English poetic genius. But that was at a moment when the atmosphere of France was not charged with the fervour of a Chateaubriand. This time, however, the spark of a second impact lighted a train which smouldered through the Revolution, exploding suddenly in *Atala*, in *René*, and in *Le Génie du Christianisme*. And Chateaubriand, now at the height of his fame, was not the man to forget what he owed to Fontanes. 'These beautiful verses,' he said of *La Chartreuse*, 'will prove to poets that their muses can profit more by dreaming in the cloister than by echoing the voice of impiety.' This is the tribute of a generous and grateful friend. Actually, Fontanes, though he dreamed in the cloister, shrank from its tragic gloom. The romantic, sepulchral glare of *Eloisa* terrified him by its excess of passion. The cloister by night fills him with dread. For he is *romanesque* but not romantic; happiest always when he moves in an atmosphere of melancholy sensibility:

> Cloître sombre, où l'amour est proscrit par le Ciel,
> Où l'instinct le plus cher est le plus criminel,
> Déjà, déjà ton deuil plaît moins à ma pensée!
> L'imagination vers tes murs élancée
> Chercha leur saint repos, leurs long recueillement;
> Mais mon âme a besoin d'un plus doux sentiment.

It was this need for a softer and sweeter sentiment which eventually drove him away from the Romanticism of Pope back to the quieter, classic sensibility of *La Grèce sauvée*. Fontanes hesitated on the brink of the precipice, looked round, and saw the beckoning finger of *la Raison*.

It is interesting in this connection to observe how small was the influence of Pope's *Eloisa* in his own country. Apart from James Cawthorn,[1] and the very classic William Whitehead,[2] *Eloisa* appears to have had no passionate admirers. The necromantics, of course,

---

[1] *Abelard and Heloise* (1746).   [2] An imitation of the same.

cultivated another sort of gloom, a Calvinistic and inspissated gloom which was actually a smoke screen designed to cloud their didactic purposes. None of their 'night-pieces' recaptures the urgent tone of *Eloisa*, because in none of them are the ideas of death and tragic love fused into poetry. For this reason, Pope was much more likely to appeal to the French *romanesques* than Young or even Gray, who was not a necromantic at all. His was, as he said, 'a white melancholy.'

The *Elegy* passed almost unnoticed on the other side of the Channel until after the Revolution. Two prose translations, a very loose one by the Swiss Madame Necker, and another by that wholesale importer, Le Tourneur,[1] excited little interest. Certainly the *Elegy* cannot be said to have left any visible trace on the French poetry of the monarchy. Delille, as he admits himself, imitates Gray in a few lines of *Les Jardins* where he lightly touches on Gray's master theme—the nobility of the common man. He left it to the later poets to copy Gray's famous:

> Some village Hampden, that with dauntless breast
> The little tyrant of his fields withstood.
> Some mute, inglorious Milton here may rest,
> Some Cromwell guiltless of his country's blood.

That idea, before the Revolution had no ring of actuality. After 1789, on the contrary, it was reproduced several times by French poets, who naturally substituted French heroes for the English ones. Indeed, it seems to have been the one feature of the *Elegy* which struck them as worthy of imitation. That is not surprising. In eighteenth-century France, nature poetry had not yet developed, and Gray, whom foreign critics will persist in regarding as a Young or a Hervey, had no thrills to offer the lovers of cypresses and tombs. The sober Delille, though he admired the humanity of Gray, was much more interested in Pope.[2]

Viewed in its correct perspective, then, the French poetry of our period, despite a few enthusiasts who were determined by hook or crook to transfuse new blood into it, opposed a strenuous and natural resistance to such efforts. Most of the reformers were theorists, not poets. And in questions of literary influence the final criterion is to be sought in the creative literature of an age, rather than in magazine articles written by persons whose motives are

---

[1] 1771. Printed along with his rendering of Hervey's *Meditations among the Tombs*.

[2] *Les Jardins*, loc. cit. and Chant IV, in which he imitates *Eloisa*.

sometimes dubious and always interested. Even translations, although no doubt they denote curiosity, do not necessarily prove that the genius of one country has been seriously affected by that of another. Thomson, Young, and Macpherson were never really assimilated by the eighteenth-century French writers. Only in so far as they already had something in common with French taste were they imitated. What was essentially English vanished in the process. Pope is in a different case. I am inclined to believe that it was through him that the religious spirit, by way of Fontanes, re-entered French imaginative literature. Hitherto, this role has been attributed by French critics to Young and Gray, on the strange assumption that Chateaubriand drew his inspiration from these Protestant sources.[1] Now Chateaubriand heartily disliked Young;[2] but quite apart from that fact it is impossible to see any connection between the strident, didactic tone of the English lay preacher and the sensuous, poetic splendour of Chateaubriand's prose. Both, it is true, write of death and of immortality, yet with what a difference!

The invasion of literature by sensibility, which becomes so very marked towards the close of Louis XV's reign, proceeded almost wholly from French sources. In this return to nature and to sentiment the influence exerted by Rousseau can hardly be over-estimated. And, Rousseau, though a born Swiss, was in every other respect absolutely a Frenchman. Now, as we have seen, the attitude displayed by the French to foreign poetry was not unfriendly. Yet, on the other hand, it can scarcely be described as enthusiastic. Even the very advanced reformers, eager as they were to abolish the *style noble* with all that it implied, could not altogether abandon their traditional respect for lucidity, symmetry, and self-discipline. Nevertheless, as we approach the close of the monarchy it is clear that French poetry has undergone a vital change. Its prevailing tone is now deeper, richer, and more sincere. The poets, too, no longer regard imagination and enthusiasm as signs of aberration.

Tentatively, the more adventurous souls turn their eyes towards the much advertised English and German models in which, it is said, the spirit of true poetry lies enshrined. As timidly, a few inspect the strange utterances of the Celtic 'bard,' only to recoil from them in puzzled dismay. There is, indeed, no lack of foreign works from which to choose. Year after year the diligent bees

---

[1] Notably M. Van Tieghem, in his *Le Préromantisme*, ii. 108.
[2] 'Young a fait une mauvaise école, et il n'était pas lui-même un bon maître.'— *Essai sur la littérature anglaise.*

L

wing their way back laden with pollen from these northern climes, only to perish before their journey's end. Meanwhile, however, the chill, dry wind of Reason abates. The gnarled old orchards of French poetry, caressed by the genial warmth of a new climate, stir with fresh life, and begin to put forth strong, sweet blossoms. A scanty yield, no doubt, but each succeeding spring brings richer promise of the great florescence that·is soon to come.

From the middle of the century until the Revolution, who are the famous French poets? Voltaire is busy with his anti-clerical propaganda. In his dramatic verse, he pays mock homage to the passing fashions, though Racine is still his god. Colardeau, Dorat, Saint-Lambert, and Roucher we know; contact with our poetry leaves no impress on their style. If anything, it serves to accentuate the contrast between the French poetic manner and our own. The 'Pindaric' Lebrun reveals an enthusiasm and passion of quite classic origin. With the slow crumbling of the barrier erected by reason against sensibility, a softer, a more elegiac, and a sincerer note steals into the erotic verse of the time. Men like Bonnard, Malfilâtre, and Gentil-Bernard still turn out graceful Ovidian trifles composed mostly in and for the boudoir. But with Léonard, Bertin, and Parny the expression of love becomes more profound and personal.

Curiously enough, although all three were born in the tropics, they contributed nothing of importance to the exoticism of their period. Their citron blossoms and pineapples come from the Jardin des Plantes rather than from Guadeloupe or Réunion. What is really new in their work derives from the fact that all were genuinely in love with love, and express their emotions with a directness which, if it is never greatly lyrical, is, at least, sincere and poignant. Nature, the generating force of lyricism, makes no deep impression on Parny, though Léonard and Bertin are sensitive to her beauties. The former, for example, in the *Journée de Printemps* strikes off a few happy lines:

> Là, des hêtres frappés d'une rougeur ardente
> Jettent sur l'herbe humide une ombre vacillante:
> Le flambeau du soleil se peint sur les étangs,
> Et sous le rideau vert des peupliers flottants
> Il glisse obliquement sa lumière inconstante.

Virgil and Thomson are his models, but Léonard is only a poet when he gives words to the sorrow from which he took refuge in nature and in poetry. In his youth, owing to a lack of fortune and

of pedigree, he was unable to marry a girl, who later died of grief in
a convent. This unhappy experience touches all his verses with
Lamartinian sadness and engenders a mood frequently recalling
that of the *Méditations*. Yet Léonard could never quite rid himself
of the jargon of conventional, pastoral poetry, though occasionally
we catch a strain which we shall later hear, more beautifully
orchestrated, in *Le Lac*:

> Souvent je crois l'entendre, et ce n'est qu'un ruisseau
> Qui baigne, en murmurant, les bords de son rivage:
> Souvent je crois la voir, et ce n'est qu'un rameau
>   Dont les vents agitent l'ombrage.
> Assis sur un rocher, et plus morne que lui,
>   J'invoque dans mon infortune
> Les astres de la nuit, et le ciel et la lune. . . .
> Ils sont sourds, et mon cœur ne trouve point d'appui.[1]

Léonard's other themes are all in harmony, all touched with the
same lilac tint of mournful resignation. It colours his *Village
détruit*, an adaptation of Goldsmith's *Deserted Village*, and recurs in
Le Bonheur and in *L'Hermitage*, which reflect the same nostalgia for
a vanished happiness. In an age that gave us no great poets,
Léonard stands in the front rank. And sometimes, by his habit
of projecting his sadness on everything that comes within his ken,
he achieves surprising and delightful results. For, although his
love of nature is never sensuous or exultant, he has an alert and
penetrating vision:

> Voyez-vous la bergère, un panier sous son bras
> Regagner lestement la route du village?
> Son ombre qui la suit s'allonge sous ses pas,
> Et les feux du couchant enflamment son visage.
>
> .   .   .   .   .
>
> Les moutons répandus le long de la prairie,
> En bêlant doucement gagnent la bergerie.
> L'âne marche entouré de ses paniers jumeaux;
> Le valet indolent qui regagne la ville,
> Siffle à demi penché sur sa mule indocile.
> Le bûcheron le suit; courbé sous ses rameaux,
> Le doux Hesper les voit, et la voûte azurée,
> Et fait briller sur eux son étoile dorée.
> Les ombres, cependant, s'élèvent dans les cieux,
> Et leurs groupes unis, toujours plus ténébreux,
> Animent lentement la tranquille soirée.

The French language is, I think, more competent than our

[1] *Soirée d'hiver.*

Anglo-Saxon to express the lingering, limpid calm of such vesper effects. Admirers of Gray will cry 'heresy,' and point to the opening stanzas of the *Elegy*, which are very lovely. Yet one wonders whether Gray could have prolonged his description beyond twenty-eight lines without having frequent recourse to words of Latin origin. It is very doubtful. Collins tried it in the *Ode to Evening*, but not with complete success. The point is of minor importance, yet it might be interesting to compare English and French elegiac poetry with this in mind.

Until we come to Burns, who arrives rather late in the century, there is no love poetry in eighteenth-century England;[1] and Burns, moreover, was not English. For that matter there was very little in France, though that country produced a surfeit of amorous and erotic verse. Now Bertin really was a 'grand amoureux,' and through the veil of his classic reminiscences[2] we discover a man who existed for love and little else. Like his bosom friend, Parny, and the lesser members of the club which met at *La Caserne*, Bertin moves in a cloud of vivid, erotic memories. For him *la bagatelle*, to use a prudish French expression, is of paramount importance. In the earlier *Élégies* of the *Amours*, which are not elegies at all, he spares us few details of his triumphs—the stolen rendezvous, the soft footfalls, the creaking doors, the delicious fear of discovery, the hurried exits through the casement, the all too swift return of dawn, and the rest. It is *Romeo and Juliet* recast by an eighteenth-century French captain of cavalry, or by Anatole France in his *Rôtisserie de la Reine Pédauque*. And indeed, Bertin's Eucharis, like Jahel, is 'une fine mouche' or, as we say in Scotland, 'a gey jiff.' Bertin, on the other hand, is a perfect Tournebroche, absurdly but credibly jealous, naïvely and impudently exigent. He is, in a word, the eighteenth-century Frenchman as he appears to those who know the age of Louis XV only through the novels of Crébillon and his disciples. But there are two Bertins. One writes in this mood:

Vous savez si son cœur alors paya mon zèle!
L'œil humide de joie, et d'amour enivrés,
Tête-à-tête à la fin tous les deux nous soupâmes.
Je tenais ses genoux entre les miens serrés.
Ce doux rapprochement semblait réunir nos âmes.
Ciel! que le moment fuit! que les plaisirs sont courts![3]

[1] With, however, the notable exception of Pope's *Eloisa*.
[2] He constantly imitates Ovid, Propertius, and Tibullus.
[3] *Les Amours*, III. xi.

The other, in more disillusioned vein:

> Plaisirs, amours, qu'êtes-vous devenus?
> Je crois errer sur des bords inconnus,
> Et ne retrouve ici que votre image.
> Dans ce bois sombre, en cyprès transformé,
> Je n'entends plus qu'un long et triste murmure;
> Ce vallon frais, par les monts renfermé,
> N'offre à mes yeux qu'une aride verdure;
> L'oiseau se tait; l'air est moins parfumé,
> Et ce ruisseau roule une onde moins pure:
> Tout est changé pour moi dans la nature,
> Tout m'y déplaît: je ne suis plus aimé.[1]

The faithless Eucharis was soon replaced, and, with admirable virtuosity, Bertin the erotic flits from the Muse who inspired *Les Baisers* [2] to her mournful sister, from whom he got the really beautiful *Aux Mânes d'Eucharis*:

> Loin de moi tous ces noms dont un amant accable
> L'objet qu'il cesse de charmer!
> Le temps a dû me désarmer,
> Et ton cœur n'est plus si coupable.
> Pour un autre que moi s'il a pu s'enflammer,
> Sans doute il était plus aimable;
> Hélas! savait-il mieux aimer?
> N'importe: sors en paix, ombre toujours chérie;
> D'un reproche jaloux ne crains plus la rigueur:
> Ma haine est évanouie.
> Tu fis, sept ans entiers, le bonheur da ma vie;
> C'est le seul souvenir qui reste dans mon cœur.

In such moments Bertin restores to France those qualities of sincerity, dignity, and tenderness which vanished from her poetry with Ronsard and from her theatre with Racine. Just as after Léonard we may expect a Lamartine, so when Bertin passes we shall not be surprised to encounter a De Musset.

From England this poet took nothing save perhaps a fondness for the careless charm of her gardens. But the landscapes which he loves are those of Feuillancour and of Burgundy, the regal province described in his *Voyage de Bourgogne*, that delightful book of impressions written by a man who loved rustic sights and manners. Somehow, here, Bertin occasionally reminds us of Cunningham, as in:

> Un essaim léger d'hirondelles,
> Rasant la surface de l'eau,
> L'effleure obliquement du sommet de ses ailes,
> Se relève et s'envole aux branches d'un ormeau.

[1] *Les Amours*, II. v.
[2] 'Dieux, que ta bouche est parfumée!
Donne-moi donc vite un baiser . . .'

But in the quiet malice of his vignettes of provincial types, he can be compared only with Cowper.

It is interesting in *Le Voyage* to note the impression made upon Bertin by mountain scenery. Writing to Parny's brother, he says: 'You have heard so often about the Pyrenees that I will not attempt to describe them. Besides, I should be at a loss to depict the astonishment, the horror, and the admiration which seized me at their approach. . . . From Lourdes to Saint-Sauveur you ascend constantly by a road cut in the rock; and always you see, two or three hundred feet below, now at your right and now on your left, a torrent which seems to have taken a thousand centuries to bore a passage through these masses of granite: and its presence is still betrayed by a horrible roar when your eye can no longer follow it to the bottom of the precipice.' Bertin is happier on the lower, more wooded slopes, where the rush of falling waters fills him with a 'sweet melancholy.' He writes: 'The flight of the waters recalls the flight of time. I think of all the losses I have sustained, even at my early age. Alas! I have seen the disappearance of the most lovable and the most beloved objects. My soul becomes gradually suffused with sadness. Soon I am drowned in tears, and, from the depths of my heart, I repeat what I rarely tell you because I fear to grieve you. O my friend, may I never survive you!' Either Rousseau or Diderot might have written that.

To describe such moods and the wild beauty of the scenes that provoked them, the Frenchmen of the seventies coined a new word, *romantique*. It meant something more distinctive than *romanesque*; more intense than *pittoresque*. Later, just before the Revolution, Marnésia [1] used the new adjective to describe the emotions aroused in him by thoughts of far-off primitive times.

Parny, unlike his friend Bertin, is not appalled by the 'horror' of the Pyrenees. On the contrary, they seem to him but a fitting cadre to his despair at the loss of his mistress, Éléonore. [2]

> Mon œil rapidement porté
> De torrents en torrents, d'abîmes en abîmes,
> S'arrête épouvanté.
> O nature! qu'ici je ressens ton empire!
> J'aime de ce désert la sauvage âpreté;

---

[1] Speaking of Bugey (Savoie), he says: 'Les sites les plus pittoresques y sont devenus romantiques *par les vestiges que les anciens peuples y ont laissés*' (my italics).

[2] She was a French girl, born in Réunion, whom his parents would not allow him to marry.

De tes travaux hardis j'aime la majesté.
Oui, ton horreur me plaît, je frissonne et j'admire.[1]

The poetry is indifferent, but the feeling it attempts to express was genuine. For in general, both in his erotic poems and in his elegies, Parny is more passionate and more spontaneous than Bertin. In his most indiscreet moments, the latter never wrote anything so frankly physical as Parny's *Délire*. Nor again, in the expression of his grief at the desertion of his mistress, does Bertin convince us, as Parny does, that he has supped the dregs of sorrow:

Le chagrin dévorant a flétri ma jeunesse.
Je suis mort au plaisir, et mort à la tendresse.
Hélas! j'ai trop aimé; dans mon cœur épuisé
    Le sentiment ne peut renaître.
Non, non, vous avez fui pour ne plus reparaître,
Première illusion de mes premiers beaux jours,
Céleste enchantement des premières amours!
O fraîcheur du plaisir! O volupté suprême![2]

There is something more in this than mere regret at the loss of physical beauty and voluptuous ecstasy. Éléonore symbolizes a critical period of Parny's life—his youth. That is the deeper cause of his despair. For, with her going, a fragment of his soul was wrenched away and the place still bleeds:

Ce cœur, hélas! que le chagrin dévore,
Ce cœur malade et surchargé d'ennui,
Dans le passé veut ressaisir encore
De son bonheur la fugitive aurore,
Et tous les biens, qu'il n'a plus aujourd'hui.
Mais du présent l'image trop fidèle
Me suit toujours dans ces rêves trompeurs,
Et sans pitié la Vérité cruelle
Vient m'avertir de répandre des pleurs.
J'ai tout perdu; délire, jouissance,
Transports brûlants, paisible volupté,
Douces erreurs, consolante espérance;
J'ai tout perdu; l'amour seul est resté.

In two elegies[3] Parny tried to persuade himself that this was not so; that friendship might bring him a more reasonable and lasting happiness. But in the simple, limpid verses to Bertin, on the death of the latter's Eucharis, he no longer pretends to cherish that illusion:

Représentons l'Amour, l'Amour inconsolable
    Appuyé sur un monument;
Ses pénibles soupirs s'échappent sourdement;
Ses pleurs ne coulent plus; le désespoir l'accable,

---

[1] *Poésies érotiques*, IV. vi.   [2] ibid., xiv.   [3] IV. xii and xiii.

L'instant du bonheur est passé;
Fuyez, plaisirs bruyants, importune allégresse,
Eucharis ne nous a laissé
Que la triste douceur de la pleurer sans cesse.[1]

Not till the nineteenth century did the French poets look back to the Middle Ages for inspiration. Before the Revolution, an odd *romance* or a rare imitation of some old English ballad [2] betrays the first glimmerings of interest in ancient poetry. In 1787 De Tressan unearthed and modernized some of the medieval chivalrous novels which he later included in the *Bibliothèque des Romans*. But eighteenth-century France had no Percy to arouse enthusiasm for her ancient literature. Voltaire's attempts in *Zaïre*, in *Tancrède*, and in *Adélaïde du Guesclin* to create an historic or national drama were superficial, and, moreover, were compromised by his irritating trick of injecting anti-clerical propaganda into everything he wrote. Rousseau, though brought up on the idealistic romances of the seventeenth century, was not interested in the Middle Ages. Still, in Bernis and in other poets, we find a growing tendency to contrast the austere, and largely imaginary, virtues of their ancestors with the sophisticated, luxurious habits of the reign of Louis XV. Again, Rousseau's *Émile* and his *Nouvelle Héloïse* created a vogue for simplicity of a somewhat artificial and extremely sentimental nature. Orthodox Frenchmen, however, stood aloof from this Rousseauistic revival of sentiment, aghast at the audacity of Jean-Jacques's heresies. This was the doing of the Church, which in its dogmatic way was as rationalistic as the Encyclopaedists. By proscribing Rousseau it let slip a valuable opportunity, since it was not until the appearance of Chateaubriand that the sentimental forces, dispersed through the scattered writings of the eighteenth-century poets and novelists, were collected and canalized for religious ends. And even then, the Catholic, like the Protestant, Church preserved her old distrust of enthusiasm and imagination.

The democratic idea, in a subdued fashion, was expressed in the poetry of Saint-Lambert, of Roucher, and others, yet never with the frankness evinced by Gray, Goldsmith, and, above all, by Cowper. For this the *philosophes* were chiefly responsible. Their social reforms aimed at nothing more radical than a tinkering with the taxation system and a fostering of the spirit of patriarchal charity among the landowners. Possibly their reluctance to encourage a

[1] *Le Tombeau d'Eucharis.*
[2] e.g. Lemierre's *Arthur et Luci*, composed in the insipid manner of the *opéras comiques*.

more democratic literature may be to some extent attributed to the censorship, but, after the seventies, that excuse is not valid. It arose really from the fact that these intellectuals were only academically interested in the lower classes. One has only to read their criticisms of such genuine democrats as Coyer to realize this truth. So in the poetry of their time we discover little of that warm sympathy for the underdog, of that imaginative understanding of the meaning of poverty and hardship which lights up *The Deserted Village* and Cowper's *The Task*.

Gilbert, who committed suicide in 1780, was justified in writing:

> L'on prêche les mœurs jusque dans *La Pucelle*,
> Je le sais; mais, ami, nos modestes aïeux
> Parlaient moins des vertus et les cultivaient mieux.

This unhappy lad, if he had lived, would have been a great lyric poet. As it was, he alienated the men of his day by the violence and the subjective tone of his writings. A French academy, packed with fish-blooded intellectuals of the D'Alembert type, recoiled in polite disgust from Gilbert's *Le Poète malheureux*, in which he naïvely laid bare the secrets of a soul tortured by poverty and neglect, and fired by boyish ambitions:

> Un dieu, sans doute un dieu m'a forgé ces malheurs
> Comme des instruments qui peuvent à ma vue
> Ouvrir du cœur humain les sombres profondeurs,
> Source des vérités, au vulgaire inconnue.

ending with the touching lines:

> Bientôt je rejoindrai ma mère
> Et l'ombre de l'oubli va tous deux nous couvrir.

This was unheard-of language, the language of *enthousiasme*, and the *Académie française*, however grandly it might theorize on the need for more enthusiasm in poetry, was shocked at Gilbert's ignoble and indelicate lack of classic restraint. The *Poète malheureux* was not crowned. Neither was the work submitted by the same author in the following year. Its title, *Le Jugement dernier*, was alone sufficient to damn it. Gilbert had his revenge in *Le Dix-huitième Siècle*, without exception the most scathing, the most pertinent, and the most illuminating criticism of the *philosophes* and of the social abuses of the age ever penned by a French eighteenth-century writer. Gilbert leaves our Churchill and Lloyd far behind. Cowper is his only rival, though the Frenchman is much more personal and more trenchant. There is no mistaking the democratic tone of Gilbert's

*L

satire. His victims are all selected from the aristocracy of rank and letters. In common justice, the *philosophes* have the first honours.

> Ce lourd Diderot, docteur en style dur,
> Qui passe pour sublime à force d'être obscur.
>
> Saint-Lambert, noble auteur dont la muse pédante
> Fait ces vers fort vantés par Voltaire qu'il vante.
>
> Et ce froid D'Alembert, chancelier du Parnasse,
> Qui se croit un grand homme et fit une préface.
>
> La Harpe est-il bien mort? Tremblons, de son tombeau
> On dit qu'il sort armé d'un *Gustave* nouveau.[1]

With fine verve and ease Gilbert moves from one subject to the next. He scarifies the

> Demi-dieux avortés qui par droit de naissance,
> Dans les camps, à la cour règnent en espérance;

the fashionable blue-stocking,

> Qui gouverne la mode, à son gré met en vogue
> Nos petits vers lâchés par gros in-octavo,
> Ou ces drames pleureurs qu'on joue incognito;

the vaporous beauty who bursts into tears if Fido hurts his paw, and fights for a front seat at public executions; duchesses who prostitute themselves; fathers who look with complacent indulgence on the debauchery of their children; dishonest bankrupts; boudoir abbés being witty about God; magistrates who sell their honour and their wives; dunderheads who sneer at Racine and Corneille. The poem is not long, but Gilbert's repertoire is extensive and well-chosen. The only poem in English which resembles *Le Dix-huitième Siècle* is Byron's *Don Juan*, which, if enormously more lengthy, does not excel Gilbert's in quality. The latter has an amazing gift for condensing a portrait or an idea in a couplet. On the other hand, he lacks Cowper's genius for the original and quaint epithet.

> Gorgonius sits, abdominous and wan,
> Like a fat squab upon a Chinese fan.[2]

is infinitely superior to:

> Entends ce jeune abbé; sophiste bel esprit,
> Monsieur fait son procès au Dieu qui le nourrit.

Again,

> La muse de Sophocle en robe doctorale,
> Sur des tréteaux sanglants professe la morale.

---

[1] A reference to his play, *Gustave Vasa*.   [2] *The Progress of Error.*

hits off the craze for *drames* very prettily, but there is a more effective slyness in Cowper's thrust at the Scotomaniacs:

> Perhaps some bonny Caledonian air,
> All birks and braes, though he was never there.

Gilbert's satire, though terribly sincere, was inspired by a sense of personal disappointment. All his poetry expresses an almost arrogant consciousness of his own worth and a despair that it will never be recognized. This is evident in his earliest poem, *Les Plaintes du Malheureux* (1771).

> Le jour fuit, la nuit naît, prompte à s'évanouir;
> Tout passe, et ma douleur paraît seule éternelle.

Gilbert curses his parents for educating him above his station, and, in an access of self-pity, exclaims:

> Et moi . . . sur un grabat arrosé de mes larmes
> Je veille, je languis par la faim dévoré.
> Et tout est insensible aux horreurs que j'endure,
> Tout est sourd à mes cris, tout dort dans la nature,
> Dans les bois, à la ville, aux champs et sur les flots.[1]

Like Rousseau's hero, Saint-Preux, he turns to nature for solace from the inhumanity of man:

> Quand tout devant mes yeux respire la tristesse
> Je ne sais quel plaisir pénètre dans mon cœur.
> Mais mon front s'éclaircit, je sens moins mon malheur,
> Je crois que la nature à mon sort s'intéresse.
> Être plaint, c'est beaucoup pour un infortuné!
> Et ce triste bonheur que l'homme lui dénie,
> En apparence au moins, dans les bois m'est donné.[2]

This is still the work of a prentice hand, but the emotions are true and deep. The pessimism of Gilbert suggests that a new theme has entered French poetry, a theme which will be later superbly exploited by De Vigny. A few days before he took his own life, Gilbert wrote his epitaph in lines that are justly famous:

> Au banquet de la vie, infortuné convive,
> J'apparus un jour, et je meurs.
> Je meurs: et sur ma tombe, où lentement j'arrive,
> Nul ne viendra verser des pleurs.[3]

With the quenching of this gallant spirit we arrive at the brink of the Revolution. And at this point, these comments on French

---

[1] Readers of *Iphigénie* will recognize the source of the last two lines.
[2] *Quart d'heure de Misanthropie* (1771).   [3] *Ode imitée de plusieurs Psaumes.*

and English eighteenth-century poetry may very fittingly conclude. On the whole, the way followed by Gilbert, by Léonard, Parny, and Bertin is that of French tradition. It is the road leading from Villon through Ronsard and Racine. Soon that road will traverse a new climate and will be flooded with radiance. Yet it will not essentially change. The great singers, De Vigny, Lamartine, Hugo, and De Musset, will march along it, whilst the smaller men, lured into foreign by-paths, will disappear into the jungle of oblivion. For it is the national or traditional quality that makes poetry great. Rarely, therefore, do the supreme masters exercise a universal or even European appeal. Language, the expressive medium of the poet, has limitations which music, painting, and sculpture scarcely know. That the genius of the translator is powerless to surmount these obstacles we have seen. And in the eighteenth century, translation from our tongue into French was in its infancy. Mostly, it was in the hands of two or three men, like La Place, Le Tourneur, and Prévost, who, indeed, admired our literature but also were obliged to translate for a livelihood. To argue that our imaginative works were rendered into French in response to an urgent and widespread demand is to misrepresent the actual situation. Translation, then as now, was undertaken in the pious hope that such a demand existed or might be created. It is undeniable that in a varying degree the French versions of Pope, Thomson, Young, and Ossian aroused curiosity: yet, with the exception of Pope, acquaintance with these English works left the French traditional genius almost intact. In reality, the early processes of the great change called *le Romantisme* resulted from internal forces which by their nature and origin were thoroughly French. And the supreme event in that change was the gradual freeing of poetry, by sentiment, from the tyranny of the rational or scientific spirit of the eighteenth century. French Romanticism is the triumph of individualism, the splendid challenge hurled by a handful of rebels at the old giants. Reason, as it was conceived by the age of Louis XIV, was discarded by the men of the eighteenth century for the reason of Newton, which they were as yet, however, unfitted to wield. So, whilst reviling Descartes, it was still to his way of thinking that they turned in their fever and in their haste to evoke a millennium.

The result of this confusion is plainly reflected in the ideology of the century, in that queer jumble of ideas of which some were derived from experience, others from the fertile minds of optimistic visionaries.

Small wonder, then, if after the Revolution, men of imagination shuddered at the name of reason, and claimed the right for each to carve out his own destiny. Systems had seen their day: rules of every kind were suspect. Rational religion and rational morality were terms that stank in the nostrils of the young men of 1820. *Le moi*, the individual soul with all its pent-up passions and its dreams, was at last free to express itself. In so doing it created a new poetry, a new literature. But this poetry was, let us not forget, essentially French. For at this moment the old genius of France, mustering all the forces at her command, discovered potentialities and talents which had long lain buried and unused. Tomes have been written to show that the France of the romantic period borrowed from her foreign allies to enrich her treasury and to increase her strength. And to some extent that is true. Yet the triumph she achieved was due, in the last analysis, to the genius of her race. The romantic crisis in France was no doubt precipitated by foreign agencies: yet its form and direction were determined by tradition. And the resistance which was opposed by her eighteenth-century poets to every serious attempt at imposing the genius of a foreign race upon their own was continued by their successors. That must be evident to any one who will review the romantic literature of France in its correct perspective. But here, precisely, is the danger that lies in wait for the student of comparative literature. Closeted for months with a single writer whose influence he seeks to trace in the thought of a foreign race, he is apt to lose all sense of relative values. His particular tree looms larger and larger, till at last the forest disappears. For this reason, such individual studies, though most valuable, have usually to be consulted with precaution. Indeed, in many cases, if we were to add up the conclusions arrived at by certain of these authors we should reach the strange result that eighteenth-century France had no native literature at all, so heavily indebted was she to our English writers.[1] If only as a corrective of such a misconception in regard to French poetry, maybe the preceding chapters have justified their existence.

---

[1] I refer to the type of study which, for convenience, we may classify as the *Jones en France* thesis. With notable exceptions, the writing of these has been too often entrusted to young students who lack sufficient general knowledge of the period from which their subject is drawn. In some cases, too, there has been a tendency to assume, *a priori*, that 'Jones' *must* have influenced French literature and, therefore, that the business of the thesis is simply to discover evidence in support of that assumption. The remedy for such a state of affairs is obvious. Subjects for doctoral theses should no longer be presented to students by well-meaning professors. No book is of any value unless the author has a strong conviction that it must be written and that he is qualified to write it.

THE NOVEL

CHAPTER XII

TWO STRANGE WOMEN

THE Elizabethan theatre was designed to satisfy the public appetite for strong and highly imaginative fiction in an age which had as yet no novels worthy of the name. Indeed, perhaps the most stupendous feature of Shakespeare's art is the nonchalance with which those elements, now considered peculiar to the novel, are alchemized into poetry and transmuted into dramatic action. In a way, then, the playwrights of the Elizabethan period almost rendered novelists superfluous. The contrary is true of the French neo-classic stage. Racine took over and perfected a type of drama that was essentially and deliberately *anti-romanesque*. His audiences, when they wanted combats, disguises, abductions, *reconnaissances*, ambushes, druggings, and duels, knew better than to expect them at the *Comédie française*. For such agreeable and facile excitants they went to the book-sellers of the Palais-Royal, and there purchased the latest romance by Camus or La Calprenède. Despite the sneers of the Abbé de Villars and others at the 'weepiness' of *Bérénice*, the theatre of Racine, in its general tone, is utterly different from the heroic fiction of the same era. With *Phèdre*, the last and greatest French tragedy of love, a chasm was opened between the theatre and the novel. Here is the quintessence of tragedy. It is tragedy purged of all the ingredients which combined to build up a European reputa-tion for Mlle de Scudéry and her followers. The spectator, lifted above time and space, has the curious illusion of gazing down into the amphitheatre of the universe. As the play of human passions unfolds, the words, the gestures, and the silences of the characters assume a strange and remote beauty. Yet everything is supremely and terribly real. No one, it is true, can imagine that he will ever again hear accents so poignant or witness passions of such intensity; but they clutch at the fibres of the heart and arouse a shudder of astonishment and awe. In contemplating the ordeal of Phèdre, we understand what Aristotle meant by drama purging us of pity and terror by means of pity and terror.   For just as men who have known the dangers of war have only to recall them so as never again to be afraid of the lesser physical calamities of normal life, so, after witnessing Racine's immortal tragedy, the spectator is granted a new vision of life.   How shamefully trivial now are the petty mishaps which we used to grandly call our 'tragedies.'   Racine gives us a new set of spiritual values to substitute for our old counterfeit tokens.   Actually for the first time, we know what pity and fear really mean: we know what is really critical in life.   That, it seems, must be the function of great tragedy.   It must be a tonic to the spirit, a sanctuary, lofty but accessible, where man can recover his lost belief in human dignity.   There one can glimpse the godlike streak in man and go back exalted and refreshed into the arena.

With this in mind, consider the temerity of Madame de La Fayette, who, one year after the appearance of *Phèdre*, calmly set out to write a novel based on an almost similar theme.   For the subject of her *Princesse de Clèves* is eminently Racinian.   It concerns the effect of an illicit passion upon the soul of a *maîtresse femme*, a woman who, like Phèdre, is incapable of juggling with moral values. And the amazing fact remains that *La Princesse de Clèves* is a masterpiece, the first great love-novel in any language.   Briefly described, this was the achievement of Madame de La Fayette.   Striking a middle way between the incredible idealization of the heroic novel, and the grotesque caricature of the comic fictions invented by Scarron and Furetière, she gave to the novel the dignity, the compactness, and the form of neo-classic drama, yet made it reveal an aspect of the human soul untouched by Corneille or Racine.   In a word, she created, by force of genius, the novel of psychological analysis.   How much that implies will be evident only to those who have read the works of Prévost, Marivaux, Laclos, Constant, Stendhal, Flaubert, and Proust.

There is no occasion to discuss the comparative merits of Madame de La Fayette and of Racine as interpreters of the sentiments and passions.   One does not ask whether *Tom Jones* is a better work than *Le Barbier de Séville*, or whether *Paradise Lost* is superior to *Hamlet*. Here we are dealing with two different types of art, and our sole purpose is to show that they are different.   *La Princesse de Clèves* is not simply Racinian drama recast in narrative prose form in the manner of some Lamb's tale.   Had our author wanted to perform this operation on a Racinian play, she could have done it in a few lines. What she wanted to do and did with *éclat*, was to present a vision of life which the neo-classic dramatist had deliberately ignored. Interested only in crises, caught up in the relentless, breathless sweep of action, Racine had no time to portray the incubation of passion, or to reveal the complex transitional process by which virtue is slowly transmuted into vice and happiness into sorrow. In his eyes, a destiny only began to be dramatic at a point which, for the novelist, marks a crisis. Had Racine, on the other hand, undertaken to dramatize the *Princesse de Clèves*, he would have opened his play just before the moment where the heroine, tortured by the consciousness of her love for Nemours, makes full confession to her husband in the futile hope that she can enlist his sympathy and aid. Actually, this crucial scene occurs more than half-way through the novel, though everything that precedes it, from the author's standpoint, is absolutely vital to our understanding of the situation. What, then, is contained in these two hundred pages that neither a Racine nor a Corneille can portray? The historic colour we can dismiss, because at this stage in the development of the novel historic colour is still something of an *hors-d'œuvre*. And yet it is quite essential to understand the social *milieu* to which Madame de Clèves belongs. Here we touch upon something quite foreign to neo-classic drama. The heroine's inner life is shaped and constricted by a mass of conventional but inescapable social obligations. The profound truth, therefore, which emerges from this novel is that to live the honourable and happy life it is not enough to possess principles and to apply them to our conduct.

In neo-classic drama, the tragedy arises from an inner conflict between duty and passion. In that respect, Phèdre is always rational. She is poignantly aware that her passion for Hippolyte is criminal, but she is swept away by the fury of love. 'C'est Vénus toute entière à sa proie attachée.' Madame de Clèves is also passionately in love. Her instinct is to avoid Nemours; but in the eyes of the world her very avoidance of him must be interpreted to her dishonour. Her tragedy is that she cannot be alone. Every day she must face her husband with a guilty secret in her heart and at every social function she hears her lover discussed. By sheer force of circumstances she is compelled to live a long and bitter lie. And when, with supreme courage, she throws herself on her husband's mercy it is with the despairing knowledge that in obeying a high and fine impulse she is committing a social crime which, in her remorse, she interprets as a moral one. Here we are no longer confronted by ultimate values.   Free will, justice, honour cease to be absolutes since, in reality, no one can live in society and claim to be free to exert his will; nor is it even possible, except at the risk of inflicting frightful pain on an innocent fellow-being, always to carry one's principles into effect.   That all these complexities are to be found in a novel and not in a play involves no criticism of Racine, who moves on another plane.   The contemplation of Madame de Clèves's destiny does not fill us with astonishment and awe, though it arouses our quick interest and sympathy.   It is tragic, but it does not leave us with that sense of inevitability, of inescapable doom which broods over Phèdre.   One can criticize the actions of Madame de Clèves but not those of Phèdre, because, with her, passion could only end in destruction. No character in a novel can ever be, I suppose, so completely individual as in great tragedy and remain credible.   Balzac is the exception that proves the rule: with Stendhal it does not somehow matter.   Moreover, it is the peculiar privilege of the dramatist to astonish us by situations which, though suddenly presented, are never challenged by an audience carried along by the rush of action.   No novelist, for example, would dare to present Phèdre's stupefying confession to her stepson without previously leading up to it.   Suddenly projected into a novel, it would strike the reader as bad art, and would be bad art, because the novelist, as narrator, has it in his power to reveal the genesis of such an act.   Thus, a great part of the *Princesse de Clèves* is devoted to the analysis of the doubts and fears, the jealousy and shame that lead to the final confession.   But in *Phèdre* all this is relegated to the unseen action of the play, to that silent zone covered by the first four scenes of the second act, where the heroine is invisible to the spectator. In a novel there can be no such unexplained periods.

We need not embark upon a detailed discussion of the minor points which further differentiate the art of Madame de La Fayette from that of Racine.   As she had not to reckon with the unities and other conventions imposed by the dramatist upon himself, Madame de La Fayette was free to move her characters at will, to choose their settings, multiply her situations, and so fortify that illusion of warm, first-hand contact with everyday life that is peculiar to great novels.   In this respect, however, she reveals admirable restraint, and therefore never allows the focal ray of interest to shift or to lose its intensity.   By stressing the importance of psychological analysis as opposed to the mere narrative of physical adventures, Madame de La Fayette plotted the master curve to be followed by later novelists. In a way, the success of the *Princesse de Clèves* necessarily retarded, in France, the evolution of the novel of manners. Its author was too seventeenth-century in her outlook to be interested in those picturesque, descriptive details which the nineteenth century was to consider so vital to the creation of 'atmosphere.' And, although excited research students never fail to draw attention to a certain *cabinet de verdure* once mentioned in the *Princesse de Clèves*, its author can scarcely be described, on that account, as a precursor of Jean-Jacques Rousseau and the nature novelists. Her achievement was, nevertheless, a great one. Out of the chaos of seventeenth-century fiction she created something that was a genuine and independent form of art, and gave to the modern French novel its shape, its substance, and its dynamic power. A full half-century elapsed, however, ere France produced, in the Abbé Prévost, a worthy successor to the author of the *Princesse de Clèves*. Over the life of this man there hangs, as over some ancient ruin, a spell of mystery and romance. Nevertheless, from the fragments so piously collected by M. Harrisse, it is just possible to divine the contours of the mind which conceived the immortal *Manon Lescaut*. And, if we cannot justly assert that all the emotional experiences of his heroes reflect those of Prévost himself, it is morally certain that they are his spiritual children. In the modern sense, Prévost the novelist was not an observer. His imagination, unlike that of Flaubert or Proust, did not work outwards. He could never, for instance, have created a Homais or a Charlus, because characters like these are spiritually detached from their authors. They are the products of an imagination controlled by intellect, an imagination which seizes upon observed material and moulds it into artistic shape. On the contrary, Prévost never worked in this objective way and all his men have unmistakable traits which betray their filiation. The fibres linking them to their author are never broken. The vital stuff which composes their character is spun from Prévost's own soul. All possess, in varying degree, a restlessness, a craving for passion and for high adventure followed by a swift sense of satiety and a nostalgia for quiet. Now these are the very qualities which drove Prévost himself from the seminary into the army, thence to the cloister; from the cloister to Holland and to England; back again to the cloister, and finally, once more into the world as chaplain to the Prince de Conti. In a sense, then, it is true to say that all his male characters are hewn from the same block, though it would be wrong to affirm that they are not sufficiently individualized. Actually, they are; since Prévost's own nature was protean in the variety of its component elements. And, if he had not the Olympian aloofness of the objective novelist, or that astounding gift of perception we find in Proust and Flaubert, these lacks were compensated for to some extent by his amazing knowledge of himself. The *esprit d'examen* was with him a natural habit of mind. To create character, therefore, he had only to look within himself, to seize and examine one of his many moods, and to brood upon it. This power of introspection, fortified by an unbridled imagination, furnished him with an array of strongly-marked characters whose fundamental absence of complexity is cleverly concealed by the fact that Prévost, having launched them into his imaginary world, thereafter gives them no rest. They are ruthlessly plunged into a bewildering maelstrom of adventures, physical and emotional. It is only after we lay down a Prévost novel and begin to reflect on the psychology of his people that we realize how one-idea'd they are. In *Manon Lescaut* this is not a defect but a virtue, since the whole object of the novel is to portray a man in the grip of a single obsession. The other works, however, fail to hold us to-day because we are no longer interested in the adventures that charmed Prévost's contemporaries; and thus, we are no longer blinded to the inherent shallowness of the characters themselves.

As is natural, the fame of *Manon Lescaut* has driven all Prévost's other works into oblivion, with the sole exception, perhaps, of *L'Histoire d'une Grecque moderne*. If one hears of *Les Mémoires d'un Homme de Qualité*, his first novel, it is because of certain precocious and interesting remarks on the England of Queen Anne. *Cléveland*, which used to make Rousseau weep, *Le Doyen de Killerine*, and *Les Mémoires de M. de Montcal* are known only to scholars. It is, however, necessary to speak of them here since they help us to a more complete understanding of Prévost's artistic methods, and besides. as M. Le Breton has shown, they contain passages that may still be read with pleasure. In common justice to the author, it should be mentioned that they were 'pot-boilers,' as he frankly admits in the preface to his *Doyen de Killerine*. But *Manon* was a labour of love.

All Prévost's heroes have an invincible and Pascalian horror of life, and this idea is at the root of all his novels. The Homme de Qualité has spent his boyhood in a foreign land, far from the world of men and action. On returning to France in order to inherit the family estates, he is suddenly struck down by a series of disasters. His sister is accidentally killed, his father retires to a Carthusian monastery, and owing to legal chicanery, the hero is deprived of all his property. With no other equipment than a set of rigid principles, he is cast into a seething whirlpool of violent experiences. Clèveland, an illegitimate son of Cromwell's, spends his boyhood in a Somersetshire cave, where he is educated by his mother according to a system based upon the teachings of the pagan philosophers. At her death, he embarks on a career that takes him to the New World, to Cuba, St. Helena, England, and France. The Doyen de Killerine, from a sense of family duty, abandons his peaceful Irish parish to follow his brothers and sisters to France, where he is caught up in a network of Jacobite intrigue and passionate adventure. M. de Montcal, an officer of a philosophic cast of mind, is lured by his chivalrous instincts into a bubbling crater of jealousy, love, and violence. Finally, there is Des Grieux, who, as it were, walks from the seminary into the arms of the mistress of his heart.

Now these characters all possess common traits, and, beyond a doubt, they present an idealized picture of the author himself. Des Grieux is almost certainly the Prévost who bolted from Holland with the mysterious Lenki, and escaped prison either by a technical error or by the kindness of his employer. Clèveland is Prévost, the *philosophe*, torn between orthodoxy and Deism. The Doyen de Killerine is the Prévost who pleads for a more humane interpretation of Holy Writ, the priest who has learned what temptation and human weakness really are. Montcal is the older, the calmer Prévost who believes, like the Homme de Qualité, that reason and honour can overcome our most violent passions. The difference, however, lies in the fact that Montcal's wisdom comes from experience, not from theory. In all these characters the attitude towards love is much the same. No novelist, it is safe to hazard, has ever paid such homage to the power of passionate love or invested woman with so much mystery. For Prévost, as for Racine, love is 'Vénus toute entière à sa proie attachée,' a violent malady, an almost pathological state which renders its victims capable of the most terrible crimes. As a result, Prévost will condone murder, rape, abduction, and the blackest perfidy provided they emanate from this grand passion. The Homme de Qualité has a pupil who, in a jealous rage, shoots an inoffensive rival. The tutor's remarkable comment is: 'Deliver yourself of love and I see you almost without a defect.' Clèveland has a queer friend,

Gelin, who falls in love with Madame Clèveland and, with Iago-like cunning, poisons her mind against her husband. Gelin persuades her to leave Clèveland, whom he later tries to murder. Yet Clèveland freely forgives Gelin and tells us that he is at heart a generous and honourable man. The Doyen's brother, Patrice, commits bigamy and murder; yet Prévost presents him always as the victim of misfortune, and Patrice ends up as a model husband and father. One could cite many such cases. Indeed, except for Cromwell and a certain Huguenot minister in *Clèveland*, who are both hypocrites, there are no 'villains' in Prévost's novels. His men commit almost every crime in the statute-book save perhaps simony and barratry, but they are merely 'the playthings of an evil Power.'

The misfortunes of all Prévost's heroes, if we except Georges in the *Doyen de Killerine* whose troubles arise from the vice of ambition, arise directly or indirectly from love. Here, however, a distinction is to be made between events that are *funestes* and such as are merely *tragiques*. Clèveland points that out. The crimes done by Gelin and by the nefarious Captain Will, who kidnaps and rapes a French widow, are tragic because they are violent. But when Clèveland falls passionately in love with a girl who later turns out to be his own daughter, that is 'une aventure funeste,' since, as he naïvely observes, it nearly leads to the wreck of his honour and virtue. It is this quaint morality which leads Prévost, in *Manon Lescaut*, to gloss over the murder of the prison turnkey, the card-sharping of Des Grieux, and the hero's tacit consent to the prostitution of Manon. To grasp Prévost's point of view, one must remember that he was extremely fatalistic. Now all his critics attribute his fatalism to the fact that he was a Jansenist, and, until recently, I myself have accepted this explanation, with the reserve that he was rather more of a Calvinist than a disciple of Port-Royal. On re-reading his works, however, I have come to the conclusion that Prévost's apparent fatalism is really superstition; and one cannot but be struck by the recurrence of his allusions to dreams and to what in Scotland we call 'fore-goes.' Beyond a doubt this author, despite his religious training—some might aver because of it—firmly believes in the existence of a Power of Evil. His heroines, in the midst of their brief spells of happiness, are invaded by the premonition of pending disaster. Someone, so to speak, is constantly 'walking over their graves.' Now that, although in the last analysis it amounts to a belief in predestination, is hardly the same as the religious dogma of a Calvinist or a Jansenist. It arises from an ingrained, morbid superstition which is reflected in various incidents. The *Homme de Qualité*, his earliest novel, is in this respect particularly illuminating. Before the death of his sister Julia, the hero is tormented by grisly nightmares, and Julia herself talks of her approaching demise with calm certainty. The Man of Quality, before learning of Louis XIV's decease, sees the whole event in a vivid dream. Clèveland, on embarking for France, is full of forebodings that are amply realized. Des Grieux, on the brink of his second and fatal lapse, has a vision of himself, as of a man lost in a dark and desolate countryside. Gelin, in despair at the coldness of Madame Clèveland, has recourse to sorcery and performs certain black and mysterious rites with some of her blood and hair, while Prévost, though condemning this 'profanation and the impieties with which the dark ceremony was accomplished,' reveals by his very horror of the occult that he believes in it implicitly. In the *Homme de Qualité*, death is often associated with some form of morbidity. When the hero loses his wife he puts her heart in a golden box, and lives for a year in a shuttered room lighted by candles, lost in gloomy contemplation of her clothes, her portrait, and the box. The marquis de Rosemont, on the death of Diana, wears her garments converted into male apparel. Patrice, the precocious romantic, whose character it is to 'feel an unsurmountable ennui in the midst of everything that bears the name of pleasure or amusement,' retires after the death of his bigamous wife to a Trappist cell hung with violet tapestries.

Everything in Prévost was extraordinary, and, in his novels, if we except always *Manon Lescaut*, life is constantly melodramatized. His characters feel and act with an intensity that is incredible, and their situations are equally inconceivable. Never, for example, does he present them engaged in the ordinary occupations of existence. His attitude toward money is typical. His people pass from opulence to poverty overnight; yet always, in some unforeseen way, they find the sinews of love, since all their wealth is squandered in the service of that passion. The Doyen and his family calmly leave their Irish estates to seek a fortune in France, and have not the slightest doubt that, on arrival, there will be generous Frenchmen eager to assure their future. Again, despite the most amazing adventures in America, Clèveland and his friends always succeed in meeting once more though divided by hundreds of miles of virgin territory. Every novel thus becomes a bewildering tangle of swift separations and miraculous reunions, a queer kaleidoscope of events so strange and varied as to baffle description. Prévost was an avid reader of English history and of travels, and, indeed, the *Histoire générale des Voyages*, which he edited with success, is borrowed largely from an English source. Without the slightest compunction, then, he allots important roles in his novels to Cromwell, Charles II, James II, the Duke of Monmouth, and the Earl of Clarendon. To give an instance of his technique, Cromwell is portrayed as a bloody and vindictive Tartuffe who tries to do away with one of his bastards, and, when foiled in the attempt, has his mistress abducted and raped by his servants. The same amiable Protector is also responsible for the ravishing of the Countess of Axminster through the friendly offices of his creature, the Earl of Aberdeen. Prévost was, it will be seen, the first successful writer of *romans-feuilleton* and the lineal ancestor of Soulié, Sue, and Dumas.

A similar recklessness is evident in his account of the emotional adventures of his heroes and heroines, who are ringed in by a chain of misfortunes, all of which the author dexterously contrives to attribute to excess of passion. Prévost's method of presenting these is remarkable, and, for his time, unique. By exploiting the fact that his stories are supposed to be related by the principal actor, and in order to lend them an air of great veracity, he often anticipates the reader's curiosity by presenting him beforehand with the key to a situation. So when Cleveland is living in Cuba with his wife, Fanni, in a state of illusory happiness, we are let into the secret that she is consumed with jealousy of a certain Mme Lallin whom her husband, out of gratitude, had rescued from Virginia and brought to Cuba. Fanni's jealousy is incessantly fed by Gelin, with whom she eventually elopes. Prévost disingenuously takes us into his confidence and informs us of the actual situation. 'I have perhaps,' he confesses, 'satisfied my readers' curiosity too soon. To make my story more interesting, to lend it the graces of a novel, I ought to have postponed till the end of the work the *éclaircissement* which I have hastened to give at this point. But am I capable of seeking to please, and have I in these memoirs promised anything else but the picture of my remorse and grief?' This trick of letting the cat out of the bag rather stimulates the interest than otherwise, since we have no very clear view of the cat itself till later on. When, for instance, with a truly royal gesture he opens *Manon Lescaut* with a picture of the heroine in chains, all he is giving us is what a lesser novelist would regard as the *pièce de résistance*. His own ending is where it should be. In other words, Prévost anticipates events only where they do not essentially matter. Where such a premature disclosure will vitally detract from the suspense of a situation he is discreetly reticent and darkly portentous. The incestuous episode in *Clèveland* is typical. Here, of course, Prévost is wading in deep waters. Somewhere in this strange and passionate account, he is obliged to prepare the reader for the shock that is to come and to ward off, if possible, a revulsion of feeling. He opens with a solemn generalization. 'I feel my hand tremble as I begin the tale of one of the most fateful adventures of my life. . . . Only a miracle of heaven could have saved me so close to the abyss.' As the narrative proceeds, Clèveland's passion is imperceptibly drained of its sexual and erotic qualities, until it gradually becomes clear that in Cécile he is really worshipping the ideal once embodied in the wife whom he now believes to be faithless. Granting the incredibility of the hypothesis on which this situation is based, it is difficult to see how any one could have handled it with more delicacy and charm. It is, indeed, the only episode in all Prévost's works where he recaptures the poetry of *Manon*. And just as in that masterpiece there are lines which defy translation, there are in the following passage certain words which must lose their secret aroma if decanted into our idiom: 'En effet, j'étais comme enchanté de la voir. L'émotion de la marche et les aventures de la nuit lui donnaient un air si fin et si brillant, que je me rassasiais aussi peu d'admiration que d'amour. . . . Il faut que le corps ait un étrange pouvoir sur nos âmes! Depuis que j'avais touché les mains de Cécile, que j'avais été seul avec elle, que je m'étais enivré, pour ainsi dire, de son haleine, et qu'elle m'avait pénétré de ses regards, je sentais hors de sa présence une vive inquiétude comme il arrive lorsqu'on se trouve dans un état violent. Je croyais m'apercevoir à tous moments qu'il me manquait une partie essentielle de moi-même.' There is no mistaking the pulsing beat of these accents. We have heard them already in the voice of the chevalier Des Grieux.

Prévost's women, like his men, live on the mountain peaks. Oddly enough, however, except for Manon, they are all constant to their love through every vicissitude. Sometimes, in fact, their very constancy is a thorn in the hero's flesh. So when Patrice is forced by the Doyen to marry Sara Fincer because her money released him from prison, his wife dogs him like a shadow even after he has subjected her to every conceivable form of ignominy. Clèveland's Fanni, although convinced of her husband's infidelity, rather than breathe a word of reproach, prefers to be considered an abandoned woman and leaves him to follow Gelin, whom she does not love but merely uses as an escort to the convent which is her objective. Rose, the Doyen's sister, has the courage to refuse Des Pesses despite the debt she owes him, and remains faithful to an ideal though taxed with ingratitude. But Prévost's most interesting women possess will-power of a more formidable cast. Lady R—— in the *Homme de Qualité*, Mme Lallin in *Clèveland*, Donna Figuerrez in the *Doyen*, and Mme de Gien in *Montcal* represent a feminine type which Prévost was the first to introduce into the novel. Seized with a violent passion, they discard every shred of reticence or modesty and boldly propose to the embarrassed object of their desire. Prévost loves describing these women, and, above all, the emotions of the man as he tries to extricate himself with honour and dignity from his unhappy predicament. His most successful picture of one of these modern Hippolytes is Montcal, who, owing to a complete lack of vanity and of worldly experience, is naturally and maddeningly obtuse. That is, however, because Mme de Gien's methods are less direct and brutal than those of the English Lady R—— and the impetuous Spaniard, Donna Figuerrez. It is interesting to observe, in this connection, that the majority of Prévost's characters are foreigners. He is, in fact, the first cosmopolitan novelist; for obviously, we need not take Le Sage's 'Spaniards' any more seriously than those of Beaumarchais. In *Gil Blas*, the Spanish veneer is so transparent as to be invisible to any one except the odd Castilian who still persists that the book is translated from an unknown and vanished Spanish original.

For various reasons, the Abbé Prévost found it useful to give his novels a strong cosmopolitan flavour. As he was quite aware how incredible were the adventures and sentiments conjured up by his excited imagination, it seemed advisable to attribute them to foreigners rather than to his own compatriots. Besides, having made two sojourns in England he realized the selling value of English 'copy' at a time when the French, having lost interest in Spain and in Italy, were beginning to be curious about Anglo-Saxon manners. In his first novel, England shares the honours along with Italy, Spain, and Turkey, but in his second, Prévost made all his leading characters English, except for the impetuous Gelin, who is French. In the *Doyen* he made them all Irish save for the implacable Donna Figuerrez. In *Montcal*, they are Irish and French, with the latter in a slight majority. In any case, it makes very little difference, since Prévost was incapable of anything so objective as the study of a foreign temperament. Actually, it was he who created the 'stage' Englishman of eighteenth-century France, a type later exploited in a dozen novels and plays. This ideal Englishman, the *honnête homme* of the period, the Lord Edward Bomston of Rousseau's *Nouvelle Héloïse*, is essentially Clèveland. Briefly resumed, the following are his outstanding traits. In the first place, he is a man of rigid principles and a melancholy or splenetic cast of mind. He is prone to analyse his feelings, and, as Cleveland says of himself, is 'idolâtre de sa tristesse.' Eminently just and reasonable, he is above ordinary prejudice and slow to yield to passion. But once aroused, as when he becomes the victim of love, he plumbs depths of misery unknown to the average man. He is in a word, an eccentric, *un original*, but an honourable and lovable one. Add to this, a morbid penchant for the *macabre*, and, at times, a tendency to suicide. Such was the French ideal of the English gentleman. Now, to a great extent, all these traits are already to be found in the Man of Quality, who is not unlike Prévost himself, and, as we have noted, his other heroes, with the exception of Des Grieux, reflect the same characteristics in varying degrees. One is, therefore, driven to the conclusion that our abbé invented the legendary Englishman of eighteenth-century France, and, what is more, created him largely after his own image. Certainly there is no model in our own country, either in reality or in literature, which he could have copied. Young had not yet written his *Night Thoughts*, and of all our eighteenth-century victims of misfortune, his hero is the only one who can pretend to compete with Clèveland for the title of 'le plus infortuné des hommes.' What of our novelists? Richardson had not begun to write, neither had Fielding nor Smollett. There remain Mrs. Aphra Behn and Defoe, neither of whom is mentioned in Prévost's magazine, the *Pour et Contre*. Mrs. Behn we may dismiss, since there is nothing in her work to suggest a resemblance to Prévost's manner, and Defoe's men, who are relatively unimportant compared to his women, have nothing of Clèveland in their temper. Reference to Defoe, however, calls to mind the fact that an enthusiastic devotee of the comparative method has written a long article [1] to show that *Manon Lescaut* is 'in part a reminiscence of *Moll Flanders*,' and that Manon herself is 'a purified version of the character of Moll.' Unhappily, the

[1] Roland Elissa-Rhaïs, 'Une Influence anglaise dans *Manon Lescaut*,' *Revue de la Littérature comparée* (1927).

arguments which he advances are so fantastic and the so-called resemblances so inept, that it is hardly possible to give serious consideration to this writer's views.[1] Nevertheless, it might be interesting at this point to compare the art of Defoe with that of Prévost, if only to show the racial and temperamental differences between the two novelists.

In Prévost's *Pour et Contre*[2] is to be found a laudatory and anonymous critique of *Manon Lescaut*. The writer is the author himself: 'Quel art n'a-t-il pas fallu,' he exclaims, 'pour intéresser le lecteur et lui inspirer de la compassion par rapport aux funestes disgraces qui arrivent à cette fille corrompue!' Of the style he writes: 'Il n'y a ni jargon, ni affectation, ni réflexions sophistiques: c'est la nature même qui écrit. Qu'un auteur empesé et fardé paraît pitoyable en comparaison! Celui-ci ne court point après l'esprit, ou plutôt après ce qu'on appelle ainsi. Ce n'est point un style laconiquement constipé, mais un style coulant, plein et expressif. Ce n'est partout que peintures et sentiments, mais des peintures vraies et des sentiments naturels.' This is admirably true; but that is not the point. It is rather that Prévost, less than a year after the appearance of *Manon Lescaut* in France, knew that he had created a masterpiece. But it is clear from the *façon* of the novel itself that in writing it, Prévost never for one moment forgot that he was producing a great work of art. *Manon Lescaut* has the integrity, the shape, and the deliberate restraint of a classic work of art. No one who has ever studied the genesis and evolution of an artistic masterpiece can fail to recognize the touch and finish of a man conscious at every line that he is an artist. The novel leaves us with that sense of aesthetic completeness which is to be obtained from a Racinian tragedy. Not a word could be altered, not an incident or an expression changed, without marring the plastic perfection of the whole. Its vitality, its beauty, and its interest rise in a crystalline jet from the well-spring of a single idea and a unique conception of life.

Now Defoe's *Moll Flanders*, although it is also a great novel, derives its greatness from quite other qualities. In reading it, one does not acquire the impression that its author ever visualized himself as the creator of a complete and artistic object, mastering and shaping his material in the light of an inner ideal. One might express the same opinion in another way. Prévost, in creating

[1] My reasons for this apparently harsh statement will be found in Appendix III.
[2] xxxvi, 1734.

Manon Lescaut, is influenced at every step by the fact that he possesses a seventeenth-century or Cartesian vision of the universe, which he regards as an organism governed by the forces of order, reason, and intelligence. In this cosmos, the passions are pre-ordained to defeat. Defoe, on the other hand, whatever lip-homage he pays to the power of morality as represented by a punishing and rewarding Deity, confines himself to the plain business of describing life as he sees it, and leaves the reader to form whatever general ideas he may from the novelist's picture of events. Given certain hypotheses, this is what happens to Moll Flanders. This is what she says and does. And gradually, the reader is invaded by the feeling that all these things are quite credible. Yet at the same time they might have been different and still credible. At almost any point in the narrative, for instance, one might perfectly well interfere and give a twist to the thread of events. The younger brother, Robin, whom Moll marries, need not have died after five years of marriage. Moll's second husband need not have been a rake who bolted to France. It was sheer bad luck, again, that the 'lovely person,' the highwayman, should have been a penniless, charming scoundrel. And out of all the men in the world why should she have wedded her own brother? Now *Manon Lescaut* has at every stage the authentic ring of the inevitable; everything that Des Grieux says or does is dictated by the fact that he is Des Grieux and not another man. Is Prévost on that account the greater novelist? Surely not. After all, when we look back over our own lives, or those of our friends, the predominating impression is one of surprise, and maybe chagrin, that so few of the outstanding events can be honestly attributed to our volition, to what we vaguely call 'character,' and so many to what with equal vagueness we call chance, luck, or fate. But the real difference between the art of Prévost and that of Defoe is due to another factor. In *Manon Lescaut,* the author presents, not a life, but an episode in a man's life. Defoe, on the contrary, traces the whole existence of Moll Flanders from the cradle almost to the grave. In its general trend, therefore, the French novel follows the curve of tragedy; the English, that of history or biography. Prévost's story is for that reason more critical, more compact, and more intense. It starts, evolves, and finishes on a different plane from *Moll Flanders.*

Examine the themes selected by the two writers. Des Grieux has almost completed his education and is ripe for a high position in the Church. The Arras stage coach arrives. He sees Manon and becomes the prey of a love so fierce, so implacable that, in one moment, the carefully-erected structure of his religious upbringing is consumed in the flames of passion. Des Grieux has no experience of life save through books; of women he knows nothing at all. Manon, on the other hand, is being sent to a convent because she has already evinced a precocious and inordinate love of life and pleasure. Had she been as inexperienced as Des Grieux, the matter might well have ended there; for it is she who acts. All that her lover knows is that he wants to go away with Manon, to be with Manon, anywhere and always. It is the girl who, by outwitting her servant, gives Des Grieux a breathing space in which to plan the elopement. Utterly transformed by his passion, the chevalier embarks on the first stage of his degradation. He makes a dupe and a tool of his faithful friend, Tiberge. The lovers spend a brief but deliriously happy period in Paris; yet Des Grieux is still haunted at moments by the spectre of his conscience. That ghost, however, he lays by the resolve to write to his father and to marry Manon. She, on the other hand, is not enthusiastic, since her realistic mind tells her that Des Grieux *père* will never consent to a *mésalliance*. Now follows one of the most powerful incidents in the novel, the betrayal of Des Grieux by his mistress, who sells herself to an elderly financier in order to satisfy her lust for pretty things. A stupid and scared little servant-girl reveals to Des Grieux what an ordinary man would have already guessed in twenty-four hours. But he is a poet, and not an ordinary man. In short, he is young and very much in love. And it is typical of the chevalier that when confronted with a fact such as this, namely that Manon is secretly entertaining another man in his absence, he cannot face the truth. It is here that one realizes the essential source of Des Grieux's tragedy: the impossibility of his ever entering into contact with the mental processes of Manon, to whom, of course, he attributes his own logic and his own sense of honour. The question that keeps pounding in his brain is: 'Why should Manon be unfaithful to me?' His actions reflect the movements of his soul. When the door is opened and the servant blurts out the truth, Des Grieux does not go in. Recoiling from the reality, he shuts the door and stumbles his way downstairs, crying gently. Why, he does not know. He goes to a café to think things out, and, of course, arrives at an interpretation favourable to Manon. The mysterious visitor must be a friend of her family who is supplying her with secret funds. That illusion vanishes when, on his return he is seized and taken home by his father's servants. Even then, he does not dream that this is the work of Mànon.

That revelation emerges later from a jocular remark dropped by his father. On learning the truth, the chevalier falls senseless. Picture now a man torn apart by conflicting emotions, by love, jealousy, hate, pride, revenge. He resumes his old life, plunging with ardour into his studies, so as to forget. The scene of the second and inevitable lapse is in the *parloir* of Saint-Sulpice. Only Prévost's own words, for no translation has ever rendered their secret power, can enable us to realize why Des Grieux sacrifices career, honour, and manhood to this woman: 'Il était six heures du soir. On vint m'avertir, un moment après mon retour, qu'une dame demandait à me voir. J'allai au parloir sur-le-champ. Dieu! quelle apparition surprenante! J'y trouvai Manon. C'était elle, mais plus aimable et plus brillante que je ne l'avais jamais vue. Elle était dans sa dix-huitième année; ses charmes surpassaient tout ce qu'on peut décrire: c'était un air si fin, si doux, si engageant! l'air de l'amour même. Toute sa figure me parut un enchantement.' Need one relate the outcome of this meeting, the reproaches, the meek submission, and the counter-reproaches of Manon? Once again, at a crucial moment, it is she who commits the practical act which launches the chevalier on his new career. Des Grieux, exquisitely alive to the misery that the future holds for him, seeing the uttermost depths of the abyss, hurls himself over its brink— a superb and tragic gesture.

To men like Des Grieux there are seven hells as well as seven heavens, and, in the months that ensue, he has ample time to explore them all. The successive stages of his spiritual *débâcle* are to be for ever graven on his consciousness. There are acts and thoughts which really gangrene the soul, and upon these Prévost lays most emphasis. Des Grieux, living on the money given to Manon by her financier, hopes that his father will conveniently die before these funds are exhausted. Des Grieux, the card-sharp, preys on society. That is sufficiently bad. But it is nothing to the sophistry with which he succeeds in convincing himself that it is moral to despoil the rich. Manon's pimp of a soldier brother points out that they need never starve so long as his sister keeps her looks, and the chevalier, who would once have smashed the words back into Lescaut's foul throat, merely replies with a sickly smile that this must be regarded as a last resource. Yet perhaps the vilest of his deeds is to feign conversion so as to persuade Tiberge to lend him his last few hundred francs. From that to the ignominy of passing himself off as Manon's brother in the grim farce which finally lands him in Saint-Lazare is not a difficult transition.

Des Grieux escapes from prison by intimidating the superior, whose sympathy he has won by pretended repentance. In this affair he murders the porter. After releasing Manon from the Hôpital, the chevalier enters on the final adventure which leads to the transportation of his mistress. Foiled in a desperate attempt to rescue her on the road to Le Havre, he follows Manon to New Orleans. Both are now changed. But by an ironic circumstance, their first attempt to conform to the ways of society leads to disaster. The governor's nephew is in love with Manon but thinks she is already married. Therefore, when Des Grieux and his mistress try to regularize their situation, they are told that the governor intends Manon for his nephew. There is a fight and a hurried flight into the wild. Here Manon dies and Des Grieux buries her in the sand. Nowhere else in fiction do I know of anything so moving and so beautiful as Prévost's account of these last moments: 'J'ouvris une large fosse; j'y plaçai l'idole de mon cœur, après avoir pris soin de l'envelopper de tous mes habits pour empêcher le sable de la toucher. Je ne la mis en cet état qu'après l'avoir embrassée mille fois avec toute l'ardeur du plus parfait amour. Je m'assis encore près d'elle; je la considérai longtemps; je ne pouvais me résoudre à fermer sa fosse. Enfin, mes forces recommençant à s'affaiblir, et craignant d'en manquer tout à fait avant la fin de mon entreprise, j'ensevelis pour toujours dans le sein de la terre ce qu'elle avait porté de plus parfait et de plus aimable; je me couchai ensuite sur la fosse, le visage tourné vers le sable, et, fermant les yeux avec le dessein de ne les ouvrir jamais, j'invoquai le secours du Ciel et j'attendis la mort avec impatience.' These lines have all the solemn sweetness of a requiem.

To suggest that *Moll Flanders* resembles *Manon Lescaut* because both novels introduce a prostitute is arrant nonsense. A prostitute, according to the Oxford Dictionary, is 'a woman who offers her body to indiscriminate sexual intercourse, especially for hire.' Now, strictly speaking, this definition applies both to Moll Flanders and to Manon Lescaut, yet it can hardly be said to throw much light on their characters. And they are, in fact, utterly unlike. Defoe and Prévost view life from completely different angles. Both, of course, discuss love in its relation to the individual and to society, but scarcely ever do they meet on common ground. Moll

Flanders is the illegitimate child of a woman transported for petty larceny, and she is brought up by a nurse to whom the parish entrusts such little waifs. By a stroke of luck, however, she interests an ex-mayoress of the provincial town where she lives, and is taken into the family as a domestic servant. Moll is well treated and is educated along with the daughters of this household. The eldest son, with whom she falls deeply in love, seduces her, and, under the eyes of his unsuspecting parents, makes her his mistress. He has, as a matter of fact, promised to marry her when he comes into the estate. Meanwhile, Robin, the younger brother, offers Moll honourable love; and her seducer, seeing a good chance of getting the girl off his hands, does everything to get her to listen to his younger brother. This is a crucial moment in the life of Moll. She is filled with horror at the suggestion, but finally, out of fear of poverty, marries Robin. Moll remains technically faithful to her husband despite her lover's ignoble advances, but, as she confesses, during all the time of her marriage she commits adultery in thought with the elder brother. On Robin's death, after five years of wedlock, Moll is a changed woman. When she remarries it is simply to have an assured social position. Her new venture is not a success. Her husband, a linen-draper and a rake, decamps to France to avoid the consequences of bankruptcy. Moll is not left penniless, but she takes refuge in the Mint as Mrs. Flanders. From this point her attitude towards the other sex is definitely that of a disillusioned woman. It is to be seen in her handling of the Virginia planter who comes courting her money. She brings him to heel with great cunning, and, by shaming him, persuades him to propose marriage although she protests that she has no fortune. This man takes her to America, where, on meeting his mother, Moll learns to her horror that her husband is no other than her own brother. This terrible episode is narrated with incredible power and naturalness. Eventually, the heroine reveals the dreadful situation to her husband, but only after every attempt has failed to persuade him to let her go back to England. At no other point in this novel does the deliberately undramatic manner of Defoe stand him in greater stead. By eschewing art he achieves an artistic triumph. With characters drawn from a higher social sphere he would have failed abjectly. As it is, the sheer brutality and directness of what is said and done and felt by Moll, by her mother and her husband, makes the reader forget absolutely that the whole situation is grotesquely incredible. That is great art.

In England, Moll, to quote her graphic expression, is 'bleeding to death' financially. Through her bawdy landlady, she strikes up a friendship with a man whom she nurses through a severe illness. This man is quite prepared to let their intimacy rest at friendship and, indeed, lives with her on this footing until, as she says: 'I exchanged the place of friend for that unmusical, harsh-sounding title of whore.' In any case, there is no question of marrying her protector, who has an insane wife. The liaison is broken after six years by the man during a fit of pious remorse induced by a long illness. It is typical of Moll that she makes no effort to hold him, although she is now forty-two and not at all well off. That is not her way with men, for she has a kind of pride. In this particular affair, moreover, she is uneasy in her conscience since it was she who played the part of seducer. On casting up her accounts, her invariable habit on such occasions, Moll finds herself with four hundred and fifty pounds this side of destitution. Her one desire, as always, is security. She therefore makes the acquaintance of a London tradesman to whom she entrusts the management of her small fortune. As Moll shrewdly surmises, the business man is touched and flattered by her confidence, and, in return, tells her about his intimate affairs. Amongst other things he is a cuckold. To cut the story short, this man offers to marry Moll after his divorce. But meanwhile, that romantic lady is being courted by an impetuous Irishman who has been led to believe by a female accomplice that he is on the track of a large fortune—an illusion which Moll cunningly fosters. They are married, and the husband, who in private life is a highwayman, learns that his wife has nothing. That, of course, is also a lie. This imbroglio, with its queer blend of tragedy and farce, forms one of the most interesting episodes in the book. Moll is really in love with her Jemmy and is sorely tempted to offer him all her goods. Prudence, however, gets the upper hand. She goes so far as to suggest that she may be able to raise three hundred pounds if Jemmy will take her to Virginia, but is rather relieved when he refuses and proposes a separation. The upshot of this strange affair is that Moll emerges with a glowing sensation of righteousness, whilst the husband, far from suspecting her craftiness, is seized with admiration for her virtue, regarding himself as little better than a hound. That is Moll's speciality.

She is, however, with child, and this brings her into contact with the 'eminent lady in her way,' later always referred to as her 'governess.' Here Defoe gives a richly documented account of

M

one of those institutions which, under various disguises, still flourish in all great cities. I mean the private lying-in establishment where social 'slips' are rectified or otherwise hushed up. Defoe, who is not handicapped by the nineteenth-century niceness of Dickens or with his penchant for sentimental exaggeration, paints his picture in gruff and true colours. Incidentally, he accentuates the relieving traits of Moll's nature, her horror of abortion and, above all, her maternal anxiety as to the fate of the child. The old beldam herself is superbly drawn. Smooth-spoken, understanding, placatory, and secret, she is a universal type, the perfect *proxénète*. Even Moll, who is not over-given to blabbing out her private matters, is as wax in the hands of Mother Midnight, who laughs away her scruples as to marriage with her London tradesman. She therefore yields to his urgent advances and a new chapter is opened in her life. For some years Moll leads the existence of a douce and respectable cit's wife. But money, that most potent of all agencies in Defoe's novel, again plays its part. Moll's husband is robbed by an embezzling clerk, and the incident preys so strongly on his mind that he dies in a decline.

Faced by the old spectre of want, no longer so sure of herself because she is no longer attractive, Moll starts her career as a petty thief. Soon she has recourse to her governess, who, in consequence of a little matter involving abduction and Tyburn, has abandoned midwifery in favour of the pawnbroking or rather the receiving business. Under her skilful tuition, Moll becomes an expert shoplifter and pickpocket. That is to say, she succeeds in keeping out of Newgate for five years. However, she is finally caught and sentenced to death. Her highwayman husband, as it happens, is also in prison pending the arrival of sufficient evidence to hang him, too. Moll is reprieved and persuades Jemmy to accept transportation. They therefore sail together for Virginia. Moll has plenty of money because, even as a thief, she has always been provident. The two settle down in the colonies as successful planters and Moll renews acquaintance with her son. At the age of about seventy, Moll and Jemmy return to England to end their days, 'in sincere penitence for the wicked lives we have lived.'

It would be hard to find two novels more completely dissimilar in colour and in tone than *Manon Lescaut* and *Moll Flanders*. Prévost, although he describes certain incidents peculiar to the lives of those who play hide-and-seek with the law, manages somehow to divest them of their ugliness whilst still conserving their reality.

To some extent, of course, this comes from the fact that such events are narrated by Des Grieux, who is a romantic and a poet. There is, indeed, a gallant kind of air about the exploits of the French adventurers which redeems them from the sordidness attaching to the experiences of Moll Flanders. When he comes to talk of the Hôpital, of Saint-Lazare, and of the Châtelet, Prévost adroitly skirts all details that would have shocked his French readers and detracted, perhaps, from the mysterious beauty of the heroine. As if unwilling to dwell upon the picture of Manon in chains, he separates this unaesthetic incident from the novel proper and hurries over it in the prologue, fearful no doubt lest it should compromise that unity of tone which is a characteristic feature of *Manon Lescaut*. To certain readers, Defoe will appear the greater realist. With his passion for detail he keeps us informed of every circumstance in the heroine's life. If she dines we know that it was 'on the sweetbread of a breast of veal,' or 'a chicken roasted and hot, with a bottle of sherry.' After each of her many marriages, Moll, like Pepys on New Year's Eve, makes an inventory of her worldly goods; and all the proceeds of her thefts are minutely described and valued. Now Defoe enters into these matters for the very reason that Prévost, wherever possible, avoids them. The fertilizing idea of the English novel is not the passion of love but the equally powerful and human instinct of self-preservation. Nearly all Moll's actions are inspired by the dreadful fear of poverty. She is not, like Manon, a *fille de joie*; she is a daughter of poverty. When Manon, to excuse her departure with G. M., writes: 'I swear to you, my dear chevalier, that you are the idol of my heart, and that there is only you in the world that I can love in the way I love you; but don't you see, my poor dear heart, that in the state to which we are reduced, fidelity is a silly virtue? Do you think one can be really loving, wanting bread?' one need not take her too literally. In reality, she knows perfectly well that she need never know hunger. By bread, she means the pretty things which to her are necessities, like Mrs. Tanqueray's expensive, out-of-season fruit. But Manon knows her chevalier's sentimental and sensitive nature. He will, of course, exclaim: 'She is afraid of hunger, God of Love; what coarseness of feeling and what a reply to my delicacy!' Nevertheless, it is effective. Despite himself, he is touched by her words. No, Manon has not Moll's personal and realistic experience of hunger. When she speaks of 'la faim' and 'le pain,' it is because she comes of a stock which, no doubt, once used words like these in deadly earnest. This atavistic element in language is profoundly interesting, persisting as it does, through the generations, in spite of social and economic changes which deprive such words of their reality, and, indeed, make them sometimes almost incongruous, as, for instance, when a wealthy Frenchman whose family has been in affluent circumstances for a century tells us: 'Il faut que je gagne mon pain,' or, when self-righteously washing his hands of a certain doubtful venture, says: 'Je ne mange pas de ce pain-là.' Do not let us, therefore, confuse Manon with Moll Flanders, every one of whose allusions to poverty means exactly what it says. At the moment when she is writing her pathetic letter, Manon, as it appears, is already in funds. All she is waiting for is a necklace and some jewellery which her doting admirer has promised for that night.

Moll is a less complex character than Manon, but that, one feels, is because Prévost deliberately surrounds his heroine with an aura of mystery. We see Moll Flanders very distinctly and directly. The dominant traits of her psychology emerge clearly from her own account of what she does and feels in each situation. Yet this self-drawn portrait offers ample scope for the play of our imagination. Between Moll's explanations of her actions and the actions themselves lies a wide field for conjecture. In the midst of her *post-factum* moralizings, the reader is continually haunted by doubts as to their sincerity. Granting, of course, that the Moll who relates the story of her life is very much older than the woman whose acts and emotions are described with such evident gusto, Moll's story, like every confession, is in the nature of a *plaidoyer*. Therefore, in a subtle way, we get a picture of two Molls, the one we are supposed to see, and the other whom we reconstruct by reading between the lines. The true Moll, one suspects, has no real connection with the woman who continuously refers to herself as a prostitute. Had she actually been one, she would never have used the 'harsh, unmusical title' which is ever on her lips, nor have remembered at a given moment that she had had intercourse with 'thirteen men.' In telling her story she dramatizes and maligns herself because Defoe, for moral reasons, will have it so. Moll is not naturally a prostitute but a married woman *manquée*. All her adventures with the other sex make that quite clear. What she wants always is security, not sexual excitement or pleasure. Take the case of the seduction of the invalid lodger. This she attributes to mere concupiscence, but that is only Defoe's moralizing after-thought. Actually, Moll is governed by her instinctive desire to establish a sense of gratitude in the man, to inspire him with a feeling of obligation, and thus, indirectly, to link his life closer to hers. So long as he refrains from sexual intimacy there is nothing marital in their relations, and Moll's nature is such that she must feel like a wife, if only in name. There is, in fact, none of that promiscuity in her composition which distinguishes the prostitute from other women. Nor, after the first girlish experience, is she ever passionate. In her life Moll had several children, and that is natural to her. Is it possible by any stretch of imagination to picture Manon as a mother?

Moll Flanders is extremely fond of referring to her principles, and as a result, leaves one with the impression that 'the lady doth protest too much.' Accept her remarks at their face value and we have the wisdom of a 'lone widow,' compelled by poverty to dissemble, as she does in money matters, solely in order to protect her little hoard from the clutching hands of rapacious male admirers. That is only partly true, for the real Moll revels in the game of pitting her cunning against the duller brains of the men whom she so easily outwits. She once exclaims, after having made a dupe of the London tradesman: 'If I had a grain of true repentance for an abominable life of twenty-four years past, it was then. Oh, what a felicity it is to mankind, said I to myself, that they cannot see into the hearts of one another!' Here we have the two Molls. The first affords an excellent example of what the French call 'le cant anglais,' since she is really able, by merely expressing contrition, to satisfy her conscience, or what she calls her conscience. Yet she has just played off the unsuspecting tradesman against the charming Jemmy with manifest enjoyment and a complacent admiration for her own cleverness. That is the other Moll. All through the novel the one is continually changing places with the other in a most disconcerting way, since no sooner has the younger Moll carried off a particularly clever *coup* than the older one qualifies it by some sententious observation. Morally speaking, she is always wanting to have her cake and eat it. On moral grounds, too, she can justify every one of her actions to herself. It is enough to weep and to say: 'Dear me! What an abandoned creature I am, and he was such a good man, too!' This is not hypocrisy, it is cant. Other people might condemn Moll's conduct as sheer duplicity, but she herself sincerely believes that contrition, if expressed with sufficient passion, removes the need for repentance of a more tangible sort. With a heart brimming with maternal fondness she presents her long-lost son in Virginia with a gold watch and chain. It is true that she stole them in London. But that, as she casually remarks, 'is by the way.' She has given up thievery and has repented. What more do you want?

She is not always so. In moments of deep emotion, what Moll says actually reflects the colour of her soul. Then she is utterly sincere. Two such moments jut out in stark relief. One is when she expresses her love for the man who seduced her. 'His words, I must confess, fired my blood; and all my spirits flew about my heart and put me in disorder enough. . . . My heart spoke as plain as a voice that I liked it.' Nor is there any doubt about her feelings when her lover hypocritically urges her to marry Robin. 'I gave him a look full of horror at these words, and, turning as pale as death, was at the point of sinking out of the chair I sat in.' That is language with the ring of truth. That is what Moll must have said. Not so the following, which is again edited by the older woman. 'Are the sacrifices I have made of honour and modesty to you no proof of my being tied to you in bonds too strong to be broken?' Here she is no longer convincing and natural. This duality of tone in the novel, leaving as it does the impression of a dual Moll, derives evidently from the two moods of Defoe himself; alternately he is moralist and artist. When he is content to abandon himself to his imagination and to live inside the skin of his creation, Moll Flanders is amazingly real. From the preface, incidentally, it appears that the author was aware of these discrepancies, since he is careful to point out that he was obliged to 'edit' the language of his so-called original. What he meant was that he had not the courage to follow his genius all the way.

In the incestuous episode, the heroine is, again, absolutely sincere. Every word she speaks is natural and unforced. Thus, describing her feelings of revulsion towards her husband, she says: 'And I think verily it was come to such a height, that I could almost as willingly have embraced a dog, as have let him offer anything of that kind to me, for which reason I could not bear the thoughts of his coming between the sheets with me. I cannot say that I was right in carrying it to such a length, while at the same time I did not discover the thing to him; but I am giving an account of what was, not of what ought or ought not to be.' Had Defoe always written so spontaneously, his portrait of Moll would have stood out sharp and clear. As it is, thanks to his misgivings, she is sometimes distorted. In Rousseau's *Nouvelle Héloïse* we have a similar example of what can happen to a finely drawn character when the author switches his attention from his work to his gallery of readers. Julie de Wolmar is different from Julie d'Étanges simply because the author, in an access of morality, broke the psychological continuity.[1] But in Defoe this is not so marked, and at no particular stage can one point to a sudden change. Besides, he has a good answer to all our objections. If the sententious Moll annoys us, the author can always allege that, as it is the heroine herself at the age of seventy who is telling the story, some allowance must be made for those sporadic attacks of piousness which are the inevitable accompaniment of old age.

The character of Manon is not projected in the same manner. In the first place, we know her only for two years, between the ages of seventeen and nineteen. Besides, the reader very seldom obtains a direct vision of this 'étrange fille,' as Prévost calls her. Strange she is, too, in another and deeper sense; for she has all the lure and mystery of the strange woman of the Old Testament. To maintain this illusion of beauty, therefore, the author keeps Manon always remote, yet never so remote as to appear unreal. That is the secret of his art. Here poet and novelist meet on common ground, a rare occurrence. To some extent, Prévost is assisted therein by the fiction that it is Des Grieux who tells the story. Through the tinted, glowing screen of the chevalier's passion we see the woman whom he calls the idol of his heart. We surprise her in several attitudes, and always she is sweet and poignantly alluring. Yet Manon sometimes speaks and then, too, she loses nothing of her charm. But is not that again because it is Des Grieux who reports her words, unconsciously endowing them with something of his own strange sadness? Her very acts are robbed of their inherent ugliness, and rendered disarming because they are narrated by a man obsessed by Manon's beauty; for Des Grieux's eloquence could lend wings to the Devil himself. In any case, Prévost achieved his object. Not only do we condone the passion of her lover; there is scarcely a man amongst us who does not envy him.

One question must often have passed through the minds of Prévost's readers. Does Manon love Des Grieux? Or rather, is she capable of loving anybody? Obviously, in her final disgrace, she does; yet that is a love born of gratitude and of wonder at his amazing constancy. Only in New Orleans does Manon realize the full splendour of the chevalier's passion and the revelation

[1] It should, however, be noted that he tried to bridge the psychological gap by imagining a spiritual conversion.

moves her to say: 'I have been light and fickle and even, loving you madly as I have always done, I was nothing but an ingrate. But you cannot realize how changed I am. The tears you saw me shed so often (on the ship) were not once for my own misfortunes.' Reading these words and looking back, one tastes really for the first time the bitterness of Des Grieux's long agony. During all those months, though he tried to assure himself that it was not so, he must have known that Manon never understood what love was. So the conviction that now at last she does is the most fateful event in his life. 'Her tears, her words, and the tone in which she pronounced them, made such an astonishing impression upon me that I thought I felt a sort of division in my soul.' What a wonderful phrase, and how perfectly does it express that sense of dualism which accompanies the most critical happenings in life, the queer sensation that one has two egos, one of which is the spectator of the other's experience! In a physical shock, as when a man is shot, he experiences an analogous, though physical, division. One part of him sees or hears the other part being wounded. Similarly, in an emotional trauma like that of Des Grieux, there is also a division, but a division of the spirit.

The girl we saw in Paris, the Manon who ruined her lover, did not know what love was. She went off with the chevalier, because, I think, she would have run off with any one to escape the convent. Besides, Des Grieux was good to look at. He was also noble, and that, to a little *roturière*, meant much in the eighteenth century. 'She was flattered,' says the hero, 'to have made the conquest of a lover such as I.' Manon's dominating passion is a love of pleasure, and, so long as she is amused, she remains faithful. Of this the chevalier becomes aware, as the result of bitter experience. 'Never was a girl less attached to money than she was; but she could not be quiet for a moment with the fear of lacking it. What she had to have was pleasure and distraction; she would never have wanted to touch a sou if amusement could be obtained at no cost.' In a word, she has the mentality of the *fille de joie*, the same animal-like faculty of living from day to day. 'She never even asked how much money we had, provided she could spend the day agreeably.' This is the very antithesis of Moll Flanders. And Manon has another trait which is peculiar to *filles de joie* and to children. She can utterly banish an unpleasant experience from her consciousness, and it is the contrast between what Des Grieux thinks she ought to be feeling and her own complete absence of any sensation whatever, which accentuates the tragedy of the chevalier. Recollect that amazing scene where the latter, having received a note in which Manon calmly informs him that she is spending the night with G. M., succeeds by a ruse in obtaining access to Manon's room whilst the *zèbre* is sent on a fool's errand. Des Grieux enters, expecting to find his mistress prostrate with anguish and remorse. Not a bit. 'Manon was busy reading. It was here that I had occasion to marvel at the character of this strange girl. Far from being terrified or seeming timid at seeing me, she merely evinced those slight marks of surprise which involuntarily escape one at the sight of a person whom one thought elsewhere.' Strange, indeed, but what superb psychology! Who else, in some fifty words, could have interpreted so marvellously the essential cause of Des Grieux's despair, his terrible awareness of that unbridgeable chasm of the spirit which separates him from the real Manon?

As if to emphasize the impossibility of any true contact between these two minds, Prévost, in this same episode, shows us a Manon who, for once, tries to think of her lover's feelings. But note the occasion. Eager to seize the opportunity of plundering G. M., which involves spending the night with that gentleman, she remembers that Des Grieux is waiting for her in a cab outside the Palais Royal. So Manon, for whom the greatest imaginable evil in the world is solitude, sends a pretty girl to console the chevalier for her absence till morning. In the stormy interview which ensues, Manon simply cannot see that her lover's rage arises from jealousy, nor can she understand why he sent the girl away. The only explanation that occurs to her is that he must have interpreted the action as a cruel jest at his expense, concocted in collusion with G. M. At least, so it would appear from her reply to the chevalier's upbraidings. But, as he himself tells us: 'Elle fut quelque temps à méditer sa réponse.' It is hard to know ever when Manon is telling the truth. She is so completely amoral, and besides, her natural instinct is always to seek the words that will most speedily end an unpleasant scene. That must constantly be borne in mind. So now in regard to the sending of the girl, just as in her letter with its pathetic allusion to the fear of hunger, she discovers a phrase which is sure to impress Des Grieux. 'The girl arrived,' says Manon; 'I thought she looked pretty, and, as I did not doubt that my absence would cause you pain, it was in all sincerity that I wanted her to help to console you. *For the fidelity I want from you is that of the heart.*' [1] This is pure romancing. The idea of sending the girl

[1] My italics.

* M

was, in fact, suggested to her by G. M. Had Manon really understood her lover's mind, had she really loved him, not for a moment
could she have entertained the thought of his intimacy with
another woman. As it is, however, she makes a virtue out of a
careless impulse, and with instinctive dexterity succeeds in turning
the tables. And Des Grieux, whilst fully aware that, despite all
her explanations, the damning fact remains that Manon did intend
to spend the night with G. M., is touched by her 'ingenuous-
ness'—ingenuity would be the better word—and by the 'frank,
open way' she related even the very circumstances that caused him
most agony. He says naïvely: 'She sins without malice, but she is
straight and sincere. Add to this the fact that love alone was
sufficient to close my eyes to all her faults.'

None of Defoe's women possesses Manon's secret charm. Moll
has admirable qualities, and even Roxana has her good points,
yet neither can be called charming. The only woman in Defoe's
novels who can approach the subtle femininity of Manon is to be met
with in *Colonel Jacque*. It is 'the lady in the house opposite' who,
'with witchcraft on her tongue,' manages, after a long pretence of
indifference and even hatred, to snare Jacque into marriage.
There is a typical French air in Defoe's account of this prolonged
sex duel. Still, once more, the woman, though she has finesse, has
no charm. Compared to Prévost, the English novelist is extremely
fleshly in his portrayal of love, and his women, for all their pretence
at being shocked, positively love to describe their bedroom adventures. One might, indeed, say that bedding and banking are their
two main interests in life. Moreover, in all their dealings with the
other sex, they reveal an Amazonian virility which is not to be found
even in Prévost's most determined man-hunters. Roxana is an
extreme case in point. In her attitude to men in general, she is
a middle-class Millamant, with a strong dash of Lillo's Millwood.
Involuntarily, she conjures up visions of those strapping, high-
bosomed females to be seen in the prints of the century. And,
secretly, Defoe admires their brutality. Therefore, he lingers long
over Roxana's contemptuous portrait of her fool of a husband, or
again, over the discomfiture of Colonel Jacque in the presence of his
trullish, drunken wives. Also, descending into a world unknown
to Prévost, Defoe gives us in Amy, the faithful servant-girl, an
astonishingly true picture of the English woman of the lower classes,
brutishly ignorant and insensitive, yet capable, in her doglike
fidelity, of murdering Roxana's obstinate and unwelcome daughter.

In all Defoe's novels there is a strong vein of physical brutality, which is much more real than the melodramatic violence of Prévost's lesser works.   In Defoe, too, we find a plebeian and unsavoury insistence on money which is quite foreign to the French novelist. A gentleman, in the eyes of Moll and of Roxana, is a drunkard and a rake.   Above all, he is a fellow who makes the guineas fly. Thrifty and avaricious themselves, Defoe's women adore the 'men of quality' because they are spendthrifts.   They are 'lovely persons.'

This sort of 'realism' is not to be found in Prévost; nor did he ever aim at it in *Manon Lescaut*, though the subject offered a tempting opportunity.   If he ever read Defoe, which is quite probable, there is nothing in his novels to suggest that he admired Defoe's manner.   It is only, indeed, within recent years that *Moll Flanders* has been translated into French,[1] though *Robinson Crusoe*, as every one knows, immediately became a European novel.   Once, however, Prévost amused himself by an essay in the 'English' manner of writing, though the author who inspired him was not Defoe, but John Lillo.   It was in the curious *Histoire de Molly Siblis*, an abbreviated parody, in the *George Barnwell* style, of his own *Manon Lescaut*.   This short story appeared in the *Pour et Contre* [2] where it was palmed off upon Prévost's compatriots as the true account of the adventures of an English harlot.   The heroine of this *relation curieuse* might be full sister to Millwood, since she glories in her crimes, and, when brought to book, displays all Millwood's royal contempt of her judges.   Yet throughout the narrative, there are echoes of *Manon Lescaut*.   Molly Siblis is captured and condemned to death for theft, but begs to be allowed to make a full confession of several other and more horrible crimes before going to the scaffold.   As a result, her sentence is commuted to transportation.   On the eve of her sailing for the colonies, a futile attempt to rescue her is made by a gang led by one who seems to be a man of quality.   This mysterious person, whose rank is known to his judges, is sent abroad in place of Molly.   After this brief preamble, which is not unlike the preface to *Manon Lescaut*, the heroine's story is unfolded.   Molly was born of decent stock, but her parents had not the money to gratify her love of pleasure.   She resolves, therefore, to sell herself to the highest bidder who will take her to London.   For this purpose she haunts the coaching-stages and, at last, falls in with a man whom she

[1] By Marcel Schwob.   On the other hand, it cannot be said that *Manon Lescaut* was popular in England in the eighteenth century.   See Appendix IV.
[2] iv, 1736.

mistakes for a gentleman. He turns out, however, to be merely a footman pimping for his master. Introduced to the latter, Molly lives with him for some months and, on his death, is again pestered by the valet. Aided by a new lover, she lies in ambush for this troublesome fellow whom she wants to kill with her own hands. 'The first blow, however, was dealt him by my second, but no sooner did I see him on the ground where he had fallen wounded, than seizing a dagger that I had on me, I tore his life out through a thousand slow and painful wounds.' Already, we have, it will be seen, a good idea of Molly's mettle.

The new lover is a gambler, and once, when luck is out, Molly suggests that he should rob one of his friends. The victim is to be invited to supper and made drunk. Whether because of his strong head or from suspicion, the guest retains his wits, whereupon Molly, in a cold rage, creeps behind him, and, with his napkin, strangles him. Seizing his money but leaving his watch and a few guineas, the couple summon the servants. The murder is passed off as an apoplectic stroke. Now Molly falls in love with the son of the murdered man, who does not respond to her tenderness. To her fury, not only does the young man refuse her offer to break with her lover, but informs the latter of her unfaithfulness. Out of revenge, Molly goes to the police, outlines the circumstances of the theft and strangling, and accuses the lad of a share in the deed. Along with Molly's lover, he is cross-examined and released, the whole affair being regarded as the concoction of a jealous and irresponsible woman.

To escape her debtors, Molly marries a soldier, a sort of Lescaut, so as to enjoy the immunity of a *feme covert*. She now sets up a high-class brothel where she ensnares a young rake. His father, however, forces him to marry in order to break this shameful liaison, and to Molly's chagrin, he becomes really fond of his wife, now enceinte. This woman Molly poisons, though, as she points out, it is with regret, since her blow was aimed only at the unborn child. She thus recovers her admirer, who is now more infatuated than ever. But Molly, in her turn, grows cool and, remembering the grief he had caused her, sets an accomplice to rob his house. To her satisfaction, he is completely ruined.

Molly's last adventure is equally sinister. She falls in love with a fascinating Frenchman. But, on the eve of the day which she has appointed as that of his triumph and of her capitulation, Molly surprises a plot between the stranger and her maid to rob and murder her. Miss Siblis handles this situation with her usual vigour and secrecy. As if nothing had occurred, she keeps her rendezvous, spends the night with the traitor, and at dawn strangles him in her bed. In this little tale, there is a savage, almost sadistic air which would have charmed Diderot, who, if only in theory, advocates this peculiar blend of crime and voluptuousness. We are accustomed to it in our Elizabethan literature, for example, in *Arden of Feversham*, and Lillo, who recast that play, betrays the same sinister quality in his *George Barnwell*. Memories of the latter and of his own *Manon* probably inspired Prévost with the impish idea of writing *Molly Siblis*. It was assuredly not imitated from Defoe, who, if he liked crime, preferred 'clean crime.' We shall not encounter anything of this sort in any of the French novelists until we come to Stendhal, Barbey d'Aurevilly, and the vicious little stories of Verlaine.

CHAPTER XIII

THE UNHEROIC HEROES

BECAUSE of its unfailing good humour, *Gil Blas* is possibly the best satire upon civilized society ever written. By comparison, Swift's *Gulliver's Travels* is a foul and brutal libel; whilst Voltaire's *Candide*, for all its astringent wit, smells too strongly of the lamp. It is too obviously a thesis in disguise. Now this cannot be said of *Gil Blas*, although, like every novel, it reflects its author's conception of life, or to employ a grander term, his philosophy. Here, perhaps, the generating idea, the idea which colours the behaviour of every character, is a rooted mistrust of sentiment and, in consequence, of imagination. Yet it is typical of Le Sage that, in deference to his reader's human weakness for the *romanesque*, he has interlarded the realistic narrative with short tales, all of which are crammed with sentiment and with imagination. These we may omit or not, at will, since they have little or nothing to do with the adventures or with the character of Gil Blas himself. On the other hand, it is perfectly clear from the novel proper that Le Sage regards both sentiment and imagination as exceedingly dangerous possessions. All the experiences which he relates have but one lesson. Fail to keep these qualities under proper control and you will fall a victim to the predatory instincts of your fellow-men. Over the gateway of Gil Blas's world should be inscribed the famous words uttered by Basile in the *Barbier de Séville*: 'Qui diable est-ce qu'on trompe ici?'

In creating Gil Blas, his author achieved a stroke of genius. Had he made him, like Don Quixote, a sentimental romantic, the whole tone of the novel would have been different and, of course, unoriginal. The hero's adventures would have assumed the form of a farcical narrative, somewhat in the manner of Smollett's *Sir Launcelot Greaves*. But Le Sage was too much of a dramatist to picture the misfortunes of an ineffable simpleton. To give complexity, subtleness, and comic force to his story, he conceived Gil Blas as the type of 'knowing cove' who has nothing to learn about the dangers of sentiment and of romantic imagination, the would-be cynic who, with a contemptuous lift of the nose, tells you 'that he has heard all that sort of thing before, and that you 'd better try another one.' One catches this note immediately on opening the novel. When Gil Blas leaves the paternal home to set out upon his Odyssey, we can see him with tongue in cheek, gravely listening with mock respect to the sententious advice tendered by his father. In this mood, he falls an easy victim to the parasite and to Corcuelo, the wily inn-keeper. Yet this first contact with the outer world teaches him nothing. 'Ah, poor Gil Blas,' he exclaims in his chagrin, 'you ought to die with shame at having given these rascals a just reason for making you a laughing-stock. . . . Your parents will, no doubt, be sorry that they wasted their homilies on a fool. Far from exhorting me to deceive nobody, they should have warned me not to let myself be duped.' Henceforth, it will be a point of honour with Gil Blas not to be a dupe. In other words, he will continue to be guided by his *amour-propre*, which is to be the real cause of all his future mishaps, though, invariably, he confuses it with wisdom or shrewdness.

The problem of experience and its influence upon character is one that interests Le Sage enormously. Writing at a time when France was much exercised by the question of education in its widest sense, Le Sage inclined to favour the seventeenth-century school of innate ideas. Without taking this matter more seriously than does the author himself, one might compare his attitude to education—which is experience codified—to the attitude of a fatalist or a Jansenist. A man is either born honest or he is not. For a time his environment will influence his conduct but, sooner or later, just as water rises to its own level, his good or evil genius will prevail. That, in the last analysis, is the case of Gil Blas. Take the edifying examples of Captain Rolando and his lieutenant. The former was a spoiled child, an idle, lying, impudent little wretch who was never thrashed. The latter, on the other hand, whilst endowed with much the same attributes, was whacked unmercifully. Both ended as brigands. Then there is the young bandit whose mother had substituted him for a baby of noble parentage, which she was nursing along with her own child. The peasant's son, as he grew up, consorted for preference with servants. He drank, gambled, wenched, and finally decamped after robbing his supposed parents. So much for the benefits of education, good, bad, or indifferent.

It will be surmised already that none of Gil Blas's associates belongs to what is called the 'public school type'; yet they all possess in common, and, moreover, naturally possess, a quality which our public schools, by a long and expensive process, only occasionally succeed in imparting to their products. I refer to the quality vaguely termed 'the sporting instinct,' presumably because it is absent from almost every form of English sport, as any fox, stag, grouse, or pheasant will tell you. All Le Sage's rascals are sportsmen in the sense that they are good losers: not because they have been trained to regard it as the 'right thing,' but because they have a keen perception of the comic in life. In all their accounts of the various little accidents which brought a carefully concocted scheme to naught and, maybe, put their necks in danger of the noose, there is a delicious vein of mockery at their own expense. Naturally enough, the joke is all the richer if it is played on someone else; but, provided there is a *mot pour rire*, Gil Blas, Scipion, Fabrice de Nuñez, and, above all, that inimitable pair of rascals, Ambroise de Laméla and Don Raphaël, are sure to hail it with shouts of delight. Read, for instance, Don Raphaël's amusing story of his discomfiture in the matter of the good bourgeois Moyadas whose son-in-law he pretends to be. Even in the presence of the constable, Don Raphaël is prepared to bluff the affair to a finish, but: 'The alguazil looked at us askance and imposed silence. I don't know why these people have such an ascendancy over us.' Consider, too, Scipion's disillusioned report of his encounter with the priest who steals the money that the innkeeper's wife stole from Scipion, who had stolen it from the good mendicant. Gil Blas himself is quickly inoculated with the same good humour, that marvellous antidote to misfortune. Experience of being duped, as he soon discovers, is not an infallible preventive. At best, it only shortens his attacks of rage and mortification when he is trapped once more, lured by a slightly different bait. After the episode of Camille and the rented house, for instance, he swears that he will give women a wide berth. But that does not prevent him from being taken in by Laure, the soubrette, or from building castles in the air about Donna Aurora. There is no such thing, he finds, as Experience: there are only experiences. By then, however, he has learned how to laugh heartily at his own simplicity, which marks the first step on the way to wisdom. No longer does he say: 'I shall not be duped,' but rather: 'I probably shall, but what does it matter?' He realizes that history, if she repeats herself, never does it twice in the same way, so that the tricks which outwitted our grandfathers will serve, with a very slight alteration, to catch their clever grandchildren.

For Gil Blas, the universe is inhabited, roughly speaking, by two sets of people: those who have wit and those who have not. All, however, are liable at some time to be exploited by their confrères, though it is only the fools who bear rancour. The fools of this world are the people who have no sense of humour: that is the hall-mark of the fool, whether he is a doctor, a pedant, a merchant, an archbishop, or a prime minister. Le Sage is an authority on fools and, according to him, the most perfect specimens are to be found in the medical profession. Was it not he who coined the devastating phrase: 'Le médecin n'est pas un animal risible'? And his most joyous, most sparkling *mots* are struck in honour of the leech. What attracts Le Sage to the professors of medicine is their astounding gravity, their cast-iron belief in methods, and their inveterate, but secret hatred of their own colleagues. After Molière, it was sheer audacity to handle this theme; but it must be admitted that in the episode introducing Dr. Sangrado, Le Sage has made a priceless contribution to the gaiety of nations: and, on the many subsequent occasions when a doctor glides forward to the bedside of a sick man in *Gil Blas*, the mock horror evinced by the author is an infallible tonic—to the reader who happens to enjoy good health. Can one ever forget that phrase which recurs in all its variants: 'A mild fever, reinforced by a good doctor, polished him off in two days'?

The rigidity of the medical mind appealed to Le Sage's comic sense, and rigidity of mind in any form appeared to him ridiculous. Gil Blas, although he is frequently duped, never strikes us as a complete fool, precisely because the essence of his character is its pliability. When he is tricked, it is always because of vanity, or because he rigidly adheres to certain principles from motives of self-interest. And, if one comes to consider the matter, is not vanity simply another aspect of that rigidity of mind which Le Sage finds so comical in his doctors, pedants, and authors? The attitudes of the vain man are always stiff and wooden. He adopts a manner, a tone of voice, a set of body, and a way of moving which never changes. Indeed, he takes a sort of comic pride in adhering to his favourite attitude under all circumstances. Always he is an actor and a bad actor, since his audience never fails to discern the contrast between the part he is playing and the true personality of the mime. For that reason, Le Sage loves to take us into the society of actors and actresses, holding the two contrasting pictures always before our eyes. With Gil Blas the valet, we pry into the intimacy of the voluptuous, debauched, and gluttonous Arsénie, as she cracks her bawdy jokes and swills down liqueurs with her infatuated admirers. Flick over a page, however, and we see Arsénie, 'fat with the smoke of her sacrifices,' installed like some oriental goddess on a white satin cushion, aping the *grande dame*, or, again, bullying some wretched playwright, who sidles humbly forward to present the manuscript of the part which she deigns to play in one of his productions. Le Sage, the author of *Turcaret*, knows how to extract the last ounce of comedy from delicious incidents like these: 'Our little lackey came and loudly announced to my mistress: "Madame, a man with dirty linen, spattered with mud from head to foot, and who, saving your presence, seems to be a poet, is asking to speak with you." "Let him be shown upstairs," replied Arsénie; "don't move, gentlemen, it is an author." . . . On entering, he bowed deeply five or six times to the company, but no one rose or even returned his salutation. Arsénie replied with a simple inclination of the head to the civilities with which he overwhelmed her. Trembling and embarrassed, he advanced into the room. He let fall his gloves and his hat. He picked them up again, approached my mistress and, presenting her with a paper more respectfully than a plaintiff presents a petition to his judge: "Madame," he said, "please accept, I beg, the part which I take the liberty to offer you." She received it in a cold and contemptuous manner and did not deign even to reply to the compliment.'

Note the woodenness, the immobility of Arsénie's attitude and that pompous rigidity which is the unmistakable sign of self-sufficiency and vanity the world over, and in every walk of life. Who has not seen it in the Foreign Office official, the American 'executive,' the French *concierge*, the German stationmaster? Gil Blas, and he cheerfully admits the fact, was sometimes a fool of that sort, and in the prison tower of Segovia had ample leisure to reflect with self-disgust on the insufferable Gil Blas, confidential friend of the prime minister De Lerme, the vain upstart who received the grocer's son from his native village of Oviedo with such cold indifference, and bundled him out of the office when the poor fellow dared to hint that perhaps Gil Blas's parents might share in their son's affluence. How does Le Sage describe the effect of vanity on his hero? 'I lost all my gaiety,' confesses Gil Blas, 'I became gloomy and thoughtful; in a word, a stupid animal.'

For Le Sage, what distinguishes man from the lower animals is the gift of laughter. Laughter is the music of life, the great solvent of care, and the marvellous antidote to evil of every sort. Solemn people alarm Gil Blas, especially after his unpleasant adventure with the grave Ambroise de Laméla, the valet who prefers a mass to a bottle. This he remembers when, as the duc de Lerme's secretary, he has occasion to engage a servant. 'The first who appeared was a fellow with such a gentle and pious look that I would have nothing to do with him. I thought of Ambroise de Laméla.' So he chooses the cheerful, lively Scipion, though he looks a bit of a rascal. The intervention of Scipion at this stage in the hero's career is most interesting, because, in many respects, he is the double of the younger, roving Gil Blas. By linking Scipion to the ambitious and avaricious Gil Blas, now elevated to unexpected grandeur and affluence, Le Sage very cleverly explains the hero's gradual reversion to his old nature. By the end of the story, the fusion of the two characters is almost complete, and we realize that Scipion was only really a 'shadow.' Imagine the novel at this point without him, and it will be seen at once that the stream of gaiety would have dried up when Gil Blas becomes a careworn and intriguing politician. As it is, through the latter's conversations with his valet, the novel recaptures its former colour and vivacity. It preserves its unity of tone. For all that, it must be admitted that the last two books of *Gil Blas* do not quite possess the old, joyous, carefree ring. Le Sage, if reproached with this, might answer very plausibly that his hero is nearing middle age, that he is married and, moreover, loses his wife. The true explanation is, more probably, that the last chapters were written in the atmosphere of a changed France, the France of that depression which succeeded the wars of the Regency, and the spectacular crash engineered by John Law and a corrupt administration.

Nevertheless, *Gil Blas* is a well of laughter, What precisely is the secret of its gaiety? There is nothing of Rabelais's hilarity in *Gil Blas*, none of his Pantagruelian zest in the purely animal functions, so wilfully distorted and magnified to epic stature. Nor do we often encounter those farcical scenes, ending in a memorable 'volée de coups de bâton,' peculiar to the lesser plays of Molière and to the novels of Scarron and Furetière. The hoary Spanish jests about innkeepers and feline rabbit-pies do occasionally crop up, but with this, and one or two similar acknowledgments to the comic genius of Spain, Le Sage rests content. His *vis comica* is absolutely his own and it is utterly French. The cruder forms of comedy, as a rule, he eschews. He is not interested in 'slapstick' comedy, in the humour which emerges from a purely physical act or situation. By a comic situation, Le Sage usually means something more subtle, involving the exercise of *esprit*. In nearly all his comic situations, humour and wit are nicely blended. The situation, as such, is in its general aspect, humorous, but at some point humour is suddenly crystallized into a sparkling, witty remark or comment which forms the crux of the comic incident. Take, for instance, the humorous episode of the gullible Gil Blas in the clutches of the rascally innkeeper and his confederate, the horse-coper. We have a vivid, animated picture of the scene. The naïve Gil Blas listening with sinking heart to the coper's disparaging remarks, as, one by one, the points of the wretched mule are criticized and coolly damned, until, says the hero in his shame: 'I would have given him my mule for nothing.' That is humour, but not wit. The wit only emerges unexpectedly when Gil Blas decides to throw himself on the horse-coper's 'good faith.' 'Then, acting the man of honour, he replied that in interesting his conscience, I was getting at his weak spot. It was certainly not his strong one, for, instead of raising the valuation to ten or twelve pistoles, like my uncle, he was not ashamed to fix it at three ducats.' There is no need to wonder why the phrase, 'la foi d'un maquignon,' like Molière's 'Vous êtes orfèvre, Monsieur Josse,' has become a byword. Then there is the immortal scene of Gil Blas and the Archbishop of Granada, who insists that our hero, under pain of losing his favour and incidentally a fortune, must tell him immediately if he notices a falling off in the quality of the archiepiscopal sermons. The prelude to the critical moment is a masterpiece of humorous description. Since Gil Blas is not a fool, we enter into all the conflicting emotions, the weighing of the pros and cons that precede his final decision; but the *bon mot* is reserved for the end, and it is the old archbishop who utters it. Cutting through Gil Blas's stammered apologies and his plunging efforts to retrieve a hopeless situation, he says: 'Je ne trouve point du tout mauvais que vous me disiez votre sentiment. C'est votre sentiment seul que je trouve mauvais. . . . Adieu, monsieur Gil Blas; je vous souhaite toutes sortes de prospérités, avec un peu plus de goût.' Here we have the finish, the 'curtain' to a scene which could only have been conceived by a born playwright like Le Sage. More often, however, the wit which suddenly immortalizes a situation that had otherwise remained on the plane of humour, comes from without, in the form of a comment by the narrator. Told by any one save Gil Blas, the account of that hero's apprenticeship to Dr. Sangrado would be rollicking fun, but nothing more. Illuminated by his marvellous comments, the various events acquire a verve and comic force almost unparalleled outside the French theatre itself. They are animated and flood-lit by the delicious asides of Gil Blas. Thus, describing the trail of death which he leaves behind him as he plies the healing craft in the lower quarters of Valladolid, our hero remarks: 'Every day, there came to the house some father calling us to account for a son whom we had removed, or else some uncle reproaching us with the death of a nephew. As for the nephews and the sons whose uncles and fathers had suffered from our remedies, none appeared. The husbands, too, were most discreet.'

In the comic of Le Sage there is the same absence of bluster, rowdyism, and grossness which distinguishes the French comedy of his period from our own. All the doings and sayings of his rascals contain an element of sang-froid, of cool and imperturbable impudence. The novelist is everywhere reinforced by the dramatist, a rare and excellent combination. Here, undoubtedly, the great exponent is Don Raphaël, whose boast it is that he specializes in 'les fourberies qui demandent de l'esprit,' which is no more than the simple truth. Aided by his faithful henchman, the solemn and pious Ambroise de Laméla, and also by a somewhat scared Gil Blas, it is Don Raphaël, disguised as an officer of the Inquisition, who plunders the Jew, Samuel; and it is again Don Raphaël and his lieutenant who conceive the brilliant plan of decamping with the funds of a monastery, an undertaking which required years of patience and duplicity. Even Gil Blas, who has shared their exploits and, to his cost, has had occasion to appreciate the artistry of their methods, is completely deceived by their latest metamorphosis, believing implicitly that at last they have seen the light. In creating Don Raphaël and Laméla, Le Sage was almost certainly inspired by memories of Tartuffe and Laurent. But in transferring that sinister couple from the stage to the novel he recast and amplified the characters. Primarily, this was due to the fact that his philosophy of life is essentially different from that of Molière. The author of *Tartuffe*, of the *Avare*, and of the *Femmes savantes* cherished a traditional, bourgeois respect for order. In the plays just mentioned, as in others, he mercilessly ridicules everything tending to disturb the harmony of *la famille*, which he regards as the unit of that larger family, the State. Le Sage, in this respect, is very modern and curiously un-French. For the family, as an institution, he cares not a button, and all his rascals, like Gil Blas himself, are strangely lacking in that veneration for parental authority which was soon to saturate the larmoyant comedies and *drames* of the age. Indeed, not until the closing books of the novel do we find our hero becoming sentimental about his old father and mother. Here a quite remarkable change of tone is evident, reflecting, of course, the invasion of French literature by middle-class ideas and taste. On the whole, however, the attitude of Le Sage to society is that of the transition period which reached a climax in the cynicism of the Regency authors. Social problems do not exist for Le Sage. Prostitution, administrative corruption, religious tolerance, and the privileges of the nobility are taken for granted. On the other hand, he views with ill-concealed delight every successful attempt on the part of his rascals to outwit or plunder the police, the regular clergy, and the Turcarets, or men of money. With the nobles he goes warily; and Gil Blas shares the opinion of Figaro in all his dealings with the duc de Lerme and the comte d'Olivarès. His policy is simple. It is to make himself indispensable to these powerful masters. If a man has no rank he can at least compensate for that disadvantage by using his brains; and by flattering the foibles or vices of his hierarchic superiors, he is certain to share in the general pillage. Whilst the duc de Lerme remains in power our hero is faithful to him and, indeed, regards him with affection. That does not, however, prevent him from writing, at the command of D'Olivarès, several able and stinging pamphlets against the administration which has just fallen. All through his political career, Gil Blas never forgets the advice given him by Melchior de la Ronda, when he urged our hero to swallow his resentment at the conduct of the Archbishop of Granada: 'Common men must always respect persons of rank, whatever motive they may have to complain of them. I admit that there are some very shabby noblemen who deserve no such consideration: but they can be harmful and must be feared.' To put it crudely, the policy of Gil Blas in his relations with nobles is that of the professional sycophant or 'trimmer.' Yet, in his defence, it must be remembered that under the existing social system no other policy was possible. Seen through the eyes of the twentieth century, Gil Blas is wholly unadmirable. Still, he does not forfeit our sympathy because he is so completely frank and cynical. 'Tout comprendre, c'est tout pardonner'; and Gil Blas never leaves us in any doubt as to the motives for his actions, most of which are dictated by self-interest or, as he would regard it, by necessity.

Gil Blas is, in fact, a queer hero for a novel. His history is that of an ordinary man confronted by a series of extraordinary circumstances; and that, it must be confessed, does not form a very promising theme. Actually however, Le Sage performs the feat of making Gil Blas's life not merely interesting but dramatic. Drama, we are commonly informed, can only emerge from a clash between character and situation. Yet the outstanding trait in Gil Blas is his marvellous skill in avoiding such rude impacts. All his instincts lead him to adapt himself, like a chameleon, to the swiftly changing hues of fortune or misfortune. He is utterly unheroic in the sense that never, if he can help it, does he once attempt to dominate the force of circumstances. Conduct of that sort he regards not as heroic, but as stupid. On the other hand, who is more alert to take advantage of a sudden veering of the wind of destiny, to trim his sails to the new and favouring breeze? Gil Blas, like most of his boon companions, is the very antithesis of Prévost's heroes, whom he would certainly dismiss as sombre imbeciles. It would be hard, for example, to discover in all literature a more violent contrast than that presented by the temperaments of Clèveland and Gil Blas. The former is dramatic and tragic because, whilst convinced that he is the predestined victim of an evil fate, he yet fights to the last barrier. Gil Blas is dramatic and completely untragic for the opposite reasons. There is, after all, an element of drama in the unfailing cheerfulness, nay, of gaiety, with which he meets reverses. In temperament, apart from the question of his sense of the grotesque, he reminds us of Robinson Crusoe, who offers a supreme example of manly courage in the face of material obstacles that would have utterly destroyed a man of more imagination or more sensitive fibre. Gil Blas has similar courage and resource, but they are lightened and mellowed by his sense of humour. He is the ordinary man who is unheroic or heroic according as you look at him, like the average *poilu* or the Tommy of the recent war. Sentimental journalists and melodramatic novelists have turned the *poilu's* history into an epic. But, told by himself, as Gil Blas relates his own life, his tale would pretty much resemble the tale invented by Le Sage. Its general tone would be anti-*romanesque*, unsentimental and disillusioned. Observe how suspicious Gil Blas is of the heroic in any form. When, in the affair of Sephora, the little surgeon with the long sword reveals himself as a man of mettle, is Gil Blas the

man to have his throat cut for a point of honour? Decidedly not.
'"That is sufficient," I said, sheathing my sword. "I am not one of
those brutal fellows who refuse to listen to reason. After what you
have told me, you are no longer my enemy."' And, like his friend,
Diego de la Fuente, he is not 'one of those intransigent lovers who
oppose a sturdy resistance to obstacles.' Yet let us make no mistake. If, as he implies, it is only quixotic fools who butt their heads
against stone walls, on the other hand, it is equally stupid to throw
up the sponge at a first defeat. 'If a man of wit falls upon evil
days, he waits in patience for better times. Never, as Cicero has
said, must he allow himself to sink to the point where he forgets
that he is a man.' That is the trait in Gil Blas which makes the story
of his adventures dramatic, and that is why, with all his unheroic
qualities, he captures and retains our sympathy. To the poetic
mind Gil Blas is distressingly unromantic. Only at one stage in
his career do we catch him in the mood to act like *un héros de roman*.
It is when, after the death of his wife, and the collapse of his protector, D'Olivarès, Gil Blas proposes to retire from the world into
a Dominican convent. Luckily, Scipion, his other self, is at hand
to dissuade him and to reflect the author's opinion upon conduct
of this sort. This, he points out, is 'une idée de malade,' a morbid
thought. And so it is, since Gil Blas does not belong to the race of
mystics.

We have already noted Le Sage's odd and almost comic aversion
to sentiment and to imagination. It is more clearly reflected in
his attitude towards women and love. Here, of course, we should
sedulously ignore in *Gil Blas* the numerous and very passionate
intercalated love stories for the excellent reason that Le Sage himself regarded them frankly as *hors-d'œuvres* of a pronounced Spanish
flavour, offered by the novelist to those who have the palate for
that sort of thing. The author's own views on these bloody and
gloomy tales, with their unreal and ardent ladies and knights, will
be found in Don Raphaël's dry comment upon the pathetic history
of Don Alphonse who has had the misfortune to kill the brother of
his lady-love. The rascal, at the moment disguised as a hermit,
listens gravely to the hidalgo's tale of woe, and remarks: 'My son,
you were most imprudent to remain so long in Toledo. I regard
with other eyes than yours, all that you have related; and you
love for Séraphine seems to me pure folly. . . . You will find, no
doubt, some other young person who will make the same impression
on you and whose brother you will not have killed.'

If we turn, however, to Le Sage's real women, it will be seen that, whilst entertaining an extremely low opinion of feminine virtue, he has a very healthy respect for the feminine intelligence. In the set frequented by Gil Blas, love is regarded as a sort of malady, 'a distemper,' to quote Diego de la Fuente, whose unlucky experience with the amorous Mergelina has cured him of any further wish to dally with the fair. Gil Blas, himself, is not amorously inclined, though, indeed, he has his weak moments. It is, however, significant that in most of his adventures with women, the compelling emotion is not love but vanity. Vanity, mingled with self-interest, leads him into the toils of the artful Camille, and vanity, reinforced by a vivid imagination, causes him to believe that the lady Aurore has arranged a secret rendezvous because of his *beaux yeux*. It is again his conceit which inspires the romantic illusion that Laure, dressed up in the finery of her mistress, is a *grande dame* smitten with his charms. Yet, when the fraud is discovered, Gil Blas is actually relieved to find in Laure, 'the laughing Laure,' a thoroughly kindred spirit. And her remark, when the bogus Don César stands revealed as a simple valet, rounds off and sums up, the situation: 'Tu es en homme ce que je suis en femme.' These two get along famously, and, if Gil Blas has his suspicions about the formidable number of Laure's 'cousins,' neither he nor the lady ever indulges in the ridiculous emotion called jealousy. 'Point de jalousie,' said Laure on one occasion; 'les jaloux chez le peuple comique passent pour des ridicules.' It is true that she was speaking of the 'profession,' but the observation applies to all Le Sage's leading characters. Laure is the typical Le Sage woman, malicious yet never vindictive; alert, voluble, and merry, regarding all men as fair game; an audacious and fluent liar, and, like Gil Blas, keenly appreciating any joke, even at her own expense. Only once did she really fall in love, in a passionate affair with the handsome Louis d'Acacer. 'We loved each other with so much fury that it seemed as if a spell had been cast over us.' But Louis was insanely jealous, so Laure broke with him. 'Will you believe,' she says, 'that the last day of our liaison was the most charming one we ever spent? Both equally worn out by the ills we had suffered, there was nothing but joy in our farewells. We were like two miserable captives recovering their freedom after a period of harsh bondage.' How very typical of Le Sage is that remark! Laure, it will be observed, is an individualist; and so are all his characters. They have an inborn horror of ties of any sort; an almost feline independence and

a feline love of wandering. Love and domesticity they regard with
comic terror, and the lives they lead are the lives they like. Valets,
strolling actors, bandits, adventurers, they are all social pariahs,
always on the move and never entirely free from police supervision.
Gil Blas, in a sense, is scarcely one of them, because, although he
leads the roving life, it is by force of circumstances rather than by
deliberate choice. One must not forget that when he left Oviedo,
it was to pursue his studies at Salamanca and there to settle down as
a pillar of the Church. There is nothing incredible, therefore, in
his final metamorphosis into a country gentleman.

Gil Blas is a novel of the open road, and yet, for all that, curiously
urban. Its types are urban types. The characters, whether they
be muleteers, innkeepers, or brigands, possess the wit, the craft,
and the subtlety of town children. In his heart, Le Sage has
all the Parisian's contempt of countrymen and the country,
and all the indifference to natural beauty which is so typical
of the seventeenth-century Frenchman. However, in his respect
for good food and drink, he is a thorough Breton. Nature he
polishes off in a few sparse allusions to the conventional clump
of trees, a bubbling spring, or a field 'enamelled' with flowers. But
if we wander with Gil Blas we are sure to meet with an inn or, at
least, a wayside halt necessitating numerous *accolades* to the wine-
skin and a devastating attack on the gigot of mutton or roast capon.
Somehow or other the reader carries away an impression of sunlit,
dusty roads, of wooded, rocky scenery, of fertile, smiling plains
studded with châteaux girt with stately trees, though, to tell the
truth, he would be hard put to it to 'furnish his references,' to employ
a favourite expression of professors and landladies. I suppose that
Gil Blas can be called an 'open-air' novel in spite of the absence of
the picturesque and rustic matter which moderns associate with literature of the open-air type. There is a certain spaciousness in *Gil
Blas* that comes from Le Sage's habit of mapping out the itineraries
followed by his roving creatures. The novel has a breeziness and
a gallant air of freedom, qualities which derive, one imagines, from
its lack of sentiment and of reflection. To be sentimental one must
really keep quite still, and preferably within four walls, whilst with
Gil Blas's friends one is barely conscious that houses and walls
exist. They are always on the move, gesticulating, talking, walking,
riding, eating, or whacking the bottle. Having been everywhere,
they know everything and everybody. In fact, it is really in these
early eighteenth-century novels, and not in our modern ones, that

we realize what a small place the world is. Gil Blas gives Captain Rolando the slip from the underground cavern but, with no surprise at all, runs across him later in a street in Madrid garbed as an alguazil. So, too, when he is assistant to Dr. Sangrado, that illustrious High Executioner, an impish fate delivers the wily Camille into his hands; for she is one of his first patients, if one may use the word in its most literal sense. All through their chequered careers, Le Sage's characters are continually faced with the truth that in life there is no such thing as a dead past. Some fragments of their past, in a very lively and sometimes very disconcerting form, is constantly jumping out at them, a fact which Le Sage exploits with gusto and wit. Thus, after many years, Gil Blas discovers that the actress Estelle, mistress of the Portuguese nobleman, Marialva, is no other than Laure, the former soubrette. So, like Manon and Des Grieux, they resolve to pass themselves off as brother and sister in order to hoodwink the naïve Portuguese. But somewhere in the troupe there is a certain humble little assistant-snuffer of candles who remembers our hero when he was valet to Arsénie and on more than fraternal terms with Laure. Casually he imparts the information to Narcissa, the deposed mistress of Marialva, and the fat is in the fire. There is nothing for it but flight, for, as Gil Blas points out: 'I was not the man to give the lie to an assistant-snuffer of candles.' Once more, therefore, he has to make one of his hurried exits, decamping from Granada at the first crow of cock. A whole chapter could be written on these 'excursions and alarums.' Le Sage loves to describe his hero's comic fear on such occasions. For, if Gil Blas usually has his imagination under good control, on the contrary, when his precious skin is in danger, he falls a prey to the most lively fancies. Of the Marialva experience, he says: 'I was assailed by a thousand thoughts. If sometimes I fell into a doze, I saw the furious marquis battering Laure's beautiful face and smashing everything in the house; or else I heard him ordering his servants to thrash me to death. Thereupon I woke with a start, and the awakening, which is usually so sweet after a frightful dream, became for me still more cruel than any nightmare.' Once out on the open road, however, his fears diminish with every mile that separates him from Granada. 'As we moved away from Granada, my mood regained its tranquillity. I began to chat with the mule-driver. I laughed at some of his funny stories and imperceptibly lost all my terrors.' In these pictures there is something Chaplinesque. One can note the same despondent droop of the shoulders, the same hare-like, apprehensive backward glance and quickened step; then, as the figure fades into the distance, the return of the old, jaunty impudence so eloquently mirrored in every gesture. It is positively heart-rending to reflect, as I write these lines, that to some of my younger readers this comparison may be completely meaningless.

If Le Sage's people refuse to lend themselves to psychological exploration, they are, on the other hand, wonderfully alive. He is an adept at situating characters and endowing them with animation. Where Balzac, very often at the expense of animation, devotes pages of minute description to details of physique, Le Sage is, as a rule, content to hit off in a few telling strokes the essential and significant trait. And by significant trait he means something quite different from Balzac. Only seldom, for caricatural and comic effect, does Le Sage offer us a passport description of his man, and give us details regarding the colour of his hair, eyes, or complexion, the shape of his nose or cheek-bones or the other features which compose a 'still' portrait. What he seizes with cinematographic alertness is the expression of his people, their gestures, their tone of voice, their posture of the moment; in a word, the reflection of whatever emotion happens to possess them. His favourite words are verbs, 'doing words.' With this in mind, examine the long and exciting narrative of Gil Blas's adventures in the brigands' cave. Its animation derives from a breathless sequence of verbs which tumble over each other in mad excitement. Nowhere in the novel do we encounter many descriptive or digressive passages of any length. That, of course, is because Le Sage the playwright and Le Sage the novelist rarely part company. It is only, indeed, after perusing *Gil Blas* that one grasps the extraordinary power and vivacity of the past definite tense, that bugbear of our schooldays. Handled by a master such as Le Sage, it makes dullness unthinkable and carries the tale along with incomparable verve. It is the vital nerve of his style.

'The disgraces of Gil Blas,' says Smollett in the preface to *Roderick Random*, 'are for the most part such as rather excite mirth than compassion: he himself laughs at them; and his transitions from distress to happiness, or, at least, ease, are so sudden, that neither the reader has time to pity him, nor himself to be acquainted with affliction. This conduct, in my opinion, not only deviates from probability, but prevents that generous indignation which ought to animate the reader against the sordid and vicious disposition of the world.' Thus, in the preamble to a work confessedly modelled on the plan of *Gil Blas*, we hit upon a fundamental dissimilarity of temperament in Smollett and Le Sage which finds a logical expression in their divergent attitudes to life and, in consequence, to the art of the novel. Detached and imperturbable, Le Sage betrays almost nothing of that 'generous indignation' which warms and enlivens the pages of Smollett, redeeming, to some extent, the defects of his style and construction. On the other hand, much of his worst writing is to be attributed to this very characteristic. Smollett is a satirist whose favourite weapons are caricature and invective. Le Sage is an ironist, and, though on occasion he will descend to caricature of a purely physical sort, his normal weapon is wit. In his particular domain Smollett has few equals, Rabelais, of course, being *hors concours* as a creator of picturesque and abusive epithets. There is nothing, however, of the Rabelaisian, epic quality in Smollett's invective, which, in all its forms, is brutal and devoid of fancy. Take, for example, those physical encounters related with such evident gusto in the early pages of *Roderick Random*. Never by any chance does the narrative rise from the level of mere ferocity to the stupendous and immortal heights attained by Rabelais when he describes the drubbing of the Catchpoles or Friar John's exploits against the Chitterlings.

Like Rabelais, Smollett revels in visions of bloody noses or black eyes, and in the joyful, soul-satisfying crack of cudgel on skull or knee-cap; yet in all this horseplay lurks an underlying note of savage, personal enjoyment and of premeditation; as if in these imaginary rough-and-tumbles, the author were meting out a vicarious revenge to his enemies. It is not exactly vindictiveness, but rather something akin to the gloating of the small boy when he sees the school bully outwitted, humbled, and soundly castigated—a quite deplorable, but lovely and heartsome sensation. One finds its reflection in the temper of Roderick Random and of Peregrine Pickle, with whom it is a point of honour never to leave an injury unavenged. Herein they differ completely from Gil Blas, who was wont to console his smarting *amour-propre* more easily, and, as we wrongly say, more philosophically, by the simple resolve never again to be caught in the same trap. Remember his comment after that unfortunate experience with the parasite: 'I merely laughed at his ingratitude and looked at him with the contempt he deserved.' Now Peregrine would have bided his time and, by catching the parasite off his guard, given that clever gentleman something to ponder over.   Scott tells us that Smollett's old school-master, Gordon, used to speak with affection of his 'callant wi' the stane in his pouch.'   The phrase aptly symbolizes Smollett's attitude to his private enemies and, in general, to every form of injustice, hypocrisy, and oppression.   Roderick Random, it will be observed, has none of Gil Blas's good humour and cynicism in the face of misfortune.   What tides him effectually over the shoals of life is a stinging and lasting resentment, coupled with the pious hope of a swift and adequate revenge.   In this first novel, there is not a trace of the Christian and incredible forgiveness later attributed to Renaldo,[1] and little of Matthew Bramble's generous tolerance.[2] On the contrary, the author lingers with diabolical glee over the narrative of Roderick's tussles with his oppressors.   With smacking lips, he describes the smashing of the chaplain's teeth by that well-directed pebble from behind the hedge.   The same ill-concealed relish is evident in the account of the schoolmaster's castigation at the hands of Tom Bowling, in the tale of O'Donnell's humiliation, and in the episode of Roderick's duel with Lord Quiverwit: 'I imagined that his weapon had perforated my lungs, and, of con-sequence, that the wound was mortal; therefore, determined not to die unrevenged, I seized his shell, which was close to my breast, before he could disentangle the point, and keeping it fast with my left hand, shortened my own sword with my right, intending to run him through the heart; but he received the thrust in the left arm, which penetrated up to the shoulder-blade.   Disappointed in this expectation, and afraid still that death would frustrate my revenge, I grappled with him, and, being much the stronger, threw him upon the ground, where I wrested the sword out of his hand; and so great was my confusion, instead of turning the point upon him, struck out three of his fore-teeth with the hilt.'   At this early stage in his career—for Smollett was twenty-seven when he wrote *Roderick Ran-dom*—all this was meat and drink to the author.   At that age no normal man believes that 'the pen is mightier than the sword.' Physical violence seems still the most natural and satisfactory way to wipe out personal grudges.   And, indeed, as Dr. Johnson felt in the case of Osborne, there are certain situations which can only be adequately regularized in this manner.

However, about half-way through *Roderick Random*, Smollett the polemist and social reformer joins forces with Smollett the novelist. The first effect of this coalition is to drive the hero into the back-

---

[1] *Ferdinand, Count Fathom.*   [2] *Humphry Clinker.*

ground, so that until the end of the novel, his character practically remains static. During the whole of the naval episode, Roderick is simply the medium through which we gaze upon a procession of new arrivals, each one of whom typifies some particular aspect of nautical life and manners in the eighteenth century. And in building up his picture, Smollett proceeds along traditionally English lines. His is the cumulative method, by which the artist rises slowly from a mass of details to the general impression which he proposes to create. Not until the last trait has been added to the smallest and humblest figure in this motley pageant, do we grasp the significance of the satire. Remove a single character, however 'minor' he may appear to be, and the whole conception will be twisted out of focus. This is in keeping with Smollett's idea of the novel as a genre, and it is set forth in *Count Fathom*: 'A novel is a large, diffused picture, comprehending the characters of life, disposed in different groups, and exhibited in various attitudes, for the purposes of a uniform plan, and general occurrence, to which every individual figure is subservient. But this plan cannot be executed with propriety, probability or success, without a principal personage to attract the attention, unite the incidents, unwind the clue of the labyrinth, and at last close the scene, by virtue of his importance.'

The weakness of such a scheme is evident. The novel itself is apt to be sacrificed or subordinated to the author's satiric purpose; and there is always a danger lest the characters may lose their human interest, eventually degenerating into mere ciphers. But whilst this is true of Roderick Random himself, so great is the multiplicity of the other figures in the book that the reader is rarely aware of Smollett's thesis. Though we know, of course, that the author's intention is satiric or even polemical, the chain of our interest is rarely broken. In the account of the siege of Carthagena, perhaps, there are heavily sarcastic references to the conduct of the military leaders which reveal the intrusion of the journalist; but they are not numerous enough to spoil our enjoyment of the fiction.

Smollett, and here he differs from Le Sage, achieves nearly all his effects by a process of mass-grouping. Unlike the Frenchman, he loves a crowded stage; and the resulting impression is curiously human and intimate. His characters, though actually shallow, are strongly individualized by their peculiar actions and idiosyncrasies of speech. They do not seem to evolve, or if they do, it is almost imperceptibly; yet the cumulative effect of their individual acts and words, which are in themselves crudely simple and even repetitious, is surprisingly potent and suggestive. Segregate, for example, Captain Oakum from the group on board the *Thunder* and examine him as an individual. He will be found totally lacking in complexity. One has, indeed, only to clap eyes on him once to recognize the breed. He is the brutal, callous bully, the typical product of the eighteenth-century public school, with just enough brains to espy and detest any evidence of intellect or culture in his subordinates. Mackshane is the type of toady who is Oakum's natural complement; for Mackshane has something resembling a mind and, in his crude way, is an intriguer. Similarly, Morgan is devoid of subtlety. The fiery little Welshman holds our attention not so much by what he says, because, like the others, his stock of ideas is limited, but largely because he expresses himself in a queer, amusing jargon. The others are simple too. Thomson is a shadowy creature, and the lovable, honest sea-dog, Jack Rattlin, is merely a lower-deck version of Tom Bowling. Nor is there anything complex in the nature of that vindictive swine, Crampley. Yet in all the naval scenes, every character, however insignificant, contributes a splash of colour, of illumination to the final pattern, the general contours of which, though we do not suspect it, were predetermined by Smollett's habitual attitude to life. Take, for instance, that apparently irrelevant incident which occurs when Crampley's ship hits a sandbank off the English coast. 'In the midst of this uproar,' says Roderick, 'I went below to secure my own effects; and found the carpenter's mate hewing down the purser's cabin with his hatchet, whistling all the while with great composure. When I asked his intention in so doing, he replied very calmly: "I only want to taste the purser's rum, that's all, master." At that instant the purser, coming down, and seeing his effects going to wreck, complained bitterly of the injustice done to him, and asked the fellow what occasion he had for liquor when, in all likelihood, he would be in eternity in a few minutes. "All's one for that," said the plunderer, "let us live when we can." "Miserable wretch that thou art," cried the purser, "what must be thy lot in the other world, if thou diest in the commission of robbery?" "Why, hell, I suppose!" replied the other with great deliberation.' This brief incident provides the ideal, final touch to Smollett's picture of eighteenth-century naval life. In no other way could the author have so vividly *realized* the brutalizing and soul-destroying effects of the system he loathed. It is the stone which closes the arch.

To a greater or less degree, every novel derives its shape, colour, and tone from the author's conception of what life should be, rather than from his immediate experience of life. In the novels which we call idealistic, the artist boldly ignores actuality and with loving intensity concentrates on his picture of a dream world, inhabited by creatures who are beautiful but incredible. And at the other end of the scale, amongst the so-called naturalists, the same process is at work, although the manner of its expression is widely different. Here, by exaggerating the ugliness of actuality, the artist strives to inspire us with the desire for an ideal, thus resembling certain preachers who, in order to awaken their hearers to a sense of the glory of God, depict the Devil in unnecessarily sombre colours. The ultimate effect produced by such novelists is one of unreality, and moreover, their works do not possess the saving grace of beauty. Yet both of these schools have a common belief in the perfectibility of man : they are all artists with a social purpose. In what relation do Le Sage and Smollett stand to these categories? In the work of the former there is nothing to justify the assumption that he possessed no inner vision of an ideal life, though this is not directly reflected in his art. The very irony of his attitude to human vice and folly seems to be born of a conviction that human nature is, as such, imperfect, and, moreover, irremediably so. By cultivating a deliberate sense of remoteness, Le Sage passed beyond the Smollett stage of resentment and seething irritation. The decision that he reached in regard to life is that nothing can be done about it. Better, therefore, look upon it as an inexplicable comedy of errors. Had he known Figaro, he would have assuredly adopted that hero's famous maxim : 'Je me presse de rire de tout, de peur d'en pleurer.' Being completely sceptical as to the regeneration of humanity by any means whatever, Le Sage the artist was careful to avoid extremes and so pictured man neither in his most animal nor in his most angelic moments. He set out to portray the mind of the average man, and his final impression, if very far from flattering, cannot on the whole be considered libellous or grotesque.

Now Smollett, with all his pretended misanthropy, cherishes a very eighteenth-century faith in the perfectibility of human nature. He is really convinced of the regenerative and tonic power of satire and of invective. His attitude to human vice and folly is not, therefore, ironical. Irony springs from a consciousness of the incurable disparity between life as it is and life as it might be, were it not for man's spiritual ugliness and intellectual blindness. The habitual ironist has no reformative intention. His irony is a purely

N

private affair, a quite selfish source of amusement. It is the intellectual's way of consoling himself for the fact that he is doomed to share with imbeciles and knaves a world governed by folly and vice. Smollett was too sentimental and too humane ever to acquire such a feeling of superiority and of isolation. In this respect, he was typical of a race and epoch which produced very few ironists. As a result, his idea of what is comic in life is utterly different from the conception peculiar to Le Sage, to Molière, to Voltaire, Beaumarchais, Flaubert, Stendhal, or Proust. Molière, for instance, could view avarice and hypocrisy as comic manias. In the same spirit, Flaubert makes us laugh at the ineffable stupidity and pedantry of Homais and his gruesome experiment on the clubfoot. Proust emphasizes the comic aspect of the invert, Charlus; and, from the traditional French point of view, nothing is more logical, because, in the eyes of Charlus, it is only normal lovers who are abnormal. A few chapters ago, in referring to *Othello*, we mentioned a French dramatist who, no doubt with memories of Molière's Tartuffe, wanted to recast Iago as a comic type. To an Anglo-Saxon, the idea seems grotesque and, indeed, it is so when we remember the fate of Desdemona and Othello. What suggested it to the Frenchman was Iago's *idée fixe* that in a world of sentimental and romantic imbeciles he is the only intellectual and realist. Our French dramatist, being unable to visualize such a character in tragedy as it was then conceived, could think of no other alternative than to make Iago a figure for *la haute comédie*. The eighteenth-century French conception of a comic character was rooted in the notion that such an individual lives in a continual, blissful illusion as to his abnormality. Like the recruit in the marching squad, he gravely notes, and with considerable pride, that all the others are out of step. It is only when he *knows* that he is abnormal and, moreover, realizes that he has not the will-power to change, that he ceases to be comic and becomes tragic. In that great novel, *Le Rouge et le Noir*, Stendhal has portrayed the transition from the one state to the other in the character of Julien Sorel.

Men of Smollett's temper cannot possibly attain to this view of the comic. An optimist, an idealist inspired with a 'generous indignation' at the spectacle of human imperfection, Smollett naïvely believed that vice and folly could be cauterized by satire; regenerated, that is to say, by reason, since satire is but a sharp reminder to the culprit that his conduct is irrational and anti-social. Smollett had all the Scotsman's fiery hatred and intolerance of injustice and stupidity even in their most trivial forms. In consequence, he is apt to attack some of his lesser fry with astonishing savagery. In the early part of *Roderick Random* nothing will satisfy him but to see them thrashed, stoned, and otherwise man-handled. As he proceeds, however, the castigation assumes a less brutal and less physical form. Yet a large part of *Peregrine Pickle* is devoted to the schemes devised by the fertile imagination of the hero in order to lure his butts into situations where they will be exposed, ridiculed, and completely humiliated. This *acharnement* of Smollett's produces grave artistic defects in his novels. To a much greater extent than his brilliant pupil, Dickens, he is betrayed by his satiric intemperance into caricature and melodrama, a fact noted by the artist Cruikshank, though perhaps overstressed. In *Launcelot Greaves* and *Count Fathom* it is very blatant. Granting that the former is an extravaganza based on *Don Quixote* there are, nevertheless, characters who are meant to be real and not *fantoches*. Yet they fail to hold our interest. For example, Ferret the party-writer and Justice Gobble, whom we are supposed to take seriously because they typify viciousness and corruption, leave us with the impression that they are unique individuals. The Gobble episode opens in a vein of mingled humour and satire, until Smollett, warming to his task, loses all restraint or sense of proportion and lapses into low farce, with the result that the 'Description of a Modern Magistrate' degenerates into the caricature of an incredible imbecile who could not possibly have existed even in the eighteenth century. Besides, by combining rancid sentimentality with his farce, Smollett concocts a hopeless pot-pourri. Such an artistic blunder Dickens was careful to avoid when he composed the famous scene immortalizing Mr. Nupkins. A like immoderation is evident in *Count Fathom*, where Smollett melodramatizes his Tartuffe into a creature so unbelievably sinister and so obviously a hypocrite that he could not deceive a schoolgirl, let alone the intelligent and high-souled Renaldo and Ferdinand's numerous lady victims.

These are, admittedly, Smollett's worst novels, but the same lack of balance is to be seen in all his works, particularly in their general looseness of texture. In adopting the novel form used by Scarron and Le Sage, Smollett tacitly recognized his own shortcomings in the art of psychological analysis. He chose a cadre eminently suited to his peculiar genius. His object was to offer a satiric picture of contemporary English manners and social institutions, and for that he needed a large canvas. In all novels of this type,

evidently, the character of the hero and even the story of his
adventures must needs occupy a secondary place. Of this Le Sage
was quite aware when he made Gil Blas almost a passive agent,
a man to whom things happen but who never deliberately courts
adventure except in so far as he is cursed with the wandering spirit.
Now Roderick and Peregrine are not passive agents. Wilfully
and often they create the situations which give rise to their troubles.
They are adventurous in a positive sense, quite foreign to the nature
of Gil Blas. Roderick Random, it is true, is pressed into the
navy, but then had he not been moving heaven and earth to become
a naval surgeon? Poor Gil Blas never really wanted to be any of
the things he did become: assistant to Sangrado, robber, valet,
secretary. He drifted into these professions on the tide of destiny.
Nor would Gil Blas have ever, like Peregrine, pursued the intriguing
lady who lived at the 'ofspital of the Anvil-heads,' or harassed the
fair Fleming, or contrived and executed the complicated series of
escapades which brighten the career of Peregrine at Oxford, Bath,
and London. The explanation is, surely, that Le Sage's object is
not, like Smollett's, to present a localized and coloured picture of
manners, but to offer a universal panorama of the human mind.
That is a cardinal point of difference between the two novelists.
It accounts, too, for the fact that Smollett's novels, like the comedies
of the Restoration, interest us to-day because of something which
has nothing at all to do with the essentials of art. They have 'an
eighteenth-century flavour,' to use a trite phrase; and this does not
entirely come from Smollett's genius. It is due rather to the circumstance that his books resemble certain wines which, although
not originally remarkable, acquire with time a charming bouquet
and mellowness. *Gil Blas* owes its excellence to no such fact,
but to an intrinsic and perennial virtue. It has no historic
colour or, at least, very little, because its people are fundamentally
as true to-day as they were in 1715. For that reason it is quite
idle to seek, as some do, the 'keys' to Dr. Sangrado, Don Gabriel
de Triaquero, and the Archbishop of Granada since all their sayings
and doings are undatable. On the whole, this is not the case with
Smollett's creations, many of whom are as extinct as the great auk.
It might be possible in some remote spot to run across a Trunnion,
a Hatchway, or a Tom Bowling. Yet even Mr. W. W. Jacobs has
not quite succeeded in doing so. Of course, the majority of these
people were oddities to begin with and, moreover, their distinguishing traits are usually physical and superficial. On the other hand—

for Smollett is encyclopaedic in the richness and variety of his observation—one can still discover in his pages certain real types which persist in English society.   It should still be feasible, for instance, to discover at Oxford the modern counterpart of Peregrine Pickle, the 'hearty,' rumbustious undergraduate who revels in 'rags.' Possibly, however, the Oxford Union now bears only a faint resemblance to the political club so humorously pilloried by Smollett. If we turn to another equally venerable yet less reputable institution, we shall find much in *Roderick Random* that is still topical.   Take, for example, the hero's encounter with the lady at the playhouse who smells of 'geneva.' She has not appreciably changed either in tactics or in language, and with slight emendations her parting shot: 'Damn you, you dog, won't you pay the coach-hire,' has an authentic twentieth-century ring. In the West End one may still meet Beau Jackson, the typical borrower with the note-book in which he conscientiously enters his obligations—a sort of Doomsday Book.   Politics and law no longer harbour Sir Steady Steerwells or Mr. Cringers; they have gone the way of highwayman Rifle and Captain Weazel. The snobbish Wagtail and the waggish Banter and the crusty Medlar are still in our midst, but Smollett's happy hunting-ground, the squirearchy, is now barren of game.   Squire Bramble would be hard to unearth, and one has a lurking suspicion that, like Dickens's Christmas, he is too splendid ever to have existed. But Gawky, Darnel, Tom Random, Timothy Thicket, and the other brutal country boobies most certainly did exist; though no one deplores their passing.   Generally speaking, Smollett's novels are richer in museum pieces than in perennial human types.   In this somewhat limited sense, therefore, they may be called classics. *Gil Blas*, on the other hand, is a classic in the fullest acceptation of the term, precisely because its author eschewed the local or evanescent, and struck boldly at the basic things in human nature. This distinction has a parallel in the divergent manners of English and French comedy at the turn of the seventeenth and eighteenth centuries. Very few of the English playgoers who flock to see a revived Restoration comedy are really impressed by its dramatic merits. What attracts them, actually, is the piquant contrast afforded by the spectacle of a twentieth-century actress expressing herself in the free idiom of a vanished epoch. Molière, on the contrary, is admired for reasons that are absolutely artistic and have nothing to do with quaintness or historic colour.

If not a profound, Smollett is an alert observer of human nature who was led by his satiric bent to cast his net very widely. He hated the right things and the right people; and if many of them have disappeared that is scarcely Smollett's fault. At least, he showed us what they were. But a great novelist portrays not only what is local and transitory in life, but also what is eternal and significant in human nature. Without Troubert, Grandet, Vautrin, and Sophie Gamard, the novels of Balzac would still be readable and amusing. Yet Balzac would not be a true classic. He rises from the picture of contemporary manners to the *comédie de la vie humaine*. Smollett gives us the picture of contemporary foibles and little else, rarely penetrating beneath the crust of his characters. Le Sage, whose psychological explorations do not go deep, yet got deeper down than Smollett, and, besides, if we were to protest that his men and women have no souls, he could reply with truth: 'Yes, exactly. That is why they are men and women.' Smollett has no such excuse. A sentimentalist and a reformer, he cannot pretend to share Le Sage's cynical opinion of humanity. And though at times he does his best to show us the souls of his characters, he never succeeds, because like some angry bee, he is instantly distracted by something going on in the next garden. The trouble with Smollett is that there are so many queer, droll, irritating, and even sinister flowers in his gardens. In his anxiety to investigate them all he buzzes to and fro, never remaining long enough in one chalice to extract its essence. Were it true that the only people whom we really know are our enemies, Smollett would be a profound psychologist; for he had many enemies. But satire, unless its roots are planted in a deep and lasting hatred, is not a great illuminant, and the satire of Smollett is diffused over so many objects. Novelists like Stendhal and Flaubert concentrate on a few, so that the light of their satire is strong and searching. Smollett's fault was to waste much of his energy on a motley array of harmless nonentities who, at most, deserve a passing crack over the knuckles. Thus he tends to lose all sense of relative values, and on meeting a Strutwell, a Mrs. Pickle, or a grandfather Random, does not seem to suspect what excellent and complex studies they might make. The novels of Smollett are full of such half-etched characters or *ébauches*, and Dickens is not our only novelist who has realized and profited from Smollett's dilettantism. The word is, perhaps, hardly adequate to describe his typical method of handling character and situation, since it does not reflect Smollett's surprising trick of veering suddenly

from the extreme of farce to the extreme of sentiment. 'Smollettry' would be a better term. All his heroes are touched with
it, and a whole novel, *Count Fathom*, is completely ruined by Smollettry.   However, as is natural, it is most evident in his accounts of
the sentimental experiences of Random and Pickle.

Le Sage, and it is one of his titles to fame, knew his own limitations, and is always careful to keep Gil Blas away from sentimental
or passionate women. Of Antonia, who became the hero's wife,
we are told nothing save that Gil Blas married her. But Smollett,
whose 'generous indignation' was fired by the thought of women
in distress, recklessly plunges into a world which, by temperament,
he was totally unfitted to understand. Roderick's Narcissa is a
complete puppet and the hero's luscious conversations with her are
deliriously funny. Listen to Roderick: 'By this ambrosial kiss,
a thousand times more fragrant than the breeze that sweeps
the orange grove, I never more will leave thee.' 'As my first
transport abated,' he tells us, 'my passion grew more turbulent and
unruly. I was giddy with standing on the brink of bliss, and all
my virtue and philosophy were scarce sufficient to restrain the
inordinate sallies of desire. Narcissa perceived the conflict within
me and with her usual dignity of prudence called off my imagination from the object in view, and with eager expressions of interested
curiosity desired to know the particulars of my voyage.' The
Renaldo-Monimia affair in *Count Fathom* is epic in its imbecility.
One may safely say, however, that no English novelist has ever
subjected his unhappy heroine to the prolonged and fiendish trials
which dog the footsteps of Monimia. And, poor girl, not even
marriage ends her troubles since, in the closing pages, we learn
that Renaldo, 'like a lion rushing on his prey, approached the
nuptial bed.' As Shakespeare would have put it: 'Well rush'd,
lion!' All our author's bridal nights are coloured by this Smollettry,
which, though infallibly amusing, is apt to disconcert the quiet
reader.   One cannot, on the other hand, forgive him for bungling
Peregrine's love affair with Emilia, because in the early part of the
novel Emilia promises to develop into a charming and subtle
feminine study. Why then does Smollett ruin a delightful picture
of youthful *dépit amoureux* by suddenly inspiring Peregrine to attempt
rape upon his fiancée? Really, our eighteenth-century ancestors
had a rape complex. No doubt Smollett had just read *Pamela*,
but that is no excuse. If anything, it aggravates his offence. Possibly, too, he wanted to satirize the popular mania for foreign travel,

and to demonstrate the pernicious effects of a petty tour on a eupeptic young Englishman of 1751. The net result of his stupidity was to transform Emilia into a creature who, at a highly critical moment, expresses herself as follows: 'Sir, you are unworthy of my concern or regret, and the sigh that now struggles from my breast is the result of sorrow for my own want of discernment. As for your present attempt upon my chastity, I despise your power as I detest your intention. . . .' There is much more of this and Peregrine deserves every yard of it. So, by the way, does the reader who, like myself, is idle enough to read it all.

Evidently, then, Smollett is not at his happiest when he tries to portray the virginal mind. His most successful feminine creations, needless to say, belong to the realm of low comedy. Here he is not, indeed, unique, but at least thoroughly in his element. Mrs. Trunnion, Tabitha Bramble, Jenny Ramper, Mrs. Hornbeck, Miss Lavement, Dolly Cowslip, Miss Snapper, and the Rosicrucian lady reveal a Smollett sadly lacking, no doubt, in gallantry, but a voracious and alert collector of female 'humorists.' In common with all the novelists and comic dramatists of his time, Smollett discovered in the old maid and in her lust for matrimony a fertile source of humour. He has since been quite overshadowed in this province by Dickens, who is infinitely more subtle and suggestive. Yet Mrs. Trunnion and Tabitha Bramble continue to hold their own. Though spurred by a common motive, these two ladies are quite different in character and in technique. For sheer aggressiveness, Perry's aunt cannot hold a candle to Tabitha, who believes in the frontal method of attack and never admits defeat. Still, there is much to be said for the Trunnion policy of envelopment by insinuation and flattery. And when once installed in the garrison, having scornfully cast aside all subterfuge, she is a Tartar. Tabitha is rather funny than humorous, since what we remember her by is her grotesque letters to Mrs. Gwyllim. Smollett perhaps tends to over-exploit this facile and purely verbal source of merriment, though it must be admitted that he does not often repeat himself. Mrs. Hornbeck, Win Jenkins, and Tabitha all maltreat the language with the same bland confidence, yet in different ways.

Without taking Smollett's funny females too seriously, let us note a trait common to them all. It is their inveterate resentment at the elusiveness of the male. As a rule, they are obliged by their economic situation to bottle up this contempt and hatred, though it fizzes out from a number of safety valves. In the case of the wealthy Miss Snapper, however, no attempt is made to conceal it. The account of her ride with Roderick, the captain, the lawyer, and the prim gentlewoman in the Bath coach is a vivid and priceless example of Smollett's satiric humour. At the same time it illustrates very well his habitual trick of creating fire and illumination in a scene by the constant friction of incompatible elements or characters. In her way, Miss Snapper is unique because of her sparkling malice; her sisters are, on the whole, merely irascible, vindictive, or stupid. She represents, in fact, our author's closest approach to the ironical Le Sagian attitude to the other sex. In general, Smollett has none of the Frenchman's ingrained respect for feminine cunning or intelligence. Gil Blas would have been quite outwitted by the wily Miss Lavement, who has no terrors for the confident and conceited Roderick. Miss Lavement, as it happens, might have developed in other hands into something more subtle and interesting than Smollett makes of her, into somebody, in fact, not unlike Miss Fanny Squeers. Miss Lavement was good for more than a few ribald jests: but on these occasions the medical student in Smollett is ever ready to dart out. So he whisks Miss Lavement from the arms of O'Donnell into Squire Gawky's nuptial couch just as she is about to be intriguing. The sudden idea, also, of giving a sentimental twist to this bawdy farce by making her falsely accuse the innocent hero of theft is but another typical bit of Smollettry.

Smollett enjoys himself most hugely in the society of ladies like Jenny Ramper, 'brisk and airy' ladies, or of bovine and bonny country wenches like Dolly Cowslip, the innkeeper's daughter, or Tabitha's servant girl, Win Jenkins. He lingers over the scene featuring Jenny, the old Jew, and Captain Weazel, obviously loving the flavour of Jenny's fluent Billingsgate and her gutter-bred cheekiness. With similar gusto, he narrates Peregrine's experiment with the 'nymph of the road' where that hero, anticipating Mr. Bernard Shaw's *Pygmalion*, transforms a street-girl into a fine lady. The account of the card-party, the nymph's sudden lapse from graciousness into her native lingo, and the quaint manner of her exit reveal Smollett in one of his most frolicsome and natural moods. In the same lightsome way he maliciously records the innocent rustic indiscretions of Win Jenkins and Dolly Cowslip or the inarticulate ardours of the former oyster wench, Mrs. Hornbeck, who, to her puzzled annoyance, is being carted over Europe by a suspicious and badgered husband. The letter to Peregrine

* N

beginning : 'Coind Sur,' with its helpful reference to the 'Calf-hay
de Contea,' is of its kind a little gem. With the ladies who hail
from the purlieus of the Covent Garden Piazza or who are to be
accosted in the corridors of inns and *auberges*, Dr. Smollett is on easy
and intimate terms, since invariably they provide an admirable
excuse for broad and rollicking farce. His old maids and the snobs
of Bath are good for a passing laugh, but he never really hits off
their foibles with Le Sagian gaiety and slyness. Even in the case
of Mrs. Trunnion, Smollett has to drag in the gin-bottle and a
lengthy, not very funny obstetrical incident, in order to make up for
his deficiencies as a psychologist. One must read Dickens to realize
how much escaped Smollett in the matter of feminine humour : but
that may be due to his ignorance of London landladies. In any
event, Smollett never shared Dickens's extraordinary interest in
women, either as objects of humour or of pathos.

Speaking of women, it is to Smollett and not to Le Sage that
one must go for these *gauloiseries* which Anglo-Saxons are wont to
regard as the unique, dynamic source of laughter in French novels.
Compared to Roderick and Peregrine, Gil Blas is extremely chaste
not only in fact but in language. The late Dr. Saintsbury refers
to Smollett as 'one of the nastiest writers in English,' an expression
which would be better applied to Sterne. The Scotsman is coarse,
ribald, and indelicate. His heroes are all more concupiscent than
sentimental. Even Pipes and the ludicrous Strap have their
carnal moments, but Smollett is never really offensive or salacious,
because in all his bawdy episodes the sexual element is submerged
in gales of laughter or in the crash and din of buffoonery. Evidently,
however, his books could find no place in an English *Bibliothèque
rose*, assuming that we ever possess such a collection. And, touching
upon this question of decency, there is a marked difference in tone
between the early novels and *Humphry Clinker*, which was not
published till 1771. By that time, the medical student has almost
disappeared and in his room we discover Dr. Smollett, the enlightened but irascible humanitarian. One is very forcibly made
aware on reading Smollett that there is no element in literature
that is apt to age quite so rapidly as humour. Wit, on the other
hand, offers a diamantine resistance to the pressure of time and
changing fashion. That is why the back numbers of *Punch* leave such
a peculiar, almost melancholy impression on the minds of the curious
who skim through their pages in dentists' waiting-rooms. If we
laugh at them it is hardly because of their humour but at the idea

that our grandfathers once found them humorous. With Smollett such is not entirely the case, though it is true of his ribald passages. As we have noted, many of his favourite butts have vanished into oblivion, carrying their laughter with them. However, Smollett never wholly relied on these oddities for his best effects, which more often depend on situation than on character. Now, whilst humour no doubt arises from the contrast between situation and character, there are situations which of themselves are funny, quite apart from the characters involved. And, though humour thus engendered is rarely very intellectual, it has its appeal even to the twentieth-century reader. To this category belong nearly all the boisterous escapades of the earlier novels. Some are frankly detestable, but it is still possible to laugh at the 'roasting' of Medlar by Jack Banter or at Crabtree clowning as an Eastern soothsayer. When he is neither medical nor scatological, Smollett uncovers a rich fund of jollity. The quakings and invocations of that egregious poltroon, Strap; the pious ejaculations of the fervent evangelist, Humphry Clinker, and his solemn and farcical attempts to win the good graces of Tabitha; the gorgeous scene in Tunley's inn where we first meet that inimitable trio, Trunnion, Hatchway, and Pipes; the hilarious revenge meted out to the curate, Sackbut; the frustrated amorous pursuit of Amanda, the fair Fleming, by Peregrine aided by the wily Capuchin; Win Jenkins's account of her misadventures in the pool at Bath—these are but a few of the excellent 'turns' in Smollett's repertory of clowneries.

Smollett ought to be read at least twice; once for the sheer fun of the thing, and again for the admirable common sense and worldly lore stored away in odd corners of his books. Like so many Scots, he was a cosmopolitan, and if he cannot vie with Fielding in penetration and in sensibility, he is less insular than the author of *Tom Jones*—for all Smollett's apparent contempt of foreign ways. Certainly, none of our eighteenth-century novelists has shown up the rottenness of contemporary English social and political conditions with more truth and contempt of accepted opinion. Smollett has been reproached for his lack of good taste: but that is sheer cant. To a certain type of Englishman, it is flagrant bad taste to attack the navy, the universities, the nobility, the law, the government, and the medical profession. Smollett, who had no sense of reverence for institutions merely because they were old, arraigned all of these and exposed their venerable corruption. It would be easy, no doubt, to convict him of frequent exaggeration and of prejudice because he was impetuous and aggressive. Yet, if he was intolerant, he was intolerant of the right things, and of how many can that be said? With the years he mellowed, until in *Humphry Clinker* we can see him for what he always was, despite his errors in taste and lapses from decorum—a warm-hearted, irascible humanitarian. Good taste is an excellent thing so long as it is not used as a bogy in order to stifle legitimate criticism or intelligent curiosity, and Smollett's lack of it must not deter us from peering into the queer world that lies within the pages of his novels. He may surprise and even shock; but as Matthew Bramble said to the Oxford under-graduate, young Melford: 'A young fellow, when he first thrusts his snout into the world, is apt to be surprised at many things which a man of experience knows to be ordinary and inevitable.' And Dr. Tobias Smollett was a man of much experience.

CHAPTER XIV

WISE VIRGINS

SOME thirty-five years ago, Joseph Texte launched the now widely accepted idea that Richardson changed the destiny of the French novel.[1] In forming this opinion, however, Texte was biased by the thesis which he was defending, and, in addition, seems to have been imperfectly acquainted with the trend of French fiction prior to the appearance of *Paméla* in France.[2] Misled, also, by the 'Englishy' titles of several novels published in his own country after the translation of *Clarissa*, he leapt to the conclusion that their authors had been inspired by Richardson and converted to the English idea of art in the novel.   A closer examination of these works would have convinced this eminent historian that the apparent English influence penetrates no deeper than the title page.   Indeed, if we except Diderot and the few anglomaniacs who could actually read our language in the original, none of Richardson's French admirers ever gained first-hand contact with his works.   The Richardson whom they knew through the translations of Prévost and Le Tourneur was, like the Shakespeare presented by La Place, the shadow of a shadow.[3]

In writing of our debt to the French novel, Texte dismissed the notion that Richardson borrowed the theme of *Pamela* from Marivaux's *La Vie de Marianne*, but, as we shall see, there are others who disagree with this opinion.   Some insist, moreover, that Fielding was indebted to Marivaux's *Le Paysan parvenu* for much of *Joseph Andrews*, a question ignored by Texte.   What really interests him is Richardson's *Clarissa* and its alleged influence upon Jean-Jacques Rousseau, a matter which is vital to his whole thesis, of which,

[1] In his original and suggestive *Jean-Jacques Rousseau et le Cosmopolitisme*.
[2] A fuller discussion will be found in my *French Novelists*, vol. i, chaps. xi–xii, together with some remarks on the novels supposed to have been influenced by Richardson.   Beyond doubt, Texte was led into error by enthusiasm for his thesis, viz., 'Cosmopolitanism was born of the fruitful union between the English genius and Jean-Jacques Rousseau.'
[3] See my article, 'Further Evidence of Realism in the French Novel of the Eighteenth Century,' *Modern Language Notes*, May 1925.   But for a detailed examination of the matter one ought to consult F. H. Wilcox, *Prévost's Translations of Richardson's Novels*, in the University of California Publications (1927).

indeed, it forms the keystone. According to Texte, who repeats and elaborates an opinion current among the *philosophes* of the eighteenth century, Rousseau imitated Richardson's *Clarissa*, and thus 'furthered the spread of English and of the northern literatures generally among the French.' This question is important enough to merit a chapter to itself. Meanwhile, let us return to the earlier Richardson, to Marivaux, and, since he has been dragged on board the galley, to Fielding.

As every one knows, *Pamela* met with an ecstatic reception in England. But, lurking in the orchestra of Richardson's public, were certain low, unregenerate fellows, whose guffaws and horse laughs struck a discordant note in the symphony of sobbings and retchings of soul. More painful still, from the author's point of view, were the clamant trumpet blasts of the intransigent Puritans whose sense of decency was shocked by Samuel's penchant for carnality. What was the attitude of the French public? Here Texte must, I fear, be consulted with some caution. 'The success of *Paméla*,' he tells us, 'was in the first place due to the fact that it impressed the reader as being at once moral in tendency, and true.' [1] In support of this statement he quotes as follows from the *Journal étranger* of February, 1755: 'An English girl, without birth or property, sets an example which might put to shame the *comtesses* and *marquises* of our most famous novelists.' Texte does not gives us the whole passage, which was written by Prévost in the course of a review of Goldoni's play, *Pamela*. Now whilst corroborating Texte's general remark that the English novel was read in the first place for its morality, Prévost condemns *Pamela* as a corrupt work. 'The English novel of this name,' he says, 'appeared in France at a time when the nation, addicted to works of imagination and sentiment, did not affect much scruple about morality. It was not shocked to see, in a book, seduction occupying an outstanding role, morality employed to justify the vilest weakness, and fortune ever faithfully crowning it. A young English girl, without birth or fortune, offered an example capable of discrediting the *comtesses* and *marquises* of our most celebrated novelists. The naïve style of M. Richardson was relished, and, despite his corruption of principles, the virtuous character which he lends to his heroine won him a great many partisans.' [2] Now, had Texte been familiar with French novels

---

[1] loc. cit., chap. v.
[2] In view of these remarks I cannot believe that Prévost, as has been claimed, had a share in translating *Pamela*.

like Crébillon's *Les Égarements du Cœur* (1738) and Duclos's *Histoire de Madame de Luz* (1741), he would have appreciated the full force of Prévost's remarks and realized why *Pamela*, in its emended French version, appealed to the French sophisticates of 1742. It had the same piquant blend of eroticism and sentimentality, which never fails to attract the extremely *blasé* or the very uneducated.

In quoting Desfontaines on *Pamela*, Texte is again disconcertingly brief. Desfontaines, it is true, praises the novelty of *Pamela*, and applauds the author for his defence of womanhood. But he also defends his low choice of a heroine by inferring, sarcastically, that Pamela's resistance would have been incredible in a *marquise*. No doubt, too, he praises the happy carelessness of Richardson's style, but Texte draws a wrong conclusion from Desfontaines's actual words. The latter did not say that *Pamela* 'was an excellent pattern to set before French authors.' On the contrary, he praises the French translator for having omitted 'the disgusting jargon of a low servant or a man of the people.' Also, he cavils at the description of Mr. B.'s attempt on Pamela's chastity. 'The attempts of milord B. necessarily offer some rather bold images which at first alarm us but leave no dangerous impression.' Madame du Deffand wrote to a friend that she was inconsolable because she could not read *Pamela* in the original, and Crébillon the younger told Chesterfield: 'But for *Pamela* we should not know what to read or to say.' We have already referred to Boissy's parody, *Paméla en France*, and to La Chaussée's larmoyant comedy on the same subject. Both were utter failures. As in England, *Anti-Pamélas* made their appearance in France.[2] Aubert de la Chesnaye des Bois, who found that Desfontaines over-praised the English work, expressed what I think is a very fair reflection of French contemporary opinion in regard to *Pamela*. 'I respect his decisions,' he says, 'but I respect still more those of the public, whom I have heard say that the *Lettres de Paméla* are drowned in a mass of insipidities which, by inspiring the reader with disgust and boredom, hide from him in several places the *naïveté* and simplicity of style which constitute the merit of the book in question.'[2] Now, considering that the one element in Richardson's work which was certainly not reproduced in the French version is precisely his style, one is led to think that the French public of 1742 can scarcely be described as converts to English taste. A great many people read *Paméla* and a few *romanesque* souls were touched by the heroine's distresses:

[1] V. Harrisse, *L'Abbé Prévost*, p. 338.   [2] *Lettres amusantes et critiques* (1743).

but apparently the majority were either bored or maliciously amused.

Actually, quite apart from the curiosity invariably aroused in a limited circle by the translation of any successful foreign work, there was no valid reason why *Paméla* should have revolutionized the French novel. Very little of Richardson's realism, which was too low for French taste, survived the ordeal of translation, and, of course, it would have required a genius to imitate the homespun texture of his language in those parts where he is not trying to write 'like a book.' On the other hand, the French reader was spared the almost nauseous smell of Richardson's sanctimoniousness and sentimentality, both of which were deodorized and diluted. *Pamela*, though less ruthlessly 'cut' than *Clarissa* or *Grandison* was, nevertheless, reduced very much in volume and in tone. To the Gallic reader of 1742, therefore, it was pre-eminently the sensational account of a squireen's clumsy and abortive attempts to violate an incredibly lettered and incredibly chaste serving-wench. Now, the French public was used to rapes and persecuted virtue through Prévost's *Clèveland* and *Le Doyen de Killerine*, where rape is, so to speak, in the ordinary way of business. It had also just finished reading Duclos's sad story of poor Madame de Luz, who was forced by a wicked judge to purchase with her honour certain documents incriminating her husband, and to crown all, was drugged and violated by her nasty director of conscience, Father Hardouin. Yet in none of these novels did the question of class distinction play any part, whereas in Richardson it is the dynamic idea. Marivaux, however, had written two novels, *La Vie de Marianne* and *Le Paysan parvenu*, on the theme of social inequality. Marianne, like Pamela, is persecuted and, like her, marries above her station. Here was a flagrant 'parallel.' The hue and cry was up! But someone remembered that Richardson could not read French in the original —ignorant fellow! This was distinctly annoying; but luckily someone else unearthed from the British Museum an English translation of *Marianne*, published in 1742, just in time for Richardson, if he could read fast, to be 'influenced' by Marivaux and to dash off his imitation called *Pamela*. Who shall say that there is no excitement in the academic groves? One enthusiastic German lady [1] drew up the 'evidence' in accusatory, parallel columns, carefully

---

[1] Frl. Schröers, *Ist Richardsons Pamela von Marivaux Vie de Marianne beeinflusst? Englische Studien* (1915–16). Her conclusion is: 'The Frenchman's work was the mine from which Richardson lifted his treasure.'

noting such damning items as that the French, like the English seducer, led up to his vile scheme by offering soft words, presents, and a little apartment. This, of course, is a unique and striking departure from the good old method of cracking the girl on the head with a club. Here, as in so many equally ingenious comparative studies, one cannot but regret that so much labour should be misspent. As we shall see, it is sufficient to read *Pamela* and *Marianne* as works of art to realize at once how they differ in atmosphere, in conception, in style, in plot, and, indeed, in everything that makes them novels, as distinct from the dead material beloved of so many aspiring doctors of philosophy.

As is usual in most classic French novels, the plot of *Marianne* is simple. As a child, the heroine loses her parents, who are evidently persons of rank, in a brutal attack made upon their carriage by highwaymen. Marianne, the sole survivor, is brought up by a village *curé* and his sister. They are cultured folk, and Marianne is, therefore, well educated. Whilst upon a visit to Paris in connection with a lawsuit, the sister, who is accompanied by Marianne, hears of her brother's death, and herself dies, leaving her ward to the care of a good religious. The latter appeals for help to M. de Climal, a wealthy and pious philanthropist who apprentices the girl to Mme Dutour, a linen-draper. Marianne, though secretly hating her new life, prefers it to the humiliation of domestic service. De Climal, however, has other designs and gradually reveals himself to be a *vieux satyre*. A silent duel ensues between the alert but dependent orphan and the amorous hypocrite who, under the cloak of a paternal benevolence, seeks to win her affections by presents. Very soon, however, it becomes impossible for her to pretend not to see the drift of his actions and conversation. Meanwhile, when returning from church, Marianne sprains her ankle, and is assisted by a young gentleman, De Valville, who turns out to be De Climal's nephew. In a dramatic scene, the uncle surprises Valville at Marianne's feet. Being De Climal, he feigns not to know her, and follows Marianne discreetly to Mme Dutour's, where in a fit of jealousy he discards all his prudence and bluntly offers to set her up as his mistress. Valville, however, is also on her trail, and discovers the two in an apparently compromising situation. Without waiting for an explanation, he dashes off, to the rage and mortification of the girl, who is now merciless to her elderly adorer.

Marianne is now in desperate straits, since Mme Dutour cannot afford to keep her. She therefore turns to the religious, with whom she finds De Climal, who impudently accuses her of lies and ingratitude. Marianne succeeds, however, in convincing the priest of her innocence, and he promises to do what he can for her. Friendless and disconsolate, she creeps into the church of a convent, hoping that the superior will take her in as a novice. She gets fine words, regrets, and nothing else. As it happens, she attracts the interest and pity of a kind-hearted lady, Mme de Miran, who adopts her. In the course of a conversation between Mme de Miran and her bosom friend, Mme Dorsin, Marianne learns that Valville is the former's son and has broken off a good match because of his infatuation for a girl whom he met outside a church. Beyond doubt, the girl in question is Marianne. This she confesses to her adoptive mother, who is deeply touched by Marianne's frankness and courage. The latter herself offers to cure Valville of his folly, and in a remarkable scene, sacrifices her love to gratitude and reason. The only result, however, is to make Valville more infatuated than ever; and finally his mother, in defiance of every social precedent, consents to the marriage. Marianne is meanwhile sent away to finish her education at a fashionable convent and passed off as a provincial cousin.

One day, whilst Marianne, accompanied by Valville, is on a visit to a school friend, Mme Dutour calls to do business and, recognizing her former apprentice, embraces her with loud cries of delight. The secret of her humble origin is now out; and soon Mme de Miran's relations intervene to prevent that lady from disgracing the family. By a trick, Marianne is taken before a *conseil de famille* and offered the choice between the veil and marriage with a man of her own class. Mme de Miran and Valville interrupt the proceedings, and after a long and interesting debate, sensibility carries the day. The minister of state, a distant relative who by virtue of his rank presides over the council, refuses to interfere, and it now seems as if all Marianne's troubles were over. But Valville conceives a violent passion for an interesting little intrigante, Mlle Varthon, a boarder in Marianne's convent, thus creating a situation which reveals Marivaux in his very element. Mlle Varthon is surprised in an attempt to elope with Valville and takes the veil. Here, unfortunately, Marivaux laid down his pen; but Mlle Riccoboni, in a marvellous imitation of his style, provided the inevitable ending. A penitent Valville returns to the Marianne whom he had never really ceased to love.

In *Pamela* we step into a different world. The heroine is a servant-girl in the house of a wealthy squire called Mr. B., whose mother, having taken a fancy to the child, taught her to read and write, to sew and strum on the spinet. As we learn in the second book, young B. had already marked down Pamela as his prey, but during his mother's lifetime, always affected to regard the girl with indifference and even dislike. The story is told in letters, and, at the outset, we catch its prevailing tone. Pamela's father, the god-fearing, self-righteous old cottager, warns his daughter to expect the worst, and Pamela, that paragon of daughters, listens with approval to daddy's words. B. starts off by giving her money and clothes and at once offers her familiarities. There was nothing whatever to prevent Pamela from walking out, yet she stays to finish a flowered waistcoat which she is embroidering for her master. With gloating eagerness, she commits to paper every tiny detail of her self-imposed martyrdom. Every epithet hurled at her by the exasperated Mr. B. is lovingly treasured and commented upon. We know what Pamela said to him and what he said to her and what Mrs. Jervis, the housekeeper, thought about these goings-on, and what dear old silver-haired Mr. Longman, the steward, said to Jonathan, the butler, about poor Pamela, and so on, for hundreds of pages.

Stripped of its verbiage and moralizings, the situation is as follows. B. is determined to rape Pamela. He tries once to do so by secreting himself in her bedroom, but is foiled by the good Mrs. Jervis. By a ruse, he gets Pamela off to his country-seat in Lincolnshire, where Mrs. Jewkes, an ex-barmaid, is in charge. This harpy keeps strict watch over Pamela, pending the arrival of Mr. B., and amuses herself by cracking bawdy jokes on her probable fate. Pamela, meanwhile, is in correspondence with B., whom she beseeches to allow her to go home. B., who, like Pamela, takes a perverse delight in torturing himself, offers to let her go if she will marry his curate, Williams. Pamela, to his rage, consents. With the able assistance of the expert Mrs. Jewkes, B. disguises himself as the cook and pretends to be in a drunken slumber on a chair in her bedroom. Richardson, thoroughly enjoying the vicarious sensations which he extracts from these descriptions, gives a long, circumstantial account of B.'s second and serious effort to violate Pamela. By fainting, she again escapes, and B. now changes his attitude, developing, indeed, symptoms of repentance. Still, he toys for a moment with the idea of a bogus marriage. He is now assured of Pamela's love, which in her childish, prattling way she coyly admits. In the meantime it should be noted that B., in a fit of jealousy, had thrown Williams into jail for an imaginary debt; enraged, too, at Jervis and Jonathan, he had dismissed them. Pamela is at last betrothed to her dear master, and her first act as the future Mrs. B. is to beg forgiveness for these poor people.

Pamela is eventually married, and in the second volume we are regaled with a long account of her incredible perfections, in the role of lady of the manor. Wherever she goes, Pamela makes conquests. All the local gentry fall in ecstasies at her feet. The one really human being in the book, B.'s sister, Lady Davers, holds out longest. She persecutes and even slaps Pamela—joyous moment!— but soon she too succumbs; for no one can come within range of Pamela without being overpowered by her meekness, her virtue, her innocence, her sensibility, her righteousness, and her eloquence. Pamela never resists her victims: she anaesthetizes them. To crown her triumph, 'the naughty Mr. B.' has a little affair with a lady he meets at a masquerade, who turns out to be a dowager countess. Need one say that her scalp is added to the others? With no great surprise, we learn also that Mr. B. has an illegitimate daughter whose mother is married to a gentleman in the Indies. With her customary tact, Pamela wins the child's affections, and receives the grateful thanks of her mother and fresh encomiums from her dear B., whom she regards as a being just one step removed from the Deity. In her spare time, for she is writing an improved version of Mr. Locke's book on education, Pamela manages the servants, converts Mr. B.'s dissolute friends, and rescues one of her maids from the predicament into which she herself would have fallen but for her stalwart belief in Providence, and her inherited, deep-rooted suspicion of men. So we take leave of Pamela, now blessed with five children, and determined to live up to the B. family tradition of seven: the perfect daughter, the perfect woman, the perfect wife, and a perfect humbug.

Were one to ransack all French and English literature, it would be impossible to unearth two novelists more completely dissimilar than Marivaux and Richardson. No one could be more French than the artist who created Marianne, no one more English than the spiritual father of Pamela. Yet each in his way reflects a new mood which in France and in England was beginning to colour the national mind. Marivaux and Richardson are both men of feeling. In the thirties of the eighteenth century, sensibility was rare in literature because it was rare in actual life. Examine the social organism of the period, French or English, and you will discover that in all its workings there is very little trace of humanity or sentiment. Petty delinquencies were confused with serious crimes and punished with insane savagery. Though Englishmen boasted about their Habeas Corpus Act, there was as much corruption in the administration of justice as in France. For if the latter had her seigneurial courts where judges were often intimidated by their local overlord, England suffered under her 'trading justices' who worked in collusion with thief-catchers in order to line their pockets. In both countries, the *peuple* and lower middle classes flocked eagerly to public executions, gazing with avid curiosity at scenes too foul to be described. In London and in Paris prostitution, disease, and poverty were regarded with indifference as necessary evils and, on the whole, the attitude of the public towards the orphan and the penniless sick was one of apathy or insensibility. A spirit of senseless brutality governed the relations between teacher and child, flogging being regarded as an indispensable adjunct to instruction. The lower classes in France, held in check by the Church and by the Law, were outwardly polite and more civilized than their English fellows. Yet one has only to read Marivaux's penetrating study on *La Populace* to realize how little they possessed of that *bonté naturelle* later attributed to them by Rousseau. The London mob was a byword in Europe for drunkenness, stupidity, and bestial violence. In the French family, more than in the English, the head of the household enjoyed and exercised despotic powers over his children and in this was supported by the majesty of the law. In England, the same tyranny was apparent, but, since there was more drunkenness, there was less filial respect. The type of conversation indulged in by Squire Western before his daughter Sophia was not at all exceptional. The authority still exercised by the Church in France certainly made for greater decency in the home, though it did nothing to encourage a warmer and more intimate relationship between parent and child. In England, as is well known, the miserable economic position of the lower clergy robbed them of any prestige whatever. In neither nation did the upper classes set an example that might be imitated with profit. The nobility of France, for all its external elegance, was morally quite as corrupt as the aristocracy of England. The bourgeoisie, French and English, constituted the moral backbone of the country, but, unfortunately this class, although decent and sober in its habits, was not remarkable for sensibility. Materialism and selfishness governed the trading and commercial population of France and England, which had few interests outside money-making, except, perhaps, a general urge amongst its more wealthy members to ape the vices of the titled. Nevertheless, this is the class which gave to England and to France most of the writers who were destined to spread the gospel of humanity and sensibility and, through their poetry, plays and novels, and miscellaneous publications, suggested the possibility of a higher, more civilized relationship between man and man. To this class belonged Marivaux, Diderot, La Chaussée, and Vauvenargues in France; Addison, Fielding, and Richardson in England.

La Vie de Marianne and *Pamela* are both idealistic novels. Marivaux depicts a kind of life which was the exception rather than the rule in France of his day; Richardson, who is much more *romanesque*, portrays a state of things quite bad enough to be credible, but offers us a *dénouement* that could have had no counterpart in reality. The two heroines are as unlike as the artists who created them; whilst the style of Richardson, compared to that of Marivaux, is as coarse wincey to Lyons silk. So it is, too, with their sensibility. Marivaux's is delicate and shot with fancy, yet it is as strong and resistant as the crude fabric woven by the English novelist. Marivaux conceives sensibility as a quality attainable by all, and one that will stand the wear and tear of everyday life. Richardson, however, makes of it something so monstrously perfect that it fills our soul with incredulity and dismay. In Pamela he embodied all the virtues, for it is certain that he never intended her to have any defects. If we take her at Richardson's own valuation she is completely uninteresting because she is, like an angel, so completely perfect as to be above criticism. In books, as in life, angels make poor company. However, in creating Pamela the author involuntarily portrays his own mind with all its repressions; and in the very actions and words that are supposed to mirror the perfections of his heroine we catch the reflection of Richardson's private views on humanity. There are, therefore, two Pamelas, the author's and our own. But there is only one Marianne, and it would require an extremely subtle psychologist to discover in Marivaux's picture of her mind any traits which that clever student of the human heart has failed to analyse and explain. Let the reader match his wits with the French novelist and, at any point in his story, attempt to anticipate his narrative of the heroine's emotions and sentiments. He will be amazed to find how obtuse he is. Now, at any stage in

Pamela it is possible, usually, to predict what the heroine will feel
and, after her first experience, what she will do. After she has
survived the original attempt at rape and remained, Pamela's
future conduct can be easily guessed. The question that keeps the
reader in suspense is not what she will do or think, but what will
happen to her. Pamela will remain noisily passive, but she will
remain; exposed to further onslaughts on her chastity, which is held
up by the author like a coco-nut for Mr. B. to shy at. That, no
doubt, provides a sort of excitement; yet, as has been suggested,
the real interest lies deeper. It does not reside in the novelist's
account of Pamela's virtues and her martyrdom, but in the answer
to the following riddle: 'What kind of mind is it that can sincerely
regard Pamela as a model of virtue, and this whole narrative as
a credible picture of the behaviour of two people in love?'

Marivaux presents his heroine through the medium called by
the French the *récit personnel*. This is the method favoured by Defoe
and Le Sage, but in the hands of Marivaux it gains enormously in
power since, in order to justify the subtlety of the heroine's self-
portrait and the penetrating quality of her comments on people and
life, the author takes full advantage of the assumption that her
story is told by a middle-aged and married Marianne. Richardson, who employs the letter-form, is never retrospective in this sense.
Pamela is sixteen when she relates the story of her persecutions
and not much older when she tells us of her married life. In any
case, there is no change, either in the style of her writing or in the
nature of her ideas or emotions, all of which are elementary and
crude. Of this, however, Richardson is blissfully unaware, and
throughout the novel his chief anxiety is to explain why a servant-
girl can be credibly supposed to express herself with Pamela's wisdom
and fluency. The effect of this, naturally, is to make the heroine
even more of a blue-stocking than she really is. No one, of course,
has ever pretended to find an interest in the Pamela of the second
volume, who is obviously a mouthpiece for the author's views on
questions of social morality and nothing else. Besides, these views
add nothing to our knowledge of life and very little to our knowledge of Richardson as he appears in his correspondence.

Since a parallel has been drawn between the scene of the
attempted seduction of Marianne and the behaviour of Mr. B. to
Pamela, this may well serve as a convenient excuse for comparing
the artistic methods and aims of the two novelists. To begin with,
Marianne is quite friendless and has the strongest possible motive

for not offending her benefactor, Climal. Pamela, at any moment, could have escaped to her parents. But Marianne has a weapon denied by Providence to Pamela. It is her acutely sensitive *amour-propre*, which, in the absence of love, forms an impenetrable barrier against all attempts to undermine her virtue. And from first to last this is the real obstacle she opposes to Climal's attacks. One might, indeed, say that in Marianne virtue and *amour-propre* are identical, since she never rants, like Pamela, about her 'precious jewel' or invokes the help of God to defend it. In the early stages of her duel with Climal she is prepared to take him at his face value and, even after knowing him to be a villain, still pretends to regard him as an elderly and paternal philanthropist. Climal unwittingly offends her at the first interview, during which she suffers the humiliation of hearing her unfortunate situation discussed with the religious. 'On avait épluché ma misère,' she tells us resentfully, and this rankles in her mind when she accepts Climal's first gifts. In a way, the account is squared; he owes her some compensation. Even when Climal, becoming more ardent, praises Marianne's beautiful hair, she makes no outcry, since he has not yet stepped outside his self-appointed part. What really enlightens her as to his true character is the incident in the cab, 'the burning flame' in his eyes, and a subtle change of tone as he throws off the mask. Therefore, when he tries to steal a kiss, Marianne is ready for him and, cleverly evading the embrace, apologizes for her awkwardness in knocking against him when jolted by the cab! Marianne is well aware of the valuable ally she has in Climal's own *amour-propre*, in the hypocrite's dread of any scandal that might destroy his carefully built up reputation as a pious and benevolent man. This card she plays to its full value. Her love of pretty things and—what is more remarkable—her fear of poverty never really place her in danger. So long as Climal 'behaves,' Marianne will suffer and blandly ignore his little hints and playful ways if they afford him pleasure.

But Climal persists in offending her *amour-propre*, partly by masculine clumsiness, partly by accident. With his genius for preferring the tortuous to the straight way simply because it is crooked, he pretends to Mme Dutour that the clothes he has given to Marianne were left her by the *curé's* sister, so that when the parcel is opened and the linen-draper sees from the name on the wrapper that they are new, a scene occurs. This merely precipitates a matter which has been disturbing Marianne's conscience. The blunt remarks of

Mme Dutour and of her servant Toinon fill her with mortification and wounded pride, and she breaks into an ungovernable rage. When advised by Dutour to take what she can get from the infatuated Climal, Marianne suddenly remembers vividly all the virtuous lessons she had learned from the *curé's* sister and is really shocked. Even then, her natural common sense seeks a compromise that will satisfy virtue, self-esteem, and her girlish vanity—for it *is* a pretty dress! So she resolves to wear it to church and, at the next interview with Climal, to inform him that she cannot possibly love him. And even had he been a younger man, love would have been out of the question owing to the circumstances in which they first met. But let Marianne explain: 'I had known him only on the footing of a pious man offering to take care of me out of charity; and I do not know any way of meeting people which makes one less inclined to love them with what is called love. It is no use expecting tender sentiments from a person who has made your acquaintance in that manner. The humiliation she has suffered has closed her heart to yours in that direction. That heart preserves a grudge of which it is unconscious so long as you ask from it only the sentiments which are your just due. But if you demand of it a certain tenderness, oh! that is another affair. Then its *amour - propre* recognizes you, and you are irretrievably lost. It will never forgive you.' Can any one imagine Pamela expressing sentiments like these?

The meeting with Valville reveals to Marianne what love is and, automatically, her whole attitude to Climal is changed. Hitherto she had merely despised him since, by his hypocrisy, he had given the girl a sense of moral superiority. Now, by contrast with Valville, he seems hateful; and his love, which up till then she had regarded with a certain amused tolerance, appears ugly. It is not so much that his actions are offensive, because, as Marianne wisely remarks: 'Every day, in the way of love, people are doing very delicately things that are quite coarse. The difference between the man one loves and the man one doesn't, is not that the former is free from desire; but in him, the sentiments of the heart are mingled with the senses and they fuse together. That makes a love tender and not vicious, though, indeed, capable of vice.' In other words, the true lover respects the woman's *amour - propre*, and that is not very difficult, because it is desensitized by her love for him.

After Marianne catches her first glimpse of Valville, everything fights against Climal, and in recording these moments Marivaux displays his marvellous insight into the heart of the *jeune fille*. When the fussy old surgeon is binding her sprained ankle, Marianne has all the deliciously naughty thrill of knowing that Valville can see how pretty it is, with the virtuous satisfaction of knowing also that this cannot be helped. 'J'allais en avoir le profit immodeste, en conservant tout le mérite de la modestie.' Here is a scene describing the dawn of youthful love, that might have come straight from one of the author's comedies. Marianne has never forgotten those exquisite moments. 'It was a blend of uneasiness, pleasure, and fear; of fear, yes, fear, since at this stage in her apprenticeship a girl has no idea where all this is going to lead her. She is enveloped in a haze of unknown emotions which dominate her; emotions which possess her and which she does not possess. And the novelty of this state is alarming. True, they give her pleasure; but it is a pleasure that looks like a danger. Her modesty even is terrified. Something threatens her, bewilders her, and already begins to take hold of her.'

Yet in the midst of this wonderful day-dream, Marianne's *amour-propre* is still paramount. Valville, very naturally, takes it for granted that she is a girl of family and asks her to stay to lunch. Meanwhile, he will send a lackey to reassure her 'people.' There is the rub. How can she possibly admit that she has no family, that her address is 'chez Mme Dutour, lingère'? Marianne therefore refuses, on the plea that it would be *inconvenable*, the only occasion when she adopts the prudish language of a Pamela. Valville is pressing; Marianne bursts into tears and becomes thereby all the more adorable. But she is prepared to run the risk of never seeing her lover again rather than divulge her address. With her sensitive *amour-propre*, she can imagine the change in Valville when he learns who she is. With torturing clearness she can see herself, and 'la pudeur gémissante de la figure d'aventurière que j'allais faire.' Valville is piqued by her refusal. That is bad enough; yet it is nothing to the thought of Mme Dutour's shop. Finally, in despair, she blurts out the latter's name, and a new complication arises. Valville knows the woman, for his mother is one of her customers. 'At Madame Dutour's, the linen-draper's!' he cries, 'so it is she who will let your people know where you are. But who shall I say is sending the message?' There is nothing for it then but to confess that she lives there, and at this critical instant, Climal enters—a splendid *coup de théâtre*. He is accompanied by Mme Dorsin, who quickly grasps the situation and is amused. Climal, eaten up with jealousy, is not amused; and instinctively commits the supreme folly of pretending not to know Marianne. Valville's love sharpens his wits, which are none too blunt, and he scents a mystery.

Looking back on this experience, Marianne distinguishes between the sentiments she had then and those she ought to have had. All that really terrifies her at the moment is the fear lest Valville may hear about the shop, not the more serious question of her relations with a hypocrite. Therefore she says nothing of their having already met. That is perfectly natural, for in situations of this sort our pride is always stronger than our virtue. 'Our pride and we,' says the heroine, 'form one; our virtue and our pride are two.'

The upshot of the next interview with Climal is never in doubt, so that, when he trots out his offer of the little house, the servant, and the dancing lessons, he encounters a Marianne completely armed and inwardly revolted at the sight of him. The meeting with Valville has opened her eyes, and for the first time she sees Climal as he really is: 'his age, his wrinkles, and all the ugliness of his character.' Even then, as she is not a fool, Marianne does not break out into vituperation or reproaches. Climal gradually leads up to his proposition, depicting her loneliness and dependence with consummate cruelty veiled in the language of sensibility. But at last the *gros mot* plumps out, and Marianne, although expecting something of the kind, is so stunned by the reality that she can only ejaculate: 'So no one knows you; the priest who took me to your house told me you were such a decent man.' Now that is just the inadequate sort of remark she would have made in real life. It is only later that one remembers the tragedy-queen retort. Pamela, of course, would have blasted Climal with a sermon on chastity, poverty, and a woman's honour.

Here Marivaux, the incorrigible dramatist, introduces Valville, who, after one swift look, disappears in a rage, throwing over his shoulder the enigmatic and devastating phrase: 'Voilà qui est joli!' Instantly Marianne's *amour-propre* is stung to the quick and she is on her feet like a small but enraged tigress. In her fury, she orders Climal to bring Valville back and to exonerate her in her lover's eyes. Now Climal wilts under the storm of her outraged pride and virtue; whilst in an access of passion Marianne tears off the bonnet he has given her, to the comic alarm of the hypocrite, who, on the arrival of Mme Dutour, presents the picture of a baffled ravisher, since Marianne's beautiful hair is dishevelled and her voice is raised in anger. So Climal slinks off, a rather shoddy and unsuccessful Tarquin. We shall next meet him on his deathbed, making full reparation for his sins.

To Richardson virtue is the consciousness of being good. Unlike Marianne, Pamela is not naturally virtuous. She wears her chastity as she wears her Sunday frock, in a constant flurry lest somebody should soil it. Moreover, having been well steeped in the Old Testament, she is highly sophisticated in sexual matters. Thus, when Mr. B. is in one of his 'naughty' moods, she at once remembers the case of poor Tamar, ruined by the wicked Amnon; though Pamela, in her secret heart, must regard Tamar as a bit of a fool. On the death of her mistress, Mr. B. gives her four golden guineas. 'And he took me by the hand; yes, he took my hand before them all.' Thus, at the outset, we have the tone of the whole novel. Mr. B. is the fine, rich gentleman who stoops to notice the existence of the humble servant-girl, offering to befriend her for his dear mother's sake. But Pamela's humility is a weapon of offence, a form of moral blackmail. By constantly harping on her poverty and lowly rank, she unconsciously adopts the only tactics likely to result in the subjugation of Mr. B. Whilst ever reminding him of the social gulf that divides her 'rich and great' master from the 'poor and little' Pamela, she also reminds him how easy it ought to be to seduce her. On the other hand, she is determined to barter her 'jewel' only against a wedding-ring. Therefore, by the time the exasperated and erotic Mr. B. has exhausted all other methods and discovered that he can only possess her in marriage, he is already, heaven knows, sufficiently inured to the idea of their social disparity. Besides, in abasing herself as she does several times a day, Pamela never fails to tell him how powerful and independent he is. And after marriage, this humility of Pamela's is a splendid insurance against criticism. So very modest is she about her attainments that the gentry are amazed and delighted to find that the self-styled goose is a lovely swan.

Very early in her relations with Mr. B., Pamela is warned by her dear old father, Goodman Andrews, to arm herself against the worst; for this amiable, god-fearing man had, like Richardson, the lowest possible opinion of country squires. Apparently, too, he has no great opinion of Pamela's virtue, and already looks on her as 'ruined and undone.' That is why, after 'the sad, sad scene' in the summer-house when Mr. B. kisses Pamela 'with frightful eagerness,' Goodman Andrews urges her to return to her poor but honest parents. But

Pamela, having already tasted the delicious and fearful sensation of being mauled about, prefers to stay and finish Mr. B.'s flowered waistcoat. He has called her a *slut*, a *hussy*, a *boldface*, a *sauce-box*, and lovingly she hoards up these epithets, secretly resolved, at the first opportunity, to invite another outburst. The one thing that would really torture Pamela would be Mr. B.'s indifference. If the worst came to the worst, she would rather be raped than ignored; and if Mr. B. had not obligingly overwhelmed her with attentions, it is morally certain that his most casual acts and words would have been interpreted by her romantic imagination as veiled declarations. Richardson knew the mind of the English servant-girl.

With nauseating regularity, the words *innocence*, *virtue*, *honesty* recur on the lips of this incredible little creature, only to be immediately belied by her actions. In the trivial reasons which Pamela alleges for inviting fresh trouble, she is completely dishonest; whilst the most elementary conception of virtue, in her own orthodox sense of the word, demands the immediate removal of her person from the presence of Mr. B., who, as she well knows, is an incontinent stallion of a fellow. Even the King's Regulations of the British Army, which no one has ever described as a treatise on practical virtue, enjoin that an officer should avoid the presence of a drunken private, after arrest, lest he should induce the said private to commit the more serious crime of giving him a black eye. Judged, therefore, by the best standards, Pamela, I very much fear, must be regarded as imprudent, unvirtuous, and unchristian. As for her innocence, it is enough to repeat that she has the whole of the Old Testament at her finger-tips. Richardson confuses innocence with sex-consciousness and warmly praises Pamela for making Mrs. Jervis lie with her after the 'towsing' episode in her master's chamber, although the front door of the house was still performing its normal function.

This 'towsing' is but an *apéritif*, however, to the banquet that follows. One can visualize Richardson licking his lips as he dwelt over the account of B.'s abortive attempt to rape Pamela in the presence of his housekeeper. He really enjoys writing these scenes and, having absolutely no sense of humour, contrives to invest them with a sliminess of which he and Pamela, in their self-righteousness, are blissfully unaware. To make matters worse, his strange and twisted imagination is ever coiling back on itself, harking back to these erotic moments. With great ingenuity he manages to find an excuse for retrospective and leering allusions to the *summer-house*, the *dressing-room*, the *closet*, which are usually italicized. Thus the innocent Pamela, with Mr. B. eavesdropping, prattles over her little 'bundles' to Mrs. Jervis, on the eve, we fondly hope, of her departure. 'Now I come to the present of my dear, virtuous master; hey, you know, *closet* for that, Mrs. Jervis.' And what can dear Mrs. Jervis do but laugh merrily at her 'comical girl.'

Mr. B. is quite obviously invented in order to allow Richardson to indulge his penchant for smug salaciousness. Now, Defoe and Smollett and Fielding, whilst never hesitating to call a spade a spade, never offend any but the prudish and 'nancy-minded.' Richardson, on the contrary, has a positive genius for disgusting the most tolerant; and could make the binomial theorem sound indecent. Sterne is a master of slimy innuendo, but Richardson has not the wit to rise even to innuendo. In all his sexual jokes, Mr. B. rarely exceeds the level of a nasty-minded small boy. Besides, just in case we have had time to brush our teeth, the relentless Pamela is at hand to repeat the exact words with pious spasms in a letter to Goodman Andrews. Should any one wonder why the French coined the phrase, 'le cant anglais,' let him read *Pamela* and cease to wonder.

However, we now leave the Bedfordshire house amidst a chorus of tearful and pathetic farewells from Pamela's 'fellow-servants dear,' and follow the abducted heroine to Lincolnshire. This house, which is to be the scene of her supreme trial and of the intervention of divine grace, is well described. With enjoyable romantic terror, Pamela tells us: 'About eight at night, we entered the courtyard of this handsome, large, old and lonely mansion, that looks made for solitude and mischief, as I thought, by its appearance, with all its brown, nodding horrors of lofty elms and pines about it. Here, I said to myself, I fear is to be the scene of my ruin, unless God protect me, who is all-sufficient!' The aspect of its keeper, Mrs. Jewkes, does nothing to allay her fears; for Mrs. Jewkes, in addition to her other charms, has 'a dead, spiteful, grey, goggling eye, to be sure she has.' For the first time, we encounter the Richardson of *Clarissa*.

Now Mr. B.'s conduct becomes, to say the least, peculiar. In his absence, by the way, his able understudy, Jewkes, provides the suggestive patter that Richardson has already accustomed his readers to expect. Mr. B., apparently in order to torture himself and to play with Pamela before pouncing, suggests by letter that she should marry his curate Williams, who is given the run of the closed garden. She enlists the aid of Williams, and he tries to interest the rector and the local gentry in her case; but they cautiously withdraw. All that the wretched curate gets out of the business is a ducking in a horsepond from B.'s thugs. To cap his woes, he is jailed for a fictitious debt, his own salary, for which he was simple enough to ask no receipt. Pamela contemplates suicide, but not with any fervour, and compromises by throwing her cloak and hat into the horsepond to give the naughty Jewkes a good fright.

Tarquin himself arrives, in a towering rage that Pamela should dare to consent to marry Williams; though she had, in fact, no such intention. Samuel now girds up his dressing-gown for the grand scene, *un viol dans les formes*, at dead of night, in the old deserted house with Mrs. Jewkes listening to Pamela 'running on' about her past history, and wishing the whole business were over so that she can get to sleep. But the naughty B. is inside the fortress, snoring in a chair in her very closet, disguised as Nan, the drunken cook. 'Like a clap of thunder' the victim hears the fateful words: 'Now, Pamela, is the dreadful time of reckoning come that I have threatened.' But divine grace, in the form of a swoon and cold, dewy sweat, mercifully comes to Pamela's aid. As Mr. B. once petulantly remarked: 'She has a lucky knack of falling into fits when she pleases.' Lucky, lucky Pamela; for this is the end of her martyrdom and the beginning of her apotheosis. True, Mr. B. had thought of another device, a bogus marriage, but having meanwhile read Pamela's letters, he is quite converted. Anyhow, as he remarks incidentally with delicious *naïveté*: 'I remembered how much I had exclaimed against and censured an action of this kind attributed to one of the first men of the law . . . my foolish pride was a little piqued with this because I loved to be, if I went out of the way, my own original as I call it.'

Up to then Pamela had done a tolerable amount of praying and kneeling, but now her heart overflows with pious gratitude to God and Mr. B. She is now continually at his feet, kissing his dear hand and lifting up her eyes at his nobility and generosity. But she will not consent to his offer to have her parents in the same house. This is not inordinate, but her reasons for refusing are distinctly unusual. 'They could not perhaps serve God so well if they lived with you; for, so constantly seeing the hand that blesses them, they might, as must be my care to avoid, be tempted to look no further in their gratitude than to the dear dispenser of such innumerable benefits. 'Excellent creature!' exclaims Mr. B., accepting this as his simple due. All the same, Pamela is going to have no nonsense about the wedding, and with pretty obstinacy holds out for a proper ceremony in the chapel. 'It is a *holy* rite, sir,' said I, 'and would be better, methinks, in a *holy place.*' Methinks, too, after studying B.'s *dossier* that it had better be in the church, with a large cloud of terrestrial witnesses. Reluctantly, we must part for a moment with this fair flower of English maidenhood, after just one farewell peep into the nuptial chamber where, half an hour before the arrival of her dear lord, we discover Pamela industriously scribbling, scribbling, scribbling.

The English and, since Zola, the French public has been gradually accustomed to apply the adjective *realistic* only to what is unconventional or perhaps scabrous in literature. Certain critics, too, terrified lest they should seem to judge of art by moral rather than by aesthetic criteria, have been scared into an extremist attitude. Thus in the opinion of some, the only novelists who deserve to be called realistic are those who offer detailed descriptions of scenes which in real life are, as a rule, enacted in the greatest privacy, and who introduce into their narrative words and expressions not commonly heard in society of any kind. From such a point of view, Richardson would be held to be a greater realist than Marivaux. Actually, apart altogether from moral considerations, such is not the case, at least, in *Pamela*. That is evident when we compare the impressions left on our minds by the two episodes just described —the seduction scenes.

The final picture that emerges from Richardson's account, which is immensely longer than Marivaux's, is an extremely simple one with a very limited repercussion. The images aroused by it are purely physical and, as their sole appeal is to the senses, they do not hold the interest. Now Marivaux is, in the best meaning of the term, dramatic; Richardson is only melodramatic. The thrill we procure from Pamela's eleventh-hour escape is as brief as that excited by an averted street-accident, simply because it has nothing whatever to do with the heroine's personality. Marianne, on the other hand, eludes the designs of Climal because she is Marianne and no one else; because, in resisting his efforts at seduction, she displays all the resources latent in a remarkable intelligence and in a sensitive soul. Now Pamela has very little intelligence, and what she calls her soul is a very second-rate affair, composed largely of maxims borrowed from the Bible and other good books. She has, in fact, the soul of a canting pedant, the soul of the author at this stage in his career. The first psychological blunder committed by Richardson was in emphasizing the wholly physical nature of Mr. B.'s crude and amateurish Don Juanism. When in real life a man steps out of the way of a charging rhinoceros we do not feel disposed to regard him as a hero, since he is merely doing the instinctive and usual thing. Had he charged the rhinoceros he might begin to be heroic and dramatic. Similarly, had Pamela deliberately set out to seduce Mr. B., one might begin to look upon her as a promising and interesting study. As it is, she is simply a fool, because she has not the elementary common sense to leave the Bedfordshire house and return to her parents. In effect, all she does is to remain passive, and when, by good luck, her loutish lover bungles his plans Pamela merely wails that he is immoral and that God will punish him. What, then, creates the feeling of suspense in the spectator's mind? It is a sensational curiosity as to the probable nature of the next move, and that, we know, will throw no further light either on the character of Mr. B. or of Pamela. But the affair between Climal and Marianne is a duel of wits, in which every thrust and parry draws attention to some hitherto unobserved trait in the characters of the protagonists and, at the same time, reminds us that life is an active and complex affair. These are real people involved in a real emotional crisis. Their actions and emotions have a meaning that is more than local or ephemeral; they project shadows because their experience might easily be ours. That of Pamela, on the contrary, stirs up but a brief excitement which evaporates when we close the book and whistle to our dog.

Admirers of Richardson are apt to wonder how this squabby little recluse acquired his amazing knowledge of the feminine soul. The fact is, however, that his knowledge of the feminine soul is extremely limited, as will be quite evident to those who read him alongside Marivaux. In the case of *Pamela*, it might be urged in Richardson's defence that he is dealing only with the minds of a servant-girl and of a country squire. But it is quite obvious that our author views himself as a connoisseur in the matter of women and of love. 'Is it not strange,' says Pamela profoundly, 'that love borders so much on hate?' No doubt, yet it needs a really great observer of the feminine heart to demonstrate this truth; and Richardson, who has none of Marivaux's craft in affairs like these, never ventures into by-paths but sticks to the plain, open road. In default of personal experience, he takes as his model the brutal episode of Tamar and Amnon, which he modifies to fit his moral

o

thesis. In consequence, the picture unfolded by him is not one of love but of baffled lust. Mr. B. is not in love with Pamela but in rut for her. In all his conduct, prior to the impossible change of heart, this erotic bumpkin resembles nothing so much as one of the greater primates. There is nothing 'stark' or 'Russian' about his amorous advances and petulant outbursts of rage. Much the same behaviour may be witnessed any morning at the Zoo.

Few novelists have yarned more bowelfully over the purity and sanctity of woman than Samuel Richardson in *Pamela*; yet his conception of her place in the social scheme is, here at least, disgracefully low. Be it said, however, to his credit that he made amends in *Clarissa*. But in his first novel, the author can never see past the sex of his heroine, whom he never really regards as an individual. She is the destined instrument of Mr. B.'s pleasure, and, as that gentleman continually reminds us in his leering fashion, the potential mother of future little B.'s. Richardson's object, no doubt, was to mount Pamela on a pedestal as an exemplar to her sex, and he attributes to her all the virtues. But the price of this glory is an outrageous one because, in order to retain her lord's kindness, she is obliged to prostrate herself before him for twenty-four hours in the day. In other words, she must always remain a fawning sycophant, eternally doomed to sound the trumpet of Mr. B.'s excellence and generosity under pain of his displeasure. Richardson's idea of the perfect household makes the traditional picture of the mid-Victorian home seem like a feminine paradise, and we know from his biography that, in his quiet way, this fat little sultan of North End was a tyrant of the worst description. His heroine is brutalized and bullied before marriage and, as Mrs. B., is subjected to the most revolting form of moral blackmail—that of gratitude. With the utmost blandness, the author assumes that she enjoys being dominated, the inference being that all women ought to behave and feel like Pamela. In his perverted manner, Richardson almost persuades us that Mr. B. is a fine fellow, whose gross excesses, which should have procured him transportation for life, are but the excusable pranks of a mettlesome young man. Like the old lady who used to run from priest to priest confessing a youthful 'slip' because 'she loved to talk about it,' Pamela's husband is eager at any moment to regale the local gentry with the tale of his infamies, whilst little wifie sits meekly by ready to jog his memory. The effect of Richardson's garrulity is peculiar. By constant repetition he bemuses the reader into accepting black as white. Thus, for example, Mr. B., after each of his thwarted attempts on Pamela, never fails to insist that she should beg his 'forgiveness,' with the, odd result that eventually one is left with the uneasy impression that she really ought to, since, in some queer way, it is Pamela who is guilty.

With his genius for playing upon the baser emotions, Richardson drew floods of tears from his feminine public by a facile and maudlin pathos. Pamela has three stereotyped attitudes: she is to be discovered either kneeling in prayer for the wickedness of Mr. B., or struggling to free herself from his lustful embraces, or, with apron over her eyes, weeping at his cruelty. In the early scenes she has an admiring chorus of 'fellow-servants dear'; the good Mrs. Jervis, the wise and faithful Longman, and the venerable butler, Jonathan, all of whom wag their heads in solemn sympathy and utter the appropriate, sentimental platitudes. To reinforce the pathos, Goodman Andrews contributes an occasional letter and, at the right moment, puts in a personal appearance as the white-haired old father crying: 'Give me back my child!' Usually, however, all the limelight is focused on Pamela herself, crushed, humbled, tearful, preaching, beseeching, until the sound of her whining voice drives one to distraction. The really joyful moments in the book are when Mrs. Jewkes gives her a sound box on the ear for calling her a Jezebel, and when the exasperated Lady Davers, 'that rageful woman,' slaps her for impudence. How admirable the novel would have been if Richardson had taken his tone from these two episodes! As it is, such characters, like all the minor ones, are introduced merely to display the Christian meekness and nobility of the central figure. And in all this mawkishness, which imbrues the whole novel, there is no variety, for the excellent reason that Richardson, though he can talk till Doomsday about the beauties of sensibility, is quite incapable of telling us what it is. Marivaux, in a hundred little touches, portrays and analyses the sensibility of Marianne, of Mme de Miran, and of Mme Dorsin who are all *sensibles*, though in different ways. Sometimes his women cry, but they never snivel; and when Marianne deliberately sets out, like Pamela, to win the sympathy of her audience it is with dignity and restraint. Read, for example, her admirable appeal to the *conseil de famille*, which does not contain one forced note. Sensibility, common sense, and *amour-propre* are blended with exquisite tact. *La Vie de Marianne* is perfumed with sentiment: *Pamela* smells of rank pathos.

The characteristic differences already noted in English and

French drama are reflected in these two novels, and if, owing to the nature of Richardson's theme, there is much less local colour in *Pamela* than in the works of Smollett or Fielding, his stage is, nevertheless, more crowded than that of Marivaux, who, in the traditional French manner, likes to give his people ample room in which to develop their personality. Yet in this respect *La Vie de Marianne* marks an important advance owing to the introduction of characters such as Mme Dutour, the servant Toinon, and the Parisian 'cabby,' who is responsible for one of the most alert and amusing episodes of the book. For the first time, a French novelist presents the people in a realistic and understanding way; and in contrasting the blunt tactlessness of a Mme Dutour with the sensitiveness of his heroine, Marivaux created several pages that have never been excelled. Here is a picture of Marianne in the Dutour household:

'The word *charity* was not much to my taste: it was a little too crude for an *amour-propre* so sensitive as mine. But Mme Dutour knew no better; her expressions, like her mind, took their colour from her lack of malice and finesse. However, I made a wry face but said nothing since my only witness was the grave Mademoiselle Toinon, who was much more likely to envy me the clothes I was given than to think me humiliated by accepting them. "Oh, as for that, Mademoiselle Marianne," said she, a little jealously, "you must have been born with a silver spoon in your mouth." "On the contrary," I retorted, "I was born very unfortunate, for there is no question but that I ought to be better than I am." "By the way," she went on, "is it true that you 've got no father or mother and that you are nobody's child? That's funny." "Quite," I said, a little piqued; "it is very amusing, and if I were you I 'd congratulate me." "Hold your tongue, you idiot," said Mme Dutour to her, seeing that I was annoyed. "She is quite right to make a fool of you. Thank God for preserving your own parents! Who ever said to anybody that they were foundlings? I 'd just as lief be told I was a bastard."'

Marivaux has humour and wit, and though never so exuberant as Fielding, he is closer to the author of *Tom Jones* than to any other English novelist of the eighteenth century. Certainly, however, he is poles apart from Richardson, who herds his people into two categories, saints and sinners, and has, moreover, none of Marivaux's warm tolerance and sympathy. In consequence, his picture of contemporary society is unilluminating, whereas Marivaux, employing a very few characters, achieves an illusion of movement, variety, and truth. With the exception of Lady Davers, though she, too, succumbs to the heroine's meekness, none of Pamela's entourage can be said to possess an individuality. Mrs. Jewkes is melodramatized out of all credibility; whilst the servants, Mrs. Jervis, Jonathan, and Longman with his 'Adsbobbers!' and 'Adsheart-likins!' are all too sentimental to be real. Perhaps, however, we should except Polly, the 'bad' girl who was nearly seduced by B.'s nephew, Jackey, and if she is more credible than the others it is, I fear, only because she is naughty—a sad reflection on human nature. The truth of the matter is that Richardson's turgid morality and his fly-blown pathos obscure his vision of life. He is much more interested in situation than in character, so that his people, whilst indulging in endless conversations, do not develop. Now Marivaux, whose people talk a great deal less, say and do things that really matter. A great deal of our information comes, no doubt, from Marianne, but these indirect, psychological portraits are always reinforced by the revelations made by the other characters themselves in dialogue and action. There is a give and take in *La Vie de Marianne* which is absent from *Pamela*, where, inevitably, every remark made by a minor character is designed solely to emphasize the heroine's perfections. No one in real life would be permitted to dominate her fellow-beings as Pamela does, and, in a work of art, there can only be one reason for thus focusing all the interest on one person. In the case of Pamela it is not justified by results, since the heroine's psychology is not a complex one. Therefore it bores the reader, who does not really care very much what happens to her. But we make fresh discoveries about Marianne at every page. As she truthfully says, when the fickle Valville deserted her for the intriguing Varthon: 'Je savais être plusieurs femmes en une.'

Marivaux realized something that quite escaped the obtuse Richardson: in order to lay bare the character of a woman in love one must provide her with a rival. That is elementary. When Mlle Varthon appears on the scene, Marianne positively flowers; and a hundred subtle unsuspected traits are suddenly revealed. To understand what is meant by exploiting a situation, one must read the account of her conversation with her rival in the convent bedroom. The contrast between Mlle Varthon, blooming and triumphant from her stolen interview with Valville, and the con-valescent Marianne, languid but jealously alert, is a fine example of novel-craft. The whole episode is brilliantly prepared and wonderfully accented, evolving in an atmosphere charged with suppressed emotions, vibrant with cruelty, jealousy, hatred, and *amour-propre*. Yet to any one casually entering that room, nothing of all this would be obvious in the tone or expression of either girl. By comparison, Richardson's belated effort to show us a jealous Mrs. B., in the masquerade scene, is grotesquely inept. All that Pamela can do is to enact the hoary melodrama of the forgiving but wronged wife who will disappear from her husband's life, clutching the tiny fingers of her innocent child. Here one may fitly borrow the remark made by Lady Davers on a similar occasion: 'I hope I may not be quite sick.' The only bright moment in this long drawn out and imbecile episode is an observation of Mr. B.'s, and that, I need not say, is meant to be serious. 'I am resolved,' says Pamela, 'to do my duty, sir, if possible. But, indeed, I cannot bear the cruel suspense! Let me know what is to become of me. Let me know what is designed for me, and you shall be sure of all the acquiescence that my duty and conscience can give to your pleasure.' 'What *means* the dear creature? What *means my* Pamela? Surely your head, child, is a little affected.'

Two eminent critics, both equally at home in French and English literature, have written of *Pamela* in terms of the highest admiration. The late Dr. Saintsbury looked on this novel as 'a remarkable analysis and exposition of motive and feeling,' [1] whilst M. Cazamian says of the heroine: 'The growth of her affection for her master and persecutor, the subtle traits which reveal it to us, and the fine gradation of her expression of it to herself, belong to an order of artistic achievement and psychological truth to which English literature had hardly risen since the decay of Elizabethan drama.' [2] With much deference, I submit that, on the contrary, *Pamela* is completely lacking in subtlety or in psychological truth. How, for example, does the heroine depict the change in her feelings towards Mr. B.? Where is the 'fine gradation' of events, sentiments, or emotions that ushers the *peripeteia* of this Drury Lane melodrama? Surely, if anywhere, it is here that Richardson betrays his impotence in the domain of psychological analysis. After the final and frustrated attempt to overcome Pamela's resistance by physical means, Mr. B. has recourse to blandishment. But a gipsy woman has handed Pamela an anonymous note warning her of a

[1] Introduction to the Everyman edition of *Pamela*.
[2] *Cambridge History of English Literature*, x. 5.

projected bogus marriage. Meanwhile, however, Mr. B. has read her journal. Smitten with remorse, he allows Pamela to go, and in a letter which she reads *en route*, informs her that he has sent her away to escape the temptation of paying her 'an honourable address.' As he puts it: 'I was just upon resolving to defy all the censures of the world and to make you my wife.' Now we come to the 'subtle traits.' But Pamela must be allowed to speak for herself. 'This letter, when I expected some new plot, has affected me more than anything of *that* sort could have done. His great value for me is here confessed, and his rigorous behaviour accounted for in such a manner, as tortures me much. The wicked gipsy story is a forgery on us both and has quite ruined me. My dear parents, forgive me! But I found before to my grief that my heart was too partial in his favour; but *now*, with so much openness, affection, and *honour*, too (which was all I had doubted), I am quite overcome. This was a happiness, however, I had no reason to expect. But I must own to you, that I shall never be able to think of anybody in the world but him. "Presumption," you will say; and so it is, but love is not a voluntary thing—*Love* did I say— But come, it is not, I hope, gone so far as to make me very uneasy; for I know not *how* it came, nor *how* it began; but it has crept, like a thief, upon me, before I knew what was the matter.' To put it bluntly, Pamela is mentally kicking herself for having carried prudence and suspicion too far; and if she only now discovers why she submitted for so long to Mr. B.'s brutalities, it is because she is singularly obtuse. What is really interesting in this passage is the further light it throws on the almost sadistic conduct of Mr. B., who for once devises a mode of torture which is not purely physical. In effect, he says, holding up a vanishing wedding ring: 'See what you might have got if you hadn't been so confoundedly suspicious.' And Pamela, who has not a halfpennyworth of Marianne's pride, practically says: 'What a blessed little idiot I was!' To characterize these primitive reflections as profound psychological truths is to lose all sense of proportion. In literature and in life, there are certain characters, usually charwomen and domestic servants, who prattle on with such gusto about their doings and feelings that the listener, out of sheer self-respect, is compelled to discover some rational explanation for his own indulgence in having listened to them so long. So, instead of admitting to himself that he was overwhelmed and bemused by a torrent of verbiage, and feeling vaguely that no one could possibly have so much to say about nothing, he envisages his persecutors as 'interesting types,' talkative, of course, like all women of the people, but endowed with shrewd common sense and, maybe, wit. That is how Richardson regards his Pamela, and that, I fear, explains the praises showered upon her by so many critics, who must also, therefore, be added to Pamela's collection of scalps. Personally, at the risk of incurring the horrid reproach of insensibility, I transfer my homage to Marianne. She may be a little monkey but, at least, her head is not affected by her experiences.

It is delightful to escape from *Pamela* with its odour of unaired closets and incipient masochism into the clean, virile atmosphere of Fielding's *Joseph Andrews*. This is a story with a tonic, open-air quality which pleasantly reminds one of Le Sage, since most of its scenes have as a background the countryside. From time to time, however, we are whisked from the high road into Lady Booby's boudoir, and in these priceless moments, Fielding allows us to contemplate the havoc wrought in the heart of a lady of fashion by the fatal charms of a rustic but chaste Adonis. On the strength of such episodes, no doubt, and of two innocent references to Marivaux in the first chapter of the third book, some of Fielding's English critics have invented the legend that much of *Joseph Andrews* is imitated from *Le Paysan parvenu*. As we shall see, there is no warrant for this assumption nor for Saintsbury's statement that in his second novel, Marivaux was 'playing Fielding to his own Richardson.'

The initial theme of *Joseph Andrews*, a theme which was practically abandoned half-way through the book and resumed towards the end, bears only a spurious resemblance to the subject of *Le Paysan parvenu*. In every respect, Joseph, that sheer figure of fun, differs absolutely from Marivaux's Jacob, who is a most credible and a carefully-drawn character. Joseph is the incarnation of chastity, and because he is a man, his virtue is much more incongruous and even more ridiculous than the clamant, strouting virginity of his sister Pamela. Now Jacob is, on the contrary, a shrewd and in-continent fellow, only too anxious to barter his 'jewel' for a soft and well-paid sinecure. Joseph is absurd: Jacob, whilst amusing, is often repellent. He embodies the huge vanity of the robust, handsome male, the *bel homme* from a village in Champagne who has the cunning to divine and to exploit the effects of his devastating virility. But Marivaux's satire is not wholly directed at Jacob. He is also amused by the women who fall a prey to the charms of this well-built peasant and, from Geneviève the chambermaid to

Madame de Vambures the *grande dame*, are all eager to improve Jacob's material situation. Here, indeed, is an apparent link with *Joseph Andrews*; yet the resemblance is more fancied than real. Marivaux is far too subtle to have inspired Fielding when the latter was depicting the attempted seduction of Joseph by the urgent Slipslop and the somewhat more complex Lady Booby. In pursuing his original idea, which was to present an inverted and comic picture of Pamela, the English novelist was led quite logically to transform Mr. B. into a Lady Booby just as he had changed Pamela into Joseph. The rest follows as a matter of course. In Lady Booby's behaviour we have a humorous parody of the conduct of Mr. B., which consists in a series of passionate advances and withdrawals, accompanied by swift outbursts of baffled rage and by petulant imprecations when pride of rank gets the better of carnal desire. Happily, or as some may think, unhappily, Fielding stops short of rape; though Joseph has at least one very narrow escape from the 'violent amorous hands' of Madam Slipslop, whose passion, as she complains, has been 'resulted and treated with ironing.'

In foolery of this sort Fielding cannot be excelled even by Smollett; but there is nothing remotely like it in Marivaux. In that memorable interview where Joseph upholds the finest traditions of the Andrews family against the shameless attacks of his high-born mistress, there is nothing in the hero's language or conduct to suggest the manner of the Paysan parvenu. 'Madam,' says Joseph, 'that boy is the brother of Pamela, and would be ashamed that the chastity of his family which is preserved in her should be stained by him. If there are such men as your ladyship mentions, I am sorry for it, and I wish they had an opportunity of reading over those letters which my father hath sent me of my sister Pamela's; nor do I doubt but such an example would amend them.' How very different, how very un-English, alas! is the behaviour of Jacob in the presence of that amorous but cautious *dévote*, Mme de Ferval. Hark to the rascal himself: '"Not so loud," said she, pointing to the antechamber, 'my maid is perhaps in there. Ah! my dear boy, what have you just told me? So you are in love with me." "Alas!" I replied, "unworthy though I am, yes." "All right," she said, with a little sigh. "But you're very young, and I, on the other hand, am afraid to trust myself with you. Come closer," she added, "so that we can talk better." I am forgetting to tell you that during this conversation, she had resumed the posture in which I first discovered her; still minus that slipper and still with her legs

*o

slightly revealed, now more, now less, according to her attitudes on the sofa. The glances I cast in that direction did not escape her. "What a tasty little foot you 've got, madame," I said, moving my chair closer; for I was gradually slipping into a more familiar tone. "Never mind my foot," said she, and put on her slipper again. "We must talk about what you have just told me. Let 's see what can be done about this love of yours." "Does it by any unlucky chance happen to offend you?" I said to her. "Oh, no, La Vallée, it doesn't offend me," she replied, "On the contrary, I am touched by it. You have pleased me only too well. You are as lovely as Cupid himself.'''

This conversation, as editors say, 'must now cease.' But it is to be feared that neither in this instance nor in his dealings with another lady, Mme Fécour of the 'furieuse gorge,' can anything be noted which redounds to the credit of Jacob's morals. Considering, also, that these 'goings-on' occur within a few hours of his marriage with the prudish and plump Mlle Habert, they offer a sorry contrast to the acts and sentiments of Joseph Andrews. Would it not, indeed, be doing a grave disservice to English letters to suggest that our Fielding could possibly have gone to such an impure source for his inspiration when he erected that monument to the chastity and virtue of the English common man which is enshrined in the work known as *The Adventures of Joseph Andrews*?

The function of all great comic writers is to exercise a steadying influence upon the spirit of their age; Marivaux, like Fielding, reminded his contemporaries of the dangers that may arise from an excessive and exclusive cult of the reason or the senses or the emotions. In the province of comedy each is an undisputed master. Yet only in the most general sense can it be said that Marivaux's idea of the comic resembles Fielding's. In the latter's well-known invocation to Genius, he has outlined his comic purpose in words which apply with equal truth to Marivaux: 'Remove that mist which dims the intellects of mortals, and causes them to adore men for their art, or to detest them for their cunning in deceiving others, when they are, in reality, the objects only of ridicule for deceiving themselves. Strip off the thin disguise of wisdom from self-conceit, of plenty from avarice, and of glory from ambition.' But although Marivaux and Fielding display the same humanity and good-humoured tolerance in their attitudes to folly and vice, as comic artists they work on different planes. Fielding is direct and picturesque, choosing, as a rule, fools and rascals of the cruder sort for the purpose of his ridicule. Marivaux, however, even in his most frivolous moments, never forgets that comedy, to be really effective, must subserve the more serious business of psychological analysis. Fielding has a weakness for burlesque or humorous caricature, and it is much in evidence in *Joseph Andrews*. For that reason it is rather futile to compare this novel with *Le Paysan parvenu*, the comic temper of which is so different and so much more equable. In *Joseph Andrews* the comic effects are achieved by the method of contrasting extremes. The absurd sentimentality of Joseph and Fanny is set off by the coarse earthiness of Mrs. Tow-wouse, Madam Slipslop, and Lady Booby, none of whom would have appealed to Marivaux's subtler taste. Fielding, too, for that matter, was well aware that this vein of humour can be very quickly exhausted, and besides, he was urgently impelled to deepen and to enlarge the tone of his satire because of his anger at certain social abuses. He therefore created Parson Adams, whose amiable though laughable simplicity makes an excellent foil to the cringing rascality of lawyer Scout, the brutal avarice of Pounce, the hoggish materialism of Parson Trulliber, the sombre imbecility of the squire and his cur-like satellites, and lastly, to the transcendental asininity of Joseph Andrews himself.

In the *Paysan parvenu* there are no extreme types of this sort. On the other hand, we do not derive from it that sense of amplitude which distinguishes the Fielding panorama of life, and though, no doubt, in his second novel Marivaux has greatly enlarged his cadre, his picture of manners remains relatively meagre. Nor does he possess Fielding's remarkable gift for endowing a novel with variety, colour, and excitement. Yet it is the Frenchman who has, to a superlative degree, that quality which Fielding called 'invention,' and which he described very finely as a 'quick and sagacious penetration into the true essence of all the objects of our contemplation.' Contrast, for instance, Marivaux's superb account of the Habert household with Fielding's picture of the Western home. The latter never plumbs the 'moral density' of his characters, to use one of Flaubert's expressions. Sophia is a charming and natural creature; but she is as open as a book. Western is equally simple, though, in his irascible, profane, 'huntin' and shootin'' way, he is highly entertaining. Honour, too, is amusing but shallow, and Mrs. Western, once we know about her Hanoverian penchant for diplomacy, tends to become mechanical.

Marivaux, with fewer characters, understands the art of grading and grouping them with a view to general effect. Once he has finished with the Habert sisters and their cook, Catherine, we know exactly what is meant by a *ménage dévot*. He invests every trifle with significance. The elder Mlle Habert's half-bottle of Burgundy is more eloquent than pages of Fieldingesque description. Thus, too, when the younger Habert arrives with Jacob in tow, the argument about what she shall have for lunch betrays the whole tenor of the household. Marivaux is really dramatic, in a sense unknown to Fielding. Consider that apparently inoffensive phrase uttered by the *directeur de conscience* when he learns—unparalleled fact!— that Jacob has been engaged without consulting him: 'Vous avez été bien vite.' Dropping one by one into the silence of a room charged with suppressed emotions, the words shatter the habits of twenty years, and irrevocably change the destinies of all who are there assembled. Fielding aimed at broader effects, and his sense of the comic, though spacious, is not profound enough to embrace characters like the elder Habert, the *directeur*, or even Jacob himself. It is true that he is tolerant of Tom Jones to the point of condoning that gentleman's dubious relations with Lady Bellaston, and even applauds his cleverness in extricating himself from her clutches by a proposal of marriage. Whether he would have shared Marivaux's appreciation of Jacob's exploits is more than doubtful. Fielding, I imagine, would have seen nothing comic in the picture of Jacob's married life. Marivaux handles this with an exquisite sense of comedy, though it is difficult for the modern English reader to ignore the underlying pathos of Mme La Vallée's anxious and desperate love for her young and too attractive husband. Yet this is the very element from which Marivaux, cleverly eschewing pathos, extracts a dozen intensely comic situations. In this he is abetted by the garrulous landlady, Mme d'Alain, the supreme type of born *gaffeuse*, a wholly priceless creation. Add to the group at the supper-table the sly, insensible, and calculating daughter, Agathe, and you have all the ingredients for a banquet of mirth. Mme d'Alain rattles along in her tactless way and fatally, at every other word, drops a heavy allusion to the elderliness of Mme La Vallée. She, poor creature, sits with compressed lips, bridling or casting languishing glances at Jacob who, with a complacent smirk, is greedily collecting the sidelong looks shot at him by the demure, mischievous little monkey, Agathe, whilst Jacob's wife, by her repeated peeps at her watch and strenuous yawns, tries desperately to suggest that bedtime is now long overdue. Take again, that superb vision of Jacob, the gentleman of leisure, inordinately proud of his dressing-gown and his new suit with its red silk lining, seated alone in his room and trying hard to imagine what a gentleman does in his leisure. 'About three in the afternoon the bells rang for vespers, and my wife went to church, whilst I read some serious book or other which I could not very well understand and which I picked up only to imitate the appearance of a gentleman at home.'

All this, as readers of *Tom Jones* and of *Joseph Andrews* will at once realize, is very different from the humour of Fielding, who is vastly comic, too, but in another and less subtle way. 'The knowledge of upper life,' he tells us, 'though very necessary for preventing mistakes, is no very great resource to a writer whose province is comedy or that kind of novel which, like this I am writing, is of the comic class.' With such a statement Marivaux would not agree; and in both his novels the *vis comica* is unaffected by questions of class. Fielding, on the contrary, is comic only when he operates on types drawn from the lower and middling ranks. Give him a Tow-wouse, a Slipslop, or a Partridge and he is inimitable: there is no limit to the variety, the gusto, and the spontaneity of his humour. Fielding aims at and secures broad and massive comic effects. To outline one of his situations or to describe one of his humorous characters will convey very little, since his laughter can very rarely be traced to a particular incident or phrase. Fielding's humour distils gradually from a profusion of tiny elements which, like the esters and ethyls of a noble wine, mysteriously combine to emit a fragrant and arresting bouquet. To select but one instance, consider the episode of Tom Jones, the lieutenant, and the Upton landlady, not to speak of the silent and ghostly 'first husband,' whose alleged *obiter dicta* play no small part in this little comedy. One cannot point to any one outstanding *mot pour rire*—though the reference to the spilling of Christian blood 'in a civil way' is a gem— yet the ultimate and cumulative impression is joyous and unique. In Fielding's novels there is a foison of scenes like these and a swarm of characters all equally alive and comic. They are, however, to be viewed in the mass as Fielding, with his keen sense of the picturesque, has presented them. Isolated from their natural *milieu*, they would seem, as individuals, rather shallow and a little incredible, like the 'humorists' who crowd our eighteenth-century stage. Depicted, however, by Fielding, in their natural habitat, which is the English countryside, all these people are wonderfully real. Western reeks of tobacco, stables, and port; and his full-mouthed oaths clang in your ears long after he has stepped into the garden to bawl for Sophia. The Gargantuan appetite and easy morality of Jones pleasantly offset his almost unbelievable generosity and obtuseness; for Blifil, I fear, is too unctuous and hypocritical to take in any one but the guileless Allworthy. Molly Seagrim and her family are just what they would be; they sound and smell like eighteenth-century English villagers. English they all are, the waiting-women, the ensigns, the innkeepers, their maids and ostlers—and they could be mistaken for nothing else. The traits which Fielding has seized and immortalized are national traits. His people are comic or detestable, virtuous or vicious, brutal or sentimental in a way that is utterly and completely English. It would only be partly true to say that Marivaux's characters are exclusively French, because Marivaux still had one foot in the seventeenth century. Although he did so much to develop the modern novel of French manners, the human qualities, which he has noted and has most heavily underlined, are still more universal than local. On the surface they are French and belong to his own time; yet, by delving into their hearts, he discovered things that are fundamental and therefore common to all mankind. Fielding sometimes, but rarely, achieves this. When he does, it is because for a moment he has left the company of his imaginary people. It is, in fact, when he is no longer Fielding the novelist but Fielding the urbane, sagacious man of the world who talks to us, in the prefaces, with pregnant sense and wit about men and books and art.

CHAPTER XV

THREE SEDUCERS

THE French and English seldom fail to attribute to each other all the doubtful honours of priority in any literary innovation which appears to involve a departure from conventional standards of morality. Was it in deference to this old family custom that Joseph Texte hastened to greet our Samuel Richardson as the founder of the 'seduction novel'? In any case, it was he who first gave currency to the now popular view that Rousseau's *La Nouvelle Héloïse* and Laclos's *Les Liaisons dangereuses* had their fount in Richardson's *Clarissa*. With Laclos, Texte is not concerned, his main thesis being that Rousseau drew his inspiration from Richardson, and thus served as a channel through which the English genius flowed into French literature, inundating and refreshing the parched territories of French fiction. *La Nouvelle Héloïse*, according to this critic, is a mere adaptation of *Clarissa*, though, as he handsomely allows, Jean-Jacques has a lyrical quality for which he is beholden to no one save himself.

Few will quarrel with Texte's statement that Rousseau adopted the letter form in his novel because of the success achieved by *Clarissa*. However, it is interesting to note that Montesquieu not only used this technical artifice in his famous *Lettres persanes*, that is several years before Richardson, but also was well aware of its possibilities when he wrote: 'Besides, novels of this sort are usually successful because each character gives his own account of his actual situation; this makes the reader feel the passions more than any narrative could.' As is, however, well known, the imaginative element in the *Lettres persanes*, the novel proper so to say, is subordinated to the author's major purpose, which was social criticism. The glory, therefore, of having produced the first readable epistolary novel belongs to Richardson.[1]

By a system of 'parallels' Texte tries to convince us that each of Rousseau's characters has its prototype in *Clarissa*. Thus Julie

[1] See my 'Montesquieu the Novelist and some Imitations of the *Lettres persanes*,' *Mod. Lang. Rev.*, January 1925.

resembles Richardson's heroine; Claire, her friend, is like Miss Howe. The baron d'Étange, Julie's father, has his counterpart in Harlowe senior. Lord Édouard Bomston, Texte finds, has an 'opposite number' in Colonel Morden; whilst Wolmar, the husband of Julie, is said, with some reserves, to be the French version of Lovelace. It is almost sufficient to enumerate these so-called parallels in order to reveal how unfounded they are. Julie is seduced by, or rather seduces Saint-Preux; Clarissa, on the other hand, is violated; and the whole point of Richardson's novel is that her virtue cannot be overcome. Besides, as will become clear, the two girls are widely different in other respects. As for Miss Howe, she is no doubt, like Claire, a vivacious girl; yet these two also exhibit distinctive traits which cannot be compared. Claire, for example, abets Saint-Preux's love affair with Julie and later falls in love with him herself. That alone separates her from Miss Howe, who detests Lovelace. The baron d'Étange is an irascible nobleman who strongly objects to Saint-Preux simply because he is a *roturier*. Again, Morden and Bomston have little in common except that they are both gentlemen in the eighteenth-century sense of the word; both have had mistresses. Bomston is Saint-Preux's closest friend and mentor. Morden, however, loathes Lovelace and finally kills him in a duel. Wolmar, the atheist and *philosophe*, who marries Julie, has absolutely no resemblance to Lovelace. It would be difficult to discover a greater contrast. Lovelace is a romantic; Wolmar is the complete rationalist of the period. He was possibly suggested by Saint-Lambert, but he might have been modelled upon D'Holbach or, indeed, on any member of the philosophic sect once frequented by the author of *La Nouvelle Héloïse*.

Judged, therefore, even by Texte's comparative method, which is mechanical and valueless, the two novels seem to have little in common. To the more general assertion that Richardson, as the creator of the bourgeois novel, provided Rousseau with an idea for a middle-class setting, there is but one retort: Richardson was not the creator of the bourgeois novel. That honour is shared by Marivaux and Defoe. Nor would it be fair to Rousseau to agree that he learned from Richardson 'the art of depicting and staging his characters, the eloquence of the heart, and the tone of sentiment.' In the first place, the characters in *La Nouvelle Héloïse* are not presented in the Richardson manner, and they echo the voice of Rousseau himself. As for their passionate eloquence and the timbre of their sensibility, these also are Rousseau's. But here it becomes imperative to examine the two novels, not, indeed, as anatomical subjects, since they are living works of art. To say, as does Texte, that *La Nouvelle Héloïse* is an imitation of *Clarissa* because in both the central theme is a struggle between love and duty is unilluminating. The marvel would be to find a novel of passionate love from which such a theme is absent. Everything depends on what is meant by 'love' and 'duty.'

Clarissa was given to the public in 1749, seven years, that is to say, after the appearance of *Pamela*. In the interval, Richardson the artist had reached maturity; but Richardson the man had not essentially changed. He was still the frustrated romantic, absorbed in the contemplation of emotional experiences which he was never to know save through the medium of a vivid and erotic imagination. Paradoxical as it may seem, however, this lack of direct personal contact with human passion, which is so characteristic of Richardson the man, was destined to be the greatest asset of Richardson the artist and novelist. Rousseau, on the contrary, had lived the emotions which he ascribes to his hero, Saint-Preux.

In *Pamela* Richardson showed that he was incapable of visualizing love as a spiritual experience, and in *Clarissa* there is nothing to indicate that the author had fundamentally increased his knowledge of love and of its effects on a woman's soul. In other and lesser respects, however, his knowledge of feminine psychology is immensely greater than in *Pamela*. Yet in both novels he regards love wholly as an affair of the senses. Like Mr. B., Lovelace is a pure sensualist, and although his motives and methods are much more complex and sophisticated, his overwhelming desire is that of physical possession. Once again, too, Richardson lingers with almost sadistic enjoyment over the prolonged and painful spectacle of the heroine's persecution. On the whole, Richardson's attitude to love in both novels is that of an English eighteenth-century bourgeois reared on the teachings of the Old Testament; a man for whom chastity is not a spiritual and personal quality but a physical attribute. Richardson cannot really distinguish between virginity of the soul and virginity of the body. Once Clarissa is drugged and raped, she must die; and, when we realize the *milieu* in which Clarissa and Richardson were brought up, nothing is more credible or more tragic.

In that *Éloge de Richardson* which has been so often quoted, Diderot described *Clarissa* as a *grand drame*, and if we remember what is implied in the word *drame*, Diderot was perfectly right. In *Clarissa* the author moves upon the plane of tragedy, but of domestic tragedy. In spite of Lovelace, he is not Shakespearian; and, of course, his conception of tragedy is much too English to allow of any comparison with either Racine or Corneille. The tone of *Clarissa* is rather that of *Arden of Feversham* or of Lillo's *George Barnwell*, bordering, that is to say, on melodrama, yet never crossing the frontiers of great art. Only a great artist could have raised passion and sentiment to such a high degree of intensity whilst rendering them perfectly credible. A situation that has no counterpart in everyday life is presented within the cadre of everyday life. By sheer force of genius it is fashioned and hammered into the shape of reality; and our coldly rational doubts are triumphantly dispelled by the hypnotic power of the author's sincerity and imagination. How is such a miracle achieved?

The novel opens at a critical point. The Harlowe family is at open feud with Robert Lovelace, a notorious libertine, but the nephew of a peer. The origin of the quarrel is as follows. Lovelace had first paid his addresses to Clarissa's elder sister, Arabella, who, in the conventional manner of the day, refused his hand and then sat back complacently to await the second, more ardent proposal. This, however, did not materialize, and in a dispute with James Harlowe, junior, who is an insolent cad and coward, Lovelace wounded his man. The true reason for his lack of ardour is Clarissa and, whilst insisting upon an apology from the Harlowe family, Lovelace coolly asks leave to transfer his attentions from Arabella to her younger sister. Now, however, no such reconciliation is possible. Clarissa's natural sense of justice makes her unable to share the family's hatred of Lovelace or to endorse their exaggerated picture of his character. She is not attracted to him because she detests his morals; on the other hand, she knows that in the affair with her brother, Lovelace was not the aggressor. Moreover, as she learns from her bosom friend, Miss Howe, Lovelace is not wholly bad. He is, in fact, a just and most generous man in his relations with his tenants. Indeed, were it not for his ungovernable pride and his scabrous reputation in sexual matters, Clarissa could almost like Lovelace. At first, indeed, she is vaguely annoyed at his intransigent attitude towards her brother and her uncles.

Meanwhile, Clarissa's situation in the Harlowe family grows rapidly intolerable. Infuriated by their sister's cool indifference,

James and Arabella make her the victim of their vindictive hatred of Lovelace. James is 'an indoor insolent,' the type of domestic tyrant who trades upon his father's ill-health and his own position as eldest son to bully the women-folk of the house. Apart from the Lovelace affair, however, he has a long-standing grievance against Clarissa, whose grandfather had left her a rich estate, thereby not only depriving James of a desirable possession, but, what he regards as intolerable,'making her financially her own mistress. This inheritance plays an important part in the novel, since it explains the readiness of Clarissa's father to abet James and Arabella in their persecution of their sister. Arabella is, of course, eaten up with jealousy and mortified pride. There is an elder-sisterly quality in her hatred, a petty and untiring zeal in her nagging of Clarissa, which is kept at constant white heat by the latter's shrewd and contemptuous homethrusts. James and Arabella are terrible; but the true cause of Clarissa's despair lies in the hopeless feeling that she has lost the affection of her father and mother. That, as it develops, becomes a vital source of tragedy in the events to follow.

James and Arabella persuade the family that Clarissa is in love with Lovelace and must, consequently, be protected against herself. She finds, therefore, that she is opposed by the 'embattled phalanx' of the Harlowes, including Aunt Hervey, Uncle Harlowe, and, to quote Miss Howe, 'the creeping, old, musty Uncle Antony.' Through Clarissa's clandestine letters to her friend, and the notes sent downstairs to the various members of this sombre conclave, we are able to follow, almost hour by hour, the progress of a psychological conflict involving the fate of a strong soul. How momentous it is we know from the heroine herself. 'It is not a little thing that is insisted upon; not for a short duration; it is for my *life*.' As in all struggles that are truly dramatic, the immediate and local issue is but a microcosm. Viewed in its proper light, this crisis affects not merely the future of an imaginary individual but the social position of the eighteenth-century unmarried woman. Clarissa's real crime, in the eyes of her parents, is not so much that she is supposed to be in love with a libertine—who, by the way, was once considered good enough to marry Arabella—as that she is a rebel against tradition. In the first place she is economically independent, thanks to her grandfather. Moreover, as Anne Howe shrewdly notes, she has not the materialistic Harlowe soul; and the fine, spiritual quality in her has always irked her brother and sister, whose pent-up jealousy has now attained full ripeness. Clarissa's parents had always loved her because she was gentle and sub-missive. Her refusal to marry the family's choice, Solmes, comes to them as a sudden revelation. Having no imagination, they are puzzled and irritated. Clarissa commits the unforgivable sin of not living up to a character which was never her own, but the pro-duct of her parents' superficial judgment. As in all such cases, the daughter now appears ungrateful, obstinate, and hypocritical. She upsets her father's comfortable scale of values, and that is always distressing.

There is no real parallel, I think, in the French language for our expression: 'She was sent to Coventry.' This form of refined torture, which is probably the most fiendish ever invented by civilized man, seems to be an English institution. Clarissa is sent to Coventry; but her solitary confinement is interrupted by visits from the uncontrollable Arabella, by occasional notes from James, and the attempts at mediation made by her old governess, Miss Norton, and by Aunt Hervey. 'Poor Bella,' as Clary calls her, poor Bella with her 'plump, high-fed face,' combines with brother James to mitigate Clarissa's despair and anguish at losing her parents' love. Incidentally, the heroine is humanized by these 'scolding bouts' at a moment when she was in some danger of degenerating into an mere saint. Clarissa reveals, to our delight, that she has a pretty temper and a superb *flair* for the word and gesture best calculated to produce that 'browner, sullener glow' on Bella's high-fed countenance. These interludes serve another purpose. Without them, the prolonged contemplation of Clarissa's martyrdom would be painful and intolerable, especially when one remembers that during this time she is kept in a state of alarm by the importunities of the impetuous Lovelace and his threats against her family.

When Richardson created Lovelace, the English novel, at one bound, overleapt a century. By forcing us to believe in the reality of this character, he proved that romantic imagination had not vanished from our literature with the Elizabethan theatre. At a critical stage in the evolution of the novel; at a moment when its contours were about to be defined and limited by the 'common sense' of the age, the very writer who was doing so much to create the realistic novel of bourgeois manners, gloriously betrayed his own creed and conceived a figure whose stature entitles him to a place alongside the heroes of great drama, yet does not seem incredible in the more ordinary *milieu* imagined by the novelist.

Had Richardson been a greater poet, it would have been possible to speak of Lovelace in the same breath as Iago or of Don Juan. Like them, he has the intellectual romantic's contempt of the ethical code governing ordinary human relations, and possesses, too, a demonic belief in his own powers. But the romanticism of Lovelace is of the nineteenth century. In his pursuit of evil he is not a complete artist. His individualism harbours a lurking, superstitious fear of the divine wrath, and a germ of sensibility which produces a constant fighting in his soul. In his self-dramatization he appears to himself as a superman, the intellectual superior of the Harlowes and of his own family. The strings of their destinies are in his hands, and with Satanic glee Lovelace watches the puppets dance to his will. When, as a result of his elaborate contrivings, Clarissa is at last delivered into his power, he is beside himself with exultation. 'How it swells my pride,' he cries, 'to have been able to outwit such a vigilant charmer! I am taller by half a yard in my imagination than I was. I look *down* upon everybody now. Last night I was still more extravagant. I took off my hat as I walked, to see if the lace was not scorched, supposing it had been brushed by a star.' Yet, in reality, this episode marks the close of Lovelace's victorious career as an individualist. So far, he has plotted with the cunning of an Iago, but no Iago would have been so naïve as to imagine, as Lovelace foolishly does, that there is any lasting intellectual satisfaction to be procured from a mere physical superiority.

By capturing Clarissa and thus placing himself in daily contact with her sweetness and strength of soul, Lovelace has let the enemy within the gates of his self-esteem. Henceforth, instead of looking *down* he experiences a new and exasperating sense of moral inferiority. All his subsequent follies can be traced to this new consciousness. Richardson notes the declension when he remarks: 'There is more of the savage in human nature than we are commonly aware of.' Lovelace, beneath his veneer of sophisticated immoralism, is a savage. Hitherto, no woman has resisted him because of his superior cunning. What now maddens him is to find that Clarissa quickly sees through his artifices, despising him as a common liar and cheat.

However, Lovelace the amateur dramatist experiences a devilish thrill of satisfaction when he succeeds in luring Clarissa into Mrs. Sinclair's bagnio, the inmates of which he has carefully schooled in their parts. And after the heroine becomes aware of her terrible situation Lovelace manages to preen the feathers of his bedraggled *amour-propre* by inventing Tomlinson, the bogus intermediary between Clarissa and her father. Here he is more successful because Harlowe's curse weighs heavily upon the daughter's conscience. Yet at every stage in this strange and torturing masquerade, Lovelace has to stop and goad himself on to fresh devilries by wilfully recalling his original motive, which was revenge. Baffled by his inability to make Clarissa respond to his sensual passion, he drugs his pride with wild imaginings. In these visions a triumphant Lovelace towers above an imploring Clarissa, whose friends and relations have succumbed to the schemes of this master plotter. In one picture he beholds Miss Howe and her mother ravished at sea by Lovelace and his brother Mohocks. In another, even more arresting tableau, Lovelace is in the dock on trial for his life. All the sympathies of the audience, however, go, not to his victims but to the handsome, reckless criminal. 'Even the judges, and the whole crowded bench will acquit us in their hearts! and every single man wish he had been me.' Clarissa he visualizes in one of his erotic frenzies, 'with a twin Lovelace at each charming breast . . . full of wishes for the sake of the pretty varlets, and for her own sake that I would deign to legitimate; that I would condescend to put on the nuptial fetters.' The reproaches of his friend and quondam fellow-rake, Belford, and the curses of his uncle serve only to cocker up his self-esteem; for romantics, like small boys, love to be told how wicked they are. Besides, at this particular moment, after several fruitless attempts to impress Clarissa, Lovelace has need of such a tonic. Her words: 'I have a soul above thee, man!' somehow make all his carefully thought out contrivances appear tawdry, puerile, and dirty. Away from the footlights it is devilish hard to be a convincing Mephistopheles. So Lovelace has continually to remind himself that he is swayed by three passions: 'all imperial ones—love, revenge, ambition or a desire for conquest.'

Lovelace's last slender hold over Clarissa breaks when, after she is drugged and raped, he at last proposes immediate marriage, only to be rejected. That was a stroke of genius on Richardson's part. And Lovelace's foul act itself, which in any other context must have seemed far-fetched, is made to appear an inevitable climax to his erotic exasperation. In view of the author's peculiar technique, one must further point out that all the critical incidents of the novel are thus carefully prepared. A bare summary gives the impression that Richardson is an indifferent artist, whereas the whole secret of his genius lies in the skill with which he makes the improbable appear natural and credible. Clarissa's destiny is, as she says, 'a mysterious destiny'; but it has all the illusion of truth. Richardson makes it absolutely inescapable. That is all the more remarkable when one reflects that the net in which she is caught is a material one. A modern novelist, unless, indeed, he wrote 'thrillers,' would scorn to weave a story round the situation imagined by Richardson. A girl is lured to a bagnio masquerading as a genteel lodging-house. After repeated attempts, she escapes to Hampstead but is lured back by a trick. She escapes again, after being drugged and raped, only to be imprisoned in a sponging-house on a trumped-up charge. Finally, still hounded by her persecutor, she resigns herself to die in an apartment in Covent Garden. To write a great novel centring upon a psychological impasse is a simple affair compared to the task which Richardson set himself in *Clarissa Harlowe*.

The last two books, with their long, painful account of the heroine's preparation for death, shocked even Prévost, who omitted them from his translation. Most modern readers will applaud his good sense. Yet here again, nothing is really out of focus, not even the incident which pictures Clarissa ordering her coffin and installing it like a harpsichord in her room! Thus torn from its context and baldly reported, it sounds, no doubt, puerile and ludicrous; but no such criticism arises in our mind as we reach this point in the narrative, thanks to the subtlety with which the author has traced the heroine's gradual approach to the mystic state of rapture preceding her death. Richardson's object was to present a drama which had its *dénouement*, not on earth but in paradise. Such was his retort to the hysterical lady readers who beseeched him to spare Clarissa and grant her 'a fortunate ending'; this, too, was his reply to those who asked the same boon on the grounds of 'poetic justice.' Quite evidently, Richardson regarded the death of his heroine as a moral necessity, and he was too sensitive an artist to entertain for one moment the absurd suggestion that she should marry a converted Lovelace. The life of Clarissa, from the dramatist's point of view, falls into three acts or states. In the first, we perceive a normal but strong-willed girl, not unlike Cordelia, torn between her sense of filial duty and her consciousness of human dignity; a virtuous and reasonable individual who, for the first time, becomes aware of life's complexity. From this ordeal she emerges stronger but sadder. The second trial, painful and degrading though it must seem, is in reality much less momentous than the first. To a woman of Clarissa's sensitiveness it is, no doubt, horrible; but, despite her prepossession for Lovelace, her chastity is never in danger. Spiritually, she is immune; and the conflict in which she is engaged is actually one of wits, a duel in which all Lovelace's hypocrisy and craft are set at naught by the heroine's superior intelligence. As each one of his subtle contrivances is discovered by Clarissa, the possibility that Lovelace will trick her into a bogus marriage grows hourly more improbable. Her sole enemy at this stage is her natural anxiety to stand well in the eyes of her family and of the world. Therefore, for a time she is sorely tempted to ignore the inner voices of reason and of virtue; since marriage seems such an easy solution to all her troubles. The erotic Lovelace, by his precipitate violence on the occasion of the supposed fire at Sinclair's, reveals to Clarissa the exact state of her soul. In a flash, she realizes the true horror of her situation, which is not that she is in the physical power of Lovelace, but that she was almost betrayed by weariness and by weakness of will into marriage with a man whose vices render him unfit to be her husband. This vital fact Richardson has failed to illuminate. The question of physical chastity, it is evident, loomed in the forefront of his mind, and he lays undue emphasis upon the narrative of Lovelace's attempts to obtain carnal possession of the heroine. In the final stage, after the degrading and brutal assault, Clarissa's intellect is momentarily clouded, but she is preserved from madness by the mystic conviction that all her trials have been but a preparation for grace. Thenceforth, Clarissa, the woman, disappears to make way for Clarissa, the bride-elect of Christ. 'Love me still, however,' she writes to Miss Howe, 'but let it be with a weaning love. I am not what I was when we were *inseparable* lovers as I may say—our *views* must now be different.' Nothing earthly can now really touch her, not even the dreadful experience in the sponging-house engineered by the beldam, Sinclair. Only one thought ruffles the serenity of her mind; it is the memory of her father's curse. Her enemies, even Lovelace, she cheerfully forgives; and moreover, begs her cousin Morden not to pursue her seducer. Indeed, in her mystic exaltation she expresses gratitude to Lovelace 'for so many years of glory, as might have proved years of danger, temptation, and anguish, had they been added to my mortal life.'

Clarissa Harlowe, therefore, is not primarily a love novel, it is the dramatic narrative of a religious and mystic experience. The passion of Lovelace is too earthy, too *Paphian*, if I may borrow the author's own adjective, to justify the assumption of a real conflict between sexual love and virtue in the heroine's soul. That, as we have seen, is but a minor aspect of Clarissa's greater dilemma. Her problem is akin to that of a Cordelia or of an Alceste, complicated, however, by the heroine's inveterate respect for the Old Testament teachings to which, from the very cradle, she has been exposed. In the effort to pursue an inner ideal of truth and goodness, she finds herself in sharp and agonizing conflict with the fact that her conception of truth and goodness is unique. As events develop Clarissa becomes conscious, with growing despair, that there is not a living soul in her entourage who can understand her point of view. The family regards her as perverse, ungrateful, and insincere. Not even Miss Howe, her most passionate admirer, is to be excepted; for plainly, she looks upon her friend's refusal to marry Lovelace as a quixotic whim. Yet never for one moment is Clarissa untrue to herself and, in the end, although at the cost of her life, she preserves her immortal soul intact.

In his *Confessions* [1] Rousseau gives a brief criticism of Richardson's novels: 'Diderot has paid great compliments to Richardson upon the enormous variety of his situations and the number of characters introduced by him. Richardson certainly has the merit of having given them all distinctive characteristics; but, in regard to their number, he has the fault common to most insipid writers of romance, who make up for the barrenness of their ideas by the aid of characters and incidents. It is easy to excite interest by incessantly presenting unheard-of incidents and new faces, who pass like the figures in a magic-lantern; but it is far more difficult to sustain this interest continually by means of the same objects without the aid of wonderful adventures. And if, other things being equal, the simplicity of the subject adds to the beauty of the work, the romance of Richardson, though superior in so many other things, cannot, in this respect, be compared to mine.'

Now, as Rousseau knew Richardson only through the 'chastened' and heavily abridged translation of Prévost, there is little reason to assume that a wider acquaintance with the work of the English novelist would have altered his opinion. On the contrary, it is more probable that Rousseau's esthetic disgust for Richardson's 'unheard-of incidents' would have increased the severity of his original verdict.

[1] I quote from the Everyman translation, vol. ii, pp. 187–8.

Apart from the letter form, which he very possibly owed to English example, it is quite clear from the author's own account of the genesis of *La Nouvelle Héloïse*, that this novel, like all his works, was a necessary and spontaneous effusion, the expression of one of Rousseau's many moods. In June 1756, the author, then aged forty-five, was living at the Hermitage, near Eaubonne. Brooding upon the incidents of his past life, he realized with a torturing sense of frustration, that he, Jean-Jacques Rousseau, the Man of Feeling *par excellence*, had never experienced the passion of love. 'Consumed by the desire of loving, without ever having been able to satisfy it completely, I saw myself approaching the portals of old age, and dying without ever having lived.' This intolerable thought was reinforced, he tells us, by 'the consciousness of my inner value.' A fertile germ sprang into life. Quickened by a hot imagination, nurtured by memories of former contacts with women, it began to assume the dim contours of a work of art. Intoxicated by his dreams of an ideal world, peopled by creatures whose essence was love, Rousseau pictured two women linked by a beautiful friendship, yet different in character: 'one prudent, the other weak, but with so touching a weakness that virtue seemed to gain by it.' To one he gave a lover, 'whose tender friend the other was, and even something more.' This lover was Rousseau himself, but a younger and happier Rousseau. Later he was to be christened Saint-Preux; whilst the two girls were to be called Julie d'Étrange and Claire d'Orbe. All that now remained was to discover an appropriate setting for these dream creations. Rejecting the valleys of Thessaly because he had never been there, and the Borromean Isles because they were too theatrical, Jean-Jacques finally settled upon the shores of Lake Geneva.

At this juncture it is important to note that Rousseau's book was still in embryonic state. However, it would be a novel, a novel of passionate love, in which Rousseau, the thwarted romantic, should, in the person of Saint-Preux, vicariously consummate his love. In the late summer, however, something occurred which vitally influenced and gave definite shape to his floating, coloured, and formless dreams. This was the sudden visit of Mme d'Houde-tot, the mistress of Rousseau's friend, Saint-Lambert, the poet and *philosophe*. Mme d'Houdetot's carriage was bemired near the Hermitage, and she herself, like some vision from the pages of a romance, appeared at Rousseau's door drenched to the skin and attractively tricked out in borrowed riding boots too large for her dainty feet. She stayed just long enough to dry her clothes, to dine, and, incidentally, to provide Jean-Jacques with a real and vivid Julie. In the *Confessions*, which are far from chronologically exact, Rousseau tells us that it was not until the second visit of Mme d'Houdetot, in the spring of 1757, that he fell in love with her. But in the interval, the characters of his novel obsessed him. 'My delirium never left me.' The plan of the novel, too, hardened into shape. Now, Julie was to allow herself to be 'overcome with love, and, when wedded, should find strength to overcome it in her turn and to become virtuous again.' In a word, the dynamic idea of the work had crystallized. Julie was, moreover, to marry an atheist, a union intended to symbolize one of Rousseau's fondest dreams—the fusion of rational incredulity and orthodox Catholicism in a universal religion, the essence of which is human, natural sensibility.

In the spring and summer of 1757, Sophie d'Houdetot, Rousseau, and the absent Saint-Lambert enacted what is surely one of the strangest tragi-comedies ever chronicled. 'She came, I saw her,' writes Jean-Jacques. 'I was intoxicated with love without an object. This intoxication enchanted my eyes; this object became centred in her. I saw my Julie in Madame d'Houdetot, and soon I saw only Madame d'Houdetot, but invested with all the perfections with which I had just adorned the idol of my heart. To complete my intoxication, she spoke to me of Saint-Lambert in the language of passionate love. O contagious power of love! When I listened to her, when I found myself near her, I was seized with a delightful tremor, which I had never felt with any one else. When she spoke, I felt myself overcome with emotion. I imagined that I was interesting myself only in *her* feelings, when my own were similar. I swallowed in deep draughts the contents of the poisoned cup, of which as yet I only tasted the sweetness. At last, without either of us perceiving it, she inspired me with all those feelings for herself which she expressed for her lover. Alas! it was very late, it was very hard for me, to be consumed by a passion, as violent as it was unfortunate, for a woman whose heart was full of love for another.'

To soothe his gigantic and turbulent *amour-propre*, Rousseau suggests in the *Confessions* that Sophie, but for his high sense of honour and the obligations of friendship, might have succumbed to his passionate wooing. 'For the first time in my life, I was sublime.' The truth is less romantic. Sophie was embarrassed, scared, and possibly a little amused. Saint-Lambert, when he appeared on the scene, treated Jean-Jacques 'severely but amiably.' Rousseau was eager to retain the friendship of these two, and visualized a triangular situation analogous to that which he has immortalized in *La Nouvelle Héloïse*, where Saint-Preux, the former lover, Wolmar the cold but humane husband, and a chastened, wifely Julie live together in complete amity and mutual love upon the still warm ashes of a volcano. In reality, this ideal never materialized, and in February of 1758, the deserted Rousseau interrupted his novel to write the severe, almost Calvinistic *Letter to D'Alembert on Theatres*. However, he finished *La Nouvelle Héloïse* in the winter of 1758–9.

With this picture in mind, one cannot seriously accept the opinion that, to quote the *Monthly Review*,[1] 'the author appears to have had the writings of our celebrated Richardson in mind, and seems not only to have happily imitated his manner but to have excelled him in purity of style.' This eighteenth-century view has been accepted by Texte because it is essential to his thesis; but it has nothing to support it save a veneer of similarity. Rousseau could only have written one novel and he wrote only one: it is the lyrical narrative of a personal experience, altered and distorted in obedience to the dictates of an imperious egotism.

Saint-Preux, who is a *roturier* but the son of an officer, is employed as tutor to Julie d'Étange and Claire d'Orbe, and falls passionately in love with the former. Claire, and subsequently, Lord Édouard Bomston, an English peer, are the confidants and admirers of the two lovers. Julie, terrified at her own weakness, appeals to the chivalry of Saint-Preux, who, in a Platonic frenzy, agrees that to seduce her would be 'incest.' Julie's father, the baron, is a hot-tempered nobleman of the old school, so that marriage is not to be thought of. Her mother, although she might have sympathized, is weak and dominated by her husband. For a time the lovers taste the pure and sweet joys of renunciation. Their love is unique. It is the ideal union of two hearts predestined for each other ever since the world began. But gradually the letters of Saint-Preux reveal the struggle between the god and the man; whilst Julie is invaded by a poignant sense of pity. Soon, inspired by a spirit of revolt against the injustice of the social order, she relieves Saint-Preux of his knightly vow and herself assumes the care of their 'common destiny.' An incident now occurs which profoundly alters their relations. Julie and Claire invite their tutor to a certain

[1] November 1760.

bosquet where the lovers for the first time kiss, with devastating effects on their peace of mind.

From that moment Saint-Preux the Platonist becomes Saint-Preux the urgent, sensuous lover and poet. At Julie's request, he goes to Meillerie, in the Valais, where all nature is magically transformed into a sombre and perfect cadre to his romantic passion. A crisis is approaching, and it is reflected in the letters of this modern Abelard, with their plaintive note of sadness rising in a wild crescendo of lyrical despair. With the superb eloquence born of romantic frenzy he appeals to Julie's senses, to her religion—does not God favour their union?—to her sensibility, and finally, in darker mood, threatens to take his own life. Meanwhile, Julie has learned that she has been promised in marriage to an old friend of her father's, a man who once, indeed, had saved the baron's life. She dare not tell Saint-Preux, and her mother is already on the verge of discovering their secret. In her exaltation, Julie conceives her dilemma to be this: If she goes away with Saint-Preux her mother will die of grief, and the baron, she is convinced, will prefer death to the dishonour of breaking his word to a comrade-in-arms who holds his pledged word. But if she does not yield to her lover's appeals he will certainly commit suicide. So, to quote her own words: 'Je choisis ma propre infortune.' And in so doing, she makes Saint-Preux happy.

As Rousseau was well aware, this was the episode in the novel most likely to expose him to the attacks of the orthodox, since Julie, the frail, 'the fallen woman,' was destined to reappear as Julie de Wolmar. Outside the pages of Holy Writ the French had little use for Magdalens, and Julie de Wolmar is presented as a model wife and mother. Never before had a novelist put forward such an audacious hypothesis; and never did an artist display more consummate skill than Rousseau in portraying the spiritual transition of his heroine. Having given herself to Saint-Preux, Julie, now endowed with the sweet cunning born of love, plots to arrange another meeting; for she is now determined to have a child by her lover. Of this, however, he knows nothing. With a sophistry worthy of his powers, Rousseau introduces in Claire and in Lord Bomston an admiring chorus, whose utterances are designed to palliate the impression made on the reader by Julie's lapse from convention. This, I think, detracts from the value of the novel. Claire reminds her friend that her weakness will be effaced by the tremendous sacrifices she has made. 'Without having been vanquished,' she tells her, 'I am less chaste than you.' And later, Bomston tells the lovers that they are unique; they are linked by an 'eternal decree of heaven,' and cannot, therefore, be judged by mundane standards of morality. Here, too, Jean-Jacques interjects the Fanchon incident where Julie and Saint-Preux renounce a romantic meeting in a mountain chalet to perform an act of charity to a poor servant-girl.

The baron, though he does not know how far matters have gone, discovers to his rage that his daughter is in love with her tutor. Vainly, Bomston pleads the cause of his friend, offering to settle one-third of his fortune upon him to compensate for his lack of pedigree. The old man will not be placated, however, and in a painful altercation with his daughter, he strikes her and commands her to prepare for marriage with his friend Wolmar. As a result of this brutal scene, Julie has a miscarriage and falls into a languor. Claire informs Saint-Preux of the approaching marriage, and, in a state of indescribable agitation, he is hurried away by the generous Bomston, who offers the lovers the sanctuary of his Yorkshire estate. Tortured by the reproaches of Saint-Preux, sorely tempted, also, to accept Bomston's offer, Julie now faces the great crisis of her life. On the surface, this is a situation not unlike that of Clarissa when she is being hounded into marriage with Solmes. Essentially, however, it is quite different. Julie has the strongest possible motives for obeying her parents. After her surrender to Saint-Preux, she experiences a revulsion of feeling, not against him, but against herself. In sacrificing virtue to pleasure, she tells him, they became 'ordinary lovers,' sharing with 'the vilest mortals' the sensual experience which they now call love. With unspeakable shame she remembers that it was she who held 'their common destiny' in her hands, and that it was she who arranged for Saint-Preux to come to her room at night. This second lapse, with its distressing aftermath, accentuates her sense of self-disgust, and subtly alters her attitude towards Saint-Preux, whom she now regards with increasing and almost maternal pity. The tone of her letters changes; and Saint-Preux himself becomes weaker and more effeminate as Julie grows stronger and more virile. 'Il soupire et gémit comme une femme.' Supported by Claire, who is also about to marry, Julie preaches the gospel of Plato to her now docile lover. In yielding to his love, she tells him, she obeyed the voice of nature; but the instinct of filial gratitude is also natural and more imperious still. Until the end of the novel, then, except for an occasional passionate outbreak from Saint-Preux, such will be the relations between these two. Rousseau, the author of the stern *Letter to D'Alembert*, speaks now through the medium of Julie the *prêcheuse*; Rousseau, the suppliant lover of Sophia and the unsuccessful candidate for the goodwill of Saint-Lambert, borrows the voice of Saint-Preux. The long suite of letters exchanged between the lovers reveals an ever stronger Julie scolding Saint-Preux, who is in Paris, for his *bel esprit*; indulgently taking him to task for his lack of candour, and mourning over his folly when he confesses that he was beguiled by bad company into a disorderly house. At this point, Madame d'Étange discovers their secret and dies, though not of grief, as Claire points out to the despairing Julie. Inconsolable, and haunted by passionate self-reproaches, the latter now demands Saint-Preux's permission to marry, ignoring his plea for another hour of happiness, and treating his adulterous proposals for future meetings with the contempt which they deserve. Before the ceremony with Wolmar, Julie asks for an hour's solitude, deliberately reviews her past, and prays fervently for guidance. The result of this *examen de conscience* is a spiritual conversion. As the psychological veracity of the whole novel hinges upon this incident, it might be well to allow Rousseau himself to describe it. Julie is writing to Saint-Preux:

'The test was a sure but dangerous one. I began by thinking about you. I bore witness to myself that no tender memory had profaned the solemn pledge I had just given. I could not conceive by what miracle the persistent image of you could have left me so long in peace, with so many reasons for recalling it: had my state of mind been one of indifference or of forgetfulness I should have suspected it as too unnatural to be lasting. This illusion was scarcely to be feared; I felt that I loved you as much as, and perhaps more than, I had ever done, but this I felt without a blush. I saw that to think of you, I did not require to forget that I was the wife of another man. When I told myself how dear you were to me, my heart was moved, but my conscience and my senses were tranquil; and from that moment onwards I knew that I was really changed. What a torrent of pure joy then flooded my soul! What a feeling of peace, to which I had been so long a stranger, came to revive this heart of mine, withered by ignominy! My whole being was invaded by a new serenity. I felt myself reborn; I believed I was beginning a new life. Sweet and consoling virtue, I am beginning it anew for thee! Thou wilt make it dear to me and to thee I consecrate it. Ah! I have learned only too well what it costs to lose thee, to desert thee for a second time.'

The novelist had another delicate task to achieve. This was to portray and to make credible a situation unparalleled in literature. With varying degrees of success, modern novelists have depicted the reunion of a man with his married ex-mistress. Sometimes, too, they have assumed that the husband was aware of his wife's former relations. Yet, so far as I can recollect, the situation imagined by Rousseau is unique. Wolmar knew his wife's secret before their marriage, though Julie did not tell him until they had been wedded for six years, that is to say, after the return of Saint-Preux from a voyage round the world with Anson. Just before the arrival of the ex-lover, who is deliberately invited by Wolmar, the latter has already frankly discussed the whole situation with his wife. Thus, when Saint-Preux comes to Clarens, he has already been informed by the husband of Julie's confession. 'The wisest and dearest of women,' writes Wolmar, 'has just opened her heart to her fortunate husband. He thinks you worthy of having been loved by her, and offers you the freedom of his home. There reign peace and innocence. There you will find friendship, hospitality, esteem, and confidence. Consult your heart, and if it harbours nothing to terrify you, do not be afraid to come.'

In presenting such a situation, Rousseau was almost two hundred years in advance of civilization, since, even at this day, a Wolmar would be looked at askance by all but the few. It may be objected that such a *ménage à trois* is not uncommon among the uneducated classes, and that is perfectly true. Indeed, the modern primitivist who believes implicitly in the Rousseauistic doctrine of the *bonté naturelle* might argue triumphantly that the man of the people, just because he is uncorrupted by education or civilization, sees nothing unnatural in a Wolmar's conduct. But the vital point is that Saint-Preux, Julie, and her husband are all highly educated persons, trained and accustomed to examine the secret workings of their souls. That alters the whole question. By conceiving such a theme and, above all, by stamping it with the *cachet* of actuality, Rousseau proved himself to be a novelist of genius, and, as a psychologist, superior to Richardson. In his attitude to human relationships, he moves upon a higher and different plane. Here Rousseau but continues the tradition founded by Madame de Lafayette. Julie's confession to her husband had almost a counterpart in *La Princesse de Clèves*, a fact noted by him in the *Confessions*, where he compares the two situations and, I think rightly, considers his own to be artistically superior. Nevertheless, before Jean-Jacques, a great French novelist had struck a blow for social freedom. Madame de Clèves's behaviour was regarded as audacious and unprecedented; but it made a breach in the stagnant dam of public opinion. *Manon Lescaut* widened the breach. A great artist had the courage to see tragedy in the liaison between a nobleman and a *fille de joie*. That, again, amazed and shocked public opinion, but again it provoked discussion and thought. Madame de Lafayette, Prévost, and Rousseau were great novelists and for precisely the same reasons. All three imagined an intensely human situation involving a problem for which they offered a solution at variance with the conventional idea governing the social relationships of their time. And they have had successors to whose works the same criterion may be applied. The latest example is Proust, who, by enlarging the frontiers of the novel to admit a Charlus and an Albertine, has provoked the same sort of criticism to which Rousseau was subjected when he published *La Nouvelle Héloïse*. The quality shared by all such writers may be described as tolerance; but it is tolerance based upon a profound knowledge of human psychology; and their claim to be great novelists or artists depends entirely on the illusion of reality which they have succeeded in lending to their situations and characters. They are not to be confused with the writers of 'thesis' novels, like Zola and Bourget, who obtain their effects and prove their thesis by inventing marionettes to dance round an *a priori* idea.

Rousseau's *ménage à trois*, on the contrary, presents an illusion of veracity. It comes to pass naturally because all the characters remain, in their behaviour, faithful to themselves. The idea originates in the mind of Wolmar, who is not a sentimentalist but an atheist, and, above all, a cool and profound observer of human nature. To-day, very probably, he would be a psycho-analyst, but a psycho-analyst called upon to solve a problem involving his own future happiness. Julie herself does not really know the state of her own emotions and, still appalled by the memory of her past weakness, distrusts herself. That is reflected in her prudish treatment of the servants. Her *gynaeceum*, as Claire points out, is a foolish and unnatural institution. Nature herself has devised ways of separating the sexes; why, therefore, try to improve on nature? As for Saint-Preux, he is, as Wolmar shrewdly observes, still in love; but he is in love with Julie d'Étange and not with Julie de Wolmar.

P

With superb understanding, Rousseau depicts the actions and emotions of the former lovers at their first reunion. Saint-Preux is nervous and apprehensive. When Julie embraces him frankly and openly in her husband's presence, he is incapable of any feeling whatever. 'I received her embraces, but as my heart had just emptied itself, I merely received them.' To his painful embarrassment, far from avoiding references to their past, Julie freely discusses it with her former lover; and Wolmar, who is standing by, bluntly tells Saint-Preux, though with the greatest friendliness, that frankness is the tone of his establishment. Alone with Saint-Preux, however, Julie is no longer so confident. The lovers furtively examine each other, and to his bitter surprise, he discovers that she is more beautiful than ever. Evening comes, and Saint-Preux sadly says good night to Monsieur and Madame de Wolmar.

To Wolmar's delight, Saint-Preux treats him with cold reserve: any other attitude would have been false and dangerous. In the days that ensue, Julie and Wolmar initiate Saint-Preux into all their domestic secrets. They talk of rural economy and, above all, of the education of the children. In this way, Julie's former lover is imperceptibly led to see her more and more as a devoted wife and mother. Finally, in a conversation which, by Wolmar's arrangement, takes place in the very grove where Julie and Saint-Preux exchanged their first delirious kiss, Wolmar confesses to them that he has read all their passionate love-letters, which, indeed, he now produces. 'I saw,' he says, 'the deceptive exaltation which led you both astray; it is active only in fine souls. Sometimes it ruins them, but by a charm that seduces only souls like yours. I judged that the very inclination which had formed your union would dissolve it the moment it became criminal and that, although vice might enter into hearts like yours, it could not take root there.' Wolmar then informs them that he proposes to go off for a few days and, to Julie's dismay, asks Saint-Preux if he will stay with his wife until he returns. Saint-Preux accepts.

In a perturbed letter to Claire, Julie asks for enlightenment as to her own feelings; and Claire, with her usual subtlety, diagnoses the condition of her friend's heart. Julie is mistaking sensibility for love and she must guard against 'that dangerous virtue of humility which merely animates the *amour-propre* by concentrating it.' With delicate humour, she indicates symptoms in Julie's manner towards Saint-Preux which Wolmar, as a mere male, will certainly have misinterpreted. Such, for instance, are the furtive glances exchanged at their first meeting. These, says the wise Claire, need not perturb Julie; they are favourable signs because passionate lovers do not examine each other in that way.

Wolmar's private plan is to make Saint-Preux the tutor of his children. But first he must destroy the latter's memory of the former Julie, and convince him that Julie d'Étange is dead. The two, he feels, are still lovers; yet they are also friends. Everything now depends on what happens during his absence from Clarens. Here the two geniuses, Jean-Jacques the poet-lover and Rousseau the psychologist, coalesce to create a scene of great dramatic power and beauty. This is the crisis at Meillerie, where Saint-Preux, exiled by Julie before the first lapse, had once found solace. At Meillerie, again, amidst romantic scenes evoking memories of the former Julie, Saint-Preux makes a last passionate attempt to recapture her. It fails. They return by moonlight and, on the lake, Saint-Preux's tempestuous emotions gradually yield to feelings of a sweeter and sadder kind, finding an outlet in words touched with a Lamartinian and elegiac poignancy. For Julie, too, it seems that the crisis is over.

Why does the novel not end at this point? The lovers have survived the test, and Saint-Preux writes to Bomston that he is cured of his passion. There are two answers to this question. Rousseau wanted to depict the spiritualizing effect of Julie's natural goodness and sensibility on the atheist, Wolmar. Again, Rousseau, the romantic and egotist, felt impelled to lay the ghost of his wounded self-esteem. The real Julie, Sophie d'Houdetot, had vanished from his life, carrying Jean-Jacques's heart in fee. So, in the *Nouvelle Héloïse*, he imagined another and more honourable ending to his romance. Claire, now widowed, comes to stay at Clarens and discovers that she has fallen in love with Saint-Preux. He, at the moment, is in Italy with Bomston, disentangling the latter from a liaison with a courtesan who is dissuaded by Saint-Preux's eloquence from accepting his friend's offer of marriage. Julie's state of soul is a curious blend of mystic fervour and very human irritation at Saint-Preux's hesitation to return to Clarens, where he is to settle down as tutor to the Wolmar children. In a spirit of angelic renunciation she urges Saint-Preux to marry Claire, yet for reasons which are unflattering to him and are subconsciously dictated by self-interest. If we decode her letter, the gist of it is this. Knowing Saint-Preux's sensual and passionate temper, Julie would feel more at ease if he were married to Claire. She even hints that the servants would be safer! In brief, she proposes to use their marriage as a fire-screen, and actually takes Saint-Preux very severely to task when he replies that he has sworn never to marry.

As nearly always occurs when a lyric genius attempts to fuse an objective element with a subjective experience, the ending of the *Nouvelle Héloïse* has a disappointing ring of unreality. Julie dies as the result of a chill caught whilst saving her son from drowning. She is a 'martyr to maternal love.' In her last letter to Saint-Preux, she confesses that she has been living in an illusion. 'One day more, perhaps, and I was guilty . . . the fears I thought I had for you were, of course, fears that I felt for myself. All my trials had been overcome; but it was only too true that they might have come back again. Have I not lived enough for happiness and virtue? What further good could I derive from life? In taking it from me heaven is depriving me of nothing that I shall miss, and is putting my honour in safety. My friend, I am leaving at a favourable moment, content with you and with myself; I go away joyfully and there is nothing cruel in this parting. After so many sacrifices, I count for little the one which I have now to make; it is simply dying again.' Yet the spiritual glamour which surrounds the last hours of Julie's life must not blind us to the unreality of this *dénouement*. Julie the woman is convincing though unusual; Julie the dying martyr belongs to a different world. The death of Clarissa was inevitable and dramatic; that of Julie is theatrical and untrue.

When Richardson discovered that many of his young lady readers were actually sorry for Lovelace he was grieved and horrified. Is this another classic instance of 'le cant anglais'? Richardson was himself obviously fascinated by the child of his brain; hallucinated by this monster which had arisen from the flaming pit of his imagination. How then, sincerely or logically, could he be shocked by the *Schwärmerei* of his little schoolgirl friends? The explanation is simple. The way to hell is paved with good intentions. Richardson the moralist was betrayed by Richardson the imaginative artist. In conceiving Lovelace he opened the portals of our literature to admit one of the most attractive and dangerous figures of romance. Yet, like the good custodian he was, Richardson first satisfied himself that his visitor was a good Tory and a stout Anglican. So, with a shrug of resignation, poor Don Juan bowed to the inevitable. God and King George were safe. Luckily, however, no one would ever know of this shameful lapse from majesty, since Don Juan proposed to travel among the islanders as Mr. Robert Lovelace, and he, according to Richardson's friend, the Rev. Robert Smith, is too intelligent to be an atheist.[1]

In France, where he arrived in the seventeenth century from Spain by way of Italy, Don Juan had long been a well-known figure. Molière, that great defender of the *morale bourgeoise*, held him up to public obloquy in 1665 and, with his genius for essentials, presented the character of the Great Seducer in a few strong and massive strokes. Don Juan has a demonic pride, a monstrous *libido dominandi*, complete insensibility, and, above all, a cynical contempt for religion. Molière's play founded a tradition, and in the novels of Marivaux, Crébillon the younger, Duclos, and Neufville de Montador, we discover an uninterrupted stream of literature dealing with seduction and persecution. When, therefore, Clarissa appeared in 1751 she received a cordial welcome. But this English cousin did not exactly set the Seine on fire.[2] In the *Nouvelle Héloïse* there is no Don Juanism, although Julie, in virginal terror at the first passionate advances of Saint-Preux, writes: 'Lured by degrees into the snares of a vile seducer, I see, though I cannot stop myself, the horrible abyss towards which I am rushing headlong.' This, however, is the language of exaltation and it is unjust to her lover, who is so little of a Don Juan that he is immediately disarmed and touched by her appeal to his chivalry. In her romantic excitement, Julie is swayed by memories of the silly teachings of her former governess, La Chaillot. In her heart of hearts she knows that Saint-Preux is not a 'vil séducteur' and, when he asks her naïvely: 'Why should your fears exceed my desires?' Julie is discreetly silent.

Laclos, the author of *Les Liaisons dangereuses*, a regular manual of seduction, had undoubtedly read both Richardson and

---

[1] Texte, who had evidently not read *Clarissa* in the original, says quite wrongly of Lovelace: 'Like Don Juan, he is an atheist and glories in the fact' (op. cit., p. 184). Richardson makes it exceedingly clear that he was not. 'It has been thought . . . that if Lovelace had been drawn an infidel or *scoffer* his character . . . would have been more natural. It is, however, too well known that there are very many persons of his cast, whose actions discredit this belief. And are not the very devils in Scripture said to *believe* and *tremble*?' (*Works* (1883), v. 533–4).

[2] The *Année littéraire*, strangely enough, ignored *Clarissa*. Grimm, in his *Correspondance*, said it made more noise than was justified by its success. The *Journal étranger* (1762), in printing the burial scene left out by Prévost in 1756, said that when he omitted it he was consulting, not his own taste, but that of the public. *Clarissa* was translated by Prévost in 1751–6. A second edition appeared in 1766 and another in 1777. Le Tourneur's more complete rendering of 1751 was reprinted 1785–7.

Rousseau. It is, however, in Molière's *Don Juan* and not in *Clarissa* that we must look for the original of his Valmont. To some degree, no doubt, Lovelace resembles both Don Juan and Valmont, notably by his 'Herodian' pride and lust for domination. Like them, too, he is an artist. 'I must create beauty!' he cries, 'and place it where nobody else can find it.' Again, Lovelace and Valmont would certainly both recognize themselves in the sketch which Don Juan has given us of himself: 'For my part, beauty ravishes me where-ever I find it, and I readily yield to that sweet violence with which it draws us; that I 'm engaged signifies nothing, the love I have for one fair, does not engage my heart to do injustice to others; I have eyes to see the merit of 'em all, and to pay every one the homage and tribute that nature obliges us to. However it is, I can't refuse my heart to any lovely creature I see, and from the moment a hand-some face demands it, had I a thousand hearts I 'd give 'em all. The rising inclinations, after all, have inexplicable charms in 'em, and all the pleasure of love consists in variety. One tastes an extreme delight in reducing, by a thousand submissions, the heart of a young beauty; to see the little progress one makes in it from day to day; to combat with transports, tears, and sighs, the innocent modesty of a mind which can hardly prevail upon itself to sur-render; to force, inch by inch, through all the little obstacles she throws in our way, to conquer the scruples she values herself upon, and lead her gently whither we 've a mind to bring her. But when one is once master of it, there 's nothing more to wish; all the beauty of the passion is at an end, and we sleep in the tranquillity of such an *amour*, if some new object does not awake our desires and present to us the attractive charms of a conquest still to make. In short, there 's nothing so delightful as to triumph over the resistance of a beauty. I have the ambition of conquerors, in this case, who fly perpetually from victory to victory, and never can resolve to set bounds to their wishes. There 's nothing can resist the impetuosity of my desires; I find I 've a heart to be in love with all the world, and, like Alexander, I could wish there were other worlds, that I might carry my amorous conquests thither.' [1] But the pride of Lovelace is not the pride of Lucifer or of Don Juan. He is not prepared to do battle with the Almighty, and that, as it happens, is the particular speciality of Valmont.

Laclos was no copyist. If he imitates Richardson, it is to show how the original ought to have been written. And, despite his

[1] The Everyman *Molière*. The translation is the Baker and Miller one of 1739.

admiration for Rousseau's doctrine of natural goodness, he parodies Saint-Preux with ill-disguised mockery. To write of seduction demands experience and subtlety as well as creative imagination; and in this particular field Laclos makes Richardson seem like a blundering amateur. Molière he also surpasses, but not for the same reason. It is rather because Laclos is using another medium —the novel—which lends itself to the deft analysis of motives and emotions. His three chief characters, Valmont, Madame de Merteuil, and Madame de Tourvel, are, indeed, explored with a thoroughness and regard for *nuances* quite foreign to the dramatic method of Molière. Laclos has another title to fame. Towering above Valmont even is the original and arresting Madame de Merteuil. To find a parallel to this female Don Juan we should have to go to Lillo; though Millwood, who is in all conscience wicked enough, has none of Merteuil's artistry in crime. In creating her, Laclos displayed not only originality but also a certain disingenuousness; since he is clever enough to take full advantage of the popular belief, that a bad woman's badness knows no bounds, in order to lend an illusion of reality to several most extraordinary events. Merteuil is the ex-mistress of Valmont, and their correspondence forms the armature of the novel. Piqued at the desertion of a former lover, Gercourt, now engaged to a convent-bred *ingénue*, called Cécile de Volanges, Merteuil arranges to corrupt the girl and have her seduced, if possible, by Danceney, a romantic *chevalier de Malte*. Whilst posing as a prude and as the close friend of Cécile's mother, Madame de Merteuil wins the affection of the daughter and of the chevalier. She contrives a scheme whereby they may secretly correspond, through Valmont. But the latter is occupied with bigger game than Cécile. Nothing will satisfy him but to seduce and ruin Madame de Tourvel, a profoundly religious and sensitive woman, whose husband, a noted judge, is at Dijon, whilst she is the guest of Valmont's aged aunt, Madame Rosemonde. It is at her château that the nephew opens his campaign. Valmont is well aware that his reputation as a seducer is known to Madame de Tourvel, and he realizes, too, that her religion will prove a formidable obstacle. That, however, merely enhances the excitement of the battle: 'I will dare,' he exclaims, 'to ravish her from the God she adores . . . I shall be the true god whom she prefers.' Merteuil warns him cynically that religious women, even when they do fall, offer but *demi-jouissances*; but for Valmont it is the chase and not the banquet that counts.

Madame de Tourvel, having been informed as to the character of Valmont, is curious enough about him to order her servants to watch his movements, whilst he, having read *Clarissa*, arranges to be surprised in the act of doing good by stealth. With Tartuffian art he feigns devotion, awakens the interest and pity of Madame de Tourvel, and, after a passionate declaration of love, kisses her. At this moment, he might have achieved his object by taking advantage of the lady's agitation. But he nobly resists this *désir de jeune homme*; in an unworthy moment, in an instant of weakness, Valmont had almost sacrificed his real plan. Madame de Tourvel must be made exquisitely conscious of every step in her degradation. Nor must she have, like Julie, 'les plaisirs du vice et les honneurs de la vertu.' 'Let her surrender,' says Valmont, 'but let her struggle. Without the strength to conquer, let her have the strength to resist. She must savour at her leisure the sentiment of her weakness and be constrained to admit her defeat.' This hellish scheme he discusses in every detail with Madame de Merteuil.

After her momentary agitation, Madame de Tourvel refuses to open Valmont's letters and begs him to go. He finds out, by corrupting her maid, that his letters have produced an effect : Madame de Tourvel treasures them, and has been seen by her maid crying over them. With less pleasure, Valmont discovers that Madame de Volanges has warned Madame de Tourvel against him and depicted him in his true colours to her friend. In revenge, he resolves to ruin Cécile himself. First, however, he pretends to give way to the pleadings of Madame de Tourvel and goes to Paris, where he amuses himself by sending her, from the bed of an actress, a romantic letter which is a masterpiece of *double entendre*. To his delight, Madame de Tourvel gradually reaches the stage of despair. She admits her love, throwing herself on her lover's generosity and honour. 'The fervent prayers,' writes Valmont to his accomplice, 'the humble supplications, everything that mortals, in their fear, offer to their divinity, I receive from her.'

Merteuil, during this time, has not been idle. Danceney, whom she regards as another Saint-Preux, 'le tendre Danceney' annoys her by his timidity; he is apparently content to write despairing notes to Cécile until Doomsday. Madame de Merteuil, therefore, concocts a brilliant plan. By secretly informing Madame de Volanges of the correspondence between her daughter and Danceney she gains her entire confidence; at the same time she consoles the young lovers and arranges that Cécile shall go to Madame Rosemonde's.

Here Valmont, in his role of best friend to the chevalier, persuades Cécile to let him duplicate the key of her room in order to facilitate delivery of the chevalier's letters. The result is, of course, the seduction of Cécile, which is described in a letter to Merteuil, with cold-blooded and lingering enjoyment. Morally speaking, she is raped; but in a court of law, Valmont would come off without a stain on his character.

Suddenly, Madame de Tourvel disappears. In a pathetic letter to Madame Rosemonde, she confesses that she is in love. The old lady, in reply, writes in the tone of Claire d'Orbe to Julie d'Étange: 'However, do not lose heart. Nothing ought to be impossible to a fine soul like yours; and were you to have the misfortune to succumb (which God forbid!), believe me, my dear, you must at least remember for your consolation that you fought with all your strength. And then, divine grace, when it pleases, can achieve what human wisdom cannot do.' Valmont, in a cold rage, has put his servant on Madame de Tourvel's track; and, to while away the time, amuses himself by corrupting Cécile, for whom he prepares a catechism of debauchery. On discovering that Madame de Tourvel is in Paris, he writes to her confessor to arrange a meeting on the pretext that he has important papers to hand over to her before he himself goes into retreat. The good priest thus becomes an innocent actor in this blasphemous farce, and, by his complaisance, brings about the interview, which culminates in the total surrender of Madame de Tourvel.

In portraying this crisis, Laclos surpasses himself. After his victory Valmont is strangely disconcerted. Madame de Tourvel is like a woman in a trance, 'seeming neither to think, to listen, nor to hear.' Only when he tells her that she has made him for ever happy, is she aroused from her torpor. '"Your happiness?" she said. "Are you happy, then?" I redoubled my protestations. "And happy through me? . . . I feel," she said, "that that idea consoles and comforts me."' And in writing to Valmont's aunt, Madame de Tourvel insists that she has no regrets. 'It is not that I have no cruel moments; but in my most heart-rending hours, when I feel I cannot stand the torture any longer, I say to myself: Valmont is happy; and everything vanishes at that idea, or rather it transforms everything into pleasure.'

In all her letters, Madame de Merteuil twits Valmont with his romantic infatuation. Her contempt eventually gives way to irritation and to jealousy. In Paris, Madame de Tourvel surprises

* P

Valmont in a carriage with a *fille de joie* who, at a remark made by her companion, stares at Madame de Tourvel and bursts into raucous laughter. The latter, with death in her heart, sends him a desperate letter, upbraiding him for his treachery. The affair is, however, plausibly explained by Valmont, who plays the comedy of the outraged and misunderstood lover, which effectually brings his mistress to heel. Merteuil, to whom he relates the incident, is not at all amused, regarding the reconciliation as a sign of pitiable weakness. To Valmont she sends the draft of a brutal letter of rupture with orders to forward it immediately to his mistress. Valmont, to prove that he is not the victim of ridiculous sentimentality, sends on the note to Madame de Tourvel, who, on receiving it, goes at once into a convent.

In yielding to Merteuil's ultimatum, Valmont sacrificed Madame de Tourvel to his principles; but he is secretly enraged because, at the same time, he acted as the instrument of Merteuil's jealousy. She, meanwhile, has become the mistress of Danceney and, in her sensual infatuation, offends Valmont by refusing to forgo a rendezvous with her chevalier when her accomplice visits her in town. This elicits a summary command to give up the chevalier, 'a marital letter,' observes Merteuil with malicious amusement. In revenge, Valmont arranges a meeting between Danceney and Cécile, and Madame de Merteuil is deserted for the *ingénue*. War is now declared. From Merteuil, Danceney learns all the truth about Cécile and Valmont. A duel ensues in which Valmont is killed. On hearing the news Madame de Tourvel dies. Cécile, whose shame is now known to her mother, takes the veil, and Merteuil's crimes become public property. To avoid bankruptcy proceedings she escapes to Holland, where, hopelessly disfigured by smallpox which costs her the sight of one eye, she drags out a miserable existence.

Such, in outline, is the novel which shocked the public of 1782 by its cynical audacity, and to this day remains one of the most curious social documents of the period. The libertinism of the closing seventeenth century, against which Molière reacted with such violence in his *Don Juan*, throve and blossomed in the Regency and, later, under the Pompadour. Yet its rare fruits set and ripened in a more capricious climate, exposed alternately to the parching breath of Newtonian reason and to the humid warmth of Rousseauistic sensibility. To this dual influence *Les Liaisons dangereuses* owes its strange and bitter savour, as of intellectualism touched with decay. The libertinism of the Regency, of men like the foul

Vendôme, of women like the marquise de Prie, assumed the form of a refined and perverted eroticism, somewhat resembling the lechery of Rochester's poetry. The libertinism of Valmont and of Madame de Merteuil is more intellectual and, therefore, more inhuman. It cannot, for example, be compared even with the sadism of Richardson's Lovelace, which is mainly physical. That of *Les Liaisons dangereuses*, on the contrary, is almost spiritual. The ambition of Valmont is to rape Madame de Tourvel's soul as well as her body. He visualizes himself as the Evil One, lurking in the holy wafer. Of this *satanisme*, as the French romantic decadents were to call it, there exists not a trace in our writers of the eighteenth century, although, in the succeeding age, Byron was mildly affected by it, a fact that possibly explains his extraordinary reputation in France. In recent years, M. André Gide has founded a sort of *chapelle* by following in the track of Valmont, who is the eighteenth-century prototype of his Immoralist. It is interesting to note that both Valmont and Madame de Merteuil are vigorous exponents of what M. Gide calls, in his odd jargon, the *acte gratuit*. In plainer language, they translate their most vicious impulses into action, unrestrained by moral or social scruples. In *Les Caves du Vatican*, M. Gide pictures a sombre individual who, in order to prove to himself that he possesses free will, performs the *acte gratuit* of throwing a complete stranger out of a moving train. Valmont's brutal letter of rupture to Madame de Tourvel may also be described as an *acte gratuit*, although, to do justice to Laclos, he contrives to make it seem quite credible, in view of Valmont's previous conduct and character.

Laclos claimed that he wrote his novel with a moral object; but in the eighteenth century every one wrote with a moral object. His unfinished essay on *L'Éducation des Femmes* reveals him, however, as a fervent Rousseauist, and casts a retrospective light upon *Les Liaisons dangereuses*, which is evidently an attack levelled not merely at eighteenth-century systems of feminine education, but at a system of civilization which has resulted in the enslavement of woman by man. This idea is embodied in Madame de Merteuil, the 'new Delilah,' who was born, as she tells Valmont, 'to avenge my sex and to dominate yours.' The conduct of Merteuil represents, in an extreme degree, the feminine revolt against male tyranny. 'Having entered society,' she explains, 'at a time when, being still a girl, I was consecrated by my social condition to silence and inactivity, I seized the opportunity to observe and to reflect.' From that moment, all her energy and intelligence is employed to hide and to master her emotions and desires. Merteuil is a perfect example of the female Tartuffe. As a young widow, she establishes a reputation as a *rigoriste*, yet manages to satisfy her sexual caprices without fear of detection. 'By exploring my own heart, I saw that there is nobody who does not harbour some secret which must not be divulged.' A modern Delilah, she worms that secret from her lovers and is thus immune from scandal. Even the astute Valmont, who is involved in some dark political villainy, has been imprudent enough to confide in Merteuil. To this woman, love is an intellectual as well as a physical experience; a 'divinity' whose essence has been defiled by the false priests called lovers, whom sentimental women invariably confuse with the goddess herself. From these Madame de Merteuil stands proudly aloof. She is a true priestess who has spent a lifetime initiating herself in the mysteries of love. In her eyes all lovers are charlatans or fools, to be used only as instruments of pleasure and then discarded. Here already we have the romantic *femme fatale*, the Lélia of the eighteenth century, but not yet, like George Sand's heroine, a sexless Lélia, since it is her sensual weakness for Danceney that finally ruins her.

Cécile de Volanges is the product of convent education. Ignorant, fleshly, and insipid, she belongs to the category scornfully dismissed by Merteuil as 'machines à plaisir.' Madame de Tourvel presents a more interesting study. She is the typical *femme à directeur*, a woman whose whole life has been governed by religious principles. A thousand ordinary men might attack her virtue and fail; Valmont succeeds because he is exceptional and has examined her defences with the eye of an expert. Lovelace was defeated by Clarissa owing to his lack of patience and intelligence. In the early stages, as, for example, in contriving the 'Rosebud' comedy, he was on the right track, but abandoned it for the cruder, shock tactics of the amateur. Valmont, on the contrary, exploits Madame de Tourvel's high sense of justice, her sensibility, and Christian charity. Deceived by Valmont's little farce in the matter of the wretched, evicted family, she has a revulsion of feeling, and asks herself whether she has not committed the sin of the Pharisee. Valmont, the opportunist, is quick to profit by this weakness, and holds out an additional lure which, to a religious woman, is irresistible. Madame de Tourvel is certain that she can reclaim him. In the process, she mistakes the nature of her own sensibility and becomes the victim of her goodness of heart. In pleading the cause of the unfortunate women he has ruined, she becomes entangled in the outer meshes of the web; and when Valmont perfidiously asks for her help, and tells her that she has taught him at last to know the difference between the higher love and mere sensuality, Madame de Tourvel experiences all the glowing emotions of an evangelist. Had she pursued her original policy of 'silence and oblivion,' her destiny might have taken another course. Cécile de Volanges was ruined because her mother allowed a stranger to win her daughter's confidence. Madame de Tourvel falls because she established confidential relations with a noted libertine. In confessing her fears to Madame Rosemonde, she wilfully closes her eyes to her actual situation, knowing in her heart that she should have consulted Madame de Volanges. But Valmont's aunt will sympathize with her nephew and talk about him. That, and not advice, is what Madame de Tourvel desires.

The subtle Valmont, of course, intercepts this correspondence and plays the comedy of the devil who is sick. His indulgent aunt, alarmed at her nephew's strange melancholy and at his sinister allusion to 'la grande affaire de ma vie,' communicates her fears to Madame de Tourvel. Thus, at the fatal meeting in Paris, the dice are loaded in Valmont's favour. Convinced that he is about to go into retreat, she is torn asunder by conflicting emotions. Valmont, after all, has proved the stronger, since he can apparently renounce her without great difficulty. Yet is not this blasphemy; for is not Valmont returning to 'their common Father'? On his arrival at her house, she finds that his resolve is not a voluntary one; it was dictated by despair. The duel is hopelessly unequal. Valmont's every move has been carefully rehearsed. He knows what he wants and Madame de Tourvel does not. In an access of cleverly acted despair, Valmont delivers his heroic, farewell speech. He will make the great sacrifice and pass out of her life, even though it costs him his own. 'Whilst I spoke thus, I felt her heart beating violently; I observed the change in her expression; above all, I saw the tears that choked her, yet flowed but slowly and painfully. Only then did I resolve to pretend to go away. So, holding me back by force: "No, listen to me," she said, quickly. "Let me go," I replied. "You shall listen to me! I insist." "I must leave you, I must." "No," she cried. At this last word she rushed, or rather fell fainting into my arms.' So Madame de Tourvel is seduced and Valmont's triumph is complete. But, as Baudelaire suggests, is it not Madame de Merteuil who kills her? I wonder.

The assumption is, obviously, that Valmont, but for the gibes and stings of his accomplice, would have been gradually changed by Madame de Tourvel's love. Laclos is not such an optimist as to believe in these changes of heart. Sooner or later, Valmont would have returned to his 'principles'; and his mistress, after nameless agony, to hers. The letter was a merciful, though brutal, stab.

With the after-life of his heroine, Laclos is not concerned. That, as he would doubtless have agreed with Rabelais, is 'matter of breviary.' Richardson and Jean-Jacques made it matter of fiction and, being artists of genius, they succeeded; the latter, however, only up to a point. For I consider that the *Nouvelle Héloïse* would have been a stronger novel had the author sacrificed his celestial *dénouement*. This criticism may not be levelled, however, at Richardson, whose master theme is not love. Clarissa dies because she has the mystic conviction that her 'state of preparation' is over. In His divine goodness, Jehovah had deigned to single her out for an exemplary chastisement, as a prelude to the eternal joys of sainthood. But the central theme of the *Nouvelle Héloïse is* love. By obeying the impulse of her 'natural goodness,' and aided by divine grace, Julie conquered and spiritualized her passion. The drama is finished and, as in real life, the flame of love is smothered and quenched. Such a reality Rousseau could not contemplate; so God, in His infinite mercy, removes Julie from this earth before she has time to slide back into the pit. From this we must infer that Saint-Preux is the unconscious rival of God Himself. It is Fatime saying to Orosmane of Zaïre: 'Tu balançais son Dieu dans son cœur alarmé.' By vastly different methods, therefore, and without knowing it, Saint-Preux almost achieves the ambition of Valmont. And if he does not ravish Julie from the God whom she adores, it is because the Rousseau deity does not play fair. He has, in fact, recourse to the classic subterfuges of a Zeus, and behaves like a vulgar *deus ex machina*.

CHAPTER XVI

THE LEOPARD'S SPOTS

A PEDANT, even when he is right, is a barren creature; but the very errors of a true scholar are stimulating and fertile, because they are born of enthusiasm. Such a scholar was Joseph Texte, whose survey of Anglo-French literary relations in the eighteenth century is a pioneering feat of the first order. Yet of one thing I am morally certain. It was never Texte's intention that his book should degenerate into what Flaubert would have dubbed a *Dictionnaire d'Idées reçues*. That, however, has been its fate. A generation of industrious students has come and gone. They have embroidered upon and enlarged Texte's vast canvas, but, curiously enough, none has seriously questioned his suggestive and important theory that 'from 1760 till the end of the century almost no French novel escaped the absorbing influence of *Clarissa*.' It is, therefore, with some trepidation that I find myself diverging more and more from the route mapped out by this able investigator. At the same time, I am fortified by the reflection that in this, as in any province, scholarship is doomed to become moribund unless it continues to examine the validity of accepted ideas. Now the refuting of what one imagines to be another man's errors is a solemn and, necessarily, a rather didactic business. But, in the process, it is often possible to acquire a new angle of vision which opens up fresh perspectives. Such, at any rate, has been my experience in reviewing Texte's remarks upon Diderot, Rétif de la Bretonne and their supposed indebtedness to Samuel Richardson. To quote his actual words: 'It was again of him [Richardson] that Diderot was thinking when he wrote *La Religieuse* . . . and as for Rétif, that popular and powerful painter of common life, he wrote his *Paysan perverti* under the influence of *Pamela* and boasts of it; it is after the manner of Richardson that Rétif claims to have portrayed "the whole progress of that corruption which invades an innocent and upright heart." ' [1]

To Diderot we shall return; for the moment let us observe what Rétif de la Bretonne actually thought and said about Richardson.

[1] For a detailed refutation of Texte's views see Appendix V.

In his *Monsieur Nicolas*, possibly the most amazing and most intimate autobiography ever printed, Rétif makes the following comment upon the origins of the *Paysan perverti*.[1] 'I had begun the manuscript in 1769 after reading a detached part of *Pamela* which I found by chance at Edme the bookseller's in the Collège de Presle. It was this reading which gave me first the idea of writing rustic letters in which a peasant is supposed to relate everything that happens in town.' Rétif then proceeds to tell us what every reader of his confessions can guess for himself, namely, that all the adventures narrated in *Le Paysan perverti* and in its sequel, *La Paysanne pervertie*, are based either upon his own experiences or on those of his sister Geneviève. And in the novels, Rétif appears as Edmond; whilst Geneviève becomes Ursule Rameau. No doubt, to some extent, their misfortunes and adventures have been 'romanced' because, as it happens, the actuality was so strange and so pungent as to require such edulcoration. The point, however, to be remembered is that Rétif, the novelist, had no recourse to the imagination of Richardson. In reality, he had lived through experiences the bare recital of which would have made the author of *Clarissa* shudder with pious horror.

There is no trace in *Monsieur Nicolas* of a Rousseau's artistry, but it is written with sincerity and vigour. Nowhere does the author give evidence of that *amour-propre* which so often induced Jean-Jacques to tone down and to justify certain of his actions. On the contrary, with an exhibitionism which to many must appear scabrous, Rétif de la Bretonne derives an almost masochistic pleasure from the confession of emotions which, although more human than is generally supposed, are apt to startle even the hardened twentieth-century reader when he meets them in cold print. Probably the truest description of these confessions is that vouchsafed by the author himself: 'I wanted to write a true book, entirely true from beginning to end; to depict the events of a natural life, and to bequeath it to posterity as a treatise on moral anatomy. I am sure that I am offering an interesting and faithful reflection; faithful by the truth of its pictures, and interesting by the variety and the multiplicity of the adventures which filled my life; by my boldness in naming everything, in compromising other people, in sacrificing them to public utility. I possessed lively passions but none of the passions that brutalize; such as gluttony, drunkenness, or indolence. I have always displayed the greatest activity in love. It was the need of

[1] The original edition of 1794–7, tome viii, p. 4578.

love and sexual enjoyment which led me to desire, to seek, and to encounter that crowd of adventures which, in a single man, cause you astonishment. Well! I have omitted an infinity of unimportant, chance amours.'

Issued from an old family of peasant farmers long settled in Saci, Rétif de la Bretonne became acquainted with vice at a very early age, and, so to speak, on his father's doorstep. When a mere boy, he met the brothers Courtcou, two sadists who occasionally dabbled in that particularly foul and silly brand of the occult called diabolism. As a chorister at Bicêtre in 1746, Rétif also came into contact with homosexualists, from whose baneful influence, however, he was saved, as he naïvely tells us, by the charitable offices of an amorous nun, known as Sœur Mélanie. The lad was educated by the good brothers of Courgis, who quickly discovered that their pupil possessed an inordinate appetite for sexual pleasure. It was, indeed, at this stage that Rétif began to lay the basis of his famous *Calendrier*, a daily journal of his erotic successes containing a minute description of his mistresses and their habits.

For some years Rétif worked as a printer's apprentice in Auxerre, where he lodged with his master, Fournier, a dangerous libertine who, with his wife, occupies an important place in the *Paysan-Paysanne*. As in the novel, so also in fact, the apprentice seduced his mistress; the Madame Parangon of the book is no other than Madame Fournier. Just prior to this crisis, Rétif had come under the baleful power of an ex-Cordelier, Gaudet d'Arras, at whose suggestion it was that he violated the chastity of Madame Fournier. Gaudet encouraged the youth's natural proclivities to debauchery and, in his sinister, perverted fashion, extracted a vicarious pleasure from the spectacle of Rétif's *rage érotique*.

From 1755 until 1759, we discover Rétif in Paris, still accompanied by his Mephistopheles who introduces him to the society of prostitutes and actresses. The sudden death, in 1759, of Madame Fournier momentarily suspended the excesses of Rétif, and in the same year he married an Englishwoman, referred to in *Monsieur Nicolas* as Miss Harriet. After a sojourn in the country, in order to recover from the shock of matrimony—for his blue-eyed *ingénue* decamped with her husband's money—Rétif came back to Paris, and, nothing daunted, again plunged into wedlock. This time it was a French-woman, Agnès Lebègue, but a *fausse Agnès* who, if she made no direct raid on Rétif's coffers, presented him with several royal sets of antlers, and by her extravagance reduced her husband to absolute poverty.

Where an ordinary man might easily have taken to drink, Rétif took to scribbling, having, indeed, acquired by this time a store of experience which, for its wealth and variety, is unrivalled. This he now proceeded to alchemize into literature. The bare enumeration of his works would fill a large bibliography; it is enough, therefore, to indicate their general nature. Considered as art, most of Rétif's output is quite negligible, and only two or three of his novels, the *Paysan-Paysanne*, *La Vie de mon Père*, and *La Dernière Aventure d'un Homme de quarante Ans*, really deserve to be recommended to the modern reader. The others are rubbishy, sentimental productions, mere echoes of Prévost in his worst manner, and of Mme de Villedieu in her normal vein. Yet nothing written by Rétif can be quite ignored by the student of French eighteenth-century thought and manners. He will discover in *Les Nuits de Paris* and in *Les Contemporaines* a rich fund of attractive information on Parisian social types. The second of these books, comprising, as it does, a long series of feminine portraits drawn from every conceivable trade, is really a sort of *Midinettes' Who's Who*. *Le Pied de Fanchette*, so often reprinted and still much in evidence in the windows of Paris booksellers who cater to the odd tastes of elderly foreign gentlemen, reveals its author as what the Germans call a *Schuhverehrer*, or, as we say, a fetishist. Much more significant are the *Idées singulières*, including Rétif's pamphlets on social reform, *La Mimographe*, *Le Pornographe*, *Le Thesmographe*, *L'Anthropographe*, and *Les Gynographes*, in which he exposes his ideas on the proper governance of actresses, prostitutes, jurists, and humanity in general.

Such is the bare skeleton of an existence which, for the extent and variety of its experiences, must have few parallels. 'I was born,' confides Rétif, 'to be indebted to women for everything—for pleasure, pain, and even death.' This is the simple truth. Women dominated his entire life, affording him a joy that was not, however, wholly sensual; for his erotic fury often subsided into moments of idyllic calm. We have mentioned Madame Fournier, and there were others, like Jeannette Rousseau, whom he loved with a pure and tranquil devotion. In the *Paysan-Paysanne* one can detect echoes of this struggle between the Casanova and the Saint-Preux who wrestled for mastery in the soul of this amazing creature.

In commenting upon the genesis and the fashioning of his masterpiece, the *Paysan-Paysanne*, the author concludes: 'I saw, I felt, I transcribed; sentiment was my only guide.' Must we take him literally and agree, for instance, with his German biographer, Dr.

Dühren, that Rétif had little imagination, being, in fact, the mere stenographer of his own experience? I do not think so. It is, of course, extraordinarily hard to define exactly what is meant by the trite expression, 'creative imagination.' Certain novelists there are, like Richardson, who seem able to dispense almost entirely with personal experience; to conjure up, as it were, out of the deep, characters and situations vibrant with the illusion of reality. That kind of creative imagination Rétif did not possess; always, in his flights, he took off from the concrete runway of the actual.

It is very evident, when we read the *Monsieur Nicolas* in conjunction with the *Paysan-Paysanne*, that Rétif was endowed with imagination of a powerful sort. The autobiography has the genuine stamp of truth, but is not a work of art. Here we have raw material, picturesque yet shapeless, awaiting only the magic touch of the artist who will lend it pattern, rhythm, and that sense of inevitability which emerges from the *Paysan-Paysanne*. In their crude state, the characters and situations are as yet merely interesting; they have really no cosmic meaning. Until subjected to the illuminating and shaping influence of the author's mind, they strike one simply as odd people and unusual happenings. Gaudet d'Arras is an excellent case in point. In *Monsieur Nicolas*, he is undeniably a strong and arresting, but a shadowy figure. However, as we shall see, when the artist takes him in hand, the character of this ex-monk and pervert undergoes a tremendous change: Gaudet grows in stature, looming up at last as a gigantic, sinister, and truly Balzacian creation, as the very genius of evil working to produce good. No; Rétif did not transcribe. All his characters are composite, representing, as he confesses, the fusion of two or sometimes three originals. Thus we are confronted by an imagination which must be called creative though it differs essentially from that of a Richardson. When our author, in an effort to be dramatic, ventures too far from his base of actuality, he loses himself in a forest of incredible and luxuriant fantasies. Therefore, he very seldom wanders far afield, and, in order to achieve the illusion of reality, usually follows a road almost directly opposed to that pursued by Richardson who, in *Clarissa*, at least, sets out from a situation that is barely probable, and by sheer force of genius eventually forces us to believe in the existence of people who never did exist. There is, therefore, very little kinship between the two artists. If Rétif resembles any other novelist, it is Jean-Jacques, with the very important reserve that he has practically no lyrical gifts. So, even when he exaggerates

the actual, Rétif de la Bretonne never soars into the empyrean;
if he makes strange discoveries in human nature, if he reveals and
magnifies unsuspected motives and emotions, the habitual object
of his curiosity is the seat of the senses, and not that penumbra
which veils the shrine of the spirit.

In its general conception the *Paysan-Paysanne* is Balzacian. It
narrates the fortunes of a peasant family which, through two of its
members, Edmond and Ursule, is drawn into contact with urban
morals and manners. From this initial situation arises a jungle of
complications. How varied and numerous they are we learn from
the extensive repertory of characters appended by the author to one
of the later editions of his book. Here, again, is a Balzacian idea,
since Rétif's 'Cerfbeer and Christophe'[1] indicates very vividly the remarkable scope and precocity of his artistic method, and announces
that fertile theme of social solidarity and interdependence later
exploited by Balzac and by Zola. Rétif, too, has the gift for seeing
his characters simultaneously as individuals and as group-units.
At this stage in the development of the French novel, such a blend
of the synthetic and the analytic, such deftness in the manipulation
of psychological perspectives, can only be described as wonderful.
Besides, never once does Rétif permit us to lose sight of the genera-
tive idea, nestling at the core of the vast and complicated organism
to which he gave the name of *Le Paysan et la Paysanne pervertis*. Not
once are we allowed to forget that its leading *motif* is the inevitable
and essential contrast between the mind of the man who dwells
in cities and that of the man who tills the soil. Backwards and forwards we move between two separate climates of the soul; realizing
always that there is no intermediate, temperate zone where towns-
man and peasant can meet. To Edmond, as to Ursule, the air of
the capital is miasmal; it shrivels and poisons their souls, as it
bloats and gangrenes their bodies.

Edmond is sent to Auxerre to study painting under the direction
of M. Parangon, a lecher who has completely alienated the affections of an admirable wife by his brutality and unfaithfulness.
Parangon has, as mistress, a cousin of his wife's, called Manon
Palestine, whom he has rendered enceinte. With great cunning,
therefore, he arranges with Manon to inveigle Edmond into marriage
by playing upon the *amour-propre* of the country bumpkin, who is
accordingly treated with the utmost hauteur until, smarting under
Manon's affected contempt, he is seized with an overpowering desire

---

[1] The compilers of the indispensable *Répertoire de la Comédie Humaine*.

to gain her respect. Edmond meanwhile conceives a sympathy, based largely on common suffering, for Manon's much bullied maid, Tiennette, whom, indeed, he would have married but for the fear of his father's anger. The Rameau family honour will not permit of an alliance with a servant. Besides, Parangon stages a little tableau which convinces Edmond that Tiennette is his master's paramour and, since Manon now shows herself in a softer light, the apprentice walks into the trap.

At this point, however, Gaudet d'Arras takes the stage and the atmosphere becomes charged with portents. Gaudet is a Franciscan who has been forced into orders by his putative father. Possessing a genius for intrigue and an astonishing knowledge of human nature, two attributes which his claustral meditations have fortified and matured, Gaudet has no intention of remaining a monk, and already, on meeting Edmond, is about to renounce his vows in order to carry into practice a certain atheistic philosophy of life of which he has long dreamed in the silence of his convent. In Edmond he sees the predestined instrument of his schemes, so Gaudet resolves to mould the boy's destiny, to refashion and dominate his mind, and, incidentally, to assure his material fortune. But first of all he must be cured of his 'prejudices' and, with this in view, the monk subjects Edmond to an insidious course of training in libertinism.

Madame Parangon, a chaste but over-sentimental woman, returns now to Auxerre after a prolonged absence and quickly uncovers her husband's plot. On learning the true situation, Edmond's natural impulse is to upbraid Manon for her duplicity, but Gaudet counsels another line of conduct. The apprentice, therefore, secretly marries Manon, whose mother agrees to transfer the family fortune to her son-in-law. Manon, however, has now fallen desperately in love with her husband and makes spontaneous confession of her relations with Parangon. Gaudet contrives that she shall discover a cynical letter written to him by Edmond, with the result that the girl, on realizing that she has been used as a mere stepping-stone to her husband's material advancement, commits suicide.

Already thoroughly corrupted by his master's doctrines, Edmond visits his native village, where he seduces a young cousin, Laurette, who passes with her child into the care of Gaudet. Heavily weighed down by the parental curse, Edmond plunges recklessly into vice. His sister Ursule is also now at Auxerre as the ward of Madame Parangon who, as the monk evilly suggests, regards her with more than sisterly affection. In her anxiety to save Ursule from her

husband's lustful advances, Madame Parangon momentarily over-
looks Gaudet, who proposes to give Ursule the benefit of that
education which has already transformed the character of her
brother.

Through Ursule, Edmond learns to his delight that his passion
for his master's wife, which is, by the way, wholly unsensual, is
shared by Madame Parangon, though she is resolved never to admit
it.   Her lover, now reinstated in the family favour, revisits the country, and in order to escape his hopeless obsession, contemplates
marriage with a vine-grower's daughter.   This scheme he imparts
to Madame Parangon, who approves, although with mingled
emotions.   Her own dream had been to marry Edmond to her
sister, Fanchette, for much the same reasons which induced Rousseau's Julie to desire a union between her lover and Claire.   But
now Gaudet scornfully throws cold water on Edmond's plan and,
after delivering a characteristic homily on marriage, urges his pupil
to dismiss his prejudices and, by possessing Madame Parangon, to
rid his mind of that 'viscosity' which is interfering with his intellectual development.   In an access of lust, Edmond rapes his
mistress and she becomes pregnant.

Ursule has also turned out to be an apt pupil and, by Gaudet's
contriving, she is violated by a nobleman infatuated with her
beauty.   This situation, by the exercise of discreet blackmail, the
monk utilizes in order to extract a substantial income for his
protégée, whose child is adopted by its father's family.   Edmond's
sister, however, now disconcerts even her tutor by her extravagance
and by the intemperance of her desires.   In vain Gaudet preaches
the golden rules of prudence and moderation.   After a delirious
career as the most expensive *cocotte* in Paris, Ursule falls victim to
the vindictiveness of one of her dupes, an old Italian banker.   She
is abducted, forcibly married to a street-porter, and after being
subjected to every conceivable form of brutality, is discovered by
Edmond in a brothel.   He, too, is now in a sorry plight, for he
becomes the pimp of his own sister.   Gaudet, released at last
from his vows, comes to the rescue, and wreaks a typical
revenge on the Italian by abducting his daughter and reducing
her to the situation of Ursule.   With diabolical refinement, moreover, he arranges a meeting between the father and child in a house
of ill-fame.   Now rotten with disease, Ursule is admitted to La
Salpêtrière, whence, after many years, she returns in penitence to
her home in Burgundy.

Gaudet, now a free agent, feels that the moment is ripe for taking Edmond into partnership. Together they will embark on a grandiose scheme for the reform of social abuses, but first, however, they must have wealth. The ex-monk, therefore, marries an elderly and rich woman and persuades Edmond to wed her mother. Soon, thanks to their joint fortune, both obtain important administrative posts, and by secretly playing into each other's hands, acquire immense power and add to their riches. Unfortunately, suspicion is aroused by the sudden death of Madame Gaudet and the brothers-in-law are arrested. In a berserker rage they fall upon their guards, with the result that Edmond is condemned to the galleys, whilst his tempter, rather than face execution, kills himself. Eventually, Edmond is pardoned, and after years of wandering returns to his village where, ignorant of the fact that Ursule is married to her marquis, he murders her in order to save her soul. He himself is crushed under the wheels of his own carriage and, by a queer trick of fate, the stone that made his horses bolt was thrown by a girl whom he had ruined.

In weaving his plot, it will be seen that Rétif betrays no lack of inventive power, and, indeed, in his closing episodes he prepares us for the exuberance of the early romantic novelists. The book possesses, nevertheless, a sinewy and close-knit armature. In any case, it does not reveal any marked derivative traits, either Richardsonian or otherwise. There exists an advertisement, obviously prepared by the author himself, in which he draws attention to his originality.[1] 'The author,' says Rétif, 'has created a genre of his own, which is as remote from the *romanesque* ideality of our languorous novelists as it is from the unnatural sombreness of the anglomaniacs.' And, in fact, only in two very minor incidents can one detect an echo of Richardson. In the account of the cruel treatment shown to Ursule by the marquis after their marriage of convenience, it is possible that Rétif remembered Pamela's Mr. B., although the marquis's conduct may be perfectly well explained by the events preceding his marriage. Again, Madame Parangon's last will and testament, if very different in tone and in length from that of Clarissa, was probably suggested by the 1766 French edition of Richardson's novel, which, for the first time, included the heroine's dying injunctions. Apart from this, the *Paysan-Paysanne* is quite original and, in its prevailing colour, absolutely French. Even the rustic interludes which, according to the author himself, owe their

[1] At the end of the first part of his *Nouveaux Mémoires d'un Homme de Qualité* (1774).

raison d'être to his reading of *Pamela*, are unlike anything written by our English novelist. Inspired by an obvious half-truth, the Teutonic Grimm christened Rétif *le Rousseau du ruisseau*, implying thereby that, in matters of love, he was an artist of the gutter. In point of fact, he does remind one of Rousseau, but for reasons which the facetious and snobbish Grimm had not the wit to see.

Edmond worships Madame Parangon with a strange blend of adoration and cruel possessiveness. Immediately after his crime, his attitude recalls the mood of Saint-Preux—chivalrous, remorseful, and submissive. And Madame Parangon, though free from Julie's pedantry, has all the maternalism of Rousseau's heroine. Older and wiser than her lover, she tries desperately to shield him against the machinations of Parangon and, above all, against the corrupt teachings of Gaudet. She is, however, morally stronger than Julie, and has, indeed, a fair share of Madame de Tourvel's *rigorisme*. Rétif, it is true, intended to portray in her a virtuous woman ruined by too much sensibility, a woman in whom 'the purest virtue is allied to the most ardent passions.' He speaks of her as a frail woman, yet no frail woman repulsing the passionate advances of the man she loves could have steeled herself, as does Madame Parangon, to cry: 'Stop! If you are as fastidious as I have always believed you to be, there is one reason which must restrain you. Monsieur Parangon sometimes uses his rights over me.' Only a woman of rare force of will could thus violate her *pudeur*. Not till later, in a terribly lucid examination of her own conduct, does she realize the futility of the plea which it cost her so much to utter. 'I should neither have betrayed anger nor have accepted a reconciliation. A woman is lost when she stoops to such alternatives. "Would you consent to share me with another man?" was tantamount to saying: "If you want me, I am yours."' This is not the language of a 'frail' woman.

Edmond is Rétif himself, sensual to an incredible degree and endowed with all a sensualist's facile sentimentality. As a result of his carnal intemperance, he is naïvely unaware of the boundaries which divide sexual morality from abnormality. So familiar is he with the sexual act in all its variants that his moral contours are hopelessly besmudged; and even after his incestuous relations with his sister—for he commits this infamy—Edmond experiences no genuine horror or remorse. Tenderness, friendship, love, and lust no longer exist on different planes for him. In an access of nervous excitation, he is liable to traverse the whole gamut of the emotions in a flash.

The moral sense, that refracting agent which enables the normal man to view his conduct as in a spectrum, becomes, in the case of Edmond, atrophied, and finally ceases to perform its function.

A creature of sensations and of emotions, Edmond is as wax in the hands of the intellectual Gaudet d'Arras.   If at first the monk's evil influence is counterbalanced by his pupil's cult for Madame Parangon and by persistent memories of parental teachings, the grandiose nature of his mentor's schemes appeals to the romantic and social reformer in Edmond.   Besides, he sees too many examples of his friend's apparently disinterested love not to be tenderly grateful to Gaudet.   Extreme in everything, even after being condemned to the galleys, Edmond preserves his old habit of self-dramatization. 'They will call me,' he exclaims in a mood of self-abasement, 'the parricide, the fratricide, the ingrate, the perjurer, the chastised of God and man.   The country people, when they pronounce my name, will shudder with horror.   Trembling, they will relate my story. They will make of it a ballad which will be sung.   The mention of my name in the evenings round the fireside will terrify the young men and maidens.   The place where my comrades went with me will be deserted; they will be afraid lest they see my phantom dragging its chains.'

Until we come to Balzac, there is no character in European fiction who may be compared in stature or in originality with Gaudet d'Arras. Of this Rétif was perfectly aware when he referred to him as 'the most extraordinary man . . . in any of our novels.'   Therefore, in the *Paysan-Paysanne*, the true centre of irradiation is Gaudet d'Arras.   To him the novel owes its vitality. Directly and indirectly, he influences the destiny of every other character in the book.   An illegitimate child, thrust into a vocation which he loathes, Gaudet becomes an atheist and a deliberate libertine.   Seen from the peak of his immense intellectual pride, the world consists of two kinds of men : the *plantes mouvantes* or those who are content merely to vegetate, and the *fleurs*, who, like himself, flourish in a special climate of their own, a climate charged with the lust for action and conquest.   During his long, enforced claustration, Gaudet has meditated upon the moral laws that compose the ordinary social code, and these, in the final analysis, he rejects as negligible 'prejudices.'   The precepts he inculcates upon Edmond betray the trend of his own philosophy.   In judging of the morality or immorality of an action, it is enough to ask oneself the question : 'Can it harm my existence or in any way diminish the pleasure which I derive from life?' If not, it is good, and, says Gaudet, one must then proceed to action, ruthlessly crushing all prejudice underfoot. His second axiom is that no such thing as spiritual love can exist between man and woman; here only sensation is possible and that must be tasted in moderation. Feminine chastity, *la pudeur*, is not an instinctive attribute, but simply one of Nature's devices for conserving the human species in temperate zones. It is but an excitant to desire; and the proof is that in hot climates, what Europeans call chastity is unknown. True, chastity, in the Gaudet sense, implies merely the observance of certain necessary social and hygienic rules. Thus, for example, married women are normally to be respected; whilst sexual enjoyment, which should be natural in its origin, must only be indulged in with moderation. Gaudet's attitude to incest is equally rational and specious. To quiet Edmond's passing remorse, he tells him that the prejudice against incest is but a *loi de décence*, and therefore cannot be infringed unless the incestuous act becomes publicly known. Indeed, to show that he has the courage of his own convictions, Gaudet secretly arranges a marriage between Edmond's children by Laurette and by Madame Parangon, a circumstance which invests the closing chapters of the novel with the direful gloom of an Ibsen play. It will be readily imagined, too, that our professor of immoralism has no difficulty in soothing the misgivings of Edmond and Ursule in regard to the question of rape. To the former he blandly points out that rape, whilst, no doubt, a socially deplorable act, springs, nevertheless, from natural laws which in themselves are admirable. God, Nature, and the Universal Principle, says Gaudet, are identical; therefore all that is, is right. To Ursule, he expounds a point of view peculiar to the libertines of the eighteenth century; and his striking phrase: 'La violée est toujours intéressante' is pregnant with significance. 'The woman who has been violated is interesting because she retains a sort of virginity which men find no less delicious to pluck than the other—that of the heart's consent.' This is the very flower of decadence, and the idea which is expressed in Gaudet's words reflects a fusion of the vital forces whose workings we have observed in the eighteenth-century French mind; the rational, the sensational, and the sentimental here combine, by some strange chemistry, to produce a new element of human corruption.

To Gaudet, the besetting vice of his age is its fly-blown sensibility; his immoralism is, therefore, almost wholly intellectual and sensual.

He allows himself, however, one indulgence. This is his passionate friendship for Edmond, which absorbs all the perverted tenderness of his heart. In wilfully corrupting the peasant, the monk is not simply glutting an immense creative desire; it is his absolute conviction that he can offer no greater proof of his love than by eradicating Edmond's 'prejudices' and by refashioning him after his own image. All Gaudet's thoughts and actions in relation to his pupil are disinterested. Indeed, so obsessed is the priest by his passion that he attains an incredible degree of self-immolation; ceasing, indeed, to enjoy contact with women unless they have first passed through the purifying medium of intercourse with his neophyte. Thus, in an access of impure exaltation, he writes to Edmond of Laure: 'Je l'ai préférée fatiguée par toi et encore rouge de tes baisers à une vierge qui n'aurait jamais aimé ni joui; cette bouche qui s'est collée sur la tienne m'en paraît plus voluptueuse.' Here, it will be noted, Rétif is moving in a region never before frequented by the novelist. More than a hundred years before Gide or Proust, he stretches the confines of the novel to admit the analysis of abnormal psychology.

What inspired Rétif to create this satanic and impressive figure? Richardson we may safely leave out of the discussion. In *Monsieur Nicolas*, alluding to Gaudet d'Arras, the author says abruptly: 'I knew this man.' Yet the Gaudet of the autobiography, as I have said, is but a pale shadow of the Gaudet we meet in the *Paysan-Paysanne*, and, moreover, in the years which elapsed between the writing of the first and the second parts of this novel, it is clear that Rétif's imagination had been very active, elaborating and deepening the traits of the original. In *Monsieur Nicolas* occurs a passage which affords an interesting clue to Rétif's artistic method. The Gaudet of actual life, he says, treated him with the respect accorded by his disciples to the Mahomet of Voltaire's famous tragedy, *Le Fanatisme*, in which, it will be recollected, a religious fanatic so dominates the soul of his neophyte, Séide, as to persuade him to commit parricide. In a footnote, Rétif explains that the Gaudet of his novel is, therefore, diametrically opposed to the Gaudet of reality. Evidently, then, the memory of Voltaire's play, combined with his personal experience of the living Gaudet d'Arras, suggested to Rétif the fertile idea of a young man spiritually enslaved by an older one. In the novel, as in fact, Gaudet harbours an unholy passion for his young friend. But Rétif the artist recast that situation, and in his novel portrays a Gaudet who dominates and perverts his pupil for the latter's weal—a demonic and Balzacian Gaudet. Yet, in a later metamorphosis this character borrows certain traits from the personality of the author himself. In outlining his plan for a 'moral and physical revolution' destined to rejuvenate the human race, the ex-monk is obviously inspired by Rétif the ideologist. 'Our great objective,' he grandly announces, 'will be to introduce the reign of philosophy and to establish it everywhere. We will labour to diminish all the great fortunes, and to increase those of the peasants by gradually making them landowners. To that end we will put into vogue a type of gallantry tinged with debauchery, and thus, so far as possible, ruin the seigneurs by obliging them to sell out. We will dismember the great fiefs and arrange that they shall be auctioned in lots. We will levy a considerable tax upon every luxury, such as carriages, servants, country-houses in the neighbourhood of Paris. . . . On the other hand, we will encourage the popular, inexpensive pleasures. We will see to it that these entertainments are established in the villages. . . . We will annihilate every idea that tends to regard as criminal what is dictated by nature. It shall no longer be a dishonour for an unmarried girl to have a child; yet prostitution shall be absolutely abolished.' These reforms, together with Gaudet's scheme to suppress all convents and monasteries, might easily have been lifted bodily from the *Idées singulières*.

There is, however, no trace of the author himself in the Gaudet of the last phase, which discloses, incidentally, a new and interesting aspect of the novelist's creative method. The ex-monk is accused of having poisoned his wife and is seized, whilst Edmond is also arrested as an accomplice. Gaudet, after an unsuccessful attempt to commit suicide, is brought to trial. In court, he protests that Edmond is innocent and assumes all the responsibilities for the murder of the jailers. The corpse of his wife is examined, but the doctors are puzzled to find no trace of poison. Interrogated anew, Gaudet, now weakened by loss of blood, vouchsafes only the sardonic remark: 'They know their business, do they not?' With stubborn contempt of his judges, he adheres to his original statement. Edmond is brought to the dock and rushes into the arms of his friend, only to be roughly dragged off by his warders. For a moment, Gaudet loses his iron self-control. 'Are you men or tigers? Monsters! You prevent two doomed and unhappy men from embracing each other. Away with you! You are unfit for me to talk to and from this moment my lips are sealed.' Where

had Rétif heard words like these if not in *Othello*, when Iago, in a
mood of similar, demonic pride, exclaims:

Demand me nothing. What you know, you know:
From this time forth I never will speak word.

There is a reminiscence of Shakespeare, too, in the account of
Gaudet's supreme moments. His last speech to the despairing
Edmond is fraught with dignity and resignation: '"Take heart. . . .
To you I have always spoken the truth. At this instant I am disinterested. My friendship for you was always sincere; its sole
motive was an absolute devotion. In that I found my pleasure.
I looked on you as my son and my handiwork. Whatever physical
enjoyment I experienced was more through you than through myself;
that is the truth. Your greatest misfortune is in losing me, but
remember that you have never abased yourself. Men may readily
declare that such and such a one is dishonoured; but they cannot dishonour him. Come, Edmond! Death is nothing. That I
realize more than ever at this supreme moment." As he concluded
these words, the priest made a sign. Gaudet smiled, and, as at
the moment one of his hands was free, he stretched it out, seized
a large nail which by chance had remained stuck at the foot of the
scaffold on which they were about to behead him, and suddenly
shouted to the priest: "Look, my friend! Here is the fruit I've
culled from your sermon. They shall not kill me and my destiny
will be complete." At the same moment he stabbed himself in
the breast, over the heart. He expired at once. Nevertheless, as
he was still palpitating, they cut off his head.'

There is an Elizabethan quality in Gaudet's elemental and
unexpected gesture. Like an arrow from the unseen, it plants
itself quivering in our consciousness. In this brutal transition from
philosophic musing to swift and grim action, I wonder if there is
not an echo of that supreme moment when Othello plunges the
sword into his own heart. Be that as it may, it is certain that, in
conceiving Gaudet, Rétif strikes a chord never before sounded by
a French writer. For the first time, undismayed by the spectre of
la Raison, a French writer surrenders himself absolutely to his
imagination and presents, in bold and flaring colours, the lineaments of a man whose moral code is unique and individual. Gaudet
is more than a character of fiction; he incarnates an extreme mood
of French civilization, combining, as he does, the dual forces of
eighteenth-century rationalism and sensibility. A super-*philosophe*,
he blends the epicureanism of the earlier libertines with the fanatical

humanitarianism of materialists like Diderot and D'Holbach. For the Rousseauistic and chivalrous sentimentality of Edmond he has nothing but contempt. Sexual love, as conceived by Jean-Jacques, he despises, because it implies the sacrifice of man's individualism and, in some sort, a degradation of the intellect. That is why he urges his pupil to rape Madame Parangon; because in Edmond's infatuation, Gaudet sees the persistence of an outworn Christian cult. In his new scheme of things only man shall command; women are to be relegated to the position they held in pagan times. That is why he fosters the philosophic idea of masculine friendship as opposed to bi-sexual love. Once launched on that dangerous current, he is swept into dark and troubled waters. Of this, it seems, Rétif became conscious at the close of his novel, when he insists, rather too eagerly, on the paternal nature of Gaudet's affection for his pupil. Actually, in view of the revelations contained in *Monsieur Nicolas*, it is impossible to escape another, less normal interpretation. There is no doubt but that in the attitude of Gaudet to Edmond we have already the situation later presented by Balzac, when he wrote of Vautrin and Lucien de Rubempré. And to have anticipated Balzac is in itself a title to fame.

In a century whose men of letters were not interested in the life of the lower classes, unless perhaps, like Vadé or the comte de Caylus, they found it amusing to imitate the picturesque language of the *Halles* or of the *guinguettes*, Rétif de la Bretonne juts out in strong relief. He is at once the Hogarth and the Greuze of the eighteenth-century French novel. Hogarthian and terrible are the scenes picturing the *débâcle* of Ursule and Edmond in the stews of the capital. In this atmosphere of brothels and procuresses, Rétif has no need to use his imagination; the bare reality is sufficiently dreadful. Those whose boast it is that they like to hear 'a spade called a spade' will be able to glut their desire for 'realism' in the pages of the *Paysan-Paysanne*. It is not, however, in these urban episodes that we must seek the Rétif who knew and sympathized with the miseries, the joys, and the occupations of the working classes. Paris he had explored more thoroughly even than Mercier; [1] yet the capital held him only by its women, and his interest in women, as we have seen, was somewhat limited. Rétif's outlook is distorted by the memory of his personal experience, and he is, therefore, prone to see only what is corrupt. But his scenes of peasant life betray sympathy and profound insight and, if he

---

[1] The author of *Le Tableau de Paris*.

sometimes verges towards the idealism of Greuze or Marmontel, the air of reality surrounding all his pictures is seldom dissipated. In the hinterland of Rétif's mind stands the patriarchal and superb figure of his father, Edme de la Bretonne, whom he venerated and feared. His respect for the family saturates the whole work and, in portraying the final downfall of his hero, the author is inspired, as in that passage where he describes the wave of horror which submerges the Rameau household on receipt of the news that their son is a convicted felon. And the shock kills Edmond's parents, who cannot survive this ultimate blow to the family honour.

However, Rétif has no illusions about the eighteenth-century peasant, of whom he has left us an admirable little etching which, in its essential traits, is still valid. 'An excellent worker, a thrifty manager, he loves wine yet rarely drinks it because it is more profitable to sell it. He spends his holidays, not in tasting of the sweets of love, but in going over his accounts, visiting his neighbours, inspecting his vines—or in sleep.' And in Ursule's description of a Burgundian village courtship, we glimpse a community whose naïve animalism is held in check by a Jansenist respect of authority. 'The boy approaches the girl long before speaking to the parents and wanders sometimes for months round the house before being able to talk to her. People speak about it in the countryside and the girl learns that Pierrot or Jacquot So-and-so is prowling round the house for her. One evening, out of pure curiosity, she seeks some excuse for going out, such as having forgotten to shut the hen - house or the byre or to give the cows straw for the night. The parents are not taken in by this. If they approve of the boy, they say nothing and the girl goes out. If, on the other hand, he does not suit them, the mother or the father rises, pushes the girl back on her seat saying: "Stay where you are: I'm going myself." Then the boy, not seeing the girl come out, resolves to enter the house, saying to the parents: "Will you let me come near your daughter?" He never gets a point-blank refusal. They tell him to sit down. He takes a seat beside her and she either looks at him tenderly or otherwise, until he finally incurs a dismissal couched in these terms: "Keep to your own house." Usually the courtship lasts two or three years because during the first winter there is rarely any question of marriage, and the parents seldom dream of putting the usual question: "What do you come here for, Jacquot?" until the second winter of his frequentation.'

Rétif has none of Rousseau's lyric power, but he understands the peasant's passionate love of his village. Edmond, in the early days of his exile in the city, discovers fitting words to describe his nostalgia: 'Ah, Pierrot! Yes; I'm weary. In the morning, when I wake up it seems to me that I'm still at home. I think I hear the noise of the farm-hands in the yard, the lowing of the kine, and the whinnying of the horses. I think I hear the sheep and the crowing of the cocks; I start and rub my eyes. . . . Alas! I'm in the town. I must get up, only to endure the jaundice of boredom! This morning, dear Pierrot, I wept like a fountain, remembering one Corpus Christi eve when I was cutting lucerne alone in the valley of Vau-de-Lanard. How happy I was! Everything around me was a source of joy. The half-cloudy weather, the cry of the solitary wheatear, even the grass on the slopes had a soul that spoke to mine. The wild brambles seemed delicious and I ate some to refresh my mouth. Then the sound of the big bell fell on my ear in the profound hush of that solitude, and my heart leapt to hear it.' Rousseau could have rewritten these lines with greater art, but not with more sincerity; for this man had the country in his blood. It is interesting, by the way, to reflect that the feeling for nature enters the European novel, not through our Anglo-Saxon writers, but by way of Rousseau the Swiss, and Rétif the Burgundian. It certainly did not come from Richardson, who was almost insensible to natural beauty, and cannot hold a candle to Rétif in the portrayal of country life or manners. The villagers in *Pamela* smack of sentimental comic opera, and their language has a most theatrical twang.

When he dashed off his famous article on Richardson, poor Diderot little knew that he was signing away his claim to the title of original genius. Yet surely one can praise a writer without desiring to imitate him; and there is no valid reason for assuming that, because Diderot wrote an *Éloge de Richardson*, he should therefore have enrolled himself as a pupil of our great novelist. The Diderot who composed the eulogy was the man who once wrote to his mistress, Sophie Volland: 'The spectacle of injustice sometimes sends me into such transports of indignation that I lose my judgment, and in this delirium, I could kill, annihilate. . . .' Fired by the spectacle of Clarissa's fictitious sufferings, such was the mood in which this humanitarian and defender of individual liberty poured out upon paper the impressions burnt into his mind by Richardson's masterpiece. Does it, however, necessarily follow that the artist and creator of *La Religieuse* chose to imitate a foreign novelist's style and technique? So far, thanks to Texte and to the incuriosity of his successors, it has become a commonplace to regard Diderot's anti-clerical novel as a mere adaptation of *Clarissa*, as a work which could not have been produced but for the example set by Richardson.

Every generalization has a grain of truth, and, most probably, the success achieved by *Clarissa* opened Diderot's eyes to the potentialities of the novel in general as an instrument of moral or social propaganda. Somewhat naïvely, and with the air of one making a discovery, he declaims in the *Éloge*: 'Until this day, the word novel has meant a tissue of chimerical and frivolous events, the perusal of which was dangerous alike to morality and good taste. I should like to find another name for the works of Richardson, which elevate the mind, which move the soul, which breathe everywhere the love of good, and are also called novels. . . .' It is reasonable, therefore, to suppose that Diderot must have toyed for years with the idea of himself writing a moral novel; yet there is little to justify the assumption that, in creating it, he would slavishly copy the artistic method of Richardson.

Not until 1758 did he find a theme. Writing in that year to the novelist, Madame Riccoboni, whose *Lettres de Miladi Catesby* he had just laid down, Diderot says: 'I have a fine subject in my head; it is something that must be worked up with fire and genius.' This can only mean the subject of *La Religieuse*, which was apparently finished at La Chevrette, where the author was the guest, in 1760, of Madame d'Épinay. The reference is worth noting in view of the peculiar circumstances surrounding the composition of the novel. These were related, many years later, by Diderot's close friend, Grimm, the lover of Madame d'Épinay.

Early in 1759, to the great distress of this trio, their little society lost one of its cheeriest and most original members, the marquis de Croixmare, 'le charmant marquis par excellence,' a quixotic, warm-hearted old gentleman who left Paris to settle upon his estate in Normandy. His friends resolved, after fifteen months without his company, that this delightful man must be lured back to his old haunts. But how? Diderot remembered that before his departure, M. de Croixmare had interested himself in the case of a young nun at Longchamp who had appealed for annulment of her vows. The affair had created some excitement, but, despite De Croixmare's feverish activities on behalf of his unknown protégée,

Q

she had lost her case. Diderot's fertile mind conceived the following plan. Aided by Grimm and by Madame d'Épinay, he concocted a bogus letter, purporting to come from the nun, now supposedly at large, appealing to the marquis for help. De Croixmare, walking into the trap, wrote to the nun and offered her a post as companion to his daughter. The correspondence went on for some weeks, during which Diderot and his friends spent many a joyous evening, inventing heartrending details, and roaring with laughter at the replies of the good De Croixmare. However, seeing that the marquis was becoming obsessed by the misfortunes of the imaginary nun, Diderot hastened the *dénouement* by killing her off. 'But,' observes Grimm, 'whilst the joke was inflaming the imagination of our friend in Normandy, M. Diderot's also caught fire.' The result was his novel, *La Religieuse*, the general theme of which germinated in the author's mind as early as 1758 but hardened into shape only in the following year. Everything goes to prove that the story of Diderot's heroine and her struggles to escape from a life into which she had been driven against her will, was inspired by memories of the real nun at Longchamp. De Croixmare, when the conspirators made full confession, was, it is said, highly amused. He was evidently a gentleman of unusual tolerance.

Essentially, however, *La Religieuse* owes its genesis to Diderot's passionate hatred of religious fanaticism and, viewed in its proper light, must be regarded as one of the many weapons forged by the *philosophes* during the critical period of that bitter offensive which they waged against clericalism and other forms of intolerance. *La Religieuse* is a work of imagination, but it is also a work of propaganda; it represents art subordinated to a polemical aim, a dangerous combination of two elements which are apt to be incompatible. It remains, therefore, to be seen whether Diderot's genius achieved the miracle of a complete fusion. Do not let us forget, in this connection, that his theme was not a new one, even in the novel. Brunet de Brou, Marivaux, and that terribly fecund writer, the chevalier de Mouhy, had all employed it with more or less success.

Now this is precisely where Diderot's originality asserts itself. The enforced-vocation theme was a well-worn *cliché*. The public was familiar with the persecuted girl debarred from marrying her lover by harsh, materialistic parents. Diderot, therefore, presented a heroine, Suzanne Simonin, who has no lover and has no particular desire to marry. Her motive for wishing to renounce her vows is to escape from a career which is distasteful, and into which she has been thrust by moral blackmail. Her sole object is personal liberty, the freedom to choose her own life, and to live it according to the dictates of her own conscience.

The novel opens with a vividly drawn picture of the Simonin household: a cold, reserved father, and a mother estranged from her husband for reasons which gradually transpire. Suzanne cannot understand why her affection for her parents meets with no response, but is painfully aware that she is a source of domestic discord. To placate her mother, she tells her that her sister's fiancé is showing signs of transferring his attentions to herself, and, as a reward, is promptly bundled off to a convent. On the marriage of her two sisters, Suzanne imagines that she will now be taken home, but learns that her parents want her to take vows. This she is determined to resist. Persuaded, however, by the mother superior that it will commit her to nothing if she enters the noviciate, she does so, and for two years is petted and made much of. In every way, she is led to believe that convent life is a refuge from the outside world and its troubles. However, her instinctive fears are aroused once more by a certain incident. A mad nun escapes from confinement and Suzanne sees her dragged back, shrieking and dishevelled, to her cell. This so horrifies her that she resolves to leave at the end of her noviciate. The superior is most sympathetic, and pretends to take her part against her parents, who still insist on her entering the profession.

Suzanne is visited by her spiritual director and by the mother of the novices. Life becomes a succession of conferences with monks, priests, and interfering, pious old ladies. The day is fixed for her profession and she is put in solitary confinement for her obstinacy. Diderot now reveals a change in Suzanne's character. The effect of this treatment is to make her cunning so that, though she pretends to consider her parents' request, it is only to get an opportunity of making a public protest against this outrage on her liberty. By her duplicity, she disarms suspicion and becomes once more the darling of the establishment. The day of the ceremony arrives, and Suzanne has seen to it that the church is crowded with her friends. The officiating priest asks the fateful question: 'Suzanne Simonin, promettez-vous à Dieu, chasteté, pauvreté et obéissance?' To the consternation of the public and the rage of the conventual authorities, the answer '*Non*' rips through the veil of profound stillness. There is an uproar. The screen in front of the *grille* is lowered and the unwilling bride is hustled off to her cell.   But so great is the scandal that her parents are obliged to take her home.

With consummate realism, Diderot now depicts her mental sufferings in a house where she is treated as a pariah.   The explanation of this unnatural conduct is revealed to her by her confessor, who informs her that she is illegitimate, and a painful interview now takes place between mother and daughter.   Madame Simonin tells her daughter that she is a constant reminder, not only of her fault, but of the ingratitude and baseness of her real father.   Her presence forms an obstacle to any reconciliation with her husband, who has long suspected the truth.   Suzanne offers to renounce all legal claim to her legitim, but this is impossible.   Also, in view of the scandal at the convent she has little hope of finding a husband.   In this way Diderot skilfully disposes of every possible objection to his hypothesis.   To explain Suzanne's final capitulation he uses the one valid argument, her love for her mother, who throws herself on her daughter's mercy, asking her if she is to be tortured all her life for a sin which she has already expiated.   Suzanne is finally admitted to Longchamp as a novice.

Madame de Moni, her superior, is an indulgent woman, and the time passes pleasantly enough, for Longchamp is a centre of some culture.   However, as the end of her noviciate draws near, Suzanne's old abhorrence of the religious life becomes more intense and she confides in the mother superior.   Madame de Moni is a quietist, accustomed to deal with such cases of spiritual uncertainty.   Now, however, and for the first time, all her exhortations fail.   Perturbed and discouraged, she tries to move Madame Simonin, but with no success.   The day of the ceremony arrives and the girl, now reduced to a condition of stupor, replies automatically and in the affirmative to the momentous question.

At this stage, death removes three characters from the story, Suzanne's parents and the quietistic Madame de Moni, who is replaced by the narrow, superstitious Sœur Christine, a Jesuit and a martinet.   A new regime is now instituted.   The cilice and the scourge return, whilst the nuns are closely interrogated as to their theological beliefs.   Suzanne revolts, taking her stand on the regulations of the convent which she obeys to the letter.   The new practices, however, she will not carry out and thus becomes an object of suspicion.   She stirs up the other nuns to revolt and is therefore ostracized by order of the superior, who confines her eventually to her cell. After a period of persecution the captive manages to smuggle a letter to a lawyer, M. Manouri, appealing for annulment of her vows. As a result, he visits her and takes up her case. The fury of the superior now assumes the form of a mania and she subjects Suzanne to every conceivable kind of punishment. She is treated as an apostate, and forced to lie upon a bier surrounded by lighted candles, whilst nuns file past chanting the *Requiescat*. Offal is mixed with her food and she is deprived not only of fresh clothing but of the most necessary hygienic conveniences. The sadistic mind of the superior then hatches a diabolical plan. The rumour is spread that Suzanne is possessed of a devil, and in order to reduce her to a crazy condition, the nuns terrify her by night. When the Grand Vicar of the convent calls her before him she is dragged in by two nuns who pretend to struggle with her whilst a third slyly holds her from behind. However, it is clear from her sensible answers that a grave injustice has been done, and Sœur Christine is severely reprimanded.

Meanwhile Suzanne's case comes before the courts and is lost. The superior redoubles her tortures, and Diderot, also losing self-control, launches into a sickening recital of atrocities. For five days, the unhappy girl is made to perform an *amende honorable*. With a rope round her neck and a torch in her hand she is forced to scourge herself, and to walk on broken glass with bare feet between two rows of nuns chanting the *Miserere*. Finally, the service for the dead is read over her prostrate body, and she is actually brought to the brink of death.

Owing to Manouri's activities, however, she is removed to another convent, Sainte-Eutrope, Sœur Christine being condemned and disgraced by an ecclesiastical commission. We pass now into a different atmosphere. But if the heroine's physical trials are at an end, she is confronted by a more insidious and sinister danger. To put it bluntly, her new superior is a Lesbian, and the whole of this closing episode is devoted to a minute analysis of that distressing mania which Proust has since so vividly described in *A la Recherche du Temps perdu*. From certain strange letters written by Diderot to Sophie Volland in September 1760 it seems to me likely that the Sainte-Eutrope episode was written at this time. Diderot's abnormal jealousy of Sophie's sister, Madame Legendre, undoubtedly suggested to his feverish imagination the traits which he attributes to Suzanne's superior. That his psychological portrait has all the illusion of truth no one can deny ; whether it is scientifically accurate is a problem for the psychiatrist. Rétif, a specialist in such matters, complains of Diderot's lack of realism,[1] but as he was a bitter enemy of the author of *La Religieuse*, his judgment is suspect. 'I cannot conceive,' he wrote, 'why Diderot chose to write his *Religieuse* absolutely from imagination. The truth would have been more arresting. But he was too lazy to seek it out. Besides, Diderot was an egoist . . . a vicious, and therefore a mediocre man.'

The idea at the core of *La Religieuse* is not to be explained merely by Diderot's well-known hatred of the Catholic Church. It springs from a deeper source, from his conception of human nature and his ideal notion of human dignity viewed as a product of civilization. Note, for example, the remark made by Madame de Moni to Suzanne as she contemplates the group of sweet, docile, and innocent creatures entrusted to her care. 'There is not one, no, not one that I could not turn into a wild beast; a strange metamorphosis, the disposition for which is all the greater when they enter the cell at an early age and with but a slight knowledge of social life.' Again, at Sainte-Eutrope, the heroine herself, appalled at the results of her superior's perversion, exclaims: 'There you have the effects of the cloistered life. Man is born for society. Separate him, isolate him, and his ideas will become dissociated, his character will change, a thousand ridiculous affections will arise in his heart. Extravagant thoughts will germinate in his mind, like brambles in fallow land. Put him in a forest and man will become ferocious; in a cloister, where the idea of necessity is added to that of servitude, and it is still worse. You can get out of a forest but not out of a cloister. In a forest you are free; in a cloister, a slave. Perhaps it needs still greater force of soul to resist solitude than to stand up to hardship. Hardship degrades a man, but the claustral life makes him depraved. Is it better to live in abjectness or in madness? That is a question which I should not dare to decide; but either extreme is to be avoided.'

If *La Religieuse* had been only an attack on the monastic system, one might very well place it in the numerous category of eighteenth-century works which, like D'Argens's *Lettres juives* and Marmontel's *Bélisaire*, have no literary interest. But the genius of Diderot invests it with a deeper and wider significance. The immediate thesis recedes into the background as we gaze upon the triptych fashioned by this great author. Each panel offers the tragic image of a human soul that has been twisted, perverted, and prematurely

[1] *Monsieur Nicolas* (ed. of 1794–97), viii. 4543–4.

blasted by injudicious transplantation to a climate for which it was never intended by nature. Madame de Moni dies in an agony of mystic despair; Sœur Christine sinks to the level of a brute; the superior of Sainte-Eutrope expires amidst the horrors of madness, accentuated by lucid moments of ghastly remorse and superstitious terror. They fill the spectator with an overpowering sense of pity and of awe as he reflects upon what might have been their destiny. Actually—and here Diderot may be said to have failed, happily, in his polemical object—one does not lay down this book seized with an irresistible desire to rush out and set fire to the nearest convent. It is only too obvious that his heroines are exceptional individuals and not representative types, but they are not on that account less tragic. That the *milieu* in which these women wither and die should happen to be the convent is an affair of minor importance; there are households, professions, and boardinghouses which to-day constitute similar prisons of the spirit. When he created *La Religieuse*, Diderot builded better than he knew, and perhaps better than he deserved, for the artist in him eventually rose beyond the propagandist. It happens, too, that the character for whom the author solicits our interest, our admiration, and our pity is the least interesting, the least admirable, and the least pitiful of the four women whose destinies are here portrayed. Suzanne is unconvincing and, save at the outset, too logical, too fluent, and much too wise for a girl of her years and lack of experience. In her relations with the superior of Sainte-Eutrope, her innocence is wholly incredible, because it does not tally with the shrewdness and penetration displayed on other occasions. Really, she is very seldom Suzanne Simonin; more often she is Denis Diderot masquerading as an *ingénue*.

What of the alleged debt to Richardson? In the abrupt *dénouement* which solves the problem of Suzanne, we learn that she was abducted by a lecherous priest. Inveigled into a *maison borgne*, she escapes, however, and eventually finds employment with a laundress. To quiet the distress of the charitable marquis, Diderot composed a few letters, later appended to the novel, and in the last of these it was announced that Suzanne was dead. In these three pages, with their bald account of the heroine's fate, there is really nothing to suggest the influence of Richardson's manner, although it is quite possible, if one chooses, to assume that Diderot, in imagining the laundress episode, was haunted by memories of Clarissa's final station at the milliner's in Covent Garden. But in everything that concerns the art of the novel, these two great writers live in different worlds.

The style of Diderot is typically French, and, in presenting his characters, this author follows the tradition built up and, with variants due to their individual genius, continued by La Bruyère, Le Sage, Prévost, and Marivaux. In *La Religieuse*, Diderot evinces a racial love of form, a respect for clarity and balance. He eschews the digressive or the picturesque, avoiding, too, all suggestion of *flou* in the interpretation of ideas. Could anything be less Richardsonian, for example, than the following portrait of the superior of Sainte-Eutrope?

'C'est une petite femme toute ronde, cependant prompte et vive dans ses mouvements; sa tête n'est jamais assise sur ses épaules; il y a toujours quelque chose qui cloche dans son vêtement; sa figure est plutôt bien que mal; ses yeux, dont l'un, c'est le droit, est plus haut que l'autre, sont pleins de feu et distraits: quand elle marche, elle jette ses bras en avant et en arrière. Veut-elle parler? elle ouvre la bouche, avant que d'avoir arrangé ses idées; aussi bégaye-t-elle un peu. Est-elle assise? elle s'agite sur son fauteuil, comme si quelque chose l'incommodait: elle oublie toute bienséance; elle lève sa guimpe pour se frotter la peau; elle croise les jambes; elle vous interroge; vous lui répondez, et elle ne vous écoute pas; elle vous parle, et elle se perd, s'arrête tout court, ne sait plus où elle est, se fâche, et vous appelle grosse bête, stupide, imbécile, si vous ne la remettez sur la voie: elle est tantôt familière jusqu'à tutoyer, tantôt impérieuse et fière jusqu'au dédain; ses moments de dignité sont courts; elle est alternativement compatissante et dure; sa figure décomposée marque tout le décousu de son esprit et toute l'inégalité de son caractère; aussi l'ordre et le désordre se succédaient-ils dans la maison.'

Neither Le Sage nor Marivaux could have written these lines, yet, in collaboration, they might have produced something not unlike this style of Diderot's with its nervous, almost abrupt antitheses, impetuous yet purposeful, digging deeper than Le Sage into the mind of the subject but lacking Marivaux's subtle, antenna-like groping after nuances of emotion and sentiment. Of Richardson's patient, relentless, and cumulative manner there is not a trace; and Diderot has not our English novelist's genius for suggesting perspectives. When, for example, he tries to portray his nuns in groups, clustering round the superior in her boudoir at Sainte-Eutrope, the general impression is shadowy and ephemeral. That background which we shall later find in *Jacques le Fataliste*, is absent here; the minor characters are neither individualized nor graded, and all the illumination falls upon the central figure. How very different from Richardson! One has only to think of Clarissa at Harlowe Place, at Sinclair's, or at Hampstead to realize the shortcomings of Diderot. In dialogue, however, the Frenchman excels, and the three leading characters of *La Religieuse* are analysed with considerable power. But the truth is that, whilst Richardson is *un romancier de race*, Diderot is not. His peculiar gifts find happier expression in a work like *Jacques le Fataliste*, which, even in the loosest sense of the term, can scarcely be called a novel.

Diderot composed this book to amuse the tedium of a journey into Holland; and it was probably finished on his return to Paris in 1773, though not published until 1796, long after the author's death. It has absolutely the air of a work composed *en voyage*, reflecting as it does a Diderot in carefree, March-hare mood, chained no longer to the galley-proofs of the *Encyclopédie*, able at last to follow the idea of the moment or to abandon it; in fact, the man so aptly described in the following words of an anonymous English friend: 'It seemed that enthusiasm was become the natural turn of expression of his will, of his soul, and of all his faculties. . . . Till his thoughts had transported him beyond his ordinary feelings he was not himself, he was not Diderot.' [1] And in *Jacques le Fataliste*, there is an excitement and a certain spontaneous digressiveness which mirrors the true nature of the author better perhaps than any other of his works. In writing this holiday book he gaily threw every consideration of form or of art to the four winds, and half imitating, half parodying the manner of Laurence Sterne, wove into the tissue of an imaginary conversation between two travellers a fascinating pattern made up of brilliant comments on human nature, *contes* dramatic and bawdy, and scenes and characters vibrating with life. Of his initial debt to Sterne he makes no secret, nor need he. His two protagonists are Jacques the Fatalist and his master whose adventures, squabbles, and reminiscences form the matter of the book. From *Tristram Shandy* Diderot annexed as his spring-board the idea that Jacques, like Trim, was wounded in the knee and hence fell in love. But in *Jacques le Fataliste*, this incident is recast and much enlarged. However, like Sterne with his story of the amours of Uncle Toby and Widow Wadman, Diderot humorously keeps deferring the *dénouement*

---

[1] *To the Memory of Diderot*, a preface to the anonymous English translation of *Jacques le Fataliste* (London, 1797, 3 volumes).

* Q

of Jacques's affair with Denise, to the comic exasperation of his master; whilst Jacques himself at every interruption philosophically bows to the will of fate and, with a sentencious, 'Il était écrit là-haut,' turns for Pantagruelish inspiration to the flask which never leaves his saddle-bow.

Jacques is a rare but richly human creature. He is the privileged and faithful servant, loved for his gruff sincerity and pawkiness by a master whom he alternately infuriates and delights. He is the realist, destined always to experience the most romantic adventures, yet stubbornly refusing to regard them as dramatic or even unusual. His master, on the contrary, is a sentimentalist, whose impetuous curiosity provides an excellent foil to the valet's delicious sang-froid and mock disillusionment. However, Jacques has one weakness. He is incurably garrulous, a fault he attributes to his early environment. But let him explain matters in his own way:

> *Jacques.* My grandfather, Jason, had several children. The whole family was serious; they got up, dressed, went about their business; they came home, dined and went back again without uttering a word. In the evening they threw themselves into their chairs; the mother and the daughters span, sewed and knitted without saying a word. The boys rested, the father read the Old Testament.
> *Master.* And what did you do?
> *Jacques.* I ran about the room with a gag on.
> *Master.* And why?
> *Jacques.* Because of my repetitions, which my grandfather regarded as babble unworthy of the Holy Ghost. He said that people who repeat themselves are fools, and that those who listen to them are fools too.

As a result, no doubt, of this Spartan training, Jacques himself has acquired a rooted dislike of interruptions, a peculiarity which Diderot exploits with capital effect. Behold Jacques, in his own inimitable vein, slipping off from the high road into apparent side-tracks which prove to be detours; stolidly ignoring his master's impatient questions and moans of exasperation; maliciously, sometimes, feigning loss of memory until, pleaded with and placated, he grumpily consents to resume the broken narrative. But then, as always curiously occurs, an interruption comes from outside. The hostess has also a tale to unfold, perhaps the strange and moving story of Madame de la Pommeraye's revenge. Immediately Jacques lapses into one of his queer, sulky moods, for the hostess outdoes him in garrulity. So he stretches himself grandly in an arm-chair, where with closed eyes and hat pulled down over his ears, he resigns himself to listen; what time his master coughs, looks at his watch, and takes a pinch of rappee. The tale commences, rising in a leaping crescendo, and as the suspense grows, the listeners become animated. From downstairs comes a steady crackle of interruptions. Now it is the servant-girl asking where she is to sleep a guest; now the helpless lout of a husband shouting for the corn-dealer's account book. Always the hostess takes up the thread where she left off, never repeating herself. That is the mark of the true gossip! Soon, however, the bustle of the inn dies away. Champagne is brought in and the hours dance past, Jacques getting steadily more maudlin in his comments, and his master more sententious as each successive *cadavre* is lowered to its honourable grave beneath the table. The reader's final illusion is that he could pick out that inn amongst a thousand as surely as if he had met it in the pages of Balzac. Yet he does not know the colour of its shutters. Great art this, and, oddly enough, not at all English.

'Digressions, incontestably, are the sunshine; they are the life, the soul of reading,' exclaims Sterne; but one has to read *Jacques le Fataliste* to appreciate the justness of his remark. Sterne's own digressions are, as a rule, too abrupt, too unmotivated, and the author *will* persist, as if to aggravate the offence, in telling us how clever he is at this pleasant game of changing hobby-horses in mid-stream. Diderot manages it much better. 'I see,' he remarks casually, 'that with a little imagination and style there is nothing easier than to spin a yarn,' and thereupon pilots us through a maze of winding by-ways, wickedly arousing our expectance, gravely rebuking our childish impatience to see what lies round the corner; then, with his hand earnestly laid on our shoulder, blandly feigning to humour our whim, leads us, still talking, talking—back to the point from which we started. When Sterne mounts us on Uncle Toby's hobby-horse, he is more than charming; priceless, too, are those conversations between the eloquent and frustrated Mr. Shandy and his painfully modest brother. But his digressions are often unhappy. In labouring to imitate the erudition of that great humanist and prince of jollity, François Rabelais, poor Sterne reminds one of the ambitious frog in La Fontaine's fable. He is out of his element. What makes him most insufferable, however, is his inveterate lack of sincerity. With him one can never somehow escape the image of a fortunately rare war-time type, the jolly padre trying to tell a naughty story to the 'boys.' Now, in *Jacques le Fataliste*, Diderot is occasionally bawdy; but in his bawdry there is a humour and frankness infinitely more pleasing than Sterne's rictus, his key-hole sniggerings and salacious innuendoes. On these occasions, Diderot loses nothing of his dignity as a philosopher; Sterne, on the contrary, temporarily sinks to the intellectual level of a lascivious commercial traveller.

That having been said, let us salute, in the author of *Tristram Shandy*, one of the most alert, observant, and original artists in all English literature. No one possibly has ever excelled his power of evoking a personality by the deft and subtle exhibition of individual *tics* of speech, gesture, and expression. 'Attitudes,' he observes with his usual acuteness, 'are nothing . . . 'tis the transition from one attitude to another—like the preparation and resolution of the discord into harmony—which is all in all.' Here, it seems, is the secret of Sterne's remarkable fluidity in the presentation of character. So complete is his grasp of nuances that all his people talk, move, and evolve with amazing naturalness. They have, it is true, no depth, nor do we expect them to have any; like the 'humorists' of eighteenth-century English comedy, their *raison d'être* is to amuse us, not to make us reflect. They take their tone from the whimsical *milieu* created for them by Sterne's impish fancy. But from the purely artistic point of view, is it not annoying that Sterne, who is extraordinarily original in the matter of character creation, should have proved so very uninventive and even monotonous in his choice of situations? His peculiar obsession by the obstetrical leads him to harp on one string—a curious example of impotence in one endowed with such a prolific imagination. Reading him, one is forcibly impressed by the wisdom of Marivaux's advice to authors who propose to dabble in the licentious. It is to remember always the difference between the mood in which a book is written and the mood in which it will probably be read. The jest that amuses us over a midnight bottle is apt to look curiously frowsy in cold print at eleven o'clock on the morning after. That is not matter of breviary, but of taste and sense of proportion. A really great artist, of course, can induce or command the requisite mood: I do not find that Sterne can perform this feat.

Sterne and Diderot, though they both sat at the feet of Rabelais, have actually little in common. They present a temperamental disparity which is reflected in *Tristram Shandy* and in *Jacques le Fataliste*. Sterne's interest in human beings is essentially that of the artist, whilst Diderot's springs from a deeper source. Sterne has the simian inquisitiveness of the small boy, the same alert cocked eye for the comic or revelatory trick of speech or movement. In point of fact, he has none of that profound sympathy for humanity which glows beneath the screen of Diderot's apparent cynicism and humorous tolerance. Laurence Sterne's much advertised sensibility is a shoddy affair, for it is almost always just a reflected ray from the dark lantern of his self-pity and egotism. The pretty picture constructed by Professor Cross of Sterne in France, of Sterne the *âme sensible* and, on that account, the darling of the *salons*, is composed largely of material obligingly furnished by the author of *Tristram Shandy* and *A Sentimental Journey*. As a corrective, it might be well to quote the opinion of a Frenchman who actually met Sterne in Paris. Sterne's sentimentality, he discovered, was entirely a thing of the mind and not of the heart. 'He seemed to us,' says he, 'one of those men who possess an inordinate appetite for laughter, and for laughing at nothing and at everything indiscriminately. Now, we believe that a man with this sort of character can have very little of that sensibility of soul which is affected by Sterne in his writings.' [1] Brutal, but I think, true.

There is a spaciousness in *Jacques le Fataliste* which is not to be found in *Tristram Shandy*. Jogging along the miry roads of provincial France with Jacques, we realize that we are in the society of one of the great originals; for our fellow-traveller belongs to that noble company which includes Pantagruel, Gil Blas, Figaro, and Coignard. Our journey over, we take leave of him regretfully, as we take leave of a delightful comrade, and the smile lingers on our lips when we recall the hundred sallies, the rich, mellow cynicism of the eccentric whose philosophy is crystallized in that oft repeated 'Il était écrit là-haut!' Yet what do we know about him? Shall we recognize him again? Yes. There is the hat, 'the enormous hat, an umbrella in bad weather, a parasol when it is fine; headgear for all seasons, the tenebrous sanctuary beneath which one of the finest brains that ever existed, consulted destiny on grand occasions. Raised, the wings of the hat placed his face about the middle of his body; lowered, he could scarce see ten paces before him, and this had given him the habit of walking with his nose snuffing the wind.'

For obvious reasons, *Tristram Shandy* has never been popular in France. The peculiar quality of its style is such as to baffle the ablest translator, and it would require a very determined Anglophile to appreciate the unique flavour of Sterne's humour. On the

[1] *Journal encyclopédique*, iii (1784). This periodical, by the way, was noted for its Anglomania.

other hand, neither can it be said that *Jacques le Fataliste* has ever enjoyed a vogue in England. It is doubtful, indeed, whether it has been re-translated since 1797, though I am certain that, were it better known, *Jacques le Fataliste* would appeal to a large circle of English readers. Some years ago, the author of a doctoral thesis [1] on the influence of Sterne in France expressed the quaint opinion that Jacques and his master were mere *fantoches* and *marionnettes*; whilst he found their adventures 'insipid and boring'—a harsh verdict with which very few of Diderot's readers will agree.

To enjoy an uninterrupted view of Mr. Shandy, Trim, and Uncle Toby one must first learn how to avoid Sterne's digressions, which, as a rule, have nothing to do with his heroes. Now Diderot, on the contrary, rarely allows us to lost sight of Jacques and his master. He may, it is true, veer off at a tangent to introduce us to the duelling captain, to the ineffable Monsieur Gousse, or to the perfidious chevalier de Saint-Ouen. Or, again, he is quite liable to embark on the long, exciting story of Madame de la Pommeraye's revenge, or on the dramatic tale of Father Hudson and the young novice. Yet inevitably, by some casual word or gesture, he will contrive to add another brush-stroke to his impressionistic picture of Jacques and his master. Moreover, these characters are projected against a suggestive background of everyday people and familiar sounds. Take, for instance, the scene at the inn or the description of the convalescence of Jacques in the peasant's cottage. Here we have alert, racy interpretations of eighteenth-century village life comparable, in their warm humanity, to the work of Fielding. By contrast, the *milieu* surrounding Shandy and Uncle Toby seems curiously drab and limited.

Sterne would have agreed, no doubt, with Diderot's remark: 'Nature is so varied, especially in the matter of instinct and character, that there is nothing so queer in the imaginings of a creative artist that experience and observation do not offer a model of them in nature.' Now the people in *Jacques le Fataliste*, as in *Tristram Shandy*, are decidedly queer, but they bear the stamp of actuality; they are decidedly not *fantoches* or marionettes. Indeed, many of Diderot's characters possess astonishing depth, and are presented

---

[1] *Étude sur l'influence de Sterne en France au dix-huitième siècle*, in which the author, Mr. F. B. Barton, has found it necessary to belittle Diderot in order to magnify Sterne. Unfortunately, his severe generalizations upon *Jacques le Fataliste* are unsupported by any examples drawn from the text and therefore, I fear, possess no critical value. However, Mr. Barton's account of the various translations of Sterne in France constitutes a scholarly and exhaustive piece of research work.

with a dramatic power which is completely alien to the leisurely, whimsical genius of Sterne. Those who make the acquaintance of Madame de la Pommeraye or of that sinister, yet humorous rascal, Father Hudson, will realize how inept it is to regard the author of *Jacques le Fataliste* as the copyist or pupil of Sterne. Consider merely the tone of this passage where Diderot describes one little incident in the career of his lecherous superior: 'Parmi ses pénitentes, il y avait une petite confiseuse qui faisait bruit dans le quartier par sa coquetterie et ses charmes; Hudson, qui ne pouvait fréquenter chez elle, l'enferma dans son sérail. Cette espèce de rapt ne se fit pas sans donner des soupçons aux parents et à l'époux. Ils lui rendirent visite. Hudson les reçut avec un air consterné. Comme ces bonnes gens étaient en train de lui exposer leur chagrin, la cloche sonne; c'était six heures du soir: Hudson leur impose silence, ôte son chapeau, se lève, fait un grand signe de croix, et dit d'un ton affectueux et pénétré: *Angelus Domini nuntiavit Mariae.* . . . Et voilà le père de la confiseuse et ses frères, honteux de leur soupçon, qui disaient, en descendant l'escalier, à l'époux: 'Mon fils, vous êtes un sot. . . . Mon frère, n'avez-vous point de honte? Un homme qui dit l'*Angelus*, un saint!' This is the great tradition of French art, untinged by the influence of Sterne or of any foreign genius.

By the character of his philosophic ideas Diderot takes rank as a European figure, but, as an artist, he remains essentially French. In this he resembles all the imaginative writers of his period. Great literature is singularly reluctant to surrender the heritage bequeathed to it by tradition and, in closing this survey, I am led to the irresistible conclusion that the cosmopolitan spirit left no deep or lasting imprint upon the imaginative literature of eighteenth-century France or England. In examining the writings of two divergent races, with regard to questions of resemblance or influence, it is fatally easy to lose one's sense of perspective. The enthusiastic pursuit of 'parallels' and 'sources' often leads the keen research scholar to neglect the substance for the shadow, and thus to forget what a priceless illumination may be obtained from the comparative study of artists who resemble each other in nothing but the fact that each has endeavoured to express, in language of genius, the traditional spirit of his race and of his time. That this truth has been frequently ignored implies no criticism of the comparative method itself, the value of which has been amply proved by the works of its leading exponents. The danger to which I allude comes rather from an abuse of the comparative method, and from a prevalent illusion that the vital, delicate organism called imaginative literature will ever yield its secret under the onslaught of the 'scientific' investigator. It is not the function of literary criticism to *prove*, but to suggest and to interpret. And the critic who sets out upon his journey shackled to an *a priori* conviction is bound to return to us with an empty mind. In the last twenty years, a great many theses and articles have been devoted to the question of Anglo - French literary relations in the eighteenth century. Of these many are admirable, but there are others which, from an excess of zeal, have tended to prove too much and to suggest too little. To them the present survey owes its genesis.

APPENDICES

APPENDIX I

I FIND it impossible to agree with Professor Lounsbury's statement that Voltaire in *Zaïre* was indebted to Shakespeare for 'the general outline of the plot and its details.'[1] This author, I feel, has fallen into an error common to many students of comparative literature. He forgets that, as Boileau puts it, 'La raison, pour marcher, n'a souvent qu'une voie.' In other words, if two dramatists set out to depict the behaviour and the emotions of a jealous man, nothing is more likely than that there will be 'the same all-absorbing love on the part of the hero and heroine.'[2] In both plays, too, the jealousy will be 'unfounded on the part of the hero.' Somewhere in both works, also, there will be 'a pretext for its display'; in *Othello* it is the handkerchief, in *Zaïre*, a letter. Nor is it odd, if we recall the traditional practice of the French theatre, that Orosmane, like Othello, should have a confidant: it is the obvious way to avoid interminable monologues. But, as I have shown, there is absolutely no foundation for Professor Lounsbury's statement that Corasmin is a parallel character to Iago. The former is the usual colourless confidant of neo-classic tragedy. It is not very surprising either that in both plays the jealous hero murders the heroine, and afterwards discovers he has made a mistake. She would scarcely be likely to murder him, or he to kill himself and leave her unscathed. The unfortunate critical method adopted by Professor Lounsbury is exceedingly dangerous since it can be made to prove almost anything. By applying it to Racine and Shakespeare it would be possible, for instance, to 'prove' that the former copied half his plays from the latter, though so far this has not been asserted by the most fanatical Shakespearian.

Professor Lounsbury does not feel that 'it is straining the evidence' to assert that Voltaire's Lusignan is suggested by Shakespeare's Gloucester in *Lear*. His 'evidence' is that in both plays the old man dies of grief and joy after recognizing his long-lost offspring. To put it very mildly, this is far-fetched. Such *reconnaissances* were extremely common in French plays and novels of the seventeenth century. Lusignan dies because the author has no further use for him. He has served the purpose of Voltaire's anti-clerical propaganda and provided Zaïre with a tragic problem. After that he could only be a source of embarrassment. And, with all deference to Professor Lounsbury, it is quite credible that after twenty years in a dungeon this octogenarian should succumb to the

---

[1] *Shakespeare and Voltaire*, p. 78.
[2] This and the quotations which follow are from Professor Lounsbury's book.

shock of a sudden emotion. Nor is it strange that his son should mention the fact, since we do not see Lusignan expire on the stage.

It is difficult to discuss seriously the second 'analogy' between *Lear* and *Zaïre* advanced by Professor Lounsbury. Edmund, on hearing of the death of Goneril and Regan, says: 'Yet I was beloved.' Orosmane, who has just murdered Zaïre, learns from Nérestan why Zaïre was proceeding to the rendezvous. As Professor Lounsbury does not quote the passage, I will, in order to show that there is no resemblance whatever between the situation of Edmund and of Orosmane:

> *Nérestan.* Lusignan, ce vieillard, fut son malheureux père;
> Il venait dans mes bras d'achever sa misère,
> Et d'un père expiré j'apportais en ces lieux
> La volonté dernière et les derniers adieux;
> Je venais dans un cœur trop faible et trop sensible
> Rappeler des chrétiens le culte incorruptible.
> Hélas! elle offensait notre Dieu, notre loi,
> Et ce Dieu la punit d'avoir brûlé pour toi.

This is the *éclaircissement*. Orosmane now realizes that his jealousy was criminal and baseless. Nérestan is Zaïre's brother:

> *Orosmane.* Zaïre! Elle m'aimait? Est-ce bien vrai, Fatime?
> Sa sœur? . . . J'étais aimé?

Fatime overwhelms him with passionate reproaches, and tells him of Zaïre's struggle between love and filial duty:

> Celle qui, malgré soi constante à t'adorer,
> Se flattait, espérait, que le Dieu de ses pères
> Recevrait le tribut de ses larmes sincères.

Then Orosmane, filled with remorse and despair, ejaculates:

> Tu m'en as dit assez. O ciel! j'étais aimé!
> Va, je n'ai pas besoin d'en savoir davantage.

Nothing could be less like the situation of Edmund in *Lear*. Edmund has known for some time that the sisters loved him. The words:

> Yet Edmund was beloved:
> The one the other poisoned for my sake
> And after slew herself, [1]

denote awe and wonder mingled with a certain dreadful *amour-propre*. No two characters, no two situations could well be less analogous. Here, Professor Lounsbury is, I fear, guilty of the very fault which he so often imputes to Voltaire, that is, of misrepresenting the work of a foreign author to his compatriots. And this, as we shall see, is not an isolated example.

[1] Professor Lounsbury quotes only the first line, and to support his parallel with *Zaïre* gives us only: 'O ciel! j'étais aimé.' This, to say the very least, is misleading.

Professor Lounsbury states that in Voltaire's *Mahomet* (1742) 'occurs a direct imitation of Shakespeare.' The alleged imitation appears, we are told, in the scene where the young fanatic, Séide, under the baneful influence of the charlatan, Mahomet, kills Zopire who, as it transpires, is not merely his father, but the father of Palmyre, another fanatical adherent of Mahomet's. The latter, indeed, promises her in marriage to Séide as an additional inducement to murder Zopire. In the scene preceding that of the murder, Séide, who recoils from the deed, makes Palmyre the confidante of all his misgivings. Both are convinced that Mahomet is the mouthpiece of the Divine will; both are aware that the consummation of their love depends on Zopire's death. But Séide tries to persuade Palmyre to give him a direct command to kill Zopire:

Séide. Eh bien! pour être à toi que faut-il?
Palmyre. Je frémis.
Séide. Je l'entends, son arrêt est parti de ta bouche.
Palmyre. Qui? Moi?
Séide. Tu l'as voulu.
Palmyre. Dieu! quel arrêt farouche!
  Que t'ai-je dit?
Séide. Le ciel vient d'emprunter ta voix;
  C'est son dernier oracle, et j'accomplis ses loix.

He then rushes to commit the crime. In his frenzy he sees supernatural favourable omens—a ghost, moving shadows, blood-red flashes, in the gloomy precincts of the altar where stands Zopire. The murder is done, followed immediately by the dreadful *éclaircissement* we have mentioned. This scene, in which, of course, Voltaire's object was to portray the horrors of religious fanaticism, is regarded by Professor Lounsbury as 'an evident attempt to reproduce the effect of the tremendous situations in *Macbeth* which precede and follow the assassination of Duncan.' He pursues: 'All the accessories to the scene which are found in the one play are introduced into the other as far as the difference in plot allows them to be employed. It was the appearance of Lady Macbeth in the English tragedy, it was the part she played in it which led Voltaire to make Palmyre an associate in the murder. The conversation between husband and wife just before the commission of the crime suggested the conversation between the lovers.'

This is very dogmatic and very inaccurate. It is absurd to compare for one instant the behaviour and characters of Lady Macbeth and Palmyre. The latter is a pathetic, weak-minded child, the victim both of her love for Séide and of her fanatical awe of Mahomet. She is a characterless puppet in comparison with Lady Macbeth. Palmyre is not an 'associate' in the murder. She does not want it, but is so bewildered by the rapidity of the events and the mad exaltation of her lover that she does not know what to do. If Voltaire got the idea of this scene anywhere, it was not from *Macbeth*, but from Corneille's *Cinna*, where the woman, indeed, does deliberately excite her lover to murder and, in fact, tells him that he cannot have her unless he kills Auguste. But Voltaire,

[1] op. cit., p. 121.

as we have seen, wanted neither to imitate Shakespeare nor Corneille. As for the 'broken utterances, the abrupt inquiry, the startled comment' which characterize the conversation preceding the murder and which Professor Lounsbury calls 'the manner of Shakespeare,' equally concise utterances will be found in the critical scenes of Racine, Corneille, and of Voltaire's own earlier plays. Professor Lounsbury, it is true, does not admit that Voltaire succeeds in reproducing the 'manner' of Shakespeare but that, as he puts it indulgently, is because in the measure of French tragedy 'the restraint of time, the regular recurrence of like sounds, however fitted to impart pleasure, are little calculated to cause impressions of terror'! I think of *Phèdre*, *Iphigénie*, *Britannicus*, *Polyeucte*, and *Le Cid*, all written in that measure only 'fitted to impart pleasure.' There are certain critical judgments which render comment unnecessary. That Professor Lounsbury's should occur in a book the purpose of which is to compare the dramas of two authors, English and French, is more than unfortunate: it is disastrous.

APPENDIX II

1762. De Bissy, in the *Journal étranger* (Feb. 1762), translated the first *Night*.

1764. The same author published, in the *Gazette littéraire de l'Europe*, a translation of the second *Night*. Like the first, it is in prose.

1770. Le Tourneur's complete translation of the *Night Thoughts*.

1770–1. Colardeau turned Le Tourneur's first and second *Nuits* into alexandrines.

1771. An anonymous and fragmentary translation of the first *Night*.

1771. An obscure rhymester called Doigny de Ponceau produced a verse rendering of the fourth, twelfth, and fifteenth *Nuits*.

1779. The equally obscure L. de Limoges versified the first and fifteenth *Nuits*.

M. Van Tieghem, to whom I am indebted for much of the above information, mentions also several short extracts or adaptations which are of minor importance. Whether one can agree with this eminent scholar that the above output, which is spread over twenty years, constitutes a *succès de vogue* is doubtful. It is significant that no well-known French writer ever attempted to adapt or to imitate our *doctor atrabilarissimus*.

APPENDIX III

THE main thesis advanced by M. Elissa-Rhaïs, in his article in the *Revue de la Littérature comparée*, is that the realism of *Manon Lescaut* is to be explained by the fact that it is 'in part a reminiscence of *Moll Flanders*.' That Prévost's own experience was in itself a probable source of realism is not once taken into consideration. In any case, the realism of the French novelist, as I have shown, is not that of Defoe. However, let us select for criticism a few of the 'resemblances' which M. Elissa-Rhaïs sees in the two novels.

(*a*) Of Moll and Manon it is said: 'their age, their beauty, their precocious instinct, their knowledge of a certain uprightness in men, their facility, their ruses, their lack of conscience, their native reserve, the gay trend of their humour make of Moll and Manon the same sympathetic character, and the same easily excusable little animal.' The reply to this is contained in my comparative study of the two women. Apart from the fact that they are beautiful and attract men, they are utterly different.

(*b*) Des Grieux is compared to Jemmy the highwayman and to Robin, the younger brother, who is Moll's first husband. Why Robin comes into the matter is beyond comprehension. Nor can I understand why Jemmy is described as the faithful chevalier who follows Moll to America, where 'they promise themselves and realize a life of redemption.' The truth is that Jemmy accompanies Moll only with the greatest reluctance and, in Virginia, has to be constantly amused to keep him from getting bored and clearing off to England. He first pursued Moll for her money, and finding she had none, left her for his good and hers.

(*c*) Neither Moll nor Manon, says our critic, likes poverty. Who does? However, I have already discussed their respective attitudes to the money question.

(*d*) The most astounding 'resemblance' is that alleged between Tiberge, the faithful friend of Des Grieux, and the Bath lodger who is content to remain with Moll on a Platonic footing. Tiberge is a priest, a long-suffering comrade to the chevalier until the very end, since he follows the couple to New Orleans. The sole basis for M. Elissa-Rhaïs's amazing theory is a general remark of Tiberge's to the effect that he, too, had once had a youthful penchant for pleasure but had conquered it by reason. On the strength of this, our writer accuses him of voluptuous desires when the poor fellow, searching all Paris for Des Grieux, calls upon Manon to ask if she knows where he is!

(*e*) Of the passages in the two texts which are placed side by side by M. Elissa-Rhaïs in order to prove their resemblance, I will select only two, with this general comment: 'La raison pour marcher n'a souvent qu'une voie.' In other words, every human being, whether he be Chinese, French or English will have the same views on certain ordinary matters. Moll wants a settled life and says so. Des Grieux, in New Orleans, feels the same urge and says so. By our writer's method I would undertake to prove that any work of fiction is 'imitated' from another. But M. Elissa-Rhaïs asks us to see a resemblance between passages which, even when abstracted from their context, have absolutely nothing in common. Thus:

Then he cajoled with his brother and persuaded him what a service he had done him. (*Moll Flanders.*)	Oui, oui, se hâta-t-il de dire, c'est un fort bon service que je vous ai rendu. (*Manon Lescaut.*)

What are the circumstances? In Defoe, Moll's seducer is telling his younger brother that he has done him a good turn in persuading the family to consent to the latter's marriage with Moll. In Prévost's novel, Manon's ne'er-do-well brother is telling Des Grieux, whose violence he fears, that he has done the chevalier a good service in arranging to pass him off as Manon's brother in order to dupe G. M. Except that the two men, in their respective languages, express the conviction that they have done someone a good turn there is not one iota of similarity between their situations or characters. But there is no limit to the imagination of M. Elissa-Rhaïs. What, for example, is the conclusion he draws from the following passages?

A little awning which served as an arbour at the entrance from our house into the gardens. (*Moll Flanders.*)	Une maison écartée avec un petit bois et un ruisseau d'eau douce. (*Manon Lescaut.*)

It is quite simply (*a*) that Prévost's phrase indicates the appearance of 'verdant' nature in French fiction, and (*b*) that he owes his inspiration to the passage quoted from Defoe!

APPENDIX IV

SOME NOTES ON THE EIGHTEENTH-CENTURY ENGLISH TRANSLATIONS OF
'MANON LESCAUT'

IN the December number of *Blackwood's Magazine* for 1931, the late
Mr. R. S. Garnett, commenting on Miss Waddell's translation of the
1731 edition of *Manon Lescaut*, drew attention to the fact that she had been
anticipated in 1767 by an anonymous English translator. The full title
of his version is: *The History of the chevalier des Grieux, written by himself,
translated from the French. London. B. White,* 1767. 2 *vols.* 8*vo.* There
is no copy in the British Museum, and, although I had known of its
existence from the *Monthly Review* and other contemporary periodicals,
it was not till recently that I discovered and read a copy in the Bibliothèque Nationale (Y2 60693–94).

With Mr. Garnett, I consider it a fine translation, but in the absence
of further evidence I find myself unable to accept his suggestion that it
is from the pen of Goldsmith. To me, the rendering does not possess
the unique flavour of Goldsmith's limpid prose, nor can I believe that he
could have written the following stanzas, which serve as a preface to the
translation:

> You who have Hearts, ye Virgins fair and gay,
> Who blindly rove where Pleasure leads the Way,
> Here see the Dangers of the gay and fair,
> Here see what Manon suffered—and beware!
>
> And you, fond Youths, whose Love and Beauty warm,
> Whom flattering Vice and Dissipation charm,
> Learn from the Tale your Passions to restrain,
> Be timely wise, and Virtue's Paths regain.

With scholarly caution Mr. Garnett, whilst accepting the anonymous
translator's statement that his was the first English rendering of *Manon*,
expressed the view that there might be an earlier one although he had
not been able to find it. As it happens, there was an earlier translation
published in 1743, which, with some difficulty, I have managed to run
to earth.

In the footnote to an article on Prévost in the *Gentleman's Magazine*
for 1770 reference is made to a translation of *Les Mémoires d'un Homme
de Qualité* which was made in 1743, under the misleading title of *The
Memoirs and Adventures of the Marquis de Bretagne and Duc D'Harcourt.
Written originally in French and now done into English by Mr. Erskine.* The
critic, who did not know that *Manon* formed part of this novel, stated

474

that a reprint of it had just been made for the publishers of the *Gentleman's Magazine*. This second edition, which bears the imprint: 'Dublin. Printed for James Williams at No. 5 in Skinner-Row, MDCLXX,' I was able to consult in the British Museum. It is a good translation and consists of three volumes. On page 188 of the third, begins the translation of *Manon Lescaut*, under the title: *The History of the chevalier de Grieu and Moll Lescaut*. The substitution of Moll for Manon is not remarkable: it was the common name for a woman of doubtful life in the eighteenth century. The translation is not so fine as that of 1767, but it is faithful to the original.

Now the British Museum possesses no copy of the first edition of the *Memoirs of the Marquis de Bretagne* and, in the absence of more definite proof, I was in doubt as to whether it included *Manon Lescaut*. Fortunately, however, the situation is cleared up by an advertisement which appeared in the *Daily Advertiser* for 9 June 1743. It runs as follows: 'This Day are published Beautifully printed in three neat Pocket Volumes 12mo. The Memoirs and Adventures of the Marquis de Bretagne and Duc D'Harcourt. Or the Wonderful Vicissitudes of Fortune exemplified in the Lives of those Noblemen. To which is added. The History of the Chevalier de Grien [*sic*] and Moll Lescaut, an Extravagant Love Adventure. Translated from the original French by Mr. ERSKINE. Printed for M. Cooper at the Globe in Pater-noster Row.' Erskine I cannot identify. All that I can find about him is that he was responsible for an alleged translation from the French called: *The Travels and Adventures of Mademoiselle Richelieu, cousin of the present Duke of that name, who made the Tour of Europe, dressed in Men's Cloaths, attended by her maid, LUCY, as Valet de Chambre. Now done into English from the Lady's own manuscript. By the Translator of the Memoirs and Adventures of the Marques* [sic] *of Bretagne and Duke of Harcourt. London. Printed for M. Cooper, at the Globe in Paternoster Row. MDCCXLIV. 3 vols. small 8vo.* I know of no French novel of this name, and am inclined to doubt whether any exists.

There is still another eighteenth-century English version of *Manon*. Its full title, according to both the *Monthly Review* and the *Critical*, is: *Manon L'Escaut: or the Fatal Attachment. A French Story.* 2 vols. 6s. sewed. Cadell. 1786. There is no copy either in the British Museum or in the Bibliothèque Nationale, nor have I been able to procure it elsewhere. It is significant that both reviews appear to be ignorant of the author's name and agree that the novel is an inferior and immoral production. Apparently the translation is by no means literal, but the reviewers obtain that fact from the translator himself who, to quote the *Monthly Review* (1786), 'acknowledges that he has made considerable alterations, as to length of periods, transposition of pages, etc., but all this has been done to render the performance more pleasant to the English ear, and, after all, he fears, "the *clinquant* of the French is still very visible."'

APPENDIX V

'C'EST d'après Richardson,' says Texte, 'qu'il (Rétif) prétend peindre *toute la marche de la corruption qui s'empare d'un cœur innocent et droit* (L'Avis de Pierre . . . en tête du *Paysan perverti*.)' Now, either Texte's memory played him false or else he was carried away by enthusiasm for his thesis. In the *Avis* to *Le Paysan perverti*, Rétif says: 'Profitez de la lecture de ces lettres où vous pourrez suivre toute la marche de la corruption qui s'empare d'un cœur innocent et droit.' Nowhere in this preface does he once allude to our English novelist. In *La Vie de Monsieur Nicolas* he merely repeats the remark we have already quoted in regard to *Pamela*, but adds a striking judgment on *Clarissa* which Texte, oddly, ignores. '*Clarissa* fatigued me; I admired this work but I did not like it.'[1] He says, however, that he was attracted by Clementina, the heroine of *Sir Charles Grandison*. In a final critical survey of his own two novels,[2] Rétif feels that they are worthy to be compared with the achievements of Richardson or of Rousseau: with the former because of their scope, with the latter because of their artistic value. 'It[3] is,' he remarks with pride, 'a vast production, like *Pamela*, *Clarissa*, or *Grandison*; it is a book full of matter and of warmth, like the *Héloïse*.'

[1] Edition of 1794–7, tome v, 2775.
[2] Edition of 1792, viii. 4589.
[3] The two novels really form one work, and, in 1784, Rétif amalgamated them under the joint title, *Le Paysan et La Paysanne pervertis*.

INDEX

INDEX

The figures in heavy type indicate the important page references

479

R